Perspectives on Development in the Middle East and North Africa (MENA) Region

Series Editor

Almas Heshmati, Jönköping University, Jönköping, Sweden

This Scopus indexed book series publishes monographs and edited volumes devoted to studies on the political, economic and social developments of the Middle East and North Africa (MENA). Volumes cover in-depth analyses of individual countries, regions, cases and comparative studies, and they include both a specific and a general focus on the latest advances of the various aspects of development. It provides a platform for researchers globally to carry out rigorous economic, social and political analyses, to promote, share, and discuss current quantitative and analytical work on issues, findings and perspectives in various areas of economics and development of the MENA region. Perspectives on Development in the Middle East and North Africa (MENA) Region allows for a deeper appreciation of the various past, present, and future issues around MENA's development with high quality, peer reviewed contributions. The topics may include, but not limited to: economics and business, natural resources, governance, politics, security and international relations, gender, culture, religion and society, economics and social development, reconstruction, and Jewish, Islamic, Arab, Iranian, Israeli, Kurdish and Turkish studies. Volumes published in the series will be important reading offering an original approach along theoretical lines supported empirically for researchers and students, as well as consultants and policy makers, interested in the development of the MENA region.

Goran M. Muhamad • Nabaz T. Khayyat
Editors

Resource Management Performance: A Sectoral Analysis in the Post-Conflict Kurdistan Region of Iraq

Springer

Editors
Goran M. Muhamad
Economics and Finance Department
University of Kurdistan Hewler
Erbil, Iraq

Nabaz T. Khayyat
Technology Management, Economics, and Policy Program
Colleges of Engineering, Seoul National University
Seoul, Korea (Republic of)

ISSN 2520-1239 ISSN 2520-1247 (electronic)
Perspectives on Development in the Middle East and North Africa (MENA) Region
ISBN 978-981-97-7724-2 ISBN 978-981-97-7725-9 (eBook)
https://doi.org/10.1007/978-981-97-7725-9

This Springer imprint is published by the registered company Springer Nature Singapore Pte Ltd.
The registered company address is: 152 Beach Road, #21-01/04 Gateway East, Singapore 189721, Singapore

Contents

Part I
Introduction to the Book

Chapter 1
Integrated Approaches for Strategic Development in the Kurdistan Region: Perspectives on Resources, Strategies, Infrastructure, and Agriculture

Goran M. Muhamad and Nabaz T. Khayyat

1.1 General Overview

After World War I, with the creation of new states from the territories of the Ottoman Empire, Kurdistan was integrated into the new entities of Turkey, Iraq, and Syria, in addition to the eastern part of Kurdistan, which had already been part of the Gajar Empire in Iran (Stansfield, 2006). Although promises were made by Britain to shape independent areas called Kurdistan within the territories of the defeated Ottoman Empire under the Treaty of Sèvres in 1920, Britain, then, reneged and forced the Treaty of Lausanne in 1923 (McDowall, 2021).

After decades of fighting and extensive international communication efforts, Kurds in Iraq successfully established a self-governing region. With its rich history and cultural heritage, the Kurdistan Region of Iraq (hereafter KRI) stands at a critical juncture in its economic development and holds immense potential for economic transformation. The KRI, which is located in the northern part of Iraq, boasts significant reserves of oil and gas, alongside fertile agricultural land, a burgeoning tourism sector, and a small service sector.

G. M. Muhamad (✉)
Economic Research Centre, Soran University, Erbil, Iraq

Economic and Finance Department, University of Kurdistan Hewler, Erbil, Iraq
e-mail: goran.mustafa@ukh.edu.krd

N. T. Khayyat
Brandenburg University of Technology, Cottbus-Senftenberg, Germany

Technology Management, Economics, and Policy Program, Colleges of Engineering, Seoul National University, Seoul, Korea (Republic of)
e-mail: nabaz@snu.ac.kr

G. M. Muhamad, N. T. Khayyat (eds.), *Resource Management Performance: A Sectoral Analysis in the Post-Conflict Kurdistan Region of Iraq*, Perspectives on Development in the Middle East and North Africa (MENA) Region,
https://doi.org/10.1007/978-981-97-7725-9_1

Historically, the KRI is marked by conflict and political instability; however, the region is now poised to harness its abundant natural resources, to build a future of prosperity and stability. Despite these abundant resources, the KRI faces considerable economic challenges, including over-reliance on oil revenues, economic volatility, and a need for more sustainable development practices (Khayyat, 2019).

A resource-based economy offers a viable pathway to harnessing the KRI's natural wealth for long-term prosperity. This model emphasizes the sustainable and efficient use of natural resources to drive economic growth, social equity, and environmental stewardship. Unlike traditional extractive models that often lead to boom and bust cycles, a resource-based economy seeks to create a diversified, resilient, and inclusive economy (Zahra, 2021).

This book is a collection of 13 studies covering several areas pertinent to the current economic resources and development in the KRI. The book aims to outline a comprehensive framework for developing a resource-based economy in the KRI, focusing on sustainable practices, economic diversification, and equitable growth. The significance of this book is vital to several interested groups related to the study of post-conflict areas, namely, the KRG policymakers, international development organizations, think tanks, and the private sector. The book also offers guidance to the regional government, as well as Iraq and Syria considering reconstruction, rehabilitation, and repatriation of their displaced population; economic governance; and effectiveness of institutions. It would be of interest to academics, students, and the general public who are interested in the study of the Middle East and modern Kurdish issues.

1.2 The Kurdistan Region of Iraq Context

The Kurdistan Region is a conflict-sensitive region that has experienced civil war and long conflict with the Iraqi government (Muhamad, 2022). Since 1920, Kurds have fought for their rights with the Iraqi government. Over that period, the governments had brutally crushed the Kurds; as a consequence, Kurds faced a series of purposeful actions such as human rights abuse and genocide, who were at risk of being annihilated (Hiltermann, 2008).

The KRI is a constitutionally recognized semi-autonomous region in northern Iraq with a population of more than 6.5 million. Its government, the Kurdistan Regional Government (KRG), based in Erbil, has the right under the Iraqi Constitution of 2005 to exercise legislative, executive, and judicial powers according to the Iraqi constitution, except in what is listed as exclusive powers of the federal authorities under that constitution.

The KRI comprises three major cities (governorates), Erbil, Sulaymaniyah, and Duhok. Recently, the district of Halabja has been formed as a new governorate to become the fourth governorate in the KRI.[1]

The KRI perceived exceptional economic growth resulting from a 17% share of the Iraqi budget, investment, oil, and natural gas utilization (Khayyat & Muhamad, 2023). The KRI enjoys a degree of political autonomy with a semi-autonomous government, which provides a unique opportunity to implement tailored economic policies. The region's oil and gas reserves are among the largest in the world offering a significant source of revenue. However, heavy reliance on these resources has exposed the economy to vulnerabilities, such as fluctuating oil prices and geopolitical instability. Additionally, the region faces political and security challenges that can impact economic stability.

The region has a structural economic issue due to low capital investment, poor productivity growth, severe structural unemployment, high dependency on imports, structural inequality, monopoly in the market, the unbalanced role of the private sector compared to the public sector, and poor and traditional taxation system. Recently, there have been restrictions on freedom of expression marked as one of the factors contributing to backsliding in the region. The unemployment rate in KRI was 6.5% before the war with ISIL in 2014. This rate rose to 13.5% in 2015 but declined to 10.2% at the end of 2017. The figure as of 2018 stands at 9%.[2]

The KRI has had peace and relative security with a more liberalized economy and market-oriented policies. While its economy is dominated by the oil industry, the largest nongovernment sectors in terms of value added to the KRI were construction, wholesale and retail trade, home ownership and rental, services, and manufacturing, respectively. Although some of those sectors have been progressing, new leading economic sectors are growing. The leading economic sectors in KRI change; then more attention needs to be paid to the social changes that follow. There is a growing recognition that economic change involves massive movements from one economic sector to another and from one community to another.

The Kurdish people, known for their resilience and strong cultural identity, possess the potential to drive economic transformation. By harnessing their natural resources strategically, and having a different model of the economy, Kurdistan can achieve sustainable development and improve the living standards of its population. It is evident that the current model of the KRI's economy, which relies heavily on oil, has failed; oil export has been halted with no resumption schedule and the welfare of people is in danger. As such, the KRG requires a new model of economy that promotes economic diversification and sustainable use of resources.

Despite these challenges, Kurdistan's strong sense of identity and community resilience provides a solid foundation for building a resource-based economy. The Kurdish people have a rich cultural heritage, a strong work ethic, and a deep connection to their land, all of which can drive sustainable development efforts.

---

[1] https://krso.gov.krd/en/map/kurdistan-region/population

[2] https://krso.gov.krd/en/indicator/population-and-labor-force/labor-force-participation

1.3 The Promise of Natural Wealth

The KRI is blessed with a wealth of natural resources, particularly its substantial oil and gas reserves. These resources have the potential to drive significant economic growth and development. However, the traditional model of resource extraction and export has often led to a series of economic and social challenges, including dependency on a single sector, economic volatility, and uneven wealth distribution. To overcome these challenges, a new paradigm is necessary, one that emphasizes strategic economic diversification, institutional empowerment, and the sustainable and strategic use of natural resources (Abdullah & Gray, 2022; Muhamad, 2023; Muhamad et al., 2021).

1.4 A Resource-Based Economy

A resource-based economy is not merely about the extraction and sale of natural resources. It is about creating a holistic economic model that leverages these resources to drive comprehensive development. This involves adding value to raw materials, fostering local industries, investing in human capital, and ensuring that the benefits of resource wealth are broadly shared across society (Mhatre et al., 2021). Key elements of a resource-based economy include:

1. Value Addition: Processing raw materials domestically to create higher-value products
2. Sustainable Practices: Employing methods that preserve the environment and ensure long-term resource availability
3. Economic Diversification: Reducing reliance on a single sector by developing other industries
4. Social Equity: Ensuring a fair distribution of resource wealth
5. Environmental Stewardship: Protecting natural ecosystems and minimizing environmental damage

1.5 Vision and Goals of a Resource-based Economy in the KRI

The vision for a resource-based economy in the KRI is ambitious but achievable. It aims to transform natural resource wealth into a catalyst for sustainable, diversified, and inclusive economic growth. The key goals of this vision are:

1. Sustainable Development: Ensuring that the extraction and use of natural resources are conducted in a manner that meets the needs of the present without compromising the ability of future generations to meet their own needs

2. Economic Diversification: Reducing dependence on oil revenues by promoting other sectors such as agriculture, manufacturing, tourism, and renewable energy
3. Social Equity: Ensuring that all segments of society benefit from the region's natural resource wealth, with a focus on reducing poverty and improving quality of life
4. Environmental Protection: Implementing practices that minimize environmental impact, promote the health of natural ecosystems, and mitigate the effects of climate change

1.6 Strategic Pathways

Achieving this vision requires a multifaceted strategy that encompasses policy reform, education and training, infrastructure development, and international collaboration.

1. Policy Reform: Effective policy reform is crucial for creating an enabling environment for a resource-based economy. Key policy measures include:
    - Regulatory Framework: Developing a robust regulatory framework that promotes transparency, accountability, and sustainable practices in resource extraction and management.
    - Incentives for Value Addition: Providing incentives for businesses to engage in value-added activities, such as refining oil domestically or developing downstream industries.
    - Taxation and Revenue Management: Implementing fair and efficient taxation policies to ensure that resource revenues are collected and managed effectively. Establishing a sovereign wealth fund can help manage resource revenues for long-term stability and investment in public goods.
2. Education and Training: A skilled workforce is essential for driving innovation and efficiency in resource management. Key initiatives include:
    - Technical and Vocational Education: Expanding technical and vocational education programs to equip the workforce with the skills needed for jobs in value-added industries.
    - Higher Education and Research: Investing in higher education and research institutions to foster innovation and develop expertise in areas such as sustainable resource management, renewable energy, and environmental protection.
    - Capacity Building: Providing training and capacity-building programs for government officials, industry leaders, and community members to promote best practices in resource management and economic development.
3. Infrastructure Development: Robust infrastructure is the backbone of a diversified economy. Key infrastructure investments include:

- Transportation Networks: Developing transportation infrastructure, such as roads, railways, and ports, to facilitate the movement of goods and people and support economic activities beyond the oil sector.
- Energy Infrastructure: Investing in energy infrastructure, including renewable energy projects, to ensure a reliable and sustainable energy supply.
- Information and Communication Technology (ICT): Expanding ICT infrastructure to support digital economy initiatives and improve access to information and services.

4. International Collaboration: Engaging with global partners can provide valuable knowledge, investment, and market access. Key strategies include:

   - Foreign Direct Investment (FDI): Attracting FDI by creating a favorable investment climate and offering incentives for foreign companies to invest in value-added industries.
   - International Trade Agreements: Pursuing international trade agreements to expand market access for Kurdish products and integrate them into global value chains.
   - Knowledge Exchange: Collaborating with international organizations, universities, and research institutions to share knowledge and best practices in resource management and sustainable development.

1.7 Challenges and Opportunities

The journey toward a resource-based economy is not without challenges. Political instability, regulatory hurdles, regional conflicts, and environmental concerns are significant obstacles that need to be addressed. However, these challenges also present opportunities for innovation and resilience. For instance, addressing political instability requires strengthening governance structures and promoting transparency and accountability. Overcoming regulatory hurdles involves streamlining procedures and ensuring that policies are conducive to business growth. Managing regional conflicts necessitates fostering dialogue and cooperation among different stakeholders. Environmental concerns can be tackled by adopting green technologies and sustainable practices. Alternatively, regulating economic activities to reduce waste production will offer protection against environmental degradation (Khezri & Muhamad, 2023).

1.8 The Book Structure

This book has been divided into three areas of research: Resource management and development, resource-based strategies for development, and infrastructure and agricultural development. This book bridges the link between researchers, academicians, and practitioners. It is a good up-to-date handbook for researchers, policymakers, and governmental and nongovernmental organizations interested in studying contemporary Kurdish issues, the rehabilitation, reconstruction, and development of the Kurdistan Region. The next section will present a summary of the studies covered in this book.

Part II: Resource Management and Development

Resource management in the Kurdistan Region of Iraq (KRI) is a critical issue that impacts its socioeconomic stability and development. The KRI, with its significant oil reserves, agricultural potential, and strategic location, has faced numerous challenges due to historical conflicts, regional instability, and governance issues. Part II of this book consists of five chapters. The first chapter of this part (Chap. 2) deals with the KRI's challenges involved in state-building within the context of conflict and natural resources. The study applies a political economy perspective to consider the impact of conflict and natural resources, specifically oil, on state formation in the Kurdistan Region of Iraq. It offers an alternative approach to establish a new economic model that emphasizes economic diversification, economic governance, and reinforces institutions. Chapter 3 investigates the KRI's energy position within the new geopolitical reverberations. The study offers a new energy vision to the KRG to play a role in a new emerging regional order. Closely related to previous chapters, Chap. 4 studies the interplay between resource wealth and tax revenue. The study provides an intensive examination of dependency on natural resources and its effects on fiscal outcomes. The chapter offers policy recommendations to the KRG to stabilize economic growth and foster more significant social equity.

The role of United Nations missions and international aid has been pivotal in addressing the KRI's challenges and promoting sustainable resource management in the region. Chapters 5 and 6 study the role and commitments of international agencies in the development of the Kurdistan Region. Chapter 5 examines the factors that affect the growth of multinational corporations (MNCs) in the region and how the MNC manages to make use of local resources, technical advancements, and external factors to enhance its performance and overall growth.

UN missions, particularly through agencies like the United Nations Development Programme (UNDP), have been instrumental in enhancing governance and institutional capacity in the KRI. Chapter 6 studies the effects of the UN mission on the socioeconomic performance of the region. The UN's role has been crucial in addressing the immediate needs of the population, particularly in times of crisis.

Part III: Resource-Based Strategies for Development: Business Organizations, Technology, and Social Media

The first chapter of this part (Chap. 7) assesses the impact of civil society organizations (CSOs) on the KRI's development. The CSOs are important to the development of KRI. They contribute to several key areas such as promoting governance, providing aid, supporting economic growth, advocating for rights, enhancing services, protecting the environment, fostering civic participation, and collaborating internationally, contributing significantly to the KRI's development.

Chapter 8 studies leadership styles in the public and private sectors of the Kurdistan Region with emphasis on finding commonalities and differences in the impact of the present leadership on employee motivation and commitment to resource management in both sectors. While there are differences in leadership styles' orientation in both sectors, public sector leadership contributes less to managing employees and resources, and thus public managers' behaviors should be assessed to make their leadership best deal with the recent awareness of the workforce and managing resources.

Utilizing technology in daily work has profound effects on improving human resources management (HRM) performance. Chapter 9 focuses on analyzing how much Information and Communication Technology (ICT) can contribute to increasing the performance level of HRM staff in Higher Education Institutions in the Kurdistan Region of Iraq (KRI). This study draws attention to how recruitment, training, employee engagement, and development decisions are affected.

Chapter 10 pays attention to the digital landscape and the contemporary role of social media in shaping human experiences. Since the Kurdistan Region has become a destination for visitors, social media has an essential role as the source of information to help travelers in every stage of travel decision-making. This chapter investigates the relationship between the travel decision-making process through the use of social media, especially from the point of view of Kurdish travelers. The study offers some recommendations for the development of the tourism industry to execute marketing strategies that are more focused on the consumers.

Part IV: Infrastructure and Agricultural Development

The first chapter of this part (Chap. 11) investigates the impact of risk factors on the accuracy of project cost estimates. Project cost overruns significantly hinder the development of the KRI by straining financial resources, delaying project completion, and increasing debt levels. These overruns can divert funds from other essential initiatives, leading to economic instability and reduced public trust in government effectiveness. Additionally, they can deter foreign investment and aid, exacerbate inflationary pressures, and result in compromised project quality and scope. Addressing the causes of cost overruns, such as poor planning and inadequate project management, is crucial to ensuring sustainable development in the KRI.

While infrastructure development, especially electricity, has been part of longlasting investment in the KRI over the past few years, there are frequent power outages and no self-sufficiency in the region. Chapter 12 investigates the factors affecting residential electricity consumption in the Kurdistan Region of Iraq. The study identifies the important variables that play roles in electricity consumption and analyzes the possible impact of family behavioral changes on their electricity consumption. This helps the KRG policymakers design strategies for rational electricity consumption, establish intervention strategies, and formulate and implement targeted campaigns to inform and educate in order to promote advances and changing habits of its users, to reduce the electricity demand.

The two final chapters are related to agricultural development in the KRI. Chapter 13 examines the role of the agriculture sector in the economy of the Kurdistan

Region and considers the challenges of underdevelopment of the agricultural sector in KRI. The KRI has immense landscapes, water resources, and wilderness to raise farm animals and it has been counted as one of the most fertile lands in the area which used to be a food basket for the rest of Iraq. The study in line with the current initiative strategy of the KRG offers some policy recommendations to promote agricultural contribution to the national income of the KRI.

Chapter 14 explains the causes of agricultural decline in the Kurdistan Region of Iraq. It identifies several factors, such as the subsequent embargo period after the Gulf War, high production costs, and no protection policy for domestic producers. Additionally, the difficulties farmers experience in gaining access to markets, finance, and competition with cheaper imported items have made agriculture an underdeveloped and undiversified sector. The KRI's current economic growth strategies include two main goals: employment generation and the reduction of revenue inequity. This study assesses how the agriculture industry contributes to achieving these goals.

References

Abdullah, S., & Gray, T. (2022). Political constraints on economic diversification in the Kurdistan region of Iraq. *Energy Policy, 171*, 113274.

Hiltermann, J. R. (2008). *The 1988 Anfal campaign in Iraqi Kurdistan*. Online Encyclopedia of Mass Violence.

Khayyat, N. (2019). Technology management and policy of Kurdistan region of Iraq. *Iraqi Kurdistan's Statehood Aspirations: A Political Economy Approach*, 87–98.

Khayyat, N. T., & Muhamad, G. M. (Eds.). (2023). *Empirical studies of an internet and service based economy*. Springer.

Khezri, M., & Muhamad, G. M. (2023). Environmental effects of entrepreneurship indices on ecological footprint of croplands and grazing lands in the economy. *Journal of Cleaner Production, 414*, 137550.

McDowall, D. (2021). *A modern history of the Kurds* (4th ed.). Bloomsbury Publishing PLC.

Mhatre, P., Panchal, R., Singh, A., & Bibyan, S. (2021). A systematic literature review on the circular economy initiatives in the European Union. *Sustainable Production and Consumption, 26*, 187–202.

Muhamad, G. M. (2022). Private sector development analysis in post-conflict Kurdistan region of Iraq. *UKH Journal of Social Sciences, 6*(2), 19–32.

Muhamad, G. M. (2023). *Reducing natural resource dependency for economic growth in resource rich countries*. Springer Nature.

Muhamad, G. M., Heshmati, A., & Khayyat, N. T. (2021). How to reduce the degree of dependency on natural resources? *Resources Policy, 72*, 102047.

Stansfield, G. (2006). The Kurdish question in Iraq, 1914-1974. *The Middle East Online, 2*, 1–8.

Zahra, S. A. (2021). The resource-based view, resourcefulness, and resource management in startup firms: A proposed research agenda. *Journal of Management, 47*(7), 1841–1860.

Part II
Resources Management and Development

Chapter 2
Political Economy of State Formation in the Kurdistan Region of Iraq: Challenges and Opportunities

Goran M. Muhamad

Abstract This chapter examines the Kurdistan Region of Iraq (KRI) as a case study, providing a critical analysis of the challenges involved in state-building within the context of conflict and natural resources. The study applies a political economy perspective to consider the impact of conflict and natural resources, specifically oil, on state formation in the Kurdistan Region of Iraq. While the activity of conflict and civil wars appear to be a natural and inevitable aspect of state-building in early and modern times, the projection of natural resources in KRI could potentially shape a sustainable political process leading to a level of self-governance. However, issues such as poor institutional quality, institutionalised corruption, mismanagement of natural resources and domestic conflicts over resource management have led the Kurdistan Region, like many rentier states, to rely heavily on resource revenue, resulting in the so-called 'resource curse'. Consequently, the KRG has faced challenges in funding its economy, and thus oil-based state formation has not been successful, causing a weakening of the KRI's reputation for being relatively secure, stable and prosperous. An alternative approach would be to establish a new economic model that emphasises economic diversification and economic governance and reinforces institutions.

Keywords Political economy · Natural resources management · Diversification Policy · Kurdistan region

G. M. Muhamad (✉)
Economic Research Centre, Soran University, Erbil, Iraq

Economic and Finance Department, University of Kurdistan Hewler, Erbil, Iraq
e-mail: goran.mustafa@ukh.edu.krd

G. M. Muhamad, N. T. Khayyat (eds.), *Resource Management Performance: A Sectoral Analysis in the Post-Conflict Kurdistan Region of Iraq*, Perspectives on Development in the Middle East and North Africa (MENA) Region,
https://doi.org/10.1007/978-981-97-7725-9_2

2.1 Introduction

The study of economic development has focused on institutional and political structures that might pose obstacles to growth, and how these structures are contingent upon conflict and natural resources. The interactions between natural resources and conflict can explain features of a country's political economy (Anten et al., 2022). It is well evident that conflict and civil wars are a natural and inevitable aspect of state-building, for instance, the independence of South Sudan from Sudan, the creation of the independent state of Timor-Leste from Indonesia and the embryonic Republic of Kosovo from Serbia.

This study only considers the Kurdistan Region of Iraq (KRI). Since 1920, Kurds have fought for their rights against the Iraqi government. Over that period, the governments had brutally crushed the Kurds; as a consequence, Kurds faced a series of purposeful actions, such as genocide and putting them at risk of being annihilated (Hiltermann, 2008). After decades of fighting, the Kurdistan Regional Government (KRG) was established in 1992, and the 2003 Iraqi invasion gave Kurds an official federal region. Since it has been genuinely governing itself, there are several factors that appear vital to the development of the region's political economy, and thus the encouragement of state-building.

The region's economy has seen variations since the establishment of the KRG. At first, the region's economy was largely reliant on humanitarian aid (Natali, 2010); then the post-invasion international aid to Iraq made essential contributions to the development of the Kurdistan Region (Muhamad & Heshmati, 2021). After the establishment of the Iraqi government in 2005, the KRG received a 17% share of the federal budget based on the Kurdish population, while constituting around 23% of the Iraqi population. Despite economic stability during that time, the KRG started the exploration and development of natural resources. There has been a partial transformation from reliance on foreign aid and agriculture to industry, services and rapid urbanisation, the economy of political rent-seeking and property development (Muhamad, 2022).

However, it must be stressed that the region has experienced a developing economy. The GDP growth rate reached 12% in 2011 compared to 1.5% in 2008. Investment has dramatically boomed resulting in KRG's effort to promote investment and outstanding security situation relative to other parts of Iraq. Investment in the oil sector accounts for the major contribution to growth in the region. With over 45 billion barrels of oil reserves and 1.88 billion cubic metres of gas, the KRG attracts international oil companies, including the world's top ten global companies. Consequently, the value of resource rents ensures tensions between Kurdistan and Iraq, on the one hand, and between the KRG ruling parties, on the other hand. It has been a long double dispute between the Kurds themselves, and the KRG and Iraqi governments over resource management, territory and power-sharing.

This study tends to examine resources, conflicts and state formation in the Kurdistan Region. The political economy perspective of state formation will apply throughout the chapter, which considers the impact of conflict and natural resources that predominantly affect the formation of states. While war-making activity is an integral part of the process of state formation in early and new modern times, the projection of natural resources might design a sustainable political process that tends to attain a degree of autonomy. However, the rentier state runs into difficulties in times of decaying natural resources (Schwarz, 2008).

This chapter serves as a case study for KRI to provide a critical analysis of the variables and trends in building a state vis-à-vis conflict and natural resources. First, I will examine the role of conflict and natural resources, in particular oil, in relation to state formation in the Kurdistan Region. Then, I revisit my previous argument about how resource-rich countries can reduce the degree of dependency on natural resources (Muhamad, 2023). Finally, I summarise my original argument about how the KRG is strengthening its status by building fiscal capacity. This could be achieved by having an economic diversification policy, including a taxation system, private sector development, agricultural development and economic governance.

The establishment of the KRG is an outcome of the long-lasting fighting and the support of the international community to Kurds. The post-conflict humanitarian aid and international oil companies help the global recognition of the KRI. However, building a rentier region with the overdependence on oil and gas has made the region highly vulnerable to political and fiscal shocks and hence running into difficulties in financing its economy. Consequently, the oil state formation model of the KRI has not been successful leading to high inequality and institutionalised corruption, poor public service and institution system and thus weakening the region's stability and prosperity. It is highly recommended that the KRG establish a new model of the economy to reduce reliance on natural resources since oil and gas have caused many internal, regional and international problems.

The next sections provide a wide understanding of resources, conflict and state formation in the Kurdistan Region. Then, I will discuss the major challenges of the KRG in keeping its reputation for being relatively secure, stable and prosperous. I will discuss an alternative solution to strengthen the status of the KRI. The final section concludes the study.

2.2 Conflict and Oil State Formation in the Literature

The literature review section has been divided into two parts. The first part deals with the role that conflicts play in state-building. The section explains how oil resources relate to conflicts, and how conflict itself, along with its dynamics, helps or hinders building states. The second part briefly analyses the challenges facing new states, especially those that have oil, such as budgetary implication, expenditure, aid and relations with neighbours, by looking at some examples. In general, this section explores the relationship between the use of oil resources and state-building, more specifically, the role of oil in the expansion of legitimacy and fiscal autonomy as the most important task for investing in the capacity of the state.

2.2.1 State-Building and Natural Resources Conflict

The concept of state formation as an element of a theory of the state has changed over time. In this study 'state formation or state-building' refers to the construction of a state follwoing conflicts over natural resources. In the field of political theory, from Weber to Hobbes, many different scholars have provided their own version of the definition of state but there is no clear definition. Kukathas (2008) defines a state that is 'a form of political association'. According to Milliken and Krause (2002), the state has three principal functions, namely the provision of security, representation and welfare.

There is a wealth of literature arguing that security is the prerequisite for building a state (Baldwin, 2018; Greene, 2020), particularly for development after conflicts (Wang, 2023). However, the fact remains that security alone cannot result in state-building. Maslow's hierarchy of needs determines the fact that when the basic safety and psychological needs are satisfied, those of social and belongingness must be taken into consideration. This is where representation and welfare come into action.

According to the Montevideo Convention on the Rights and Duties of the State in 1933, the ability to create relationships with other governments and provide viable services for its people are important duties of the state. States need certain institutions or assemblies to mobilise legitimacy or to conduct foreign activity (Elbasani, 2020). These encourage sovereignty, which is the primary objective of post-conflict reconstruction activities. Further, the state or the government has the responsibility of distributing wealth, social security or other benefits to ensure the welfare of its citizens. This duty can be performed through the creation of mechanisms, regulatory frameworks and institutions that contribute to an increase in the aggregate capacity of the state (Titumir, 2022).

Over the past few decades, there has been a renewed interest in the dictum 'War makes States', with the formation or creation of many independent states such as the embryonic Republic of Kosovo from Serbia and South Sudan from Sudan. While the activity of conflict and civil wars appear to be a natural and inevitable aspect of state-building in both early and modern times, wars are essentially, in one way or another, fought over control of natural resources. Scholars have linked natural resources to conflict. Afriyie et al. (2020) investigated resource conflict in South Sudan and natural resources have been identified as one of the factors contributing to the conflict. Hansen (2011) believed that 'wars have been suspiciously connected to natural resources, in particular oil'. For instance, natural resources, especially oil, have motivated, financed and shaped conflicts in the Middle East.

On the other hand, using natural resources, in particular oil, in making a state is primarily dependent upon prioritising goals and activities. These priorities should ensure security and the provision of viable services to build legitimacy and then precede sovereignty. The abundance of natural resources seems to have indirect state consequences through the efficiency of the three principles.

2.2.2 Oil and State Formation

Much of the debate in the existing state-building literature emphasises the role of conflict in bringing independence. However, the projection of natural resources might design a sustainable political process that tends to attain a degree of autonomy. If the process is endowed with a sufficient degree of legitimacy, oil is more likely to be a sustainable source for building a state. The expansion of legitimacy and fiscal autonomy is the most important task for investing in the capacity of state-building. Legitimacy is the determining factor behind state resilience and successful institution-building in the transition to statehood (Börzel & Risse, 2021).

Development as a process of the expansion of wealth (economic growth) that can be achieved through the maximisation of oil revenue is essential to state formation. Revenue maximisation can then bolster the stability of new states and even expand the possibilities of external linkages. Furthermore, in designing a viable economy, infrastructure needs to be addressed and investment is required. The opinion of Schwarz (2008) is that the maximisation of oil revenue positively affects the function of the modern state in providing welfare and wealth to its citizens. He demonstrates the link between state-building and high levels of revenue. He finds that the expenditure side of public revenues is most clearly linked to a state-building agenda of creating societal peace and political acquiescence.

Schwartz describes the degree of stability that oil-rich economies can attain. He believes that oil state-building is generally stable since the availability of resource abundance helps to preserve traditional loyalties and thereby renders state formation into a legitimate process. Accordingly, this state model remains stable as long as the government can provide welfare for its citizens. Crucial to the process of state formation is building trust between the citizens and state institutions through providing public services; the state would thereby increase its sovereignty. However, Schwartz acknowledges that this model of state formation faces many challenges and different political and societal dynamics as compared to other countries. He provides an example of most Middle Eastern oil-rich countries, which are relatively weak states with little or no dependence on domestic taxation; transparency and accountability have remained absent for the most part in these states. He concludes his study with the major challenge that a rentier state or oil state formation runs into difficulties in times of declining natural resources and when there is absence of long-term economic development.

Other issues surrounding oil state formation include budgetary and the management of public finance and relationships with neighbouring countries. Additionally, the challenges of managing macroeconomic issues during oil price fluctuations cause oil-rich countries to suffer from revenue insecurity (Eregha & Mesagan, 2020). A further issue is mismanaging expenditure since they are a single commodity dominated by oil. Progress in improving non-oil revenues is very slow and characterised by the lack of economic diversification (Muhamad et al., 2021). Such an economy is described as 'a classic payroll economy' where the majority of the government budget goes to salary (Kameir, 2011).

The nature of political institutions in post-conflict state-building, which is crucial for the state institutional framework, is another issue. The state-building literature recognises the importance of the nature of established institutions, which determine democracy and legitimacy (Justino, 2022; Murtazashvili & Murtazashvili, 2020). Institutions refer to the judiciary system, armed forces, government effectiveness and rule of law. The major difference between developed and other nations is that the former establishes strong institutions, while the latter falls apart because of a lack of institutions (Acemoglu, 2015; Wimmer, 2023). Furthermore, the role of institutions in directing the objectives of state-building is crucial and affects economic stability. Muhamad et al. (2021) found that resource-rich countries that benefit from having institutional quality adjust towards a better diversified economy to reduce natural resource dependency than countries with poor institutions.

2.3 Conflict and State Formation in the Kurdistan Region

The consequences of the downfall of the Ottoman Empire during World War I recognised southern Kurdistan as a part of Iraq. Changing international policies towards Iraq and a concurrent successful Kurdish revolution contributed to empowering Kurds. Kurds in Iraq benefited from the establishment of their own government with the decision of the federal region announcement following the 1990 Gulf War. The decision has not formally been welcomed, either locally or internationally but the considerations of self-governing have increased Kurdish responsibility for their own fate (Bengio, 2012; Kaplan, 2020).

2.3.1 The Background of the Conflict

Over the last century, Kurdish people have clashed with a series of Iraqi governments fighting for their rights, stability and independence. During World War I, the Kurds started to formulate Kurdish independence demands. They gained a measure of international approval in the Treaty of Sèvres in 1920, which promised autonomy and the option of an independent Kurdish state. The promise, however, was scrapped by the 1923 Treaty of Lausanne, which divided Kurds into four separate minorities in Turkey, Iran, Iraq and Syria (McDowall, 2021); the Kurdish struggle has been widespread since then.

In 1970, in the immediate aftermath of the Kurdish–Iraqi war, the Kurds and Iraqi government reached an agreement: the first Kurdish constitutional autonomous region was announced. The agreement formally ended hostilities at that time, but it did not essentially bring peace to a conflict-affected country. The peace plan for Kurdish autonomy eventually fell, and thus the Kurdish–Iraqi battle began again. The abundant availability of resources especially oil assisted Iraq's large military. The government then took advantage of the role of military technology to combat the Kurds. Consequently, the Kurds faced a series of purposeful actions, such as displacement and genocide, and were at risk of being annihilated.

Kurds in Iraq faced genocide and chemical attacks; thousands of people including women and children were killed. It was a serious attempt to completely destroy the Kurdish people to put an end to the Kurdish aspiration towards greater autonomy or independence (Hiltermann, 2008). The aim of the process was not only the mass killing of Kurds but also the complete destruction of its economy. The Kurdistan economy at that time was largely dependent on agriculture and livestock. Personal damaged property belonging to the genocidal people has financially been estimated at roughly 8 billion dollars (KRG-MOMA, 2008).

2.3.2 Kurdish State Formation and the Role of the International Community

The 1990 Gulf War gave a golden opportunity to the Kurdish rebellion, which enabled the release of three governorates out of four. Yet, when the Iraqi troops were driven from Kuwait, they were deployed in the distinguished Kurdish region. Thus, around three million Kurds fled to the border with Iran and Turkey, which appeared to be one of the largest, most rapid movements of refugees in history; thousands died as a result of disease and starvation.

The effective reaction of the United Nations Security Council was to create an immediate intervention for humanitarian purposes in Iraq, which adopted Resolution 688 on 5 April 1991. As a consequence of the Resolution, the United States and its allies posted armed forces to create a relatively secure environment and non-fly zone for Kurds. Then, aid agencies could safely contribute to the humanitarian relief operations; the Kurdistan of Iraq seemed a separate faction within the integrity of Iraq. In fact, the role of the UN and the international community was effective in creating a relatively stable environment that allowed economic recovery and institution-building. It also offered the region forms of recognition, external patronage and internal sovereignty that promoted quasi-statehood (Natali, 2010).

Nevertheless, in the emerging post-conflict environment neither humanitarian intervention nor deployment of UN agencies led to addressing the root of conflict but created a sustainable internal capacity. The chronic conflict between the Kurds and Iraqi governments has a key root which might be related to identity, land or the economy. It is argued that economic causes can agitate different groups on a larger scale but not always take them towards war, as many other factors might play a fundamental role in this regard. One important issue is that the Kurds have never viewed themselves and their land as a connected part of Iraq.

On the other hand, the Iraqi point of view tends to highlight the fact that Kurdish demand would endanger Iraq's land and economic unity. Bengio (2012) illustrates the largest fear of any Iraqi government vis-à-vis Kurdish demand for the division of its territorial integrity into three small states: a Kurdish state, an Arab-Sunni state and a Shi'i state. She also argues the geographical importance of Kurdistan in terms of its valuable resources. She points to oil and rich agricultural land as being potential avenues for increasing fear in the Kurdish demand. In fact, Kurdistan territories dominate plenty of rich Iraqi areas, which have relatively large natural resources and even wealth in terms of fresh waters.

2.3.3 The Dual War and the Kurdish Quasi-State

The focus of Kurds in the post-conflict time of the invasion of Iraq in 2003 has shifted from fighting against Iraq to leading it. They assist in establishing a governance system and improving security, thus making new Iraq a classical rentier state. With this shift, the Kurdish character has played a major role in rebuilding Iraq. It has widespread opportunities to strengthen its semi-autonomous region, both domestically and internationally, which had suffered from the diversity of the economic blockade by the Iraqi government, on the one hand, and economic sanctions in Iraq imposed by the UN, on the other, over the period 1991–2003.

During the Kurdish revolutions in Iraq, however, the sole goal that Kurds have been fighting for was secession from Iraq, but in 2003 they intended to persist as part of it. Galbraith (2006) believes that the incentive of the advantages that would accrue to Kurdistan from revenue-sharing of Iraq's massive resources encourages Kurds to remain within Iraq.

The 2003 war in Iraq has brought both benefits and losses for Kurds. The most beneficial achievement was the legitimate recognition of the Kurdistan Region. The valuable involvement of Kurds in the negotiations of Iraq's Transitional Administrative Law (TAL) secured the legal recognition of the de facto Kurdish quasi-state within a state in Iraq. Simultaneously, the TAL has made large improvements to the circumstances of Kurds in Iraq by making serious pledges, such as securing a 17% share of Iraqi oil revenues and leading KRG control of its forces. Furthermore, it allowed displaced Kurds, dislodged from Kirkuk by the Arabisation programme to other provinces of Iraq, to return to their homes and recognise Kurdish as one of Iraq's two official languages. Moreover, Kurds have gained the promise of a future referendum to decide control of the contested territories that had to be held formally by the end of December 2007. These have been viewed as an outstanding political achievement of Kurds within Iraq. Those pledges were recognised later in the Iraqi constitution in 2005. However, those agreements and recognition did not necessarily bring the automatic restoration of a functioning state based on power-sharing between Kurds and Arabs. In fact, a number of pledges were exclusively acting until the strength of the Iraqi military, which always threatened the Kurds. For instance, the Iraqi army brutally attacked Kerkuk and some other areas that had been run by Kurds since 2003 as a consequence of the Kurdish Referendum.

It must nonetheless be stressed that the past of the Kurds had been marked by the loss of their land and powers. As Kurds, in the bargain of 1970, acknowledged a four-year plan to address the fate of Kirkuk, they offered a chance to strengthen

Iraqi military power. Kurds have repeated history when lately held a controversial independence referendum in 2017, while this should have been held earlier after the collapse of Saddam Hussein. The Iraqi government has seen the referendum as a serious attempt of Kurds to leave Iraq, and thereby called for cancelling the results, rejected to have a dialogue with the KRG about the outcome of the referendum, established a regional embargo with the support of neighbouring countries on Kurds, and finally with the aim of protecting the unity of Iraq, an immediate military conflict was taking place. Consequently, the KRG lost control over almost half of its territories, including Kirkuk and other disputed areas.

To conclude, it appears that the invasion of Iraq has created a perfect political environment for Kurds within Iraq, resulting in the achievement of a quasi-state within the recognition of the federal state of Iraq. This provides the KRG authority with freedom of action and self-governing politically and financially and assists Kurds in attaining semi-independence. It can be concluded that the first persistent Kurdish semi-autonomy resulted from the 1990 Gulf War. Likewise, the recognition of Kurdistan as a federal region and the establishment of a quasi-state was an outcome of the 2003 Iraqi invasion. The indication is therefore that the dual warfare and its consequences were the key to Kurdish semi-state formation, using a variety of sources in favour of powering their state. However, in the post-conflict time, the region was in desperate need of finance to start its journey towards building the most basic state institutions, infrastructure and development. The foreign aid, then, recorded quite significant success in the development of the region.

2.4 Resources and Kurdish State Formation

The KRI has been de facto independent since 1991. Kurds commonly preferred independence rather than being integrated with Iraq, but in 2003 they accepted coexistence as an autonomous region rather than being truly independent. Galbraith (2006) believes that the benefits of revenue-sharing of Iraq's massive resources incentivise the Kurds to remain within Iraq. However, Natali (2010) describes this choice as an understanding by the Kurds of the danger of proclaiming secession in Iraq. The Kurds realise that protecting their current stability and their future success will considerably evolve within the federation of Iraq. However, intractable disputes between the Iraqi central and KRG over a number of issues imply that the federation in Iraq would not be successful, or at least not stable. The most important issues are disputes over resources, territory and power-sharing. In modern Kurdish history, those factors have encouraged and pushed Kurds vastly to secede from Iraq. Nevertheless, the mismanagement of natural resources has weakened the position of the Kurds locally and internationally; the oil and gas industry turns its blessing into a curse for the nation as is the case in many underdeveloped oil-rich countries (Auty, 2007; Rodriguez & Sachs, 1999; Sachs & Warner, 2001).

While Kurds are expected to use the projection of natural resources in establishing a sustainable political and financial process that tends to strengthen the state of the KRG, as this has been the case in some gulf countries like the Emirates, Qatar and Saudi Arabia, oil state formation has not been successful. Such a model of the economy, while not being able to provide generous welfare systems for the people of Kurdistan, has brought a political curse and put the KRG at risk of losing political power (Abdullah & Gray, 2022).

2.4.1 Resource Management and Disputes

The oil dispute is one source of tension between the KRG and the Iraqi federal government. In the beginning, it was an issue regarding who has the right to sign contracts with international oil companies. Later, this dispute was extended when the KRG started independent crude oil export through Turkey in 2013. While the volume of the exporting was small and delivered by track, it was a rational move towards financial autonomy and greater economic independence. The rationality of this decision comes from the fact that Kurds have always been uncertain about the future of federal government funds to the region; therefore, they have primarily started, with international oil companies, to establish economic sovereignty. Additionally, to further strengthen the fiscal autonomy, the KRG started building its pipeline to export oil without Iraqi jurisdiction and oil transportation began via the newly built pipeline to Turkey in 2014. Soon later, the value of resource rents ensured further tensions between them, and consequently, the Iraqi government cut the 17% share of the Kurds in the Iraqi budget.

The agreement of the federation in Iraq had left plenty of promises that might cause more problems in the ambiguous future of Iraq. The intergovernmental control over oil and gas has a direct implication for the hydrocarbon legislation debate based on the Iraqi Constitution. The Constitution, indeed, grants the KRG authority to manage resources in the region. While Iraq does not have a hydrocarbon law, the KRG, in harmony with the Constitution, passed the regional hydrocarbon law in 2007 and began negotiating with foreign companies. Two years later, the KRG discussed over 30 contracts by estimation of more than $10 billion in investment with European, American and South Korean companies. The disputes over resource management thus began. The Iraqi government considers that resource operations in the region need their approval and, therefore, furiously restates the illegality of those contracts. As a result, a series of reactions have been undertaken.

However, the KRG has succeeded in bringing reputable foreign companies into the region by offering them more incentives than Iraq in designing fiscal terms for leases, licences or concessions. While the licence in the rest of Iraq was based on Risk Service Contracts (RSCs), the KRG negotiated with foreign companies based on Production Sharing Contracts (PSCs). This guarantees as much as 25–35% versus 15–18% in other parts of Iraq for fixed-fee output-boosting and start-up deals for unproven fields for the companies.

Furthermore, while Kurds have relentlessly shared their political and economic experience to reconstruct Iraq in post-conflict times, they were left desperate. It seems that many of the tensions between both sides have deeper political roots, some of them relating to those that had caused the physical conflicts. Others relate to the recent history of the Kurds in Iraq. They have been enjoying more than a federal government, although the Iraqi government has behaved centrally.

2.4.2 *State Capacities and Economic Structure*

One of the strongest aspects of the evolution of political economy in the KRI during its first self-rule was building a region as a kind of self-governing entity with a variety of contemporary state abilities. The region already had some statehood features according to the Montevideo Convention on the Rights and Duties of the State in 1933, such as having a limited population, geography, ability to create relationships with other governments and providing viable services for their people. Whereas the KRG, after the collapse of Saddam Hussein, started to invest in state capacity, it benefited from greater internal sovereignty. State capacity investments guarantee the performance of the state, which standardises the basic functions in the interest of residents at a given level of economic development (Anten et al., 2022). Nevertheless, the region has not been successful in building economic sovereignty in supporting the position of the KRI. The way the KRG built its economy was not in favour of the region. As such, the region's political system has been at risk and the people's angriness towards the political system has increased. In this section, we will discuss a range of structural challenges that have caused stagnation to the KRI's economic development in general, and in particular, they became critical constraints in the establishment of KRG's fiscal autonomy.

2.4.2.1 The High Dependency on the Oil Sector

Oil and gas have played a vital role in the political and economic life of the KRI, which contains a large reserve of both. The region has 1.88 billion cubic metres of gas and an estimated 45 billion barrels of oil reserves—more than one-third of the federal total of 143 billion—which means that if the region were independent, it would possess the world's sixth-largest oil reserves (Gunter, 2011). This has made the KRI's decision-makers attach the future of Kurds to only the oil and gas sector. This is reflected in the KRG's hydrocarbon law in which the fiscal system has been designed to maximise the value of oil and gas revenues. Therefore, oil investors have been offered a strong incentive to invest quickly, leading to the generation of a net profit share of about 10–12%. This incentive attracts companies and leads the KRG to increase oil production in a pipeline from 100,000 in the beginning to around 5 billion bpd in 2025 (Fig. 2.1).

Initially, the KRG enjoyed success in attracting smaller companies such as DNO of Norway and Gulf Keystone Petroleum of Britain. Gradually, larger well-known companies were also attracted. However, the law clearly sets out some of the

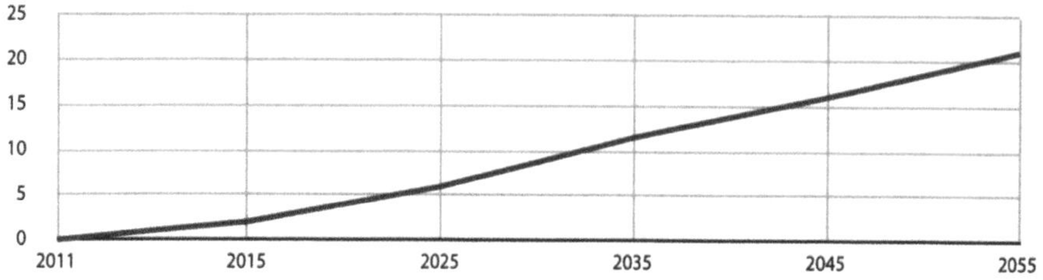

Fig. 2.1 Kurdistan Region cumulative oil production (billion barrels). Sources: Smith and Valentin (2009)

responsibilities of contractors in favour of the region. The KRG tried to connect oil contracts with services in Kurdistan. Based on this, the KRG guarantees 10% of royalties and around 15–80% share revenue from the contracts that would not be added to Kurdistan's budget because they would be subtracted from the budget by the Iraqi government. The KRG spent some of this money on infrastructure development, such as water projects, road construction, public schools and accommodation for family victims of Peshmarga and genocide.

The structure of the economy was built on oil and gas, which has become the major share of the KRG's revenue accounting for more than 85% of all fiscal revenues. This has left the KRG to face continuous revenue volatility and has brought about uncertainties and stagnation in the region. While the region, over the last few decades, has seen remarkable economic growth, a lack of economic diversification alongside mismanagement of the oil sector resulted in an inefficient and unstable economy. As described by Kolstad and Søreide (2009) such an economy lacks innovation and thus commercial enterprise is replaced by rent-seeking. There has been a severe economic condition in the region since the global oil shock and the cutting of its budget by Baghdad in 2014, poor governance and a large government sector without real attempts to diversify the economy. This condition has been troublesome for the region for almost a decade, especially macroeconomic performance indicators.

Years of de facto autonomy have relatively developed the region's economy, while it has been unable to survive from the dependency on Iraqi oil revenue. Figure 2.2 presents the amount of money the KRG received as a 17% share of the budget from Iraq, which increased from $1.4 billion to over $12.8 billion annually in the period 2005–2012. The economy has substantially grown from that period; the per capita economic growth increased to $7000 in 2013 from only $400 in 2002. There was a large expansion in the economy with 8% annual growth resulting in an economic boom; the size of the economy expanded from $3 billion in 2004 to $26.5 billion in 2013 (Sumer & Joseph, 2018).

The overdependence on oil and gas has made the KRG, similar to Iraq, have an excessive role in the economy. Even the method of spending the budget tends to be worse than its dependency. The imbalance between operational and capital expenses during 2005–2012 has created the major failures of the KRG. Around 70% of the budget is allocated for operational uses, while only 30% is specified for capital

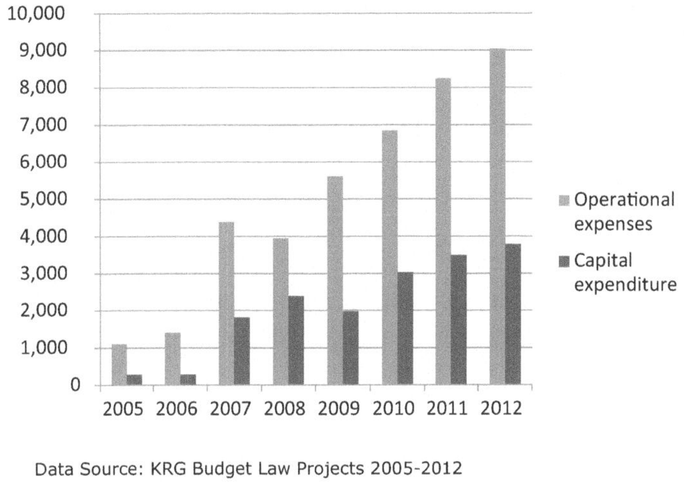

Fig. 2.2 KRG budget (2005–2012) in million US$. Data Source: KRG Budget Law Projects 2005–2012

investment. A large majority of the workforce is employed in the public sector accounting for 70% (Alavi & Ghafour, 2019) in which their salaries, pensions, social assistance and subsidies take 70% of the operational budget (The World Bank, 2016). This economy is essentially described as a classic 'payroll' economy, where the civil servants' wages drive almost all expenditure. Several services have been subsidised which were financially costly and resulted in a large deficit of the KRG's budget; fuel subsidy compared to the key component of the budget from 2010 to 2013 was 10.8% (Muhamad, 2022).

The mismanagement of natural resources and lack of financial capacity have made the KRG fall into difficulty in the time of global oil price shock. This condition with the cutting of its share from the Iraqi budget and the war against ISIS has deepened the economic downturn. Consequently, the KRG was unable to pay civil servants' salaries, finance the investment projects and thus experienced a massive budget deficit and reliance on others for recovery.

The KRG responded to the economic downturn by increasing oil exports, borrowing debt from local and external sources, and austerity policy to cut many of the finances. Even though this temporary strategy saved the KRG from a severe economic collapse, it showed the volatility of its economy and resulted in around $14.9 billion budget deficit (Fig. 2.3).

2.4.2.2 Economic Governance and Regulatory Framework

Generally, the weak institutions and underperformance of collective actions have provided less space for economic governance in the Kurdistan Region. Economic governance includes several collective actions carried out within institutions to

Fig. 2.3 The KRG budget deficit in billion IQD

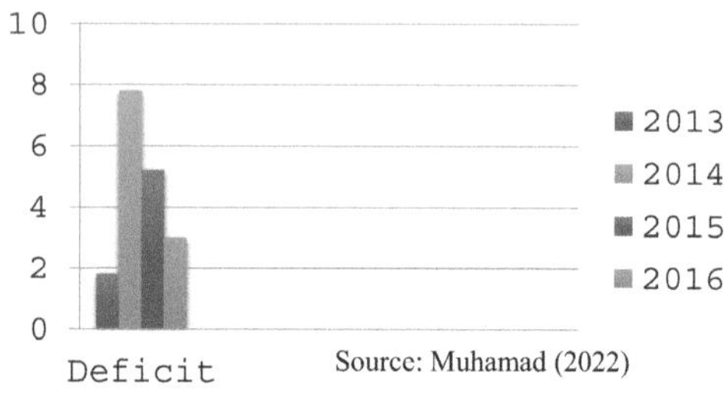

protect property rights, enforce contracts and provide infrastructure development aiming at improving economic performance in different conditions (Dixit, 2008).

How the region's economic governance has changed depends on the existence and effectiveness of institutions that make collective decisions about the economy. The region established modern state institutions, such as parliament and government in 1992, but its economy was established after the 2003 Iraqi invasion, where the region had the first budget law in 2005. However, the political condition of the region has made it difficult to run the economy. Several factors are causing damage to the economic governance of the region.

First, the Iraqi Constitution guarantees the right of the KRI to continue practising foreign policy to promote its economic, cultural and educational interests but there is no constitutional support for fiscal autonomy. This has been the major challenge for the KRG to practise different economic policies in favour of the region without the Iraqi government's jurisdiction. While the KRI has institutional power to issue various economic laws, it is limited to those that are not in conflict with the Iraqi laws. There is also a significant gap in the laws and regulations promoting economic governance of the region, such as intellectual property rights. However, the KRI, particularly its parliament, does not have the capability to resolve those economic and financial issues that might affect its fiscal independence.

Second, internal conflict between the KRG's ruling parties has made the economic governance of the region impossible. While the government has several specific organisations to take collective actions towards the economy, the region has long been divided into two economic and political areas, namely the Yellow Zone and the Green Zone. They refer to the KDP and PUK ruling areas, respectively, that have more power than the government. Each party has the power to scrap or implement any decisions. This has negative consequences on the development of those areas, equal opportunities and the economic governance of the region.

Another challenge to the economic governance of the region is political consideration in the way of doing business. The ruling parties have run almost all the leading private and profitable companies (Muhamad, 2022). While they have left little opportunities for others, they have had less commitment to improving the economic performance of the region. Furthermore, although several strategic plans for sectoral development and diversification have been provided, such as KRG Vision 2020, 2030, agricultural and industrial strategy development, tourism and other non-oil development, Abdullah and Gray (2022) found that economic diversification policy cannot be implemented in the region because the political elites see its consequences as a threat to their power.

2.4.2.3 Lack of Modern Economic Structure

The macro level of the KRI economy reports a lack of modern economic structure. The KRG has not been able to invest in the modern economic structure of the region to support fiscal independence. There are several factors behind the lack of modern economic structure, mainly structural issues, weak financial system, large informal economy and corruption.

The major structural issues of the KRI economy are low capital investment, poor productivity growth, severe structural unemployment, high dependency on imports, structural inequality, monopoly in the market, the unbalanced role of the private sector compared to the public sector and poor and traditional taxation system.

Capital investment is the expenditure of money to finance a country's development and long-term growth and objectives. The KRG capital expenditure as a share of the budget reported in Fig. 2.2 shows that 42% of the budget from 2005 to 2013 was spent on capital investment. This has largely contributed to the rebuilding and infrastructure development of the region. Since then, the war against ISIS, the drop in oil prices and suspending the KRG's share from the Iraqi budget caused the fall of this investment to zero points. Currently, while it is unknown how much is capital expenditure, low capital investment is a critical factor behind poor productivity growth, the next structural issue, thus causing severe structural unemployment.

The Middle East and North African countries (MENA) have recorded on average the lowest labour productivity rate of 0.3% compared to the rest of emerging and developing nations from 2013–2018 (The World Bank, 2020). The KRG has had poor post-conflict productivity growth in the region. The notion of labour productivity refers to the value of work from the region's workforce supply to the economy generated at the national level. While there is no figure to rely on, the productivity growth is driven by natural resource activities. Fatah and Pasławski (2023) study the determinants of labour productivity in the construction sector of the Kurdistan region and report 'Economic condition in the country' as a major factor. There are many critical explanations for poor productivity growth in the region, but wars, poor education system, traditional management, lack of skilled workers and political consideration towards the workforce sector are among the main reasons.

The continuous conflict and crisis in the region have brought several consequences, including structural unemployment and high-income inequality. From 1992 to 2003, the Kurdish civil war and the dual economic embargo on the region caused substantial damage to workforce development and offered no opportunities. Nevertheless, 2003 onward openness to the region was noted which has brought a range of opportunities (Khayyat & Muhamad, 2023). Noori (2012) reports inheritance inequality in the Kurdistan Region from 2004 to 2010 resulting from the economic and political system. However, public policies, nepotism, corruption and the traditional structure of the labour market contributed to the expansion of income inequalities and societal divisions.

Nonetheless, it seems to be very naïve to ignore the existence of corruption and lack of transparency within the recent economic development of the KRI. Despite some efforts the KRG made, corruption remains a significant risk to the development and economic independence of the region. Iraq, including the Kurdistan Region, scored low rank on Transparency International's Corruption Perception Index in 2023; it was 157th of 180 countries. Additionally, the informal economy and monopoly have made it difficult for the KRG to establish a modern economy to help towards economic sovereignty. Muhamad (2022) explained the growth of the informal economy and less contribution of the private sector to the economy of the region because of the existence of poor synergy between the public and private sectors. This is mainly because the ruling parties have run almost all the profitable sectors of the economy and have had less commitment to improving the economic performance of the region.

2.4.3 Opportunities to Strengthen Fiscal Autonomy

The indications are therefore that securing a diversified economy and downsizing the public sector are principal acts for strengthening the status of Kurds in the Kurdistan Region. The KRG must progressively act to build a secure economy to move ahead in planning for powering its fiscal autonomy. Thus, expanding opportunities for the private sector would enable the KRG to improve its economic performance. Sumer and Joseph (2018) who discuss the paradox of linking Kurdish independence to its economic collapse believe that economic reliance on neighbouring countries is against the KRG's model of state formation and suggest an establishment of economic autonomy. Abdullah and Gray (2022) who study internal political pressure on the Kurdistan Region's economic diversification suggest the leading role of the private sector in developing the region's economy while highlighting the challenges of the private sector in leading this diversification which is seen as a threat to the KRG's ruling parties' political power. Several other studies have suggested economic diversification to reduce natural resource dependency (Muhamad, 2023; Muhamad et al., 2020, 2021). We follow the latter studies to suggest a new model of the economy that strengthens the status of the KRG in improving economic performance as well as establishing fiscal autonomy.

The past years of the KRI are evidence that resource dependency and lack of economic diversification have negatively affected the status of the region and its economic development. As such, the KRG has limited options, but to apply a new economic model aiming at establishing an economic structure that is supported by diversification and a strong institution system. This diversification must contain several economic strategies, such as taxation, private sector development, agricultural development and economic governance.

2.4.3.1 Taxation System

Generally, the KRG, which generates revenues from natural resource rents, is unlikely to rely on taxes; the current contribution of taxes to the KRG's total revenue is 4.7%. However, establishing a tax system might lead to reduced natural resource revenue dependency, thus deriving long-lasting economic stability and strengthening the government's accountability. Muhamad (2023) identifies the determinants of taxation in 110 resource-rich countries, including Iraq which relies on privatisation, in other words, smaller public sector, the quality of institutions and tax capacity.

The KRG increasingly has begun to move away from a state-controlled economy to a market-oriented one. In these attempts, the KRG has privatised several government-owned industries, but monopoly power in profitable sectors has remained a topical economic and political issue. The lack of competition coupled with the lack of adequate economic regulations has made this transition fail. Therefore, this transition should be highly regulated and political parties are not allowed to engage in the process.

Furthermore, a weak level of institutions has been identified as one of the major causes of having a volatile economy in resource-rich countries. Muhamad et al. (2021) found that natural resource dependency reduction relies on the quality of institutions. It is, therefore, an opportunity for the KRG to strengthen the institutional structure so as to empower the tax capacity of the region. Muhamad (2023) reports a causal relationship between tax system and tax capacity; taxation is proportional to tax capacity, the more tax capacity the region builds, the higher the level of tax revenues it can collect.

2.4.3.2 Private Sector Development (PSD)

The KRG's economic diversification strategy must contain private sector development and entrepreneurship development. In fact, the KRG has long been engaged in private sector development, but political consideration has limited the contribution of the PSD to the KRI economy. Muhamad et al. (2020) investigated the determinants of PSD in resource-rich countries, including Iraq. Accordingly, the KRG must have a flexible tax regime that has both implications for the KRG's fiscal revenue and significant incentives for the effective engagement of the private sector. However, the KRG has several times undertaken the wrong tax policy resulting in adverse effects on the economy. For instance, during the very first recovery time from the COVID-19 effects, the KRG, unlike the global economy, increased taxation. This has devastating effects on the private sector resulting in several private companies leaving for other parts of Iraq that are offering more incentives.

Another factor to support the PSD is improving workforce skills and capabilities to support development. For the KRG, knowledge-based development at this stage would be much more supportive of the economy than the traditional economic engagement of physical labour and the production of raw materials. While the KRG had effective human development policies, such as attracting a reverse human capital flight during the economic boom of 2009–2013, the establishment of several English language teaching institutions and a substantial improvement in human resource development, the consequences of lack of equal opportunities, income inequality and political support to unqualified people have demotivated many and caused a critical brain drain. Therefore, the KRG is advised to further enhance human abilities by offering equal opportunities and enhancing positive relationships by suspending political consideration of unqualified people. This would affect the development of the private sector and its engagement in the economy.

A further factor to positively contribute to the private sector development in resource-rich countries is Foreign Direct Investment (FDI). Since the very beginning of its development, the KRG has attracted foreign enterprises and investment. In 2006 the KRG passed an investment law, one of the most liberal in the Middle East. Given the advantage of the law and outstanding security, multi-million investment projects in the region have been constructed. Since then, 1124 projects with a capital of $67 billion, including housing, tourism, manufacturing, banks, agriculture, health and education, have been established in the region. Whereas the largest investment comes from the national investment, foreign investment accounts for almost 18% with an investment of $12 billion mainly coming from the UAE, Turkey, Lebanon, United States, Germany and Saudi Arabia.

The period 2006–2012 investment in the region increased gradually by approximately 12.9% with a total capital of $21.8 billion marking Erbil fifth amid the top Middle East governorates for potential FDI by FDI Magazine, a subsidiary of *Financial Times*, in March 2011. Nonetheless, the 2014 consequences of the ISIS attack, global oil price shock, and cutting the KRG's share of the budget have dramatically damaged investment projects in the region.

Despite essential improvement in the business environment and high potential return, investment in the Kurdistan Region is challenging. The major challenges for foreign investors are security and lack of economic governance. Therefore, the KRG must continue attracting foreign investment through enhancing economic governance where competition, equal opportunities and protection of intellectual property are promoted. An investment strategy must be designed in response to the needs of the region where the new economic model for development is supported.

2.4.3.3 Agricultural Development

Another area for building fiscal autonomy in the Kurdistan Region is agricultural development. The region, similar to other resource-rich countries, has the ability and potential to successfully enhance small-scale agriculture development to overcome the high dependency on imports from the neighbouring countries, especially Turkey and Iran. Agriculture is the most important sector after oil, which has good revenue in the region. The region used to be a food basket for Iraq, but the series of conflicts and wars have destroyed its natural capacity. Before the oil dominance of resource revenue, the sector productivity provided around 27% of the Kurdish needs. This capacity, however, declined and currently contributes around 10% of the region's economy.

Nevertheless, to regain the capacity of becoming a basket of food for Iraq and the wider regions, the KRG has launched an initiative project to export several organic foods, such as pomegranates, potatoes, grapes, figs and honey, by supporting local farmers in increasing their agricultural productivity. While this is a good opportunity for expanding the agricultural sector and diversification of revenue, the focus must be on production for domestic use first. This would benefit the region in several ways, especially if it helps to reduce high reliance on imported foods.

Furthermore, the KRG must protect domestic production while promoting free trade. The KRG 2030 vision identifies the promotion of free trade as a way to diversify revenue. While free trade is globally promoted, theoretical and empirical evidence suggests that free trade is not of benefit to small economies because of dumping strategy by others. Therefore, the KRG must have policies to face the dumping strategy of the neighbouring countries. Such strategies have injured the KRI's domestic economy and largely affected its economic sovereignty. For instance, the incapacity to produce its food puts the region at a disadvantage when negotiating with the neighbouring countries that feed them (Natali, 2010).

Additionally, the domestic private sector is significantly weak and small due to the economic and political consequences of the region, the high dependency on imports and the crowding-out effects of the public sector. This condition necessitates an effective anti-dumping strategy for the region to support PSD, diversification and entrepreneurial spirit.

2.4.3.4 Economic Governance

Building economic governance requires the functioning of institutions which has been very challenging for the KRI. It is the major requirement of strengthening the status of the KRG, particularly, fiscal autonomy. Economic governance requires the application of law in all economic activities, economic integration across the region and institutionalisation of business activities. Although the Iraqi economic environment generates a range of challenges for the KRI, precise and direct instructions have not been followed. However, the most central challenge of economic governance in the Kurdistan Region has been the lack of institutionalisation. The KRI needs political cooperation to strengthen the economic governance of the region. The major agreement could be economic integration of the region and political stability.

Furthermore, the KRG must have a yearly budget law to improve transparency and better management of public finance. One of the main achievements of the KRG is cutting the size of the cyclical budget deficit which remains high due to financial inability. This prevents the continuous rise of the KRI national debt. However, the weakness of the KRG is that it is incapable of finding other sources of revenue. Having the annual budget law enables the KRG to better manage the source of revenues and spending, thus encouraging transparency.

On the operational yearly spending, a large budget spend on security accounts for almost half, and the civil servant drives almost the remaining expenditure. As such, there have been few public investment programmes and substantial imbalances in the budget. This has increasingly empowered military intervention in many aspects of governance, such as the judiciary system, businesses and the social life of people. Consequently, corruption, nepotism, inequality and rent-seeking are intimately intertwined and feed into one another as major constraints that hamper the effective functioning of the state institutions in KRI.

Despite the importance of oil and gas, two explanations principally benefit the Kurdistan Region in favour of empowering its status. First, foreign oil companies play a major role in the future of Kurdistan. The KRI has gained a reputation for signing contracts with good-quality oil companies. The KRG's contracts have had significant implications for Kurdistan's march towards economic autonomy. However, the recent Paris-based arbitration court decision in favour of Baghdad against Turkey and the Kurdistan Region might demotivate international oil companies investing in the region.

If one considers internal links, the KRI can benefit its economy by seeking non-oil revenue such as PSD, agricultural development, taxation system and improved labour productivity in the interests of the fiscal autonomy being built. In addition, it needs to prepare interregional forms of cooperation with Baghdad, particularly in terms of technical assistance and society to strike the tension between them.

Another opportunity for the KRG to build economic governance to strengthen financial capacity is the development of natural gas for domestic use. A decade after oil export in 2023, with an initiative to export natural gas in the future, the KRG expands the domestic gas pipelines network to provide more energy supply. However, this development must be for domestic use rather than export. The reason for this is that, while energy export put the KRG in a further complicated position, the global demand for oil and natural gas will gradually decline, especially within the European countries, due to its environmental implications and cost-effectiveness of alternative renewable energy (Timilsina, 2021; Zheng et al., 2019). Nevertheless, providing energy domestically across Iraq will strengthen the fiscal position of the KRG and enhance its economic governance within Iraq.

2.5 Conclusion and Policy Implication

This chapter reviewed the political economy of state formation in the post-conflict Kurdistan Region of Iraq considering the potential contribution of war and natural resources. The Kurds are clearly in a dilemma over how to establish a viable state. On the ground, Kurds made the decision towards secession in Iraq, but they were unsuccessful. Evidence suggests that the disputes and chronic conflicts between Iraqi governments and Kurds have prevented Iraq from achieving unity. Therefore, allowing the Kurds to remain within the Iraqi fragile state means a strengthening of the Kurds, a phobia that Iraq has been doing its best to tackle. The political development and the importance of natural resources have nonetheless evolved a radical change of the fate of Kurds from absolute statelessness to de facto independence in Iraq. As such, the solution to the disputes is the key that has to be considered regarding the tension of resource management, contested territories and power-sharing.

The KRI oil export has been halted since March 2023 and there is no progress to resumption. The major issue with this decision is that the KRG might not be allowed to resume oil export independently any longer. As such, the oil state formation model of the KRG has failed. This is mainly due to (1) the geopolitical condition and the way the KRG has managed oil extraction and exporting resulting in the political curse, and (2) the economic model of the region has not ensured the welfare of its citizens. Additionally, running the KRG into difficulties in financing its economy, inequality and institutionalised corruption, poor public service and institution system caused weakening of the region's stability and prosperity. Therefore, the KRG must turn these challenges into opportunities to strengthen the economic governance, institutions and fiscal capacity of the region. There are three priorities for the KRG. First, the KRG should in the short term focus on developing a detailed understanding of what it now owns and what the long-term prospects are for its oil industry. Second, the KRG should, unlike most rentier states, reduce its dependence on natural resources revenue through private sector development, national taxation system, agricultural development and economic governance to build a diversified economy. Third, it must make the best use of its revenues for development and strengthening fiscal capacity. These priorities tend to ensure fiscal security, which implies a political claim of legitimacy, since in the post-conflict state capacity, security and political legitimacy are very closely connected (Mittiga, 2022).

Kurds failed in building a model of oil state formation; building a rentier region with the overdependence on oil and gas has made the region highly vulnerable to political and fiscal shocks and hence running into difficulties in financing its economy. The mismanagement of natural resources has caused the region to experience highly organised corruption and rent-seeking and undermined the effectiveness of the sector in bringing fiscal autonomy to the region. Consequently, the region has become a dumping ground for imported products; its economy has been weak and inefficient, unable to pay its civil servants' salaries with having large budget deficits and owing billions of dollars to oil companies on one hand. On the other hand, the disbursement of the region's revenue for personal and political gain has increased the people's disloyalty towards the ruling parties and thus to the political system as a whole. Therefore, the KRG needs to make a radical change in its administration and resource management, in particular the cohesiveness of political institutions, potential development of transparency and investment in the institutional power of the government rather than political power.

The KRG has been successful in finding cooperation. Kurds have had a long political issue with Turkey, but economic cooperation has assisted, paving the way for resolving some political differences. The KRG is advised to apply a balanced strategy to build trust and relationship with Baghdad and an economic balance relationship with neighbouring countries, especially Iran to further strengthen its economy and sovereignty. If reliable access to the existing export network is not authorised, the KRG should build varied thriving forms of regional cross-border cooperation with neighbouring states to strengthen economic sovereignty.

Another significant strategy to support current agricultural initiative development and diversification and get rid of overdependence on imported products is to establish an effective anti-dumping strategy for the region. This will support the development of small-scale private sectors and domestic producers against unfair competition by traders, thereby strengthening the fiscal capacity of the KRG.

Thinking about exporting natural gas might bring many more challenges to the region. Despite the geopolitical conditions of the KRI, the demand for fossil fuel energy will gradually decline since many of the developed nations have a net zero emissions target policy. This will change the position of the KRG from a potential energy provider to a struggle with energy exporting. As such, the new model of the economy of the KRG must focus on empowering fiscal sovereignty by targeting its energy policy to domestic use, private sector development and the development of a national taxation system.

References

Abdullah, S., & Gray, T. (2022). Political constraints on economic diversification in the Kurdistan region of Iraq. *Energy Policy, 171*, 113274.

Acemoglu, D. (2015). Why nations fail? *The Pakistan Development Review, 54*(4), 301–312.

Afriyie, F. A., Jisong, J., & Yaw Appiah, K. (2020). Comprehensive analysis of South Sudan conflict: Determinants and repercussions. *Journal of Liberty and International Affairs, 6*(1), 33–47.

Alavi, H., & Ghafour, S. I. (2019). A study of challenges in entrepreneurship development and potential role of public sector in mitigating them–evidence from Kurdistan region of Iraq. *Multidisciplinary Aspects of Production Engineering, 2*(1), 589–599.

Anten, L., Briscoe, I., & Mezzera, M. (2022). *Political economy of state-building in situations of fragility and conflict: From analysis to strategy*. Clingendael Institute.

Auty, R. M. (2007). Natural resources, capital accumulation and the resource curse. *Ecological Economics, 61*(4), 627–634.

Baldwin, D. A. (2018). The concept of security. In *National and International Security* (pp. 41–62). Routledge.

Bengio, O. (2012). *The Kurds of Iraq: Building a state within a state*. London Lynne Rienner Publishers.

Börzel, T. A., & Risse, T. (2021). *Effective governance under anarchy: Institutions, legitimacy, and social trust in areas of limited statehood*. Cambridge University Press.

Dixit, A. K. (Ed.). (2008). *The new Palgrave dictionary of economics*. London Palgrave Macmillan.

Elbasani, A. (2020). State-building or state-capture? Institutional exports, local reception and hybridity of reforms in post-war. In *Kosovo international-led Statebuilding and local resistance* (pp. 1–16). Routledge.

Eregha, P. B., & Mesagan, E. P. (2020). Oil resources, deficit financing and per capita GDP growth in selected oil-rich African nations: A dynamic heterogeneous panel approach. *Resources Policy, 66*, 101615.

Fatah, R. H., & Pasławski, J. (2023). Factors affecting labor productivity on construction in Kurdistan of Iraq: Web survey. *Journal of Engineering, 29*(1), 14–41.

Galbraith, P. (2006). What went wrong? In B. O'Leary, J. McGarry, & K. Salih (Eds.), *The future of Kurdistan in Iraq*. University of Pennsylvania Press.
Greene, O. (2020). Human security, peacebuilding, and state-building in conflict-affected societies. *Journal of Human Security Studies, 9*(2), 15–24.
Gunter, M. M. (2011). Economic opportunities in Iraqi Kurdistan. *Middle East Policy, 18*(2), 102.
Hansen, B. (2011). *Ecowar: Natural resources and conflict*. BoD–Books on Demand.
Hiltermann, J. R. (2008). *The 1988 Anfal campaign in Iraqi Kurdistan*. Online Encyclopedia of Mass Violence.
Justino, P. (2022). *Wartime governance and state-building trajectories in post-conflict societies*. WIDER Working Paper.
Kameir, E. W. (2011). *The political economy of South Sudan: A scoping analytical study*. African Development Bank. Available online at http://www.afdb.org/fileadmin/uploads/afdb/Documents/Project-and-Operations/2011%20Political_Economy_South_Sudan_-_24_October_20111.pdf
Kaplan, M. L. (2020). Foreign support, miscalculation, and conflict escalation: Iraqi Kurdish self-determination in perspective. In *A century of Kurdish Politics* (pp. 29–45). Routledge.
Khayyat, N. T., & Muhamad, G. M. (2023). *Empirical studies of an internet and service based economy: The case of the Kurdistan region of*. Springer Nature.
Kolstad, I., & Søreide, T. (2009). Corruption in natural resource management: Implications for policy makers. *Resources Policy, 34*(4), 214–226.
KRG-MOMA. (2008). *The estimation of the damaged property in Anfal campaign*. Documentary Evidence. Ministry of Martyrs and Anfal Affairs-KRG.
Kukathas, C. (2008). *A definition of the state, conference presentation*. University of Wisconsin, Madison, March, 29.
McDowall, D. (2021). *A modern history of the Kurds*. Bloomsbury Publishing.
Milliken, J., & Krause, K. (2002). State failure, state collapse, and state reconstruction: Concepts, lessons and strategies. *Development & Change, 33*(5), 753.
Mittiga, R. (2022). Political legitimacy, authoritarianism, and climate change. *American Political Science Review, 116*(3), 998–1011.
Muhamad, G. M. (2022). Private sector development analysis in post-conflict Kurdistan region of Iraq. *UKH Journal of Social Sciences, 6*(2), 19–32.
Muhamad, G. M. (2023). *Reducing natural resource dependency for economic growth in resource rich countries*. Springer Nature.
Muhamad, G. M., & Heshmati, A. (2021). *Aid in the development of the Kurdistan region of Iraq*.
Muhamad, G. M., Heshmati, A., & Khayyat, N. T. (2020). The dynamics of private sector development in natural resource dependent countries. *Global Economic Review, 49*(4), 396–421.
Muhamad, G. M., Heshmati, A., & Khayyat, N. T. (2021). How to reduce the degree of dependency on natural resources? *Resources Policy, 72*, 102047.
Murtazashvili, J., & Murtazashvili, I. (2020). *Bottom-up state-building*. Springer.
Natali, D. (2010). *The Kurdish quasi-state: Development and dependency in post-Gulf War*. Syracuse University Press.
Noori, N. N. (2012). *Faces of economic inequality in the Iraqi Kurdistan (2004-2010): The role of regulation*. University of Exeter (United Kingdom).
Rodriguez, F., & Sachs, J. D. (1999). Why do resource-abundant economies grow more slowly? *Journal of Economic Growth, 4*, 277–303.
Sachs, J. D., & Warner, A. M. (2001). The curse of natural resources. *European Economic Review, 45*(4–6), 827–838.
Schwarz, R. (2008). The political economy of state-formation in the Arab Middle East: Rentier states, economic reform, and democratization. *Review of International Political Economy, 15*(4), 599–621.
Smith, R., & Valentin, G. (2009). *The oil &gas year: The who's who of the global energy industry: Kurdistan Region of Iraq*. Retrieved from France.

Sumer, F., & Joseph, J. (2018). The paradox of the Iraqi Kurdish referendum on independence: Contradictions and hopes for economic prosperity. *British Journal of Middle Eastern Studies, 45*(4), 574–588.

The World Bank. (2016). *The Kurdistan region of Iraq - Reforming the economy for shared prosperity and protecting the vulnerable* (106132). Retrieved from https://documents.worldbank.org/en/publication/documents-reports/documentdetail/672671468196766598/main-report

The World Bank. (2020). *Labor productivity in the Middle East and North Africa: Trends and drivers.* Retrieved from global economic prospects; Middle East and North Africa. https://thedocs.worldbank.org/en/doc/677761588268272641-0050022020/original/GlobalEconomicProspectsJanuary2020Box241.pdf

Timilsina, G. R. (2021). Are renewable energy technologies cost competitive for electricity generation? *Renewable Energy, 180*, 658–672.

Titumir, R. A. M. (2022). *State building and social policies in developing countries: The political economy of development*: Routledge.

Wang, H. (2023). 'Security is a prerequisite for development': Consensus-building toward a new top priority in the Chinese Communist Party. *Journal of Contemporary China, 32*(142), 525–539.

Wimmer, A. (2023). *Nation building: Why some countries come together while others fall apart Survival 60.4* (pp. 151–164). Routledge.

Zheng, J., Mi, Z., Coffman, D. M., Shan, Y., Guan, D., & Wang, S. (2019). The slowdown in China's carbon emissions growth in the new phase of economic development. *One Earth, 1*(2), 240–253.

Chapter 3
Charting the Course: Geopolitical Dynamics and Market Realities in the Iraqi Kurdistan Energy Sector

Bahrooz Jaafar Jabbar

Abstract The Iraqi–Kurdish conflict consisted of a series of wars and rebellions by the Kurds against the central authority of Iraq in the twentieth century. However, after the fall of Saddam Hussein's dictator regime in 2003, the new Iraqi constitution was adopted under the supervision of the US administration, and the Kurdistan Regional Government (KRG) was officially recognized. Later, the conflict turned into a dispute over oil and gas and an attempt to break the will of the Kurdistan Region of Iraq (KRI). As a result, the KRI's political economy of hydrocarbon has faced turbulence in recent years: the continual internal political divisions, the Iraqi federal government's inclination to keep KRI away from energy negotiation, regional pressure, and the decision made by the International Court of Arbitration (ICC) in Paris, and ruled in Baghdad's favor against the Kurdistan Region's independent crude oil exports through Turkey in March 2023. This study serves as a case study to investigate the KRI's energy position within the new geopolitical reverberations, such as those supposed to connect the Eastern Mediterranean Gas Project and the Gulf energy basin as a new emerging regional order. To this effect, the research assumed a more realistic approach to show how the regional powers' threats to the KRI's oil and gas fields and the KRI's energy sector require the support of superpowers such as the United States and Europe. Finally, this effort calls for the KRI's ruling parties to bring a new energy vision and activate institutions so that the global economic market looks exuberantly forward to the Kurdistan Region during the Russian–Ukrainian war.

Keywords Geopolitics · Oil and gas · Regional pressure · Kurdistan region of Iraq

---

B. J. Jabbar (✉)
Mediterranean Institute for Regional Studies, Sulaymaniyah, Iraq

G. M. Muhamad, N. T. Khayyat (eds.), *Resource Management Performance: A Sectoral Analysis in the Post-Conflict Kurdistan Region of Iraq*, Perspectives on Development in the Middle East and North Africa (MENA) Region,
https://doi.org/10.1007/978-981-97-7725-9_3

3.1 Introduction

Inflation and rising fuel prices, especially in Europe and the United States, are among the most significant consequences of the Russo-Ukrainian War that began on February 24, 2022. Achieving energy security at the global level remains a primary priority for all countries to maintain their stability and enhance their security, which creates a real challenge, especially in light of the growing demand for energy (oil and gas) in the first place, which is offset by a decline in supply due to the difference in energy strategies and policies adopted by countries. This has led to an escalation of competition between the major countries, whose policy priorities are the continuous and increasing flow of energy. Thus, today, the primary driver of conflicts has become closely linked to the "geopolitics of energy," and "energy" has become the fuel of many conflicts worldwide.

The Middle East and Eastern Mediterranean regions have increasingly garnered strategic importance from a Western perspective due to their location bridging Asia, Europe, and Africa. Notably, the Middle East serves a critical role in global energy markets by providing oil and natural gas, thus maintaining balance within the energy sector. In this context, the Kurdistan Region of Iraq (KRI) emerges as a significant player in the Middle East's hydrocarbon landscape. Analyzing its role in the exportation process from Iraq and the Kurdistan Region to Turkey and Mediterranean ports becomes imperative. Such analysis not only fosters economic and political connections but also shapes future dynamics in the region.

Moreover, adopting a political economy framework offers a more comprehensive understanding of the Kurdistan Region of Iraq's economic dynamics. This approach underscores the inseparable link between politics and economics, emphasizing that political factors play a central role in shaping economic outcomes. Consequently, economics significantly influences the functioning of political systems (Sorenson, 2010; Wiseman, 2024).

Although Kurds are without their autonomous nation-state, one can say without any fear of contradiction that Kurds remain the largest ethnic group territorially concentrated in the Middle East. However, the population of the KRI seems to be different since it has been striving to create its managerial trajectory to establish an independent political order for more than a century. The net effect of this action is that the Kurdish region in the north of Iraq is a high-ranking candidate when speculating about forming several new states in the Middle East. The visible events since Baghdad have lesser influence in the region, given that the Iraqi Kurds have established and empowered a government of their own, administration, armed forces, and a parliament that is independently pursuing their policies contrary to the will of their parent state (Jüde, 2017).

Kurdistan remains a semi-autonomous region of Iraq, with a proven 45 billion barrels of oil and a natural gas reserve of 200 trillion cubic feet (5.7 trillion cubic meters). This economic strength in terms of natural resources has motivated and triggered other states along the Mediterranean and Europe to rush into the formation of economic relationships (Ismael, 2018). During the Atlantic Council's Global

Energy Forum in Dubai in March 2022, the Prime Minister of the KRG Masrour Barzani announced that "We will become a net export of natural gas to Iraq, Turkey and Europe soon."

To this effect, a Kurdish–Turkish energy relationship exists between Europe and Russia. How have the natural resources of the KRI mentioned above acted as a motivation to the Eastern Mediterranean bloc? The KRI's energy capacity has the potential to transform geopolitics significantly. However, political divisions among the KRG's ruling parties and ongoing and long disputes between the KRG and the Iraqi government have complicated the process of realizing this possibility. Baghdad has also traditionally leveraged its energy sector control to secure concessions in political disputes critical to the Kurdistan Regional Government's (KRG) existence. Nevertheless, both Iraq and Iran realize that Iran's gas supplies are insufficient for Iraq's energy needs, which heightens the importance of Kurdish gas reserves and raises the imperative of a compromise (Alaaldin, 2023). The presence of the Kurdistan Region in the regional chessboard is required, like asking how can the Kurdistan Region demonstrate its willingness to form a strategic triangle with the Gulf Corporation Council and Turkey.

This chapter aims to inspect the KRI's oil and gas industry to determine its actual condition. Moreover, the study offers a new idea to see the KRI's hydrocarbon resources as a common ground in world affairs as realists and neorealists focus on the readiness of powerful countries as unitary players. Therefore, all actions can only uphold oil and natural gas when the powerful states push them. Threats on oil and gas resources, water resources, renewable energy, and electrification, for example, are assumed to be oriented and promoted by the most powerful states to administer some form of order in international systems. Therefore, the Kurdistan Region likely needs to be a part of the new regional and global order to maintain its energy security and promote the Kurdish entity. Consequently, this study recommends procedures that may help avoid disappointing outcomes for the KRI's oil and gas industry.

3.2 A Comprehensive Overview of the Kurdistan Region

The significant global shifts following the Cold War, coupled with the collapse of the Iraqi Baath Regime during the 1991 Second Gulf War, were pivotal moments leading to the establishment of the KRG. The oppressive policies of the Baath regime resulted in a surge of refugees, predominantly Kurds, drawing attention from international bodies such as the United Nations, as well as nations like the United States, France, and Britain. In response, the United Nations addressed the dire situation through Security Council Resolution 688 (Rogg & Rimscha, 2007). Meanwhile, Britain, the United States, and France implemented no-fly zones over the northern and southern regions of Iraq, conducting numerous flights totaling around 225,000 sorties between 1991 and 2003 (France withdrew in 1996).

The perpetual fighting between the Kurds and Iraqi forces did not stop until October 1991, when the Iraqi forces eventually left the Kurdish region. The region assumed an independent status, and after that, proclaimed a de facto autonomous power with the formation of a Kurdish Regional Government and a regional parliament in 1992. Therefore, the Kurdistan Region of Iraq is the territory located on the northeastern border of Iraq. However, per the 2005 constitution Iraq is legally known today as a federal region. The region is one of its kind, given that it is multi-ethnic and multi-religious, which is an attribute that distinguishes it from the other regions of Iraq.

The Kurdistan's economy was initiated as a result of this autonomous formation relying mainly on international aid and local resources (Muhamad & Heshmati, 2021). While changes have taken place, the region has experienced a partial transformation from reliant on foreign aid and agriculture to industry and services. Yet, the contemporary economy of the region is reliant on oil and gas and is highly dependent on neighboring countries (Muhamad, 2022).

Geographically, the KRI encompasses four governorates: Erbil, Sulaymaniyah, Duhok, and Halabja administered by the KRG. Notably, Article 140 of the Iraqi Constitution (2005) was established to address the contentious issue of disputed lands between the KRG and the federal government. These disputed areas lie within the provinces of Diyala, Kirkuk, Nineveh, and Saladin (Washington Kurdish Institute, 2021). Erbil, serving as the capital of the Kurdish Regional Government, holds historical significance as a key stop on the Silk Road and ranks among the oldest continuously inhabited cities globally. Moreover, due to its size and stability, Erbil has become a prominent hub for humanitarian organizations.

The Kurdistan Region of Iraq is four times the surface area of Lebanon and more extensive than the Netherlands. By the end of 2021, the KRG Ministry of Natural Resources (MNR) estimated the region's reserves at 45 billion barrels of oil and 25 trillion cubic feet (Tcf) of proven gas reserves, around 25 percent of Iraq's total. It also has up to 198 Tcf of unproven gas (Baram, 2022), which could make the region the world's eighth-largest oil reserve, had it been fully independent and internationally recognized (Ismael, 2020) (Fig. 3.1).

3.3 The KRI's Hydrocarbon Dynamics: Curbed or Geopoltical Shift?

The natural resources, specifically oil and gas, situated within the region's geographical confines have rendered the autonomous territory a focal point of interest for various countries in the Eastern Mediterranean, particularly Turkey and Greece, as well as Europe and the United States. Under the governance of the KRG, the region has experienced a degree of stability and tranquility not mirrored in Iraq's central government. Despite the political tumult within Iraq, the KRG has fostered economic and diplomatic ties with Turkey, Europe, the United States, China, and

Fig. 3.1 Administrative map of the Kurdish Region of Iraq (Mohammed et al., 2019)

numerous other nations across the globe. Turkey, in particular, exhibits a significant interest in Kurdistan's oil and gas resources, primarily to facilitate transit to Europe and address domestic scarcity. In 2013, Turkey solidified a historic 50-year pipeline agreement, granting Turkish Energy Company licenses for exploration across 12 blocks in the Kurdistan region. The subsequent operationalization of the pipeline, transporting Kurdish oil to Türkiye's Ceyhan port in 2014, has positioned the KRG as a substantial exporter of oil and gas to Turkey and the European market via the Ceyhan port in the Eastern Mediterranean (Alaaldin, 2023).

Azerbaijan has also emerged as a new supplier to Europe. It is drawing in Kurdistan to partake in the trans-Anatolian natural gas pipeline to reinforce the Shah-Deniz gas field pipeline, which was designed to transport natural gas to Southern European countries. The scarcity of energy supply and the quest to jettison Russia's monopoly in the European market are the biggest worry for Europe.

As a remedy to the aforementioned challenge, the European Union has initiated efforts to diversify both supplier countries and routes for natural gas, thereby highlighting the significance of Kurdistan for Southeastern Europe and the EU as a whole. Consequently, starting from 2007, prominent international oil and gas companies such as ExxonMobil, Genel Energy, Dana Gas, Total, British Petroleum, BOTAS, and Gazprom have forged economic agreements with the KRG for the exportation of oil and gas (Ismael, 2020). The strategic geographical position of a country can indeed prove advantageous, as evidenced by the case of the Kurdistan Region of Iraq.

The KRI faces a geographical challenge as it is landlocked without access to water bodies that could facilitate direct transport to major markets along or across the Mediterranean via sea routes. This situation raises questions regarding the strategy and role of the Kurdistan Regional Government in the oil and gas landscape. Importantly, Iraq has a history of one religious and ethnic community oppressing another, and since 2003, the state and its institutions have not functioned effectively. Consequently, Kurdish officials have viewed their oil and gas sector as a means to garner support from global and regional powers for their longstanding Kurdish aspirations and concerns (Paasche & Mansurbeg, 2014).

The Kurdistan region is the border with Iran to the east, currently being sanctioned by the international community; Syria to the west of the region under aggravated civil war since 2011 in a deeply divided society; and the south and southwest by Iraq, controlled by the centralized government in Baghdad which has constantly been in dispute over territory, degrees of autonomy the KRG has, its budget, and power as well as the quest to control the oil and gas reserves in the KRI. With this utterly landlocked territory, the greatest challenge of the KRG is the possibility of exporting oil to international markets. But with Iranian support, Baghdad is trying to keep the Kurdistan Region away from the energy issue. These factors arguably impede satisfactory agreement for the KRG over transport routes. As a result of the geopolitical mix-up, the KRG is left with one easy option, Turkey, in the north a viable and reliable partner for the export of KRG's natural resources (Alaaldin, 2023).

Again, we cannot set aside the fact that the Kurdistan Region is still officially part and parcel of the Republic of Iraq, which is trapped in a perpetual geopolitical power struggle of sectarian nature in the Middle East region spreading from Iran to Lebanon and Yemen. Therefore, this posed a problem in negotiating new alliances within this tense atmosphere and warranted the KRG to endeavor and demand consideration of rational nature. What sensible considerations can be put in place to minimize the above predicament to guarantee the smooth exportation of oil and gas by the KRG authority? The next paragraphs will address this question.

3.4 Exploring the Realities of KRI's Oil and Gas Industry

Article 117 of the Iraqi Constitution (2005) unequivocally recognizes "Kurdistan" as a federal region with an autonomous government. The Kurdistan Regional Government has official institutions, including ministries and a parliament. Policy-making responsibilities regarding water, health, education, and decision-making within the public sectors are shared between the Iraqi Federal Government and the KRG, with decentralization extending to the latter (Aresti, 2016).

Methodically, the oil and gas sector of the KRI has experienced remarkable development since 2003, having signed approximately 60 production-sharing contracts with international oil companies. Numerous factors have been put forth to explain the allure of the Kurdistan oil and gas sector for these international entities

(Heshmati & Auzer, 2018). Notably, there has been a steady increase in oil production, with projections indicating exports of 430,000 barrels per day by 2021 (Rudaw, 2021).

Contrary to the instability in Iraq, the maintenance of relative peace and security in the Kurdistan Region has permitted the regional government to embark on oil sector developmental projects and the leasing of land to international and local companies for exploration. According to the production sharing contract (PSC), the host state gives a specific area or field to the oil companies, and the government does not assume any financial risk initially. Once the company can extract oil and the wells are commercially helpful, the host state or government determines its shares, property, taxes, and production costs. Conversely, if the oil company cannot discover enough oil to be commercially viable, it will take all the responsibility and leave (Heshmati & Auzer, 2018).

The oil and gas sector of the KRI has grabbed significant political and strategic attention in recent years. The long turmoil in Iraq allowed the KRG to take advantage of oil and gas activities. Consequently, the KRG used the sector in the development of the region. The region's information technology, housing, electricity, healthcare, water supply, and education are being developed mainly because of the oil and gas industry. However, the business activities of the sector caused an increase in internal political conflict, lack of transparency, corruption, and social injustice simultaneously. This condition caused economic instability in the region and possessed a serious barrier for private businesses (Kuruüzüm, 2022; Muhamad, 2022).

As Auzer (2017) discussed, the main hydrocarbon basins of Iraq are located in the Zagros fold belt in the Kurdistan Region, the Widyan Basin interior platform (western desert), and Mesopotamia Fore deep (central and southern Iraq). Zagros and Taurus fold belts (see Fig. 3.2) harbor the resources of the Kurdistan region, i.e., about 45 billion barrels of oil reserves, which could place the region among the tenth wealthiest countries in terms of oil and gas reserves, if the region was an independent country (Auzer, 2017; Sherwani & Ahmad, 2023).

The crude oil production capacity in the Kurdish Regional Government (KRG) areas exceeded 500,000 barrels per day in December 2015, based on monthly averages. However, this capacity saw a significant decline on October 16, 2017, following the Iraqi military's invasion and capture of the Kirkuk oil fields, which had been under KRG control since the outbreak of the Islamic State in Iraq and Syria in 2014.

Subsquentially, one of the main problems started when Britain and France divided the legacy of the Ottoman Empire in the region after WWI based on oil and natural resources. However, Turkey is still involved in the matter of Kurdistan and Kirkuk's oil, in addition to the fact that the ISIS blew up the Kirkuk-Ceyhan oil pipeline in 2014. Since then, the Kirkuk oil has been transported to Turkey's Ceyhan port through the Kurdistan pipeline, and from there, buyers transport it to the global market.

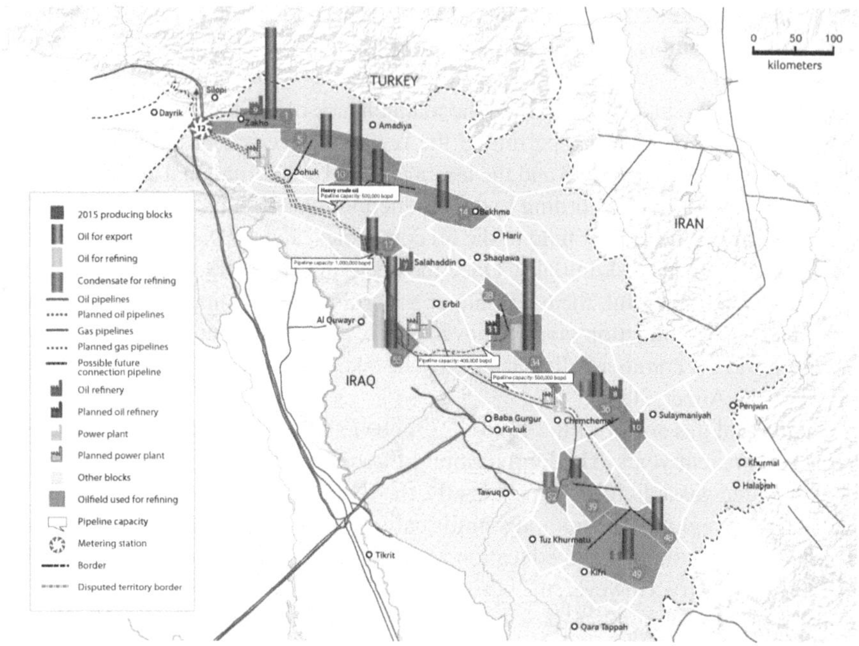

Fig. 3.2 Structural domain of the Kurdistan Region's oil and gas resources (Ministry of Natural Resources, 2013)

3.4.1 Categorizing Kurdistan Region's Oil and Gas Fields

There are several methods to categorize the oil and gas fields in the KRI, which can depend on their current operational status, whether they are actively producing or still in the development phase. Additionally, the quantity of production and reserves can be used as criteria for classification. Furthermore, fields can be grouped based on the certainty level of their reserves, resources, and activities. Some fields may have more certainty regarding their reserves than others. Consequently, efforts have been made to classify the fields using these criteria, ensuring a comprehensive approach to their categorization.

There are 52 oil blocks in the Kurdistan Region, and currently, only 9 are in production; 8 of the leading oil production blocks are in Erbil province. To this effect, the KRI's oil and gas blocks will be classified as follows.

3.4.1.1 Major Fields

The major fields are considered the largest significant oil and gas reserves, and there is some certainty about their future.

Tawke and Peshkabir Fields

Tawke oil field is located in Duhok province. The Tawke field produced about 109,000 barrels of oil daily in July 2017. However, its output has steadily declined, reaching 88,000 in April 2018 and 80,000 in October 2018. At the end of 2011, DNO (Norwegian oil and gas firm) put 13 wells in this field into production, and they continue to effectively contribute about 20% of the KRI's total oil production. Additionally, the field's operator is a transparent corporation (DNO) that frequently discloses and updates information about its reserves and output (Wali & Jaafar, 2019). Peshkabir is located in the western part of the Tawke PSC; the gross production at the Tawke and Peshkabir license averaged 107,090 bopd in 2022. In the Q2 of 2023, there was no production due to the closed KRI's export pipeline.

Khurmala Field

Khurmala Dom is the northern section of the Kirkuk field and is located 35 km southwest of Erbil, the capital of the KRI. The field is one of the other main oil fields in the KRI in Erbil Province. It has been under the control of the Kurdistan Regional Government since 2007. The KAR Group, a Kurdistan-based oil services company, operates the field. Transparency and access to data in this company are complex and almost locked. According to Wood Mackenzie Report, processing capacity at the field is 200,000 b/d following an expansion in 2018. Oil is delivered to the Erbil refinery and the export terminal at Ceyhan via Kurdistan (Mackenzie, 2023).

Shaikan Field

This is also one of the largest oil discoveries in the Kurdistan Region of Iraq and has been in production since July 2013. As of March 2023, Gulf Keystone Petroleum and MOL Hungarian Oil and Gas are the operators of the Shaikan Field, situated around 60 km to the northwest of Erbil, the largest city in the Kurdistan Region of Iraq, covering an area of 280 km^2. In December 2018, the field produced 32,000 bpd, and in Q1 of 2023, increased the average production to 55,000 bpd, with gross average production increasing by 40% between 2018 and 2022 (Gulf Keystone Petroleum, 2023).

Khor Mor Field

It is the largest nonassociated gas field in Iraq, administratively located in the Sulaymaniyah province, southwest of Chemchemal district and the epicenter of the Qadir Karam sub-district. In 2007, Dana Gas and Crescent Petroleum (UAE energy service firm) signed a contract with the KRG for the exclusive rights to assess, develop, produce, market, and sell hydrocarbons from the Khor Mor and Chemchemal fields in the KRI. This agreement gave rise to Kurdistan's gas project. Khor Mor supplies Chemchemal and Hawler electric power plants with natural gas. Its daily gas production until August 2018 was about 305 Mcf and 13,000 bpd condensate (Wali & Jaafar, 2019). In Q1 of 2023, Dana Gas announced the production average increased to 500 Mcf, aiming to reach 600 Mcf per day in 2024 (Dana Gas, 2023).

As tensions in Iraq escalate, attacks on the Kurdistan Region's oil and gas fields become an expected topic; Khor Mor has suffered from rocket and drone attacks by the Iraqi Shiite Militia due to the field's close geographic connection, which was struck three times in 2022 and 2023 (Alaaldin, 2023).

Atrush Oil Field
Atrush oil field is one of the leading new KRI oil fields, located near Duhok province and 85 km northwest Erbil; production started in 2017, operated by the Atrush production sharing license which was previously owned by Abu Dhabi National Energy Company—TAQA (39.9%), KRG (25%), ShaMaran Petroleum (20.1%), and Marathon Oil (15%). In July 2017, the field produced around 27,000 bpd (Wali & Jaafar, 2019). According to a report by ShaMaran Petroleum Corp (2023), the gross average production of approximately 66.8 Mbopd in Q1 of 2023 resulted in an increase in oil sales to $43.4 million, which was 12% more than in Q1 of 2022.

3.4.1.2 Mid-Sized and Less-Productive Fields

Apart from the main influential oil and gas fields, several other oil blocks are under the control of the KRI, which are considered mid-sized, less-productive but promising fields.

Firstly, the Taq Taq license area has a tedious story compared to other KRI fields. The block has a relatively long production history, and it is operated by Genel Energy and started producing in 2006, reaching a record high of roughly 140,000 bpd in 2015. The Taq Taq licensing area is 120 km northwest of the Sulaimaniyah province, 60 km northeast of the Kirkuk oil field, and 85 km southeast of Erbil. The Taq Taq licensed area has a gross size of about 951 square kilometers. According to the company's report, the field has been experiencing geological problems for years. Therefore, the production level has decreased remarkably, averaging 3610 bopd in Q1 of 2023 (Genel Energy, 2023).

Chia Surkh is one of the oldest oil wells in the Middle East, located in the village of Chia Surkha in Garmian. The field was discovered and operated in 1901 by the Anglo-Iranian Oil Company. The Chia Surkh oil field is operated by Petoil Turkish company, consistently producing 2000–3000 bpd between 2020 and 2022; the company halted its operation in the Chia Surkh on Aug 1, 2023, due to the decision of the International Court of Arbitration in Paris to stop the KRI's oil export. Petoil is the first oil company to enter the Kurdistan Region of Iraq. In January 2003, Petoil signed a PSA with the KRG, covering a large area, which was subsequently reduced to the current Shakal Block (Petoil, 2023).

The north of Kalar Bawanoor, Sarqala, and Shekh Tawil subdistricts is covered by a Garmian block close to 1780 square kilometers with an estimated oil of about 33 million barrels and 24 bcm or 847 billion cubic feet (bcf) of gas. Gazprom Neft is the operator of this block with a 40% stake, Western Zagros Ltd. with 40%, and the KRG back-in interest (B.I.) 20% thoroughly carried. Repsol (Talisman) has 40%

of this block, and Western Zagros B.I. has 40% and 20% wholly carried to the KRG (Salih & Yamulki, 2020).

Furthermore, several additional fields could receive funding and development to reach the point of production in the upcoming years. Relatively abundant reserves of some of these fields, installed infrastructures, and the upward trend of oil prices may reinforce these fields' future. Among those fields, Kurdamire possesses appropriate contingent petroleum resources of 366 million barrels of oil and 1.8 tcf of natural gas.

Chemchemal is another promising field with proved and probable condensate reserves of 119 million and 6.6 tcf of natural gas, and Miran with contingent oil resources of 23 million and 6.6 tcf of natural gas. In addition, Bina Bawi also possesses a contingent oil resource of 37 million and 8.2 tcf of natural gas besides Benenan, with proven and probable oil reserves of 57 million77. If these fields are brought to adequate production level, they may ramp up overall KRI oil production to around 500,000 bpd and 1.5 bcf of gas (Wali & Jaafar, 2019).

Lastly, Erbil block, which is located in the western part of the KRI, covers the northwest of Erbil and the Bastora area. This block is 313 square kilometers with an estimated one billion oil barrels (Salih & Yamulki, 2020). Conflict over hydrocarbon may sometime emanate depending on the differences in the characteristics of the resource in question. High-value resources like oil and gas in the KRI, which are not renewable, are primarily located in an area geographically limited. Hence, the location with types of resources is vulnerable to conflicts (Muhamad, 2023; Muhamad et al., 2021).

3.5 When Energy Is Surrounded by Regional Threats: The Superpower Must Intervene

In line with systematic approaches in international relations literature, particularly the "neorealist theory," which suggests that threats primarily originate from external sources and underscores the anarchic nature of the international system characterized by interests and power struggles. Iraq and the Kurdistan Region find themselves amidst regional transformations, with the "gas and oil" issue acting as a pivotal catalyst (Belser, 2021; Niakoee & Pirmohammadi, 2020). Consequently, Kurds must actively engage in navigating their political and economic challenges by strategically positioning themselves on the regional chessboard. The petroleum industry entails not only stages such as contracting, exploration, extraction, and refining but also encompasses critical phases like establishing export routes (in the realm of energy geopolitics), engaging in lobbying efforts, researching the global economic landscape, managing public relations, and understanding the political ramifications of these processes. Moreover, a pertinent question arises regarding the sustainability of their political economy beyond the oil and gas era.

One of the key assumptions in this academic endeavor of the study is that the Iraqi Kurdistan Region will become a regional player through natural gas and oil and then enter the global energy map. While Kurds still lack an independent political state, they have had autonomous regions and benefited from active foreign relations and diplomacy at state levels.

Generally, there are two sensitive issues in the Middle East. The first is the issue of combating violence and terrorism, the solution to which is to improve coexistence and combat terrorism. The second is related to issues with oil and natural gas. While the Kurdistan Region has been marked safe specifically for other religious and ethnic communities such as Yazidis, Christians, Turkmen, Arabs, and Shabaks, terrorism remains a persistent threat to the region since the upcoming of Islamic State of Iraq and Syria (ISIS) in 2014.

In terms of energy, the Kurdistan Region will export 45,000 barrels of oil per day in 2022 through the Kurdistan-Ceyhan Turkish Pipeline in the Mediterranean Sea and then to global markets. When the world was suffering from a natural gas crisis in early 2023, the KRI's gas production set a new record; the gas production exceeded 500 million cubic feet per day, with plans to reach 1 billion cubic feet per day in 2025.

The KRG's energy sector, on the other hand, faces significant challenges. As pro-Iranian groups have dominated the Iraqi government, economic, and military sectors since the fall of Saddam Hussein in 2003, the Iraqi government has opposed the Kurdistan Region's oil processes from the outset, claiming that "Kurdistan oil is being sold to Israel" and that "the Kurdistan Region is a position for Israel and the US to attack Iran from.". In reality, Iraq and Iran want to keep the Kurds out of the energy debate (Salih, 2022). As a result, from 2007 to 2023, the KRG oil has been sold in global markets at a lower price. This is mainly to attract buyers, while oil importers and buyers continue to be hesitant to purchase oil from the KRG (Wahab, 2023).

Iran has a cultural, military, political, and economic hegemony in Iraq. Iran does not want to develop an alternative energy source to supply oil and gas in the region (Salih, 2022). This made Iran to act aggressively against the Kurdistan Region exporting sector; the KRI's energy fields, the Kurdish oil and gas business leaders, and the general energy infrastructure have been subjected to missile attacks by Iraqi Shiite militia forces and recently by the Irani government itself.

Iran generally considers Iraq as its hegemonic zone, but Turkey and the UAE are actively involved, and the US administration supports them. Nevertheless, Iran has put pressure on KRI's energy sector in various ways. The Federal Supreme Court in Baghdad ruled on February 15, 2022, that "the KRG's Oil and Gas Law is unconstitutional, citing Articles 110, 111, 112, 115, 121, and 130 of the 2005 Iraqi Constitution." Whil this decision put the KRI's autonomy in danger, it has implications for the the region's economic prosperity (Smeekens & Keil, 2022). However, there have been controversies about the legitimacy of the Federal Supreme Court and its composition since the decision was made. The Iraqi constitution outlines how the Federal Supreme Court should be established. According to Section 2 of Article 92, the Court is formed by the decision of two-thirds of the members of parliament. Article 87 also confirms the impartiality of the members of the judiciary and the courts in general. Therefore, the decision of the Federal Supreme Court was seen as politically motivated and biased against Kurds.

This condition in Iraq can be explained with the application of neorealism theory on power. Accordingly, the reality of power relations is a prominent factor in international relations. Structural realism or "neorealism" is an approach to international relations that confirms the role of "power politics" in international relations, views conflict and competition as the two main characteristics, and believes that cooperation has limited possibilities. Kenneth Waltz, the father of the Neorealism School, believes that "competition" and "conflict" are the core of international relations (Waltz, 1993).

The distribution of power among countries and the existing anarchic state of international relations literature are considered two main pillars of international politics, namely, offensive realism and defensive realism. In these two types, the reality of the regional and international systems is anarchy since each country is struggling to gain more economic, political, military, and diplomatic power. Ultimately it will be the reason for embodying "security and stability." Therefore, the principle of this international chaos must be decentralized, which means all the power should not be gathered in one center or in one specific point. The reality of offensive realism insists that the state must gain power and create this chaos to impose its dominance through power and provide security. Nevertheless, defensive realism confirms that this anarchy structure should encourage the state to protect the balance of power and security more softly (Behravesh, 2010).

3.5.1 The KRI's Mandate to Stay Resilient: What Happens When Heating a Piece of Iron?

Spanning across the sovereign states of Turkey, Iran, Iraq, and Syria, Kurds represent the most significant ethnic minority in the Middle East. Kurds have benefited from changes in the Middle East over the last decades. The downfall of Saddam Hussein positioned them as primary beneficiaries in Iraq, and the collapse of Syria facilitated the establishment of an autonomous region for them. Despite their political differences, there is an existence of a growing sentiment of solidarity among Kurds, characterized by the sharing of moral, material, and human resources across Turkey, Iraq, Iran, and Syria. Their political aspirations are deeply intertwined across these nations (Akbarzadeh et al., 2020; Dudlak, 2024).

Following World War I, South Kurdistan (Northern Iraq) was incorporated into Iraqi territory, forming the modern Iraqi state. From 1921 to 2022, the Kurdish population in the region were engaged in persistent conflict and warfare with successive Iraqi governments. In 1975, Saddam Hussein's regime in Iraq signed the Algiers Agreement with Iran, ostensibly to quell the Kurdish armed revolution. In a brutal campaign known as the Anfal process in 1988, Saddam Hussein's regime perpetrated mass killings, claiming the lives of over 200,000 Kurds and decimating their villages.

After the Cold War ended, the global atmosphere became more open under the leadership of the United States, and this led to another Kurdish uprising against the Iraqi Ba'athist regime in 1991. Later, the United States, Britain, and France established no-fly zones for northern Iraq. On April 5, 1991, the UN Security Council adopted Resolution 688, which states in its preamble: the Council bears full responsibility for ensuring world peace and security and expresses concern about the repression of the Iraqi people.

During the outbreak of the Arab Spring in 2011, the regime of Bashar al-Assad in Syria lost control of its territory. Therefore, the Kurds in Syria were able to establish an autonomous entity that benefited from having military forces and various political and cultural institutions with the support of the United States and its allies. Later, in 2014, when the ISIS was formed and became a threat to global and regional security, the Kurds in Iraq and Syria became the leading force in the fight against terrorism in the region (Frappi, 2016; Mohammed & Alrebh, 2020).

Thus, the issue of energy and the fight against terrorism has advanced the Kurdish issue in the international community. Of course, Iran has significant interests with a strong presence in Iraq and will not allow the Kurdistan Region's natural gas to replace the Iranian gas in the region. As an influential regional power, Turkey needs oil and natural gas to meet its domestic needs. Without its signature, it will not allow the Kurdistan Region or West Kurdistan (Northern Syria) to reach the Mediterranean basin for energy.

In short, the birth and growth of the KRGs stemmed from the regional change consequences; the KRG's weakening and disappearance would also be due to global change. Likewise, the shape can be changed when a hot iron is beaten with a hammer; after the fall of Saddam Hussein in 2003, the Kurds were strong in Iraq, and the Iraqi government did not have an oil and gas law. However, when the Kurdish position in Iraq weakened in 2023, Baghdad took steps to intensify its efforts to pass an Iraqi oil and gas law.

3.5.2 How Can There Be a Turning Point in Kurdistan's Energy Geopolitics?

The leadership of the KRG has made use of this regional autonomy by having opted for choices that have set its oil industry on a very different path from that of Baghdad's government. Although the KRG was constitutionally recognized in 2005, Baghdad insisted that all production and oil exploitation contracts must be structured in partnership with the federal government. The KRG refuted this position and proceeded to sign more than 50 contracts with international oil companies (IOCs) from 2006 to 2013, and all were considered illegal by Baghdad. This aggressive economic behavior from Baghdad encouraged the KRI population to believe that the time of an independent Kurdistan was drawing near. Due to this antagonism between the KRG and Baghdad over absolute control of hydrocarbon, the KRI saw this as an opportunity, quickly reinforcing its historical trajectory and gathering more aspirations for self-determination (Fendi et al., 2020; Klich, 2012).

This relation has appeared to fuel and foster the Iraqi Kurds' economic autonomy. The stability of the region has attracted foreign investors and private enterprises. Turkish businesses are being invested in the autonomous Kurdish Region of Iraq, which has developed into a thriving trade relationship, with US$12 billion in the KRG–Turkey trade in 2011. To this effect, the Turkish trade with Syria, Lebanon, and Jordan was lesser than the trade with the KRI in 2010, becoming a center of the KRG's economic future and a more significant opportunity for potential independence (Dargin, 2007).

The KRG has and is in control of its security force and military and maintains border crossings, and among other things, the KRI has the power to enact legislation on issues where the federal laws of Iraq are silent. However, Mills (2016) believes that the KRI's hydrocarbon resources act as a motivation contributing efficaciously to the visible potential independence of the KRI in several ways. Firstly, the existence of the KRI autonomous power—born from a conflict that was arguably triggered by the abundant hydrocarbon resources in the KRI—has now given the KRG the right to enter into, sign, and approve oil and gas contracts with influential international companies. This encouraged many oil and gas companies to shift from Baghdad to the KRI. An obvious example is when American independent oil firm Hess was prohibited from getting the most recent licensing from Iraq when it signed a production sharing contract (PSC) with the KRG.

The KRG has used its autonomous power to put in place favorable exploration terms to firms, pushing some firms, including ExxonMobil and Total, to shift their allegiances toward the KRG (Gray, 2012). The KRG has gained some support in developing their oil and gas reserves from Europe and the United States in trying to counterweight Russian gas. Nonetheless, Russia has no control on oil and gas being exported to Europe from the Middle East countries (Stern, 2003).

Russia is the source from which the vast majority of European natural gas is being piped. In trying to jettison this effect, the European Union and the United States are planning to establish a pipeline that, if realized, will transport Kurdish gas directly to European markets. This project will increase interdependency between Iraqi Kurdistan and the European Union while waiving any control from Baghdad. The Kurdish will then gain an outlet for their natural gas that will no longer be transported through the Kirkuk-Ceyhan pipeline (often controlled by Iraq) to Turkey. This will limit Baghdad's ability to undercount its exports and withhold its gas revenues, which may give the KRG more aspirations for potential independence (Mills, 2016).

On the other hand, within the context of the Iraq–Kurdish conflict, controlling the hydrocarbon-rich area means controlling the political and economic power. Therefore, the control over oil flow was never limited to financial gain because it is also an indication of influence over political power and the control of the land. The oil reserves under the control of the KRG have been the main driving force behind the diplomatic and military efforts of the KRI. This explains why, after the fall of Saddam Hussein's regime, Kirkuk's oil became a point of contention between the Iraqi government and the KRG. If the KRG had control over the oil reserves in the KRI, it would have a powerful economic and political tool to pursue Kurdish autonomy and eventual independence.

Caspersen (2013) has propagated five characteristics for a territory to be considered a de facto state: The territory must be in control of the majority of its claimed territory; external and internal legitimacy must be increased by building state institutions; a clear demonstration of the aspiration for independence or a formal declaration of independence; the territory is still void of international recognition; and the territory must have existed for at least 2 years.

In general, the issue of Kurdistan's natural gas, both as an opportunity for further support to the Kurdistan Region and as a geopolitical turning point, includes the following points: First, gas is a more critical turning point than oil. Despite several political events from 2011 to 2022, the energy issue in the Kurdistan Region has proven to be multidimensional and very complex. For the Kurds, the oil and gas issue has always been viewed not only as an energy or financial source but also from many other perspectives.

Secondly, will the significant changes affect the historical situation of the Kurds? This requires an understanding of two essential stages. The first is the Kurdistan Region's reliance on its agreement with Turkey, signed in early November 2013 and known locally as the 50-year agreement. The second stage is the war against ISIS. While the target of the war against ISIS was to weaken or even destroy the Kurds, finally, it strengthened the Kurds. On the other hand, the Kurdistan independence referendum in 2017, which was supposed to strengthen the Kurds, had yet to have the outcome they wanted finally. These two political events have a direct impact on the situation of the Kurdistan Regional Government and the possibility of change. As a result, the changes in the KRG are an overall process and do not just involve the existence or construction of the energy sector.

Third, we can proclaim, "Welcome to the gas era!" The Russian–Ukrainian war in 2022 has brought more energy geopolitics to the forefront and complicated the condition. The European Union no longer sees Russia as a reliable partner in natural gas after the Ukraine war. As such, it is the KRG's intention to offer energy supply to Europe.

Fourth, regional powers see the development of the Kurdistan gas sector as part of strengthening the Kurdistan Regional Government. The United States supports the Kurdistan Region's energy sector. For example, the Kor Mor field, one of the KRI's major gas fields, which has 4.3 trillion cubic feet of approved gas, produces about 2000 megawatts of electricity for the Kurdistan Region through three power plants. The United States financed earlier development of the field by allocating $250 million. Additionally, when the Iraqi Federal Court on February 15, 2022, declared the oil contracts and processes in the Kurdistan Region as unconstitutional and blacklisted some oil companies operating in the area. The US administration has repeatedly called for a solution to this problem through official and diplomatic means. While the lack of institutions in the Kurdistan Region and continued internal divisions have complicated the status, the United States has reaffirmed its defense of the Kurdistan Region (Jaafar, 2022).

Fifth, the Kurdistan Region is under military, security, and geopolitical pressure from Iran and the Iraqi Shiite militia. Iran does not want Kurdistan's natural gas to be treated as a substitute for Iranian energy since that would strengthen Israel. Russia also opposes exporting energy from the Kurdistan Region to avoid the Mediterranean block. However, the intention of the KRG to export gas to Europe has been reconfirmed by the KRG deputy Prime minister Qubad Talabani subject to resolving the KRG's legal issues with Baghdad (Rudaw, 2022).

Ultimately, the Kurdistan Region of Iraq has owned an oil pipeline built at the end of 2013; Rosneft holds a 60% stake in the pipeline, while KAR Group, an Iraqi Kurdistan-based company, holds the remaining 40%. The concession period is 20 years with an option to extend for 5 years. The pipeline has a designed oil transport capacity of about 950,000 bpd and a length of about 420 km. The KRG's intention and potential to develop the energy sector need further infrastructure development. As such, these conditions must be established and reorganized for the new KRG's energy vision.

3.5.3 Iraq and the Kurdistan Region: The Epicenter of the New Silk Road to the Mediterranean

The discovery and extraction of natural gas in offshore Cyprus, Israel, Lebanon, and Syria since 2010 has had significant geopolitical consequences. As a result, several energy giants have entered the Eastern Mediterranean region to leverage the natural gas discovery. These include Noble Energy, ExxonMobil, British Petroleum (BP), French Total, Italian Eni, Israeli Delek Drilling, and German DEA. Over the past 11 years, these companies have invested heavily in terms of technical, financial, and diplomatic resources to pursue their interests in the region. The construction of a 1900 km underwater pipeline network costing approximately $7 billion is a major undertaking in a sensitive geographical area (Chondrogiannos, 2022).

Therefore, since 2010, the Eastern Mediterranean gas project has been viewed as an alternative to Russian natural gas in Europe or at least reduces Europe's dependence on Russian energy. Also, the event has turned Israel from an importer of natural gas to an energy exporter. Furthermore, these changes encouraged other regional powers and countries to move forward in the region. For instance, the UAE, although not geographically linked to the Eastern Mediterranean, has joined as a member of the East Mediterranean Gas Forum (EMGF) and Israel has sold a 22% stake in the Tamar gas field to the UAE's Mubadala Petroleum for 1.2$ billion. While Turkey is an influential regional power in the eastern Mediterranean and the Middle East, on the one hand, it requires a lot of oil and natural gas to meet its domestic needs. On the other hand, it desires to pass energy pipelines in the region through its territory. Nevertheless, Turkey has rejected joining the eastern Mediterranean gas project due to stubborn policies toward Greece, Cyprus, Israel, Egypt, and Syria in the last decade.

Iraq, and the Kurdistan region, is the epicenter of a new Silk Road to the Mediterranean. However, it is cumbersome to derogate from the fact that, even though Turkey has complex energy relations with Iraq, it has always been at the forefront of playing a crucial role in the oil and gas development in KRI. Traditionally, the critical aspect of Turkey as a territory in transit of oil from federal Iraq to the Mediterranean is also critical. It goes with the recent affirmation that while Turkish investors play an enormous role in developing hydrocarbon resources in the KRI, federal Iraq is witnessing Turkish companies constantly seeking significant commercial opportunities in Bagdad (Roberts, 2018). Encouraged by the fact that Northern Iraq is a landlocked territory, its oil transportation has always been successful through transnational pipelines to the coast of the Mediterranean, where it was accessible to the European market.

The production and transportation of Iraq's oil through pipelines via Syria to Europe were controlled by a consortium of British, French, American, and Dutch oil companies under what was known as the Iraq Petroleum Company (IPC) from 1929 to 1972. The IPC pipelines closed in 1976. This has allowed Turkey to develop and stretch its economic tentacles to Iraq in general and the KRI in particular (Honigman, 2022; Yilmaz, 2023).

Hydrocarbon resource transactions through the two pipeline projects are not limited to oil and gas. However, a political and economic influence embedded in the energy deal with the KRG is also highly considered. Turkey had to ensure an adequate and permanent energy supply to meet an increase in demand coupled with a fast expansion of its economy. In addition to the fact that Russia and Iran were the only source of Turkey's power generation, the Syrian crisis also acted as a rift between Turkey, Russia, and Iran. This connection allowed the Turkish economy to be trapped by the region's dynamics and price shocks. To remedy these predicaments and decrease its dependency on Iran and Russia, Turkey needed to scramble in search of alternative energy resources. Turkey had no choice but to urgently resolve its Kurdish problem and capitalize on the openings in KRI to cultivate energy ties with the KRG (Tol, 2014).

The Kirkuk-Ceyhan Pipeline (Fig. 3.3), the largest pipeline for transporting crude oil, was operated successfully until 1990, before the outbreak of political turmoil in Iraq. While negotiations were going on for constructing a new pipeline between Kirkuk and Turkey, ISIS interrupted the pipeline and rendered it nonoperational. As such, Turkey bypassed Iraq and established a new economic relationship with the KRG in 2013, which led to the construction of a new pipeline from Khurmala to the Turkish border (Bowlus, 2017).

The Khurmala-Ceyhan Pipeline, with an initial capacity of handling 450,000 bpd, was later increased to 700,000 bpd in 2015. The KRG consolidated control over all of the major oilfields in the north, including Bai Hassan and Avana domes, even with the invasion of ISIS in 2014. This pipeline has permitted the KRI oil and gas transportation from KRI directly to Turkey without any influence from Baghdad, thereby setting up the KRG as a competitive supplier of crude oil to Turkey. This

Fig. 3.3 The Kirkuk-Ceyhan oil pipeline (Panagiotis & Georgia, 2013)

action angered Baghdad, and it immediately responded by filing a request for arbitration against Ankara to the International Commercial Arbitration (ICC) in Paris because Ankara had given Kurds an independent pipeline. According to Baghdad, Ankara has violated the Iraq–Turkish pipeline agreement that was agreed upon in 1973 and updated in 1976, 1985, and 2010 (Knights, 2019).

The KRG reported exports of 400,000 barrels per day, with an increased capacity of up to 1 million barrels in 2018. This has expanded infrastructural development in the KRI with outflows that could rise to 1.5 million. However, Baghdad desires to have control over the revenue and has demanded the distribution of the proceeds according to an agreement with Erbil, which has been reached after the fall of Saddam Hussein's regime in 2003. Baghdad fears that if the arbitral award is rendered in favor of Turkey, the KRI could achieve energy autonomy and eventually seek political independence (Kraemer, 2019).

The new 2013 oil pipeline, masterminded by Turkey, was born from the fact that KRG was prompted to formulate its hydrocarbon law in 2007 after a successive failure of Baghdad and Erbil to reach an agreement on a unified hydrocarbon law. The 2007 KRG's hydrocarbon law completely changed the strategy of the major international oil companies, altered Kurdish aspirations for autonomy, and changed the landscape for transporting oil from northern Iraq. To this effect, ExxonMobil, Total, Gazprom Neft, Chevron, and TAQA signed production sharing contracts for exploratory blocks in the KRI from 2011 to 2012, transporting oil directly from the KRI without Baghdad's involvement (Bowlus, 2017).

Turkey's successful crude oil relationship with KRG is due to Turkey's strategic role as an energy-transit country. Three reasons are accountable for this successful relationship. First, Turkey's security can perpetually guard a pipeline such that even if opposing groups like the Kurdistan Workers' Party (PKK) were to damage the pipeline, repairs could be made expediently, and pipelines could restart in a matter of days. Secondly, in addition to the fact that Turkey has the largest military in the Middle East, it is willing to employ force when its interests are threatened. Again, the growing economy of Turkey has made the country eager to secure its demand for oil and gas. Lastly, Turkey can avoid the vicissitudes of intra-Arab politics that have plagued previous transnational pipelines in the region, given that Turkey is a non-Arab country. Therefore, the problem may be interpreted as an internal conflict between Baghdad and Erbil. However, Ankara is an essential factor that can either stabilize or spoil this affair (Natali, 2013).

3.6 Conclusion and Policy Recommendation

This study delved into the energy position of the KRI as a case study within the new geopolitical reverberations. The investigation extended to analyze the current and future opportunities of the KRG in relation to the energy sector. The Kurdistan Region, with its proven reserves of 45 billion barrels of oil and 200 trillion cubic feet of natural gas, has attracted significant political and strategic attention in recent years. This natural resource economy has motivated and triggered other states along the Mediterranean and Europe to rush into the formation of economic relationships.

Despite the political turmoil within Iraq, the KRG has managed to establish economic and diplomatic ties with Turkey, Europe, the United States, China, and numerous other nations across the globe. The subsequent operationalization of the pipeline, transporting Kurdish oil to Turkey's Ceyhan port in 2014, has positioned the KRG as a substantial exporter of oil and gas to Turkey and the European market via the Ceyhan port in the Eastern Mediterranean.

The energy sector in the Kurdistan Region faces several significant challenges, including (a) Political consideration: Iran's influence in Iraq poses a threat to Kurdistan's oil and gas sector. The Iraqi Federal Court has declared the entire oil operation in the Kurdistan Region of Iraq (KRI) illegal. (b) Geographical consideration: The KRI is landlocked without access to water bodies, which makes it difficult to transport oil and gas to major markets. (c) Governance issues: Despite efforts to address the issues of transparency, corruption, and mismanagement, they continue to plague the energy sector, resulting in division among the Kurdish elites. (d) Internal Kurdish relationships: The relationship between the major ruling political parties in the Kurdistan Region has deteriorated, leading to economic and political instability. (e) Disagreements over resource dynamics: There is critical domestic disagreement between the KDP and PUK regarding plans to export KRI's natural gas overseas. These issues alongside the long-lasting dispute between the KRI and Iraqi government may cause oil companies to leave the Kurdistan Region.

Despite these challenges, Kurdistan's oil and gas have the potential to be an alternative for the East Mediterranean gas project and replace Russia's energy to the West. However, political, economic, and social stability in the Kurdistan Region cannot be achieved without internal reforms. Therefore, (1) the KDP and PUK must work together to formulate a new energy vision and manifest to maintain KRI's national security. Iraq and the Kurdistan Region are facing significant political and economic challenges due to regional changes. To navigate these challenges, (2)

Kurds need to actively engage and strategically position themselves on the regional chessboard. The Kurdistan Region is geographically complex, sharing borders with Iran to the east and Syria to the west. The former is currently under international sanctions, and the latter has been engulfed in a civil war since 2011. As a result, (3) the KRG must resolve disagreements on oil and gas with Baghdad at any cost. Alternatively, (4) they can consider Turkey as a viable and reliable partner for exporting natural resources from the region's north. With the Russian–Ukrainian war bringing energy geopolitics to the forefront, the European Union no longer considers Russia a reliable partner. Hence, (5) the KRG can take advantage of this opportunity and reframe its energy vision by supplying gas to Europe through pipelines. This could be a turning point for Kurdistan's energy geopolitics, but it requires domestic unity and the backing of superpowers like the United States, Europe, and the Mediterranean block. Finally, it is highly recommended that (6) the KRG promotes necessary actions to strengthen transparency and reduce environmental impacts on air, water, soil, and ecosystems to make the oil and gas industry sustainable.

References

Akbarzadeh, S., Laoutides, C., Gourlay, W., & Shahab Ahmed, Z. (2020). The Iranian Kurds' transnational links: Impacts on mobilization and political ambitions. *Ethnic and Racial Studies, 43*(12), 2275–2294.

Alaaldin, R. (2023). *The geopolitics of Iraqi Kurdistan's gas reserves: Challenges and prospects*. Retrieved from https://mecouncil.org/publication/the-geopolitics-of-iraqi-kurdistans-gas-reserves-challenges-and-prospects/

Aresti, M. L. (2016). Oil and gas revenue sharing in Iraq. *Natural Resource Governance Institute*, 1–24.

Auzer, K. A. (2017). *Institutional design and capacity to enhance effective governance of oil and gas wealth: The case of Kurdistan region*. Springer.

Baram, A. (2022). *Iraq at a crossroads: Kurdish energy competition with Iran*. Retrieved from https://www.gisreportsonline.com/r/kurdish-energy-competition-iran/

Behravesh, M. (2010). *Realism and Neorealism: An investigative overview*. Retrieved from https://www.e-ir.info/2010/12/19/realism-and-neorealism-an-investigative-overview/

Belser, E. M. (2021). *A failure of state transformation rather than a failure of federalism? The case of Iraq federalism as a tool of conflict resolution* (pp. 55–73). Routledge.

Bowlus, J. V. (2017). A crude marriage: Iraq, Turkey, and the Kirkuk–Ceyhan oil pipeline. *Middle Eastern Studies, 53*(5), 724–746.

Caspersen, N. (2013). *Unrecognized states: The struggle for sovereignty in the modern international system*. Wiley.

Chondrogiannos, T. (2022). *The climate hypocrisy behind the East-Med pipeline*. Retrieved from https://www.investigate-europe.eu/en/2022/the-climate-hypocrisy-behind-the-eastmed-pipeline/

Dana Gas. (2023). *Dana Gas announces increase in Kurdistan Region production* [Press release]. Retrieved from https://www.danagas.com/media/press-releases/

Dargin, J. (2007). Hydrocarbon development in the Iraqi Kurdistan region petroleum sector. *Energy Exploration & Exploitation, 25*(2), 139–149.

Dudlak, T. (2024). Perspectives on Kurdish international relations: Cross-border Kurdish agency between Turkey and Iraqi Kurdistan. *Asian Journal of Middle Eastern and Islamic Studies, 18*, 1–14.

Fendi, P. A., Basir, S. M., Findi, H. A., & Rahman, H. O. (2020). The right to self-determination of Kurds in Iraq; perspectives international law. *International Journal of Psychosocial Rehabilitation, 24*(05), 2384.

Frappi, C. (2016). *The energy factor: Oil and state-building in Iraqi-Kurdistan* (pp. 91–121). Kurdistan. An Invisible Nation. Milano.

Genel Energy. (2023). *Taq Taq*. Retrieved from https://genelenergy.com/operations/production/taq-taq/

Gray, C. W. (2012). *Petrocapitalism in Iraqi Kurdistan: Leveraging oil and Gas firms in post-war Iraq*. (Bachelor of Arts). Claremont McKenna College. https://scholarship.claremont.edu/cmc_theses/337/. Retrieved from https://scholarship.claremont.edu/cmc_theses/337/

Gulf Keystone Petroleum, G. (2023). *Shaikan—a giant, long-life field with a proven track record of low-cost production and significant growth potential*. Retrieved from https://www.gulfkeystone.com/operations/

Heshmati, A., & Auzer, K. (2018). The role of natural resources in Kurdistan regional government's economic development. *UKH Journal of Social Sciences, 2*(1), 1–14.

Honigman, J. (2022). Never mind betrayal. *Journal of Strategic Security, 15*(1), 54–74.

Ismael, H. (2018). *The geopolitical challenge of Iraqi-Kurdistan's natural gas*.

Ismael, H. (2020). Kurdistan's role in European energy security. *Journal of Geography, Politics and Society, 10*(1), 33–41.

Jaafar, B. (2022). *A perspective in order to protect energy security in the Kurdistan Region*. Retrieved from https://www.mirs.co/KU/details.aspx?jimare=242: https://www.mirs.co/KU/details.aspx?jimare=242

Jüde, J. (2017). Contesting borders? The formation of Iraqi Kurdistan's de facto state. *International Affairs, 93*(4), 847–863.

Klich, S. (2012). Dependent yet defiant: The implications of unilateralism in Iraqi Kurdistan. *The ANU Undergraduate Research Journal, 5*, 68–72.

Knights, M. (2019). *Iraq-Turkey pipeline arbitration: Avoiding a policy train wreck*. Retrieved from https://www.washingtoninstitute.org/policy-analysis/iraq-turkey-pipeline-arbitration-avoiding-policy-train-wreck: https://www.washingtoninstitute.org/policy-analysis/iraq-turkey-pipeline-arbitration-avoiding-policy-train-wreck

Kraemer, R. (2019). *The Iraq-Turkey pipeline dispute: Opportunity in an arbitration*. Retrieved from https://www.justsecurity.org/65893/the-iraq-turkey-pipeline-dispute-opportunity-in-an-arbitration/

Kuruüzüm, U. (2022). *Iraqi Kurdistan as a capitalist frontier building from scrap: War, recycling, and labor in Iraqi Kurdistan* (pp. 29–68). Springer.

Mackenzie, W. (2023). *Khurmala Dome*. Retrieved from https://www.woodmac.com/reports/upstream-oil-and-gas-khurmala-dome-11916490/: https://www.woodmac.com/reports/upstream-oil-and-gas-khurmala-dome-11916490/

Mills, R. (2016). *Under the mountains–Kurdish oil and regional politics*. Oxford Institute for Energy Studies.

Ministry of Natural Resources, M. (2013). *The Raod to 1 Million Barrels per Day*. https://archive.gov.krd/mnr/mnr.krg.org/index.php/en/the-road-to-1-million-barrels.html: Ministry of Natural Resources, KRG Retrieved from https://archive.gov.krd/mnr/mnr.krg.org/index.php/en/the-road-to-1-million-barrels.html.

Mohammed, J., & Alrebh, A. (2020). Iraqi Kurds: The dream of nation state. *Digest of Middle East Studies, 29*(2), 215–229.

Mohammed, H., Jaff, D., & Schrock, S. (2019). The challenges impeding traffic safety improvements in the Kurdistan region of Iraq. *Transportation Research Interdisciplinary Perspectives, 2*, 100029.

Muhamad, G. M. (2022). Private sector development analysis in post-conflict Kurdistan region of Iraq. *UKH Journal of Social Sciences, 6*(2), 19–32.
Muhamad, G. M. (2023). *Reducing natural resource dependency for economic growth in resource rich countries*. Springer Nature.
Muhamad, G. M., & Heshmati, A. (2021). *Aid in the development of the Kurdistan region of Iraq*.
Muhamad, G. M., Heshmati, A., & Khayyat, N. T. (2021). How to reduce the degree of dependency on natural resources? *Resources Policy, 72*, 102047.
Natali, D. (2013). The Kurdistan region of Iraq: Stabilizer or spoiler? *Georgetown Journal of International Affairs*, 71–79.
Niakoee, A., & Pirmohammadi, S. (2020). Iraq's fragile state and intervention of regional and trans-regional powers (2011-2018). *Iranian Research Letter of International Politics, 8*(1), 191–216.
Paasche, T. F., & Mansurbeg, H. (2014). Kurdistan Regional Government–Turkish energy relations: A complex partnership. *Eurasian Geography and Economics, 55*(2), 111–132.
Panagiotis, S. I., & Georgia, P. (2013). Transportation of energy resources in the Middle East and Central Asia. *International Journal of Energy Economics and Policy, 3*(4), 127–139.
Petoil. (2023). Kurdistan Region of Iraq. Retrieved from https://www.petoil.com.tr/en/briefhistory.html
Roberts, J. M. (2018). Turkey and the Kurdistan region of Iraq: Strained Energy relations. *Turkish Policy Quarterly, 17*(3), 99–109.
Rogg, I., & Rimscha, H. (2007). The Kurds as parties to and victims of conflicts in Iraq. *International Review of the Red Cross, 89*(868), 823–842.
Rudaw. (2021). *SOMO: The Kurdistan Region exports 430,000 barrels and the 2021 budget obliges it to deliver 250,000*. Retrieved from https://www.rudawarabia.net/arabic/kurdistan/020120218
Rudaw. (2022). *Deputy PM Talabani addresses Erbil-Baghdad issues at Greece economic forum*. Retrieved from https://www.rudaw.net/english/kurdistan/090420221
Salih, D. (2022). *IRGC: View of the relationship with Kurdistan Region*. Retrieved from https://epc.ae/en/details/featured/irgc-view-of-the-relationship-with-kurdistan-region
Salih, R. S., & Yamulki, A. (2020). Reforms feasibility in Kurdistan Region petroleum contracts, triggered by the new regional blocks divisions. *International Journal of Business Social Science, 11*(5), 35–56.
ShaMaran Petroleum Corp. (2023). *Shamaran reports strong first quarter results*. Retrieved from https://shamaranpetroleum.com/news/shamaran-reports-strong-first-quarter-results-122840/: https://shamaranpetroleum.com/news/shamaran-reports-strong-first-quarter-results-122840/
Sherwani, H., & Ahmad, W. (2023). An exploratory study of economic factors that hinder economic development of Kurdistan region. *International Journal of Social Sciences & Educational Studies, 10*(1).
Smeekens, D., & Keil, S. (2022). *The Iraqi oil and gas dispute between Baghdad and Erbil*. IFF Working Paper Online No 31.
Sorenson, D. S. (2010). *Interpreting the Middle East: Essential themes*. Westview Press.
Stern, J. (2003). Natural gas in Europe– The importance of Russia. *Centrex Europe Energy & Gas AG*. http://www.centrex.at/en/files/study_stern_e.pdf, 24, 2014.
Tol, G. (2014). Untangling the Turkey-KRG energy partnership: Looking beyond economic drivers. *Global Turkey in Europe II*, 69.
Wahab, B. (2023). *Tipping point of the Iraq-KRG energy dispute*. Retrieved from https://www.washingtoninstitute.org/policy-analysis/tipping-point-iraq-krg-energy-dispute
Wali, H. H., & Jaafar, B. (2019). *Stubborn Kurdish Petroleum Resources: Surveying Actual data and investigating the declared Numbers*. Retrieved from https://www.mirs.co/details.aspx?jimare=137: https://www.mirs.co/details.aspx?jimare=137
Waltz, K. N. (1993). The emerging structure of international politics. *International Security, 18*(2), 44–79.
Washington Kurdish Institute, W. (Producer). (2021, 15/3/2024). Kirkuk and Its Arabization; Historical Background and Ongoing Issues in the Disputed Territories. Retrieved from https://

dckurd.org/wp-content/uploads/2021/04/Kirkuk-and-Its-Arabization-Historical-Background-and-Ongoing-Issues-in-the-Disputed-Territories.pdf.

Wiseman, H. (2024). Political systems: Some sociological approaches.

Yilmaz, A. (2023). *Kurdistan-Iraq and Turkey between diplomacy and non-diplomacy: Foreign relations of Kurdistan-Iraq and Palestine* (pp. 239–262). Springer.

Chapter 4
The Interplay Between Resource Wealth and Tax Revenue: Implications for Fiscal Policy and Institutional Development in the Kurdistan Region

Mohsen Khezri

Abstract This chapter comprehensively reviews the empirical and theoretical literature on the relationship between natural resource revenues and non-resource tax performance. It systematically examines how reliance on natural resources influences fiscal outcomes, highlighting the adverse effects on non-resource tax revenues in the context of the "resource curse." This review explores the fiscal substitution effect, where high-resource incomes lead governments to deprioritize other tax efforts. It discusses how resource abundance fosters a political environment undermining tax policy efficiency and governmental accountability. The role of institutional quality in mediating these relationships is critically analyzed, demonstrating that strong governance can counterbalance the negative impacts of resource dependence by enhancing tax revenue mobilization and supporting sustainable fiscal practices. The chapter draws on diverse case studies and statistical evidence to outline the economic and political dynamics at play, offering insights into how volatility in resource incomes can destabilize fiscal systems. Finally, it provides policy recommendations for resource-rich nations including the Kurdistan Region of Iraq (KRI). It suggests that enhancing institutional frameworks and implementing comprehensive tax reforms are essential for stabilizing economic growth and fostering more significant social equity.

Keywords Natural resource management · Institutional quality · non-resource revenue · Kurdistan Region of Iraq

M. Khezri (✉)
Department of Geography and Environment, London School of Economics and Political Science (LSE), London, UK

Department of Business and Management, School of Management and Economics, University of Kurdistan Hewlêr, Erbil, Iraq
e-mail: m.khezri@lse.ac.uk

G. M. Muhamad, N. T. Khayyat (eds.), *Resource Management Performance: A Sectoral Analysis in the Post-Conflict Kurdistan Region of Iraq*, Perspectives on Development in the Middle East and North Africa (MENA) Region,
https://doi.org/10.1007/978-981-97-7725-9_4

4.1 Introduction

Some studies have investigated the positive effects of non-resource income on countries' economic growth and development (Melina & Poplawski-Ribeiro, 2020; Odhiambo & Olushola, 2018). These studies highlight how diversifying income sources beyond natural resources can lead to more stable and sustainable economic growth. Melina and Poplawski-Ribeiro (2020) examine the macroeconomic impacts of non-resource revenue mobilization in the Central African Economic and Monetary Community (CEMAC). Their findings suggest that shifting the focus from resource-based revenues to non-resource income, such as taxes and other forms of government revenue, can lead to enhanced fiscal stability and reduced vulnerability to global commodity price shocks. This shift stabilizes the economy and provides a more predictable revenue stream, allowing for better long-term economic planning and investment in public goods and services, which are crucial for sustainable development. Odhiambo and Olushola (2018) explore the relationship between taxation and economic growth in Nigeria, a resource-rich country heavily dependent on oil revenues. They argue that relying excessively on resource income can lead to economic volatility and growth instability. Their study demonstrates that effective taxation policies and broader tax bases can mitigate these issues by providing a more consistent and reliable revenue source. This, in turn, enables better infrastructure, education, and healthcare funding, which are essential for fostering economic development and improving living standards. These findings underscore the importance of developing robust non-resource revenue streams to promote economic resilience and sustained growth, particularly in resource-rich countries often subject to volatile commodity markets.

By focusing on diversified revenue sources, countries can achieve a more balanced and inclusive economic growth trajectory, reducing their dependence on fluctuating resource incomes and enhancing their overall economic stability and development. Therefore, investigating the factors influencing the increase of such non-resource revenues is essential for countries rich in alternative natural resources. However, the relationship between natural resources and non-resource revenues such as taxes lacks theoretical and empirical consensus. According to some studies, revenue from natural resources can lead to increased non-resource revenues through specific mechanisms, while other studies show a negative relationship between the two. Smith (2004) argues that oil-rich countries invest windfall resource revenues in building government institutions such as tax administrations to maximize their revenues. This argument hinges on the idea that resource wealth provides the financial means for governments to strengthen their fiscal apparatus, which can enhance the efficiency and effectiveness of tax collection. As governments invest in developing tax departments in the resource sector, positive tax management can be created in other sectors of the economy, leading to higher tax revenues (Knebelmann, 2017). This is supported by the concept that a well-functioning tax administration can spill over into non-resource sectors by improving overall compliance and reducing evasion. Abdelwahed (2020) concludes that enormous oil discoveries result in a temporary boost in tax collection, which results from greater efforts on income and foreign trade taxes. This suggests that during periods of high-resource revenue, governments might be more motivated or have more resources to enforce tax compliance, leading to higher non-resource revenues. However, this effect is often temporary and may not lead to sustained improvements in tax collection over the long term.

On the contrary, most of the existing studies emphasize the negative role of natural resources in non-resource revenues. There is a big body of literature that shows that dependence on natural resources results in weak tax revenue performance (Abdelwahed, 2020; Bornhorst et al., 2009; Crivelli & Gupta, 2014; Keller, 2022; Mawejje, 2019). These findings underscore the complex and multifaceted relationship between natural resource and non-resource revenues. While resource wealth can provide opportunities for strengthening tax administration, it also poses significant risks of fostering fiscal complacency and dependency on volatile resource markets.

This chapter meticulously peruses the empirical and theoretical corpus on the nexus between natural resource revenues and non-resource tax performance. It methodically probes how dependence on natural resources sways fiscal outcomes, accentuating the deleterious repercussions on non-resource tax revenues within the framework of the "resource curse." The discourse scrutinizes various modalities through which reliance on natural resources can impair tax collection initiatives and debilitate broader fiscal structures. By analyzing an array of case studies and cross-national evaluations, the manuscript illuminates the intricate nature of the resource curse, underlining its manifestation in disparate economic, political, and institutional milieus. The exposition further delves into the role of governance, institutional caliber, and policy interventions in ameliorating the adverse fiscal ramifications associated with natural resource wealth. Additionally, the chapter evaluates the interconnection between natural resource revenues and non-resource tax policies, exploring how governmental reliance on resource-derived income can engender complacency in the cultivation of robust and diversified tax frameworks. It reflects on the consequences for enduring economic stability and sustainable development, notably in resource-abundant developing nations.

4.2 Resource Incomes and Non-resource Tax Revenue Relationship

Theoretically, there are several reasons for the negative relationship between resource incomes and non-resource tax revenues. James (2015) presented a theoretical model showing that government revenues from natural resources were used for public spending, future consumption, and/or reducing non-resource tax revenues, lowering non-resource tax rates, and implementing generous tax exemptions by resource-rich countries. This is often referred to as the fiscal substitution effect, where increased resource revenues lead governments to reduce efforts in collecting other forms of taxes. Additionally, abundant resource revenues can create a political environment where leaders feel less accountable to taxpayers, resulting in less efficient tax policies and administration (Knack, 2009). Besides, literature on resource abundance shows that a sudden increase in incomes from natural resources leads to a decrease in entrepreneurial activities and investments (Bjorvatn & Selvik, 2008; Papyrakis & Gerlagh, 2006; Torvik, 2002), which means lowering the tax base. This phenomenon is part of the broader "resource curse" theory, which suggests that resource-rich countries often experience slower economic growth than resource-poor ones. The influx of resource wealth can lead to rent-seeking behavior, where individuals and businesses focus on obtaining a share of the resource wealth rather than engaging in productive economic activities (Torvik, 2002). This shift can crowd out other sectors of the economy, particularly manufacturing and services, leading to a less diversified economic base and reducing the overall taxable income from non-resource sectors (Mehlum et al., 2006).

Furthermore, the volatility of resource prices can lead to fiscal instability. Governments that rely heavily on resource revenues may face significant budget shortfalls during periods of low-resource prices, which can force sudden and severe cuts in public spending or abrupt increases in non-resource taxes (James, 2015). Fiscal instability can deter long-term investments and strategic economic planning, thereby reducing the overall tax base (Papyrakis & Gerlagh, 2006). Conversely, resource-abundant nations that effectively manage their resource wealth through mechanisms like sovereign wealth funds can mitigate these adverse impacts by stabilizing resource income over time and ensuring fiscal stability (Mehlum et al., 2006). The inverse relationship between resource-derived incomes and non-resource tax revenues can be explained by several factors: fiscal substitution, diminished accountability and efficiency in tax administration, the crowding out of non-resource sectors, and the fiscal instability caused by volatile resource prices. Therefore, effective resource wealth management, transparent governance, and diversified economic strategies are essential for mitigating these negative effects and achieving sustainable economic growth in resource-rich countries.

Research by Bornhorst et al. (2009) demonstrated that countries with substantial natural resource revenues often experience a significant reduction in domestic tax revenues. This phenomenon, commonly known as the "resource curse," suggests that resource-rich countries frequently underperform economically compared to their resource-poor counterparts. The heavy reliance on resource revenue can result in a neglect of other economic sectors, reducing the government's incentive to develop efficient tax systems and diversify the economy. Similarly, Crivelli and Gupta (2014) found that a 1% increase in GDP from resource revenue led to a 0.3 % decrease from non-resource revenue, primarily due to lower taxes on goods and services. This substitution effect suggests governments may reduce efforts to collect taxes from other sources when significant resource revenues are available. Mawejje (2019) substantiates the negative correlation between natural resource revenues and tax revenue, highlighting that resource-rich countries often encounter governance issues, such as reduced transparency and accountability in managing resource revenues, which impede efficient tax collection efforts.

Additionally, the Extractive Industries Transparency Initiative (EITI) has been shown to enhance governance and tax revenue mobilization in sub-Saharan Africa, suggesting that better resource governance can alleviate some negative impacts on tax revenue. Gnangnon (2020) reveals that the volatility of resource income diminishes non-resource revenue volatility only when resource revenues constitute less than 18% of total public revenues. Beyond this threshold, greater resource revenue volatility exacerbates non-resource revenue volatility, underscoring the destabilizing effects of heavy reliance on volatile resource revenues and complicating budget planning and fiscal stability. Keller (2022) demonstrates that the average non-resource tax per capita is 14% lower in oil-exporting countries, primarily due to the commodity price boom in the 2000s. This effect is particularly pronounced in nations with poor institutional quality heavily dependent on oil and prefer tax instruments over non-tax ones. The commodity price boom can induce fiscal policy complacency, leading governments to rely more on resource revenues while neglecting to broaden the tax base or enhance tax collection mechanisms. According to Prichard et al. (2018), natural resource wealth has an anti-democratic effect, driven significantly by changes in government revenue. They argue that dependence on non-tax revenue from natural resources reduces government accountability to citizens, as there is less need to impose taxes on the populace, thereby weakening the social contract and democratic governance structures. Von Haldenwang and Ivanyna (2018) examine the impact of exogenous shocks on government income, finding that resource-dependent nations are more vulnerable to such shocks. Their research indicates that reliance on natural resources heightens susceptibility to global commodity price fluctuations, leading to significant revenue instability and difficulties maintaining consistent public services and investments.

The research consistently shows that reliance on natural resource revenues can adversely affect domestic tax revenue mobilization, fiscal stability, and governance. These impacts are particularly pronounced in countries with poor institutional quality and high dependency on volätile resource incomes, emphasizing the need for improved governance, diversification of revenue sources, and enhanced fiscal policies to mitigate the adverse effects of the resource curse. Khezri et al. (2022) highlighted the importance of sustainable public investment and tax reforms to mitigate the resource curse and promote economic diversification so that policy implications suggest strengthening state institutions and reducing reliance on natural resources to enhance economic stability and social security.

4.3 Institutional Quality and Tax Revenue

Botlhole et al. (2012) considered institutional quality as a factor in the relationship between natural resource incomes and tax revenue performance. They argued that strong institutions enhance tax revenue mobilization in sub-Saharan Africa by effectively managing resource incomes. Good governance and institutional frameworks are crucial in transforming natural resource wealth into sustainable fiscal revenue reducing dependency on volatile resource markets. According to Kolstad and Søreide (2009), proper management of natural resource consumption is essential in curbing corruption in countries with abundant natural resources. They highlighted that corruption often arises from the mismanagement of resource revenues, which undermines economic stability and equitable growth. Therefore, effective resource management policies are essential to ensure transparency and accountability, ultimately leading to better economic outcomes. Muhamad et al. (2021) discovered that institutional quality and human development are crucial for lowering a country's reliance on natural resource revenues and accelerating its transition to an optimum degree of diversification. They emphasized that countries with robust institutions and high levels of human capital are better positioned to diversify their economies away from natural resources, fostering long-term economic stability and growth. A large body of literature confirms the negative correlation between tax revenue and corruption (Besley & Persson, 2014; Tapsoba et al., 2017; 2008), emphasizing the role and importance of the structure of the economy in tax revenues generated (Drummond et al., 2012; Mawejje & Francis Munyambonera, 2016). Tapsoba et al. (2017) argued that corruption erodes the tax base by reducing compliance and encouraging tax evasion. Besley and Persson (2014) noted that developing countries often struggle with low tax collection due to institutional weaknesses and corruption. Thornton (2008) found that corruption alters the composition of tax revenue, skewing it toward easier-to-collect taxes and away from more complex, growth-enhancing ones. Therefore, resource dependence can lead to a weak institutional system and financial corruption due to a lack of public accountability, which reduces the government's capacity to boost tax revenues (McGuirk, 2011; Ross, 2015).

McGuirk (2011) showed that resource-dependent countries often experience a "resource curse" where resource wealth leads to reduced accountability and weaker institutions. Ross (2015) reviewed the literature on the resource curse, concluding that poor institutional quality is a significant factor in the negative impact of resource wealth on economic performance. These studies align with research that focuses on the political economy's interpretations and the correlation between oil and weak institutions (Bjorvatn & Naghavi, 2011; Bjorvatn & Selvik, 2008; Bulte et al., 2005; Papyrakis et al., 2016). Bjorvatn and Naghavi (2011) explored how rent-seeking behavior in rentier states undermines regime stability and institutional quality. Bjorvatn and Selvik (2008) examined factionalism and rent-seeking in Iran, highlighting the destructive competition for resource rents. Bulte et al. (2005) analyzed the relationship between resource intensity, institutions, and development, finding that resource-dependent economies often suffer from weak institutional frameworks. Papyrakis et al. (2016) discussed the Extractive Industries Transparency Initiative (EITI) and its role in reducing corruption in the extractive sector by promoting transparency and accountability.

In conclusion, the literature consistently shows that strong institutions and good governance are critical to effectively managing natural resource wealth. These factors help mitigate corruption, enhance tax revenue mobilization, and support economic diversification. Policymakers should, therefore, focus on strengthening institutional quality and human capital development to ensure sustainable economic growth and reduce dependency on natural resources.

4.4 Policy Implications for the Kurdistan Region, Iraq

The Kurdistan Region of Iraq (KRI) is a territory abundant in natural resources, especially petroleum, which constitutes a major portion of its income. While this wealth in resources has endowed the region with considerable fiscal capacity, it also engenders challenges such as economic volatility and a dependence on oil revenues. Based on extant literature and empirical evidence regarding the interplay between resource income and non-resource revenue, several policy implications can be delineated for KRI to advance sustainable economic growth and development.

Diversification of Revenue Sources

1. Broadening the Tax Base:

   The Kurdistan Region should prioritize broadening its tax base beyond the petroleum sector. Implementing effective taxation policies and extending the scope of tax collection to other economic activities can yield a more stable and reliable revenue stream. This involves augmenting the capacity of tax administration and instituting reforms to curtail tax evasion and enhance compliance. Drawing on the findings of Melina and Poplawski-Ribeiro (2020) and Odhiambo and Olushola (2018), KRI can stabilize its economy by depending on more predictable non-resource revenues, facilitating superior long-term economic planning and investment in public goods and services.

2. Encouraging Entrepreneurship and Investment:

   To counteract the adverse impacts of the resource curse, KRI should cultivate a favorable environment for entrepreneurship and investment in non-petroleum sectors. Policies aimed at reducing bureaucratic barriers, providing incentives for startups, and investing in infrastructure can stimulate growth in industries such as agriculture, manufacturing, and services. This diversification will not only broaden the tax base but also reduce the economic volatility associated with fluctuating petroleum prices (Bjorvatn & Selvik, 2008; Papyrakis & Gerlagh, 2006).

Strengthening Institutions and Governance

1. Enhancing Institutional Quality

   Robust institutions are pivotal for effective resource management and tax revenue mobilization. KRI needs to fortify its institutional frameworks to ensure transparency and accountability in managing resource revenues. This can be accomplished through capacity-building programs, adopting international best practices, and implementing stringent legal frameworks to combat corruption (Kolstad & Søreide, 2009; Muhamad et al., 2021). Ensuring that resource wealth is utilized to construct and reinforce tax administrations will augment overall tax compliance and collection efficiency.

2. Implementing Transparent Resource Management Practices

   KRI should adopt measures such as the Extractive Industries Transparency Initiative (EITI) to foster transparency in the extractive sector. Transparent reporting and accountability in the management of petroleum revenues can diminish the likelihood of corruption and mismanagement, thus enhancing the overall governance of resource wealth. This, in turn, can lead to better economic outcomes and higher non-resource tax revenues (Gnangnon, 2020; Prichard et al., 2018).

Mitigating Economic Volatility

1. Establishing a Sovereign Wealth Fund:

   To mitigate the fiscal instability precipitated by volatile petroleum prices, KRI should contemplate establishing a sovereign wealth fund. This fund can help stabilize resource income over time, ensuring a steady flow of revenue even during periods of low petroleum prices. The fund can be employed to support strategic investments in infrastructure, education, and health care, fostering long-term economic stability and growth (Mehlum et al., 2006; James, 2015).

2. Developing Long-term Fiscal Strategies:

   KRI needs to develop comprehensive and long-term fiscal strategies that incorporate scenarios of fluctuating petroleum prices. These strategies should emphasize the importance of maintaining fiscal discipline, diversifying the economy, and investing in human capital development. By planning for the long term, the region can better withstand economic shocks and ensure sustainable development (Bornhorst et al., 2009; Crivelli & Gupta, 2014).

Enhancing Human Capital

1. Investing in Education and Skills Development:

   A workforce imbued with extensive education and advanced skills is imperative for the diversification of the economy and the augmentation of productivity in non-oil sectors. KRI ought to allocate resources toward education and vocational training schemes to endow its populace with the requisite competencies to engage in a multifarious economy. This will not merely augment the tax base but will also bolster the overarching economic fortitude of the region (Besley & Persson, 2014; Tapsoba et al., 2017).

2. Fostering Innovation and Research:

   Encouraging innovation and research possesses the potential to propel economic diversification and bolster competitiveness. KRI should advocate for research and development enterprises, foster collaborations between academic institutions and industry, and furnish funding for groundbreaking projects. Such initiatives will engender novel economic opportunities and attenuate the reliance on oil revenues (Bjorvatn & Naghavi, 2011; Papyrakis et al., 2016).

In summary, the Kurdistan Region of Iraq can exploit its natural resource affluence to construct a more resilient and variegated economy by enacting comprehensive policies that enhance revenue diversification, fortify institutional quality, mitigate economic fluctuations, and invest in human capital. These stratagems will foster sustainable economic expansion and progress, thereby diminishing the region's reliance on capricious resource incomes and enhancing overall economic stability.

4.5 Conclusion

The manuscript scrutinizes the correlation betwixt non-resource income and economic proliferation in oil-exporting territories, accentuating the benefits of diversifying income streams distant from natural resources. Research evinces that transitioning from dependence on resource-based revenues to more extensive income origins, such as levies, cultivates more stable economic amplification, augments fiscal steadiness, and diminishes exposure to global commodity price volatility. Such diversification augments long-term economic strategies and investments in public services, imperative for sustainable development.

Nevertheless, the interactions between natural resources and non-resource revenues are convoluted and persist as a topic of theoretical and empirical discourse. Certain scholars hypothesize that resource wealth can enhance tax administration capabilities, thus augmenting non-resource revenues via improved tax compliance and enforcement. Contrarily, numerous analyses highlight the adverse impacts of heavy dependence on natural resource revenues, such as fiscal laxity, enervated tax administration, and neglect in developing non-resource tax bases.

Theoretically, elevated resource incomes might instigate fiscal substitution, whereby governments attenuate efforts in non-resource tax collection and abate tax rates, relying more extensively on resource revenues. This phenomenon can precipitate a decline in accountability, tax administration efficiency, and entrepreneurial ventures, thereby diminishing the tax base. Oscillations in resource prices can exacerbate fiscal instability, culminating in budget deficits and complications in economic planning.

Effective resource management, robust institutions, and prudent governance are paramount to mitigate these deleterious outcomes. Empirical evidence suggests that nations with solid institutions and advanced human capital are better poised to diversify their economies and reduce dependence on erratic resource markets. Corruption, frequently associated with poor resource revenue management, hampers tax revenue collection and economic stability.

In conclusion, oil-exporting nations ought to diversify their revenue streams by enacting efficacious tax policies to perpetuate economic growth and ensure stability. This encompasses establishing robust institutions, fostering operational transparency, and significant investment in human resource development to optimize the benefits of natural resource wealth while alleviating the adverse effects of the resource curse. By broadening their economic base beyond resource-dependent revenues, these nations can mitigate their susceptibility to volatile natural resource profits, thereby fortifying their economic security and progress.

Nations reliant on oil exports necessitate broadening their financial bases to advocate for stable and continuous economic expansion. A cardinal approach entails overhauling their taxation frameworks to generate more reliable revenues by widening the tax base and enhancing enforcement. These initiatives necessitate investments in fortifying tax administrative systems, elevating the skills of tax personnel, and enacting extensive tax reforms to diminish evasion and heighten efficiency. Thoughtfully devised tax policies are indispensable for financing vital public services such as infrastructure, education, and health care, fostering economic growth, and elevating living standards. Furthermore, resource-rich countries should emphasize enhancing the quality of their institutional frameworks and governance. Sound governance is crucial to managing resource wealth effectively and combating corruption that often undermines tax collection. Initiatives to amplify transparency and accountability, such as adopting the Extractive Industries Transparency Initiative (EITI), are vital in securing public trust and ensuring the proper application of resource revenues.

Moreover, the creation of sovereign wealth funds can serve as a strategy to stabilize income from resources by evening out revenue variations over time, thereby supporting consistent fiscal policies and bolstering long-term economic strategies. A pivotal policy focus is the drive toward economic diversification. Excessive reliance on natural resources can induce economic fluctuations and impede consistent growth. Consequently, governments should promote the development of other sectors, like manufacturing and services, to construct a more robust and resilient economy. This objective can be attained through targeted investments, attractive business environments, and incentives for entrepreneurial ventures. Curtailing reliance on resource revenues enables countries to alleviate the negative repercussions of the resource curse and strive for more inclusive economic development. Lastly, the development of human capital is indispensable for supporting diversified economic growth. Investments in education and training can enhance the workforce's skills, rendering the economy more adaptable and capable of sustaining varied industries. Policymakers should prioritize developing educational programs and vocational training tailored to the requirements of a diversified economy. Augmenting human capital aids economic diversification and enhances overall productivity and competitiveness.

References

Abdelwahed, L. (2020). More oil, more or less taxes? New evidence on the impact of resource revenue on domestic tax revenue. *Resources Policy, 68*, 101747. https://doi.org/10.1016/j.resourpol.2020.101747

Besley, T., & Persson, T. (2014). Why do developing countries tax so little? *Journal of Economic Perspectives, 28*(4), 99–120. https://doi.org/10.1257/jep.28.4.99

Bjorvatn, K., & Naghavi, A. (2011). Rent seeking and regime stability in rentier states. *European Journal of Political Economy, 27*(4), 740–748. https://doi.org/10.1016/j.ejpoleco.2011.05.007

Bjorvatn, K., & Selvik, K. (2008). Destructive competition: Factionalism and rent-seeking in Iran. *World Development, 36*(11), 2314–2324. https://doi.org/10.1016/j.worlddev.2007.11.002

Bornhorst, F., Gupta, S., & Thornton, J. (2009). Natural resource endowments and the domestic revenue effort. *European Journal of Political Economy, 25*(4), 439–446. https://doi.org/10.1016/j.ejpoleco.2009.01.003

Botlhole, T., Asafu-Adjaye, J., & Carmignani, F. (2012). Natural resource abundance, institutions and tax revenue mobilisation in sub-Sahara Africa. *South African Journal of Economics, 80*(2), 135–156. https://doi.org/10.1111/j.1813-6982.2011.01305.x

Bulte, E. H., Damania, R., & Deacon, R. T. (2005). Resource intensity, institutions, and development. *World Development, 33*(7), 1029–1044. https://doi.org/10.1016/j.worlddev.2005.04.004

Crivelli, E., & Gupta, S. (2014). Resource blessing, revenue curse? Domestic revenue effort in resource-rich countries. *European Journal of Political Economy, 35*, 88–101. https://doi.org/10.1016/j.ejpoleco.2014.04.001

Drummond, P., Daal, W., Srivastava, N., & Oliveira, L. (2012). Mobilizing revenue in sub-Saharan Africa: Empirical norms and key determinants. *SSRN Electronic Journal*. https://doi.org/10.5089/9781475503296.001

James, A. (2015). US state fiscal policy and natural resources. *American Economic Journal: Economic Policy, 7*(3), 238–257. https://doi.org/10.1257/pol.20130211

Keller, M. (2022). Oil revenues vs domestic taxation: Deeper insights into the crowding-out effect. *Resources Policy, 76*, 102560. https://doi.org/10.1016/j.resourpol.2022.102560

Khezri, M., Heshmati, A., Ghazal, R., & Khodaei, M. (2022). Non-resource revenues and the resource curse in different institutional structures: The DIGNAR-MTFF model. *Resources Policy, 79*, 103120. https://doi.org/10.1016/j.resourpol.2022.103120

Knack, S. (2009). Sovereign rents and quality of tax policy and administration. *Journal of Comparative Economics, 37*(3), 359–371. https://doi.org/10.1016/j.jce.2009.04.001

Knebelmann, J. (2017). *Natural resources' impact on government revenues* (9292562347).

Kolstad, I., & Søreide, T. (2009). Corruption in natural resource management: Implications for policy makers. *Resources Policy, 34*(4), 214–226. https://doi.org/10.1016/j.resourpol.2009.05.001

Mawejje, J. (2019). Natural resources governance and tax revenue mobilization in sub saharan Africa: The role of EITI. *Resources Policy, 62*, 176–183. https://doi.org/10.1016/j.resourpol.2019.04.001

Mawejje, J., & Francis Munyambonera, E. (2016). Tax revenue effects of sectoral growth and public expenditure in Uganda. *South African Journal of Economics, 84*(4), 538–554. https://doi.org/10.1111/saje.12127

McGuirk, E. F. (2011). The illusory leader: Natural resources, taxation and accountability. *Public Choice, 154*(3–4), 285–313. https://doi.org/10.1007/s11127-011-9820-0

Mehlum, H., Moene, K., & Torvik, R. (2006). Institutions and the resource curse. *The Economic Journal, 116*(508), 1–20. https://doi.org/10.1111/j.1468-0297.2006.01045.x

Melina, G., & Poplawski-Ribeiro, M. (2020). Macroeconomic impacts of non-resource revenue mobilization in CEMAC. *Applied Economics Letters, 28*(9), 721–726. https://doi.org/10.1080/13504851.2020.1772456

Muhamad, G. M., Heshmati, A., & Khayyat, N. T. (2021). How to reduce the degree of dependency on natural resources? *Resources Policy, 72*, 102047. https://doi.org/10.1016/j.resourpol.2021.102047

Odhiambo, O., & Olushola, O. (2018). Taxation and economic growth in a resource-rich country: The case of Nigeria. *Taxes and Taxation Trends*. https://doi.org/10.5772/intechopen.74381

Papyrakis, E., & Gerlagh, R. (2006). Resource windfalls, investment, and long-term income. *Resources Policy, 31*(2), 117–128. https://doi.org/10.1016/j.resourpol.2006.09.002

Papyrakis, E., Rieger, M., & Gilberthorpe, E. (2016). Corruption and the extractive industries transparency initiative. *The Journal of Development Studies, 53*(2), 295–309. https://doi.org/10.1080/00220388.2016.1160065

Prichard, W., Salardi, P., & Segal, P. (2018). Taxation, non-tax revenue and democracy: New evidence using new cross-country data. *World Development, 109*, 295–312. https://doi.org/10.1016/j.worlddev.2018.05.014

Ross, M. L. (2015). *What have we learned about the resource curse?* (Vol. 18).

Smith, B. (2004). Oil wealth and regime survival in the developing world, 1960–1999. *American Journal of Political Science, 48*(2), 232–246. https://doi.org/10.1111/j.0092-5853.2004.00067.x

Tapsoba, S., Kimani, E., Gupta, S., & Baum, A. (2017). Corruption, taxes and compliance. *IMF Working Papers, 17*(255), 1. https://doi.org/10.5089/9781484326039.001

Thornton, J. (2008). Corruption and the composition of tax revenue in Middle East and African Economies1. *South African Journal of Economics, 76*(2), 316–320. https://doi.org/10.1111/j.1813-6982.2008.00176.x

Torvik, R. (2002). Natural resources, rent seeking and welfare. *Journal of Development Economics, 67*(2), 455–470. https://doi.org/10.1016/s0304-3878(01)00195-x

von Haldenwang, C., & Ivanyna, M. (2018). Does the political resource curse affect public finance? The vulnerability of tax revenue in resource-dependent countries. *Journal of International Development, 30*(2), 323–344. https://doi.org/10.1002/jid.3346

Chapter 5
The Impact of Resource Management on the Growth of Multinational Corporations in the Kurdistan Region of Iraq

Ahang Kawany

Abstract The Kurdistan Region of Iraq (KRI) has gone through rapid development in many areas, especially the internationalization of its emerging market. However, in recent years, the performance of multinational corporations (MNCs) in the region has been suppressed due to some factors within the region such as the war against ISIS, political instability, and global economic hardship. This chapter examines the factors that affect the growth of MNCs in the KRI. The study considers how the MNC manages to make use of local resources, technical advancements, and external factors to enhance its performance and overall growth. In doing so, a mixed methodology of quantitative and qualitative approach is applied including a confirmatory factor analysis to reduce the number of variables under each group of factors. We combined several variables, and thus, one latent variable is created and called performance. The results indicate that while competitive advantages along with human capital and technology are the leading factors that positively affect the growth of the MNCs in the Kurdistan Region of Iraq, external and environmental factors have had less impact on a firm's performance. A regression analysis on the performance of MNCs is applied, and the results reveal that all the factors under performance, namely, knowledge, capability, experience, technology, and political factors, organizational culture, and firm reputation, have a positive outcome. However, legal factors appeared to have a negative effect on a firm's performance. Further research on this topic is recommended in the future with a larger sample size and involving more industries.

Keywords Resource management · multinational corporations · mixed methodology · Kurdistan Region of Iraq

---

A. Kawany (✉)
University of Kurdistan Hawler, Erbil, Iraq

G. M. Muhamad, N. T. Khayyat (eds.), *Resource Management Performance: A Sectoral Analysis in the Post-Conflict Kurdistan Region of Iraq*, Perspectives on Development in the Middle East and North Africa (MENA) Region,
https://doi.org/10.1007/978-981-97-7725-9_5

5.1 Introduction

The impact of resource management on the firm's performance has become an important theme of research. Scholars argue that improvement in firms' performance is mainly attributed to better management of their existing resources, technological advancements, and coping with externalities such as political and legal factors (Bouncken et al., 2015; Das & Kapil, 2015; Hitt et al., 2012; Sirmon et al., 2007).

The process of creating an advantage in performance is in line with the resource-based view (RBV) theory of an organization. Scholars argue that firms will have higher performance than their competitors when they put into practice a value-creating strategy (Almeida Costa & Zemsky, 2021; Jell-Ojobor & Raha, 2022). Others find that the competitive advantage of a firm results in better performance, which is initiated by owning eminent resources and capabilities that are responding to several conditions such as value, rareness, imitability, and non-substitutable (VRIN) (Arend & Lévesque, 2010; Azeem et al., 2021; Farida & Setiawan, 2022). Nevertheless, the scarcity of those resources tends to lead to perfect competition, as they are possessed by fewer firms due to the cost and non-sustainability of those resources (Arend & Lévesque, 2010; Farida & Setiawan, 2022).

Several factors affect the management of various entities in various sectors across the different levels of the productivity process which are internal and external factors such as human capital, technology, environmental, legal, and political factors. Hence, it is important to understand how multinational cooperations (MNCs) in the Kurdistan Region of Iraq (KRI) adopt these factors to secure their marketability and remain in the region.

The KRI has gone through rapid development in many areas, especially internationalization as an emerging market. The performance of MNCs has been suppressed due to some external factors, namely, the war against ISIS, political instability, and global economic hardship. According to the Kurdistan Board of Investment, from 2014 to 2019, around 30% of multinational companies have uncompleted and outstanding projects worth a total of 7.2 billion US dollars. The major reasons for such disruption have been identified as internal conflict, and political and economic instability (Muhamad, 2022). Gaur et al. (2011) state that a lack of political and environmental securities in foreign emerging markets leads to financial instability in this economy and, as a result, MNCs will not be encouraged or may avoid launching their business investment.

This chapter aims to examine the impact of resource management and the use of resources such as human capital, technology, and external resources for the growth of the MNCs in the KRI. The analysis is extended to investigate the relationship between resource management and growth and the arbitrating role of competitive advantage of international companies.

In doing so, a mixed method of quantitative and qualitative is used. In the quantitative section, a survey questionnaire is conducted on 80 selected senior employees of 8 companies in 5 different industries of the KRI in the following sectors:

energy and oil, distribution, telecommunication, education, and retail. As for the qualitative section, 5 senior staff members are interviewed, and they each represent a sector. Then, a confirmatory factor analysis is applied to reduce the number of variables under each group of factors.

The results indicate that competitive advantages along with human capital and technology are the leading factors that positively affect the growth of the MNCs in KRI. However, external and environmental factors have less impact on a firm's performance. Further results of regression analysis on the performance of MNCs reveal that all the factors under performance, namely, knowledge, capability, experience, technology, political factors, organizational culture, and firm reputation, have a positive outcome. However, legal factors appeared to hurt a firm's performance.

This study contributes to the existing knowledge as it is the first attempt to investigate the effect of different factors and resources on MNCs' growth in the KRI. Hence, this study (a) contributes to the fields of practice, management, and policymaking of companies and organizations; (b) will benefit foreign companies in all industries in KRI to evaluate their current resource management that enhances higher productivity and better performance; and (c) will help the existing MNCs in KRI to comprehend the meaning of proper consumption of available resources through resource management and will also help those foreign companies intended to enter the market.

The chapter is organized as follows: The next section reviews the existing literature on the impact of managing firms' resources on the firm's growth and the relationship between MNCs and host governments. Section 5.3 presents the methodology of the study. Section 5.4 presents an analysis of data and an interpretation of results. Section 5.5 concludes.

5.2 Theoretical and Empirical Literature

5.2.1 The Theory of Resource-based View (RBV)

Resource-based view is defined as an attempt of a firm to achieve a competitive advantage. It depends on tangible and intangible resources or assets that should be heterogeneous and immobile and need to have value, rare, imitable, and organization (VRIO) characteristics to become VRIO resources, which then provides a competitive advantage to the firm (Barney, 1991; Rothaermel, 2012). According to the scholars that support RBV theory, an organization or a firm must look inside the company to find a competitive advantage instead of looking at the competitive environment for it. In other words, an inside-out approach is suggested to be followed where a firm uses the internal and existing resources to reach a higher organizational performance rather than attaining new resources.

The first scholar to recognize the importance of resources to a firm's competitive position was Edith Penrose (Penrose, 1959). Penrose argued that a firm's internal and external growth through merger, acquisition, and diversification is due to the method in which its resources are working. She began by arguing that a firm contains a collection of productive resources with the suggestion that these resources may only contribute to a firm's competitive position to the extent that they are exploited to such a method that their potentially valuable services are made available to the firm (Newbert, 2007).

The argument of the recourse-based view was not a sensible matter for active managers till the 1990s. The view was extended by some immediate signs of progress which approved the perspective. On the theory side, there was a development for a better understanding of specific resources such as culture (Gerhart & Feng, 2021; Hossain et al., 2022).

5.2.2 Firm's Resources

Human Capital

Chiang et al. (2017) emphasized the transfer and diffusion of human resource management (HRM) as a complex phenomenon. With the fact of incomparable growth in MNCs and the adequate increase in the number of foreign subsidiaries to achieve competitive advantage and sustainability in the market, it has become a modern business approach for such organizations to apply the most effective and possible human resource management practices in their geographically dispersed network of operations. This requires transferring the confirmed human resource management practices from headquarters to their overseas subsidiaries.

According to Williams and Lee (2016), dispersed knowledge of the organization's workforce is one of the most critical strategic resources available for multinational corporations. It has been suggested that subsidiary or company managers need to pay specific attention to human resource management practices within the company if they want to integrate the company within the internal MNC network, especially for those companies based and established in an emerging market.

To compete in the market, firms continue investing in innovative activities and creating knowledge and technological capabilities. Specifically, they tend to depend more on external sources of knowledge, such as customers, competitors, suppliers, universities, and research centers. Firms revise internal innovation and creativity by examining and taking benefit from external sources of knowledge (Ferraris et al., 2017; Khayyat & Lee, 2015).

Technology

According to Ferraris et al. (2017), both theoretical arguments and empirical research recommend that developing a firm's research and development system is beneficial for innovative performance to a certain point. However, if a firm depends on external sources of knowledge, the cost of research, coordination, and monitoring will increase and may lead to creating a path toward dependent knowledge stocks. As an alternative to closed innovation, new models recommend an open innovation example, where the research and development structure is seen as an open system (Chesbrough & Bogers, 2014; Ferraris et al., 2017).

Backman et al. (2017) have introduced the governance, information management, systems, and technology (GISTe) model as a new methodological tool of RBV for analyzing how climate change impacts mitigating strategy. The GISTe model is imperative for firms' positioning, as it lets individual companies place themselves and their competitors in the market with other nations. The GISTe model aids companies in improving their performance under a government's authority, while it allows separating the public policy priority areas by identifying different groups of companies working under special resource rules. According to the GISTe model, any new public policy measure can now be evaluated in terms of expected "performance" in the possible changes of business attitude regarding governance, information management, system capabilities, and technological investments.

Political and Legal Factors

Panibratov et al. (2017) argue that political strategies have a specific significance for MNCs in emerging economies of the countries that traditionally play an important role in business affairs. To bargain with the authorities, MNCs invest in their political capabilities, not only to reach out to their benefits in host countries but also to gain home government support for their external investments.

To study and understand the government policies and ownership structures of MNCs especially in China, He et al. (2016) explain that when an emerging country liberalizes and encourages its firms toward internationalization, most of them may not succeed in the international market, due to strong competition from the existing firms. However, many of the Chinese firms have been successful in the global market, as those MNCs that were able to align with and influence Chinese government policies to gain access to resources can derive greater benefits from their owners toward better performance and gaining competitive advantage.

Through RBV theory, Eniola and Entebang (2016) described financial literacy as a particular problem of small and medium enterprises (SMEs) as there are companies that may have a higher rate of occupation progress. Yet, they may go out of business or remain small due to having problems with institutional and financial literacy.

Culture and Reputation

According to Brouthers et al. (2008), differences in nations' institutional environments may impact the applicability of resource-based advantages. As such, the effectiveness of such advantages may vary across nations. The country image can be used as an asset or liability for attracting applicants to apply for MNC since there is a chance that an applicant may have a negative or positive bias and understanding about a particular country. Thus, a company may benefit and take advantage of recruiting employees who favor one country rather than the others (Chen et al., 2017).

Tulung (2017) identified the availability of several resources required for strategic objectives: First, the resources held by local firms, such as assets, local customer base, reputation, and distribution channels. Second, the resources held by the investor, such as transferable knowledge, financial capital, and managerial services.

Third, the resources available in the market, which includes human resources skills, real estate, and access to utilities.

5.2.3 The Impact of Managing Resources on Firms' Growth

Strategic resources are categorized by their scarcity, similarity to key success factors in the business, resilience, the difficulty of substitution or imitation of products, and the suitability of generated charges. Based on the main hypothesis of RBV, only firms with certain resources and capabilities with special characteristics will gain competitive advantages, and therefore, achieve greater performance. The uniqueness of an aspect depends on its scarcity, value, resilience, non-substitutability, immutability, and appropriability of generated rents (Camisón & Villar-López, 2014; Peteraf, 1993).

Furthermore, to evaluate the impact of RBV, Barney et al. (2001) analyzed the impact of RBV on specific subject areas and identified five fields of study, namely, human resource management, entrepreneurship, economics, marketing, and international business. The important effect of the institutional environment that a firm operates on the strategies they peruse has been focused on with emphasis on smaller firms that also need to acquire critical resources to create a sustained competitive advantage (Barney et al., 2001). However, Penrose and Penrose (2009) stated that firms grow by combining internal and external resources. Tulung (2017) believed that firms grow and expand into foreign markets by combining different types of resources mentioned above to gain a competitive advantage as indicated by the RBV theory.

The RBV does not only serve as the main theoretical basis in the scholarly literature review but is rather included in all major textbooks on the subject of strategic management, research, teaching, and consulting. These fields are gradually dominated by the assumption that rare, inimitable, non-substitutable resources, capabilities, and core competencies can deliberate competitive and performance advantages to the firm (Newbert, 2007).

5.2.4 The Relationship Between MNCs and Host Governments

MNCs–host government relations (MGRs) improve when resources are invested by MNCs. This relationship is more complementary to institutional needs which strengthen personal relations with officials, firms are more responsive to indigenous social demands, and organizational reputation and trustworthiness are superior.

Luo (2001) examined cooperation-based relations between MNCs and host government, through theorizing four building blocks including resource commitment, personal relations, political accommodation, and organizational credibility. A host government intervention policy executes severe restrictions on MNC's strategies and operations within the host country. It has also been noted that the actual amount of government intervention does vary distinctly from one MNC to another within the same host country, or even within the same industry (Moon & Lado, 2000).

To analyze the relationship between MNCs and host governments, many researchers have implemented the bargaining power framework. The general logic of this framework is that the result of MNC–host government interactions reflects the relative bargaining power of the MNC over the host government. However, according to this framework, MNCs with larger bargaining power are likely to gain more promising terms in negotiations with host governments and have less probability of facing the sting of the host government (Moon & Lado, 2000).

Furthermore, with its clear focus on a firm's internal resources as sources of performance, the resource-based view not only makes the theoretical connection between bargaining power and performance but also provides a coherent theory for understanding the bargaining power relationship within a wider theoretical framework.

5.3 Methodology

The focus of this study is to analyze the actual impact of resource management on the firm's growth, with the use of human resources, technology, environment, and external resources. In doing so, a mixed methodology of quantitative- and qualitative-based approaches is applied. In this type of research, a researcher combines quantitative and qualitative research techniques, methods, approaches, concepts, or language into a single study (Strijker et al., 2020). A mixed-method design combines the strengths of both quantitative and qualitative research methods and minimizes the weaknesses (Dawadi et al., 2021).

To do the investigation different industries such as energy and oil fields (35%), telecommunications, education, and retail were identified. The reasons for selecting those industries are (1) these industries have had a higher impact on rapid economic growth in KRI, and (2) the selected retail company has dominated the retail market in Iraq in general and KRI specifically. Those who were reached out are professionals in their field of work, as they are all experts, executives, and senior-level employees and have had several years of work experience in the mentioned positions.

This study implemented two research instruments in the development of the study, which is a questionnaire survey and interview with key persons of the selected industries. We selected those participants based on the rule of thumb suggested by White (2002) since the population number of the categories was not evident at the beginning of the study. This limitation has resulted in adopting a sample size of 60 participants who responded to the online and paper questionnaire survey out of 80 preselected participants.[1] Considering the questionnaire survey, a one-to-one

[1] The questionnaire is attached to the appendix.

interview method is undertaken as a qualitative technique for the study with five selected senior staff members, each of which represents an industry.

5.4 Analysis of Data and Presentation of Results

5.4.1 Analysis of the Questionnaire Responses

This section presents the collected data to achieve the aims and objectives of the study. The demographic background and information of the survey participants are reflected in this section. Table 5.1 reports information about the participants of the questionnaire in which 48% of the participants were managers and executives, while 14% were admin staff or having other job categories. Furthermore, it was necessary to ensure that the respondents were actually from the decision-maker circle and professionals. Having high-level qualifications and expertise in the field of management and business administration improves the management level of a firm. Table 5.1 indicates that around 65% of the participants have a university degree.

The duration of employees of the participants in the company shows that more than 50% have been working between 6 and 10 years in the same company and more than 28% have worked in the company for more than 10 years. According to Berger and Berger (2011), an employee is not capable of staying in the employment of the same company for more than 5 years if they have not accomplished the

Table 5.1 Participants' information

Response selections	Percentage
Executive/manager	46
Supervisor/officer	40
Admin staff/others	14
Education background	
Up to high school	33.3
College degree	64.9
Master/higher diploma	1.8
PhD/others	0
Duration of employees	
Less than 5 years	21.1
Between 6–10 years	50.8
More than 10 years	28.1
Industry information	
Oil and energy	35
Telecommunications	37
Distribution companies	17
Education	10
Retail	10

required level of performance, especially in the perceived delicate function of the firm. A further reason is reported to be related to age, gender, and years of experience with compensation and benefits (Kethan, 2022).

With regard to the organizational biographical information, the distribution of the respondents reports the following, respectively: 35% from the oil and energy sector, 27% from the telecommunication sector, and 10% from each of the education and retail sectors.

Another part of the organizational biography is the establishment year of the company either in the original country and/or in the Kurdistan Region. Table 5.2 reports on the establishment year of the multinational corporations that have been selected to undertake the survey. Accordingly, the highest percentage of companies established in the Kurdistan Region of Iraq is between the years 2011 and 2015 with a percentage of 48%. This is an indication that MNCs were interested in investing in the Kurdistan Region during that time due to the availability of resources and some other factors that are discussed in the next section.

Table 5.3 presents the steps undertaken before launching their companies and 34% of the survey respondents reported taking action to define their target customers. Additionally, having agreements with the government is another step that 32% of the survey participants agreed with and 20% have had agreements with other companies. This indicates that using external resources has been taken into consideration before launching the company.

The first two sections of the questionnaires are auxiliary (controlled) variables, which control the other questions. These questions determine how the participant is responding to the other questions. Regarding the selected company's performance, questions were asked concerning the company's profitability, from the scale of strongly disagree to strongly agree. Table 5.4 presents the performance of the companies which introduced new products and high levels of customer care were scaled to be the highest factors in increasing companies' profitability with 63%. About 47% of the participants reported that having different products increased the company's profitability, while only 22% reported a reduction of the company's profit as a result of high-cost operations. Nevertheless, there are some external factors that will affect and reduce the profitability of a firm, and it is shown in Table 5.5 that 50% of the participants agreed on this point.

Table 5.5 shows the importance of transparency in communication with employees and rewarding hard workers with the percentage of 58%. This factor that improves the company's performance is related to internal factors called human

Table 5.2 Establishment year of the company

Company establishment year	In original country (%)	In Kurdistan (%)
Before 2000	53	7
2001–2005	20	22
2006–2010	15	28
2011–2015	N/A	48

Table 5.3 Steps undertaken before launching the company

Response selections	Percentage
Defining our target customer	34
Knowing the problem, we are solving	13
Having an agreement with the government	32
Having agreements with other companies	20
Having joint venture(s)	12
No steps have been taken	44

Table 5.4 Order or the responses

Statement	1 (%)	2 (%)	3 (%)	4 (%)	5 (%)
With our differentiated products, our firm's profitability is increased	3	7	27	45	2
We have introduced new products, and this has increased the profitability	3	7	25	40	23
Our company's profitability increased due to high level of our customer/supplier care	2	10	23	45	18
Because of the high cost of operation, our company's profitability is reduced	8	32	37	15	7
Our company's profitability is reduced due to external factors	0	18	30	38	12
Our company's profitability reduced due to the growth of other companies in the same industry.	12	3	27	18	8

Note: 1, 2, 3, 4, and 5 represent strongly disagree, disagree, neutral, agree, and strongly agree, respectively

Table 5.5 Reasons for the company's good performance

Description	1 (%)	2 (%)	3 (%)	4 (%)	5 (%)
Regular promotional offers to customers.	6	13	37	20	22
Prices discrimination	10	17	38	17	17
Promotion and advertisement	7	8	23	30	30
Constant improvement in our communications with other companies	5	13	40	20	20
As an employee, keeping fair and transparent communication with our employees and rewarding the most hardworking ones	2	8	30	20	38

Note: 1, 2, 3, 4, and 5 represent not important, less important, important, a little important, and very important, respectively

Table 5.6 Type of resources used during the launch phase

Respondent's selection	Resources used during the launch phase (%)	Most successful resources (%)	Unsuccessful resources (%)
Technology	66	63	14
Brand name	49	32	19
Efficient business process	46	54	10
Expat skilled labor	58	49	7
Internal skilled labor	53	49	9

resources. Thus, through the better use of human resources, the performance of a company improves.

Resources

The survey asked questions regarding the type of resources that were used during the launch of the company. Results in Table 5.6 show that *technology* ranked the highest among other selected resources at 66%, and *expat skilled labor* with 58% ranked the second highest, while the *efficient business process* with 46% ranked the least resources that have been used during the launch of the participated companies.

In comparing the resources according to their usefulness, the companies who preselected technology to be a resource used for launching their company were successful in their strategic planning and were able to manage their resources consequently. Although efficient business process is ranked as the least used resource for launching the company, it has been ranked as the second most useful resource.

To investigate the ability of the selected companies to turn the existing resources into capabilities and take the company to the next level, around 70% of the respondents confirmed that they were able to turn their resources into capabilities to a great extent.

Human Capital

Human capital, which is one of the main aspects that this study, will lead a company toward better growth if it has been managed appropriately. To identify whether human capital affects the growth of international companies in the Kurdistan Region, the outcome shows outstanding results. With regard to knowledge sharing among and within employees of a company, Table 5.7 shows that 46% agreed on having enough knowledge about the areas of their company. Similarly, 54% of participants also agreed on being free to share knowledge among and within the company.

Furthermore, the respondents rated their capability for solving the company's problems without revealing them with 70% agreement. At the same time, 65% of the participants agreed that the company management team is capable of finding the gaps for future accomplishment. As for having a sense of responsibility during the challenges that face the company, they agreed with 70%. This indicates that the company knows how to deal with their employee's needs for improvement and promotes knowledge sharing to lead them toward better growth and higher

Table 5.7 Human capital as a resource

Knowledge	1 (%)	2 (%)	3 (%)	4 (%)	5 (%)
As employees, we have enough knowledge about all areas of our company	5	18	28	33	13
We are all free in sharing the knowledge within the company	10	15	20	42	12
We as employees know about our company's job better than anyone	2	7	22	43	25
We have mentorship plans to enable knowledge sharing among our employees	12	12	25	40	10
In our company, we care for job rotation to obtain skills	7	17	27	32	17
Our employees take training on a regular basis	10	15	27	32	10
Our company inspires us for a continuous learning	3	17	20	32	27
Our company believes in having a fair skill development program	5	8	33	32	20
Capability					
Our company's management team is capable of finding the gap for future accomplishments	3	13	17	42	23
Our employees have the sense of responsibility toward the company to take the right decision when the company is facing challenges	2	8	18	40	30
We have employees who are capable of solving the company's problems without revealing them	0	8	20	43	27
Our employees are strictly following business process to improve capability	2	13	23	38	22
Experience					
Fresh graduates with no experience are important for us, and they can easily adapt to company's business process	5	17	28	37	12
Our previous employees have been successful in obtaining new jobs in other companies through knowledge transfer	0	3	30	47	18
We apply the principle of learning from interdepartmental interaction than theory of how to function our procedure efficiently	2	10	35	47	5
The area of specialization is important to us, and that's why we hire people accordingly	5	10	23	43	17
We apply the principle of know-how	0	13	27	40	18

Note: 1, 2, 3, 4, and 5 represent strongly disagree, disagree, neutral, agree, and strongly agree, respectively

performance. To this end, the analysis of the survey outcome can give an accurate and rational answer to the question of *how human capital* affects the growth of MNCs in KRI with around 63%.

Table 5.8 Technology as a resource

Technology	1 (%)	2 (%)	3 (%)	4 (%)	5 (%)
Our employees have innovation capability	2	5	33	50	8
Our ways of service offerings vary due to technology variations	3	13	30	38	13
Our customers feedback about our IT system and development of our services matter to us	5	8	13	53	18
Customers feedback analyses are the source of most of our new and innovative products	2	15	27	40	15
In our company, we care for our customer innovation opinion	3	10	30	37	18
With our customer lifestyle, we change our technology	2	22	15	53	7
Our research and development division always involved in most of our events and actions	7	18	27	32	13
Our company supports and invests in inventions	3	22	18	37	27
Our company always keeps the IT resources updated and efficient	3	10	7	40	38
Most of the plans of our services require high technological machine which we benefit from it	3	15	15	38	27

Note: 1, 2, 3, 4, and 5 represent strongly disagree, disagree, neutral, agree, and strongly agree, respectively

5.4.1.1 Technology

Table 5.8 shows the survey participants' opinions regarding their level of disagreement and agreement on the statements raised to investigate on how technology affects the growth of MNCs in the Kurdistan Region of Iraq. Interestingly, most of the participants opined that with the use of technology and technological awareness, companies grow better and enhance profitability. About 58% of the respondents agreed to have innovation capability as employees. As well as 71%, 55%, 62%, and 60% are the rates of agreement by the participants on customer feedback about IT systems, and customer feedback analysis as the source of their new and innovative products. Consequently, it can be inferred that technology has a high impact on the growth of MNCs in the Kurdistan Region of Iraq with a rate of 72%.

External and Environmental Factors

Analysis to investigate whether external factors may affect the growth of international companies in the Kurdistan Region shows that 91% of respondents agreed that their company faced some external and environmental factors that affected their growth. According to Table 5.9, the highest rate of the external factor with 87% of the participants agreed on the political situation, which includes the war against ISIS, security, political and governmental conflicts inside of Iraq and Kurdistan, and some legal factors that will be explained further. Price and oil price have ranked as the second external factor with 58% of participants agreeing that it has affected the company's growth and productivity.

The outcome of the participant's responses in this section confirms the impact of political factors as an external factor on the company's performance. Concerning

Table 5.9 External/environmental factors

Response selections	Percentage
Price/oil price change	58
Economic growth	33
Political situation	87
Environmental change	22
Others (resistance)	8

Table 5.10 Political and legal factors

Description	1 (%)	2 (%)	3 (%)	4 (%)	5 (%)
Political factors					
Our performance is always affected by political situation in the country	3	18	18	32	27
Decentralization has condensed our company's performance	8	13	43	27	7
As any kind of stability, political stability improves our company's performance	0	7	25	35	32
Legal factors					
We form our company's policies to be aligned with government requirements	2	0	26	35	33
The government backs the industry to access information needed	3	6	23	35	20
Company's performance favors the government competition rules	2	8	33	37	18
The industry is well protected by the government law	5	18	26	37	13
Foreign direct investment (FDI) laws favor our business	8	18	35	23	13

Note: 1, 2, 3, 4, and 5 represent strongly disagree, disagree, neutral, agree, and strongly agree, respectively

Table 5.10, the extent of participants' agreement with the provided political and legal statements, the indications show that 57% agree that the company's performance is always affected by political situations in the country, while 67% agree that political stability improves the company's performance like any kind of stability.

To explore more on the external factors affecting the firm's performance, participants responded to the survey statements raised for the legal factors section with 68% agreement on the point that their companies form their policies to be aligned with the government requirement. In the same instance, 55% agreed on having the government support the industry to access the needed information and 50% of the participants agreed that the government rules are well protecting the industry.

The outcome confirms the impact of external resources and environmental factors on the company's performance and growth. External factors such as political and economic factors lead a company toward reducing the profit and striking the growth of the company, whereas the external factors of legal factors improve the profitability and performance of a company due to the support and collaboration that exist between the government and the company.

5.4.1.2 Competitive Advantage

The firm must look inside the company to find a competitive advantage instead of looking at a competitive environment for it, meaning that an inside-out approach needs to be used, in other words, using the internal and existing resources to reach higher organizational performance rather than attaining new resources. However, a firm can use the same existing resources but in different ways and for different opportunities especially since the COVID-19 pandemic (Eggers, 2020; Klein & Todesco, 2021). In this essence, a question was raised in the survey to investigate if the selected companies were able to convert their existing resources into a competitive advantage through resource management, the outcome was *Yes* with around 90%.

Henceforth, some statements were raised in the survey questionnaire to see the level of disagreement and agreement of the participants to explore more on the points that impact the competitive advantage. The outcome of Table 5.11 indicates that when a company's values and standards are clear to everyone in the community and if there is a continuous studying of the values to fit the market with involving employees in company's policy makings and important decisions, they will gain competitive advantage. This was the result of 78%, 74%, and 71% of the agreement by the respondents.

Table 5.11 Competitive advantage

Description	1 (%)	2 (%)	3 (%)	4 (%)	5 (%)
Organizational culture					
Our company's values and standards are clear and comprehensible to everyone in the community	0	7	13	48	30
We continue studying our values to fit the market changes	2	7	17	42	32
Our employees involve in making company's policies and important decisions	3	10	13	48	23
We care for each one of our employees' ideas when we introduce new policies and programs	3	13	22	38	22
We have faith in working within the established goals and aims of our company	2	8	2	38	32
Business reputation					
Even when we are not effective enough and less productive, our customers still tolerate us	3	13	33	42	7
The information we provide to our customers is reliable and believable to them than to our competitors	3	0	23	47	25
Our company conducts programs to promote the brand name and gain customer loyalty	2	7	18	48	23

Note: 1, 2, 3, 4, and 5 represent strongly disagree, disagree, neutral, agree, and strongly agree, respectively

Table 5.12 Sustaining in the maturity phase

Response selections	Percentage
Through improving customer care/after service programs	57
Through advertisement campaign	39
Through offering price discrimination	25
Through development of new product and services	59
Through improving BM	39

Table 5.13 Analysis for resources and factors

Main factor	Sub-factors	Effect (%)	Average (%)
Human capital	Knowledge	56	63
	Capacity	75	
	Experience	58	
Technology	Technology	72	72
External factors	Political	63	55
	Legal	47	
Competitive advantage	Organizational culture	75	74
	Reputation	73	

The final two questions have been asked during the survey to understand if the companies are the maturity phase and how they can sustain there. Around 70% of respondents stated that their companies are in the maturity phase. As for sustaining in the maturity phase, Table 5.12 indicates that 57% of the participants agreed that they can sustain in the maturity phase through improving customer care and after service programs, whereas 59% agreed that they can sustain through developing new products and services.

5.4.2 *Data Analysis and Regression*

Table 5.13 shows the final result of the questionnaire responses about the resources, i.e., the main factors and sub-factors that have impacts on the growth and performance of the companies. The result indicates that human capital as the main factor has a 63% impact on performance. It is important to state that the highest percentage of the human capital sub-factors is capacity with a rate of 75%. As for technology, according to the survey, it has an impact of 72% on the growth of MNCs in Kurdistan. Moreover, external and environmental factors have less impact on performance with a rate of 55% due to the legal sub-factor that has a negative impact on performance with a rate of 47%. To this end, competitive advantage ranked the highest among other factors of growth with 74%.

All the factors (questions) in the survey have been subjected to correlation analysis. Confirmatory factor analysis is applied to reduce the number of factors under each set into one latent variable in each set. Accordingly, the variables that measure the performance of a company are knowledge, capability, experience, technology, political, legal, organizational culture, and reputation and have been reduced to one, and it is called *Performance*.

The final eight latent variables have been subjected to a multiple linear regression analysis to study the causality effects of those latent variables on the firms' performance where the dependent variable is *Performance*, and the independent variables are knowledge, capability, experience, technology, political, legal, organizational culture, and reputation. The results of the regression analysis are reported in Table 5.14.

The multiple regression analysis is conducted based on the latent variables to evaluate the individual effects of each latent variable on the performance. Table 5.14 reports the results of the estimation. Accordingly, most of the coefficients that capture the effects of different resources of the firm on performance are positive and significant. This indicates that these factors have contributed to the firm's well-being. In other words, these factors have a great role and in increasing the performance, enhancing the growth of foreign companies and MNCs in the Kurdistan Region of Iraq.

The coefficient of EYK (establishment year in Kurdistan) is negative but it is highly significant indicating that companies that established earlier in Kurdistan are performing better than others. Furthermore, according to the survey results the respondents agreed that their companies have faced external and environmental factors at the rate of around 92%. These factors were mainly economic and security issues as a result of the ISIS war. These will cause at least a slight decrease in the company's growth and performance that has been seen in recent years.

Knowledge is considered a strong potential to increase organizational performance. The interpretation of this result is that knowledge has a positive impact on performance and its coefficient shows that an increase in the level of knowledge of

Table 5.14 Regression analysis results

Variable	Coefficient	Standard error	*P*-value
Knowledge	0.059	0.114	0.0076
Capability	0.035	0.143	0.0002
Experience	0.0491	0.155	0.0006
Technology	0.529	0.131	0.0002
Political	0.031	0.106	0.0008
Legal	−0.129	0.091	0.0099
Org culture (Oc)	0.099	0.159	0.0005
Reputation	0.379	0.117	0.0022
Establishment year in original country (Eyoc)	0.102	0.058	0.0905
Establishment year in Kurdistan (Eyk)	−0.016	0.082	0.0003
Steps before launching the company (Sblc)	0.078	0.047	0.0004

Note: R-squared = 0. 835, *P*-values: <0.05 and <0.001 show statistically significant and highly statistically significant, respectively

1% will increase the performance by 0.059. This result is in line with previous studies, for example (Abbas et al., 2020; Ferraris et al., 2017; Li et al., 2020). Similarly, the coefficient of capability shows that an increase in the level of capability by 1% leads to improvement the performance by 0.034. As such, it has a positive impact on performance. This finding is similar to the finding by Gupta et al. (2020).

Experience has a positive impact on performance, and a direct interpretation of the coefficient is that increasing the experience by a unit in a year will cause an increase in the performance of the organization by 0.049. Similar results have been reported earlier explaining how a well-experienced employee has a great impact on performance, for instance, by Anwar and Abdullah (2021). However, the legal factor has a negative impact on performance as the coefficient shows that increasing the level of legal by 1% will decrease the performance by 0.129.

The positive impact on performance has been the case for other factors such as technology, political, organizational culture, and reputation. Their coefficients indicate that any unit increase by those factors will add to the performance of MNCs positively.

5.5 Conclusion and Policy Recommendations

This chapter examined the factors that affect the growth of MNCs in KRI. The study looked at how MNCs manage to make use of local resources, technical advancements, and external factors to their overall growth. A discussion of the existing resources was made in light of the RBV theory. Then, to investigate the objectives of the study, a mixed methodology of quantitative- and qualitative-based approaches was applied. Different industries have been included such as energy and oil fields, telecommunications, retail, education, and distribution companies. We implemented the rule of thumb to determine the sample size of the study suggested by White (2002). As such, two research instruments in the development of the study were implemented, a questionnaire survey and interview with key people of the selected industries.

The survey results indicated that competitive advantages along with human capital and technology are the leading factors that positively affect the growth of the MNCs in the Kurdistan Region of Iraq, while external and environmental factors have less impact. A regression analysis on the performance of MNCs was applied, and the results revealed that all the factors of underperformance such as knowledge, capability, experience, technology, political factors, organizational culture, and firm reputation have a positive outcome. However, legal factors appeared to have a negative effect on an MNC's performance.

The main policy implications of this chapter are that the Kurdistan Regional Government can create a set of rules and regulations that can enhance the growth and performance of multinational corporations by improving their productivity, for example, forming different programs and incentives for MNCs such as enhancing tax schemes for MNCs, so they will not pay tax for the first few years. KRI needs to focus on the quality control and importation of products as a support to international companies by preventing the importation of fake and low-quality products and importing high-quality products through MNCs. Furthermore, the government should try to stabilize the political situation and avoid any kind of instabilities and uncertainties. This relative stability will enhance the activity and then the performance of multinational corporations. The improvement in those factors would shed light on the advantage of low-cost labor and a low-rate tax system. As such, factors such as pull factors influence the MNC management in KRI. The pull factors can be, for example, low wages and cheap labor fees as KRI can attract the MNCs through its low-cost country or region for production through low-cost labor.

This study has several limitations which might be considered for future studies. The indicators used in this study have not covered measures such as profit, employment rate, innovation capabilities, or self-sufficiency. Due to lack of data and confidentiality, for example, international companies would rather keep their financial status and profit confidential, and this was the reason for not including the financing and budgeting to the questionnaire survey and the interviews with key persons. The size of the collected and empirical data from the selected participants of the survey questionnaire was limited as five different industries with eight companies to participate in the survey do not provide a very accurate result that can be generalized to all the industries in KRI. A further limitation is the geographical restraint as the study only included seven companies from Erbil and one company from Sulaymaniyah. Thus, future studies may widen the survey to include other cities within KRI and possibly consider representatives throughout all of Iraq. Therefore, conducting additional research with a larger size of collected data and including more industries and companies on a similar case and topic will provide more empirical evidence and an authentic result that will strengthen this research's understanding and findings as to how resource management and gaining competitive advantage can lead the MNCs to more growth and better performance.

Appendix 1: Questionnaires (Resource Management)

Part One: Demographical Information

1. Specify your job category:
   (a) [ ] Executive
   (b) [ ] Manager
   (c) [ ] Supervisor/officer
   (d) [ ] Other, please specify
2. Duration of your job experience:
   (a) [ ] Less than 5 years
   (b) [ ] Between 6 and 10 years

(c) [ ] More than 10 years.

3. Your highest level of education:

(a) [ ] Up to high school
(b) [ ] College degree
(c) [ ] Master/high diploma
(d) [ ] PhD/others

Part Two: Organizational Biographical Information

4. Please write the name of your company:
   ……………………………..
5. The company's establishment year in original country:

(a) [ ] Before 2000
(b) [ ] 2001–2005
(c) [ ] 2006–2010.
(d) [ ] 2011–2015
(e) [ ] After 2015
(f) [ ] N/A

6. Establishment year of your company in Kurdistan:

(a) [ ] Before 2000
(b) [ ] 2001–2005
(c) [ ] 2006–2010
(d) [ ] 2011–2015
(e) [ ] After 2015
(f) [ ] N/A

7. Have you had any steps before the launch of your company?

(a) [ ] Yes
(b) [ ] No

8. What were the steps you took before the launch of your company? (please tick the appropriate—more than one can be selected)

(a) [ ] Defining our target customer.
(b) [ ] Knowing the problem, we are solving.
(c) [ ] Having an agreement with government.
(d) [ ] Having agreements with other companies.
(e) [ ] Having joint venture(s).
(f) [ ] No steps have been taken.

9. When did you feel that your company started to grow? How many years after the launch?

(a) [ ] 1-2 years
(b) [ ] 3-4 years
(c) [ ] 5-6 years
(d) [ ] 7-8 years
(e) [ ] more than 9 years

10. What was the nature of your company's growth? (please tick the appropriate—more than one can be selected)

(a) [ ] Customer-motivated growth
(b) [ ] Adapting easily
(c) [ ] Intelligent hires (high-skilled labor)
(d) [ ] Boosting the top line (revenue of the business with better product or service)
(e) [ ] Increasing the bottom line (profitability of the process by diminishing the cost)

Part Three: Company's Performance

11. To what extent do you agree with the following statements concerning your company profitability?

1= strongly disagree 2 = disagree 3 = neutral 4 = agree 5 = strongly agree

	Statement	1	2	3	4	5
a	With our differentiated products, our firm's profitability is increased					
b	We have introduced new products and this has increased the profitability					
c	Our company's profitability increased due to high level of our customer/supplier care					
d	Because of the high cost of operation, our company's profitability is reduced					
e	Our company's profitability is reduced due to external factors					
f	Our company's profitability is reduced due to the growth of other companies in the same industry					

12. Which one of the below are the reasons for company performance? (rank in order).

1 = not important 2 = less important 3 = important 4 = a little important 5 = very important.

	Description	1	2	3	4	5
a	Regular promotional offers to customers					
b	Prices discrimination					
c	Promotion and advertisement					

	Description	1	2	3	4	5
d	Constant improvement in our communications with other companies					
e	As an employee, keeping fair and transparent communication with our employees and rewarding the most hardworking ones					

Part Four: Resources

13. What kind of resources used during launch phase? (please tick the appropriate—more than one can be selected)

    (a) [ ] Technology
    (b) [ ] Brand name
    (c) [ ] Efficient business process
    (d) [ ] Expat skilled labor
    (e) [ ] Internal skilled labor

14. To what extent you were able to turn the existing resources into capabilities to take your company to the next level?

    (a) [ ] To high extent
    (b) [ ] To little extent
    (c) [ ] To no extent

15. Which one of the resources were most successful? (please tick the appropriate—more than one can be selected)

    (a) [ ] Technology
    (b) [ ] Brand name
    (c) [ ] Efficient business process
    (d) [ ] Expat skilled labor
    (e) [ ] Internal skilled labor

16. Were you able to convert your resources into competitive advantage through resource management?

    (a) [ ] Yes
    (b) [ ] No

17. Which one was unsuccessful? (please tick the appropriate—more than one can be selected)

    (a) [ ] Technology
    (b) [ ] Brand name
    (c) [ ] Efficient business process
    (d) [ ] Expat skilled labor
    (e) [ ] Internal skilled labor

(f) [ ] N/A

Section One: Human Capital

Identify your answer for the following statements with ticking the appropriate.
1= strongly disagree 2 = disagree 3 = neutral 4 = agree 5 = strongly agree.

	Statement	1	2	3	4	5
	Knowledge					
a	As employees, we have enough knowledge about all areas of our company					
b	We are all free in sharing the knowledge within the company					
c	We as employees know about our company's job better than anyone					
d	We have mentorship plans to enable knowledge sharing among our employees					
e	In our company, we care for job rotation to obtain skills					
f	Our employees take trainings on a regular basis					
g	Our company inspires us for a continuous learning					
h	Our company believes in having a fair skill development program					
	Capability					
i	Our company's management team is capable of finding the gap for future accomplishments					
j	Our employees have the sense of responsibility toward the company to take the right decision when the company is facing challenges					
k	We have employees who are capable of solving the company's problems without revealing them					
l	Our employees are strictly following business process to improve capability					
	Experience					
m	Fresh graduates with no experience are important for us, and they can easily adapt to company's business process					
n	Our previous employees have been successful in obtaining new jobs in other companies through knowledge transfer					
o	We apply the principle of learning from interdepartmental interaction than theory of how to function our procedure efficiently					
p	The area of specialization is important to us, and that's why we hire people accordingly					
q	We apply the principle of know-how					

Section Two: Technology

18. Please specify your agreement or disagreement with the following aspects relating to your company technology and sustainability of competitive advantage.

1 = strongly disagree 2 = disagree 3 = indifferent 4 = agree 5 = strongly agree.

	Description	1	2	3	4	5
	Technology					
a	Our employees have innovation capability					
b	Our ways of service offerings vary due to technology variations					
c	Our customers feedback about our IT system and development of our services matter to us					
d	Customer feedback analyses are the source of most of our new and innovative products					
e	In our company, we care for our customer's innovation opinion					
f	With our customer lifestyle, we change our technology					
g	Our research and development division always involved in most of our events and actions					
h	Our company supports and invests in inventions					
i	Our company always keeps the IT resources updated and efficient					
j	Most of the plans of our services require high technological machine which we benefit from it					

Section Three: External/Environmental Factors

19. Has your company faced any external/environmental factors?

    (a) [ ] Yes
    (b) [ ] No

    If Yes, which one of the below:

(c) [ ] Price/oil price change
(d) [ ] Economic growth
(e) [ ] Political situation
(f) [ ] Environmental change
(g) [ ] Others, please specify.......................................

20. The below table contains the environmental factors that may face any company; please indicate the extent of your agreement of the statements:

1 = no extent 2 = small extent 3 = reasonable extent 4 = to a big extent 5 = to a huge extent.

	Description	1	2	3	4	5
	Political factors					
a	Our performance is always affected by political situation in the country					
b	Decentralization has condensed our company's performance					

	Description	1	2	3	4	5
c	As any kind of stability, political stability improves our company's performance					
	Legal factors					
d	We form our company's policies to be aligned with government requirements					
e	The government backs the industry to access information needed					
f	Company's performance favors the government competition rules					
g	The industry is well protected by the government law					
h	Foreign direct investment (FDI) laws favor our business					
i	It is easy to get license for the business					

Section Four: Competitive Advantage

21. How far you agree or disagree with the below statements regarding the competitive advantage?

 1 = strongly disagree 2 = disagree 3 = indifferent 4 = agree 5 = strongly agree.

22. Is your company in maturity phase?

 (a) [ ] Yes
 (b) [ ] No

23. If you are in maturity face, how you can sustain there?

 (a) [ ] Through improving customer care/after service program
 (b) [ ] Through advertisement campaign
 (c) [ ] Through offering price discrimination
 (d) [ ] Through development of new product and services
 (e) [ ] Through improving BM

	Description	1	2	3	4	5
	Organizational culture					
a	Our company's values and standards are clear and comprehensible to everyone in the community					
b	We continue studying our values to fit the market changes					
c	Our employees involve in making company's policies and important decisions					
d	We care for each one of our employees' ideas when we introduce new policies and programs					
e	We have faith in working within the established goals and aims of our company					
	Business reputation					
f	Even when we are not effective enough and less productive, our customers still tolerate us					

	Description	1	2	3	4	5
g	The information we provide to our customers is reliable and believable to them than to our competitors					
h	Our company conducts programs to promote the brand name and gain customer loyalty					

References

Abbas, J., Zhang, Q., Hussain, I., Akram, S., Afaq, A., & Shad, M. A. (2020). Sustainable innovation in small medium enterprises: The impact of knowledge management on organizational innovation through a mediation analysis by using SEM approach. *Sustainability, 12*(6), 2407.

Almeida Costa, A., & Zemsky, P. (2021). The choice of value-based strategies under rivalry: Whether to enhance value creation or bargaining capabilities. *Strategic Management Journal, 42*(11), 2020–2046.

Anwar, G., & Abdullah, N. N. (2021). The impact of human resource management practice on organizational performance. *International Journal of Engineering, Business and Management (IJEBM), 5*.

Arend, R. J., & Lévesque, M. (2010). Is the resource-based view a practical organizational theory? *Organization Science, 21*(4), 913–930.

Azeem, M., Ahmed, M., Haider, S., & Sajjad, M. (2021). Expanding competitive advantage through organizational culture, knowledge sharing and organizational innovation. *Technology in Society, 66*, 101635.

Backman, C. A., Verbeke, A., & Schulz, R. A. (2017). The drivers of corporate climate change strategies and public policy: A new resource-based view perspective. *Business & Society, 56*(4), 545–575.

Barney, J. (1991). Firm resources and sustained competitive advantage. *Journal of Management, 17*(1), 99–120.

Barney, J., Wright, M., & Ketchen, D. J., Jr. (2001). The resource-based view of the firm: Ten years after 1991. *Journal of Management, 27*(6), 625–641.

Berger, L. A., & Berger, D. R. (2011). *The talent management handbook: Creating a sustainable competitive advantage by selecting, developing, and promoting the best people*. McGraw-Hill.

Bouncken, R. B., Gast, J., Kraus, S., & Bogers, M. (2015). Coopetition: A systematic review, synthesis, and future research directions. *Review of Managerial Science, 9*(3), 577–601.

Brouthers, K. D., Brouthers, L. E., & Werner, S. (2008). Resource-based advantages in an international context. *Journal of Management, 34*(2), 189–217.

Camisón, C., & Villar-López, A. (2014). Organizational innovation as an enabler of technological innovation capabilities and firm performance. *Journal of Business Research, 67*(1), 2891–2902.

Chen, J.-S., Vemala, P., & Totten, J. W. (2017). Country of origin, familiarity, the perceived difference and MNC attractiveness. *International Journal of Work Organisation and Emotion, 8*(1), 24–40.

Chesbrough, H., & Bogers, M. (2014). *Explicating open innovation: Clarifying an emerging paradigm for understanding innovation. New frontiers in open innovation* (pp. 3–28). Oxford University Press.

Chiang, F. F., Lemański, M. K., & Birtch, T. A. (2017). The transfer and diffusion of HRM practices within MNCs: Lessons learned and future research directions. *The International Journal of Human Resource Management, 28*(1), 234–258.

Das, A., & Kapil, S. (2015). The role of technological innovation in managing through business cycles: A study on Indian ICT Firms. In *Managing in recovering markets* (pp. 427–439). Springer.

Dawadi, S., Shrestha, S., & Giri, R. A. (2021). Mixed-methods research: A discussion on its types, challenges, and criticisms. *Journal of Practical Studies in Education, 2*(2), 25–36.

Eggers, F. (2020). Masters of disasters? Challenges and opportunities for SMEs in times of crisis. *Journal of Business Research, 116*, 199–208.

Eniola, A. A., & Entebang, H. (2016). Financial literacy and SME firm performance. *International Journal of Research Studies in Management, 5*(1), 31–43.

Farida, I., & Setiawan, D. (2022). Business strategies and competitive advantage: The role of performance and innovation. *Journal of Open Innovation: Technology, Market, and Complexity, 8*(3), 163.

Ferraris, A., Santoro, G., & Dezi, L. (2017). How MNC's subsidiaries may improve their innovative performance? The role Of external sources and knowledge management capabilities. *Journal of Knowledge Management, 21*(3), 540–552.

Gaur, A. S., Kumar, V., & Sarathy, R. (2011). Liability of foreignness and internationalisation of emerging market firms. In Geisler Asmussen, C., Pedersen, T., Devinney, T. M., & Tihanyi, L. (Eds.) Dynamics of globalization: Location-specific advantages or liabilities of foreignness? (Advances in International Management, Vol. 24, pp. 211–233). Emerald Group Publishing Limited, Leeds. https://doi.org/10.1108/S1571-5027(2011)0000024016

Gerhart, B., & Feng, J. (2021). The resource-based view of the firm, human resources, and human capital: Progress and prospects. *Journal of Management, 47*(7), 1796–1819.

Gupta, S., Drave, V. A., Dwivedi, Y. K., Baabdullah, A. M., & Ismagilova, E. (2020). Achieving superior organizational performance via big data predictive analytics: A dynamic capability view. *Industrial Marketing Management, 90*, 581–592.

He, X., Chakrabarty, S., & Eden, L. (2016). The global emergence of Chinese multinationals: A resource-based view of ownership and performance. *Asian Business & Management, 15*(1), 1–31.

Hitt, M. A., Ireland, R. D., & Hoskisson, R. E. (2012). *Strategic management cases: Competitiveness and globalization*. Cengage Learning.

Hossain, M. S., Hussain, K., Kannan, S., & Kunju Raman Nair, S. K. (2022). Determinants of sustainable competitive advantage from resource-based view: Implications for hotel industry. *Journal of Hospitality and Tourism Insights, 5*(1), 79–98.

Jell-Ojobor, M., & Raha, A. (2022). Being good at being good—The mediating role of an environmental management system in value-creating green supply chain management practices. *Business Strategy and the Environment, 31*(5), 1964–1984.

Kethan, M. (2022). A study on the factors affecting employee retention in information technology sector. *The Journal of Contemporary Issues in Business and Government, 28*(4), 980–996.

Khayyat, N. T., & Lee, J.-D. (2015). A measure of technological capabilities for developing countries. *Technological Forecasting and Social Change, 92*, 210–223.

Klein, V. B., & Todesco, J. L. (2021). COVID-19 crisis and SMEs responses: The role of digital transformation. *Knowledge and Process Management, 28*(2), 117–133.

Li, C., Ashraf, S. F., Shahzad, F., Bashir, I., Murad, M., Syed, N., & Riaz, M. (2020). Influence of knowledge management practices on entrepreneurial and organizational performance: A mediated-moderation model. *Frontiers in Psychology, 11*, 577106.

Luo, Y. (2001). Toward a cooperative view of MNC-host government relations: Building blocks and performance implications. *Journal of International Business Studies, 32*(3), 401–419.

Moon, C. W., & Lado, A. A. (2000). MNC-host government bargaining power relationship: A critique and extension within the resource-based view. *Journal of Management, 26*(1), 85–117.

Muhamad, G. M. (2022). Private sector development analysis in post-conflict Kurdistan region of Iraq. *UKH Journal of Social Sciences, 6*(2), 19–32.

Newbert, S. L. (2007). Empirical research on the resource-based view of the firm: An assessment and suggestions for future research. *Strategic Management Journal, 28*(2), 121–146.

Panibratov, A., Ermolaeva, L., & Pantic, B. (2017). The role of international institutions in MNC-host country relations.

Penrose, E. (1959). *The theory of the growth of the firm*. Wiley.

Peteraf, M. A. (1993). The cornerstones of competitive advantage: A resource-based view. *Strategic Management Journal, 14*(3), 179–191.
Rothaermel, F. T. (2012). *Strategic management: Concepts and cases*. McGraw-Hill Education - Europe.
Sirmon, D. G., Hitt, M. A., & Ireland, R. D. (2007). Managing firm resources in dynamic environments to create value: Looking inside the black box. *Academy of Management Review, 32*(1), 273–292.
Strijker, D., Bosworth, G., & Bouter, G. (2020). Research methods in rural studies: Qualitative, quantitative and mixed methods. *Journal of Rural Studies, 78*, 262–270.
Tulung, J. E. (2017). Resource availability and firm's international strategy as key determinants of entry mode choice. *Jurnal Aplikasi Manajemen, 15*(1), 160–168.
White, B. (2002). *Writing your MBA dissertation*. Cengage Learning EMEA.
Williams, C., & Lee, S. H. (2016). Knowledge flows in the emerging market MNC: The role of subsidiary HRM practices in Korean MNCs. *International Business Review, 25*(1), 233–243.

Chapter 6
How the UN Mission Affects the Socio-economic Performance in the Kurdistan Region of Iraq?

Azheen Falah Mustafa

Abstract The Kurdistan Region of Iraq (KRI) is facing a complicated crisis compounding concurrent and mutually aggravating security, political, economic, and social risks. It has been impacted by three multifaceted disasters within a short period, namely the Syrian civil war in 2012 which resulted in a mass refugee inflow to the KRI, the Islamic State of Iraq and the Levant (ISIL) crises in 2014, and lastly, the KRI and the federal government of Iraq dispute that led to KRI budget crisis. The United Nations' involvement in the Kurdistan Region of Iraq has remarkably impacted its social and economic progress. By helping to resolve conflicts and promote peace, it has helped create a stable environment for businesses to thrive. The UN has also provided aid to those in need, helping them recover from the effects of war and displacement. The United Nations mission in the Kurdistan Region of Iraq has been instrumental in tackling the challenges faced by internally displaced persons (IDPs) and migrants. This research focuses on the effect of the International Organization for Migration (IOM) and the United Nations Development Programme (UNDP) on the performance of the Kurdistan Regional Government (KRG) in terms of refugee care. This research will cover the humanitarian assistance provided during the crisis facing KRG by the IOM, and how this assistance helped KRG perform better during the hard times. In addition, it will discuss the programs conducted by the UNDP during the post-conflict situation to improve the human kills, raise awareness on different aspects, and increase the economy of the KRG. A mixed methodology is applied to achieve the stated aim of this research. Twenty interviews were conducted to attain the primary data, and relevant literature was reviewed to obtain the secondary data. This study will help the government assess and evaluate the work conducted by international organizations.

Keywords Humanitarian assistance · International organization · Development · Kurdistan region

---

A. F. Mustafa (✉)
Consultancy Corner, Erbil, Iraq

G. M. Muhamad, N. T. Khayyat (eds.), *Resource Management Performance: A Sectoral Analysis in the Post-Conflict Kurdistan Region of Iraq*, Perspectives on Development in the Middle East and North Africa (MENA) Region,
https://doi.org/10.1007/978-981-97-7725-9_6

6.1 Introduction

The KRI is facing a complicated crisis compounding concurrent and mutually aggravating security, political, economic, and social risks. It has been impacted by three multifaceted disasters within a short period, namely the Syrian civil war in 2012 which resulted in a mass refugee inflow to the KRI, the Islamic State of Iraq and the Levant (ISIL) crises in 2014, lastly, and the KRI and the federal government of Iraq dispute that led to KRI budget crisis. A sudden population increase in only 2 years in KRI resulted from the influx of more than 25,000 Syrian refugees that added to the more than three million IDPs in the whole of Iraq due to the conflict with ISIL, in addition to nearly one million seeking refuge in the KRI (International Organization for Migration, 2017).

As such, about 17% of the population residing in the KRI are displaced persons from Syria and the rest of Iraq. These crises are seriously challenging the social, economic, and political conditions of KRI as the host community, which may not only halt but also reverse development gains.

While KRI continues to steadily recover from years of conflict, thousands of vulnerable families across the country remain displaced and in acute need of protection and assistance. As of September 2021, around 99% of the Syrian refugees, 50% of IDPs, and 50% of other nationalities are residing in the KRI only in the three KRI governorates, namely, Erbil, Sulaymaniyah, and Duhok (Timilsina, 2021) (Table 6.1).

According to a study conducted by Mather III et al. (2018), the stability of a region is related to the economy. When the economy is growing, the region is more stable because of more employment, better income for individuals, more security, and more provision of medical treatments. The author further argued that other factors may affect the stability, in this case ISIS. When a nation is facing war and is economically unstable, it needs international aid (Chun, 2018).

This research will focus on the humanitarian assistance that was provided by both IOM and UNDP during and after the conflict period. In this research, the work

Table 6.1 Number of IDPs and migrants in KRI and Iraq (IOM, September 2021 and UNHCR, January 2020)

Governorate	IDPs	Syrian Refugee	Non-Syrian Refugee
Erbil	239,052	124,182	9557
Sulaymaniyah	139,614	30,511	4745
Duhok	319,584	88,251	5790
Rest of Iraq	716,382	2866	21,047
Total	1,414,632	245,810	41,139
% KRI	49.36	98.83	48.84
% Erbil	16.90	50.52	23.23
% Sulaymaniyah	9.87	12.41	11.53
% Duhok	22.59	35.90	14.07
% Rest of Iraq	50.64	1.17	51.16

of UNDP and IOM will be discussed. Most of the work conducted by the UNDP is known as innovation. On the other hand, the work and projects done by IOM are known as emergency assistance. According to research, there exists a strong link between economic growth and innovation (Freeman et al., 2018); while implying the quota of the UNDP, it is clear that the organization will help in the economic growth, in different aspects which will later on be discussed in this research.

Furthermore, IOM's mission reveals that it supports in many aspects, such as providing humanitarian aid, safety, and security, capacity building, and job training, and these lead to better physiological and healthier lives for the refugees, IDPs, and local community.

The UNDP may contribute to economic growth through the direct job creation, development of new services and industries, workforce transformation, and business and entrepreneurship.

The advantages of the IOM which provides humanitarian assistance are to provide hope to vulnerable people, provide shelter, food, and security to IDPs and refugees, reduce the financial and administration pressure on the government, and help people migrate legally.

This research aims to study how IOM and UNDP are helping KRG in times of conflict and the post-conflict situation. The research is conducted to show whether IOM and UNDP took part in providing for the needs of IDPs, refugees, and the local community. The specific objectives of this study are summarized as follows:

1. To investigate the mechanisms IOM applied to help assist the refugees, IDPs, and returnees to provide them with their basic needs
2. To investigate and identify the tools used by the UNDP in providing capacity building to the refugees, IDPs, and local community
3. To investigate the effects of IOM and UNDP activities on the economics of KRG

Finally, the importance of this study can be summarized as follows:

- Explains how intergovernmental organizations, reacted during the ISIS era, as the latter is considered one of the significant topics in the world today, it is important to research how different entities react to overcome this challenge that is being faced globally.
- Adds more knowledge on what intergovernmental organizations perform, before conflict, during conflict, and in the post-conflict situation and how they have assisted everyone living in the region; the refugees, IDPs, returnees, and house community.
- Another important aspect is finance management, how the money that is donated by the donors is being spent. This is the most important topic for donor countries, sponsors, and governments to know if corruption exists or not.
- Helps the Kurdish scholars to examine and investigate this area of interest, it will also encourage them to join such organizations, even as volunteers since it will lead to helping a society and providing hope to the people in need or enhancing their skills.

- Helps policymakers and governments also to appreciate the work conducted by international organizations.

6.2 The UN Mission

6.2.1 Introduction

As much development in the world is witnessed, challenges will be witnessed too, one of the challenges is conflicts of war, and a consequence of war is the destruction of cities, towns, homes, and infrastructure (Latar, 2018). During these challenges, civilians are displaced and emergency assistance is needed. The Humanitarian assistance and development training provided to the displaced is when IOM, UNDP, and other agencies come in; however, each agency presents for some time to solve a specific issue and work on a different program (Beresford & Pettit, 2019).

Assistance ranges from providing basic needs such as water, food, and shelter, to reconstruction of the destructed areas. In between, there are several livelihood programs.

IOM and UNDP are both United Nations agencies, they are considered intergovernmental organizations, and they have 193 member states and 2 observer states. IOM and UNDP have been the agencies that continuously supported the displaced people of Iraq since 2014, during the war against ISIS (Manis, 2018). According to governments and the international community, UN agencies provide a better hope for all, while according to some citizens and activists, such agencies exist only for personal benefit. Of course, this view is not considered valid, as researchers have been tracking the work of those agencies and have seen their actions on the ground. These agencies were able to respond to the emergency needs of the displaced.

During war, the challenges are many, needs are enormous and resources are scarce; that is why all the agencies need to work together to provide the required assistance to the displaced communities. Displacement has been the faith of many people around the world due to the continuous prolonged conflicts in different parts of the world. War has been one of these conflicts, and displacement is the consequence of it.

In 2014, when the fight against ISIS started, research showed that the Kurdistan region of Iraq had the largest number of internally displaced people (IDP) and refugees in the past few years, and the number is yet to increase (Baker et al., 2019).

Throughout Iraq, many people were forced to flee their homes and leave their whole lives behind because of the fear of death. In addition to the IDPs, thousands of Syrian refugees were displaced to Kurdistan, seeking safety, and security (Alipui & Gerke, 2018). This made the economic situation of Kurdistan even worse because Kurdish Peshmergas' had to fight ISIS, KRG had to assist such food and shelter, and clothing for the IDPs and ensure that the economy of the region would not get worse, as the Iraqi government had cut off the 17% budget it provided to the region.

When the Iraqi government cut the budget, the Kurdistan region mainly depended on the income from producing and selling crude oil until the price of crude oil had decreased in the global market. This is when the KRG started seeking the assistance of the international community to assist in providing the basic needs for the displaced people (Sümer & Joseph, 2019).

Around four million people were displaced, and thousands of others were killed. The displaced people had only seen violence and war for the past few years, and this had a lot of consequences, their need was not only food and shelter but also medical and psychological treatments (Phillips, 2018).

They needed to believe that tomorrow would be better than today because some had their family members killed in front of them, while others were raped by ISIS or beaten up. Despite the economic challenges the KRI was facing, the government was able to welcome all the refugees and IDPs.

Through the Department of Foreign Relations (DFR) the government sent letters to different countries to stress the humanitarian crisis and the need for assistance (Dionigi, 2019). Luckily the KRG was able to receive humanitarian assistance from the international community; the donor countries, the United Nations agencies, and other international NGOs (Bache, 2018). Although many organizations and countries helped KRG during this crisis, this was still not enough, and more donors and more assistance are still needed as the situation of most refugees is still unstable.

As the period of war ended and the KRG was in the post-conflict stage, the UNDP interfered to help refugees, IDPs, and the local community continue with their normal lives, increase their capacity-building skills, become more creative, or even turn them into entrepreneurs (Baser, 2018).

6.2.2 The IOM's Projects in the KRI

Since 2003, when the IOM started operating in Iraq, the IOM Iraq has been able to build a strong network of offices in all the governorates of Iraq. Since 2014, the IOM office in Erbil has been expanding drastically and operating more than any of the offices, because most of the refugees and IDPs are assisted through the Erbil office. The IOM Iraq can support its operations in the northern, central, and southern regions of Iraq (Rashid et al., 2019). The IOM has sub-offices in the Kurdistan Region, in Erbil, Sulaymaniyah, and Duhok, and it currently has more than 400 staff.

The IOM's activities in the KRI were as follows:

- Responding to the Humanitarian Emergency needs. IOM is a member of the United Nations Humanitarian Country Team (HCT) and is closely working with the KRG Joint Crisis Coordination Centre's Humanitarian Coordination Forum, IOM provides humanitarian assistance in different priority sectors including non-food items such as; fuel, mattresses, kerosene, hygiene kits, blankets, kitchen sets, shelter like tents and sealing off kits for unfinished buildings, protection such as psycho-social support primary health care in the KRI (Warda et al., 2018).

In addition, since January 2014, the IOM has been studying the internal displacement in Iraq through the Displacement Tracking Matrix (DTM) (Nikolaev et al., 2019) to identify the locations, needs, and vulnerabilities of IDPs and returnees throughout all 18 governorates.

The DTM is used to evaluate the overall humanitarian response of the KRG, UN, international NGOs, and local NGOs working in the KRI. The IOM's DTM Team worked closely with the Kurdistan Regional Statistics Office (KRSO) of the Ministry of Planning, regarding the population number in the KRI (Al-Hamadani et al., 2019). Starting in 2016, the IOM's DTM identified millions of IDP and refugee families living within the Erbil, Duhok, and Sulaymaniyah governorates.

- Facilitating community stabilization in conflict-affected communities

- to facilitate the recovery of the communities affected by conflicts, IOM's community stabilization program provides a wide range of individual and community-based services. IOM works with other UN agencies such as the UNDP, and several government partners from the KRG, including the Directorate of Police (MOI), MOLSA, Governor's offices, and technical ministries such as Electricity and Agriculture and Water Resources. The program has four essential components:
- Social cohesion operates by providing psychosocial support for vulnerable people affected by conflict (especially women and youth) through sports/recreation activities, cultural, and community-driven peacebuilding, and solving housing problems.
- Provide vocational training, supporting business development, apprenticeships, and job training for individuals to strengthen livelihoods and generate income.
- Rebuild infrastructure and important services through community-led rehabilitation of physical infrastructure like schools and hospitals, and renovation of basic services (water, electricity) (Berger, 2018).
- Develop conflict mediation and community policing forums by using native conflict resolution structures and methods to strengthen security in post-conflict communities.
- Managing the Migration of KRI citizens. The IOM also maintains the KRG with assisting and training on migration management on different migration topics such as immigration and border management, human trafficking and smuggling, and labor migration through a wide range of programs to ensure 'safe' migration for the individuals who want to migrate (Chiu et al., 2018).

The IOM has launched a campaign to raise awareness of the risk of irregular migration and promote safe migration and local opportunities because many migrants have understood the concept wrong, and they expect something different during their arrival to Europe. This campaign was very essential for the youth, as it gave them a better understanding of how hard the process of illegal migration is (Smith, 2018).

In addition, the IOM's offices in Erbil, Sulaymaniyah, and Duhok have been assisting the KRG for many years through the return and reintegration of Iraqi migrants to the KRI mainly from different countries in Europe. The IOM's Assisted Voluntary Return and Reintegration (AVRR) program not only provides logistical and transportation services but also supports returnees with finding employment and other livelihood choices through job coaching, placement services, business development, and education (Palmer, 2018).

As the KRG is fighting ISIL and struggling with the fiscal crisis, agencies target to assist the KRG in managing the huge number of IDPs and refugees in the KRI and facilitating the return of IDPs through support to IDPs and host communities (Dalay, 2015). Agencies also work closely with the KRG and the UNDP to develop contingency plans for potential new displacements in the KRI to help the vulnerable IDPs and refugees. The IOM assists those vulnerable displaced people under different programs and departments.

The IOM has three main departments to respond to the needs of the people, the Department of Operations and Emergencies, the Department of Migration Management, and the Department of International Cooperation and Partnership where each department works on different programs to provide as much assistance as possible (Warda & Almaffraji, 2020).

The IOM took part in providing humanitarian assistance such as shelter, medical treatment, protection, early recovery, logistics camp coordination, and camp management, which are the most important needs because the displaced people fled their homes and had nowhere to go and nothing to eat (De Torrente, 2004). The IOM worked to improve the living conditions of the displaced by acting as the camp management agency to monitor and ensure that all families had shelter, and in coordination with other agencies, it made sure that all families got an adequate amount of food to live.

Furthermore, to the assistance provided in camps, the IOM has a resettlement program, which helps in the migration of refugees and IDPs to a country that can host them. This resettlement program is in partnership with the UNHCR, QANDIL, and the hosting country, where employees of these organizations visit the camp to register the cases of individuals who would like to migrate to another country, then the cases are sent to the hosting countries, and based on the emergency of the case, hosting country decides which case to host first. Those displaced people are sent through the IOM to the hosting country, to ensure that the process goes as smoothly as possible, employees in the operation department are in direct contact with the hosting country to ensure that the displaced people will have a home, job, and school ready for them before they migrate. The operation team also applies for their visa, and residency card, books their tickets, does their exit permit takes them to the airport, and escorts them until they arrive at their destination in the hosting country (Miller, 2016).

Before the migrants are sent to the hosting country, they undergo medical checks and cultural orientation training, where the migrants are taken by the IOM staff to the hospital to do medical checkups to check their medical condition and analyze if any doctor is needed on board or if any medication is needed to be provided by the hosting country. While in the Cultural Orientation, they are taught the basic words of the language, what to expect when they go there, what the country's food is like, how their people are, etc. So that the families are prepared do not get shocked once they start living in the hosting country. The resettlement department has been working with Canada, the UK, Australia, France, and many other European countries very closely during the past 4 years, and through this program, thousands of displaced people were able to migrate and they have now started a new life where they feel safer (Farhan, 2019).

While some of the displaced people register their cases and migrate, others believe that the situation can get better and do not want to migrate, they prefer staying in their homeland and waiting for the situation to improve (O'Donnell & Newland, 2008). The IOM, in cooperation with the UNDP, assists them as well under different programs such as the Economic Recovery and Livelihoods program and the community policing program. The IOM took part in those programs to improve the safety, security, and stability of the Kurdistan region and Iraq as a whole: to make the displaced people feel safe once again by protecting their human rights, ensuring that the international community is aware of the instability in the region, so they can send troops and forces to help fight ISIS which caused harm and destroyed their homes (Fitzpatrick, 2021).

The IOM works to recover the economy of the people and provide them with jobs needed, or training needed to start that job, and in case, the people are too young or are unable to work, the IOM provides them with a small amount of funds so that they can live (Mawani et al., 2021).

For this program, the IOM works in partnership with the Ministry of Labor and Social Affairs, the Ministry of Agriculture, Ministry of Municipalities and Planning, and this is done to increase the access of IDPs, refugees, and even local communities to sustainable and decent jobs.

It was obvious that KRG was not able to provide medical treatment for all the displaced with its bad economy and limited resources, but with the help of IOM, they were able to assist the vulnerable displaced people who had risks to their health. Their main aims are as follows:

1. To improve access to health services through referrals and assisted transportation. They provide two types of transportation: emergency transportation provides ambulance services all the time to take the patients from the camp to the nearest hospital if urgent, and non-emergency transportation, which provides a bus or car in the camp to take patients who feel well to the doctor during the day.
2. Provide health services in the camps for the displaced if they do not feel well such as Static Clinics, and raise awareness on the importance of health, for example, what they should eat, what or who they should stay away from, or what to do when one of the displaced gets ill. The IOM did not only focus on improving the health system of the displaced but also of the house community, it assisted in the rehabilitation, and revitalization of hospitals in the KRG, and in capacity building, support, and training of the staff in the hospital to strengthen the ability

of health workers so they can perform with the highest quality standards and provide the best services to the patients.

Among the displaced people, there were Yazidi families who faced the Genocide. In an interview with a civilian who faced the Yazidi Genocide, the situation of the people was discussed. She stated that "the genocide led to massacres that killed thousands of Yazidi Kurds, and the abduction of Yazidi women during the time where ISIS tried to exercise what is known as The Forced Conversion." With tears in her eyes, she stated that "the Yazidi victims included 6500 abducted girls and women, 350,000 displaced Yazidi civilians, and 1500 killed and executed." For these reasons, they needed special care and psychological support (Omarkhali, 2016).

Research showed that almost all the Yazidi civilians were facing posttraumatic stress and depression and they needed special assistance, so the IOM provided psychological therapy for the people, especially for the children and women. The women were used as sex slaves and the children had to watch their mother or sister being raped, while other children watched ISIS their father or elder brother being killed. With the help of the international community, the IOM was able to help some of the victims overcome depression, but not all the victims can overcome and forget this very easily. The refugees state that the war is over, but their consequences are not, they still do not feel safe and they face different psychological problems every day (Nicolaus & Yuce, 2017).

In addition to providing health services, the IOM was able to provide help building schools or classrooms inside the camps to emphasize the importance of education for the children. The education projects were carried out in partnership with UNICEF, and their main aim in providing education for children is to teach them that violence is not the only way to solve issues and to ensure that they do not get brainwashed by the ideology of ISIS. The education provided for children also helps the displaced to adapt to their normal school lives easier once they return home or migrate to another country (Ogunode et al., 2022).

The IOM not only assisted the refugees and IDPs only but also helped to boost the economy of the Kurdistan region as a whole, it helped the KRG's economy by at least lowering the budget which had to be provided by the region for the displaced, such as providing the food, shelter, clothing, medical treatments, and heating materials it also helped in migration, so each person who migrated meant the government could spend less money for the displaced (Eklund et al., 2016).

In addition to assisting the refugees and the IDPs, the IOM has an Assisted Voluntary Return and Reintegration program. This program is where migrants who voluntarily return to their home country are helped in different ways such as purchasing tickets to their home country and transportation to their destination in their home country after the IOM provides cash, training, startup business ideas, and location based on the needs of the family. This helps boost the economy as it is a result of more local businesses and providing them with cash and housing so it will lower the rate of poverty and in some cases incidents such as stealing (Burnam et al., 2009).

According to research, there is no durable solution to the displaced people in Iraq, but he IOM's chief of Mission indicated that there are solutions, rebuilding their destructed homes, finding them jobs, and providing them with the necessary health treatments is a solution. While studies have shown that 75% of the displaced live in rented homes or camps, more and more financial support is needed from donor countries.

6.2.3 The UNDP's Project in the KRI

Livelihood programs are essential for everyone in the region, to have the necessary skills, knowledge, and capacity to work and generate income. These livelihood programs are usually carried out by international organizations, especially the UNDP which is seen as an umbrella. It is important to realize that the contribution of the UN is needed during peace and war, at peace there is more focus on development issues while during the war the focus is mainly on humanitarian assistance (Pohlmann et al., 2007).

According to UNDP Country Director for Iraq, the first step to stability is reconstructing and recovering the destructed towns, and then returning the IDPs to their homes De Santisteban (2005). The first step that the UNDP takes is to reconstruct and lead to stable development, followed by reconciliation of security sector reform. These are considered the main aims of the UNDP in the post-conflict situation.

In addition to the two main aims, the UNDP has other projects helped in providing the necessary programs, training, and equipment to reconstruct the destructed areas and to help the local communities and displaced increase their income by providing them with job training, raising their awareness on important factors which affect the region as a whole, such as the environmental factors, the importance of water, and saving clean energy. They support youth and even elders by funding their initiatives. They increase the creativity of children by launching educational camps and playgrounds. They also train locals on creative innovation; sometimes they even provide funds to support the startup of a job.

The UNDP has programs on governmental and political level. To ensure that both the government of Iraq and KRG work together for the peace, stability, and well-being of their citizen and that is why governance codes are being conducted. One of the most important programs that is being conducted by the UNDP is the Local Area Development Program in Iraq (LADPI), to make the lives of Iraqi and Kurdish citizens better. LADPI program which is working in partnership with other agencies and is funded by the European Union started in February 2015 and operated until the end of 2018, so this program was operating during the period when the fight against ISIS was still ongoing. This livelihood program during the time of war was very crucial as it provided hope that a better life was to come and that the future would be better than the past.

Examples of projects conducted by the UNDP include assisting women and making sure that their voice is heard, they established a Women's Center where different types of assistance were provided to the women who faced violence, and since 2015 around 2000 women have been assisted. Furthermore, building institutions such as anti-corruption institutions and institutions of peace and stability, to prevent corruption and raise awareness of what a peaceful and stable society is. Another aim of the peace and stability institution is to erase the extremism ideology of ISIS, in case the victims or children who were kidnapped by ISIS were brainwashed.

Putting all the work done by the UNDP aside, some activists think that training and empowerment are not necessary during the war stage and that the money spent on such activities should be given to the families in cash, while others think that such programs are provided to give them a promise that tomorrow will be a better day and prepare them for the post-conflict situation so that they can start working even when they are away from home. Doctors and therapists think that such programs are not only essential but also mandatory, as every individual has been affected and hurt; they need to be kept busy and trained to generate income, become independent, and have feeling of being useful to themselves (Ensler, 2016).

While the United Nations Development Programme (UNDP) with the slogan "Empowered Lives, Resilient Nations" is operating to connect the world, its experiences, and knowledge to create a better life for all (Gregoratti, 2010).

The UNDP is committed to supporting the government and the people of a country during the transition toward reconciliation, reform, and stability. The support ranges from providing emergency livelihood to helping stabilize liberated areas. The UNDP usually works to support the governance of reform. The UNDP has many different programs in the transition state of Iraq, the programs mainly being conducted in Iraq and KRG, in particular, focusing on responding to disasters and building for the future. The programs include support on housing, rehabilitation, and secure tenure for the returnees in Sinjar, rebuilding the Mosul University Library, recovery and stability through local development, and mobilizing parliament on achieving the sustainable development goals and targets in Iraq so that government is more prepared for finding the right paths to achieve the goals.

The UNDP supports the government and private sector to promote job creation, as it is one of the main challenges facing the region. In addition to that, the UNDP helps the public and private sectors implement its economic reform. According to the head of the UNDP, they aim to increase revenue and minimize losses due to corruption but also promote an inclusive growth approach to achieve the 2030 agenda of the SDG (Kaul et al., 2003).

Based on the findings and the collected data through primary and secondary research, it reveals that IOM and UNDP alongside other organizations were able to provide huge assistance to the refugees, IDPs, returnees, and local community through different projects. These projects did not only provide a living to these people but also houses, training, psychosocial support, and hope for a better future. In addition to that, according to government officials, these organizations helped reduce the pressure on the government, and if these organizations did not exist the pressure would be more on the government and it would lead to bigger problems and the people would not be assisted to this extent.

6.3 Methodology

6.3.1 Research Approach

A survey approach was used which is based on primary data collection through interviews with the different stakeholders (i.e., UN officials, KRG officials, and informant interviews with community leaders), and secondary data were collected from a survey conducted by IOM and UNDP to obtain quantitative data using a triangulated research approach and find out how the livelihood programs have helped the refugees, IDPs, and local community.

The secondary data were collected from the Head of Programs of UNDP and IOM (specifically, individuals who benefitted from the UN program and interviews with the vendors) aiming at obtaining feedback on how beneficiaries were helped to find the effectiveness of the programs.

6.3.2 The Dependent and the Independent Variables

The dependent variable for this research is defined as "Livelihood programs of the UNDP and the IOM. These are programs that assist before, during, and post-conflict situations to ensure that the lives of citizens get better and that they receive their basic needs. In this research, demands for projects in the KRI are measured through the numbers of the different groups fleeing to the region, such as IDPs (internally), refugees, and returnees moving to the region from neighboring countries."

The independent variables are refugees, IDPs, returnees, the local community, and the KRG, they are known as dependent because they depend on the programs that are conducted by the organizations and the help they provide.

The programs include several sections, such as sewage projects, water projects, shelter, food, education, such as schools, and many more. Based on the collected data, after it is analyzed, the host country (its government) in cooperation with the United Nations agencies asks for funds required to be able to assist the people in need.

Sometimes, these projects face shortages, for example, a project might require $1000,000 while only $20,000 is provided, and the other remaining $80,000 is the shortage of the project. Moreover, in the next upcoming sections, the conceptualization and operationalization of both dependent and independent variables will be elaborated on in detail.

The data were collected in 2019; it included before conflict, during conflict, and post-conflict. It studies how the livelihood support provided by the IOM, the UNDP, and other agencies throughout the KRI has helped sustain and strengthen social networks.

Four governmental entities and two non-governmental entities have been selected to collect the primary data and 400 beneficiaries for collecting secondary data.

Furthermore, the primary and secondary data have been collected from non-governmental entities: IOM, UNDP, and governmental entities, including, the Joint Crisis Coordination Centre (JCC), Governorates of Erbil, Sulaymaniyah, and Duhok, the Ministry of Interior, the KRG Department of Foreign Relations.

6.4 Data Analysis

6.4.1 Field Observation and Interviews with the Vendors

A total of six vendors were interviewed during the follow-up visit, who were engaged in the implementation of the project as toolkit providers through the electronic smart card system.

They were asked various questions like: *"How did the assessment stage take place? How you were identified?"*, *"Do you see that the beneficiary selection was fair?"*, *"Did you face any challenges? If yes, do you have any recommendations?"*

The vendor stated that they were selected through a market assessment and due to the variety of the items that they can deliver, they were satisfied with the service, the vendor stated that there were some challenges in the provision of the tools, as some of the targeted beneficiaries have required lower quality tools with lower prices not available in their stores, and some other requested second-hand tools. Some vendors stated facing challenges in opening bank accounts as it took a long time.

6.4.2 Interviews with the BSP Beneficiaries Through Phone Calls and Field Visits

One of the primary aspects of the follow-up was measuring the impact of the project on the Beneficiaries' living conditions. The interviews focused on the following aspects:

- Service satisfaction
- Employability
- Functionality of the business and income increase
- Improvement of access
- Improvement of social cohesion
- Recommendations

The age of the surveyors was from 25 to 55 years old. All the beneficiaries were fully satisfied with the BDS training services stating that they fully recommend the services to friends and neighbors, and 97% of them reported using the skills learned in the BDS training. Additionally, most of them agreed that marketing and business management were the most useful topics.

Ninety-eight percent of the respondents showed high satisfaction with the smart card system used for purchasing the tools. Forty-seven percent of the respondents stated that the vendor's prices were higher than market prices, and sixty-six percent of them claimed that the prices were not negotiable as they thought that only one vendor was identified to buy the tools from, while more than one vendor identified for each type of tools.

The finding showed that 85% of the supported businesses are still operational 2 months after the project closure, and there has been a noted improvement in the employment status of the targeted beneficiaries, as the percentage of unemployed and employed on daily wages decreased, and the rate of beneficiaries having businesses increased, comparing before and after 2 months of the project.

6.4.2.1 Skills and Experience Gained

The UNDP and the IOM provided training that helped refugees, IDPs, and the local community build skills and made it easier for them to find jobs or start their businesses. In a study done, it was shown that the skill which was mostly learned was marketing, by a rate of 60%, 40% business and management skills, 20% learned the production plan, and less than 10% learned the supply chain skills. A total of 90% of the people used the skills they had learned and were able to find a job (see Fig. 6.1).

6.4.2.2 Living Experiences

To find out how much their lives have changed and what they were doing in their previous lives to generate income, this question was asked:" What did you do previously for a living?"

9% were employed on wages, 22% had their own small business, 47% of them were doing business with partners, and 22% were unemployed (see Fig. 6.2).

6.4.2.3 Current Living

During the war, all the refugees and IDPs were unemployed and they had to wait for humanitarian aid to even find food. After the KRG allowed the refugees and IDPs to work in the region, with the help of IOM, UNDP, and other organizations, most of the previously employed people were able to find a job, and the unemployment rate decreased from 22% to 8%, as through these programs even more women started working; the women were producing handmade products. The IDPs were able to be transferred and they were employed on wages at a rate of 6%, 31% were able to start

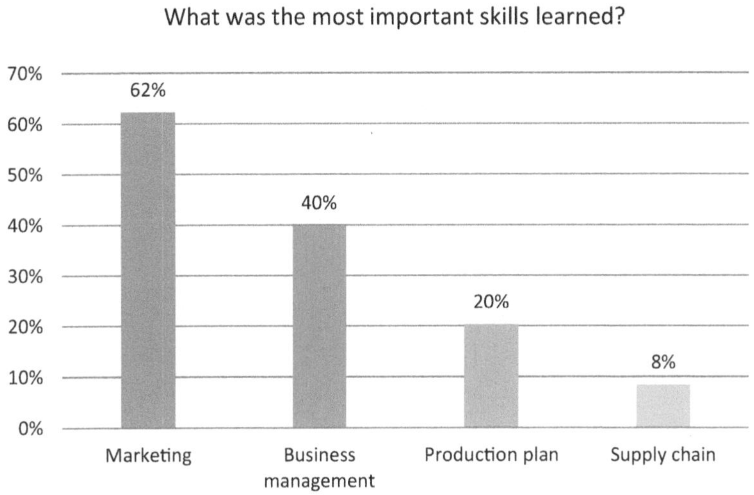

Fig. 6.1 Skills learned

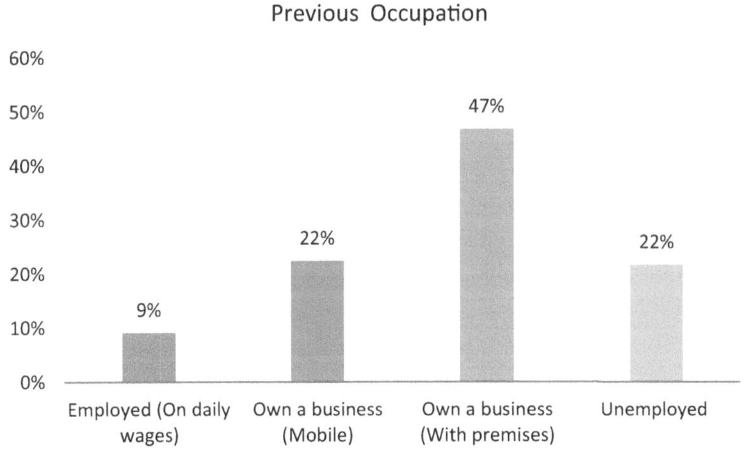

Fig. 6.2 The respondents' past job

their businesses after being trained, 55% of them started businesses with a partner, and only 8% were left unemployed (See Fig. 6.3).

6.4.2.4 Future Business Plans

Through this project, the involvement of the beneficiaries in income-generating activities and running businesses reduced their vulnerability, reportedly, the average net profit of the businesses is around 370,000 IQD per month, while the current

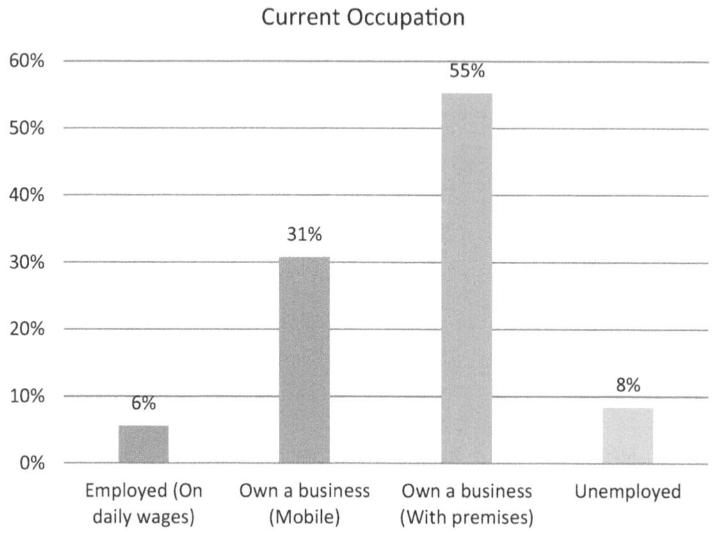

Fig. 6.3 Current job

business net profits are still not enough to cover the family expenses of 45% of the beneficiaries, and the average family expenses are around 460,000 IQD per month. At the same time, only 10% of the beneficiaries have other sources of income (other working family members).

More than 50% of the targeted beneficiaries are planning to expand their businesses, and around 42% of them are not planning to make any change, while few beneficiaries are planning to close their businesses, due to the burden of the shop rents and not having a profitable business, and few plan to move their premises to other places (Fig. 6.4).

6.4.2.5 Life After Receiving Services

Reportedly, 80% of the beneficiaries confirmed having an increase in their income due to the services they received (see Fig. 6.5).

In general, with the increased income, the targeted beneficiaries were found to have improved access to employment, healthcare, education, housing, and basic services, as a result of the services delivered. Figure 6.6 shows which sector has shown improvement and in what percent.

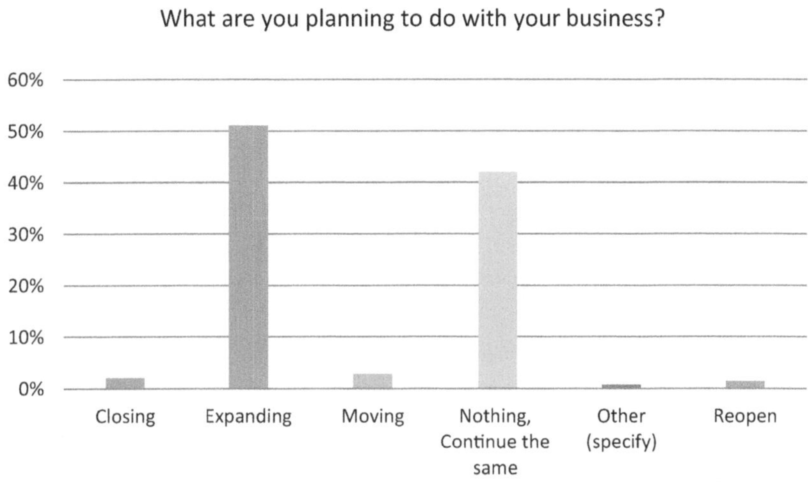

Fig. 6.4 Business plan

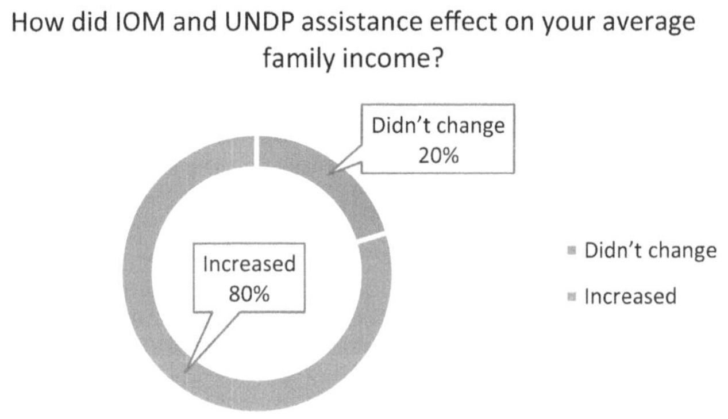

Fig. 6.5 IOM and UNDP assistance role

6.4.2.6 Interviews with the Transportation Beneficiaries Through Phone Calls

Out of 168 beneficiaries who received transportation assistance ($M = 73$, $F = 95$), a total of 136 beneficiaries were followed up on, where 75 (55%) of them were females while the rest were males.

The follow-up consisted of various questions like; "How did you access your school/work before IOM provided you with transportation assistance?", "How likely you will recommend our service to a friend, neighbor, or family?", and "Did your access to education increase?"

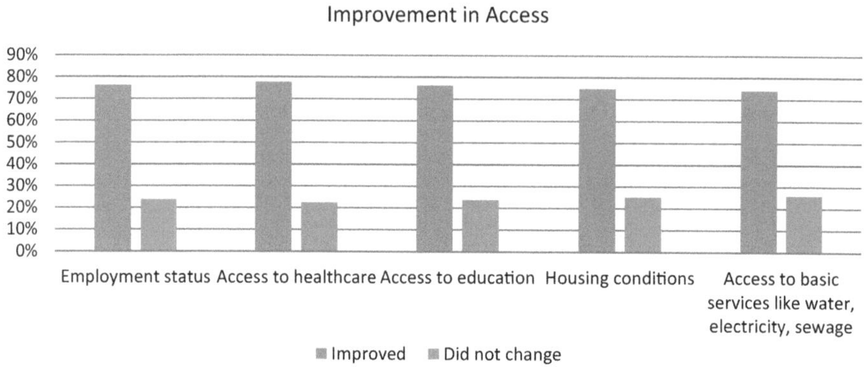

Fig. 6.6 Improvement in access

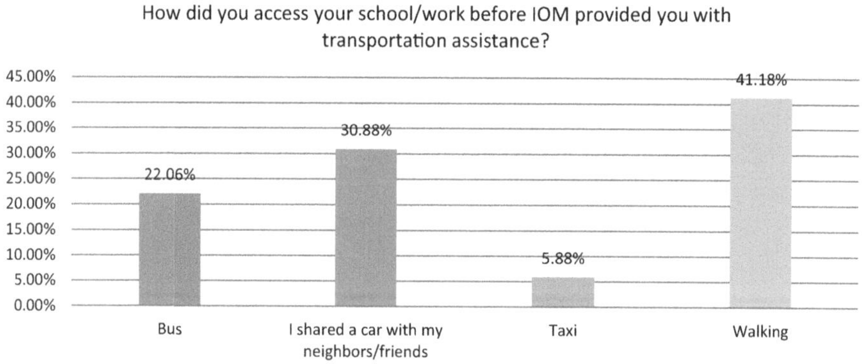

Fig. 6.7 Access to work before IOM assistant

The findings showed that before the assistance, 41% of students were walking long distances to access their schools, while the others were sharing cars with neighbors or paying for taxis and buses (Fig. 6.7).

Generally, the targeted beneficiaries were satisfied with the details of the service, as over 75% of them indicated that the timing of the transportation was accurate, and over 85% indicated that this service was meeting their daily mobility needs (Fig. 6.8).

Reportedly, 94% of the beneficiaries indicated improved access to education due to this service and also stated that they would highly recommend this service to friends, neighbors, and family members. At the same time, around 6% of them might recommend or will not recommend respectively, because of the service's short period, which was 3 months, and for some of them only 2 weeks (as two beneficiaries stated) (Fig. 6.9).

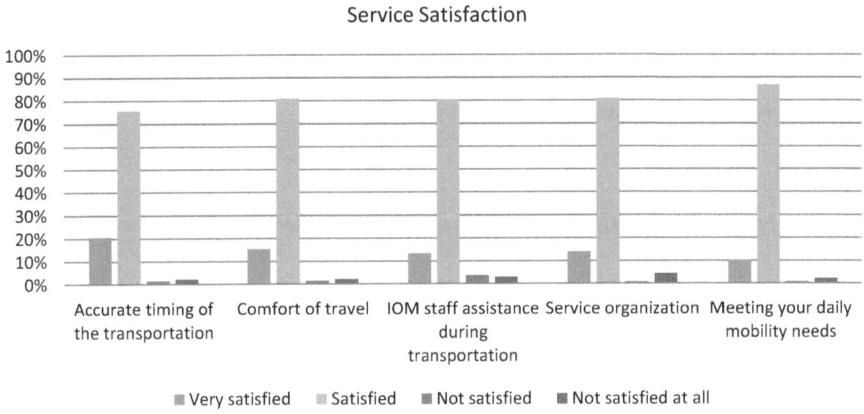

Fig. 6.8 Service satisfaction

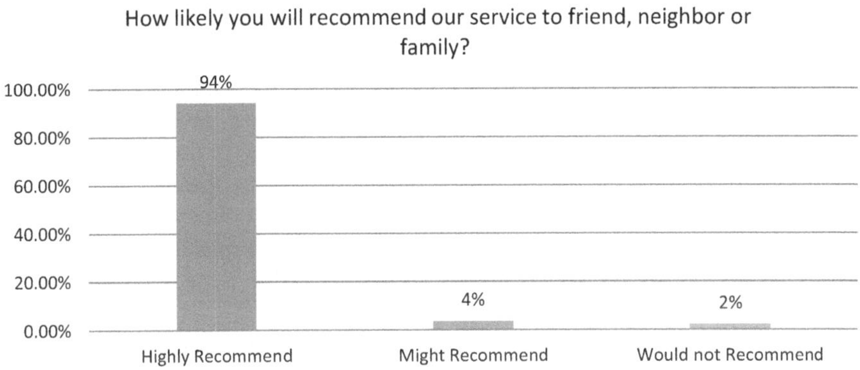

Fig. 6.9 Service recommendation

6.4.2.7 Interview with the IOM (AVRR) Team

Monitoring of the returnees is carried out from 3 to 6 months after returnees receive an in-kind grant through field visits or phone calls depending on the donor's request and the accessibility of the return location of the returnee.

Some vulnerable cases, such as minors, female-headed households, and returnees with a disability, are given priority, and sometimes, they are monitored twice.

During the monitoring process in 2017, 83% of the beneficiaries were reached after receiving reintegration assistance. The success rate was around 69%. IOM Iraq considers cases successful when returnees have reached levels of economic self-sufficiency, social stability within their communities, and psychosocial well-being.

Through IOM's Assisted Voluntary Return and Reintegration (AVRR), IOM Iraq continues to support returned migrants. The number of AVRRs in Iraq is still considerably high; over 12,500 in 2016, over 7000 in 2017, and 5600 during Jan–Dec

2018. During 2018, IOM Iraq received returnees from 30 host countries with EU member states forming the majority.

The percentage of female migrants has returned during the reporting period was 28%, while male migrants were the majority at 72%.

6.4.3 Interview with the IOM and the UNDP Staff

A total of five IOM staff members and five UNDP staff members were interviewed during the follow-up visit who engaged in the implementation of the project.

The follow-up consisted of various questions like; "*In your opinion, what are the weaknesses and strengths in the project design?*", "*What are the main lessons learned from this project?*" These questions focused on most of the aspects of the project like; Design, Relevance, Effectiveness, Efficiency, Impact, and Sustainability, staff provided their inputs and recommendations.

The project implemented primarily targeted the individuals who started their business under the previous phase of the program, the business enhancement services were tailored with a slight change in the modality, instead of receiving toolkits only, they received 1000 USD through the smart card system to buy toolkits, and 500 USD through cash to address other needs like; shop rents or other urgent needs. According to the staff member's point of view, the project achieved its aims by improving the living conditions of the targeted beneficiaries.

The capacity-building training was found effective, as external business advisors were selected to train the beneficiaries on different skills in marketing, business management, and supply chain.

Despite the good results of the project, the limited implementation period had put pressure on the implementation team, having more time flexibility will improve the efficiency of the processes and eventually the quality of the program.

6.4.4 Key Informant Interviews with Community Leaders

Key informant interviews were conducted with ten community leaders all over the Ares of the intervention, to better understand the impacts of the project on the targeted population, local economy, and also the social cohesion of the targeted groups.

The interviewed community leaders of IOM and UNDP stated that they selected these communities based on the high needs there, the project had a strong impact on improving the social cohesion of the refugees and IDPs, by enhancing their businesses which contributed to expanding their businesses and also increasing their income, leading to empowerment of the refugees in the community, and increasing their access to services.

Having the supported businesses functional and expanding them through this assistance, had impacts on the local economy and also improvement of access for community members to the services that they provide, such as barber, smothery, markets, carpenters, tailors, etc., affecting a wider community as compared to before assistance.

6.4.5 General Observation

The individual livelihoods services were observed useful and expected to have good impacts on the beneficiaries' living conditions and improve beneficiaries' and community members' access to services within the targeted areas.

It was observed that all the engaged parties from the community, community leaders, and selected beneficiaries are satisfied with the services, and they prefer livelihood services for being more sustainable than other services; all parties were recommending delivering more of these services targeting a higher number of refugees and IDPs.

All the beneficiaries were satisfied with the business training services stating that they fully recommend the services to friends and neighbors, and 97% of them reported using the skills learned in the BDS training. Through this project, the involvement of the beneficiaries in income-generating activities and running businesses reduced their vulnerability. Reportedly, 80% of the beneficiaries confirmed having an increase in their income due to the services they received.

And 94% of the beneficiaries who were provided with transportation assistance reported improved access to education.

6.5 Conclusion, Recommendations, and Policy Implications

6.5.1 Conclusion

The IOM and the UNDP have provided individual livelihood assistance activities in Duhok, Erbil, and Sulaymaniyah governorates of Iraq, to strengthen income generation capacity and alleviate poverty and debt among supported beneficiaries and their families.

The field follow-ups took place in all three governorates, interviewing most of the parties engaged in the project.

The individual livelihoods services were found useful having impacts on the targeted beneficiaries' living conditions and improving access to some services for community members within the areas of coverage. All the engaged parties from the community, community leaders, and selected beneficiaries are satisfied with the services, and they favor livelihood services for being more sustainable than other services, all parties recommended delivering more of these business support services targeting a higher number of Refugees. The livelihood programs were useful and they had a great impact on the lives of the beneficiaries.

All the engaged parties from the community, community leaders, and selected beneficiaries are satisfied with the services, and they prefer livelihood services for being more sustainable than other services, all parties were recommending delivering more of these services targeting a higher number of Refugees and IDPs.

All the beneficiaries were satisfied with the business training services stating that they fully recommend the services to friends and neighbors, and 97% of them reported using the skills learned in the BDS training. Through this project, the involvement of the beneficiaries in income-generating activities and running businesses reduced their vulnerability. Reportedly, 80% of the beneficiaries confirmed having an increase in their income due to the services they received 94% of the beneficiaries who provided transportation assistance reported improved access to education.

In addition to that, the KRG officials were satisfied with the emergency humanitarian assistance which was provided by UN agencies. Furthermore, they stated that if it were not for the help of the United Nations and the International community everything would be much harder for the KRG to deal with.

IOM and UNDP Managers also stated that under their programs they were able to assist thousands of people and provide them with their basic needs and training and even help them in migrating. All in all, the existence of such organizations is important for every country, whether they are facing conflict or they are in a post-conflict situation. Their programs did not only help the ones in need but also the unemployed individuals who were searching for a job because when these organizations operate, more local staff and international staff will be employed.

This research shows that these organizations are very important for the stability of a region and for providing emergency assistance and reconstruction in post-conflict situations.

6.5.2 Recommendation and Policy Implementation

Just like any kind of program, many aspects can be done in a better way to serve more people better. During the research, some points were made which were thought to help improve the performance of the projects and to reach more people. The recommendations are as below

- Planning projects with longer periods, especially for the assessments stage, which would allow for improved evidence-based programming.
- Raise awareness among the beneficiaries about their right to buy from more than one vendor and their right to negotiate prices, and increase the number of vendors.
- Improve the market analysis and control of inflation.
- Continue in the provision of business support packages targeting young jobless community members.

- Improving coordination with authorities and community leaders, for better identification of needs.
- Longer period for implementation of activities, especially for the assessments stage.
- Continuous improvement and developing new implementation modalities, to better meet the needs of the targeted population.
- Supporting a higher number of beneficiaries.
- Extension of their contracts to deliver these services in future projects.
- Expanding services and targeting young jobless community members with business support packages.
- Provision of training with more variety of subjects in different sectors.
- Better improvements in coordination with the area representatives for better Programs, as there are huge gaps in some areas that need assistance that occurs due to the high mobility of the refugees.
- The lack of schools remains as one of the most critical needs, and the expansion and rehabilitation of schools should be one of the main priorities of all projects.
- The increase in the provision of toolkits, cash for shop rents, and also more training for making the services better, while the female beneficiaries recommended the provision of childcare services and transportation for more encouragement of women to work.

References

Al-Hamadani, A. S., Jaff, D., & Edwards, M. (2019). The factors impeding health system reform in Iraqi Kurdistan region. *Medicine, Conflict and Survival, 35*(1), 80–102.

Alipui, N., & Gerke, N. (2018). The refugee crisis and the rights of children: Perspectives on community-based resettlement programs. *New Directions for Child and Adolescent Development, 2018*(159), 91–98.

Bache, C. (2018). Mutual economic interdependence or economic imbalance: Turkish private sector presence in the Kurdistan region of Iraq. *Middle East Critique, 27*(1), 61–75.

Baker, P. M., Rao, Y., & Mizumori, S. J. (2019). Transient input-specific neural plasticity in the lateral Habenula facilitates learning. *Neuron, 102*(1), 1–3.

Baser, B. (2018). Homeland calling: Kurdish diaspora and state-building in the Kurdistan region of Iraq in the post-saddam era. *Middle East Critique, 27*(1), 77–94.

Beresford, A., & Pettit, S. (2019). Humanitarian aid supply chain management. In *Contemporary operations and logistics* (pp. 341–364). Springer.

Berger, P. L. (2018). *The limits of social cohesion: Conflict and mediation in pluralist societies*. Routledge.

Burnam, M. A., Meredith, L. S., Tanielian, T., & Jaycox, L. H. (2009). Mental health care for Iraq and Afghanistan war veterans. *Health Affairs, 28*(3), 771–782.

Chiu, L. Y., Kim, H., Muench, P. H., & Seshadri, S. (2018). *Cache migration management in a virtualized distributed computing system*. Google Patents.

Chun, J. (2018). Is it possible to overcome nation-centric histories? Rewriting memories of colonization and war in history textbooks. *Interventions, 20*(4), 567–585.

Dalay, G. (2015). *Regional Kurdish politics in the post-ISIS period*. Retrieved June, 14.

De Santisteban, A. V. (2005). Sanctions, war, occupation and the de-development of education in Iraq. *International Review of Education, 51*(1), 59–71.

De Torrente, N. (2004). Humanitarian action under attack: Reflections on the Iraq war. *Harv. Hum. Rts. J., 17*, 1.
Dionigi, F. (2019). The Syrian refugee crisis in the Kurdish region of Iraq: Explaining the role of borders in situations of forced displacement. *International Migration, 57*(2), 10–31.
Eklund, L., Persson, A., & Pilesjö, P. (2016). Cropland changes in times of conflict, reconstruction, and economic development in Iraqi Kurdistan. *Ambio, 45*(1), 78–88.
Ensler, E. (2016). Yazidi activist Nadia Murad speaks out on the 'Holocaust' of her people in Iraq. *Time Magazine, 3*.
Farhan, S. (2019). *The making of Iraqi Doctors: Reproduction in Medical Education in Modern Iraq, 1869-1959*.
Fitzpatrick, J. (2021). *Human rights protection for refugees, asylum-seekers, and internally displaced persons: A guide to international mechanisms and procedures*. Brill.
Freeman, J., Ricciardone, M., Sullivan, R., & Vedham, V. (2018). *The influence of social determinants of health on primary and secondary cancer prevention health seeking behaviors among refugees in Middle East and North Africa Host Countries*. American Society of Clinical Oncology.
Gregoratti, C. (2010). UNDP, business partnerships, and the (UN) democratic governance of development. In *Democracy and public-private partnerships in global governance* (pp. 190–210). Springer.
International Organization for Migration, I. (2017). *Displacement Report 78*. Retrieved from Iraq https://dtm.iom.int/reports/iraq-—-displacement-report-78-august-2017
Kaul, I., Conceicao, P., Le Goulven, K., & Mendoza, R. U. (2003). *Providing global public goods: Managing globalization*. Oxford University Press.
Latar, N. L. (2018). New journalistic story telling covering conflict zones. *Robot Journalism: Can Human Journalism Survive?, 93*.
Manis, A. (2018). *Cost-effectiveness in humanitarian aid and development: Resilience programming*.
Mather, R. C., III, Nho, S. J., Federer, A., Demiralp, B., Nguyen, J., Saavoss, A., Larson, C. M., et al. (2018). Effects of arthroscopy for femoroacetabular impingement syndrome on quality of life and economic outcomes. *The American Journal of Sports Medicine, 46*(5), 1205–1213.
Mawani, F. N., Gunn, V., O'Campo, P., Anagnostou, M., Muntaner, C., Wanigaratne, S., An, A., et al. (2021). COVID-19 economic response and recovery: A rapid scoping review. *International Journal of Health Services, 51*(2), 247–260.
Miller, S. D. (2016). The international humanitarian response who is doing what on Syrian refugees? In *The "cluster political and humanitarian responses to Syrian displacement* (pp. 67–89). Routledge.
Nicolaus, P., & Yuce, S. (2017). Sex-slavery: One aspect of the yezidi genocide. *Iran and the Caucasus, 21*(2), 196–229.
Nikolaev, A., Hansen, H. H., de Jong, L., Mann, R., Tagliabue, E., Maris, B., Sechopoulos, I. et al. (2019). *Ultrasound-guided breast biopsy of ultrasound occult lesions using multimodality image co-registration and tissue displacement tracking*. Paper presented at the medical imaging 2019: Ultrasonic imaging and tomography.
O'Donnell, K., & Newland, K. (2008). The Iraqi refugee crisis: The need for action. *Migration Policy Institute*, 1–24.
Ogunode, N. J., Chijindu, O. E., & Jegede, D. (2022). Provision of education services for internally displaced persons in IDPs camps in Nigeria: Challenges and way forward. *International Journal on Integrated Education, 5*(5), 14–22.
Omarkhali, K. (2016). Transformations in the Yezidi tradition after the ISIS attacks. An interview with Ilhan Kizilhan. *Kurdish Studies, 4*(2), 148–154.
Palmer, W. (2018). Back pay for trafficked migrant workers: An Indonesian case study. *International Migration, 56*(2), 56–67.
Phillips, D. L. (2018). *The great betrayal: How America abandoned the Kurds and lost the Middle East*. Bloomsbury Publishing.

Pohlmann, A. R., Cruz, L., Mezzalira, G., Soares, L. U., Silveira, N., & Guterres, S. (2007). Structural model of polymeric nanospheres containing indomethacin ethyl ester and in vivo antiedematogenic activity. *International Journal of Nanotechnology, 4*(5), 454–467.

Rashid, N. H., Toma, D. S., & Qadir, S. A. (2019). Fragile but resistent schools in Iraqi Kurdistan in times of crisis. *Bildung und Erziehung, 72*(2), 187–199.

Smith, C. (2018). Independent without independence: The Iraqi-Kurdish Peshmerga in international law. *Harv. Int'l LJ, 59*, 245.

Sümer, F., & Joseph, J. (2019). Compatibility of the Kurdistan region of Iraq's institutions and economic development within Iraq. In *Iraqi Kurdistan's statehood aspirations* (pp. 27–54). Springer.

Timilsina, G. R. (2021). Are renewable energy technologies cost competitive for electricity generation? *Renewable Energy, 180*, 658–672.

Warda, W. K., & Almaffraji, H. S. (2020). *Reception policies, practices and responses–Iraq Country report.*

Warda, W. K., Al-Maffraji, H., Toma, Y., Arif, N., & Samoeel, A. (2018). *Iraq–Country Report: Legal and policy framework of migration governance.*

Part III
Resources-Based Strategies for Development: Business Organizations, Technology, and Social Media

Chapter 7
Assessment of Business Membership Organizations in the Kurdistan Region, Iraq: Analysis with Recommendations for Action

Nabaz T. Khayyat and Goran M. Muhamad

Abstract Business membership organizations (BMOs) are essential for the growth and success of businesses in the private sector. They offer space for collaboration, advocacy, and access to resources that can drive businesses forward. These organizations, such as chambers of commerce, trade associations, and industry groups, unite companies from different sectors to tackle challenges and pursue common objectives. This chapter delves into the significance of business membership organizations in private sector development and their crucial roles in fostering business growth and economic advancement. This study aims to assess the BMOs in the KRI, and the objective is to assist them in developing business advisory services that will foster private sector growth and employment in the region. To achieve the stated objectives, 10 KRI BMOs were assessed across the region. Seven design principles in terms of dimensions (indicators) were used to assess the associations: overall organizational capacity, advocacy capacity, other BMOs offered services capacity, staff capacity, and professionalism, alignment with the Private sector development (PSD) goals and approach, BMOs' reputation among their affiliates, and the level of the indecency of BMOs from political influence and government structure. Unfortunately, BMOs in KRI have not historically performed a good job in promoting a better business environment. The majority of the BMOs in KRI offer basic and mostly administrative services only, and they lack an understanding of the basics of

N. T. Khayyat (✉)
Brandenburg University of Technology, Cottbus-Senftenberg, Germany

Technology Management, Economics, and Policy Program, Colleges of Engineering, Seoul National University, Seoul, Korea (Republic of)
e-mail: nabaz@snu.ac.kr

G. M. Muhamad
Economic Research Centre, Soran University, Erbil, Iraq

Economic and Finance Department, University of Kurdistan Hewler, Erbil, Iraq
e-mail: goran.mustafa@ukh.edu.krd

G. M. Muhamad, N. T. Khayyat (eds.), *Resource Management Performance: A Sectoral Analysis in the Post-Conflict Kurdistan Region of Iraq*, Perspectives on Development in the Middle East and North Africa (MENA) Region,
https://doi.org/10.1007/978-981-97-7725-9_7

advocacy. However, only a few have dedicated advocacy managers; possibly, the head of the BMO is acting as an advocacy manager. Five BMOs stood out for having the highest final score: KIU, IKEU, DCCI, KAHR, and SKPI. These BMOs demonstrated strong organizational and administrative capacity, adequate level of advocacy understanding, and have experienced advocacy activities with their members, have positive impressions among their affiliates, and are enjoying a sort of independence from political and governmental influences.

Keywords Business membership organizations · Private sector development · Economic growth · Kurdistan region

7.1 Introduction

Business membership organizations generally refer to organizations with companies or individual entrepreneurs as members. These organizations include business associations, chambers of commerce, employers' clubs, trade unions, and more. BMOs unite businesses rather than individuals. While larger businesses may have a degree of power, and may also have the resources and inclination to lobby the government directly, many businesses (especially smaller businesses) see the need to come together to raise their concerns (Hall & Soskice, 2001).

To be a strong and reputable representative of the private sector to the public sector, BMOs must have the following characteristics:

- Ability to advocate member interests and concerns
- Ability to lobby, establish, and maintain government relations and high-level public–private dialogue (PPD)
- Ability to respond to member needs by delivering high-quality and affordable services and information

The designation "business membership organization" mirrors the outstanding importance of the members as the base of strength and power of this kind of business association. The main role of BMOs is to promote the growth and prosperity of their members and related business actors. In doing so, BMOs act both as service facilitators or providers and as a representative body,[1] making processes to create a more favorable business environment.

Support and strengthening of BMOs are important as they support the development of the private sector. In this area, they hold a distinctly advantageous position, as they transmit information between two major sectors—public and private sectors. BMOs, on the one hand, should be well aware of the private sector's problems and needs and have a strong organizational structure to be able to have frequent,

[1] Members join the BMOs because they want to access business development services and have influence on the political decision.

consistent, and mutual communication with their member and nonmember companies (Molnár, 2020).

On the other hand, through high qualification and proper communication, BMOs should gain government agencies' trust, which is necessary to conduct dialogue with the public sector and participate in the formation and introduction of the regulatory framework. As a result, they can significantly influence the business support environment and put pressure on the government to create more democratic and participatory governance. According to the World Bank's definition, BMOs have several common management features. First, they are nonprofit legal entities. This does not imply that they do not have the right to offer commercial business services; however, their primary goal should be to make their member/nonmember businesses more active and involve them in collective activities. Also, member-based associations are managed democratically by their member companies (or by representatives elected by members). It is open to any business that wants to become a member of an association. Finally, business associations finance their activities from various sources such as membership fees, donations, service fees, and state or various donor subsidies. Our research targets organizations that are based on these principles (Bennett, 1995).

The role of strong BMOs is especially significant in solving the problems and needs of Small and medium enterprises (SMEs). The SMEs' capabilities and constraints differ from those of large companies. SMEs are less competitive due to such factors as limited resources, lack of economies of scale, weak management, small market, and lack of access to technologies (Tiwasing & Sawang, 2022). However, BMOs can contribute to increasing their capacity and become more competitive in the market.

Business membership organizations are essential for the growth and success of businesses in the private sector. They offer space for collaboration, advocacy, and access to resources that can drive businesses forward. These organizations, such as chambers of commerce, trade associations, and industry groups, unite companies from different sectors to tackle challenges and pursue common objectives (Sack, 2022).

BMOs play a vital role in facilitating networking and collaboration among businesses. As mentioned by Ackers (2015), by bringing together companies from various sectors, these organizations offer opportunities for sharing best practices, exchanging information, and forming partnerships that can result in new business ventures. Events such as networking gatherings, workshops, seminars, and conferences organized by these groups enable businesses to connect with potential clients, suppliers, and collaborators, thereby promoting growth within the local business community.

BMOs not only encourage collaboration among businesses but also have a crucial role in representing the interests of their members at different levels. By voicing the concerns of businesses in the private sector, these organizations can have an impact on government policies and decisions that affect businesses and the economy. Through advocacy activities such as lobbying and public policy research, BMOs can contribute to creating a favorable environment for entrepreneurship, innovation, and economic development (Doner & Schneider, 2000; Dumez & Renou, 2020).

Moreover, BMOs offer essential resources and services to assist their members in overcoming challenges and reaching success (Sullivan & Bettcher, 2007). This includes training, mentorship, funding access, market insights, and other business support services. These organizations provide diverse resources to help businesses enhance operations, grow their markets, and boost competitiveness. By providing customized support and guidance to businesses across various industries and sizes, business membership organizations play a key role in the advancement of the private sector.

Business membership organizations are essential for private sector development as they offer space for businesses to work together, fight for their needs, and access crucial resources and services for success (Muhamad et al., 2020). By promoting collaboration, advocating for businesses, and providing valuable support, these organizations greatly contribute to the growth and longevity of the private sector and economy as a whole. As businesses navigate a complex and competitive environment, the role of BMOs in assisting businesses and fostering economic growth becomes increasingly crucial.

The private sector must grasp the significance of BMOs in stimulating economic progress and establishing a favorable setting for businesses. This study will examine the various functions of BMOs in fostering private sector development and their influence on businesses and communities. BMOs offer essential resources and support. They provide networking opportunities, training programs, and access to market intelligence. Networking events and conferences help businesses connect with members, partners, and customers, leading to new opportunities. Training programs improve skills and knowledge, expanding market reach. Furthermore, BMOs offer market research and industry trend information to help businesses make informed decisions and stay competitive.

BMOs play a crucial role in promoting entrepreneurship and innovation (Sanders et al., 2024). By backing startups and small businesses, BMOs play a critical role in nurturing innovation and inspiring fresh concepts and strategies. BMOs offer guidance, financial support, and connections to valuable resources that empower entrepreneurs to transform their visions into thriving ventures. By championing entrepreneurship, BMOs play a key part in generating employment opportunities, stimulating economic expansion, and advancing prosperity within the community.

This study delves into the significance of business membership organizations in private sector development and their crucial roles in fostering business growth and economic advancement in the Kurdistan Region of Iraq.

7.2 The Kurdistan Region of Iraq

7.2.1 Synopsis of Macroeconomic Analysis

The KRI is a constitutionally recognized semiautonomous region in northern Iraq with a population of more than 6.1 million (2020 estimate).[2] Its government (the Kurdistan Regional Government (KRG)), based in Erbil, has the right under the Iraqi Constitution of 2005 to exercise legislative, executive, and judicial powers according to the Iraqi constitution, except in what is listed as exclusive powers of the federal authorities under that constitution.

The KRI comprises three major cities (governorates): Erbil, Sulaymaniyah, and Duhok. Recently, the district of Halabja was formed as a new governorate to become the fourth governorate in the KRI, although it has not been approved yet by the Federal Iraqi Parliament.[3]

The KRI has had peace and relative security with a more liberalized economy and market-oriented policies in comparison to the rest of Iraq. While its economy is dominated by the oil industry, the largest nongovernment sectors in terms of value added to the KRI were construction, wholesale and retail trade, home ownership and rental services, and manufacturing (Muhamad et al., 2020).[4]

The KRI is facing a complicated crisis, compounding concurrent and mutually aggravating security, political, economic, and social risks. It has been affected by three multifaceted disasters within a short period, namely, the Syrian Civil War in 2012 and the Islamic State of Iraq and the Levant (ISIL) crises in 2014; both resulted in a mass refugee inflow to the KRI and imposed severe macroeconomic and fiscal challenges and had a ripple negative impact on all productive and social sectors. The third distress was the dispute between the KRI and the federal government of Iraq, which led to the KRI budget crisis in 2014 and added more severity to the KRI's distress.

The COVID-19 pandemic has also triggered an economic contraction in KRI, doubling the financial loss. Lockdowns and pandemic-related safety measures led businesses to close and thousands of jobs to be lost resulting in a decrease in the average household income by 29%.[5] Among the worst hit were the vulnerable people. An assessment of 893 SMEs conducted by International organization for migration (IOM) in Iraq revealed that 38% of female workers and 25% of male workers have stopped receiving salaries temporarily, while 10% of female workers and 4% of male workers have been laid off.[6] Furthermore, since the pandemic, the income

---

[2] https://krso.gov.krd/en/statistics/population

[3] https://krso.gov.krd/en/map/kurdistan-region/population

[4] For the list of KRI industries, visit: https://krso.gov.krd/content/upload/1/root/e22.pdf

[5] https://www.unicef.org/iraq/media/1181/file/Assessment_of_COVID-19_Impact_on_Poverty_and_Vulnerability_in_Iraq.pdf

[6] https://edf.iom.int/Content/Cov19/Food 20and 20Agriculture.pdf

of most refugees has decreased, which resulted in a 21% increase in poverty among Syrian refugees and IDPs in KRI ("Iraq Country Chapter 2021-2022," 2020).

The unemployment rate in KRI was 6.5% before the war with ISIL in 2014 and has been fluctuating since then between 13.5% in 2015, 10.2% at the end of 2017, and 9% in 2018.[7] The KRI suffers from high public spending on wages, as the employment rate in the public sector is about 11.5% of the total population and a very high rate of spending on public pensions.[8] Thus, in addition to the economic slowdown of the KRI due to the KRG fiscal crisis, coupled with ISIL, which resulted in the influx of refugees and IDPs, the capacity of KRG to diversify its rentier economy, reform and promote the private sector, and create more job opportunities has been weakened (WBG & UNHCR).

7.2.2 *The Business Environment in Iraq and the KRI*

Iraq and the KRI have a challenging business environment, especially for microenterprises. In 2020, the World Bank ranked Iraq 171st out of 190 countries for the ease of doing business (Rogge & Archer, 2021). The weak business environment in Iraq makes it harder for the poor to earn their way out of poverty and find decent jobs.

The laws, policies, and regulations that shape a country's business environment can be seen as the outcome of a negotiation between the public and private sectors. Business associations act as key intermediaries between the public and private sectors (Yao et al., 2022). When they work effectively, they tend to identify pressing constraints in the business environment, formulate evidence-based policy proposals, advocate for business-friendly laws and regulations, and engage the government in substantive and constructive dialogue.

7.3 Methodology

7.3.1 *Introduction*

To support the design and implementation of related measures in the KRI, an analysis of the BMO's environment in the KRI as well as an assessment of key BMOs is conducted. This study is based on a desk review complemented by interviews and relevant cross-checks and includes the following two parts:

1. Analysis of the general BMO environment along a set of guiding questions as follows:

[7] https://krso.gov.krd/en/indicator/population-and-labor-force/labor-force-participation

[8] https://us.gov.krd/media/1317/social-protection-strategic-framework.pdf

- Which types of BMOs exist?
- What is the legal and historical background of BMOs in the KRI?
- Which functions do they generally serve and what services do they offer?
- Which institutional linkages generally exist between BMOs and public sector entities?
- Are they generally open or selective in their representation?
- How well do they generally serve the private sector needs? How does it differ across sectors?
- How effective are they as intermediaries? Are there any particular accomplishments (e.g., successful case studies of public–private dialogue formats)?
- What is the general perception of interaction with the public sector; are they perceived to be open to private sector concerns? How does it differ across institutions?

2. Description and specific assessment of key nonpolitical/government-affiliated BMOs in KRI about advocacy and business advisory services

7.3.2 *Approach*

A two-stage approach is implemented to collect the data and analyses. The first stage includes desk research to collect data and information from different sources, NGOs and UN documents, research institutions, and published literature. The second stage of the methodology is based on the findings from the desk research and a field survey involving the stakeholders' engagement and informant interviews.

7.3.3 *Desk Research Phase*

The scoping assignment began with desk research, and data were collected through telephone interviews and online meetings with the stakeholders. Preliminary findings from initial interviews combined with the desk research that covers the overarching context for BMOs, demand- and supply-side constraints, and benchmarking against other BMO suppliers' interventions in other similar contexts were prepared for further analysis.

7.3.3.1 Inception Phase Meetings

To understand the background of the study, the researcher undertook a sequence of meetings online and by phone with stakeholders, i.e., business associations, and other stakeholders such as the directorate of not-for-profit organizations. A draft interview sheet guide was developed and aimed at guiding the interview process for the next phase of the assignment. The interview sheet guide can be found in Annex 1.

Table 7.1 List of BMOs interviewed

No.	BMO name	BMO acronym
1	Development of Industry and Trading of Iraq Businessmen Association Kurdistan Region	DTDA
2	Erbil Chamber of Commerce and Industry	ECCI
3	Sulaymaniyah Chamber of Commerce and Industry	SCCI
4	Duhok Chamber of Commerce and Industry	DCCI
5	Halabja Chamber of Commerce and Industry	HCCI
6	Kurdistan Federation of Chamber of Commerce and Industry	KFCCI
7	Kurdistan Associations of Hotels and Restaurants	KAHR
8	Union of Importers and Exporters of Kurdistan Region of Iraq	IEKU
9	Kurdistan Investors Union	KIU
10	Syndicate of Kurdistan Pharmacists/Iraq	SKPI

7.3.3.2 Cluster Selection

The following nonpolitical/government-affiliated BMOs were selected to assess the capacity. See Table 7.1.

7.3.4 The Analytical Framework

The analysis undertaken in the second phase of the methodology was guided by a framework based on a set of international indicators.[9]

The indicators are used to assess the BMOs' performance against seven design principle dimensions, and each was evaluated based on a set of subindicators spanning quantitative and qualitative aspects of BMOs' capacity. For the assessment purpose, a weighting value was assigned to each subindicator. Accordingly, the score of a main indicator is the average of the values assigned for its subindicators. Moreover, the total score of all the seven main indicators is considered the final score of a BMO, in which a comparison between the BMOs is made based on BMO's final score. Table 7.2 summarizes the seven main indicators along with their subindicators.

[9] https://www.bmo.com/pdf/Measuring_performance.pdf

Table 7.2 Indicators used to assess the BMOs' performance

No	Main indicator	Subindicator
1	Overall organizational capacity	Number of members
		Organizational setup
		Services offered to members
		Source of financing
		Impression of members
2	Advocacy capacity	Dedicated department
		Dedicated staff
		Dedicated instruments to collect views
		Dedicated advocacy instruments
		Ready understanding of important challenges of members
		Experience of advocacy work
		Impression of members on advocacy work
3	Other service capacity	Scope of other service
		Impression of members on other services
4	Staff capacity/professionalism	Number of staff
		Qualification of staff
		Specialization of staff
5	Alignment with PSD goals and approach	Importance attached to advocacy work
		Openness to cooperation
6	Reputation among members	Impression of members
7	Independence	Independence

7.3.5 Data Collection and Field Visit Phase

Following the desk research and inception phase, the field visit was undertaken for the scoping assessment. This included ten interviews with BMO key informants: 21 interviews with BMO members and one interview with the KRG director of not-for-profit organizations at the Erbil Governorate. The field visit was conducted between January 20 and April 17, 2022. The key informants in all the locations were asked several open-ended questions on their current needs, the type of services provided to (or received by) business associations, and their business members.

7.4 Findings from the Inception Phase

7.4.1 Business Membership Organization: An Overview

7.4.1.1 The Emergence and Legal Development of BMOs in the KRI

Before 2003, the only official trade union in Iraq was the state-sanctioned General Federation of Trade Unions. After 2003, workers and unionists took advantage of the new political climate and opportunities to reorganize and establish trade unions (Majed & Aljabiri, 2020). While nearly all pre-2003 laws were abolished in Iraq after 2003, those related to workers' rights and trade unions survived and remained in place.

The Iraqi government has attempted to impose one centralized trade union as the formal and legal one, which represents all workers, depriving workers from forming their unions independently and freely. This brought many trade unions together to defend their right to organize separately, lobbying the Iraqi government to allow the workers to create their unions and to organize in the public sector (Isakhan, 2023). However, it was only on November 20, 2017, that the House of Representatives voted in favor of a draft law that allows the Republic of Iraq to join the Freedom of Association and Protection of the Right to Organize Convention No. 87 of 1948.[10]

After 1991, the Kurdistan region of Iraq was formed administratively, and the trade unions that were affiliated with the headquarters in Baghdad began to separate from them successively. Thus the initial scenes of trade unions began to form, and their headquarters moved to Erbil and their branches in Dohuk and Sulaymaniyah.

7.4.1.2 Law of NGOs in KRG

In the KRG, under the Law of Nongovernmental Organizations in the Iraqi Kurdistan Region of 2011, Article 13 Section 4 states: The Organization may obtain income from "The Organization's share of any allocation in the Region's annual budget, and any other grants or assistance provided by the Government in support of the Organizations' projects." However, this law has never been implemented.

Most of the debate about governmental grants to NGOs in Iraq centers on how humanitarian needs and developmental priorities can be served without imposing any control on the space of NGOs' work.

7.4.1.3 The Genesis of BMOs in the KRI

In the KRI, the BMOs vary in geographical coverage, size, sector, type of activity, maturity, and dynamism and come in all different shapes and sizes, from grassroots organizations representing a few hundred smallholder farmers or microtraders to sophisticated BMOs with national secretariats and dozens of regional chapters. The

[10] http://www.industriall-union.org/iraqi-parliament-approves-ratification-of-ilo-convention-87

BMOs are carrying out different functions, including lobbying on a small scale, government relations, and public–private dialogue. Much of the activities of BMOs are about delivering business services to members, and the revenue from such activities allows them to be financially independent and self-sustaining. The BMOs in the KRI can be classified into four main types.

1. *Employers' Organizations*

Most of these organizations are public; however, they are independently developing and often as a counterpart to trade unions. Moreover, there are many individual syndicates in different professions. Some of these syndicates are public, and some others are private and self-funded associations.

2. *Trade Unions/Chambers of Commerce/Chambers of Industry*

These public organizations typically represent entities from specific industries and sectors and have close relationships with the KRG.

3. Leagues of Associations

This type of association unites several business organizations by sector and governorate, enhancing their negotiation power and interacting with the KRG at the senior level. There are two leagues of associations in the KRI: the Kurdistan United Workers Union (KUWU) and the Kurdistan Federation of Chambers of Commerce & Industry (K-FCCI). Women's organizations also develop from the need to alleviate economic biases against a certain group of entrepreneurs. In many ways comparable to small-scale enterprise associations, they focus more on women-specific concerns and engage in gender-related advocacy. Currently, there is one women's association called the Kurdistan Association of Business Women (KABW).

4. *Civil Society Organizations and Nongovernmental Organizations*

Most KRI businesses that have membership belong to provincial chambers of commerce, followed by the Leagues of Associations, the Iraqi Business Union, and others.

7.4.1.4 The Main Functions of BMOs

The laws, policies, and regulations that shape a country's business environment can be seen as the outcome of a negotiation between the public and private sectors. BMOs act as key intermediaries between the public and private sectors. When they work effectively, BMOs identify pressing constraints in the business environment, formulate evidence-based policy proposals, advocate for business-friendly laws and regulations, and engage the government in substantive and constructive dialogues.

BMOs have important potential for supporting SMEs and promoting a better investment climate in Iraq, especially in the Kurdistan region. Based on the researcher's preliminary observation, unfortunately, BMOs in the KRI have not historically performed a good job in promoting a better business environment. The majority of BMOs lack an understanding of the basics of advocacy.

However, only a few have dedicated advocacy managers or teams. Most BMOs have weak financial capacity, meaning they are unable to fund advocacy activities. This stems from inadequate fundraising skills and ineffective member communications and services.

The activities of the BMOs differ according to the type of BMOs. BMOs in the KRI help businesses to get registered, establish bank linkages, and be compliant with the law although the registration process is very long due to the presence of a huge bureaucratic environment and lack of technology-based instruments to facilitate the registration. Examples of BMO activities are listed below:

- The KFCCI acts as a representative for the interests of industrial and businessmen and local and foreign owners of private companies. K-FCCI tends to keep pro-business policies at the forefront of the legislative agenda, where the role of the Federation is manifested as legal assistance and acting as a lobby to get laws that are favorable to commercial and industrial activities.
- The KUWU focuses on protecting and promoting the rights and interests of local workers. These include getting better pay and better working conditions (especially in terms of safety and security), a fair social security plan, a good pension plan, and a necessary health insurance plan in coordination with the KRG Ministry of Labor and Social Affairs. Another activity is raising awareness and educating the working class on the importance of union organizations and their rights within existing labor laws, and being involved in drawing up economic policies and plans for KRG.
- The Erbil Chamber of Commerce: it has a variety of activities in the region, for example, organizing workshops and capacity development, providing advisory services on how to establish and operate a project, and finally organizing meetings and seminars and mentorship for entrepreneurs.

The chamber of commerce is somehow engaged in serving the Micros, smalle, and medium enterprises (MSMEs) by providing business counseling and facilitating the long process of business registration. However, it is a disappointing reality that the chambers of commerce have not been very effective in finding reasonable solutions to the impediments faced by SMEs.

Low memberships of SMEs, poor leadership and shortage of skilled staff, inadequate finance, nonacceptance as full partners by the government, and organizational instability and inefficient administration lead to their poor performance.

7.5 Findings from the Field Visit

7.5.1 BMOs' Profiles

Two sets of activities were implemented to collect the data in this phase: interviews with target associations and interviews with businesses that are members of these associations. Engaging with both associations and businesses was important for the sake of developing insight not only on associations' operations but also on their impact on perception among their primary stakeholders.

Executives and representatives of ten business associations were interviewed for a duration of 90–120 min. Different types of data were collected such as the mission, goals, and strategic orientations of BMOs, their membership and outreach, internal operation and source of financing, BMOs' organizational capacity and in-house expertise, and functions, activities, and services offered to their members.

In addition, 21 business owners have been interviewed for 45–60 min. The type of data collected was centered around their awareness, experience, satisfaction, and perception of the BMOs in addition to their opinions and suggestions for improving BMOs' activities. According to the interviews' results, a BMO profile is created, which contains general information about the BMO, its mission and objectives, functions, and some other information about its structure, memberships, and sources of financing. In addition, the BMOs' profiles have been prepared and assessed based on the five indicators mentioned in Table 7.2 in the previous section.

1. *Erbil Chamber of Commerce (ECCI)*

   Mission and Objectives

   To promote and defend the general interests of trade, industry, and services of the members. The objectives of the ECCI formation are to have an active role in the KRI policy formation related to the trade and service sectors and to promote trade and service sectors through SMEs.

   Functions

- Hold conferences, workshops, and events aiming at establishing business linkages between the members and finding new business and networking opportunities
- Provide advisory services on how to establish a project and operate it
- Resolve disputes of entrepreneurs at home and abroad

Membership

The total number of members is 28,476 members, of which 20,036 members are merchants, 6036 members are companies, and 2405 are industrialists. It is composed of three classes (A, B, and C), each corresponding to a certain capital range.

Summary About ECCI

Due to the issuance of commercial licensing on behalf of KRG, companies and businesses become members. Thus, it relies on membership dues as the primary source of revenue to cover the overall operating costs. However, starting in the year 2022, KRG's commercial licensing will be issued a directory from the Ministry of Trade and Industry. KFCCI membership will become voluntary. The challenge, thus, will be how to retain the existing members. ECCI is typically seen as a government-supported entity which affects its capability and willingness to advocate for its members.

Table 7.26 in Appendix 1 and Fig. 7.1 show the assessment conducted for ECCI based on the indicators and their subindicators.

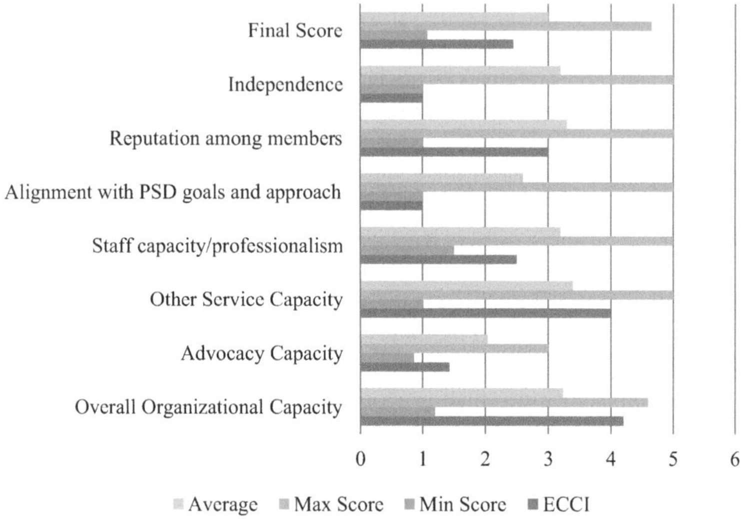

Fig. 7.1 Indicators used to assess ECCI performance

Assessment Summary About ECCI

- Below-average staff capacity and qualification
- Good performance in serving the affiliated members in terms of providing data, information, and studies that would contribute to investment decision-making in the governorate
- Absence of planned and continuous training programs for its affiliates that keep pace with the latest developments in the business environment
- Average reputation among its affiliates
- Alignment with PSD goals is below average
- Moderate level of qualified staff and capacity
- Weak advocacy capacity
- ECCI's final score for the assessment is 2.447
- Minimum score of BMOs: 1.937
- Maximum score of BMOs: 3.957

2. *Sulaimany Chamber of Commerce and Industry (SCCI)*
   Mission and Objectives

To develop the private sector to be the major partner in sustainable economic development. The SCCI objectives are to have an active role in KRI policy formation for SMEs and support the SMEs through encouraging creative projects and businesses.

Functions

- Provide consulting services in preparation of constituent instruments for the registration of businesses
- Promote business linkages internally, regionally, and internationally
- Advocate and solve disputes for its affiliates with the local, regional, and federal government

Membership

Total number of affiliates: 41,154, of which 30,281 are merchants, 5800 are companies, and 5073 affiliates are professionals.

Summary About SCCI

SCCI relies on mandatory membership dues as its primary source of revenue to cover the overall operating costs as it issues commercial licensing on behalf of the KRG. In 2020, SCCI membership will become voluntary. The challenge, thus, will be how to retain the existing members. SCCI acts as a liaison between the private sector and the KRG. The SCCI participates actively in different local government events. SCCI organizes meetings and establishes business contacts between economic agents. However, SCCI is a semi-government-supported entity which affects its capability to advocate for its members.

Table 7.26 in Appendix 1 and Fig. 7.2 show the assessment conducted for SCCI based on the indicators and their subindicators.

Assessment Summary About SCCI

- Good level of staff capacity and high qualification.
- Average reputation among its affiliates.
- Alignment with PSD goals is below average.
- Low level of advocacy capacity.
- Overall institutional and organizational capacity is seen to be above average.
- SCCI's final score for the assessment is 2.988.
- Minimum score of BMOs: 1.937.
- Maximum score of BMOs: 3.957.

3. *Chambers of Commerce and Industry in Duhok (CCID)*

   Mission and Objectives

To promote and defend the general interests of trade, industry, and services of the members. The chamber's responsibility is to cooperate through dialogue with the

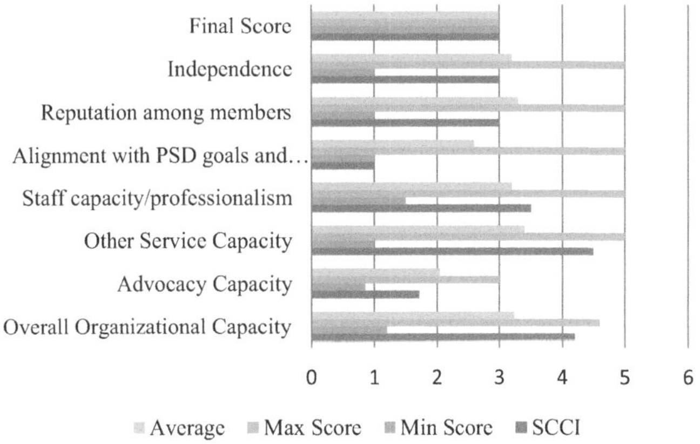

Fig. 7.2 Indicators used to assess SCCI performance

KRI's different private and public sector bodies in Duhok and play an advisory role for the private sector and businesses.

Functions

- Represent the general interest of the business community in Duhok and provide information and advice to its members
- Provide market information and economic statistics in coordination with the KRG Ministry of Planning
- Promote foreign direct investment and facilitate international trade

Membership

Number of affiliates: 38,450, of which 3755 are companies, 1294 are merchants, 2507 are real estate, and 158 are businesswomen-registered businesses.

Summary About CCID

CCID relies on mandatory membership dues as its primary source of revenue. In 2020, CCID membership will become voluntary. The challenge, thus, will be how to retain the existing members. CCID studies commercial situations and meaningful remedial suggestions for economic development. CCID takes a proactive role in business matching by initiating buyer/seller meetings and other supporting activities. CCID also offers in-house consultation services on industries, trade, and environmental issues.

Table 7.26 in Appendix 1 and Fig. 7.3 show the assessment conducted for CCID based on the indicators and their subindicators.

Assessment Summary About CCID

- Very good reputation among its affiliates
- Very good staff capacity and high qualification
- Low level of alignment with PSD goals
- Good level of advocacy capacity
- High level of overall institutional and organizational capacity

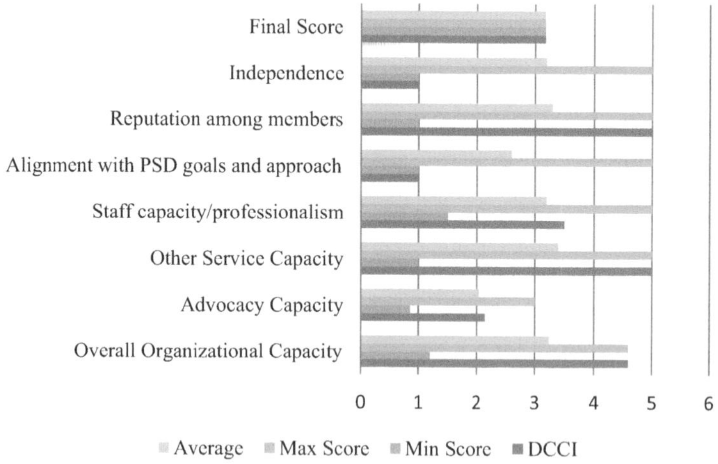

Fig. 7.3 Indicators used to assess CCID performance

- CCID final score for the assessment is 3.178
- Minimum score of BMOs: 1.937
- Maximum score of BMOs: 3.957

4. *Halabja Chamber of Commerce and Industry (HCCI)*
   Mission and Objectives
   To advocate policies, stimulate trade and investment, connect businesses, sustain economic growth, and expand member opportunities. The objectives of the HCCI are to have an active role in KRI policy formation related to the trade and industrial sectors and promote trade and industrial sectors through small and medium enterprise development.
   Functions

- Organizes workshops within and outside the region and takes advantage of the capacity of trained personnel to train others
- Provides advisory services on how to establish the business
- Networks to establish and develop social and business relations

Membership
The total number of members is 800 members.
Summary About HCCI
HCCI relies on mandatory membership dues as its primary source of revenue. In 2020, HCCI membership will become voluntary. The challenge, thus, will be how to retain the existing members. HCCI provides Business development services (BDS) to grow members' businesses, connect them to legislators, and provide valuable savings on benefits and services. HCCI provides advisory services to the local government of Halabja. It also acts as a liaison between the private sector and the KRG.

Table 7.26 in Appendix 1 and Fig. 7.4 show the assessment conducted for HCCI based on the indicators and their subindicators.
Assessment Summary About HCCI

- Average staff capacity and qualification.
- Satisfied reputation among its affiliates.
- Low level of alignment with PSD goals.
- Weak advocacy capacity.
- Low level of overall institutional and organizational capacity.
- HCCI's final score for the assessment is 2.222.
- Minimum score of BMOs: 1.937.
- Maximum score of BMOs: 3.957.

5. *Kurdistan Federation of Chambers of Commerce and Industry (KFCCI)*
   Mission and Objectives
   To promote and defend the general interests of trade, industry, and services of the members. Its primary responsibility is to cooperate through dialogue with the KRI's different private and public sector bodies to play an advisory role for the private sector and businesses and to cooperate and coordinate activities of the regional and local chambers of commerce and industries.

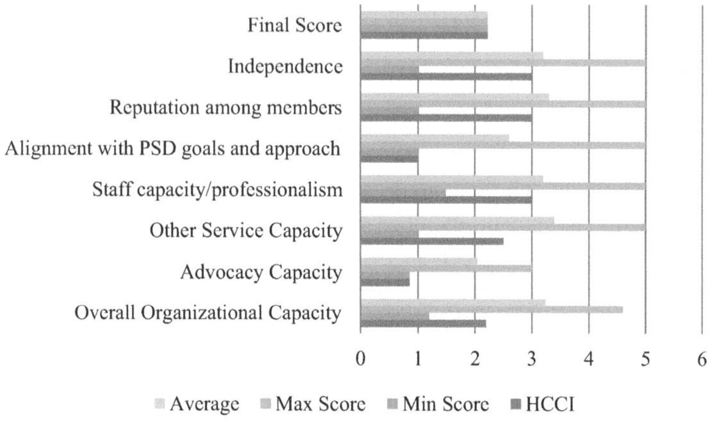

Fig. 7.4 Indicators used to assess HCCI performance

Functions

- Offer training to develop trade, businesses, and small enterprises
- Contribute to the promotion of investment in its geographical jurisdiction
- Resolve disputes that arise between its members or between members and the government
- Express opinions on draft laws and regulations related to trade and submit proposals that are deemed appropriate

Summary About KFCCI

KFCCI was established in 2007 in coordination with the Chambers of Commerce and Industry of Erbil, Sulaymaniyah, and Duhok to represent them in the KRI. Although KFCCI does not have a clear strategy on ways of systematic advocacy and lobbying to reach policy-makers to influence change, different activities are performed, such as:

- Provision of training facilities for international NGOs to train business members on different topics
- Conduct/support trade fairs and exhibitions and liaise with foreign consulates in KRI for business facilitation of the KFCCI members

Table 7.26 in Appendix 1 and Fig. 7.5 show the assessment conducted for KFCCI based on the indicators and their subindicators.

Assessment Summary About KFCCI

- Weak reputation among its affiliates.
- Very good staff capacity and high qualification.
- Good level of alignment with PSD goals.
- Average level of advocacy capacity.
- Good level of overall institutional and organizational capacity.
- KFCCI's final score for the assessment is 2.428.

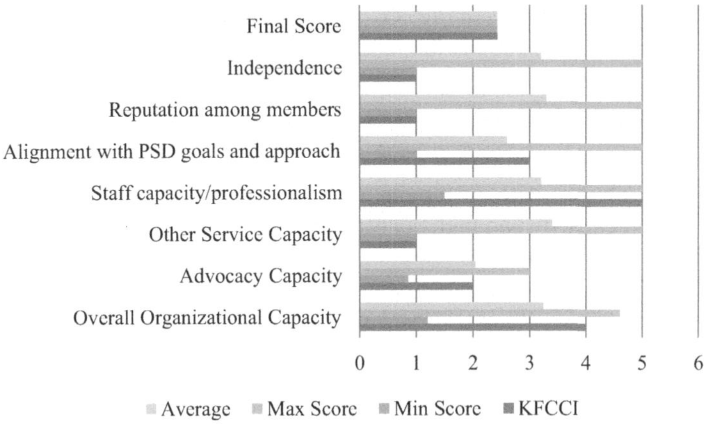

Fig. 7.5 Indicators used to assess KFCCI performance

- Minimum Score of BMOs: 1.937.
- Maximum score of BMOs: 3.957.

6. *Kurdistan Investors Union (KIU)*

Mission and Objectives

To be a platform to address the needs and grievances of investors, take their voice to the respective forums or regulatory bodies, and develop sustainable solutions to meet the emerging needs of the investor community.

Functions

- Provide research and legal and economic advice to investors and KRG to promote the economic infrastructure in coordination with the relevant government institutions and departments
- Attract international capital and investors by providing information and coordination services and matching them with local investors of the same interest
- Regulate the relationship with governmental and private banks to provide letters of credit (L.C) and other banking operations to facilitate the implementation of commercial business related to import–export and investment

Membership

The total number of members is 400.

Summary About KIU

KIU relies on membership dues as its primary source of revenue although it is not a mandatory membership. Members benefit from the wide range of services and support offered by the union. KIU is active in policy advocacy to obtain results for its affiliates' interests. KIU creates opportunities to network, make valuable connections, and gain knowledge, which creates and improves business relationships for all in the industry. KIU is in close liaison with the BOI and offers its consultancy and advisory services for matters related to granting investment opportunities, lands, and FDI by the KRG rules and regulations.

Table 7.26 in Appendix 1 and Fig. 7.6 show the assessment conducted for KFCCI based on the indicators and their subindicators.

Assessment Summary About KIU

- KIU is an independent entity that has an independent legal personality in front of official and unofficial authorities.
- KIU enjoys a high reputation among its affiliates.
- Average staff capacity and high qualification.
- High level of alignment with PSD goals.
- High capability for advocacy activities.
- Average level of overall institutional and organizational capacity.
- KIU's final score for the assessment is 3.957.
- Minimum score of BMOs: 1.937.
- Maximum score of BMOs: 3.957.

7. *Union of Importers and Exporters of Kurdistan Region of Iraq (IEKU)*

Mission and Objectives

IEKU works as a bridge between KRG and industry. Seeks the consensus of the industry, makes policy recommendations, promotes member's interests, and helps importers, exporters, and businesses tap into the global market.

Functions

- Defend the rights and protect importers and exporters from market impediments and crises, especially from industrial replicated production
- Offer facilitations to its members to attend international exhibitions and commercial conferences to expand and raise their knowledge

Membership

There are over 11,000 members in the KRI.

Summary About IEKU

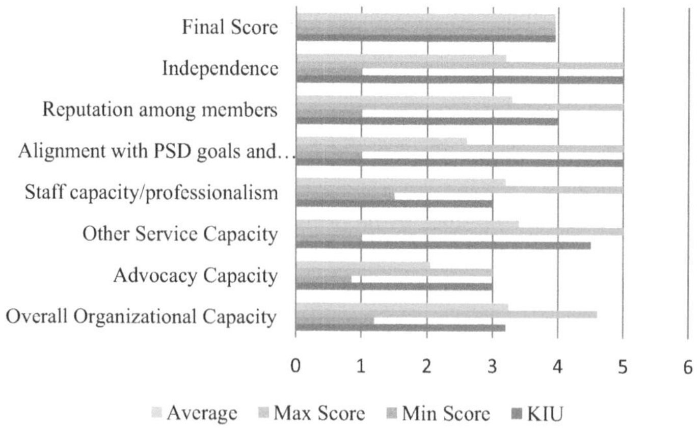

Fig. 7.6 Indicators used to assess KIU performance

Two sources of financing are board member's financial support and voluntary membership fees. IEKU is the pillar of KRI business and merchants from influencing business policy to encouraging the debate on the industries and engaging with policy-makers and civil society. IEKU provides the platform for networking and building consensus within and across sectors. From advocating for the national production protection law, the KRG has reactivated the law in 2019. IEKU advocacy resulted in the reform of KRG-regulated tariffs on imported goods and stopped the custom exemption.

Table 7.26 in Appendix 1 and Fig. 7.7 show the assessment conducted for IEKU based on the indicators and their subindicators.

Assessment Summary About IEKU

- IEKU is an independent entity not influenced by the government.
- KIU enjoys a good reputation among its affiliates.
- Weak staff capacity.
- High level of alignment with PSD goals.
- Good capacity for advocacy activities.
- Good level of overall institutional and organizational capacity.
- IEKU's final score for the assessment is 3.953.
- Minimum score of BMOs: 1.937.
- Maximum score of BMOs: 3.957.

8. *Kurdistan Association of Hotels and Restaurants (KAHR)*

Mission and Objectives

To pioneer the development of the tourism sector and improve the service standards in KRI. The main objective is to develop the tourism industry through activities such as education and training, research and publication, and annual conventions to promote interaction with different stakeholders.

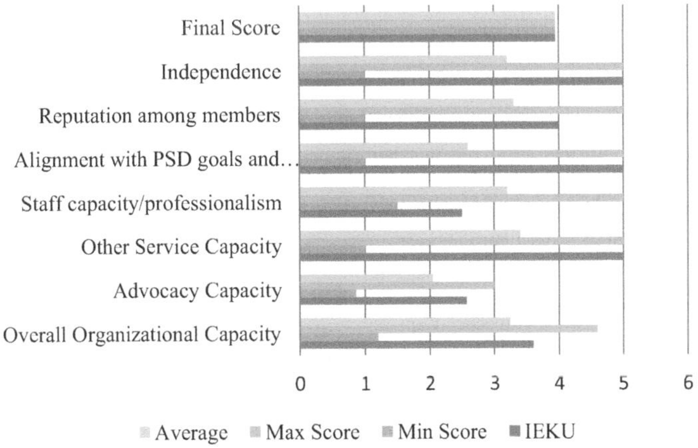

Fig. 7.7 Indicators used to assess IEKU performance

Functions

- Raise the level of practicing the profession, deploy tourism awareness for its members, and develop and revitalize the KRI tourism sector
- Offer training to HR in the tourism sector
- Collect and classify tourism information and data and share them with its members and the authorities

Membership

There are over 2000 members, of which around 920 members are restaurants and hotels that are classified as A, B, C, and D (one to four stars classification), and the rest are individual restaurants and food shops that have no classification.

Summary About KAHR

KAHR relies on mandatory membership dues as its primary source of revenue. In 2020, KAHR membership will become voluntary. The challenge, thus, will be how to retain the existing members. KAHR continued to build networking commercial relationships with the international community helping merchants to obtain franchises. KAHR is also conducting business linkages through its regular conventions and annual conferences.

Table 7.26 in Appendix 1 and Fig. 7.8 show the assessment conducted for KFCCI based on the indicators and their subindicators.

Assessment Summary About KAHR

- KAHR is an independent entity.
- KIU enjoys a good reputation among its affiliates.
- Average staff capacity and qualification.
- Good level of alignment with PSD goals.
- High capacity for advocacy activities.
- Good level of overall institutional and organizational capacity.
- KAHR's final score for the assessment is 3.296.

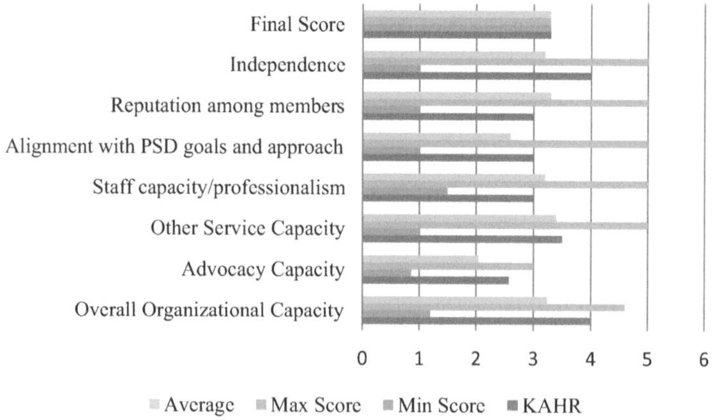

Fig. 7.8 Indicators used to assess KAHR performance

- Minimum score of BMOs: 1.937.
- Maximum score of BMOs: 3.957.

9. *Development of Industry and Trading of Iraq Businessmen Association (KURDDTA)*
   Mission and Objectives
   To support communication between businessmen and investors in Iraq to strengthen the Iraqi development and reconstruction process and to advance and lay the correct foundation for industrial and commercial activities.
   Functions

- Encourage investment inside the region by foreign trade, industry, agriculture, tourism, and other types of investments
- Advise KRG with issues related to investment and trade
- Design principles and direction for dialogues with developmental, national, and foreign institutions for investment

Membership

The total number of members is 350 across the Kurdistan region.

Summary About DTA

DTA relies on membership dues as its primary source of revenue. DTA supports Iraqi industrialists, traders, and businessmen by organizing conferences and seminars that discuss the development and growth of the region's economy. DTA leads businessmen and industrialists to deliberate policy issues with KRG to develop legislation that would create a favorable business climate.

Table 7.26 in Appendix 1 and Fig. 7.9 show the assessment conducted for KFCCI based on the indicators and their subindicators.

Assessment Summary About DTA

- DTA is a fully independent entity from political affiliations and government.
- Weak reputation among its affiliates.

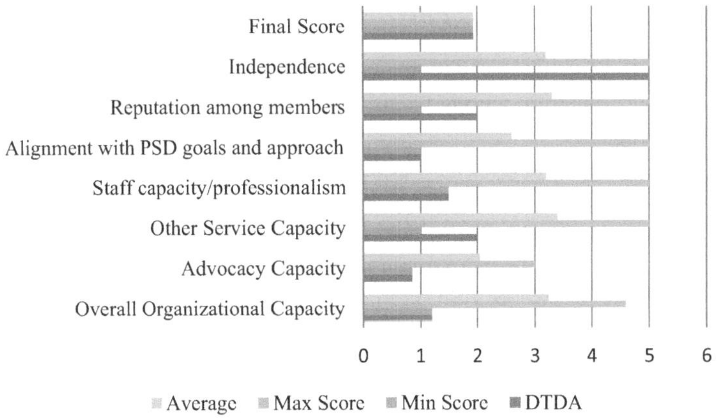

Fig. 7.9 Indicators used to assess DTA performance

- Weak staff capacity and qualification.
- Low level of alignment with PSD goals.
- Weak capacity for advocacy activities.
- Low level of overall institutional and organizational capacity.
- KAHR's final score for the assessment is 1.937.
- Minimum score of BMOs: 1.937.
- Maximum score of BMOs: 3.957.

10. *Syndicate of Kurdistan Pharmacists (SKPI)*

Mission and Objectives

To promote the profession of pharmacy and maintain its dignity in the scientific and professional level of pharmacists and raise the level of pharmaceutical services.

Functions

- Lead the profession and equip members for their role as medication experts in team-based, patient-centered care
- Disseminate timely relevant information and state-of-the-art tools and resources
- Raise societal awareness about the role of pharmacists as essential in patient care for optimal medication use

Membership

Total number of affiliates: 4550. Number of registered pharmacies: 2400.

Summary About SKPI

SKPI relies on mandatory membership dues as its primary source of revenue. In 2020, SKPI membership will become voluntary. The challenge, thus, will be how to retain the existing members. SKPI advocates giving its members a voice in decisions that affect their future while promoting their undeniable value to healthcare teams. Regular attempts to combat price differences and unify the prices across the region in coordination with the Ministry of Health and quality control bodies.

Table 7.26 in Appendix 1 and Fig. 7.10 show the assessment conducted for KFCCI based on the indicators and their subindicators

Assessment Summary About SKPI

- SKPI's degree of dependency on the government and political affiliation is low.
- High level of reputation among its affiliates.
- Good staff capacity.
- Low level of alignment with PSD goals.
- Good level of capacity for advocacy activities.
- High level of overall institutional and organizational capacity.
- SKPI's final score for the assessment is 3.267.
- Minimum score of BMOs: 1.937.
- Maximum score of BMOs: 3.957.

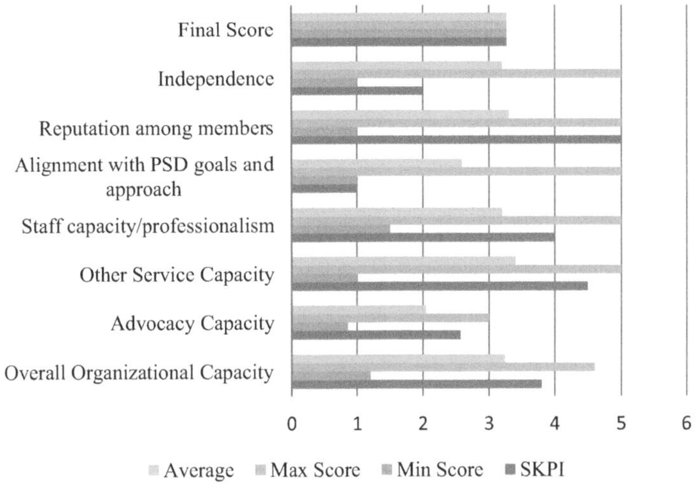

Fig. 7.10 Indicators used to assess DTA performance

7.5.2 *Findings from the Individual Design Dimensions*

As mentioned in the analytical framework section, the indicators are used to assess the BMOs' performance against seven design principle dimensions that have been evaluated based on a set of subindicators. The score of a main indicator is the average of the values assigned for the subindicators. The subindicators were assessed based on a 5-Likert scale, with being 1 the lowest and 5 being the highest.

7.5.2.1 Overall Organizational Capacity

According to Fig. 7.11, DCCI, SCCI, and ECCI are among the BMOs with the highest level of organizational capacity, followed by KFCCI, KAHR, and SKPI. This can be attributed to the financial capacity as membership in these BMOs is still mandatory by the KRG. HCCI scored low compared to its counterparts as the organization is newly established and is in the growing stage.

7.5.2.2 Staff Capacity/Professionalism

Figure 7.12 shows the assessment of BMOs based on their staff capacity and qualification, and it can be noticed that the majority of the BMO employees have acceptable skills and qualifications, with KFCCI scores the highest and DTDA the lowest.

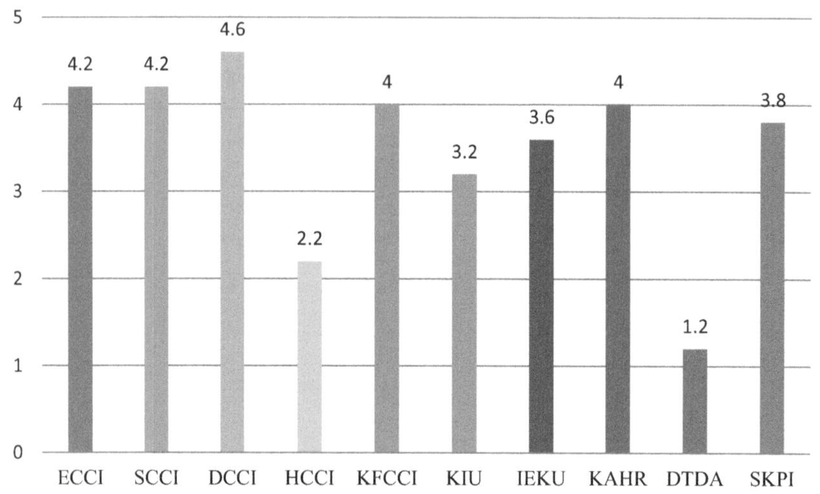

Fig. 7.11 Overall organizational capacity

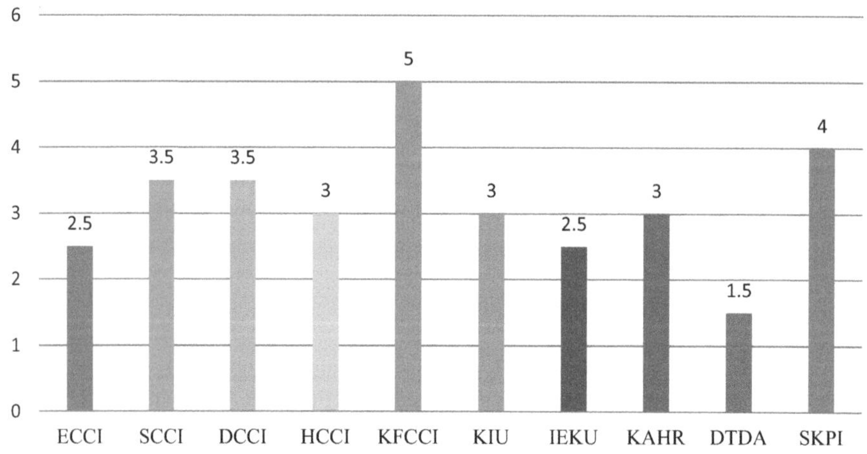

Fig. 7.12 Staff capacity/professionalism

7.5.2.3 Advocacy Capacity

The major objective for most BMOs is to give their members a voice, for example, a proactive advocacy representation that their members have neither the time nor resources to provide for themselves. Advocacy is challenging to evaluate and measure. Policy changes usually result from a combination of strategies and actions by multiple constituencies. It can be difficult to show cause and effect between one specific organization's advocacy activity and a policy change. Because policy change is usually a long-term prospect, producing incremental results along the

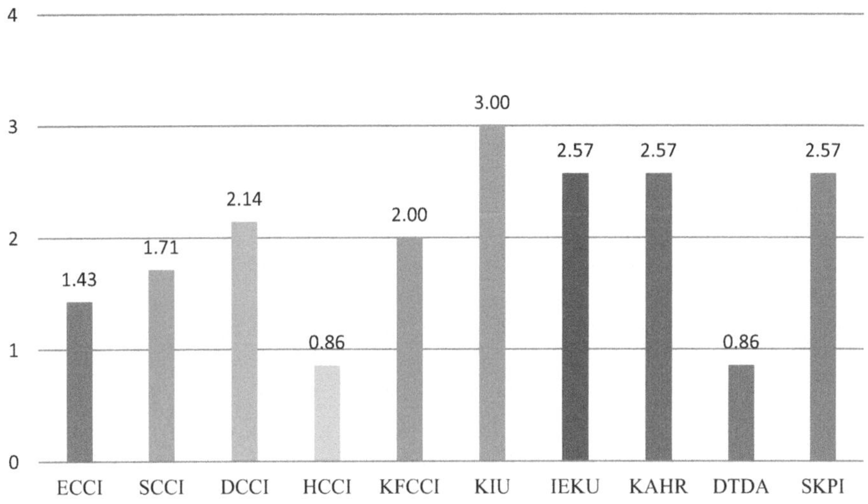

Fig. 7.13 Advocacy capacity

way, advocacy organizations must have the capacity to sustain their activities over time.

Based on the current study, unfortunately, only KIU scored an acceptable level of advocacy capacity with a score being 3 out of 5, followed by IEKU, KAHR SKPI, and DCCI scoring relatively higher than others but scored less than 3 (see Fig. 7.13). It is worth mentioning that no BMO in this study scored 4 or 5 (good and very good level of advocacy).

7.5.2.4 Other Services Capacity

Aside from the advocacy services capacity, the BMOs were assessed based on their capacity to offer other services to their members such as business networking opportunities, credibility, and referrals, for example, supporting letters for visas and for governmental administration businesses. According to Fig. 7.14, the majority of the BMOs under this study are characterized by offering the mentioned services to their affiliates with DCCI and IEKU being the top BMOs in offering the services and KFCCI and DTDA being the less in this category.

7.5.2.5 Reputations Among BMO Members

Based on the BMO members' survey, this indicator was developed to evaluate the overall level of BMO's reputation among their affiliates. The result in (Fig. 7.15) show that DCCI and SKPI are enjoying a high reputation for their members' satisfaction, followed by KIU and IEKU, while KFCCI scored the lowest level of satisfaction among its affiliates.

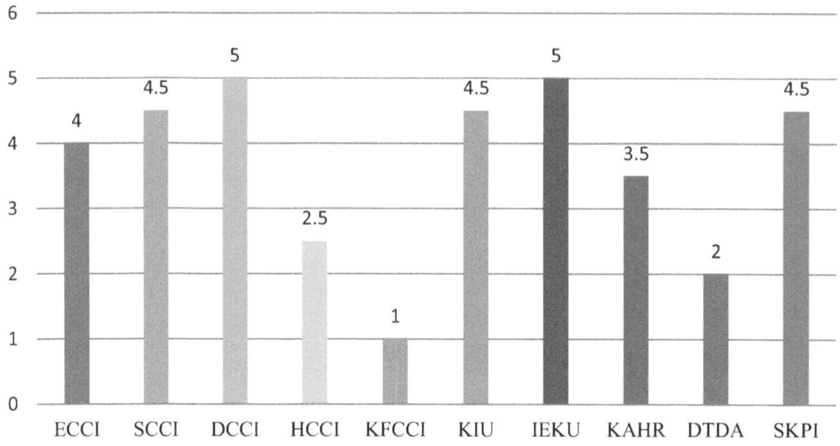

Fig. 7.14 Other services capacity

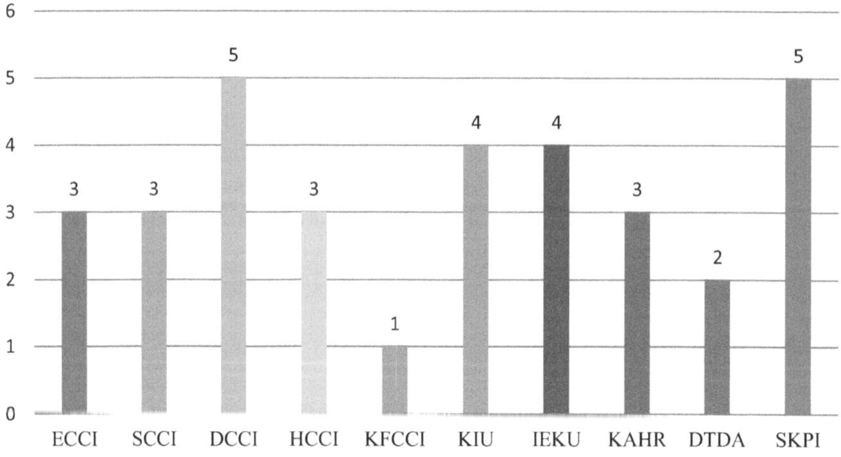

Fig. 7.15 Reputation of BMOs among their members

In reality, KFCCI is not acting as an individual chamber of commerce and industry; it acts as a representative body for all the CCIs in KRI where the individual CCI offers the services to their members.

7.5.2.6 BMO's Level of Independence

This study also assessed the BMO's level of independence from the KRG or any political affiliates. In general, the scope of this study was to select only the independent nongovernmental business associations. However, some BMOs although

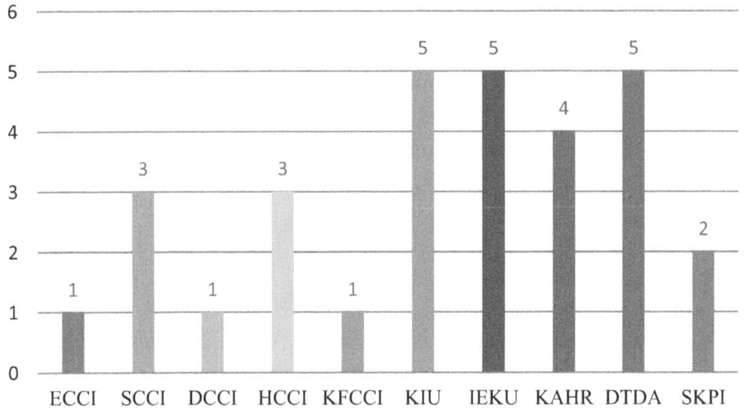

Fig. 7.16 BMOs level of independence

claimed to be independent somehow in practice have some sort of relation with the KRG. According to Fig. 7.16, three BMOs appeared to be fully independent of the government: KIU, IEKU, and DTDA, followed by KAHR.

7.5.2.7 Alignment with PSD Goals and Approaches

For this main indicator, two subindicators were used for the assessment: importance attached to advocacy work and openness to cooperation. Figure 7.17 shows that IEKU and KIU are the leading BMOs under this study that are well aligned with the PSD goals and approaches, followed by KFCCI and KAHR.

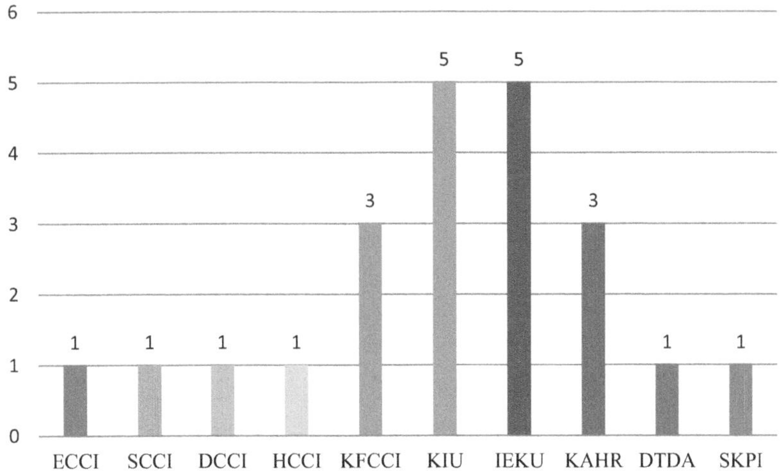

Fig. 7.17 BMOs alignment with PSD goals and approaches

7.5.3 BMO Members' Survey

A total number of 21 businesses from different sectors of the economy have been interviewed to understand their needs and their opinion about the BMO they are affiliated with. The aim was to understand the demand side from the members' voices.

7.5.3.1 Summary Statistics

The questionnaire for this interview is attached in Annex 2, and below are the summary statistics for 21 selected businesses and their responses to the questions.

Question 1: What type of association membership do you have?

When asked about the type of membership affiliation they have, 42% of the businesses have dual membership, 41% have company/business membership, and 17% have both individual and business membership.

An example of reasons why some of the businesses have dual memberships is that the business owner may have another business registered or the owner has obtained land from an investment board for a business that is registered with the chamber (see Fig. 7.18).

Question 2: The main reason behind joining a BMO

The majority of business members are joining the BMO for its benefit programs, followed by those who aim at developing networks to promote their business, while the third reason is that membership is mandatory by the KRG for administration, security, and financial issues. About 33% of the respondents emphasized joining the business associations for the sake of establishing networking for business linkages and new business opportunities. See Fig. 7.19.

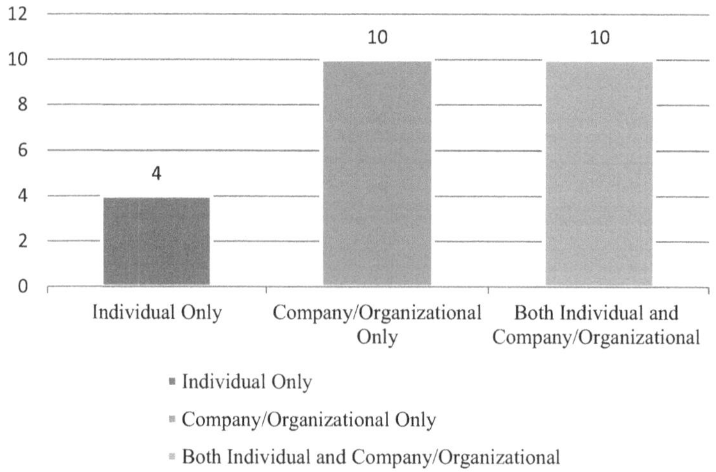

Fig. 7.18 Type of association membership

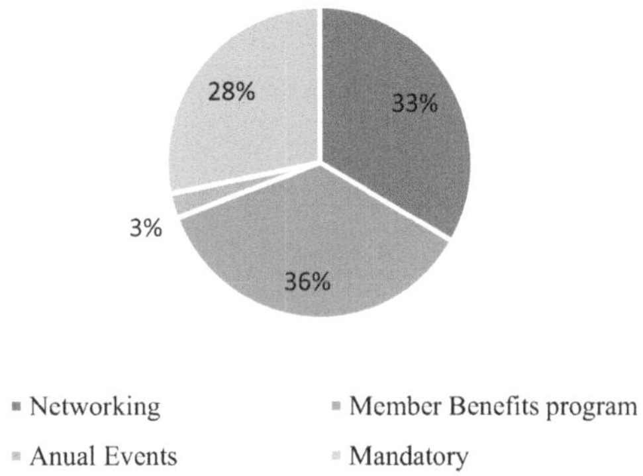

Fig. 7.19 Reasons for joining BMO

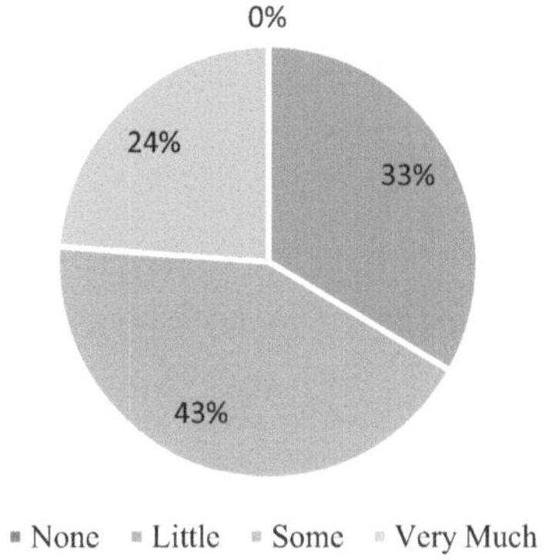

Fig. 7.20 Values of membership for organization development

Question 3: How much value do you think the association membership adds to you or your organization's development?

By looking at Fig. 7.20, it is evident that all of the respondents agreed about the contribution of membership in the association for business/organization development, and the contribution ranges from little to very much.

Question 4: Do you attend BMO's events, if yes, Question 5 what type of events?

The types of BMO events are categorized in this study into four categories: networking, annual, special one-time events, and others. According to Fig. 7.21, business members are mostly in favor of attending organized events one time, followed by networking events, annual events, and other events.

Question 6: How does the price of the association events compare with the value that you derive from them?

A 5-Likert scale is used to address the respondents' reply to this question as follows (See Fig. 7.22):

1. Not enough value for the money
2. A little value for the money
3. Some value for the money
4. A lot of value for the money
5. More value than I would expect for the money

Fig. 7.21 Type of BMO events attending

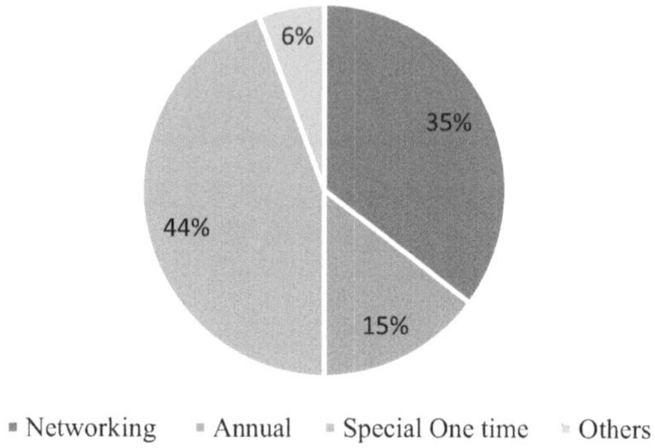

Fig. 7.22 Price of association events compare with the value driven

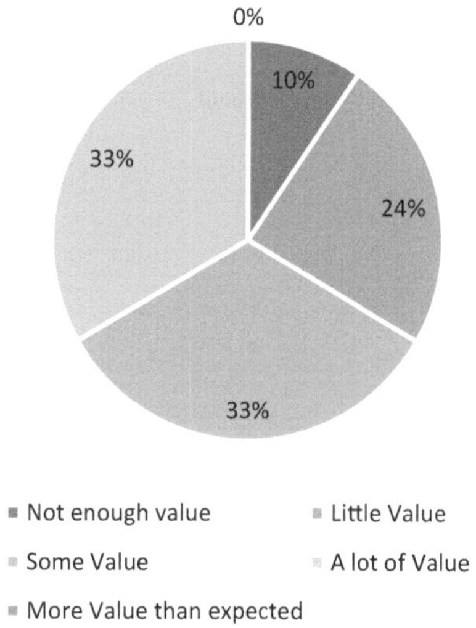

About 33% of the respondents agree that the events organized by their BMOs have more value compared to the price, another 33% reported some value, 24% little value, while 10% of the respondents reported that the price of the events is more expensive than its value, and these respondents are members of ECCI and KPS.

Question 7: How can the association make events more valuable to you? Please feel free to share any suggestions regarding future topics, formats, locations, speakers, duration, or any other event component that is important to you.

This was an open-ended question; once the answers were received, they were categorized based on 13 themes as follows (see Table 7.3):

Moreover, Fig. 7.23 summarizes the themes based on the respondents' answers.

Question 8: How does the cost of the annual association membership compare with the value that you derive from it?

The same 5-Likert scale is used for Question 6. See Fig. 7.24.

Respondents' opinions were varied in this regard; however, no respondent gave more value than expected for the price of annual membership but the majority

Table 7.3 Identified themes for Question 7

No	Theme
1	Regular updates about KRG rules and regulation to be shared, and prices and quality control activities to be shared with us
2	New ideas, laws, and regulation
3	Investors law are always changed, new regulations are issued, it is better if the union share with us the new rules and regulations on a regular basis
4	Promotion of export business, marketing, and international relations
5	Share up-to-date information about business opportunities and challenges
6	Engagement of members in events to make speeches and share their success and failure stories
7	Regular events involve chambers and other associations to have business linkages and support
8	Regular events on information sharing about the updated instructions for import/export activities
9	Events should not be during working hours; preferably weekends are a good time for events
10	I don't usually attend events, but the association is very inactive in events, I have never been invited to any, once I participated in an event in Baghdad
11	We are businessmen, we need to contiguously create networks. AITEB should be very active in making networking events on a regular basis, this is where the business opportunities emerge. Exchange experts in business is a new topic that AITEB should raise
12	We are new companies; the BMOs should have special events and sessions for small and startup companies to offer advice and share with us all business information and market. Also, to hold more networking events to establish businesses with others
13	We need statistics per season to prepare for the demand

Fig. 7.23 Themes summary for Question 7

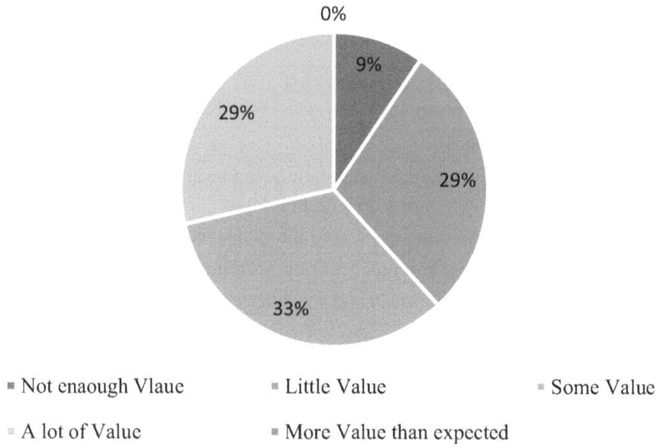

Fig. 7.24 Cost of annual membership to its value

agreed that becoming a member of a BMO has value for its annual membership fee.

Another open-ended question was asked to the members of BMOs to give their opinions and suggestions on how to improve the BMOs' organized events. The following themes were extracted that reflect the members' willingness to improve the BMOs' organized events by having more of the following subjects:

1	B2B matchmaking
2	Job fair
3	Advocacy
4	Training/marketing/ management/women empowerment
5	Information sharing
6	Networking
7	BDS
8	Market statistics

Moreover, part of businesses who already are members of one or several BMOs indicated that despite existing consultations and information delivered to them, they would like to receive the following additional services: sector information, including information on technologies, support in access to finance loan and grants, support in networking and coordination with other market participants, and training and consultations on sector-related issues they need. It can be assumed that it is more important for member businesses to obtain more narrow and specific knowledge and information.

7.6 Conclusion and Actionable Recommendations

7.6.1 The Performance of KRI BMOs in Promoting a Better Business Environment

Unfortunately, most of the BMOs in KRI have not historically done a good job of promoting a better business environment. The following points were observed:

- BMOs rarely conduct robust research, meaning that they do not understand the issues in sufficient depth and fail to formulate credible policy proposals.
- BMOs tend to present the government with shopping lists, or make vague demands for funding or "government support," which does little to address key constraints facing members.
- BMOs tend to have a poor record of engaging the media, forming coalitions, and communicating persuasively.
- BMOs often lack credibility with the government or are seen as unrepresentative due to the political duality leading the KRG.

This is especially true of grassroots BMOs and BMOs representing informal and microbusinesses. Many such BMOs in KRI have no experience in advocacy at all, and they suffer from low credibility and visibility. This weakness is doubly damaging for small businesses who cannot advocate directly to the government.

Some of them appear rather dormant, and others are very much active. Some of the more interesting activities are the organization of trade fairs, the creation of sectoral groups, and the dialogue with the public sector as well as the provision of referral and training services. The associations are often trapped in the cycle of not being able to offer services to their members due to cash problems and members not willing to pay their membership contribution for lack of advantages.

There are a variety of reasons for the poor advocacy performance of KRI BMOs both internal to the organizations and external.

Internal Factors

- *Advocacy capacity*: The majority of KRI BMOs lack an understanding of the basics of advocacy. Few have dedicated advocacy managers or teams, and there are few available external sources of support or advice.
- *Organizational capacity*: Apart from advocacy capacity, general organizational capacity is often weak, resulting in poor project management skills and dysfunctional internal systems.
- *Financial capacity*: Aside from a few long-established BMOs and compulsory-membership BMOs, most BMOs in KRI have very weak financial capacity, meaning they are unable to fund advocacy activities. This stems from weak fundraising skills, KRG's limited budget, poor member communications, and poor services (which results in low revenue generation and high default rates on member dues).

- *Governance issues*: Governance in the majority of BMOs is weak. This creates a disconnect between the BMO and its members and opens up the BMOs to elite capture. A narrow member base and poor governance also undermine the credibility of the government.
- *Cooperation*: Levels of cooperation among BMOs are generally low, not only because of a lack of trust but also because of a paucity of networking platforms. Coalitions are rare, and BMOs lack the opportunity to learn from and support each other.

External Factors

- *Policy-making environment*: The policy-making process in KRI is often haphazard and conducted behind closed doors. There are few inclusive public–private dialogue platforms such as the Private Sector Development Council (PSDC). This limits the opportunity for BMOs to openly engage in decision-making.
- *Socioeconomic factors*: The overwhelming reliance of the KRG on natural resource rents weakens the social contract and reduces the incentive for the government to engage constructively with business. Patronage politics limits the scope for substantive discussion and results in rent-seeking behavior by the private sector and BMOs. A history of military dictatorship has also weakened accountability and governance structures.

7.6.2 Challenges Facing BMOs in the KRI

- Most associations in KRI are weakly organized and highly politicized.
- The real influence of business groups on economic policy-making is weak, as larger enterprises prefer dealing directly with the government.
- Lack of weak networks of coordination and cooperation with unions and federations although the national federal laws are the same in Kurdistan, and thus affect the Kurdish workers' movement similarly.
- Women have very little role in decision-making or leadership within KRI BMOs although most of the BMOs claim to respect gender balance, youth representation, sexual harassment in the workplace, and child labor.
- An atmosphere of mistrust between private sector organizations and public bodies leads to more political interference and supervision.
- Insufficient capacity to monitor the policy-making process, analyze the impact of proposed laws and regulations on their membership, and prepare informative position papers.
- A fragmentation of private sector interests and mushrooming of voluntary BMOs.
- An informal style of interest representation favors influential bigger businesses and leads to frequent, unpredictable policy changes.
- A closed-shop mentality on the part of many BMOs (especially established chambers), which may not be too willing to accept SMEs or outsiders, and therefore cannot be regarded as genuinely representative bodies.

- Vested interests of influential members and executives, which may lead to self-serving behavior and politicization of BMO advocacy efforts.

However, in general, some of the BMOs in KRI tend to strengthen business relationships with peers abroad, provide advocacy for achieving societal and business sector goals, and disseminate information about local laws and relevant information.

Two main functions of business associations are of particular importance to smaller firms, whether export-oriented or operating in the domestic market. First, there is the "government-business relations" function, which is a two-way relationship with several dimensions. Unfortunately, in the KRI, BMOs are having poor performance in lobbying the KRG for reforms to benefit their members. Also, BMOs in the KRI are mostly unable to influence the KRG to prioritize and design reforms that will strengthen the private sector and help generate equitable economic growth.

However, some unions in KRI such as the engineering union, lawyers' union, teachers' union, and doctors' union deliver information from the KRG to their members; this is because these unions' administration structures are politically supported.

The second function is the "member services" function. It is about what individual benefits members can receive from their associations. These also include "market complementing" activities to make up for imperfect and costly information, low public investment in training, and so on.

Some examples of member services include legal advice, training and capacity building, industry promotion, such as trade missions, market information, training and capacity building, coordination among members, and dispute settlement. So far in KRI, only the three chambers of commerce in the three governorates are providing some of these services, as they are connected and supported both by political leaders and the KRG.

Effective BMOs tend to be nongovernmental initiatives led by firms. They are organized on market principles and they are self-funded and self-governed. Since strong BMOs should strive to be self-funded and offer value for money to their members, services need to be provided alongside the government-relations function. Services are very specific benefits that a member can see and give value for money daily:

- KRG needs to take ownership of the public–private dialogue (PPD) process and the involvement of the full range of private sector interests. Involving SMEs in the process is particularly critical for broad-based economic growth and the creation of income opportunities and jobs.
- Political parties' interference plays a key role in weakening trust and curtailing BMOs' freedoms. The lack of a contemporary law on BMOs significantly affected the organizations' work and freedoms. Government delays issued instructions and procedures to implement some of the laws that affected and affected workers' rights and trade union freedoms because some laws contain articles and rights for workers and union freedoms, and delays in implementation adversely affect those rights.

- Guarantee of BMOs' freedom through the enactment of a law that guarantees freedoms and by international standards in a way that guarantees the independence and pluralism of BMOs.
- Work to reduce political parties' interference, expand the scope of BMOs' freedom, encourage civil society organizations to work on labor and trade union issues, and build relationships and joint projects in service of workers' rights and union freedoms.
- Enhance the internal democratic life of BMOs and the youth to lead BMOs, build their capacities, and raise their awareness by opening courses and workshops and developing special training manuals in Iraq and the Kurdistan region.

7.6.3 BMO's Final Assessment Score

Figure 7.25 presents the final score for BMOs obtained by weighting the average of the indicators and subindicators used for the assessment. The final scores range from 1.937 being the lowest (DTDA) to 3.957 as the highest score (KIU) obtained. Accordingly, the top five BMOs have been identified as potential partners to work with GIZ, as they are aligned with the PSD goals and have adequate institutional capacity and advocacy capability. The top five BMOs are the *Kurdistan Investors Union, Importers and Exporters Union, Kurdistan Association of Hotels and Restaurants, Syndicate of Pharmacists,* and *Duhok Chamber of Commerce and Industry*.

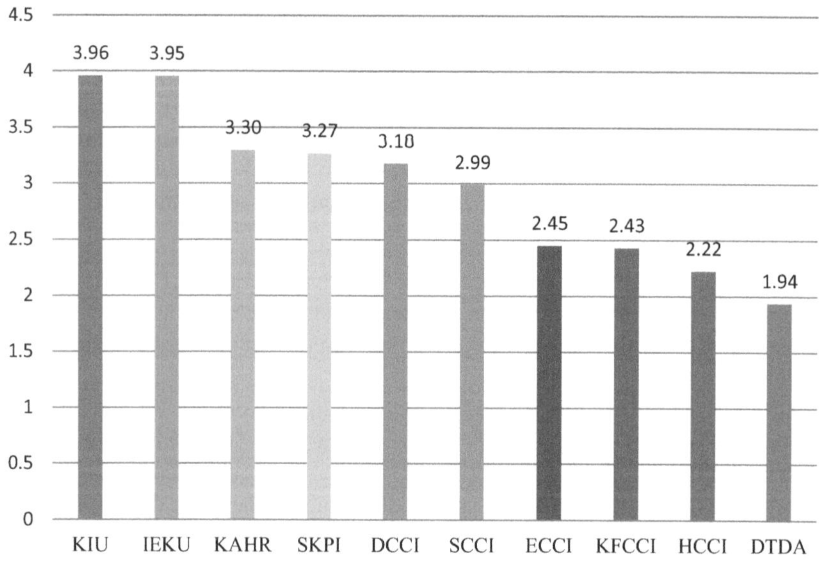

Fig. 7.25 BMOs' final assessment score

More details about BMOs' obtaining scores and the indicators and their subindicators are presented in Appendix 1 Table 7.26 and Fig. 7.27.

7.6.4 Proposals to Improve the BMOs

In light of the outputs of the assessment, the following pillars are suggested for the process of development and improvement that should be adopted to assist the BMOs in developing and institutionalizing their work. The BMOs would be better equipped to serve their affiliates and play a key role in developing the related sector in the Governorate in general. These pillars are as follows:

First: Developing the BMO's Institutional Structure Through:

1. Preparing a strategic plan, which defines the BMO's future vision, strategic orientations, and role in achieving the national and local goals, and preparing annual implementation work plans.
2. Developing an organizational structure that clarifies the chain of command, the relations among the different units, tasks at various levels, and job descriptions, to guarantee role distribution and authority delegation and decrease centralization.
3. Creating institutional mechanisms that assist the BMO in identifying the needs of its affiliates, monitoring their problems and suggestions, such as establishing a suggestion box, and holding periodic meetings between Board of Directors members and the affiliates to discuss the obstacles and problems facing the business sector in the Governorate.

Second: Strengthening Institutional Capacity Through:

- Providing excellent training services to the BMO's affiliates to improve their efficiency and productivity to achieve the desired development of the SMEs.
- Providing training services to the BMO's employees since training, rehabilitation, and development activities are among the most important services that demonstrate the BMO's ability to support and encourage SMEs.
- Developing a management information system that helps to provide accurate and complete information about the business sectors. This is deemed useful to the BMO's affiliates, investors, researchers, and those working in the fields of trade, industry, and production. In turn, they would be able to prepare periodic reports and studies on various economic issues at the macroeconomic level and economic sectors, and at the Governorate level, in collaboration with the universities, and research institutions, and also benefiting from the university students' trainees.
- Creating and developing a communication plan to market the BMO's activities and services to the business sector in particular and to the community in general. This could be done through informational bulletins, advertisements, and periodi-

cals that explain the BMO's activities and the available investment opportunities.
- Offering a digitalization mechanism, and the necessary grant to upgrade computers in the BMOs, computerize work, and archive records, files, correspondence, and minutes of meetings, in an organized manner to make them easier and more accessible when needed.

Third: BMO Management

BMO structures in many countries are of very limited use for SME development. On the one hand, numerous organizations are willing to act as chambers, federations, or business associations, but they are also wasting resources by competing with each other and are too weak and unstable to represent SMEs effectively. The established larger BMOs, on the other hand, are often dominated by large-scale enterprises because they are easier to organize and bring in more economic power and political influence.

Based on that, BMOs should develop their organizational strength and management capacities to become more effective and ensure their long-term prospects. Better organized BMOs are more focused, enjoy greater membership participation, and improve their public recognition and acceptance. They can fulfill their responsibilities for the whole—small and large—business community and can therefore be regarded as genuine representatives of the private sector.

Bad management practices and organizational weaknesses will be reflected by the following typical problems of BMOs:

1. Low membership
2. Poor leadership (lack of mission statement and strategic planning)
3. Lack of administrative skills
4. No clear-cut division of tasks between honorary representatives and secretarial staff
5. Negligible influence on government policy
6. Weak communication and public relations
7. Unattractive services
8. Inadequate funds and income generation

It is important to realize that these problems should not be seen in isolation: by reinforcing each other, they cause a vicious circle of poor BMO management. The central problem of many BMOs lies in the lack of knowledge of what they should do now (mission) and what they want to become in the future (vision). In the absence of a meaningful mission and vision, BMOs will attract only a few members. Thus, they often have to cope with insufficient financial resources that in turn limit the scope for good services and advocacy. Without attractive benefits of membership, however, companies will abstain from joining the BMO or decide to quit. Therefore, efforts to strengthen a BMO's management capacity have to be considered in the course of GIZ intervention, even when the primary objective of the promotional activity is to enhance service delivery and/or policy advocacy. Capacity building is a gradual process. Therefore, BMO management capabilities will also develop incrementally.

Appendix 1

Main Indicator	Indicators	ECCI	SCCI	DCCI	HCCI	KFCCI	KIU	IEKU	KAHR	DTDA	SKPI	Average Score	Min Score	Max Score
Overall Organizational Capacity	No of Members	5	5	5	2	5	1	4	3	1	3	3.4	1	5
	Organizational Setup	4	4	4	3	5	3	3	5	1	2	3.4	1	5
	Services	4	3	4	1	3	4	5	4	2	5	3.5	1	5
	Financials	5	5	5	3	5	3	2	4	1	4	3.7	1	5
	Impression of members	3	4	5	2	2	5	4	4	1	5	3.5	1	5
	Average Score	4.2	4.2	4.6	2.2	4	3.2	3.6	4	1.2	3.8	-	-	4.6
Advocacy Capacity	Dedicated department	0	0	0	0	0	0	0	0	0	0	0	0	0
	Dedicated staff	0	0	0	0	0	1	0	1	1	1	0.4	0	1
	Dedicated instruments to collect views	0	1	0	0	1	1	1	1	0	1	0.6	0	1
	Dedicated advocacy instruments	3	3	4	1	4	5	4	3	1	3	3.1	1	5
	Ready understanding of important challenges of members	3	3	4	2	3	5	5	4	2	5	3.6	2	5
	Experience of Advocacy work	2	3	4	1	4	5	4	4	1	4	3.2	1	5
	Impression of members on advocacy work	2	2	3	2	2	4	4	5	1	4	2.9	1	5
	Score	1.4	1.7	2.1	0.9	2.0	3.0	2.6	2.6	0.9	2.6	-	-	3
Other Service Capacity	Scope of other service	5	5	5	4	1	4	5	5	2	4	4	1	5
	Impression of members on other services	3	4	5	1	1	5	5	2	2	5	3.3	1	5
	Score	4.0	4.5	5.0	2.5	1.0	4.5	5.0	3.5	2.0	4.5	-	-	5
Staff capacity/professionalism	Number of staff	4	5	4	2	5	2	2	2	1	3	3	1	5
	Qualification of staff	1	2	3	4	5	4	3	4	2	5	3.3	1	5
	Score	2.5	3.5	3.5	3	5	3	2.5	3	1.5	4	-	-	4
Alignment with PSD goals and approach	Importance attached to advocacy work	1	1	1	1	3	5	5	3	1	1	2.2	1	5
	Openness to cooperation	1	1	1	1	3	5	5	3	1	1	2.2	1	5
	score	1	1	1	1	3	5	5	3	1	1	-	-	5
Reputation among members	Score	3	3	5	3	1	4	4	3	2	5	3.3	1	5
Independence	score	1	3	1	3	1	5	5	4	5	2	3	1	5
FINAL SCORE		2.447	2.988	3.178	2.222	2.429	3.957	3.953	3.296	1.937	3.267	2.967	1.937	3.957

Fig. 7.26 BMOs assessment and indicators' scores

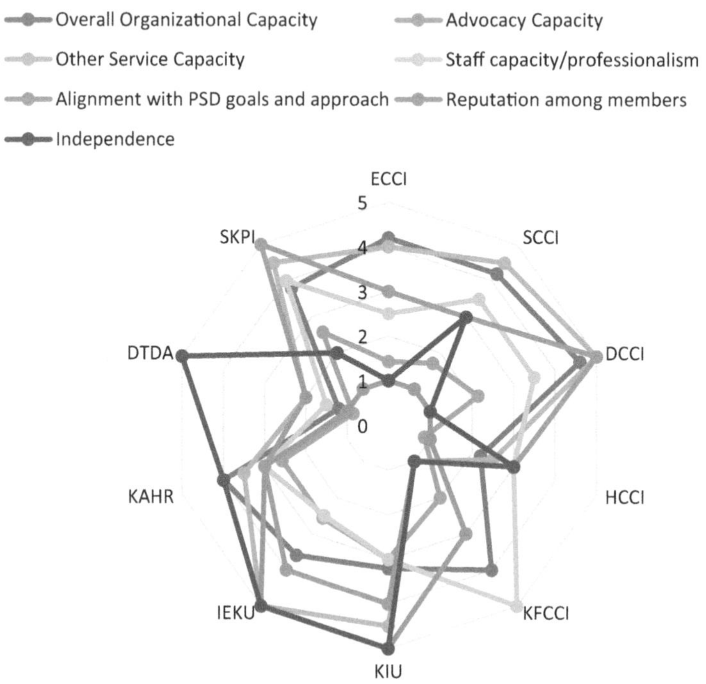

Fig. 7.27 BMOs' score obtained based on seven indicators and their subindicators

Appendix 2

Associations' Member Survey

1. What type of association membership do you have?
   - Individual only
   - Company/organizational only
   - Both individual and company/organizational
2. What was your primary reason for joining [ORGANIZATION]
   - Networking
   - Member benefit programs
   - Annual events discount
   - Others
3. How much value do you think the association membership adds to you or your organization's development?
   - None
   - A little
   - Some
   - Very much

4. Do you attend any association events?
    - Yes
    - No
5. Which of the following events have you attended?
    - Networking events
    - Amulas
    - Special one-time events
    - Others
6. How does the price of the association events compare with the value that you derive from them?
    - Not enough value for the money
    - A little value for the money
    - Some value for the money
    - A lot of value for the money
    - More value than I would expect for the money
7. How can the association make events more valuable to you? Please feel free to share any suggestions regarding future topics, formats, locations, speakers, duration, or any other event component that is important to you.
8. How does the cost of the annual association membership compare with the value that you derive from it?
    - Not enough value for the money
    - A little value for the money
    - Some value for the money
    - A lot of value for the money
    - More value than I would expect for the money
9. What benefits does the association membership best provide?
    - Not at all
    - A little bit
    - Somewhat
    - Very much
    - Extremely
10. To date, to what extent have you been able to develop professional relationships with other organizations due to your association membership?
    - Not at all
    - A little bit
    - Somewhat
    - Very much
    - Extremely

11. To what extent have these professional relationships contributed to your business activities, for example, by generating leads?
    - Not at all
    - A little bit
    - Somewhat
    - Very much
    - Extremely
12. What suggestions do you have to help improve BMO?

References

Ackers, P. (2015). Trade unions as professional associations. *Finding a Voice at Work*, 95–126.

Bennett, R. J. (1995). The logic of local business associations: An analysis of voluntary chambers of commerce. *Journal of Public Policy, 15*(3), 251–279.

Doner, R. F., & Schneider, B. R. (2000). Business associations and economic development: Why some associations contribute more than others. *Business and Politics, 2*(3), 261–288.

Dumez, H., & Renou, S. (2020). *How business organizes collectively: An inquiry on trade associations and other meta-organizations*. Edward Elgar Publishing.

Hall, P. A., & Soskice, D. (2001). An introduction to varieties of capitalism. *Debating varieties of capitalism: A reader*, 21–74.

Iraq Country Chapter 2021–2022. (2020). Retrieved from http://www.3rpsyriacrisis.org/wp-content/uploads/2021/04/Iraq_2021.pdf

Isakhan, B. (2023). *Civil society in hybrid regimes? The case of Iraq.*

Majed, R., & Aljabiri, J. (2020). Contemporary social movements in Iraq: Mapping the labor movement and the 2015 mobilizations.

Molnár, G. T. (2020). What do business associations do? *Corvinus Journal of Sociology and Social Policy, 11*(1), 73–101.

Muhamad, G. M., Heshmati, A., & Khayyat, N. T. (2020). The dynamics of private sector development in natural resource dependent countries. *Global Economic Review, 49*(4), 396–421. https://doi.org/10.1080/1226508X.2020.1821745

Rogge, N., & Archer, G. (2021). Measuring and analyzing country change in establishing ease of doing business using a revised version of World Bank's ease of doing business index. *European Journal of Operational Research, 290*(1), 373–385.

Sack, D. (2022). Organized business and trade unions in local governance. In *Perspectives on local governance across Europe: Insights on local state-society relations* (pp. 281–299). Springer.

Sanders, M., Stam, E., & Thurik, R. (2024). The entrepreneurial state cannot deliver without an entrepreneurial society. *Moonshots and the New Industrial Policy: Questioning the Mission Economy*, 259–270.

Sullivan, J. D., & Bettcher, K. E. (2007). Business associations, business climate, and economic growth: Evidence from transition economies. Kim Eric, Business Associations, Business Climate, and Economic Growth: Evidence from Transition Economies (February 2007).

Tiwasing, P., & Sawang, S. (2022). Does membership of local chambers of commerce networks enhance rural SME performance? An empirical analysis. *International Journal of Entrepreneurial Behavior & Research, 28*(2), 368–385.

WBG, & UNHCR. *Compounding Misfortunes: Changes in Poverty Since the Onset of COVID-19 on Syrian Refugees and Host Communities in Jordan, the Kurdistan Region of Iraq and Lebanon (English)*. World Bank Group.

Yao, N. C., Guo, Q., & Tsinopoulos, C. (2022). The bright and dark sides of institutional intermediaries: Industry associations and small-firm innovation. *Research Policy, 51*(1), 104370.

Chapter 8
Impact of Leadership Styles on Employee Motivation and Commitment in Public and Private Sectors in the Kurdistan Region of Iraq

Dlvin Sabah Mahmood

Abstract In the Kurdistan Region of Iraq, the public policies are articulated, but the rigidity of public management policies and procedures has hindered the managers from effectively contributing to managing employees and resources. The mass in public leadership has drawn the attention of people toward comparing leaders in the public sector with those in the private sector. Leadership in the private sector is considered to be more effective in human resource management than leadership in the public sector. This chapter aims at studying leadership styles in the public and private sectors of the Kurdistan Region with an emphasis on finding commonalities and differences in the impact of the present leadership on employee motivation and commitment to resource management in both sectors. We apply both quantitative and qualitative methods in the use of questionnaires and interviews across both sectors. We find differences in leadership style orientation in both sectors; transformational leadership is found to positively relate to employee motivation and commitment in public sector organizations, and transactional leadership is found to positively relate to employee motivation and commitment in the private sector. The major recommendation of the study is that the Kurdistan Regional Government (KRG) should induce an evaluation and assessment system that examines the behaviors of public managers to make their leadership best deal with the recent awareness of the workforce and managing resources.

Keywords Leadership styles · Employee motivation and commitment · Public and private sectors' resource management · Kurdistan Region of Iraq

D. S. Mahmood (✉)
University of Kurdistan Helwer, Erbil, Iraq
e-mail: dlvin.sabah@ukh.edu.krd

G. M. Muhamad, N. T. Khayyat (eds.), *Resource Management Performance: A Sectoral Analysis in the Post-Conflict Kurdistan Region of Iraq*, Perspectives on Development in the Middle East and North Africa (MENA) Region,
https://doi.org/10.1007/978-981-97-7725-9_8

8.1 Introduction

The workforce is the core force in shaping the success of any organization. The more active the employees are, the more improved the organization becomes. The contributions that are generated from an active workforce result in developed processes and advanced organizational performance. Managers are sought to be responsible for managing organizations including their workforce. It is the leader's responsibility to oversee the processes and make sure that the organizational goals are achieved. Each leader or manager follows a different approach to people management. For any manager, it is important to keep the employees committed and motivated at the same time. Hence, the style of leadership a manager deploys affects the employee's behaviors and attitudes in the workplace. Leaders in public and private organizations need to practice a particular leadership style that fits organizational objectives in order to have the desired impact on their subordinates.

There is a noticeable gap in leadership orientation and personnel management that incorporate employee commitment and motivation in public sector institutions in the Kurdistan region, causing a waste of time and resources. Managers in the public sector in the Kurdistan region tend to imply bureaucratic mechanisms of leadership which reduce employee involvement and increase routine work (Hamawandy et al., 2021). The lack of employee evaluation and performance systems in the public sector has obstructed employees from putting all their efforts into the job on the one hand and maintaining an effective performance as they get rewarded on the other hand.

Additionally, the horizontal hierarchy and rigid organizational structure of the public sector have misled the flow of information across the organizational layers. Ultimately, this has led the managers to follow set procedures that are not adequate for citizens' needs nowadays.

Furthermore, no acts of diversity, psychological health, and inclusion are incorporated in the working strategies which result in creating a rigid working environment for employees and has relatively reduced employee motivation in the public sector and in some private sectors as well where old mechanisms of management are practiced.

As such, bureaucratic systems, lack of performance management, and reward systems have resulted in reducing employee commitment and motivation in the public sector in the Kurdistan region compared to the private sector. The kind of leadership that does not incorporate employee commitment and motivation has resulted in two key issues in the public sector. First, it has led to low organizational performance in terms of effectiveness and efficiency. Second, it has reduced the people's trust in the government's services in terms of resource allocation and service provision.

This chapter aims to study leadership styles in the public and private sectors of the Kurdistan Region with an emphasis on finding commonalities and differences in the impact of the present leadership on employee motivation and commitment to resource management in both sectors. There are different types and styles of leadership that are adopted by public and private organizations. Each style has a different impact on employee motivation and commitment. This study only focuses on transactional and transformational leadership styles.

Transactional leadership attributes generate ground for predetermined expectations, negotiating contracts, assigning specific tasks and affording rewards and acknowledgments, and setting standards and norms. It highlights obligations to gain the set goals and performance level between leaders and subordinates. Transformational leaders inspire, motivate, and encourage their followers to renovate to help the organization grow and shape its success. Executive-level managers can contribute to shaping such culture in an organization by designing corporate culture and strengthening employee ownership and independence. Managers under a transformational leadership style follow up on processes and implementation by inspiring and motivating employees instead of micromanaging them. Trusting the capabilities of their employees to take the lead over decisions in their assigned tasks is the key for those managers (Abbas & Ali, 2023).

We apply both quantitative and qualitative methods in the use of questionnaires and in-depth interviews across both sectors. Several organizations in the public and private sectors were chosen for collecting data, such as local companies, universities, and international organizations in Erbil. On the one hand, seven private organizations are targeted including two local companies, one international company, one international university, two international organizations, and a media agency. On the other hand, the public organization includes the Ministry of Planning, the Erbil Governorate, the Kurdistan Board of Investment, and the Ministry of Education. The sample size for this research is 300 employees, and it is equally distributed between the private and public sectors. While 36% of the total sample size consists of leaders from both sectors, a portion of this percentage is interviewed using qualitative research methods, and the remaining 74% consists of subordinates of those leaders.

This study reports that transformational leadership may play a more significant role in driving public organization employees toward being motivated and more committed than it typically has done in the past, while the transactional leadership style could better serve private organization employees' motivation and commitment. This is significant for public policymakers in the Kurdistan Region of Iraq to pay attention to deploying laws and regulations that contribute to employee motivation and commitment in both public and private sectors' resource management.

The main contribution of this chapter is that it combines employee commitment and employee motivation in a study, deploying a qualitative research method in studying the effects of leadership styles and providing a compressive study that compares leadership styles in public and private organizations in the Kurdistan region. It also contributes to broadening the understanding of leaders in the region and will help them determine which style they are following and also identify their weaknesses and strengths in motivating their staff. The employees from both sectors can similarly benefit from this study by having a clearer picture of their importance in developing the organization.

The next section reviews the related literature. Section 8.3 provides a methodology and data section of the study and then discusses the main findings. Finally, constrictive recommendations are presented for the organization to follow to improve human resource management, positively make good use of talents available, and eventually increase organization performance in the Kurdistan region.

8.2 Review of the Relevant Studies

Personnel management has attracted the attention of managers in general and human resource managers in particular. Nguyen et al. (2020) claim that the key obligation of human resource directors is to identify the elements that build employee commitment and motivation and use that knowledge to control employee retention and productivity.

Most of the literature on employee commitment has been driven through social identity theory and its related elements of research (Japor, 2021). Correspondingly, according to Khan and Iqbal (2020), social exchange theory is an effective theory that explains employee commitment, and it actively contributes to employee commitment. Leader–member exchange theory is also one of the philosophies that human resource scholars base their research on while investigating employee commitment. The quality of leader–member exchange linkages has a positive correlation with employee commitment (López-Ibort et al., 2020).

Regarding employee motivation in the workplace, the basic and most popular theories of motivation are the equity theory of motivation, expectancy theory of motivation, and job characteristics theory of motivation.

The following sections discuss the abovementioned theories to understand employee commitment and motivation to manage resources that are affected by organizational leadership toward human resource management.

8.2.1 Employee Commitment

This section provides discussions about existing literature on employee commitment including the importance of committed employees, its causes and effects, and what strategies could be implied to increase employee commitment in any institution.

8.2.1.1 Value of Employee Commitment

Employee commitment is the attitude that results in higher firm performance. Scholars describe employee commitment through employee behaviors such as attending work regularly, working full day, willingness to perform extra work, citizenship behavior, high work performance, and considering to be part of the vision and mission of the organization (Alansaari et al., 2019; Puni et al., 2021).

Employee's job-related attitude in an organization is generally affected by the degree to which the employees are committed to the organization. It is also defined as the employee's truthfulness to the organization, the willingness to employ positive tools in representing the organization, and the employee's willingness to stay with the organization (Cabrera & Estacio, 2022). It is theorized that employee commitment toward the organization and organizational commitment toward employees is a joint relationship where each party formulates one side of the correlation. It provokes the unrestricted effort of employees which results in increased efficiency, improvement, innovation, reduced costs, and eventually greater organizational performance.

It is stated that commitment is not only aimed at the job and its factors. Nonetheless, it is also directed to the organization itself and the organizational goals. Chatzopoulou et al. (2022) explore that employee commitment is a key factor to favorable organizational outcomes. This aligns both the employee goals and those of the organization.

Relatively, it has been clearly approved by academics and claimed by executives that it is the sharing of collective goals that has a positive influence on improved organizational performance (Eldor, 2020). This is what differs in employee commitment from employee engagement as employee engagement is concerned with the job and not the organization and its goals. It is predicted that employee engagement is changeable over time, while employee commitment is a long-term and unchangeable attitude toward the organization (Ashfaq et al., 2021). The alignment of employee and organizational goals and the initiatives of the organization lead to better performance from the process to the end outcomes of the firm.

Employee commitment is a significant HR principle that has a significant role in determining important human resource management-related issues such as absenteeism, evaluating organizational corporate culture, and employee behaviors (Ashfaq et al., 2021). Researchers state that commitment increases employee productivity. Because the feeling of being part of the organization fosters a high level of commitment and increased efforts. Consequently, it is predicted that organizational culture and leadership could affect employee commitment (Chatzopoulou et al., 2022). Committed employees have a higher willingness to produce extra products and have more creativity and innovation in their work, which in return makes the organization competitive (Alansaari et al., 2019; Puni et al., 2021).

8.2.1.2 Employee Commitment Improvement

As discussed earlier, endless studies have found positive relationships between employee commitment and organizational behaviors such as better employee effort, increased retention, reduced absenteeism, and improved citizenship behavior. Furthermore, it is argued that in today's competitive and vibrant business environment, it has become difficult for organizations to guarantee long-term employees.

This has made the concept of employee commitment even more important. Thus, it is in the organization's best interest to invest in employee commitment.

Organizations can therefore increase commitment through human resource management (HRM) practices and strategies (Haldorai et al., 2022). To maintain commitment, organizations need to make employees feel valued and recognized. Effective communication, clear feedback, smooth reporting, and flow of information between management and employees are effective tools to increase this feeling of the workforce. Management needs to keep communication channels open to achieve better communication that makes employees feel valued (Haldorai et al., 2022).

Furthermore, recruitment and selection play roles in granting employee commitment. By providing accurate job information while announcing a post, applicants will have a clearer insight about the job to determine whether they align with its goals or not. At the same time, during the hiring process, the management will have a clearer view of the applicant that best fits the job through some sort of testing, for example, psychometric testing (Abdalla Hamza et al., 2021).

8.2.2 Employee Motivation

This section provides discussions about existing literature on employee motivation at work including the importance of motivated employees, its causes and effects, and what strategies could be employed to increase employee motivation in any organization.

8.2.2.1 Why Employee Motivation Matters

Employee potential is the key contributor to the organization's well-being and outstanding. Successful organizations understand the importance of the workforce and work on ways to better motivate them. They are uniquely helping the success of the company to meet its goals (Katsaros et al., 2020). Additionally, the current advancements in technology and global interdepends have made the human resource the most competitive advantage for firms.

Nowadays, human resource management (HRM) has become a strategy that contributes to the suitability of businesses. Researchers state that a successful human resource management strategy is empowered by employee motivation (Amjad et al., 2021). Motivation is the internal driving factor that pushes employees to behave in a particular way, and it also can be expressed as desire, welling, cause, or reason that drives employees to perform their work. It could be expressed as the process that keeps employees' intensity, efforts, direction, and staying in accomplishing job objectives (Baskoro et al., 2021).

One of the significances of motivation is that through motivated employees, organizational goals can be achieved. The maximum level of human skills and abilities is utilized when the workforce is motivated which accelerates productivity. Coordination and cooperation are other aspects that result from motivated employees, reduced costs, and greater efficiency. Employees who are motivated are more autonomy-oriented and self-driven, while those employees who are less motivated tend to be less active. Additionally, motivation drives employees to be more engaged and involved in tasks, more likely to take on challenging tasks, and have more responsibilities (Engidaw, 2021).

8.2.2.2 Strategies to Achieve Employee Motivation at the Workplace

Employee motivation should be supported by setting clear organizational goals that evolve employee participation. The organization needs to aim at promoting motivational programs that guarantee the optimal use of available skills. The applied motivation strategies should emphasize both the psychology and the financial condition of employees. There are different tools that organizations can use to promote their employees' motivation.

Some scholars consider money (salary, bounces, and promotions) as the main tool that leads to employee motivation toward better performance. Reward management system is another approach that is used by institutions to achieve their organizational goals. Such systems attract, retain, and motivate employees and lead to high levels of performance. Paais and Pattiruhu (2020) state that rewarding is a strong means to employees, whether extrinsic or intrinsic. Reward management system could be in the form of extrinsic or intrinsic rewards: financial rewards such as salary and bonus. Nonfinancial rewards are recognition, title, promotion, appreciation, praise, job security, decision-making participation, flexible working hours, social rights, feedback, and work design (Uzair & Mehmood, 2021).

Some researchers state that while planning for strategies to improve employee motivation, the management needs to consider the employee's age (Kollmann et al., 2020). Furthermore, Pessach et al. (2020) argue that an employee's position is crucial to be considered in this process. For example, employees in managerial positions may not gain motivation by financial factors; instead, granting them authority and freedom in decision-making could better motivate them.

Intrinsic reward motivates employees to put more effort into the job. Intrinsic reward is concerned with employees' satisfaction with their work emerging out of the pleasure of working in a firm that recognizes their hard work. It is what the person experiences after the accomplishment of the task such as joy and pride in a certain task or work. Extrinsic motivation is what they gain from outside sources of motivation such as salary, money, and job grades.

Realistic and achievable goals, employee engagement, staff empowerment, granting responsibility, proper feedback, effective leadership style, and smooth flow of information are considered approaches to motivation (Canavesi & Minelli, 2022).

8.2.3 Leadership

This section provides discussions about existing literature on leadership. Different leadership styles and their characteristics, their implications, and how they are related to employee motivation and commitment in managing resources are discussed.

8.2.3.1 Transformational Leadership Style

Researchers have observed that leaders who follow relational and transformational styles in leading are more influential than those who practice autocracy. Some leaders in transformational leadership impose idealized influence on their followers. They are concerned with followers' needs and practice shared risk-taking sense with employees (Berkovich & Eyal, 2021). Some others use inspirational motivation and intellectual stimulation as a technique to influence followers to achieve the set organizational goals and be more creative in problem-solving. Idealized influence or charisma is also one of the main attributes that transformational leaders follow, which inspires subordinates to consider their leader as a role model (Purwanto, 2020).

Inspirational motivation is one of the key segments of transformational leadership style. It refers to behaviors of leaders that focus on followers' consciousness, aligning employees toward the mission and vision of the organization. Instead of suffocating employees, a leader with this style inspires the employees in the organization to pursue drawing the best out of them.

Leaders who adopt this style inspire their staff by rendering more autonomy and encouraging them to make decisions without supervision by providing them with the tools to make (Tian et al., 2020). The leaders who follow this ideology set high standards for employees, transfer their vision in a clear picture, and inspire them to develop outside the normal conditions for organizational growth (Purwanto, 2020).

Successful executives are always active with their people by inspiring, rewarding, and correcting them and by replacing them if they fail, thereby creating opportunities for others. In short, leaders with inspirational motivation behavior create a vision, establish communication, and manage challenging workers by encouraging, working with employees, and giving them autonomy.

Intellectual stimulation, leaders with characteristics intellectually stimulate subordinates, produce creativity, and accept challenges. Those leaders have high levels of emotional balance and rationality and promote similar habits in their followers.

Another main element of behaviors in transformational leadership is individualized consideration. When leaders refer to individuals as the main contributors to work, employee's needs and concerns are considered and they provide coaching to employees. Transformational leadership is concerned with real-time problems, introduces new standards, and shapes the behavior of followers to achieve goals and improve employee performance (Rafia & Achmad Sudiro, 2020).

8.2.3.2 Transactional Leadership Style

Transactional leadership attributes generate ground for predetermined expectations, negotiating contracts, assigning specific tasks, affording reward and acknowledgment, set standards and norms. It emphasizes obligations to gain the set goals and performance level between leaders and subordinates (Hussain et al., 2017; Skopak & Hadzaihmetovic, 2022). This style makes clear what systems and norms employees need to follow in order to gain organizational goals (Jaqua & Jaqua, 2021).

Leaders with transactional leadership style fulfill the need and deal with followers through acknowledgment, interchange, or rewards when achieving the agreed objective as stated in contracts between the two sides. It is argued that the transactional leadership style is the most effective style for creating a working environment that promotes knowledge sharing and coordination among the leader and subordinates and the employees as well (Jaqua & Jaqua, 2021). Initially, in the planning process from task assigning to reward setting both the leader and employees are included. Transactional leaders monitor processes, announce consequences for failure in obtaining standards, engage employees in social and economic exchange processes, and increase employees' continuance of organizational commitment (Skopak & Hadzaihmetovic, 2022).

The motivation that is caused by this style is derived by doing what is predicted by the leader to avoid penalty, to receive contingent rewards, and to avoid corrective action specifying that a mistake is about to occur. The transactional style of leadership endorses obedience and reliance on the leader and their decisions. This leadership style does not promote employees to look for solutions to current problems (Hussain et al., 2017; Skopak & Hadzaihmetovic, 2022).

There are two types of transactional leadership: transactional active actions (active management by exception) and transactional passive actions (passive management by exception). In transactional active actions (active management by exception), the leader applies control over subordinates and takes direct counteractive action when mistakes happen. In transactional passive actions (passive management by exception), the leader acts only when they know about an issue to provide punishment. Thus, leaders enacting transactional behaviors monitor the performance to control the process (Jaqua & Jaqua, 2021).

8.2.4 Theories on Employee Commitment

There are many theories on employee commitment that are proposed by different social scholars. The most relevant theories include the following.

8.2.4.1 Social Exchange Theory

The origins of social exchange theory (SET) go back to 1958 when George Homans framed social relationships in his research. Then it was applied by Blau, the American sociologist, in 1964 to frame organizational behaviors within a workplace framework (Mugizi et al., 2015). The notion of the theory is that a relationship between two people/groups or more is based on cost-benefit links that both sides put into their relationship. The theory determines the amount of effort an individual puts into a relationship. The metrics as "give and take" are the basis of its analyses and it is all about cost and reward in a relationship.

The review of this theory has reached the conclusion that social exchange theory (SET) applies to the relationship between employees and organizations. Human resource management (HRM) practices build a basis of an exchange relationship in organizations, where employees reciprocate positive behaviors toward the positive financial or/and nonfinancial rewards they receive from their organizations (Mugizi et al., 2015).

According to the SET, employees perceive substantial human resource management (HRM) practices from the organizations as input, in turn, they show a positive attitude toward the organization and their job. Job design, employee involvement, performance appraisal, promotion and rewards, job security, and training are sorts of inputs that the organization puts in the relationship with their employees. In exchange, employees show commitment toward the organization (Oparaocha, 2016). SET supporters have referred to employment as an exchange of effort and loyalty for financial and socioemotional benefits (Blau, 1964).

8.2.4.2 Leader–Member Exchange Theory

The leader–member exchange theory (LMX) was proposed in 1976 by Dansereau, Graen, and Haga. LMX studies the relationship between leaders and their team members and the ways in which this relationship may affect the behaviors and attitudes of both parties. This theory is also known as the theory of vertical dyad linkage (Mugizi et al., 2015).

According to LMX, a member of any team goes across three stages in his/her relationship with the team leader or manager. The three phases include role taking phase, role making phase, and lastly routinization phase. Normally, during the first stage, members of the team are grouped into two groups by the manager or the leader. The two groups are referred to as "in and out groups."

In-group members receive more attention, more improvement opportunities, and training chances from their manager. This group have relatively easier access to the organization's resources because they are favored by the manager. In contrast, the out-group members receive less attention from their managers and have less face-to-face interaction with them. Individuals in this group have few opportunities for advancement with limited access to the resources in the organization (Mugizi et al., 2015).

LMX suggests that leadership is a collection of several dyadic links that connect the leader with subordinates. The degree of this relationship depends on the degree of mutual attitudes such as trust, loyalty, respect, commitment, obligation, and support that each one has for the other (Liden & Maslyn, 1998). The provision of such resources motivates employees to reciprocate to the leader through loyalty, voluntary behaviors, and the feeling of obligated to be committed to the organization. Accordingly, a leader's relationship quality varies from one subordinate to another.

8.2.4.3 Social Identity Theory

Social identity theory (SIT) was initially presented by Tajfel in 1978 and advanced in 1979 by Tajfel and Turner. They attempted to examine the psychological root of discrimination between one group of people and another (Hornsey, 2008). He concluded that people perceive the emotional values of their groups based on their understanding of their value in that organization and comparing the characteristics of their own organizations with other groups or organizations. Members in one group share the same values, believes, some emotional involvement, and a common definition of themselves. They work toward social consensus regarding developing their groups and their membership in them.

The theory of SIT is established on the notion that individuals contribute their behaviors in a group according to their membership in that group. According to SIT, people categorize others and themselves into different groups based on prototypical personal characteristics such as organizational membership, age, gender, and religious afflictions. Personal characteristics identified in social identity theory could be age, educational level, gender, marital status, job position, and job experience (Suman & Srivastava, 2012).

Scholars have different views on SIT and employee commitment. Hall et al. (1970) believe that based on SIT the organizational identification develops once the objectives of the employee and the organization integrate. Van Knippenberg and Sleebos (2006) state that SIT lays in shared loyalty, support, and characteristics among employees and the organization. Equally, O'Reilly and Chatman (1986) believe that involvement is the core identification in organizations.

Moreover, members categorize their membership based on roles and relationships within the group. Individuals categorize themselves based on individual personalities and features. Hence, those employees who share goals, beliefs, and attitudes with their organization show positive implications such as commitment to the organization (Mugizi et al., 2015).

8.2.5 Theories on Employee Motivation at Work

There are many theories on employee motivation that are proposed by different social scholars. The most relevant theories include the following.

8.2.5.1 Equity Theory of Motivation

The equity theory notion is based on equity assumptions as a determinant of motivation in the workplace. This theory was proposed by Adam in 1963 which focuses merely on human motives. The key determinants of equity are the inputs and the outputs. Employees compare their job's inputs with the outcomes they receive. In case of perceiving inequity, they reduce their efforts or become less interested in work which is equivalent to demotivation.

According to this theory, an employee's degree of motivation is influenced by his or her perception of being treated fairly compared to other employees. Salaries, wages, bonuses, promotions, and disciplinary acts form the balance that employees look for and think should be maintained by the employer. Hence, theorists have indicated that this theory works best for managers to determine what motivates their employees and how to balance employees' inputs with their outputs (Watters, 2021).

8.2.5.2 Expectancy Theory of Motivation

The expectancy theory of motivation was propositioned by Vroom in 1964. This theory suggests that employees perform based on self-interest and the assumptions that maximize outcomes and minimize loss (Van Knippenberg & Sleebos, 2006). They link the expectancy theory of motivation with leadership concepts as this theory provides predictions driving employees' motives toward the leaders. This theory serves as a process theory of motivation. Valence, instrumentality, and expectancy are the key components of the theory.

Valence, Expectancy, and Instrumentality (VEI) refers to the satiation where each employee gets motivated by a different reward. Some might be motivated by financial compensation and some others by time compensation. Valence is the way an employee perceives the outcome or reward of completing a specific task. Instrumentality is the assumption that employees' efforts should be rewarded by valued outcomes, while expectancy is the assumption that better efforts will result in better performance.

Ultimately, employees use the three assumptions above to decide on their level of effort and relatively get motivated by the outcomes of those assumptions. On the other hand, leaders can apply these assumptions to increase motivational tools which increase employee performance.

8.2.5.3 Job Characteristics Model of Motivation: Hackman and Oldham

Job characteristics theory by Hackman and Oldham (1976) defines the correlation between job characteristics and employee responses to work. Based on the job characteristics model, employees are expected to thrive in their work. The theory has five job dimensions encouraging three psychological situations that lead to valuable personal and work outcomes. It also includes employees' different variables as arbitrators of the relationship between the characteristics and the outcome variables.

The theory presents five main characteristics of a job: (1) Multitask refers to the extent to which a job involves multiple different activities, namely different skills. (2) Task identity refers to the extent the job needs completion of the work and accomplishing an identifiable part of work with a visible outcome. (3) Task significance is the extent to which the job has a considerable impact on others. (4) Autonomy refers to the extent the job affords freedom, objectivity, and preference to the employee to plan the work and to identify the approaches in which the work could be performed. (5) Job feedback refers to providing the employees with straight and flawless information about the efficiency of their performance (Taylor, 2015).

8.2.6 Leadership Styles and Employee Commitment

The linkage between adopted leadership style and employee's level of commitment has attracted scholar's attention for years. Studies reveal that there are factors such as religion, culture, and social setting that leaders need to concede in applying a specific leadership style to gain employee commitment (Hung et al., 2018).

The level to which the leader has knowledge on those factors will promote the type of leadership that the management will imply that best contributes to employee commitment. Depending on those factors, leaders will have an effective insight into choosing transformational leadership, transactional leadership, or any other type of leadership. Dariush et al. (2016) state that each leadership style has a different correlation with employees' perceptions and behaviors. He also indicates that the relationship of leadership styles might be positive or negative deepening the attributes of the style.

A study done by Cemaloğlu et al. (2012) showed that salary as a financial motivation that is practiced in transactional leadership style did not affect employee commitment which has led to the conclusion that extrinsic motivation does not contribute to employee commitment. Ahmad et al. (2015), on the one hand, identified that transformational leadership has relatively a positive correlation with both effective and continuance employee commitment types, whereas transactional leadership positively affects normative commitment only. On the other hand, Dahie et al. (2017) revealed that employee commitment is positively correlated with both transformational and transactional leadership styles. Equally, Dariush et al. (2016) investigated the relationship between leadership styles and employee commitment. We comparatively found out that both transformational and transactional leadership styles have a positive effect on employee commitment, while laissez-faire leadership has a relatively negative effect on employee commitment.

Multiple leader qualities (MLQ) that consist of charisma, individual consideration, inspirational motivation, idealized form, and intellectual stimulation have both positive and negative impacts on employee commitment. Megawaty et al. (2022) prove a positive relationship between leadership qualities with employee commitment. For example, intellectual stimulation and autonomy and employee job satisfaction lead to employee commitment to the organization. Furthermore, the setting of goals and task orientation also positively impacts commitment. The allocation of responsibilities likewise determines the confidence of the leaders in their subordinates and leads toward committing to the organization and the work.

8.2.7 Leadership Styles and Employee Motivation

The success of every organization depends on the workforce willingness to thrive through their effort's persistence. Leaders initiate efforts to recruit a new employee and they proceed through the entire induction process and continue every day. The adopted leadership style by a business and its management have an important role in employee optimism and job satisfaction.

Leadership is the constant process of driving employees toward a certain attitude or defined objective. Ahmad et al. (2015) define leaders as individuals who direct and help employees gain their loyalty and drive them toward gaining organizational desires. They also state that leadership and motivation is a two-way communication where leaders issue decisions in accordance with subordinates' mutual understanding and followers obey to implement. In their study, Ahmad and his coauthors discover that employee motivation could be achieved by social activities and informal attitudes among peers. There is a stronger positive relationship between leadership styles that promote social activities and norms such as transformational leadership style and motivation of employees. Transformational leadership behaviors are linked with employee needs and wants, idealized influence, intellectual stimulation, and inspiring that ultimately generate motivation in employees.

Another study by Haryono and Sulistyo (2020) discover that transformational leadership style influences employee job satisfaction in a positive way. Likewise, Qing et al. (2020) state that ethical leadership styles such as transformational leadership constructively have a significant relationship with job satisfaction. Similarly, Haryono and Sulistyo (2020) found a lean and tough positive relationship between job satisfaction and employee motivation. Those studies support this notion and predict that there is always a suggestive positive link between motivation and job satisfaction. Ultimately, the job satisfaction that is produced from a proper leadership style leads to employee motivation.

Chipunza et al. (2011) support this by determining that transformational leadership behavior that is considered as inspirational motivation encourages employees toward a variety of outcomes such as extra effort, ethical behavior, and learning orientation. According to Haryono and Sulistyo (2020), transactional leadership has a lower effect on motivation. In contrast, Khuong and Hoang (2015) believe that transactional leadership behaviors that consist of responsibility, fairness, honesty, and promise-keeping promote employee motivation. They also argue that the moral legitimacy of transactional leadership depends on fairness, contingent rewards, and the relationship between finishing certain tasks by the followers against receiving rewards from leaders; correspondingly, receiving punishment in case employees fail to perform certain tasks. Those behaviors of transactional leadership style are consistent with the assumptions of a justice approach and principles of fairness in exchange which contribute to employee motivation.

8.2.8 Leadership in Public and Private Organizations

Leadership is sought to be the main factor contributing to organizational well-being in the public and private sectors (González-Navarro et al., 2018). The importance of an effective leader lays in his or her ability to persuade followers to accept and work on organizational goals and try to modify their own goals accordingly. When organizations aim at outperforming others, a transactional style is preferable; however, a transformational style would achieve better results, while learning and growth are the desired results.

Surbhi (2015) reports that the public sector work environment is not set to be competitive. This supports the idea that the transformational leadership style is more practiced by public leaders, and the transactional style is more practiced by private leaders. However, several social science scholars argue that there are factors such as structural characteristics that hinder the potential for transformational leadership in public organizations through reducing the need for leadership by using organizational design features to provide adequate tools and to guide employee behavior (Wright & Pandey, 2010). Nevertheless, González-Navarro et al. (2018) point out that the institutional environment of public organizations drives public leaders more toward normative leadership behaviors. Eventually, they practice the transformational leadership style. Because employees in the public sector are not affected by extrinsic rewards as much as they are motivated by intrinsic values. The leaders in the public sector have limited resources for rewards that could be used as a tool to affect employee behaviors such as commitment and motivation.

In contrast, the organizational environment in private sector organizations and the availability of material rewards allow leaders to follow transactional leadership (Khuong & Hoang, 2015). De Gennaro (2019) discovered that public and private sector employees do not have the same motivational and commitment layers. Thus, the leaders in both sectors need to follow different styles that align with the inspiring factors of that sector. For instance, Waris et al. (2018) state that career surplus and financial reward can motivate an employee in a private organization, while in the public sector, this interaction is not applicable due to structural and moral issues. Factors such as personal feelings are in effect to motivate employees in public organizations. González-Navarro et al. (2018) state that leader–member exchange notion is less effective in the private sector because private firms are less focused on values and more focused on economic benefits.

Meanwhile, attitudes such as trust and respect are strong means for public organization employees. They also indicate that public managers value the implication of advisory practices in decision-making process, whereas private managers prefer the use of analytical practices to affect their employees' performance and well-being. Ultimately, leaders in the public sector are more into transformational leadership, while private leaders follow the transactional leadership style (Haryono & Sulistyo, 2020).

8.3 Methodology and Data

8.3.1 Methods

This study uses both quantitative and qualitative methods. It targets populations from both public and private sectors in the Kurdistan region. The targeted population are long-term employees from different levels regardless of their departments or sectors.

We use a purposive sampling technic in selecting the sample. The sample size is 300 employees of which 150 are public sector employees and 150 are private sector employees. While 36% of the total sample size are leaders from public and private organizations, a portion of this percentage is interviewed using qualitative research methods. The rest 74% are subordinates of those leaders. About 48% of the public sector and 31% from private sector participants were female. More than 37% of the whole population were female participants, and 63% were male respondents (Table 8.1).

Several limitations were undertaken during data collection such as the availability of the selected sample size due to COVID-19 health instructions. It was difficult to find a specific time to conduct the survey at the public organizations due to the crowds and business. Not all the participants were English speakers. Furthermore, participants were not comfortable sharing their emails or contact information to use electronic forms. There was a low response rate through electronic questionnaires.

The targeted population are long-term employees from different levels (managers and subordinates) regardless of their departments or sectors. This study targets populations from both public and private sectors. The public sectors include the Ministry of Planning, Ministry of Education, Board of Investment, and Erbil Governorate. The private sectors include local companies, universities, and international organizations in Erbil.

Table 8.1 Sample size

Sample size	Public sector sample size		Private sector sample size	
Research methods	Leaders	Subordinates	Leaders	Subordinates
Survey (questionnaire)	34	110	34	110
Interview	6		6	

8.3.2 Data Collection

Two sets of questionnaires and interviews are used as research tools for collecting primary data in this study. The questionnaire was designed with open-ended and close-ended questions. Each respondent completed one of two questionaries. The leader or manager completed the leader form (Form #1 Leaders form), and the regular employees or staff completed the employee form (Form #2 Employee form) (see Appendices 1 and 2). The forms were tested before announcing them, and several changes were made.

The questionnaire (Form #1 Leaders form) identified the leadership style of the managers, and the employee form (Form #2 Employee form) tested employee motivation, commitment, and their perception of manager's leadership behaviors in public sectors, several private organizations, and international NGOs. To support the information and data collected from the questionnaires and to put further a human voice to the trends in results, interviews were conducted in parallel. On the other hand, 12 managers form both sectors were interviewed. The data were collected manually through coding, and the interviews were recorded (see Appendix 3).

The questionnaires identified the leadership style of the managers and tested employee motivation and commitment from three ministries, several private organizations and international NGOs. The questionary also collected more data on the observation of the employees to the leader's features such as extra effort put, efficacy, and their leaders' behaviors.

In the final steps, the reliability of the questionary was tested. Triangulation was used as a method to rise the trustworthiness of the results (Aguilar Solano, 2020; Farquhar et al., 2020). Triangulation combines theories, methods, and observers in a study to guarantee any sort of bias that may arise from the use of a specific method, or a certain observer is avoided. Furthermore, a pilot study was managed to test the validity and credibility of the research.

In this study, data triangulation and theory triangulation are used. Data triangulation is the process of using different sources of data and/or information by categorizing each group or type of population under investigation including an equivalent number of participants per group in the study. Theory triangulation refers to the use of different professional perspectives in interpreting a set of data. A key strategy in this type of triangulation is bringing together people from different disciplines. Individuals from different backgrounds or places bring in different perspectives. Consequently, if each evaluator from a different background decodes the data in the same manner and draws the same conclusions, it means that the validity of the study is proven.

8.4 Data Analysis and Discussion

This section consolidates collected analysis, data, and findings and brings out the spirit of the analysis through descriptive considerations. It offers a clarification of the findings and explains how they are correlated to the literature.

8.4.1 Demographic Data

The majority of the population in this study from both Form #1 and #2 were aged between 31 and 40 years old. However, we noticed that the private sector population are younger than the public sector employees. This is due to the fact that the Kurdistan Regional Government (KRG) has held off the employment process in public organizations since 2014 as the result of the economic crises and the political instability in the region.

Respondents from Form #2 correspond the higher number of women in the public organization compared to men, while males are dominant in all other sectors compared to females.

The participants represent an educated population. About 63% of public employees who completed the leader survey form hold bachelor's degrees, 6% hold doctorate degrees, 12% hold diplomas, and 19% were master's degree holders. Meanwhile, about 53% of private employees who completed the leader survey from private organizations hold bachelor's degrees, 18% hold doctorate degrees, 5% hold diplomas, and 24% were master's degree holders.

Figure 8.1 shows the line management of the participants. About 38% of public managers who filled out the questionary were first-line managers, 54% were middle-line managers, and 8% were top managers, whereas the majority of them (42%) were employed by their current employer for the length of 6–10 years. About 5% of private managers who filled out the questionary were first-line managers, 47% were middle-line managers, and 47% were top managers, whereas the majority of them (42%) were employed by their current employer for 11–15 years.

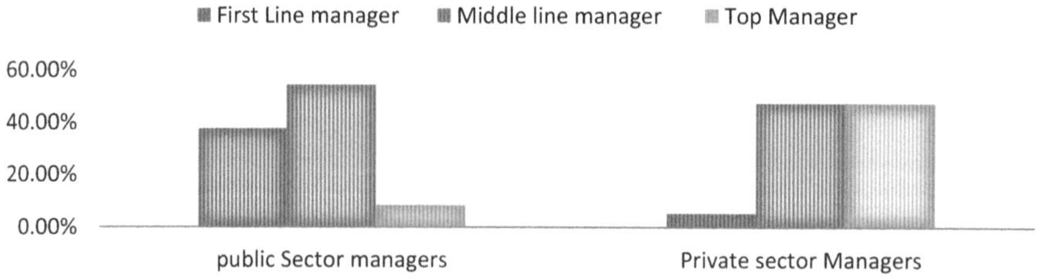

Fig. 8.1 Line management

8.4.2 *Employee Motivation Data*

Subvariable of Motivation (1)

The first three items used to test respondent's motivation toward their organization were basic needs, affiliation needs (social satisfaction), and self-actualization.

Table 8.2 demonstrates that only 8.7% of participants who are employed by the private sector and 20% of those employed by the public sector identified basic needs as their main motivating factor. Basic needs fall under existence needs in Alderfer's theory. Existence needs concern basic material requirements for living that also boosts motivation in employees in the early stages of their careers (Mohammed et al., 2020). While 63.77% of the participants employed by the private sector indicate that their main motivation to work is affiliation and social satisfaction needs, 50% of public employed participants indicate affiliation and social satisfaction needs as their main motivation factors. Based on Alderfer's theory, affiliation and social satisfaction are under the relatedness needs category. This is related to the importance of maintaining interpersonal relationships. Meanwhile, about 27% of private employees and 30% of public employed participants have identified self-actualization as their primary motivation factor toward working. Alderfer's theory assumes that self-actualization is linked to the growth category of needs which positively affects increased employee motivation.

A relatively small population of respondents in the private sector were motivated by basic needs, while a larger population from the public sector were motivated by basic needs. Although the majority of both public and private sector employees have passed the basic needs, shelter and hunger are not the reason why they are motivated to work. This could be the result of good standards of living in the region, the wealth that their families own, or it is because of the amount of time they have spent in their careers.

A relatively similar population in both public and private organizations have stated that they gain motivation through self-actualization. Yet, more of those publicly employed respondents were motivated by this factor as there is a huge competition in the private sector which makes it difficult for the employees to develop themselves or get promotions easily, while in the public sector seniority at work gives a chance to employees to receive more responsibilities and even get promotions.

Subvariable of Motivation (2)

Recognition and appreciation, clear and achievable goals, and challenging jobs were among the items that were used to test participant's sense of achievement that results in their motivation.

Table 8.2 Employee's main motivation factor, sector-wise by percentage

Motivation factors	Public employees (%)	Private employees (%)
Basic needs (hunger and shelter)	20	8.7
Affiliation needs (social satisfaction)	50	63.8
Self-actualization	30	27.5

Recognition and appreciation, clear and achievable goals, and challenging job were the main three components that were identified by the participants which boosted a sense of achievement in them (see Table 8.3). According to Chi et al. (2023), recognition and appreciation are nonfinancial parts of the reward system but have significant roles in the professional work of employees. Table 8.3 shows that 31.88% of the participants who were employed by the public sector and 52.50% of the participants employed by the private sector specified that recognition and appreciation boost their sense of achievement, which motivates them to put more effort into work. About 31.19% of public and 30% of private sector employees perceive working toward goals that are clear and achievable boost a sense of achievement in them. About 44.93% of participants from public employees and 17.50% of participants from private employees preserve challenging jobs and less routine work as one of the tools that drives them to become more motivated. A challenging job could keep employees engaged and interested in their role.

The table shows that the interests of public and private sector employees differed in terms of achievement indicators. There is a very high degree of routine work in public institutions. Therefore, nearly half of the population of public employees chose challenging jobs and less routine work as a tool that they wish to have in their work that will increase their motivation, while more than half of the employees in the private sector chose recognition and appreciation as the most powerful tool to increase or boost their sense of achievement. This is relevant to the stability of jobs in both sectors. As it is obvious, the public sector in the Kurdistan region is a lifetime employer. Hence, employees want to practice new ways, undertake new tasks, and experience different working habits than those they have always been stuck to. Moreover, the private sector in the Kurdistan region does not provide job security or job stability, on the one hand; the employees have the chance to switch to another employer, on the other hand; especially since there are no effective laws that promote employee rights in the private sector. Ultimately, employees are interested in receiving recognition and appreciation, and this factor motivates them to work harder and stay longer with their organization.

Subvariable of Motivation (3)

Financial rewards, nonfinancial rewards for a job well done, training and development, opportunities to grow within the company (organization), and feedback on work performance were tested to examine participants' sense of power.

Table 8.4 demonstrates that 22% of the participants from public organizations and 38% of the participants from the private sector identified financial rewards for

Table 8.3 Indicators of sense of achievement in employees (sector-wise)

Achievement indicators	Public employees (%)	Private employees (%)
Recognition and appreciation	31.88	52.5
Clear and achievable goals and challenging job	23.19	30
Challenging job and less routine work	44.93	17.5

Table 8.4 Participants' power resource tool by percentage

I feel powerful by my company's	Public employees (%)	Private employees (%)
Financial rewards for a job well done	22	38
Nonfinancial rewards	5	7
Training and development	13	15.22
Opportunities to grow within the organization	58	30

their good performance. About 5% from public and 7% from private organizations were found to feel powerful when they receive nonfinancial rewards such as achievement, progression, autonomy, growth, credit, responsibility, and the work itself. While 13% of publicly and 15.22% of privately employed participants have identified their organization's training, development plans, and strategies positively affecting their feelings about their job, 58% from the public organization and only 30% from private organization gain motivation by career development management and opportunities to grow within the organization. Lastly, only 2% of publicly employed and 9.42% of privately employed participants indicated coaching, mentoring, and feedback to be motivating factors for them.

Those figures indicate that public employees are mostly motivated by career development and opportunities to grow within their organizations. This includes promotions and uprisings in the organization. In the private sector, employees are more motivated by financial rewards. This is because private employers in the region are not lifetime employers, and there is a weak retirement system, thereby employees seek to gain as much financial benefit as they can while they are employees to guarantee their future. While in the public sector, employees are informed about their future and that they are going to be retired after a certain age, and hence they look for promotion rather than financial benefits.

8.4.3 Employee Commitment Data

As presented in Table 8.5, 56.25% of public and 40% of private sector employees agreed to spend their career life within their organization. It also indicates that 93.75% of public and 35% of private sector employees expressed their happiness to work for their company, and a large majority from both sectors reported that there were good options if they left the organization. Participants largely see jumping from one organization (company) to another as normal where 68.75% of participants are public and 65.22% are private sector employees.

It is uncovered by the findings that the majority of employees of the public organizations had continuance commitment toward their organizations. Meanwhile, the majority of private employees had an affective commitment toward their organizations. This means in the private sector there is more room for comparing the

Table 8.5 Employee commitment by percentage

Questions	Public employees		Private employees	
	Yes (%)	No (%)	Yes (%)	No (%)
Happy to spend my career life with this organization	56.25	43.75	40	60
Happy that I work for this company	93.75	6.25	35	65
There are good options for me if I want to leave this organization	87.5	43	79.71	20.29
This place has a great deal of personal meaning for me	25	75	16.67	83.33
One of the reasons I do not leave this place is the scarcity of available resources in the organization	68.75	31.25	65.22	34.78

financial and nonfinancial benefits of staying with a particular organization and leaving it or switching to another one. Organizational commitment is a concept that is defined as multidimensional and includes affective commitment, normative commitment, and continuance commitment. The three main types of commitment were identified using the survey questionnaire.

Continuance commitment is concerned with the employees who assess the costs of leaving the organization and compare it with the costs of staying in the same institution. It is the difference in the costs and benefits that are associated with leaving the organization. About 44% of the employees from the public sector and 38% from the private sector indicated that they do not have better options to leave so they would rather stay with their current organization. This indicates that this portion of respondents have continuance commitment toward their organization.

Affective commitment is concerned with employees' emotional connection to their organization. Those employees who have affective commitment remain with the organization by their full willingness and desire. About 31% of the employees from the public sector and 45% from the private sector showed that they are happy with their organizations and have positive feelings toward their workplace.

Normative commitment is about feelings of obligation to the organization. It appears when staff feel an obligation to their organizations, even in case they are not happy with the job or want to secure a better opportunity. About 25% of the employees from the public sector and 17% from the private sector stated that one of the reasons they do not leave their current organization at the current time is the scarcity of available resources in the organization to replace them and that they perceive jumping from one organization to another as an unethical attitude.

8.4.4 Leadership Data

Subordinates were given the chance to show their perception of their supervisors/managers or directors' behaviors in terms of leadership practices. Figure 8.2 presents leader characteristics perceived by the participants by percentage. About 43%

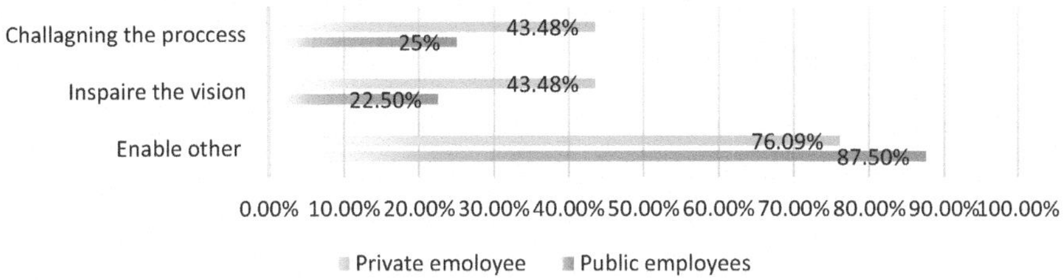

Fig. 8.2 Leader characteristics perceived by the participants by percentage

Table 8.6 Employee perception of their managers' leadership behaviors

Questions	Public employees (%)		Private employees (%)	
	Yes	No	Yes	No
My manager treats others with dignity and respect and actively listens to diverse views	87.5	12.5	76.09	23.91
He/she searches outside the formal boundaries for new tools to develop our work	40	60	79.71	20.29
Is your work monitored?	43.75	56.25	80.43	21.01
Does your manager share the future shape of the organization with the team?	22.5	77.5	43.48	56.52
My manager challenges people to use new or improved strategies in working	25	75	43.48	56.52

of privately and only 25% of publicly employed participants declare that their leaders challenge work processes to increase their motivation. About 43.48% of private and 22.5 of public sector employees agreed that their managers inspire them by sharing the organizational vision with the team. About 76% of private and nearly 87% of public sector employees believed that their managers put too much effort into enabling them (employees).

The participants were tested to provide their observations of their managers in terms of monitoring, rewards and punishment preservation, moral values maintained by managers, encouraging and offering help from managers, and the clarity, achievability, and measurability of the goals set by their managers/leaders. They were tested to determine the leadership style implied by their managers and to examine to what extend they are satisfied with their leadership style.

Table 8.6 presents employee perceptions of their managers' leadership behaviors. About 81% of the participants who were employed by the public sector stated their work is closely monitored, and the rest of 19% stated that they do not observe any monitoring from their managers. About 85% of those employees stated that their managers monitor their work in order to detect mistakes to make sure that the work is done according to the set process. About 8% of them indicated that they are monitored to detect mistakes. Nevertheless, 7% of them indicated that their managers monitor their work to study the possibility of any future mistakes.

Fig. 8.3 Manager perceived encouragement tool by percentage

About 80% of the participants who were employed by the private sector stated their work is closely monitored, and the rest of 20% stated that they do not observe any monitoring from their managers. About 55% of those employees stated that their managers monitor their work in order to detect mistakes to make sure that the work is done according to the set process. About 20% of them indicated that they are monitored to detect mistakes. Nevertheless, 25% of them indicated that their managers monitor their work to study the possibility of any future mistakes.

About 37% of public employees indicate that their managers encourage them to achieve organizational goals by reward and punishment, and 63% of public organizations state that their managers encourage them toward organizational goals through higher values and moral values. About 75% of private employees indicate that their managers encourage them to achieve organizational goals by reward and punishment, and 25% of them state that their managers encourage them toward organizational goals through higher values and moral values (Fig. 8.3).

8.4.5 Determining the Leadership Style of the Leaders in Both Public and Private Organizations

As shown in Table 8.7, 76% of public and 35% of private leaders indicated that they try to challenge employees to try new and innovative ways to do their work. This behavior is referred to as intellectual stimulation which is one of the characteristics of the transformational leadership style. It is where leaders challenge assumptions, take risks, and solicit employees' ideas. Managers recognize their employees through stimulation, creativity, and innovation. The leader encourages and cooperates with the employees as they try new methods and develop innovative ways of dealing with organizational issues. The leader encourages followers to think out on their own and to think independently so that they become autonomous.

Table 8.7 Transformational leadership style behaviors by percentage

Transformational leadership behaviors	Public sector (%)	Private sector (%)
I try to challenge employees to try new and innovative ways to do their work	76	35
I help the team to understand problems and issues and clarify situations for them to perform better	45	10
I share the future of the organization with their employees	67	32
I use higher ideals and moral values	90	76

About 45% of the participants from public organizations and 10% from private organizations identified their approaches to management that they help their team to understand problems and issues and clarify situations for them to perform better. This indicates that those managers or leaders practice individualized considerations. Individualized consideration is the extent to which a manager tries to understand each employee's needs and helping and support, and they provide coaching or guidance accordingly. He/she listens to the concerns of each team member and is empathic to each person's situation and case. When practicing individualized consideration, the managers are aware of the unique talents that each team member brings to the work and encourage them in developing and demonstrating these key skills. This pushes the employee to aspire to develop further. Theoretically, individualized consideration is one of the characteristics of the transformational leadership style.

Table 8.7 shows that 67% of the participants from public and 32% of the participants from private organizations identified that they inspire their followers by sharing an exciting dream of the future with their employees. They articulate an appealing vision that motivates employees to perform beyond expectations. Leaders with inspirational motivation behaviors are said to have high standards and expectations for their team members. They are positive about employee's ability to meet goals and provide meaning to their team members by showing the importance and clarifying all duties and responsibilities. Moreover, they can motivate their followers to have a strong sense of purpose to drive their group forward. This encourages followers to invest more effort in their tasks to be enthusiastic about the future and to invest in their own capabilities. This is said to be transformational leadership in nature. Other 33% from public and 78% from private organizations were found to have less interaction with their followers in sharing any future vision with them that will motivate them.

When participants were asked about monitoring purposes, 60% of public and 70% of private organization leaders stated that as leaders they emphasize the corporate culture of the organization in leading and directing the employees. By stating that, they monitor their team's performance to make sure that the work is done according to the set process. This is one of the fundamental traits of transactional leadership that focuses on hierarchy, and employees are acknowledged ahead of time of what is anticipated from them. Team members are afforded a road map that contains clear instructions. They are projected to follow a chain of command. About

78% of public leaders and 64% of private leaders stated that they monitor their teams to detect mistakes only, which revels that this portion of leaders are passive in their behaviors. Because of the sole focus on the status quo, they react to events after they have happened and they lack the foresight to anticipate problems due to limited resources. Passiveness is also a trait of a transactional leadership style.

About 25% of the leaders from public and 36% of the leaders from private indicated that they communicate with subordinates to describe how assignments must be done and let them know that there will be rewards for a job well done. This is solely under the transaction leadership style. Transactional leaders operate under rigid rules, and they do not take the emotions of employees into consideration. Instead, employees are given detailed and definite instructions, and a timely manner with perfection (see Table 8.8).

About 25% of public and 36% of private stated that they use reward and punishment to encourage their subordinates, which is a transactional leadership behavior. In order to elicit the predetermined goals, this interprets into the element that employees obtain rewards for behaving in a predetermined manner. The relationship uses obvious instructions, disciplinary orders, and incentives, such as bonuses, perks, praise, or promotions, to motivate subordinates. It is fundamental that employees are clear about what they receive for their efforts, and that they inherently work harder when incentivized. Besides, employees need to know in advance what they must do to receive that incentive. The manager must be coherent in rewards and punishments. If employees realize that their managers are biased, any motivation offered by him/her will fail to inspire the team members.

We interviewed six leaders from public organizations (deputy and departmental managers) and six from private organizations (CEOs, departmental managers, and assistants) to gather qualitative data for the findings of this study.

The qualitative findings support the quantitative part of this study. The interviewees from private organizations indicated that their organizations push leaders to practice rational-legal, because there is a huge desire for consistency, certainty, and equity in place. Leaders or managers can apply customized approaches of leading. They rely on structural mechanisms to limit individual preference and promote uniformity in how employees interpret and respond to work situations. Those characteristics encourage them to work based on the manifestation of individual differences

Table 8.8 Transactional leadership behaviors by percentage

Transactional leadership behaviors	Public sector (%)	Private sector (%)
I emphasize the corporate culture of the organization in leading and directing the employees	60	70
I monitor their teams to detect mistakes only	78	64
I monitor the process to make sure things are processed according to the system	55	86
I communicate with subordinates to explain processes and rewards when tasks are done accordingly	25	36
I use reward and punishment to encourage their subordinates	25	36

and attitudes. They also revealed that clear goals, clear performance management systems, and set reward and punishment systems are in place, in a way they can use those systems as tools to motivate their followers to act and perform in certain ways toward organizational goals. Lastly, the private interviewees stated that there is a huge sense of competition internally (among employees) and externally (among one organization and another) that affects the way they deal with their team and how they communicate the organizational vision to them.

Those are all characteristics of a transactional leadership style. Those findings determine the conclusion that private leaders apply transactional leadership practices, and this is in line with the findings of quantitative data gathered from surveys.

On the other hand, interviewees from public organizations stated that practices such as participating in social activities, using personal connections, and considering each employee individually are the main mechanisms they can use to make a positive influence on their teams. Additionally, those managers and leaders uncovered the reality that their organizations have hard-to-measure functioning objectives as well as weak relations between extrinsic rewards and employee performance. They also mentioned that as managers they have no access to resources that they can use to encourage their staff. One more point is that there seemed to be no sense of competition among teams in the public sector that could affect the way employees are dealt with by their managers/leaders.

Those are all characteristics of a transformational leadership style. Depending on the results of the interviews, it is predicted that public leaders are restricted from applying transactional leadership practices, and this is again in line with the findings of quantitative data gathered from surveys.

8.4.6 *Testing Hypotheses*

This study tackled the field of leadership, employee motivation, and employee commitment in public and private organizations. This section allocates with testing those hypotheses using correlation coefficient analysis.

Figure 8.4 shows that there is a solid positive correlation coefficient between transformational leadership style and employee motivation in public organizations. Correlation coefficient is significant at the 0.77 level. Likewise, there was a strong positive correlation coefficient between the transformational leadership style and

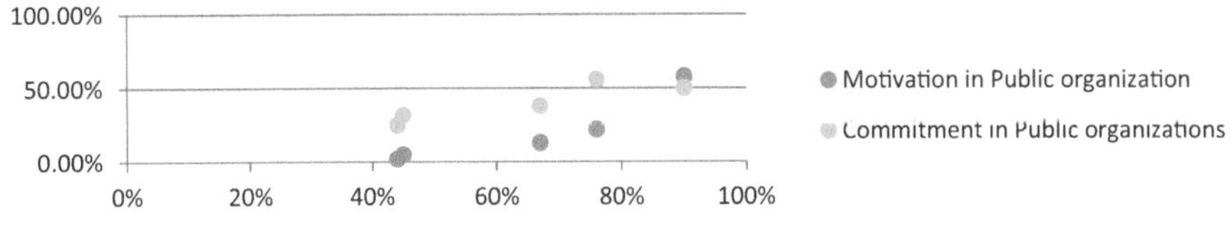

Fig. 8.4 Correlation between transformational leadership style, motivation, and commitment in public organizations

employee commitment in private organizations. Correlation coefficient is significant at the 0.82 level.

As shown in Fig. 8.5, there was a perfect positive correlation coefficient between the transactional leadership style and employee motivation in private organizations. Correlation coefficient is significant at the 0.99 level. Likewise, there was a strong positive correlation coefficient between the transactional leadership style and employee commitment in private organizations. Correlation coefficient is significant at the 0.77 level.

Table 8.9 presents the significance level of the relationship based on a 0.05% significance level. It would conclude that the correlation coefficient is statistically significant between transformational leadership and employee motivation in public organizations since *p*-value <0.05. This shows that transformational leadership has a direct positive impact on employee motivation in public organizations as attributes of transformational leadership increase the level of employee motivation increases.

Similarly, the *p*-value of 0.001 indicates that transformational leadership style has an effective power over employee commitment. Hence, transformational leadership has a direct positive impact on employee commitment in public organizations as attributes of transformational leadership increase the level of employee commitment increases.

We also found that the correlation coefficient is statistically significant between transactional leadership and employee motivation in private organizations. Accordingly, transactional leadership has a straight constructive impact on employee motivation in private organizations as attributes of transactional leadership increase the level of employee motivation increases.

The p-value of the last hypothesis reports that the transactional leadership style has an applicable influence over employee commitment in private organizations. Transactional leadership has a straight progressive impact on employee commitment in private organizations as attributes of transactional leadership increase the level of employee commitment increases.

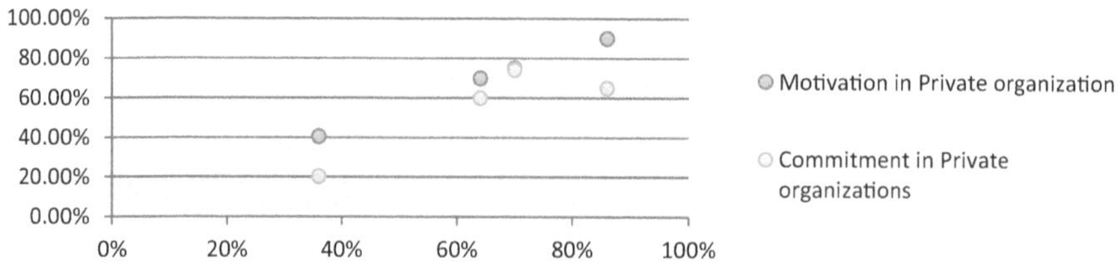

Fig. 8.5 Correlation between transactional leadership style, motivation, and commitment in private organizations

Table 8.9 Hypotheses results

Hypothesis	*T*-value	*P*-value	Results
H1: Transformational leadership style has a positive impact on employee motivation in public organizations	3.9	0.031	Confirmed
H2: Transformational leadership style has a positive impact on employee commitment in public organizations	0.5	0.001	Confirmed
H3: Transactional leadership style has a positive impact on employee motivation in private organizations	4.33	0.022	Confirmed
H4: Transactional leadership style has a positive impact on employee commitment in private organizations	9.1	0.043	Confirmed

8.5 Conclusions and Recommendations

This study investigated the extent to which a leader with a specific leadership style can affect employee motivation and commitment in the public sector compared to the private sector. The findings concluded that employees from public and private sectors have different tests of behaviors. Similarly, managers from both sectors follow different leadership styles. The results showed a positive correlation between transactional style on employee commitment and motivation in the private sector. In contrast, a positive correlation was found between transformational leadership style and employee motivation and commitment in the public sector.

We found that public employees are mostly motivated by career development and opportunities to grow within their organizations. This includes promotions and uprisings in the organization. In the private sector, employees are more motivated by financial rewards because private employers are not lifetime employers and there is a weak retirement system.

The study found out that public sector organizations endure transformational leadership style, while private sector organizations endure transactional leadership. We showed that transformational leadership is positively related to employee motivation and commitment in public sector organizations. Conversely, transactional leadership is positively related to employee motivation and commitment in the private sector.

Job stability is another notion that supports the results of this study. In the public sector, job security is high due to civil service laws and organizational governance. Contrariwise, employment within the private sector is entirely at will, and employees can be dismissed for any given reason. Hence, a leader can use reward and punishment behaviors (transactional leadership practices) in the public sector to impact the attitude of their employees. Leaders in the public sector have limited control over the very well-structured procedures that they may use to affect their subordinates' attitudes. Thus, inspiring tools (transformational leadership practices) are more attractive for employees in the public sector of the Kurdistan Region. Nevertheless, public organizations endure traditional bureaucratic mechanisms, and some other characteristics associated with public sector organizations influence the emergence of transformational leadership.

The lack of managerial discretion needed to link rewards to performance are key concerns that require greater attention when trying to understand leadership in public organizations. But when performance is not easily measured, as is the case in the public sector organization in the Kurdistan region, it is difficult to institute clear reward contingencies that allow leaders to link extrinsic rewards with their employees' performance.

We found that there are differences between the public and private sectors that affect the leadership styles adopted in each sector. Those differences include but are not limited to the public sector workplace is not designed to be competitive, while the private sector needs to meet commercial goals which drives it to be competitive in nature. There are job security and retirement packages in the public sector, whereas there are competitive salary packages in the private sector.

The major recommendation of the study is that the Kurdistan Regional Government should induce an evaluation and assessment system that examines the behaviors of public managers to make their leadership best deal with the recent awareness of the public population. It is also recommended that the KRG develops or activates its public policy that can serve the workers in both public and private sectors in a way that the worker rights are secured. Finally, the KRG must place monitoring and evaluation units in all its directorates in order to better design rewards and punishment systems. This will help in better management of resources and staff.

This study can be expanded by including culture and individual background as variables to study leadership and its impact on employee motivation and commitment in both sectors. Scholars also might concentrate on different features of both sectors in the Kurdistan region to figure out if these characteristics demand particular leadership styles.

Appendix 1

Form #1 Leaders Form Survey Questionnaire

Section One: Demographic Questions

1. Age: 23–30, 31–40, 41–50, 51–60, 61 and over
2. Gender: Female , Male
3. Level of education:
   Primary, Secondary, Diploma, Bachelor, Master, PhD, Vocational training
4. How long have you been working for your employer?
   1–5, 6–10, 11–15, 16–20, 20+
5. Your current position: Top manager, Middle manager, First-line manager
6. Sector (department) of work………..

Section Two: Leadership

1. Do you search outside the formal boundaries of your organization for innovative ways to improve the work? (Yes/No)
2. Do you communicate with subordinates to explain how a task must be done and let them know that there will be rewards for a job done well? (Yes/No)
3. I share an exciting dream of the future with my employees (Yes/No)
4. Do you monitor your team's work? (Yes/No)
5. Do you seek out challenging opportunities that test your own skills and abilities? (Yes/No)
6. I try to challenge people to try out new and innovative ways to do their work (Yes/No)
7. **It is important to set goals that are:**
   - Achievable
   - Concrete
   - Measurable
   - All the above
8. **I monitor my team's work to:**
   - Make sure that the work is done according to the set processes
   - To detect mistakes
   - To ensure about possibility of any future mistakes
9. **I encourage the team to achieve organizational goals by**
   - Reward and punishment
   - Higher ideals and moral values
   - Based on the situation and the person I am dealing with
10. **"I" as a manager...**
    - Help my team understand problems and issues, and I clarify situations for them to perform better
    - Monitor and then correct my team if necessary, to perform better

Appendix 2

Form #2 Employee Form Survey Questionnaire

Section One: Demographic Questions

7. Age: 16–20, 21–30, 31–40, 41–50, 51–60, 61+
8. Gender: Male Female
9. Level of education:

Primary, High school, Diploma, Bachelor, Master, PhD, Vocational training
10. How long have you been working for your employer? 1–5y, 6–10, 11–15, 16–20, 20+
11. .
12. Your current position: (Regular employee, Middle manager, Supervisor)
13. Sector (department) of work

Section Two: Questions on Employee Motivation

1. **What is your main motivation to work?**
   (1) Basic needs as (hunger)
   (2) Affiliation needs as (social satisfaction)
   (3) Self-actualization
2. **Which one of the below indicators boosts a sense of achievement in you?**
   (1) When my work is recognized and appreciated
   (2) Working toward goals that are clear and achievable
   (3) Less routine work and challenging job
   (4) All of above
3. **I feel powerful and motivated by my company's:**
   (1) Financial rewards for my performance
   (2) Nonfinancial rewards for my performance as (empowerment, recognition…)
   (3) Training and development practices
   (4) Opportunities to grow within the company (organization)
   (5) Feedback on my work performance

Section Three: Questions on Employee Commitment

1. I will be happy to spend the rest of my career with this organization (company). (Yes/No)
2. I am happy that I work for this company. (Yes/No)
3. There are good options for me if I want to leave this organization (company). (Yes/No)
4. This place has a great deal of personal meaning for me. (Yes/No)
5. One of the reasons I do not leave this place right now is the scarcity of available resources in the organization (company) to replace me. (Yes/No)

6. Jumping from one organization (company) to another is normal to me. (Yes/No)

Section Four: Questions on Leadership

1. My manager treats others with dignity and respect, and actively listens to diverse points of views. (Yes/No)
2. He/she searches outside the formal boundaries for innovative ways to improve the work. (Yes/No)
3. Is your work monitored? (Yes/No)
4. Does your manager share an exciting dream of the future with the team? (Yes/No)
5. My manager challenges people to try out new ways to do their work? (Yes/No)
6. **The goals set by your manager are:**
   (1) Achievable
   (2) Measurable
   (3) All of the above
   (4) None
7. **My manager monitors my work to:**
   (1) Make sure that the work is done according to the set processes
   (2) Detect mistakes
   (3) To study the possibility of any future mistakes
8. **My manager encourages me to achieve organizational goals by:**
   (1) Reward and punishment
   (2) Higher ideals and moral values
9. **To perform better my manager...**
   (1) Helps me to understand problems and issues and clarifies situations for me
   (2) Monitors and then corrects me when necessary

Appendix 3

Leader's (manager's) interview sample questions

Communication

1. Do you spend time and energy making certain that the people you work with adhere to the principles and standards agreed on?
2. What do you think of future trends that will influence how your work gets done?
3. How an organization's long-term interests can be realized by enlisting in a common vision of employees?

4. What do you think about the diversity of points of view in your organization?

Reward and Punishment style

5. How often do you communicate with your subordinates to explain how a task must be done and let them know that there will be rewards for a job done well?
6. What kind of rewards do you offer?
7. How mistakes are detected for punishment?
8. In what ways do you reward your employee's contributions to the success of projects?

Self-education

9. Are there any challenging opportunities that test one's skills and abilities in your position as a manager?
10. What do you think if your employees try out new and innovative ways to do their work?
11. Can you search outside the formal boundaries of your organization for innovative ways to improve the work?

Monitoring

12. How important it is to ensure that employees grow in their jobs, earning new skills and developing themselves?
13. What do you do to let your employees know about your confidence in them?
14. Why do you monitor your team? To make sure they work based on set systems or to investigate mistakes that might occur in the future?

References

Abbas, M., & Ali, R. (2023). Transformational versus transactional leadership styles and project success: A meta-analytic review. *European Management Journal, 41*(1), 125–142.

Abdalla Hamza, P., Jabbar Othman, B., Gardi, B., Sorguli, S., Mahmood Aziz, H., Ali Ahmed, S., Anwar, G., et al. (2021). *Recruitment and selection: The relationship between recruitment and selection with organizational performance.*

Aguilar Solano, M. (2020). Triangulation and trustworthiness: Advancing research on public service interpreting through qualitative case study methodologies. *FITISPosInternational Journal., 7*(1), 31–52.

Ahmad, A., Abdul Majid, A. H., & Mohd Zin, M. L. (2015). The measurement of the effectiveness of leadership styles for organizational commitment in Pakistan. *Asian Social Science, 11*(25), 135–143.

Alansaari, O., Yusoff, R., & Ismail, F. (2019). The mediating effect of employee commitment on recruitment process towards organizational performance in UAE organizations. *Management Science Letters, 9*(1), 169–182.

Amjad, F., Abbas, W., Zia-Ur-Rehman, M., Baig, S. A., Hashim, M., Khan, A., & Rehman, H.-U. (2021). Effect of green human resource management practices on organizational sustainability: The mediating role of environmental and employee performance. *Environmental Science and Pollution Research, 28*, 28191–28206.

Ashfaq, F., Abid, G., & Ilyas, S. (2021). Impact of ethical leadership on employee engagement: Role of self-efficacy and organizational commitment. *European Journal of Investigation in Health, Psychology and Education, 11*(3), 962–974.

Baskoro, B. D., Widjaja, B. T., & Sudarmadji, S. (2021). The nexus of transformational leadership, compensation and knowledge management towards employee performance: Mediation role of work motivation. *Management and Entrepreneurship: Trends of Development, 1*(15), 41–64.

Berkovich, I., & Eyal, O. (2021). Transformational leadership, transactional leadership, and moral reasoning. *Leadership and Policy in Schools, 20*(2), 131–148.

Blau, P. M. (1964). Justice in social exchange. *Sociological Inquiry, 34*(2), 193.

Cabrera, W., & Estacio, D. (2022). Job attitude as a factor on employees performance. *International Journal of Economics Development Research (IJEDR), 3*(1), 13–35.

Canavesi, A., & Minelli, E. (2022). Servant leadership and employee engagement: A qualitative study. *Employee Responsibilities and Rights Journal, 34*(4), 413–435.

Cemaloğlu, N., Sezgin, F., & Kılınç, A. (2012). Examining the relationships between school principals' transformational and transactional leadership styles and teachers' organizational commitment. *The Online Journal of New Horizons in Education, 2*(2), 53–64.

Chatzopoulou, E.-C., Manolopoulos, D., & Agapitou, V. (2022). Corporate social responsibility and employee outcomes: Interrelations of external and internal orientations with job satisfaction and organizational commitment. *Journal of Business Ethics, 179*(3), 795–817.

Chi, H., Vu, T. V., Nguyen, H. V., & Truong, T. H. (2023). How financial and non–financial rewards moderate the relationships between transformational leadership, job satisfaction, and job performance. *Cogent Business & Management, 10*(1), 2173850.

Chipunza, C., Samuel, M. O., & Mariri, T. (2011). Leadership style, employee motivation and commitment: Empirical evidence from a consolidated retail bank operating in a depressed economy. *African Journal of Business Management, 5*(20), 8337.

Dahie, A. M., Mohamed, A. A., & Mohamed, R. A. (2017). Leadership style and organizational commitment: Case study from University of Somalia. *International Journal of Engineering Science, 7*(9), 14838–14843.

Dariush, L., Choobdar, G., Valadkhani, P., & Mehrali, E. (2016). Leader facilitating organizational commitment of employees (Tehran). *International Journal of Economics, Commerce and Management, 4*(5), 640–655.

De Gennaro, D. (2019). Transformational leadership for public service motivation. *Journal of Economic and Administrative Sciences, 35*(1), 5–15.

Eldor, L. (2020). How collective engagement creates competitive advantage for organizations: A business-level model of shared vision, competitive intensity, and service performance. *Journal of Management Studies, 57*(2), 177–209.

Engidaw, A. E. (2021). The effect of motivation on employee engagement in public sectors: In the case of north Wollo zone. *Journal of Innovation and Entrepreneurship, 10*(1), 43.

Farquhar, J., Michels, N., & Robson, J. (2020). Triangulation in industrial qualitative case study research: Widening the scope. *Industrial Marketing Management, 87*, 160–170.

González-Navarro, P., Zurriaga-Llorens, R., Tosin Olateju, A., & Llinares-Insa, L. I. (2018). Envy and counterproductive work behavior: The moderation role of leadership in public and private organizations. *International Journal of Environmental Research and Public Health, 15*(7), 1455.

Hackman, J. R., & Oldham, G. R. (1976). Motivation through the design of work: Test of a theory. *Organizational Behavior and Human Performance, 16*(2), 250–279.

Haldorai, K., Kim, W. G., & Garcia, R. F. (2022). Top management green commitment and green intellectual capital as enablers of hotel environmental performance: The mediating role of green human resource management. *Tourism Management, 88*, 104431.

Hall, D. T., Schneider, B., & Nygren, H. T. (1970). Personal factors in organizational identification. *Administrative Science Quarterly, 15*, 176–190.

Hamawandy, N. M., Omer, A. J., Salih, H. A., MustafaAli, R., Abubakr, Z. A., Jamil, D. A., & Heayyiz, D. D. (2021). Role of internal audit in the public sector in Kurdistan Region of Iraq. *The Journal of Contemporary Issues in Business and Government, 27*(1), 3046–3057.

Haryono, S., & Sulistyo, B. A. (2020). Effects of work motivation and leadership toward work satisfaction and employee performance: Evidence from Indonesia. *The Journal of Asian Finance, Economics and Business, 7*(6), 387–397.

Hornsey, M. J. (2008). Social identity theory and self-categorization theory: A historical review. *Social and Personality Psychology Compass, 2*(1), 204–222.

Hung, L.-M., Lee, Y.-S., & Lee, D.-C. (2018). The moderating effects of salary satisfaction and working pressure on the organizational climate, organizational commitment to turnover intention. *International Journal of Business & Society, 19*(1).

Hussain, S. T., Abbas, J., Lei, S., Jamal Haider, M., & Akram, T. (2017). Transactional leadership and organizational creativity: Examining the mediating role of knowledge sharing behavior. *Cogent Business & Management, 4*(1), 1361663.

Japor, J. E. (2021). Organizational career growth: Literature review and future agenda. *International Journal of Business and Administrative Studies, 7*(1), 12–24.

Jaqua, E., & Jaqua, T. (2021). Transactional leadership. *American Journal of Biomedical Science and Research, 14*(5), 399–400.

Katsaros, K. K., Tsirikas, A. N., & Kosta, G. C. (2020). The impact of leadership on firm financial performance: The mediating role of employees' readiness to change. *Leadership & Organization Development Journal, 41*(3), 333–347.

Khan, A. J., & Iqbal, J. (2020). Training and employee commitment: The social exchange perspective. *Journal of Management Sciences, 7*(1), 88–100.

Khuong, M. N., & Hoang, D. T. (2015). The effects of leadership styles on employee motivation in auditing companies in Ho Chi Minh City, Vietnam. *International Journal of Trade, Economics and Finance, 6*(4), 210.

Kollmann, T., Stöckmann, C., Kensbock, J. M., & Peschl, A. (2020). What satisfies younger versus older employees, and why? An aging perspective on equity theory to explain interactive effects of employee age, monetary rewards, and task contributions on job satisfaction. *Human Resource Management, 59*(1), 101–115.

Liden, R. C., & Maslyn, J. M. (1998). Multidimensionality of leader-member exchange: An empirical assessment through scale development. *Journal of Management, 24*(1), 43–72.

López-Ibort, N., González-de la Cuesta, D., Antoñanzas-Lombarte, T., & Gascón-Catalán, A. (2020). The correlation between leader–member exchange and organisational commitment among Spanish registered nurses: The moderating role of sex and hospital size. *International Journal of Environmental Research and Public Health, 17*(3), 721.

Megawaty, M., Hamdat, A., & Aida, N. (2022). Examining linkage leadership style, employee commitment, work motivation, work climate on satisfaction and performance. *Golden Ratio of Human Resource Management, 2*(1), 01–14.

Mohammed, H. O., Aziz, A. I., Sadq, Z. M., & Othman, B. A. (2020). The impact of transformation leadership on employee's effectiveness (The case of Ministry of Higher Education and Scientific Research, Kurdistan regional government, Iraq). *International Journal of Multicultural and Multireligious Understanding, 7*(11), 201–217.

Mugizi, W., Bakkabulindi, F. E., & Bisaso, R. (2015). Framework for the study of employee commitment. *Makerere Journal of Higher Education, 7*(2), 15–47.

Nguyen, H. N., Le, Q. H., Tran, Q. B., Tran, T. H. M., Nguyen, T. H. Y., & Nguyen, T. T. Q. (2020). The impact of organizational commitment on employee motivation: A study in Vietnamese enterprises. *The Journal of Asian Finance, Economics and Business, 7*(6), 439–447.

Oparaocha, G. O. (2016). Towards building internal social network architecture that drives innovation: A social exchange theory perspective. *Journal of Knowledge Management, 20*(3), 534–556.

O'Reilly, C. A., & Chatman, J. (1986). Organizational commitment and psychological attachment: The effects of compliance, identification, and internalization on prosocial behavior. *Journal of Applied Psychology, 71*(3), 492.

Paais, M., & Pattiruhu, J. R. (2020). Effect of motivation, leadership, and organizational culture on satisfaction and employee performance. *The Journal of Asian Finance, Economics and Business, 7*(8), 577–588.

Pessach, D., Singer, G., Avrahami, D., Ben-Gal, H. C., Shmueli, E., & Ben-Gal, I. (2020). Employees recruitment: A prescriptive analytics approach via machine learning and mathematical programming. *Decision Support Systems, 134*, 113290.

Puni, A., Hilton, S. K., & Quao, B. (2021). The interaction effect of transactional-transformational leadership on employee commitment in a developing country. *Management Research Review, 44*(3), 399–417.

Purwanto, A. (2020). The effect of transformational leadership dimensions on job satisfaction and organizational commitment: Case studies in private university lecturers. *Solid State Technology*.

Qing, M., Asif, M., Hussain, A., & Jameel, A. (2020). Exploring the impact of ethical leadership on job satisfaction and organizational commitment in public sector organizations: The mediating role of psychological empowerment. *Review of Managerial Science, 14*(6), 1405–1432.

Rafia, R., & Achmad Sudiro, S. (2020). The effect of transformational leadership on employee performance mediated by job satisfaction and employee engagement. *International Journal of Business, Economics and Law, 21*(5), 119–125.

Skopak, A., & Hadzaihmetovic, N. (2022). The impact of transformational and transactional leadership style on employee job satisfaction. *International Journal of Business and Administrative Studies, 8*(3), 113.

Suman, S., & Srivastava, A. K. (2012). Antecedents of organisational commitment across hierarchical levels. *Psychology and Developing Societies, 24*(1), 61–83.

Surbhi, J. (2015). Cost-effectiveness of training programmes in insurance sector of India. *Management Dynamics in the Knowledge Economy, 3*(3), 533–551.

Taylor, G. (2015). Hackman and Oldham's job characteristics model. *Teaching Business & Economics, 19*(2), 7.

Tian, H., Iqbal, S., Akhtar, S., Qalati, S. A., Anwar, F., & Khan, M. A. S. (2020). The impact of transformational leadership on employee retention: Mediation and moderation through organizational citizenship behavior and communication. *Frontiers in Psychology, 11*, 513537.

Uzair, Z., & Mehmood, A. (2021). Impact of non-financial rewards on employees motivation in banking sector of Peshawar, Pakistan. *The Journal of Contemporary Issues in Business and Government, 27*(5), 2396–2406.

Van Knippenberg, D., & Sleebos, E. (2006). Organizational identification versus organizational commitment: Self-definition, social exchange, and job attitudes. *Journal of Organizational Behavior: The International Journal of Industrial, Occupational and Organizational Psychology and Behavior, 27*(5), 571–584.

Waris, M., Khan, A., Ismail, I., Adeleke, A., & Panigrahi, S. (2018). *Impact of leadership qualities on employee commitment in multi-project-based organizations*. Paper presented at the IOP Conference Series: Earth and Environmental Science.

Watters, E. R. (2021). Factors in employee motivation: Expectancy and equity theories. *Journal of Colorado Policing, 6*(1), 4–8.

Wright, B. E., & Pandey, S. K. (2010). Transformational leadership in the public sector: Does structure matter? *Journal of Public Administration Research and Theory, 20*(1), 75–89.

Chapter 9
Exploring the Impact of ICT on Human Resources Management Performance

Dilber Yousifi

Abstract In the present fast-changing commercial environment, technology serves as a key driver that is changing how organizations take care of their most important property: human resources. Merging traditional human resource practices with digital technologies resulted in efficiency as well as marked changes in employee connectedness, recruitment of good employees, and attracting the best candidates for specific jobs. This study discusses the profound effects of technology on improving performance in human resources, explaining its complicated meaning through different HR roles. The integration of technology into human resources practices has catalyzed a paradigm shift in the way organizations manage their workforce, driving efficiency, agility, and innovation. By leveraging digital tools and data-driven insights, HR professionals can navigate the complexities of the modern workplace landscape, unlock the full potential of their talent pool, and drive sustainable business growth. This study focuses on analyzing how much information and communication technology (ICT) can contribute to increasing the performance level of HRM staff in higher education institutions in the Kurdistan Region of Iraq (KRI). This study explains the role of ICT in HRM performance once integrated into HRM operations, drawing attention to how recruitment, training, employee engagement, and development decisions are affected. A quantitative approach based on a survey questionnaire is conducted to gain a clear overview of where the higher education institutions stand in the KRI in terms of the usage of ICT in the HRM field. The overall finding suggests that ICT may have positive effects on the performance level of HRM staff in higher education institutions in the KRI. Furthermore, the level of ICT usage in the KRI is not at a level where the individuals of HRM are well aware of ICT developments and E-HRM as well as the usage of computerized HRM.

Keywords Information and communication technology · Human resource performance · Higher education institutions · Kurdistan Region

D. Yousifi (✉)
University of Kurdistan Hewler, Erbil, Iraq
e-mail: d.akram@ukh.edu.krd

G. M. Muhamad, N. T. Khayyat (eds.), *Resource Management Performance: A Sectoral Analysis in the Post-Conflict Kurdistan Region of Iraq*, Perspectives on Development in the Middle East and North Africa (MENA) Region,
https://doi.org/10.1007/978-981-97-7725-9_9

9.1 Introduction

Human resources or human capital is the most valuable asset in any organization, and humans are the steering wheel behind any practices functioning inside an organization. Human resource management is very important in today's business. In the business environment, all organizations face a constant state of competition, and the difference can come from the human capital (Yousifi & Khayyat, 2019).

In the 1990s and even in the latter half of the 1980s, the business world saw the emergence of a new knowledge area, which was personnel management, nowadays referred to as human resource management (HRM) (Dulebohn et al., 1995; Legge, 1995; Hendry, 2012; Cipd, 2015). It is acknowledged by the majority that employees play a significant role in achieving competitive advantage for organizations; therefore, it is important and recommended for organizations to adopt HRM practices to gain the finest from their employees (Fey & Björkman, 2001; Lengnick-Hall & Lengnick-Hall, 1988; Armstrong & Taylor, 2006; Sparrow et al., 2016).

The HRM is defined by Cipd (2015) as follows:

> The highest level of performance can be achieved by the management of people through the design, implementation, and maintenance of strategies.

It means that for an organization to meet its strategic objectives, its employees need to be managed, and the approach to apply such management is HRM. The overall assigned corporative objectives need to reflect with functional objective of HRM since the main aim of HRM is to build the finest human resources to achieve the organization's goals (Cipd, 2015).

The keyword behind HRM is strategy, and HRM is a strategic approach to meeting the business goals. HRM designs a variety of tools to support the organization's strategy, and those tools consist of workforce planning, recruitment and selection, training and development, rewarding and motivating staff, communication, and roles and responsibilities (e.g., organization structure). Heathfield (2010) states the meaning of HRM as the process of recruitment and selection, giving induction and orientation, training and development of continuous employee performance assessment, giving benefits and compensation for motivational purposes, keeping a proper relationship between employees and maintaining employee safety, keeping safe workplace, welfare, and health measures under the labor laws.

Nowadays, information and communication technology (ICT) has become the backbone of numerous modern organizations in processing their business operations and activities (Hakeem, 2013; Adewoye, 2012). HRM has also been affected by the tremendous increase in ICT usage within the organization. The World Wide Web has transformed the HR practice, for example, human resource planning, recruitment, selection, performance management, workflow, training, and compensation.

Many organizations nowadays are using new systems in HR departments to gain supreme services to all the stakeholders, and most importantly reduce the administrative burden for HR professionals (Stone & Dulebohn, 2013). The systems used within the HR department are mainly referred to as human resource management systems (HRMS) or electronic human resource management (E-HRM). These systems are built to provide the organizational stakeholders with the ability to have access to HR information via the Internet and intranet to have effective and efficient information in decision-making (Noerman et al., 2021).

The primary responsibility of a human resource information system (HRIS) is to enhance the efficiency with which data on human capital and human resource activities are collected. The second is strategical enhancement; it facilitates the accessibility of data to managers, which allows them to make better decisions regarding human resource planning (Rainer et al., 2020).

Tokundu (2021) emphasizes the parallel between the evolution of information technology and the evolution of human resource development (HRD) as key managerial tools within organizations. Essentially, the authors first argue that both ICT and HRD have evolved from technical tools into strategic management tools with similar stages along this progression.

Human activity in nearly every field has been drastically altering the way things are done because of the revolution of ICT. The global economy faces competitive pressure in compelling countries and the business world to use ICT at a high speed for competitive advantage in improving the quality of life (Adewoye, 2012). Building an information technology-oriented society can only be achieved when the government actively builds an information infrastructure and restructures the education systems. HRM mainly conquers human resources development, which has been perceived globally as essential to the development of information technology-based economies to gain global competitiveness.

ICT is important in changing many functions of organizations, especially HRM because of how it has made them better. This study explains what happens to HRM performance after including ICT in its operations, drawing attention to how recruitment, training, employee engagement, and development decisions are affected.

The recruitment process has been revolutionized by ICT. It enhances the reach and efficiency of talent acquisition efforts. Recruitment is nowadays paperless, thanks to online job boards, social media networks, and applicant tracking systems which all facilitate it, making sure that HR professionals reach a wide audience when looking for employees to fill vacancies. Furthermore, senior analytics enable HR managers to analyze recruitment data, develop sourcing strategies, and predict future hiring requirements (Sharma et al., 2023).

In addition, ICT facilitates continuous learning and development through innovative e-learning platforms and virtual training modules. With remote work and distributed teams being on the rise, HRM has taken advantage of ICT to provide tailored training experiences that are meant to aid in skill development and the promotion of lifelong learning. Software that integrates virtual reality hardware or augmented reality software enhances education by creating worlds that can be interacted with, regardless of distance limitations (Amutha, 2020).

By promoting clear communication channels and program tools for remote cooperation, information technology improves the participation of members of staff and their cooperation. From enterprise social networks to digital feedback platforms, HRM leverages ICT to nurture a culture of open communication, facilitate knowledge sharing, and strengthen team cohesion across dispersed work environments. The use of performance feedback mechanisms may enable employees to improve their skills, and thereby they easily identify their objectives with those of their company (Hu & Oh, 2021).

Furthermore, data-driven decision-making in HRM is facilitated by ICT which is a strategic facilitator. With the use of big data analytics and predictive modeling, human resource managers can gain useful information about productivity trends within their workplaces as well as talent retention strategies. This enables them to formulate evidence-based strategies based on this kind of analysis in terms of HRM for their respective companies because it also helps them look into what will be needed tomorrow when it comes to skills, thus making it possible to prevent possible losses (Garcia-Arroyo & Osca, 2021).

This study explores the impact of ICT on HRM performance. It will conduct an empirical study to gain a clear overview of where the higher education institutions stand in the Kurdistan Region of Iraq in terms of the usage of ICT in the HRM field. Also, it will study whether ICT enhances the performance of HRM staff as well as the overall performance of higher education institutions. This study will further assess the level of ICT usage in the higher institutions in the KRI, and whether the usage of ICT has helped the level of the HRM staff performance in those institutions to increase or not.

This research combines the elements of HRM to predict the potential or consequences that ICT will have on employees' skills and performance as stated by Heslina and Syahruni (2021). The place for creating dissemination and knowledge is of course higher education institutions. The research investigates an ongoing debate about whether the adoption of ICT has a factual impact on human resource management performance or not. Therefore, the aim of this study is to unveil the impact of ICT in relation to human resource development.

In the findings, the level of ICT within the HRM function in KRI in the higher education sector will also indicate the level of ICT—within HRM that relates to the performance, the performance that will affect the overall development and performance of KRI. The main aim behind higher education institutions is thought to be to enhance the knowledge and learning experience of students. Therefore, the graduates of those institutions will contribute toward an innovative future with competitive excellence.

The main focus of the study relies on the empirical assessment since there are limited number of studies in this area for KRI. Thus, it can be argued that the motivation for this study stems from the fact that no previous research has been conducted on this particular topic on which no other studies have been conducted about.

9.1.1 Contribution of the Study

Unfortunately, no previous study investigates the impact of ICT on the HRM performance in the KRI. The findings and the results of this study will serve as a first guide to the policymakers of business in general and the KRG Ministry of Higher Education in particular. In addition, this will encourage Kurdish scholars to research in this field of study by providing more reliable scientific measurements for describing and assessing the impact of ICT on the performance of HRM and the overall organizations' performance. This research can be the source for the policymakers to make decisions based on the results of this research conducted.

Furthermore, the findings and the results of this study will provide invaluable information to allow the relevant parties to provide suggestions and advice to improve the quality of HRM performance through the usage of ICT in the region.

9.2 Previous Literature

9.2.1 Introduction

The human resource department is one of the key players in any organization, as it is responsible for one of the most important assets which is the human workforce. Many scholars stated that humans are assets for organizations because the organizations' performance, growth, and development depend on the human assets. HRM is composed of several policies, which are used for organizing work within the employment relationship, and it also centralizes the management of work and the management of people who take part in this field (Al-Qudah et al., 2020).

Human resource planning is another important aspect. HRM in organizations ensures that human resource planning is in their best interest to have the finest employees to fulfill the needed position in order to determine the organization's goals. Human resource planning is essential because it deals with the systematic and constant process of analyzing the organization's human resource needs by mutating conditions, improvement, and development of workforce policies that will gain suitable long-term effectiveness of the organizations (Al-Qudah et al., 2020).

The ICT is expected to improve the performance of HRM. It has been acknowledged that ICT has the potential to improve efficiency and productivity in many aspects and, therefore, it has received significant attention in many countries (OECD, 2015; Walsham et al., 2007). From the 1980s, business processes were rapidly shifting toward the application of information technology. Information technology has been recognized as having a vital role in moving human resources management roles from administrative toward strategic business partners.

Many scholars have been attracted and engaged in e-HRM research, which targets two large domains: (1) HRM and (2) ICT (Adewoye, 2012; Agarwala, 2002; Allen et al., 2007; Ardichvili & Alexander, 2002; Armstrong & Taylor, 2006;

Bagozzi et al., 1992; Ekwoaba & Anthony, 2012; Silverstone et al., 1991; Tar & Lawrence, 2011; Zhou et al., 2022). It is challenging to bring these two finest descriptive theories together. To bring out the interlink between these two areas, ICT's purpose is to support in achieving the overall HRM goals. The goals of E-HRM have been broken down into three types: (1) cost-effectiveness, (2) improving services, and (3) addressing the strategic objectives of the organization. Ruël et al. (2004) added the fourth goal which is E-HRM to improve the overall global orientation of human resources management.

Lakhwani et al. (2020) stated that in order for modern organizations to survive, they need to focus and increase competition and globalization by adopting the cost-effective and time efficiency of ICT. Welbourne (2010) argues that historically the field of human resource management was inundated with bureaucracy and administration. Therefore, E-HRM was introduced to restructure the core HR process as well as to reduce costs and enhance efficiency. He adds on saying that for HRM to be fast and efficient it should go beyond adding technology to a few of its tasks and simply putting HRM on the web.

Welbourne (2010) refers to HRM as a lens that will put forward different methods to strive toward a strategic base; therefore evolving E-HRM will strive for an innovative HRM. Heshmati (2007) stated the mechanisms of testing the technology acceptance (TA) are as follows: measure of technology creation, diffusion of recent innovations, diffusion of old innovations, and human skills.

9.2.2 *Information and Communication Technology (ICT)*

Nwokolo (2015) defines ICT as another term for information technology that is unified communications, integration of telecommunications, i.e., telephone lines and wireless signals, middleware, storage, computers, enterprise software, and audiovisual systems that give the users the ability to gain access to store, transmit, and manipulate information.

Zuppo (2012) emphasizes the above point and has created an ICT hierarchy that indicates each level of hierarchy to some degree of interconnection in the field of technology that enables the transfer of information and many different types of electronically mediated communications.

In summary, ICT plays an important role in fostering human development across different domains by enhancing access to information, facilitating communication, and enabling innovation. In today's interconnected world, ICT empowers individuals by providing them with tools for education, healthcare, economic opportunities, and social inclusion. Furthermore, ICT contributes significantly to the global economy, with its share in value-added activities steadily increasing over the years. From manufacturing to services, ICT permeates every sector, driving efficiency, productivity, and competitiveness, thereby fostering sustainable growth and development on a global scale. Figure 9.1 shows the list of OECD countries that gained value from the ICT sector in 2021.

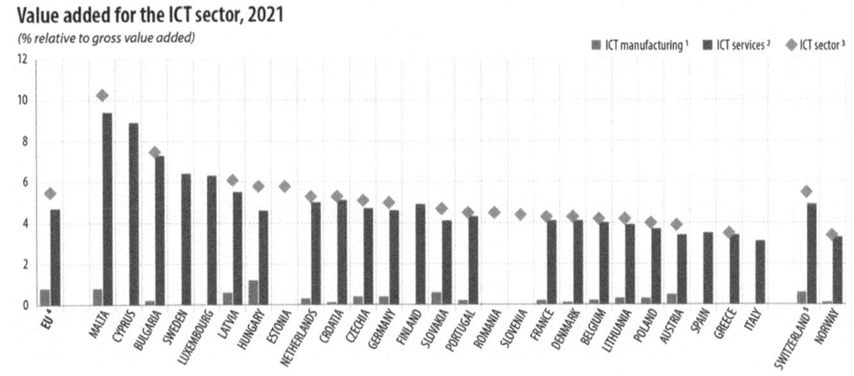

Fig. 9.1 Share of ICT sector in total value added, 2021 (EuroStat, #163)

9.2.3 Human Capital Management

Defining HRM leads to two different perspectives. HRM's first definition is that it is a procedure of managing humans within the organization in an organized and systematic manner. The second definition of HRM concludes the management of humans within the organization from a macro perspective by means of managing humans in forms of cooperative manner between employees and management (Kramar, 2022).

The difference between modern and traditional HRM is that traditional HRM focuses on fulfilling management objectives of providing and deploying humans and the greater emphasis is on planning, monitoring, and controlling. However, no matter which definition is used, the answer to the question "What is HRM?" is that it is all about managing and organizing people/humans/employees of the organization. No wonder that some multinational corporations (MNCs) call the HR managers as people managers, people enablers, and the practice of people management (Kambur & Yildirim, 2023).

In modern organizations, the HR manager or the people manager is no longer seen as someone who takes care of the activities described in the traditional way. In fact, most organizations have different departments dealing with staffing, payroll, and retention. Guest (2021) states the primary focus of HRM is managing employees by building policies in a systematic approach.

Paauwe and Boon (2009) indicate that the HR department has five main responsibilities: (1) overseeing and designing employee benefits, (2) recruiting employees, (3) developing and training employees, (4) performance management or in other words performance appraisal, and (5) rewarding employees systematically.

Klerck (2009) mentioned that HR has a role in organizational change and industrial relations, which means organizational practices are balanced with the collective requirements put forward by bargainers and from governmental laws. At first, it was subjugated by transactional work, which was payroll and benefits administration; however, due to globalization, organization consolidation, technological expansion, and continued research in the HR field, the focus of HR has come to strategic initiatives such as mergers and acquisitions, talent management, succession planning, industrial, and labor relation as well as diversity and inclusion.

9.2.4 Consequences of ICT on HRM: Current Debates

Some of the positive impacts of E-HRM are reducing cost, speed administrated processes, and effective and efficient performance. These are some of the foundations that drive organizations to adopt E-HRM; therefore, it has become an important topic for scholars to study. In order to analyze the consequences of E-HRM, the work of several scholars is reviewed.

Waheed et al. (2020) stated that an organization adopting E-HRM will achieve positive functional consequences; for instance, it will give the organization the ability to access, collect, and distribute required information, as well as provide individuals with wider accessibility to information related to job opportunities, performance feedback, and benefits. However, the authors also indicated that there may be some negative consequences of E-HRM; for instance, these systems might lead the organization to many dysfunctional consequences; e.g., there is a possibility that E-HRM will decrease social interaction which affects the quality and accuracy of information about the organization expectation negatively as well as the performance and compensation. They further argue that such systems are built to increase accessibility to many; therefore, it will affect the perceived control of the information and will lead to invasive of privacy and reduce effectiveness.

Rathee and Bhuntel (2021) examined the dysfunctional consequences of using E-HRM in the following areas: attract, select, and manage the performance of employees. The results indicated that Western cultures are behind many developments of E-HRM systems; therefore, these systems fit the meritocracy and individualism of the Western culture and values. They concluded that other cultures and nations with alternative HR processes might not gain the effective usage of E-HRM systems.

Shamout et al. (2022) studied E-HRM usage as a strategy toward achieving competitive advantages. The research was done on the four most competitive firms in Mexico in order to find out how they implement their E-HRM strategies. As a result, the study showed that in order to gain enough relevant knowledge regarding how E-HRM is utilized in the firms of emerging economies, it is most important to consider the full understanding of the local characteristics.

Khan and Talib (2023) stated that there has been an ongoing debate in the academic literature on whether a transformational impact of E-HRM is achievable or not. They mentioned that researchers indicate the impact of E-HRM depends on the structure HR function is oriented toward whether it is business partner-oriented or administrative-oriented.

According to Sparrow (2010), HR departments within organizations want to implement HR systems that will shift the people-related activities to be automated; therefore, the systems can provide service to those people without having to go through the hands of HR functions. The problems arise when E-HRM is implemented without having the required knowledge of the process of the implementation of E-HRM especially if even the consequences and HR functions are not well understood by HR professionals/managers (Sparrow, 2010).

In addition, Sparrow et al. (2016) put forward four ICT developments that have added success and potential unique competitive advantages for HRM departments within organizations, such as the advent of shared service thinking, the removal of various intermediaries in the delivery of HR services, the continued adoption of ERP system, and finally, the e-enablement of HR service delivery and more toward self-service models. Sparrow (2010) discusses further by stating that these developments will impact the current international HR functions significantly as well as affect the work of personnel, and he also indicates that the implementation of E-HRM will result in the fragmentation of HR function in MNCs.

9.3 Methodology and Data Description

9.3.1 Research Approach

This study combines the two approaches of quantitative and qualitative known as a mixed method. As this study measures the performance of HRM from the impact of ICT, an empirical quantitative approach will be used for collecting data, and in this study, logit models are used, which is a qualitative approach.

A quantitative method is used by conducting a stratified survey among the HRM departments in the higher education institutions in the Kurdistan Region of Iraq. This will be used as the major philosophy to obtain quantifiable data that can be statistically analyzed as well as identify unanticipated phenomena and influences. The research strategy is survey/questionnaire-based.

Ordinal logit models have been applied to show how they relate to the general derivation of all choice models and how they differ within this derivation. Different choice models are derived under different specifications of the density of unobserved factors.

Several aspects of the behavioral decision process affect the specification and estimation of any discrete choice model. The issues can be summarized easily in two statements: "Only differences in utility matter" and "The scale of utility is arbitrary." The implications of these statements are far-reaching, subtle, and in many cases, quite complex (Train, 2003).

Furthermore, the same issue affects the way that socio-demographic variables enter a model. Attributes of the alternatives, such as the time used and cost of mobile phone service on different modes, generally vary over alternatives. However, the

Table 9.1 Names of universities

Public universities	Private universities
1. University of Salahaddin, Erbil	14. Cihan University, Erbil
2. Erbil Polytechnic University, Erbil	15. Ishik University, Erbil
3. University of Kurdistan Hewler, Erbil	16. Lebanese French University, Erbil
4. University of Duhok, Duhok	17. International University of Erbil, Erbil
5. Duhok Polytechnic University, Duhok	18. Hayat Private University for Science and Technology, Erbil
6. University of Halabja, Halabja	19. Bayan University, Erbil
7. University of Garmian, Kalar	20. Komar University of Science and Technology, Sulaimani
8. University of Koya, Koya	21. American University in Iraq-Sulaimani, Sulaimani
9. University of Raparin, Ranya	22. University of Human Development, Sulaimani
10. Soran University, Soran	23. American University of Duhok Kurdistan, Duhok
11. University of Sulaimani, Sulaimani	24. Nawroz University, Duhok
12. Sulaimani Polytechnic University, Sulaimani	
13. University of Zakho, Zakho	

attributes of the decision-maker do not vary over alternatives. They can only enter the model if they are specified in ways that create differences in utility over alternatives.

The survey is distributed to the HR employees in the higher education institutions in the region as they are the main target of the study which will best service this research. The higher education institutions in the region are asked the survey questions as shown in Table 9.1.

The focus and particular interest and the population of this study are the HRM staff members within the higher education institutions in the Kurdistan Region of Iraq with probability sampling representative.

The population considered for the study was thus limited to the public and private universities in the Kurdistan Region of Iraq. Furthermore, to overcome geographical constraints, the survey forms were distributed in three different governorates: Erbil Governorate, Sulamaniya Governorate, and Duhok Governorate in the Kurdistan Region.

In order to collect a nonbiased and representative sample of respondents, the number of HRM staff within all the universities in the Kurdistan Region was

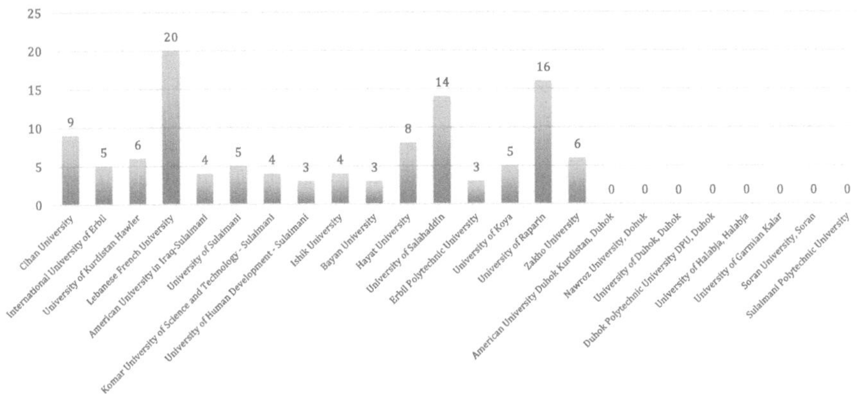

Fig. 9.2 Name of universities that participated in the research

unknown; therefore, a number of 600 questionnaires in two different languages, English and Kurdish, were circulated among 23 public and private universities. At the end of the survey process, 16 universities participated in the study and a number of 115 usable questionnaires were received, of which 9 of them are from Gihan University, 5 from International University of Erbil, 6 from University of Kurdistan Hawler, 20 from Lebanese French University, 4 from American University in Iraq-Sulaimani, 5 from the University of Sulaimani, 4 from Komar University of Science and Technology—Sulaimani, 3 from University of Human Development—Sulaimani, 4 from Ishik University, 3 from Bayan University, 8 from Hayat University, 14 from University of Salahaddin, 3 from Erbil Polytechnic University, 5 from University of Koya, 16 from University of Raparin, and 6 from Zakho University. The American University Duhok Kurdistan was not willing to participate in this research because of a confidential matter; as for the other universities no response was received from them: Nawroz University 0, University of Duhok 0, Duhok Polytechnic University 0, University of Halabja 0, University of Garmian 0, Soran University 0, and Sulaimani Polytechnic University 0 (Fig. 9.2).

9.3.2 The Independent and the Dependent Variables

The independent variable "information communication technology" is measured through the following indicators:

- The first indicator is ICT usage in higher education institutions which will be measured by asking the following questions: Are your organization's daily HRM operations heavily reliant on computers and IT? Does your organization have a separate department or division (e.g., information systems or information technology department)? Does the organization *outsourcing in order to receive usage of information system or information technology?

- The second indicator is E-HRM which will be measured by asking the following questions: Does your organization keenly keep track of innovative usage of technology by competitors? Does your organization believe E-HRM application is a strategic need to strive in the industry? To what level does the Higher Education Ministry, donors, sponsors, and the KRG have the overall operational practices in your industry pressure you to adopt E-HRM? Is your organization in the process of adopting (or being trained in) a new ICT that has been deemed essential for its competitiveness?

As defined by Schuler et al. (2001) "Human resource management is a distinctive approach to employment management, which seeks to achieve competitive advantage through the strategic development of a highly committed and capable workforce, using an integrated array of cultural, structural and personnel techniques."

The dependent variable will be measured through the following indicators:

- The first indicator "impact of ICT" will be measured by asking the following questions: after adopting and diffusing new e-HRM technologies within the organization, the organization gradually began to operate more effectively than before. To what extent or degree were the outcomes and aftereffects of the new e-HRM technologies implemented? Improvement in the quality of HR "deliverables." Reduction of human error in HR "deliverable."
- The second indicator "results of the implementation of ICT" will be measured by asking the following question: How do you feel the IT has impacted your tasks compared to before the IT was implemented? Has the e-HRM, in your view, made your role more efficient? How satisfied are you with the e-HRM?

9.3.3 Questionnaire Design

The questionnaire for this study consists of two parts as following.

Part 1 consists of the biographical information of the surveyed. gender (male 0/ female 1); the variable age is categorized into four groups: (1) 21–32, (2) 33–44, (3) 45–56, and (4) 56+. Educational level is questioned in four categories: (1) secondary, (2) diploma, (3) degree, and (4) postgraduate. The years of work experience have been questioned in five categories: (1) 1–5 years, (2) 5–10 years, (3) 10–15 years, (4) 15–20 years, and (5) 20+. The name of the organization and term of employment have been asked in two categories: (1) temporary and (2) permanent. The employment level is questioned in four categories: (1) entry level, (2) mid-level, (3) manager level, and (4) director/top management level. The job title of the surveyed and monthly salary is questioned in three categories: (1) 100–500, (2) 500–1000, and (3) 1000+.

Employees in the organization, indicating which sector the surveyed is working for, have been questioned in two categories: (1) public and (2) private. The question for how long the surveyed organization has been operating in the Kurdistan Region has been put into three categories: (1) 1–5 years, (2) 5–10 years, and (3) 15+ years.

City of residence is questioned in three categories representing the main three governorates of the region: (1) Erbil, (2) Duhok, and (3) Sulaymaniyah.

Part II consists of 27 questions specifically on information communication technology and human resource management.

Part II covers questions such as "When did your organization first adopt its major ICT system(s)?", "Are your organization's daily HRM operations heavily reliant on computers and IT?", "Could you please indicate which of the stages of HR technology reflects your organization?", "What type(s) of IT tool(s) are used to accomplish HR function?", "Which of the following E-HRM and social media technologies or tools are used in your organization specifically for human resource management purposes?", "Which of the following HRM practices are at least partially automated through your organization's E-HRM system(s)?", "To what extent or degree were the outcomes and aftereffects of the new E-HRM technologies implemented?", "How do you feel the IT has impacted upon your tasks compared to before the IT was implemented?", and " How satisfied are you with the E-HRM?". Moreover, based on the previous researches, Moore and Benbasat (1991), Liao et al. (2007), and Pagani (2004), the perceived usefulness is questioned in this part of the questionnaire.

As the target respondents are the HR staff members within higher education institutions in the Kurdistan Region of Iraq, the questionnaire is designed in two versions: one in English and one in Kurdish. The English version is created first as it is easier and more convenient for the adaptation of the original format initiated by Parasuraman et al. (1985). Then, it is translated into the Kurdish language, considering that the Kurdish version would ensure the correct understanding of the target respondents, as well as a clearer psychological interpretation of the questions.

9.3.4 Descriptive Statistics

The survey provided data on different demographic control variables, such as age, gender, education level, occupation, and the city of residence, which brings the characteristics of the respondents to light (Fig. 9.3).

The statistical yearbook 2007 released by the KRG Ministry of Planning represents the percentages of the population according to the demographic groups' percentages of the Kurdistan Region.[1]

The research covered both public and private universities; out of 23 universities under the study, 13 are public and 11 are private. The responders from the questionnaire indicate 58 are from public universities and 57 are from private universities.

---

[1] http://www.mop-krg.org/default.aspx?page=articles&c=highlight&id=6&l=1

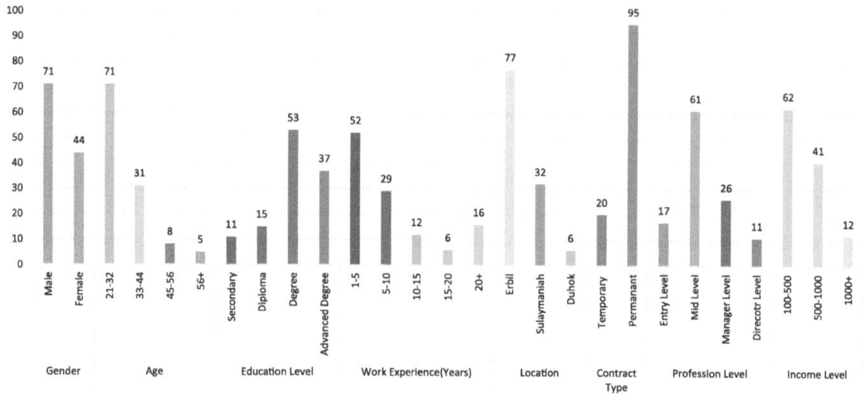

Fig. 9.3 Distribution of the survey demographic data

9.3.5 Classification of the Higher Education Institutions in the Kurdistan Region

From the withdrawal of the Ba′ath regime from the North of Iraq and the establishment of the semiautonomous Kurdistan Region, KRG has been working on changing the education system from Arabic to Kurdish and developing the education system of the region as it is considered the key for the development of the nation (Green, 1997; Gylfason, 2001; Enders, 2004). At this moment, the Kurdistan Region has 13 public universities and 11 licensed private universities.

The public universities are authorized under the Higher Education Council and chaired by the Prime Minister. Previously, the higher education institutions were managed by the Higher Education Council of Iraq; however, after the Iraq's liberation, the fifth Cabinet was formed in the year of 2006. As of today, the KRG has a vital role in running the region's higher education system. The Iraq higher education model is still being operated in the Kurdistan Region's higher education institutions even though they are not under the Iraqi higher education authority. The Kurdistan Regional Government's Ministry of higher education has its agenda to restructure the education system, since the current system is bureaucratic and, in order to enhance the ability to improve the quality, it is very inherently limited.

Higher education institutes in the Kurdistan region currently have 94,700 aggregate numbers of students, and 48% of them are female students, which is a very positive point in gender discrimination in education. The public universities have no tuition fees, which is another very positive matter for the Kurdish society to gain motivation and have no barriers to achieving the desired education.

The Ministry of Higher Education has established universities in nine cities within the Kurdistan Region: Erbil, Sulaimani, Duhok, Zakho, Koya, Ranya, Soran, Halabja, and Kalar. The public universities include University of Duhok—Duhok, University of Koya—Koya, University of Raparin—Ranya, University of Kurdistan Hawler—Erbil, University of Salahaddin—Erbil, Soran University—Soran,

University of Sulaimani—Sulaimani, Sulaimani Polytechnic University SPU—Sulaimani, University of Zakho—Zakho, Duhok Polytechnic University DPU—Duhok, Erbil Polytechnic University—Erbil, University of Halabja—Halabja, and University of Garmian—Kalar. The private universities include Komar University of Science and Technology—Sulaimani, American University Duhok—Duhok, American University of Iraq Sulaimani—Sulaimani, Cihan University—Erbil, Ishik University—Erbil, BMU Lebanese French University—Erbil, International University of Erbil—Erbil, University of Human Development—Sulaimani, and Nawroz University—Duhok.

Among these universities, there are four that are the largest: Salahaddin University—Erbil, University of Suleimani, University of Duhok, Hayat Private University for Science and Technology—Erbil, and Bayan University—Erbil. They provide studies in numerous subjects that lead to specialized diplomas, bachelor's and master's degrees, and doctorates (American University of Iraq Sulaimani, 2016; Bayan University, 2017; Cihan University of Erbil, 2015; Duhok Polytechnic University, 2015; Hayat Private University for Science and Technology, Invest in Group, 2013; Ishik University of Erbil, 2015; Komar University of Science and Technology, 2016; Koya University, 2014; Lebanese French University; Salahaddin University—Erbil, 2017; Soran University, 2015; Sulaimani Polytechnic University, 2017; The American University of Kurdistan; University of Duhok, 2016; University of Garmian; University of Halabja, 2017; University of Human Development in Sulaimani, 2013; University of Kurdistan Hewler, 2017; University of Raparin, 2014; University of Sulaimani, 2017; University of Zakho, 2016).

9.4 Model Specification and Findings

The discrete choice model is explained in this section and the findings of the study are presented.

9.4.1 Information Communication Technology

In this section, the questions of the survey that were related to ICT will be shown with the results collected from the surveyors to clarify their responses to each question.

9.4.2 ICT Usage

Table 9.2, Figs. 9.4 and 9.5 summarize the respondents' answers to the questions related to ICT usage in their organization.

Table 9.2 Respondents' answers related to ICT usage

1. Does your organization have daily HRM operations heavily reliant on computers and IT?			
Yes	No		
105	10		
2. Does the organization outsource in order to receive usage of information system or information technology?			
Yes	No		
69	46		
3. When did your organization first adopt its major ICT system?			
Never	Recent 5 years	More than 5 years	
16	72	27	
4. Indicate which of the stages of HR technology reflects your organization?			
Stage1: Paper based	Stage 2: PC usage	Stage 3: Database MIS	Stage 4: Web-based
19	38	50	8
5. When the organization first adopted the ICT system, specifically for HRM purposes?			
Never	0–2 years	2–5 years	5+ years
20	36	33	27
6. Does the organization keenly keep track of innovative usage of technology by competitors?			
Yes	No		
83	32		

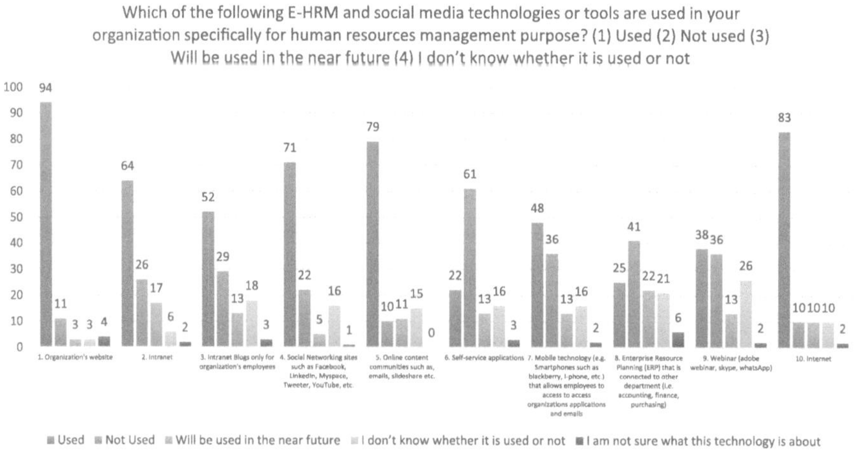

Fig. 9.4 Which of the following E-HRM and social media technologies or tools are used in your organization specifically for human resources management purposes?

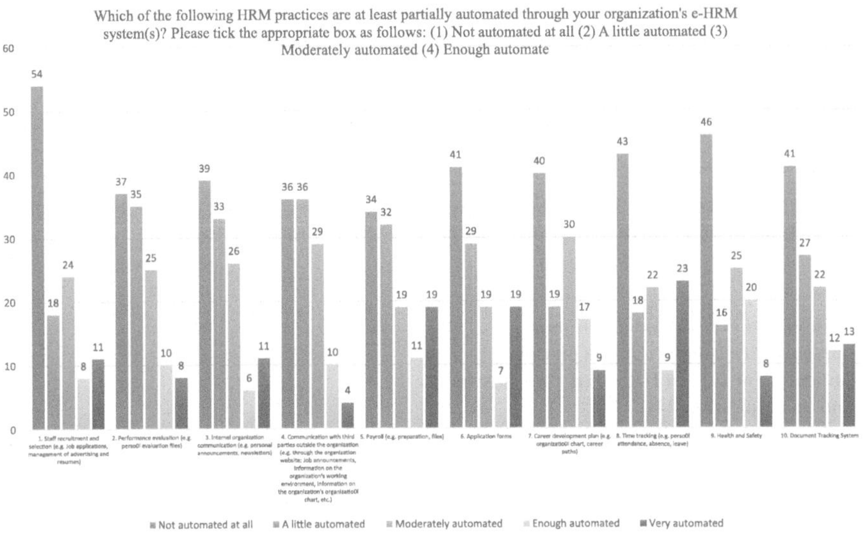

Fig. 9.5 Which of the following HRM practices are at least partially automated through your organization's e-HRM system(s)?

9.4.3 E-HRM

Table 9.3 summarizes the respondents' answers to the questions related to existence and usage in their organization.

9.4.4 HRM Performance

Table 9.4 summarizes the respondents' answers to the questions related to HRM performance in their organization.

Table 9.3 Respondents' answers related to E-HRM

(1) Does your organization believe E-HRM application is a strategic need to strive in the industry?			
Yes	No		
92	23		
(2) To what level does the Higher Education Ministry, donors, sponsors, and KRG have the overall operational practices in your industry pressure you to adopt E-HRM?			
Low	Medium	High	Never
24	64	17	10
(3) Have you ever attended seminars, courses, or training programs on the application of ICT in HRM? (if your answer is no go to question 24)			
Yes	No		
48	67		
(4) How many specialized hours of training did you receive on the application of ICT in HRM?			
1–5	5–10	30+	Never
22	19	17	57
(5) Is your organization in the process of adopting (or being trained in) a new ICT that has been deemed essential for its competitiveness?			
Yes	No		
75	40		
(6) The organization has a wide network of computerized human resource information systems with the latest software			
Yes	No		
57	58		
(7) What type(s) of IT tool(s) are used to accomplish HR functions? (you may choose more than one)			
Applications	Information system	HR System	All
63	6	20	26
(8) Did your organization change their administration structure to match with the IT software system?			
Yes	No		
75	40		
(9) Did your organization ask to customize the IT function to match the organization's structure?			
Yes	No		
86	29		
(10) When your organization first became interested in the adoption of ICT for HRM purposes, how experienced and knowledgeable in these technologies were your potential users?			
No Knowledge and Experience	Little Knowledge	Moderate Knowledge	Enough Knowledge
15	45	35	20

Table 9.4 Respondents' answers related to HRM performance

(1) How easy do you find the IT usage within HRM to navigate?				
Very easy	Easy	Neutral	Hard	Very hard
31	32	29	16	6
(2) How do you feel the IT has impacted your tasks compared to before the IT was implemented?				
Much easy	Easy	No change	Hard	Very hard
50	47	7	6	5
(3) Has the E-HRM, in your view, made your role more efficient?				
Yes	No			
95	20			
(4) Do you believe that E-HRM supports privacy and data security?				
Agree	Disagree			
100	15			

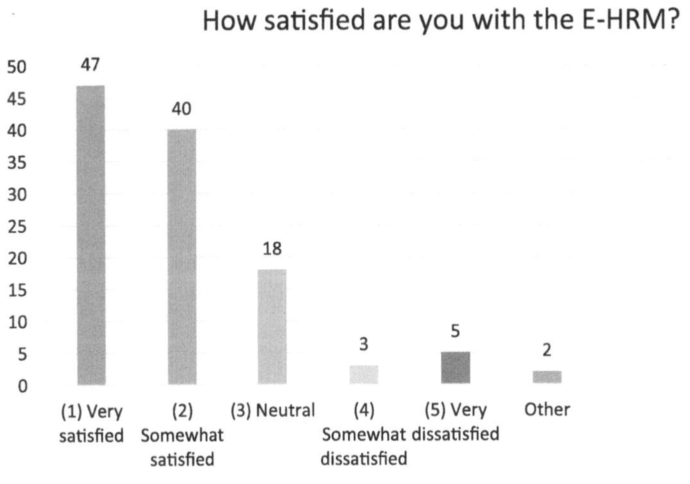

Fig. 9.6 How satisfied are you with the E-HRM?

9.4.5 *The Results of the Implementation of ICT on HRM*

Figures 9.6, 9.7, and 9.8 present the respondents' opinions about the inclusion of ICT in the HRM.

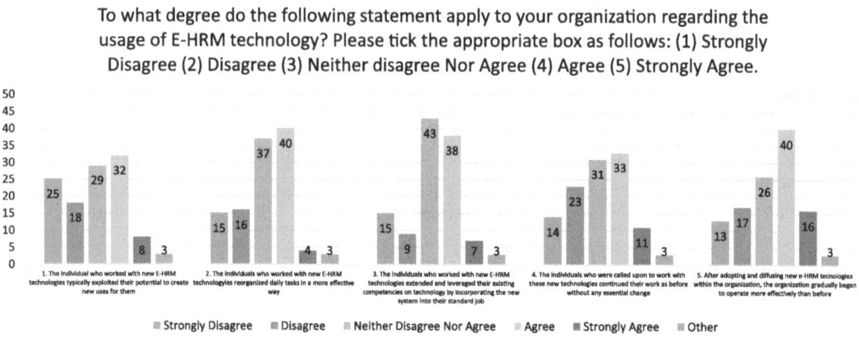

Fig. 9.7 To what degree does the following statement apply to your organization regarding the usage of E-HRM technology?

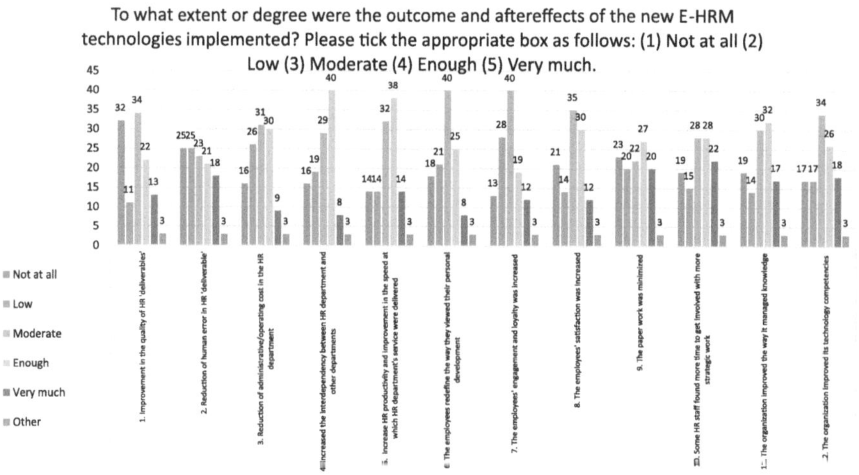

Fig. 9.8 To what extent or degree were the outcomes and aftereffects of the new E-HRM technologies implemented?

9.4.6 The Choice Experiment

The modeling choice technique is primarily based on the random utility theory (Bergmann et al., 2006). The outcomes of the choice experiment according to McFadden (1974) are modeled in the random maximization utility. The theory of random utility according to Johnson (2007) is coming from the perspective of having limited alternatives (discrete). Expecting an individual is following the utility maximum and is rational and making the decision of choosing alternatives that create the highest level of satisfaction, and individuals select alternatives based on the maximum level of utility (Yousifi & Khayyat, 2019).

As indicated by Khayyat and Heshmati (2012) and Khayyat and Heshmati (2013), logistic models are used to construct a relationship between a discrete dependent variable and the independent variables. The independent variables are supposed to have an impact on the choice or category, or the choice maker, and represent a priori beliefs about the causal elements important in the choice or classification process.

The logistic regression can be simply explained following the definition of Train (2009) as follows: a decision-maker *i* needs to make a choice *J* among a set of alternatives ($j = 1, 2, \ldots, J$). Each alternative presented to the decision-maker will have a utility denoted by *U*j. According to the theory of utility maximization, the decision-maker will make a choice that leads to maximum satisfaction. The utility of the *n*th individual for alternative *i* can be written as follows:

$$U_{ni} = \beta' x_{ni} + \varepsilon_{ni}, \tag{9.1}$$

where *i* refers to an identified alternative under consideration from the set of alternatives *J*, and x_{ni} is related to alternatives chosen from the vector of the variables observed. β denotes the estimated parameter of the vectors of unknown, and ε is a random error which is unknown researcher, but known to the individuals.

The choice of an individual can be explained by an analyst only up to the alternative probability of *i* being chosen (Hensher et al., 2005). Equation (9.2) creates the probability of selecting alternative *i* to be equal to the probability in which the utility of alternative *i* is greater than or equal to the utility associated with alternative *j* after it is evaluated every and each alterative.

$$\begin{aligned}\text{Probability}\, i = \\ \text{Probability} \\ \left[\left(\beta' \mathrm{X}_{ni} + \varepsilon_{ni}\right) \succ \left(\beta' \mathrm{X}_{nj} + \varepsilon_{nj}\right) \forall j \in j = 1,;2\ldots,;i,;\ldots,;J,;i \neq j\right]\end{aligned} \tag{9.2}$$

According to Brown (2003), Eq. (9.2) is the basis of maximum likelihood function estimation to observe the choice patterns that are actually made by the individual. The likelihood function is formed by the assumption of the distribution of the error term $\sum \varepsilon_{ni}$.

The following is the general form of the multinomial logit model (Hensher et al., 2005):

$$\text{Probability}\,\text{i} = \frac{\exp\left(\beta' X_{ni}\right)}{\sum_{j=1}^{J} \exp\left(\beta' X_{nj}\right)}, j = 0,..i..,J; i \neq j \tag{9.3}$$

where β represents the vector of parameters to be estimated, while the vector X represents variables influencing the decision-maker.

In this study, an ordered logit model is specified to rank the degree of effectiveness of E-HRM. The model is constructed as functions of the different data characteristics.

To examine how well the model fits the data, the log-likelihood ratio test (LR test) is used to compare the model without restriction (the full model) and with the model with restriction (the null model). The utility maximization that is subjected to restriction will not imply a larger maximum when it is compared with utility maximization subjected to no restriction (Gujarati, 2004).

In this chapter, an ordered logit model is specified to rank the degree of employee's belief of E-HRM effectiveness in the organization's HR operation once the system is adopted. This model is considered a special case of a general model of utility maximization (Green, 2008). The model allows us to make inferences and identify the factors affecting employees' decisions in choosing the degree of effectiveness.

An assumption is imposed in the model that the control variables consist of a set of individual employee characteristics (demographic information) such as age, income, education, and employment type. These are the same for all the choices regardless of rank chosen. The observational setting is the individual's choice among a set of alternatives, where it is assumed that an individual's characteristics determine his or her choice. The degree of effectiveness denoted by (effect) has 5 values: 0,1,2,3, and 4, where (0) represents strongly disagree, (1) disagree, (2) neither disagree nor agree, (3) agree, and (4) strongly agree. The full specification is as follows:

$$\begin{aligned} efect_i = {} & \alpha_0 + \beta_{Q3} Q3_i + \beta_{Q4} Q4_i + \beta_{Q10} Q19_i + \beta_{Q20} Q20_i + \beta_{Q35} Q35_i + \beta_{Q36} Q36_i + \\ & \sum_j \beta_{jQ321_{ji}} + \sum_j \beta_{jQ322_{ji}} + \sum_j \beta_{jQ323_{ji}} + \sum_j \beta_{jQ324_{ji}} + \sum_j \beta_{jQ325_{ji}} + \sum_j \beta_{jQ326_{ji}} + \\ & \sum_j \beta_{jQ327_{ji}} + \sum_j \beta_{jQ328_{ji}} + \sum_j \beta_{jQ329_{ji}} + \sum_j \beta_{jQ320_{ji}} + \sum_j \beta_{jQ3211_{ji}} + \sum_j \beta_{jQ3212_{ji}} \end{aligned}$$

The category (0) strongly disagree, which is the first option in the questionnaire, is selected as a reference group for the dependent variable effect. Q3 represents education, and its reference group is the first option secondary, Q4 is the employee's work experience, and the first option 1–5 years is the reference group, and so on.

To test the fit of the model, the predictive value for the five alternatives is (8 + 4 + 16 + 40 + 7)/115 = 65.2%, which implies that around 65% of the choices are correctly predicted by the model (see Table 9.5). For the option (0), the model predicted 80% of the total outcome, 67% for the option (1), 76% for the option (3), and so on.

An LR test is defined as the test statistics: $\lambda = 2$ (LRu - LRr), where LRu is the log-likelihood of the model with no restriction, and LRr is the log-likelihood of the restricted model. λ follows a chi-square distribution with a degree of freedom which is equal to the number of restrictions imposed by the null hypothesis. The difference between LRu and LRr indicates whether the restrictions are correct or not (Khayyat & Heshmati, 2013).

The likelihood ratio (LR) in this model is 147.2 (see Table 9.6). With 21 degrees of freedom, it indicates that the effects in model specification are statistically highly significant at the 99% level of significance. The null hypothesis (the model with only intercept) is rejected, and the independent variables are jointly significant.

Table 9.6 presents the ordered logit regression coefficients. The standard interpretation of the ordered logit coefficient is for a one-unit increase in the predictor and the response variable level is expected to change by its respective regression coefficient in the ordered log-odds scale, while the other variables in the model are held constant. Interpretation of the ordered logit estimates is not dependent on the subsidiary parameters; the ancillary parameters are used to differentiate the adjacent levels of the response variable. However, since the ordered logit model estimates one equation over all levels of the dependent variable, a concern is whether this one-equation model is valid or a more flexible model is required.

Table 9.5 Number of actual and predicted outcomes from the estimated model

	Predicted alternative ranks				
Actual alternative ranks	(0) Strongly disagree	(1) Disagree	(2) Neither disagree nor agree	(3) Agree	(4) Strongly agree
(0) Strongly disagree	**8/10 (80%)**	0	0	3	0
(1) Disagree	1	**4/6 (67%)**	3	4	1
(2) Neither disagree nor agree	1	2	**16/21 (76%)**	10	0
(3) Agree	0	0	2	**40/66(61%)**	4
(4) Strongly agree	0	0	0	9	**7/12 (58%)**
Col. sum.	10	6	21	66	12

Table 9.6 Parameter estimates

Variable	Coefficient	P[|Z| > z]	Mean of X	Variable	Coefficient	P[|Z| > z]	Mean of X
ConstantI	2.497	0.000***	–	Q329	0.093	0.473	2.087
Q3	−0.062	0.067**	2.009	Q320	−0.062	0.666	2.243
Q4	−0.154	0.061**	1.174	Q3211	0.116	0.556	2.200
Q321	0.35	0.007**	1.843	Q3212	0.058	0.724	2.174
Q322	0.173	0.052**	1.922	Q351	−0.693	0.000***	1.287
Q323	0.258	0.038**	1.991	Q361	−0.427	0.001***	0.861
Q324	0.315	0.089**	2.122	Q37	−0.845	0.021**	0.826
Q325	−0.105	0.444	2.287	Q71	−0.198	0.515	−0.826
Q326	−0.174	0.236	1.939	Q19	0.54	0.032**	0.722
Q327	−0.118	0.030**	1.983	Q20	−0.066	0.836	0.800
Q328	0.003	0.985	2.061	Q211	−0.033	0.811	1.113

Threshold parameters for the index

Variable	Coefficient	P[|Z| > z]
Mu(1)	0.802	0.000***
Mu(2)	1.623	0.000***
Mu(3)	2.895	0.000***

Note. Standard errors are robust
* $p < 0.10$, two-sided test. ** $p < 0.05$, two-sided test. *** $p < 0.01$, two-sided test

The estimates for the logit imply the following:

$$y^* = 2.497 - 0.062Q3 - 0.154Q4 + 0.35Q321 + 0.173Q322 + \ldots + \varepsilon$$

$$y = 0\, if\ y^* \le 0$$

$$y = 1\, if\ 0 < y^* \le 0.802$$

$$y = 2\, if\ 0.802 < y^* \le 1.623$$

$$y = 3\, if\ 1.623 < y^* \le 2.895$$

$$y = 4\, if\ y^* > 2.895$$

It is difficult to directly interpret the ordered logit coefficients. Neither the sign nor the magnitude of the coefficient is informative about the result above, so the direct interpretation of the coefficients is essentially vague. In order to interpret the parameters, one typically refers to the partial effects (marginal effects) in the ordered choice model. The marginal effects give the effects on the specific probabilities per unit change in the regressor.

For example, for the education variable Q3, the marginal effects for the ordered logit model for the five cells of are 0.007, 0.011, 0.007, −0.014, and 00.11 (see

Table 9.7), which give the expected change on the probabilities per additional level of education. For the years of experience (Q4), the marginal effects for the ordered logit model for the five cells of are 0.016, 0.027, 0.018, −0.034, and −0.028, which give the expected change on the probabilities per additional level of experience; either the signs nor the magnitudes of the coefficients are directly interpretable in the ordered choice model (Green, 2008). It is necessary, hence, to calculate marginal effects to interpret the model meaningfully. The only certainties in the signs of the marginal effects in this model are as follows, where a variable with a positive coefficient is considered:

- Increases in that variable will lead to an increase in the probability in the highest cell and a decrease in the probability in the lowest cell.
- The sum of all the changes will be zero. (The new probabilities must still sum to one.)
- The effects will begin at Pr(0) with one or more negative values and then change to a set of positive values; there will be one sign change.

The reverse is true for a variable with a negative coefficient. Daykin and Moffatt (2002) argue that in psychology applications with attitude scales, If the statement is one with which most people are either in strong agreement or strong disagreement, it would expect the cut points to be tightly bunched in the middle of the distribution. Thus, in the absence of other information, this suggests that the threshold parameters can reveal some information about the preferences of the respondents (Green, 2008).

Table 9.7 Marginal effects

Variable	Y = 00	Y = 01	Y = 02	Y = 03	Y = 04	Variable	Y = 00	Y = 01	Y = 02	Y = 03	Y = 04
Q3	0.007	0.011	0.007	−0.014	−0.011	Q_320	0.007	0.011	0.007	−0.014	−0.011
Q4	0.016	0.027	0.018	−0.034	−0.028	Q_32E	−0.012	−0.021	−0.013	0.026	0.021
Q_321	−0.037	−0.062	−0.040	0.077	0.063	Q_32T	−0.006	−0.010	−0.007	0.013	0.010
Q_322	−0.008	−0.013	−0.008	0.016	0.013	Q35	0.074	0.123	0.080	−0.153	−0.124
Q_323	−0.006	−0.010	−0.007	0.013	0.010	Q36	0.045	0.076	0.049	−0.094	−0.076
Q_324	−0.033	−0.056	−0.036	0.069	0.056	Q37	0.059	0.126	0.131	−0.110	−0.206
Q_325	0.011	0.019	0.012	−0.023	−0.019	Q7	0.021	0.035	0.023	−0.044	−0.035
Q_326	0.019	0.031	0.020	−0.038	−0.031	Q19	−0.055	−0.079	−0.039	0.104	0.070
Q_327	0.023	0.039	0.025	−0.048	−0.039	Q20	0.007	0.012	0.008	−0.014	−0.012
Q_328	0.000	−0.001	0.000	0.001	0.001	Q21	0.004	0.006	0.004	−0.007	−0.006
Q_329	−0.010	−0.017	−0.011	0.020	0.017						

9.5 Conclusion, Recommendations, and Policy Implications

Due to the limited size of the survey sample, it was difficult to derive precise implications based on the information obtained. However, as was expected from the literature review and proven by the statistical results, there is a positive relationship between the independent variables representing ICT usage and the dependent variable HRM. This suggests that ICT increases the performance of human resource management staff. The level of ICT usage is high within HR departments. The HR departments within the universities in the Kurdistan Region of Iraq use ICT in their daily activities.

Regardless of the above, the overall coefficients of all the responses to the survey are significant. This indicates that ICT has a positive effect on increasing the performance of the HRM. This is in line with the findings of other research (see, for example, Václav et al., 2011, Rahman et al., 2020, Lekic & Vukosavljevic, 2021, Karanja et al., 2018, Mohammadi et al., 2021).

Furthermore, ICT may help increase the level of performance in the higher education institutions in the KRI. Based on the responses, most of the higher education institutions in the KRI are outsourcing IT. Also, 63% of the respondents replied with the answer of applying IT in their institutions in the past 5 years. This means that the KRI higher education institutions are still new to IT to be implemented in HRM.

The highest percentage of the responses to E-HRM usage in higher education institutions is "not being familiar with the E-HRM," which indicates that the higher education institution staff are not familiar enough with computerized HR. Furthermore, the highest rate of responses to the question of whether the HRM practice is automated or not are "not automated at all." This proves that higher education institutions are not using technology in their HRM systems.

To summarize the above discussion, it can be said that ICT is not being well used in higher education institutions in the KRI. To conclude the results, the following points are presented:

- There is a positive relationship between ICT and HRM performance, which means that ICT can have a positive impact on the performance level of HRM staff in higher education institutions in the KRI.
- The level of ICT usage in the KRI is moderate; however, it is not at a level where the individuals of HRM are well aware of ICT developments and their link to E-HRM.
- The usage of ICT does help to make the daily tasks much easier according to the survey responses, which increases the level of performance of the HRM staff in higher education institutions.

Below are the main recommendations that are believed to serve the HRM staff in the higher education institutions in KRI:

- The HRM staff in the higher education institution need to be well introduced to ICT to fully understand the usage of ICT and the influence that ICT can have on HRM performance.
- ICT may help HR process to decrease the costs of getting the best out of the available staff and reach the best candidates in the market to fill the vacancies available in their institutions.
- Self-service systems can be used within higher education institutions which can help the organization to always have up-to-date information about their employees, which will facilitate the work of HR staff within the organization.
- ICT can be used to facilitate cooperation and collaboration among the different levels of management to which the tasks can be delegated easily, as well as the decisions can be made automatically while the staff is away or not capable of making a decision.
- ICT can help institutions find better employees, create a flexible encouraging schedule, and better data management, conflict resolution, training and development, and information resources.
- As the world is moving toward globalization and organizations tend to get bigger and larger in size, this requires the implementation of E-HRM to help the HRM staff to have up-to-date and exact information available in the organizations.

Appendices

Appendix 1: Survey Questionnaire [English]

Section A: Biographical Information (please tick where appropriate)

1. Q1 Gender
    - Female (   )
    - Male (   )
2. Q2 What is your age (   )
3. Q3 Highest attained educational level:
    - Secondary (   )
    - Diploma (   )
    - Degree (   )
    - Postgraduate (   )
4. Q4 How many years of work experience do you have?
    - 1–5 years (   )
    - 5–10 years (   )
    - 10–15 years (   )
    - 15–20 years (   )
    - 20+ (   )

5. Q5 What is the name of the organization you work for?-------------------------------
6. Q6 Term of employment
   - Temporary (   )
   - Permanent (   )
7. Q7 What is your employment level?
   - Entry level (   )
   - Mid-level (   )
   - Manager level (   )
   - Director level (   )
   - Top management level (   )
8. Q8Whatisyourjobtitle?--
9. Q9 Monthly salary range (USD)?
   - 1000–2000 (   )
   - 3000–4000 (   )
   - 5000–6000 (   )
   - 6000+ (   )
10. Q10 Total number of employees in the organization (   )
11. Q11 In which sector is your organization?
    - Public (   )
    - Private (   )
12. Q12 How long the organization you work for has been operating?
    - 1–5 years (   )
    - 5–10 years (   )
    - 10–15 years (   )
    - 15–20 years (   )
    - 20+ (   )

Section B: ICT and HRM-Specific Information (Please tick where appropriate)

13. Q13 Are your organization's daily HRM operations heavily reliant on computers and IT?
    - Yes (   )
    - No (   )
14. Q14 Does your organization have a separate department or division (e.g., information systems or information technology department)?
    - Yes (   )
    - No (   )

15. Q15 Does the organization *outsourcing in order to receive usage of information system or information technology?

    - Yes ( )
    - No ( )

(*The delegation of specified work to a third party for a specified length of time, at a specified cost, and a specified level of service)

16. Q16 When did your organization first adopt its major ICT systems(S)?

    - Never ( )
    - In the past 5 years ago ( )
    - Over 5–10 years ago ( )
    - 10+ ( )

17. Q17 Could you please indicate which of the stages of HR technology reflects your organization?

    - Stage 1: Paper-based system ( )
    - Stage 2: Early personal computer (PC) technology ( )
    - Stage 3: Electronic database systems ( )
    - Stage 4: Web-based technology ( )

18. Q18 When did your organization first adopt ICT system(s) specifically for HRM purposes?

    - Never ( )
    - 0–2 years ( )
    - 2–5 years ( )
    - 5+ ( )

19. Q19 Does your organization keenly track innovative usage of technology by competitors?

    - Yes ( )
    - No ( )

20. Q20 Does your organization believe E-HRM application is a strategic need to strive in the industry?

    - Yes ( )
    - No ( )

21. Q21 To what level does the Higher Education Ministry, donors, sponsors, and KRG have the overall operational practices in your industry pressure your organization to adopt E-HRM?

    - Low level ( )
    - Medium level ( )
    - High level ( )
    - Never ( )

22. Q22 Have you ever attended seminars, courses, or training programs on the application of ICT in HRM?
    - Yes ( )
    - No ( ) If your answer is no go to question 24
23. Q23 How many specialized hours of training did you receive on the application of ICT in HRM?
    - 1–5 ( )
    - 5–10 ( )
    - 20–30 ( )
    - 30+ ( )
    - None ( )
24. Q24 Is your organization in the process of adopting (or being trained in) a new ICT that has been deemed essential for its competitiveness?
    - Yes ( )
    - No ( )
25. Q25 The organization has a wide network of computerized human resource information systems with the latest software
    - Yes ( )
    - No ( )
26. Q26 What type(s) of IT tool(s) are used to accomplish HR functions? (you may choose more than one)
    - Q261 Application software (such as DBMS, spreadsheets, and data warehousing) ( )
    - Q262 Information system software (such as decision support systems and executive information systems) ( )
    - Q263 Human resources information system (HRIS) which is used by the HR function mainly for specific HR processes (i.e., payroll, performance, and management) ( )
    - Q24 All of the above ( )
27. Q27 Did your organization change their administration structure to match with the IT software system?
    - Yes ( )
    - No ( )
28. Q28 Did your organization ask to customize the IT function to match the organization's structure?
    - Yes ( )
    - No ( )

29. Q29 Which of the following e-HRM and social media technologies or tools are used in your organization specifically for human resources management purposes?

30. Q30 Which of the following HRM practices are at least partially automated through your organization's e-HRM system(s)?

Please tick the appropriate box as follows: (1) Used. (2) Not used. (3) Will be used in the near future. (4) I don't know whether it is used or not. (5) I am not sure what this technology is about.	1	2	3	4	5
Q291 Organization's website					
Q292 Intranet					
Q293 Intranet blogs only for organization's employees					
Q294 Social networking sites such as Facebook, LinkedIn, Myspace, Twitter, YouTube, etc.					
Q295 Online content communities such as emails, SlideShare, etc.					
Q296 Self-service applications					
Q27 Mobile technology (e.g., smartphones such as blackberry, I-phone, etc.) that allows employees to access organizations' applications and emails					
Q298 Enterprise resource planning (ERP) that is connected to other departments (i.e., accounting, finance, and purchasing)					
Q299 Webinar (adobe webinar, skype, and WhatsApp)					
Q2910 Internet					

Please tick the appropriate box as follows: (1) Not automated at all. (2) A little automated. (3) Moderately automated. (4) Enough automated. (5) Very automated.	1	2	3	4	5
Q301 Staff recruitment and selection (e.g., job applications, management of advertising, and resumes)					
Q302 Performance evaluation (e.g., personal evaluation files)					
Q303 Internal organization communication (e.g., personal announcements, and newsletters)					

Please tick the appropriate box as follows: (1) Not automated at all. (2) A little automated. (3) Moderately automated. (4) Enough automated. (5) Very automated.	1	2	3	4	5
Q304 Communication with third parties outside the organization (e.g., through the organization website: job announcements, information on the organization's working environment, information on the organization's organizational chart, etc.)					
Q305 Payroll (e.g., preparation and files)					
Q306 Application forms					
Q307 Career development plan (e.g., organizational chart and career paths)					
Q308 Time tracking (e.g., personal attendance, absence, and leave)					
Q309 Health and safety					
Q3010 Document tracking system					

31. Q31 To what degree do the following statements apply to your organization regarding the usage of e-HRM technology?
32. Q32 To what extent or degree were the outcomes and aftereffects of the new e-HRM technologies implemented?

Please tick the appropriate box as follows: (1) Strongly Disagree. (2) Disagree. (3) Neither Disagree nor Agree. (4) Agree. (5) Strongly Agree.	1	2	3	4	5
Q311The individuals who worked with new e-HRM technologies typically exploited their potential to create new uses for them					
Q312 The individuals who worked with new e-HRM technologies reorganized daily tasks in a more effective way					

Please tick the appropriate box as follows: (1) Strongly Disagree. (2) Disagree. (3) Neither Disagree nor Agree. (4) Agree. (5) Strongly Agree.	1	2	3	4	5
Q313 The individuals who worked with new e-HRM technologies extended and leveraged their existing competencies in technology by incorporating the new system into their standard job					
Q314 The individuals who were called upon to work with these new technologies continued their work as before without any essential change					
Q315 After adopting and diffusing new e-HRM technologies within the organization, the organization gradually began to operate more effectively than before					

Please tick the appropriate box as follows: (1) Not at all. (2) Low. (3) Moderate. (4) Enough. (5) Very much.	1	2	3	4	5
Q321 Improvement in the quality of HR " deliverables"					
Q322 Reduction of human error in HR " deliverable"					
Q323 Reduction of administrative/ operating costs in the HR department					
Q324 Increased the interdependency between the HR department and other departments					

Please tick the appropriate box as follows: (1) Not at all. (2) Low. (3) Moderate. (4) Enough. (5) Very much.	1	2	3	4	5
Q325 Increase HR productivity and improvement in the speed at which the HR department's service was delivered					
Q326 The employees redefine the way they view their personal development					
Q327 The employees' engagement and loyalty was increased					
Q328 The employees' satisfaction was increased					
Q329 The paperwork was minimized					
Q3210 Some HR staff found more time to get involved with more strategic work					
Q3211 The organization improved the way it managed knowledge					
Q3212 The organization improved its technology competencies					

33. Q33 When your organization first became interested in the adoption of ICT for HRM purposes, how experienced and knowledgeable in these technologies were your potential users?

    - No knowledgeable and experienced (   )
    - Little knowledgeable and experienced (   )
    - Moderately knowledgeable and experienced (   )
    - Enough knowledgeable and experienced (   )

34. Q34 How easy do you find the IT usage within HRM to navigate?

    - Very easy (   )
    - Somewhat (   )

- Neutral ( )
- Somewhat difficult ( )
- Very difficult ( )

35. Q35 Currently what is your level of computer usage?

- Low level ( )
- Moderate level ( )
- Higher level ( )

36. Q36 How do you feel the IT has impacted your tasks compared to before the IT was implemented?

- Much easier ( )
- Somewhat easier ( )
- No change ( )
- Somewhat harder ( )
- Much harder ( )

37. Q37 Has the e-HRM, in your view, made your role more efficient?

- Yes ( )
- No ( )

38. Q38 How satisfied are you with the e-HRM?

- Very satisfied ( )
- Somewhat satisfied ( )
- Neutral ( )
- Somewhat dissatisfied ( )
- Very dissatisfied ( )

39. Q39 Do you believe that E-HRM supports privacy and data security?

- Agree ( )
- Disagree ( )

References

Adewoye, J. (2012). *The impact of information technology (it) on human resource management (Hrm): Empirical evidence from Nigeria banking sector*. Case Study Of Selected Banks From Lagos State And Oyo State In South-West Nigeria.

Agarwala, T. (2002). Human resource management: The emerging trends. *Indian Journal Of Industrial Relations*, 315–331.

Allen, D. G., Mahto, R. V., & Otondo, R. F. (2007). Web-based recruitment: Effects of information, organizational brand, and attitudes toward A web site on applicant attraction. *Journal of Applied Psychology, 92*, 1696.

Al-Qudah, S., Obeidat, A. M., & Shrouf, H. (2020). The impact of strategic human resources planning on the organizational performance of public shareholding companies in Jordan. *Problems and Perspectives in Management, 18*, 219.

American University Of Iraq Sulaimani. (2016). *About, working for Auis* [Online]. Retrieved January 5, 2017, from http://auis.edu.krd

Amutha, D. (2020). *The role and impact of Ict In improving the quality of education*. Available At Ssrn 3585228.

Ardichvili & Alexander. (2002). Knowledge management, human resource development, and internet technology. *Advances in Developing Human Resources, 4*, 451–463.

Armstrong, M., & Taylor, S. (2006). *Human resource management practice*. Kagan.

Bagozzi, R. P., Davis, F. D., & Warshaw, P. R. (1992). Development and test of A theory of technological learning and usage. *Human Relations, 45*, 659–686.

Bayan University. (2017). Retrieved December 11, 2017, from http://bayanu.edu.iq/en/

Bergmann, A., Hanley, N., & Wright, R. (2006). Valuing the attributes of renewable energy investments. *Energy Policy, 34*, 1004–1014.

Brown, T. C. (2003). *Introduction to stated preference methods. A primer on nonmarket valuation*. Kluwer Academic Publishers.

Cihan University Of Erbil. (2015). *About, Faculties* [Online]. Retrieved November 12, 2016, from http://erbilcihan.edu.krd/en/#.WkdzurirOdu

Cipd. (2015). *History of human resource management (Hr)* [Online]. Cipd. Retrieved

Daykin, A. R., & Moffatt, P. G. (2002). Analyzing ordered responses: A review of the ordered Probit model. *Understanding Statistics: Statistical Issues In Psychology, Education, And The Social Sciences, 1*, 157–166.

Duhok Polytechnic University. (2015). *About Dpu, E-learning, E-university, human Resource* [online]. Retrieved December 18, 2016, from http://dpu.edu.krd

Dulebohn, J. H., Ferris, G. R., & Stodd, J. T. (1995). The history and evolution of human resource management. *Handbook Of Human Resource Management*, 18–41.

Ekwoaba, J. O. & Anthony, I. D. (2012). The role of human resource planning in recruitment and selection process Francis C. Anyim Ph. D Fcipm., Fnim., Fabs, Fcai. *Differences,* 6.

Enders, J. (2004). Higher education, internationalisation, and the nation-state: Recent developments and challenges to governance theory. *Higher Education, 47*, 361–382.

Fey, C. F., & Björkman, I. (2001). The effect of human resource management practices on Mnc subsidiary performance in Russia. *Journal of International Business Studies, 32*, 59–75.

Garcia-Arroyo, J., & Osca, A. (2021). Big data contributions to human resource management: A systematic review. *The International Journal of Human Resource Management, 32*, 4337–4362.

Green, A. (1997). *Education, Globalization and the Nation State*. Springer.

Green, W. H. (2008). Discrete choice modelling. *Palgrave handbook of econometrics,* 2. Available At Ssrn: https://ssrn.com/abstract=985611

Guest, D. E. (2021). *The role of line managers in the Hrm process*. Edward Elgar Publishing.

Gujarati, D. (2004). *Basic econometrics*. United States Military Academy, West Point. Tata Mcgraw-Hill.

Gylfason, T. (2001). Natural resources, education, and economic development. *European Economic Review, 45*, 847–859.

Hakeem, I. (2013). *Impact of information and communication technology on goods' clearance operations in West Africa; A case study of Nigeria customs service clearance operations*. Master Thesis, University Of Liverpool.

Hayat Private University for Science and Technology. *About Us, University Faculties* [Online]. Retrieved December 5, 2016, from Http://Hpust.Com/English/Content.Aspx?Id=2

Heathfield, S. M. (2010). *What is human resource management*. Retrieved October, 24, 2010.

Hendry, C. (2012). *Human resource management*. Routledge.

Hensher, D. A., Rose, J. M., & Greene, W. H. (2005). *Applied choice analysis: A primer*. Cambridge University Press.

Heshmati, A. (2007). *A model for industrial development of the Federal Region of Kurdistan: Science and technology policy, instruments and institutions*.
Heslina, H., & Syahruni, A. (2021). The influence of information technology, human resources competency and employee engagement on performance of employees. *Golden Ratio of Human Resource Management, 1*, 01–12.
Hu, D., & Oh, I.-S. (2021). Beyond individuals' use of information and communication technologies (Icts): A multilevel approach in research on Icts. *Industrial and Organizational Psychology, 14*, 441–443.
Invest In Group. (2013). *Knowledge is power: Education* [Online]. Retrieved January 15, 2017, from http://investingroup.org/review/246/knowledge-is-power-education-kurdistan/
Ishik University Of Erbil. (2015). *About, job application* [Online]. Retrieved November 25, 2016, from http://www.ishik.edu.iq
Johnson, T. R. (2007). *Applied choice analysis: A primer*. Cambridge University Press. 742+ Xxiv Pp. Us $60.00. ISBN: 0-521-60577-6. Psychometrika, 72, 449–450.
Kambur, E., & Yildirim, T. (2023). From traditional to smart human resources management. *International Journal of Manpower, 44*, 422–452.
Karanja, D., Sang, A., & Ndirangu, M. (2018). Influence of integration of Ict on human resource management in Kenyan public universities. *International Journal of Sustainability Management and Information Technologies, 3*, 73.
Khan, K. A., & Talib, N. (2023). Relating E-Hrm practices with transformational E-Hrm outcomes: The mediating role of proximal outcomes: Relating E-Hrm practices with transformational E-Hrm outcomes. *Journal of Workplace Behavior, 4*, 1–25.
Khayyat, N. T., & Heshmati, A. (2012). Determinants of mobile phone customer satisfaction in the Kurdistan region. *Journal of Knowledge Management, Economics and Information Technology, 2*, 1–7.
Khayyat, N. T., & Heshmati, A. (2013). Determinants of mobile telecommunication adoption in Kurdistan. *International Journal of Communication, 7*, 27.
Klerck, G. (2009). Industrial relations and human resource management. In D. G Collings & G. Wood (Eds.), *Human resource management: A critical approach* (pp. 238–259). Routledge.
Komar University of Science and Technology. (2016). *About Kust, work at Kust* [online]. Retrieved January 5, 2017, from http://www.komar.edu.Iq
Koya University. (2014). *The University, Faculties* [Online]. Retrieved January 15, 2017, from http://koyauniversity.org/node/19
Kramar, R. (2022). Sustainable human resource management: Six defining characteristics. *Asia Pacific Journal of Human Resources, 60*, 146–170.
Lakhwani, M., Dastane, O., Satar, N. S. M., & Johari, Z. (2020). The impact of technology adoption on organizational productivity. *The Journal of Industrial Distribution & Business, 11*, 7–18.
Lebanese French University. *Our University, Applying For Job* [Online]. Retrieved November 6, 2016, from Http://Www.Lfu-Bmu.Net
Legge, K. (1995). *What is human resource management?* Human Resource Management. Springer.
Lekic, N. J., & Vukosavljevic, D. D. (2021). The importance of human resources in the development of ICT enterprises. *Kultura Polisa, 18*, 293.
Lengnick-Hall, C. A., & Lengnick-Hall, M. L. (1988). Strategic human resources management: A review of the literature and a proposed typology. *Academy of Management Review, 13*, 454–470.
Liao, C.-H., Tsou, C.-W., & Huang, M.-F. (2007). Factors influencing the usage of 3g mobile services in Taiwan. *Online Information Review, 31*, 759–774.
Mcfadden, D. L. (1974). Conditional logit analysis of qualitative choice behavior. In P. Zaremba (Ed.), *Frontiers in econometrics*.
Mohammadi, S., Taghipour, M., & Mahboobi, M. (2021). Investigating the role and impact of using ICT tools on evaluating of the performance of service organizations. *Iranian Journal Of Information Processing And Management, 37*, 1–26.

Moore, G. C., & Benbasat, I. (1991). Development of an instrument to measure the perceptions of adopting an information technology innovation. *Information Systems Research, 2*, 192–222.
Noerman, T., Erlando, A., & Riyanto, F. D. (2021). Factors determining intention to continue using E-Hrm. *The Journal of Asian Finance, Economics And Business, 8*, 1079–1089.
Nwokolo, C. P. (2015). Standardization of education in Nigeria through information communications technology (Ict). *Journal Of Educational Policy And Entrepreneurial Research, 2*, 38–49.
OECD. (2015). *OECD Digital Economy Outlook 2015*. OECD Publishing.
Paauwe, J. & Boon, C. 2009. Strategic Hrm: A critical review.
Pagani, M. (2004). Determinants of adoption of third generation Mobile multimedia services. *Journal of Interactive Marketing, 18*, 46–59.
Parasuraman, A., Zeithaml, V. A., & Berry, L. L. (1985). A conceptual model of service quality and its implications for future research. *The Journal of Marketing, 49*, 41–50.
Rahman, M. H., Mutsuddi, P., Roy, S. K., Al-Amin, M., & Jannat, F. (2020). Performance efficiency evaluation of information and communication technology (ICT) application in human resource management during Covid-19 pandemic: A study on banking industry of Bangladesh. *South Asian Journal Of Social Studies And Economics, 8*, 46–56.
Rainer, R. K., Prince, B., Sánchez-Rodríguez, C., Splettstoesser-Hogeterp, I., & Ebrahimi, S. (2020). *Introduction to information systems*. Wiley.
Rathee, R., & Bhuntel, M. R. (2021). A study on employee perception about the use of E-Hrm in it. *Scms Journal of Indian Management, 18*, 37–47.
Ruël, H., Bondarouk, T., & Looise, J. K. (2004). E-Hrm: Innovation or irritation. An explorative empirical study in five large companies on web-based Hrm. *Management Revue*, 364–380.
Salahaddin University-Erbil. (2017). *About Su, Colleges* [Online]. Retrieved January 18, 2017, from http://su.edu.krd
Schuler, R. S., Jackson, S. E., & Storey, J. (2001). Hrm and its link with strategic management. *Human Resource Management: A Critical Text*, 114–130.
Shamout, M., Elayan, M., Rawashdeh, A., Kurdi, B., & Alshurideh, M. (2022). E-Hrm practices and sustainable competitive advantage from Hr practitioner's perspective: A mediated moderation analysis. *International Journal Of Data And Network Science, 6*, 165–178.
Sharma, N., William, P., Kulshreshtha, K., Sharma, G., Haralayya, B., Chauhan, Y., & Shrivastava, A. (2023). Human resource management model with ICT architecture: Solution of management & understanding of Psychology of human resources and corporate social responsibility. *Journal For Reattach Therapy And Developmental Diversities, 6*, 219–230.
Silverstone, R., Hirsch, E., & Morley, D. (1991). Listening to a long conversation: An ethnographic approach to the study of information and communication technologies in the home. *Cultural Studies, 5*, 204–227.
Soran University. (2015). *About* [Online]. Retrieved February 2, 2017, from http://www.soran.edu.iq
Sparrow, P. (2010). *Handbook of international human resource management: Integrating people, process, and context*. Wiley.
Sparrow, P., Brewster, C., & Chung, C. (2016). *Globalizing human resource management*. Routledge.
Stone, D. L., & Dulebohn, J. H. (2013). *Emerging issues in theory and research on electronic human resource management (Ehrm)* (Vol. 23, p. 1). Elsevier.
Sulaimani Polytechnic University. (2017). Retrieved February 17, 2017, from https://www.unipage.net/en/18953/sulaimani_polytechnic_university
Tar, U. A., & Lawrence, J. E. (2011). The potentials of ICT infrastructure in A developing economy: The case of small businesses in Kurdistan region, Iraq. *Information, Society And Justice Journal, 4*, 101–119.
The American University Of Kurdistan. *About The University* [Online]. Retrieved December 15, 2016, from Http://Auk.Edu.Krd
Tokundu, M. (2021). *The effect of technological advancement on human resources performance: A case study of the office of the prime minister, Republic of Namibia*. Stellenbosch University.

Train, K. (2003). *Discrete choice methods with simulation*. Cambridge University Press.
Train, K. E. (2009). *Discrete choice methods with simulation*. Cambridge University Press.
University Of Duhok. (2016). *About, Academic, Job Center* [Online]. Retrieved January 24, 2017, from http://web.uod.ac
University Of Garmian. *About Us* [Online]. Retrieved December 20, 2016, from Http://Garmianuniv.Net/About.Aspx?Jimare=14
University Of Halabja. (2017). *About, Colleges, Units* [Online]. Retrieved December 19, 2016, from http://halabjauni.org/en/default.aspx
University Of Human Development In Sulaimani. (2013). Retrieved February 17, 2017, from http://www.bordeglobal.com/foruminv/index.php?showtopic=165163
University Of Kurdistan Hewler. (2017). *About, Staff, Vacancies* [Online]. Retrieved February 17, 2017, from https://www.ukh.edu.krd
University Of Raparin. (2014). *About Uor, staff* [online]. Retrieved January 15, 2017, from Http://Www.Raparinuni.Org
University Of Sulaimani. (2017). *About* [Online]. Retrieved December 28, 2016, from http://univsul.edu.iq/en/
University Of Zakho. (2016). *About Uoz, University Council, Directories & Centers* [Online]. Retrieved December 18, 2016, from http://uoz.edu.krd
Václav, O., Antonín, P., & Petra, J. (2011). Processes, performance drivers and ICT tools in human resources management. *Journal of Competitiveness, Issue*, 58–70.
Waheed, A., Xiaoming, M., Waheed, S., Ahmad, N., & Tian-Tian, S. (2020). E-Hrm implementation, adoption and its predictors: A case of small and medium enterprises of Pakistan. *International Journal of Information Technology and Management, 19*, 162–180.
Walsham, G., Robey, D., & Sahay, S. (2007). Foreword: Special issue on information systems in developing countries. *MIS Quarterly, 31*, 317–326.
Welbourne, T. M. (2010). From E-Hrm to fast Hrm opportunities for research and practice innovation. In *Proceedings of the Third European Academic Workshop On Electronic Human Resource Management*, Bamberg.
Yousifi, D., & Khayyat, N. T. (2019). How information and communications technology affects the performance of human resources management in the higher education? *Ukh Journal of Social Sciences, 3*, 36–49.
Zhou, Y., Cheng, Y., Zou, Y., & Liu, G. (2022). E-Hrm: A meta-analysis of the antecedents, consequences, and cross-national moderators. *Human Resource Management Review, 32*, 100862.
Zuppo, C. M. (2012). Defining ICT in a boundaryless world: The development of A working hierarchy. *International Journal Of Managing Information Technology, 4*, 13.

Chapter 10
How Social Media Affect Vacation Travel Planning?

Naseem Issa Azeez

Abstract In an era where the digital landscape intertwines seamlessly with human daily lives, the role of social media in shaping human experiences has become increasingly pronounced. Nowhere is this more evident than in the realm of vacation travel planning. As travelers seek inspiration, advice, and validation for their wanderlust-fueled dreams, social media platforms have emerged as indispensable tools in crafting the perfect getaway. The purpose of this study is to find out the relationship between the travel decision-making processes through the use of social media, especially from the point of view of Kurdish travelers. The theoretical background of this study is based on the concept of consumer behavior, specifically the theory of travel planning behavior, and also on the concept of the usage of information and trusting the information on social media. Data were collected through survey questionnaires with travelers in tourist spots. The main result of this study shows that social media has an essential role as the source of information to help travelers in every stage of travel decision-making. At each step, the traveler uses the information to carry out specific activities undertaken. The study concluded with some recommendations for the scope of theoretical academics with the model of the travel decision-making process through the use of social media, as well as for the tourism industry to execute marketing strategies that focus more on the consumers.

Keywords Social media · Travel decision-making process · Consumer behavior · Tourism · Kurdistan Region

10.1 Introduction

In an era where the digital landscape intertwines seamlessly with human daily lives, the role of social media in shaping human experiences has become increasingly pronounced. Nowhere is this more evident than in the realm of vacation travel

N. I. Azeez (✉)
School of Geography, University of Nottingham, Nottingham, UK
e-mail: lgxni5@nottingham.ac.uk

G. M. Muhamad, N. T. Khayyat (eds.), *Resource Management Performance: A Sectoral Analysis in the Post-Conflict Kurdistan Region of Iraq*, Perspectives on Development in the Middle East and North Africa (MENA) Region,
https://doi.org/10.1007/978-981-97-7725-9_10

planning. As travelers seek inspiration, advice, and validation for their wanderlust-fueled dreams, social media platforms have emerged as indispensable tools in crafting the perfect getaway (Oliveira et al., 2020).

This study explores the multifaceted influence of social media on vacation travel planning, delving into its ability to ignite wanderlust, streamline research processes, and redefine the notion of discovery. From the allure of visually stunning destinations showcased on Instagram to the real-time recommendations shared by fellow travelers on Twitter, social media has fundamentally transformed how individuals conceptualize, organize, and embark on their travel journeys.

Embarking on a vacation is no longer just about reaching a destination; it is about immersing oneself in a curated narrative of exploration and discovery. Through the lens of social media, travelers can glimpse into the experiences of others, gathering insights, tips, and insider knowledge that enrich their adventure (Liu et al., 2020). From immersive travel blogs to captivating YouTube vlogs, the digital landscape offers a treasure trove of narratives that inspire and inform, empowering individuals to craft personalized itineraries that cater to their unique preferences and interests.

Moreover, social media platforms have democratized the travel planning process, dismantling traditional barriers to information and access (Karlovitz, 2020). With a few taps on a smartphone screen, travelers can access a wealth of resources, from crowd-sourced reviews on TripAdvisor and booking.com to virtual tours on Facebook and YouTube. This democratization of information empowers individuals to make informed decisions, enabling them to navigate unfamiliar terrain with confidence and ease.

However, amidst the allure of picture-perfect destinations and envy-inducing snapshots, social media presents a paradoxical challenge: the pressure to curate an idealized version of one's travel experiences. As travelers strive to capture the perfect shot for their Instagram feed or craft the most engaging narrative for their travel blog, there is a risk of prioritizing aesthetic appeal over authentic experience. In an age where likes and shares serve as currency, the quest for validation can overshadow the intrinsic value of exploration and discovery (Kapoor et al., 2022).

In light of these complexities, it is evident that the role of social media in vacation travel planning is both transformative and nuanced. As one navigates the digital landscape in search of inspiration and connection, it is essential to strike a balance between curated content and authentic experience, leveraging the power of social media to enrich rather than detract from travel journeys. By embracing the opportunities afforded by social media while remaining mindful of its pitfalls, travelers can embark on adventures that are as enriching as they are memorable, weaving together the threads of digital storytelling and real-world discovery to create a tapestry of unforgettable experiences.

Social media emerges as a powerful catalyst shaping customer behavior within the tourism sector. Platforms such as Instagram, Facebook, and TripAdvisor serve as virtual marketplaces where travelers seek inspiration, gather information, and share their experiences with a global audience. The democratization of content creation empowers individuals to become influencers, storytellers, and brand ambassadors, wielding influence that transcends traditional marketing channels. From virtual tours and user-generated reviews to influencer endorsements and destination marketing campaigns, social media permeates every facet of the travel journey, profoundly shaping perceptions, preferences, and purchase decisions (So et al., 2021).

In this exploration of the nexus between the tourism sector, customer behavior, and social media, it becomes evident that their interconnectedness forms the cornerstone of a dynamic ecosystem. By recognizing the importance of each component and its interplay, stakeholders can leverage this synergetic relationship to drive sustainable growth, foster meaningful connections, and enrich the millions of travel experiences around the globe.

By emphasizing the holiday trip planning model developed by Matikiti-Manyevere and Kruger (2019), this study aims to establish a relationship between social media and holiday travel planning among travelers of the Kurdistan Region of Iraq.

As the popularity of social media grows, the tourism industry, like any other industry, has taken advantage of the vast development of social media. However, there has been a negligible quantity of studies that have been conducted in this industry, while social media and marketing are becoming more interesting every day.

The significance of this study is to help readers and future scholars understand the impact of social media on Kurdish travelers. In addition, this study will help tourism marketers analyze digital marketing campaigns. Similarly, it will provide insight into customers about their decisions on the travel destination.

In addition, this research will explore the way information and communication technology is changing tourism marketing while the usage of social media sites for promoting tourism in the Kurdistan Region is markedly growing.

10.2 Literature Review

10.2.1 Social Media: Concepts and Categories

In the last decade, the world has witnessed a rapid proliferation of a new type of information technology known as social media. It has been defined in various ways. It is defined as a "platform to create profiles, make explicit and traverse relationships" (Boyd & Ellison, 2007). Social media is an internet-based platform that supports interpersonal communications and connections. The most well-known websites are Facebook, LinkedIn, and Twitter, which are used by millions of users around the world (Grover et al., 2022).

Social media platforms include social networking sites such as Facebook, media-sharing sites such as YouTube and Instagram, professional networking sites such as LinkedIn, blogs and forums, and commerce communities such as Amazon.com.

New social media platforms might increase with more technology advancement. By the end of 2024, it is estimated to be 5.17 billion total social media users worldwide.[1]

According to the literature on social media, there have been multiple considerable arguments about the definition of social media and the way it is interpreted. As the use of social media continues to evolve, the description of social media also recurrently changes. Van Looy (2022) emphasized several definitions of social media from various sources. Based on that, social media can be defined as the following:

1. An online platform, network, application, tool, and media that depend on information technology
2. A peer-to-peer channel of communication that allows the creation of online content and enables collaboration among individuals, public, organizations, and communities
3. Social media connect individual users to form a virtual community by providing cross-cultural platforms and, as a result, influencing an individual's behavior

In recent years, the use of social networks has become an extensive cultural, social, and economic phenomenon (Bessarab et al., 2021). Millions of people adopted social networks to perform social activities, creating virtual communities and conducting various activities of interest including personal events such as wedding ceremonies, vacations, and gossiping.

However, despite the wide adoption of social media for interpersonal communication, their application for marketing, knowledge management, and organizational purpose has just started. While social network technologies have adapted across different cultures and different industries, businesses have just realized the importance of social media sites for their organizations.

10.2.1.1 Social Media Types

Social Networking Sites

Social networking is a website where individuals can meet and communicate online by creating an account in order to make relationships, communicate, and get connected with users that they might not even know. However, some authors refer to all social media websites with different features such as video- and photo-sharing capabilities as social networking sites (Miller, 2020). Moreover, some of the social networking sites are niche-oriented and are built for a particular group of users.

Blogs and Microblogs

Blogs are defined as websites where personal experiences and insight of bloggers about a particular topic can be read. Readers can interact with bloggers by posting comments and keeping logs (Reinhardt, 2019). Blogs could be text, image, audio, or video based, depending on the blogger's preference. In addition, Miller (2020)

[1] https://sproutsocial.com/insights/social-media-statistics/

defined microblogs as a slighter form of blogs that can be used for the same purpose of sharing experience by bloggers, but only to a different extent, that microblogs are only text-based, along with a limited number of characteristics.

Content Community Sites

Content community sites are the type of social media sites that present modified material from the original work of the uploader. Generally, the modified content consists of text, photos, videos, or slide presentations (Mainolfi et al., 2022). According to Cheung et al. (2021), content community sites are unlike other social media sites since content community sites do not require the creation of a personal profile to be able to share or use its modified materials.

Virtual Worlds

A virtual world is an online application that presents the real world in three dimensions. As a result, it enables users to communicate with each other. However, the virtual worlds are sometimes restricted by gaming rules that limit the interactions (Eraslan & Kukuoglu, 2019).

10.2.1.2 Types of Tourism Related to Leisure

Leisure (Holiday) Tourism

Holiday tourism is a period of total rest usually held in a tranquil area with some attractions in the nearby areas in which everyday activities are replaced by others. Leisure holiday predominates among all other types of tourism because this type of tourism is widespread among the urban population, especially those in major economic centers due to accumulated stress deployed in the dynamic economies of today. Quite the opposite, among rural residents, this type of tourism is not practiced very much yet, relatively due to low-income status as well as reduced mobility among people (Lehto et al., 2024).

Recreation to Health Care Tourism

The oldest type of tourism is recreation related to health care. The economic and social aspects of modern life have led to the amplification of this type of tourism. In addition, there are several other factors, which have led to the need for this type of tourism and recovery of health. These factors are pollution in urban areas, the sedentary lifestyle of towns, and illnesses manifested from lack of natural nutrition. The demand for this type of tourism is linked to the diversification of services in a specific area, and the duration of such a trip is linked to the need for treatment according to a medical prescription. Also, the period of such tourism is usually above 3 weeks (Şengül & Çora, 2020).

Tourism Visitation

Tourism visitation consists of several types of tourism. It is also recreational tourism while keeping a strong cultural side. The traveler choosing this type of tourism is mainly intellectual and desires to broaden his/her horizon or general cultural knowledge. Unlike two previous types of travelers, tourism visitation consists of a small number of participants. Moreover, tourism visitation occurs more in the summer season, and the trip routes can be modified easily because of relative factors of climate changes during spring. Tourism visitation is also practiced during weekends, normally in close areas to the location of tourists (Khairi & Darmawan, 2021).

10.2.1.3 Role of Social Media in Traveling

The development of information technology has significantly increased the usage of social media, which considerably affected customer behavior and their decision-making process. In more detail, social media has affected the decision-making process of customers in every aspect of purchasing a product or service to planning a holiday trip. Social media is denoted as a communication channel that conveys tourist-generated information to other prospective tourists (Liu et al., 2020). Analysis of Spyridou et al. (2022) showed that tourist customers usually check online reviews and specialized blogs, and pages before planning a trip, and in general, tourist customers trust online information rather than any other sources.

Currently, the majority of tourist customers rely on social media to search, evaluate, and select a specific destination. In addition to this, they also rely on social media to share their travel experience and stories with others. Fortunately, all social media applications enable the users to share messages, photos, videos, and their comments and feedback that serve as a source of testimonials to know about problems and facilities available within the destination.

The findings of other scholars indicate that travelers mostly use social media after returning home from a trip to share their travel experience. Therefore, a strong relationship is shown between the impact made by social media and changes made in a holiday plan for several times before making the final decision (Corral-Gonzalez et al., 2023).

According to Tsiakali (2018), user-generated content is perceived to be more trustworthy compared to official websites of the travel agencies or mass media advertisement. For example, Oliveira et al. (2020) conducted an investigation to indicate how social media affect traveler's perception and emotions before the end of a trip. According to their study, it is confirmed that a social media page such as Facebook could influence traveler's perception and emotions, and therefore, it resulted in improving their traveling experience.

10.2.1.4 Implications of Social Media Use in the Tourism Industry

Based on the literature review of social media, there are a number of implications associated with social media for travelers in the tourism industry. Generally, this study suggests that social media influences travelers. However, the influence sometimes might be negative, which might come from the implication associated with social media platforms. First of all, from the perspective of technological innovation, some issues have been raised with the innovation potential of social media platforms. In addition, as for any other online platform, social media can constraint its users due to language barriers.

As a result, it lacks the information dissemination. In this English language-dominated world, non-English-speaking travelers are constrained to use international platforms for travel planning, and this also hinders the non-English-speaking practitioner in the tourism sector from reaching the international market (Pung et al., 2022).

However, many international social media platforms are taking advantage of difficulty by attracting more customers to use their platforms by adding multiple languages to their websites, so it is easier to be practiced by all users. Thus, social media platforms with multiple languages will be beneficial for both supply and demand purposes. In contrast, current search engines fail to leverage information produced on different social media platforms entirely. Therefore, this requires designing the websites and innovation to evolve social media development and to share information on different social media sources (Pasquinelli et al., 2023).

Moreover, from the perspective of social media management in the tourism industry, there are plenty of drawbacks associated with using social media either in trip planning or tourism management. Social media generated electronic word of mouth (E-WOM) can be a source of negative influence from the dissatisfied customers (Chopra et al., 2022). Thus, today the tourism industry is facing more difficulty after the advent of social media. If not managed properly, the dissatisfied customer can make a negative influence as the way satisfied customers do.

10.3 Methodology

10.3.1 Introduction

This research adopted the deductive/quantitative method. Simultaneously, it adopted a positivistic paradigm using a survey questionnaire. Since the quantitative approach has been used, this research mainly is based on primary data. A survey questionnaire was conducted in five tourism spots in Erbil governorate. The questionnaire was conducted through personal interviews. In this sense, a judgmental sampling technique was applied. Data are collected from 400 respondents who traveled abroad at least once in their past 12 months.

For analyzing the data, descriptive statistics has been used to analyze the personal profile and demography of respondents. Two data analysis methods are employed which were canonical correlation analysis (CCA) and factor analysis (FA) (principal component analysis). Canonical correlation analysis is applied to find the relationship between variables to predict the impact of social media on travelers' decision-making stages and travel planning. At the same time, principal component analysis (PCA) with varimax rotation was applied to identify the factors that influenced the tourist's destination selection decision. For analyzing the data, SPSS IBM has been used.

10.3.2 Population, Sampling Technique, and Data Collection Method

The target population was customers of five selected tourism spots in Erbil who traveled abroad at least once for any reason in their past 12 months to investigate their holiday travel planning. Tourism is defined as "the activities of a person traveling outside his or her usual environment for less than a specific period and whose main purpose of travel is other than exercising an activity remunerated from the place visited" (Page & Connell, 2020). This concept was employed to differentiate travelers from the public quickly.

This study employed a nonprobability sampling technique. The Cochran formula is used to determine the sample size (Cochran, 1963; Nanjundeswaraswamy & Divakar, 2021). The calculation takes into account the desired level of accuracy, the desired level of confidence, and the estimated proportion of attributes presented in the population. For a large population, Cochran developed the below equation, which yields an ideal sample for this research.

$$n_0 = \frac{z^2 pq}{\mathrm{e}^2}$$

- e indicates the margin error or the desired level of precision.
- p is the proportion of the population that has the attribute in the research,
- q is equal to $1 - p$.
- Z2 is the abscissa of the standard curve, and this value can be found in Cochran's statistical table, which consists of the area under the curve.

As a result of a calculation based on the Cochran formula with a 95% desired level of precision, and 5% accepted marginal error, a total of 400 travelers were selected. The target population was based on the total number of travelers departed or landed in Erbil airport from January to May, 2019, which were 731,220 travelers.[2]

A questionnaire tool is used to collect the primary data for this research, as it is the most suitable instrument for collecting data (Adinegara et al., 2017).

For ethical considerations, the researcher explained the objective of the research to the surveyors. The link to the Google survey was shared with the participants, and an overview of the study was described at the beginning of the questionnaire to direct the importance of their participation. The participants were also aware that their responses would remain confidential as it was for academic research. To keep

[2] https://krso.gov.krd/content/upload/1/root/air-transportation-statistics-report-at-the-kurdistan-region-airports-2022.pdf

respondents' feeling trusted about the investigation, no personal questions have been asked. Ethical standards have also been critically observed while conducting the pilot study. The right to privacy was also ensured by giving the respondents the option not to submit their responses at the end if they have been deemed necessary to withdraw.

10.3.3 Conceptualization and Operationalization of the Variables

According to Cicciola et al. (2014), conceptualization refers to the process, whereby the main constructs of the study are given theoretical meaning. The two main constructs of the study, social media, and holiday travel planning have been theoretically defined in the literature review.

The independent variable for this study (social media) is defined as a platform to create profiles and make explicit and traverse relationships (Ellingson & Sotirin, 2020). The essential variable of this study (holiday travel planning) is defined as the three stages of travel planning which are pre-trip stage, during-trip stage, and post-trip stage (Matikiti-Manyevere & Kruger, 2019).

The independent variable comprises several subvariables: social media usage and trust in social media. The following variables are measured through indicators such as the number of hours social media is used, source of information, types of social media, information search, personal factors, and E-WoM. On the other hand, the dependent variable of the study, holiday travel planning, was measured based on the three stages adopted from Manyevere and Kruger's model.

10.4 Data Analysis and Interpretation of Results

10.4.1 Descriptive Analysis

The survey questionnaire was divided into four sections, and the analysis has been conducted in the same order (the questionnaire is attached in the appendices).

The sections are as follows:

Section One: Personal Information of Respondents and Use of Social Media.
Section Two: Travelers and Social Media Information.
Section Three: Social Media Usage Levels and Purpose of Use during the Holiday Planning.
Section Four: Trusting Social Media and its Influence on Holiday Planning.

Personal Information of Respondents and Usage of Social Media
The personal information of the respondents is presented to understand the demographic characteristics of the participants. The participants are nationals of the Kurdistan Region who had at least one trip in the last 12 months. The personal information of respondents is presented in Table 10.1.

According to the data collected, 58.5% of participants were male, and 41.5% were female.

Unsurprisingly, given the cultural factors, females are as independent as males in the Kurdistan Region when it comes to traveling. According to IOM (2018), KRI is a gender-balanced community.

Table 10.1 Personal Information of Respondents

		Frequency	Percent
Gender	Male	234	58.5
	Female	166	41.5
Age category	18–24 years	53	13.25
	25–34 years	238	59.5
	35–44 years	92	23
	45–54 years	15	3.75
	55 or above	2	0.5
Education level	Primary school	6	1.50
	High school	15	3.75
	Undergraduate	59	14.75
	Graduate	303	75.75
	Postgraduate	17	4.25
Occupation	Employed	316	79
	Self-employed	48	12
	Unemployed	36	9
Income	Less or equal to 500,000IQD	36	9
	Between 500,000 to 1000,000IQD	60	15
	Between 1000,000 to 1500,000IQD	88	22
	Between 1500,000 to 2000,000IQD	80	20
	Equal or above to 2000,000IQD	136	34
Use of social media per day	30 min or less	19	4.75
	1 h	70	17.50
	1–2 h	117	29.25
	2–3 h	103	25.75
	3 h and more	91	22.75
Frequency of travelling per year	Once a year	148	37
	Twice a year	104	26
	Three times a year	48	12
	More than three times	64	16
	Not sure	36	9
Total		400	100

59.5% of the respondents aged 25-34 years old, 23% of the respondents aged between 35 and 44 years old, 13.25% of the respondents aged between 18 and 24 years old, 3.75% of the respondents aged between 45 and 54 years old, and 0.5% of the respondents are equal or above to 55 years old.

Also, most respondents have at least one educational degree. People with a bachelor's degree usually use social media more compared to people who are in high school or have a higher education degree.

Three hundred and three respondents (75.75%) hold a graduate degree, 59 respondents (14.75%) are undergraduate students, 17 respondents (4.25%) are the holder of a postgraduate degree, 15 respondents (3.75%) are high school students, and 6 respondents (1.5%) are primary school students. These findings of the education level of respondents are in line with Jacobsen and Forste's (2011) research, as they stated that university students and degree holders are mostly active on social media platforms such as Facebook, and they are mainly generators of online content by reviewing and providing feedback in the online communities.

In this research, 317 respondents (79.25%) are employed, while 49 respondents (12.25%) are self-employed, and 34 respondents (8.5%) are unemployed.

Many studies emphasized on the positive and significant relationship between income and usage of social media. The higher the income, the more social media is used per day. In this research, the majority of respondents earn 2000,000 IQD or above per month. In addition, scholars such as Gretzel and Yoo (2017) stated that both demographic characteristics such as income and level of education even differ with the type of social media used. For example, users of LinkedIn tend to be more educated as well as higher-paid compared to users of Facebook. The users of social media pages such as Facebook tend to be more students, while users of LinkedIn tend to be more full-time employees.

In addition, the use of social media by respondents is investigated. Seventy respondents (17.5%) use social media for 1 h per day. Also, 117 respondents (29.25%) use social media 1 to 2 h per day. One hundred and three respondents (25.75%) use social media 2–3 h and more per day. However, during a day, 91 respondents (22.75%) use social media for 3 h and more per day. Furthermore, 19 respondents (4.75%) use social media for half an hour or less during a day. This information presents that majority of the respondents use social media between 1 and 2 h per day (Fig. 10.6).

Travelers and Social Media Information

One hundred and fifty respondents (37.5%) travel abroad once a year. One hundred and three respondents (25.75%) travel abroad twice a year. Fifty respondents (12.5%) travel abroad three times a year, and 63 respondents (15.75%) travel abroad more than three times a year. However, 34 respondents (8.5%) were not sure how many times they travel per year.

In this section, the purpose of the frequent travels of respondents has also been examined. Two hundred and forty four respondents (61%) frequently travel to have leisure. Also, 65 respondents (16.25%) travel to reunite with their families. Also, 64 respondents (16%) travel for work purposes. Fourteen respondents (3.5%) travel to

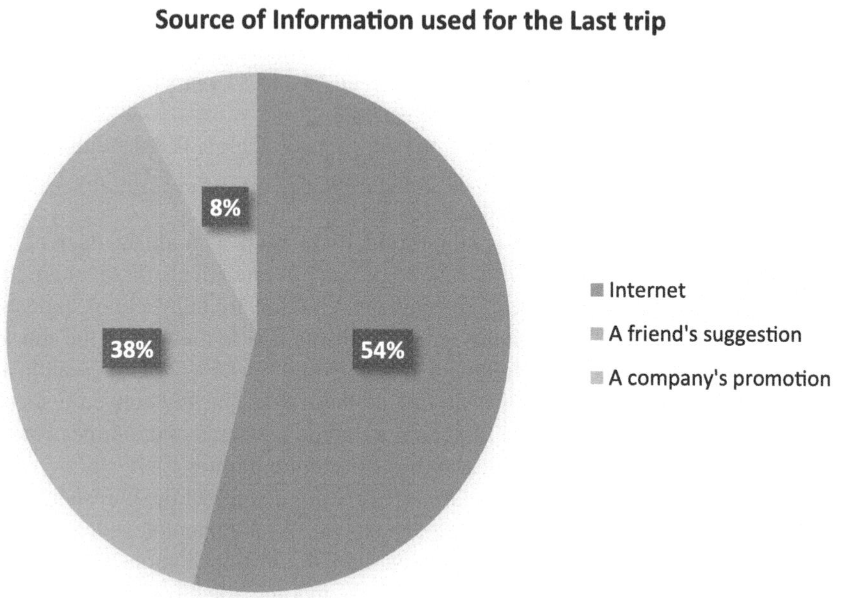

Fig. 10.1 Source of information used for the last trip

receive medical treatment. Thirteen respondents (3.25%) travel to attend educational courses or conferences.

In the survey, the used source of information for last trip planning by travelers have also been explored. Generally, 216 respondents (54%) relied on the Internet for their whole travel planning. One hundred anf fifty two respondents (38%) relied on their friend's suggestion for their travel planning. However, the company's promotions also played a role in the trip planning of travelers as 32 respondents (8%) have relied on promotions made by companies on their last trip (Fig. 10.1).

More specifically, 212 respondents (53%) used Booking.com during their last trip. Following that, TripAdvisor has been the mostly used travel arrangement application by 111 respondents (27.75%). In addition, Airbnb has been used by 17 respondents (4.25%), and Trivago has been used by 25 respondents (6.25%). However, other 35 respondents (8.75%) of the total have relied on different sources for their travel arrangement such as local agencies, eDream application, Google Trips, travel websites, or relied on the family plan. (Fig. 10.2).

Social media has become a popular tool for searching information among people due to different reasons. According to data collected, 215 respondents (53.75%) search for information on social media due to its ease of access. In comparison, 99 respondents (24.75%) use social media searching for information since it has multiple sources of information. However, in a small group of respondents, 22 respondents (5.5%) find social media reliable searching for information. Twenty four respondents (6%) use social media searching for information since social media information is trustworthy to them. Furthermore, 25 respondents (6.25%) use social

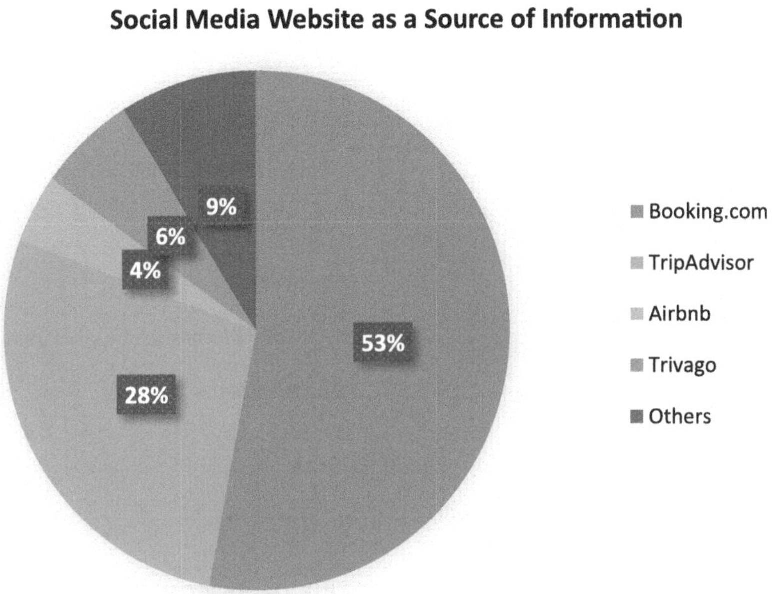

Fig. 10.2 Social media website as a source of information

media searching for information because they can collect feedback from other social media users with a similar interest. Fifteen respondents (3.75%) do not use social media searching for information at all (Fig. 10.3).

In the following part, factors influenced the last trip of travelers are investigated. The level of importance has been categorized as very important, medium important, less important, and not crucial toward each factor of the duration of trip, budget of the trip, shopping purpose, leisure, treatment purpose, and adventure, as it is presented in both (Fig. 10.4).

The question was: "which one of the following factors prioritized your last trip?"

In answer, the respondents presented that budget of the trip has been the most important factor in prioritizing the last destination by travelers. In contrast, receiving medical treatment has been the least important factor in prioritizing the last destination by travelers and having leisure time. Two hundred and forty five respondents (61.25%) have considered the budget of the trip as the most important factor in prioritizing their last trip, and 2 respondents (0.50%) have considered leisure and medical treatment as the least important factor for prioritizing their last trip (Table 10.2).

> I check on the experience of other travellers on social media by checking their comments, reviews and feedback after they have been to a specific destination.

According to Hede and Kellett (2012) and Thevenot (2007), social media-generated electronic word of mouth (E-WOM) could be a negative source of

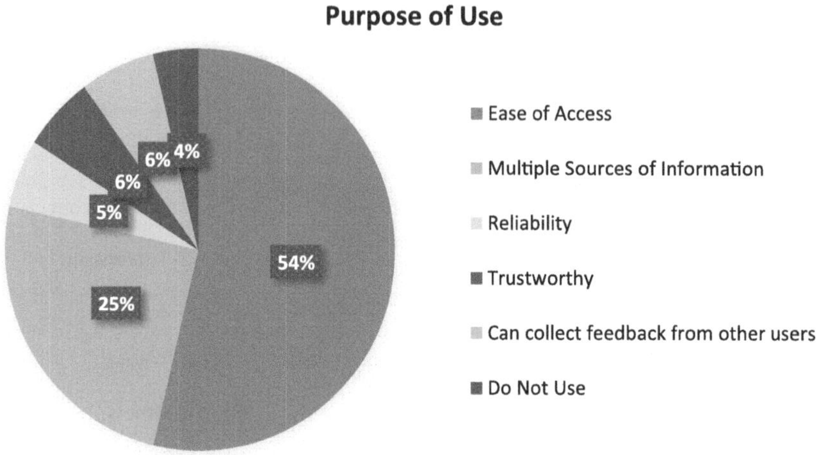

Fig. 10.3 Information search on social media

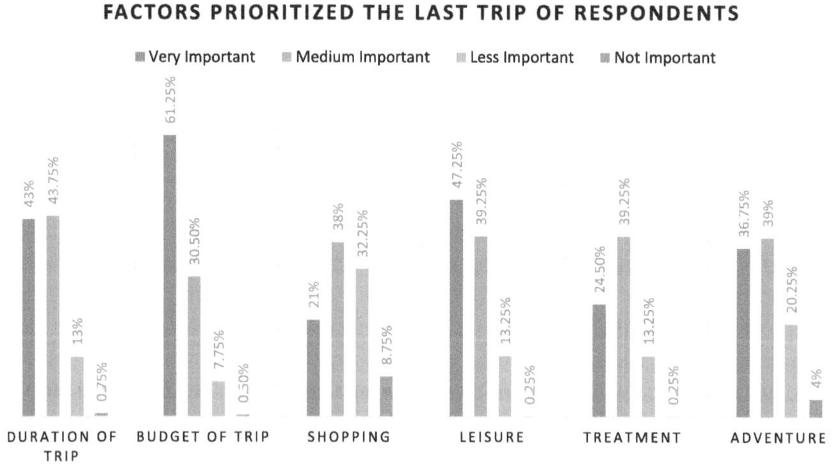

Fig. 10.4 Factors prioritized the last trip of respondents

Table 10.2 Factors prioritized the last destination of respondents

Level of Importance	Duration of Trip	Budget of Trip	Shopping	Leisure	Treatment	Adventure
Very important	172	245	84	189	98	147
Medium important	175	122	152	157	163	156
Less important	50	31	129	53	84	81
Not important	1	2	35	1	55	1
Total number of respondents	400	400	400	400	400	400

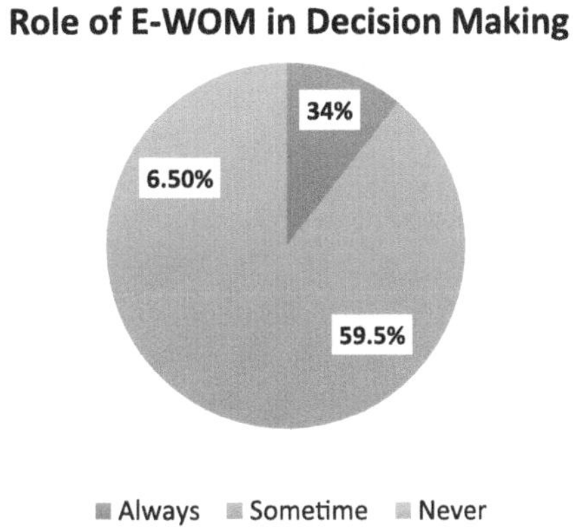

Fig. 10.5 Role of electronic word of mouth in decision-making

influence from the dissatisfied customers. Thus, today the tourism industry is facing more difficulty after the advent of social media websites. When it is not managed appropriately, the dissatisfied customer can make a negative influence as the way satisfied customers do. In this regard, the respondents are questioned if they check the experience of other travelers and reviewed their comments and feedback.

In answer, 136 respondents (34%) indicated that they always check on the experience of former travelers before making a decision. Two hundred and thirty eight respondents (59.5%) sometimes check on the experience of others while only 26 respondents (6.50%) never check on reviews and comments of others (Fig. 10.5).

Do you make comments, reviews and feedback on social media after your travel experience?

In general, commenting and reviewing on social media pages has become a standard approach for providing feedback about a service or product. In this sense, 245 respondents (61.25%) sometimes provide feedback about their experience after a trip, and 35 respondents (8.75%) always review and comment about their experience after a trip. However, 120 respondents (30%) indicated that they never comment, review, or give feedback after their travel experience (Fig. 10.6).

Social Media Usage Levels and Reasons for Use During Holiday Planning

In this section, the uses of social media for three levels of holiday planning are tested. In the first stage, which is the pre-trip decision-making process, 210 respondents (52.50%) showed that they use social media mostly for collecting information about selected destination and accommodation, 127 respondents (31.75%) use social media to review feedback and comments of former travelers before going to a specific destination, and 63 respondents (15.75%) use social media searching for a new destination before making a decision (Fig. 10.7).

During the trip, travelers use social media for other different reasons. One hundred and ninety six respondents (49%) use social media to share and post their travel experience with others during the trip. However, 113 respondents (28.25%) use social media to stay connected with their family and friends during their journey,

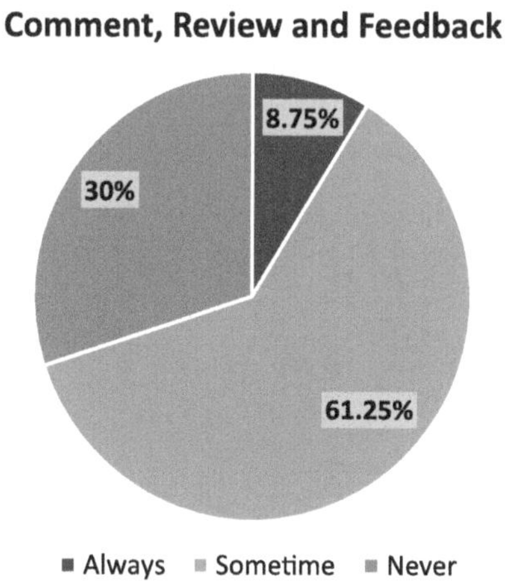

Fig. 10.6 Comment, review, and feedback

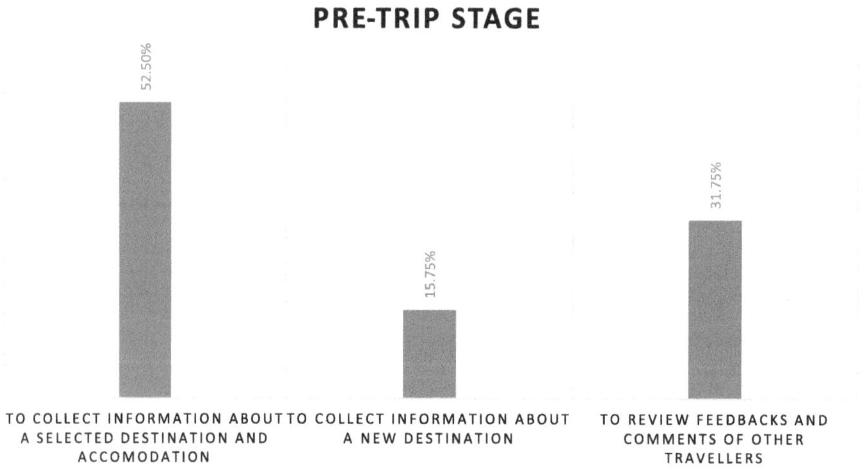

Fig. 10.7 Pre-trip stage

and 91 respondents (22.75%) use social media to find more travel-related information (Fig. 10.8).

According to a ComScore report (Hakeem), after the trip, 45% of the travelers' post travel-related information on social media, write online reviews, and create social media-generated content. In this study, 139 respondents (34.75%) use social media to provide feedback and comments about the destination in general. Besides, 172 respondents (43%) use social media to give feedback and comments about the tour services and accommodations they relied on the destination during the trip. In addition, the other 89 respondents (22.25%) use social media to share their travel experience with others (Fig. 10.9).

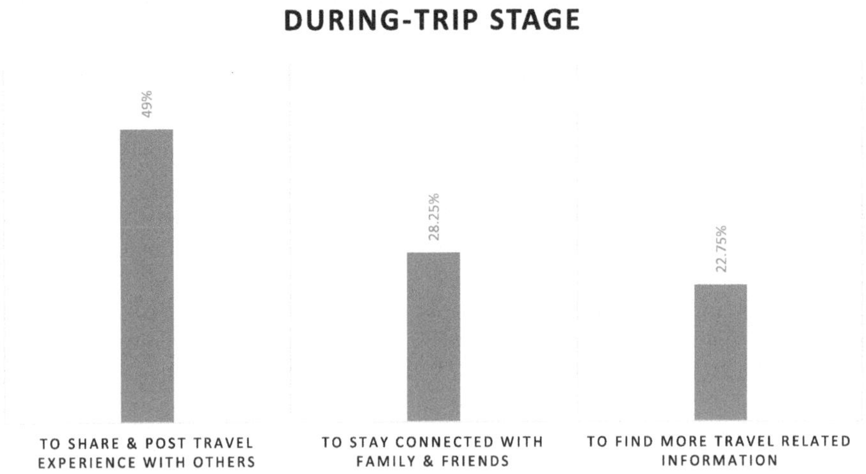

Fig. 10.8 During-trip stage

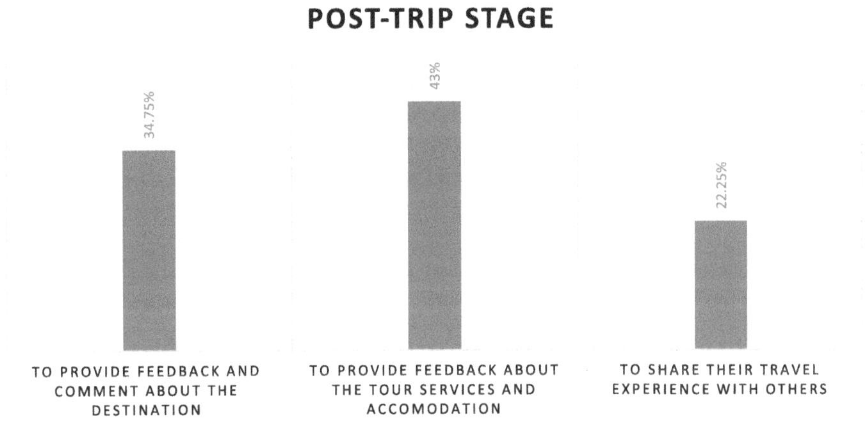

Fig. 10.9 Post-trip stage

Trust on Social Media and its Influence on Holiday Plan
In this section, the influence of social media on holiday plan of travelers has been examined. The participants have been allowed to indicate their level of satisfaction with the following sentence "during holiday planning, social media affects my plan." In response, 213 respondents (53.25%) indicated that they were very satisfied with this statement, which shows that social media has a huge impact on the planning of travelers. Also, 149 respondents (37.25%) were satisfied with the statement. However, 19 respondents (4.75%) have been neutral on the statement and could not indicate their level of satisfaction with the statement. On the contrary, ten

respondents (2.50%) have been dissatisfied with the statement that social media affects their planning, and nine respondents (2.25%) have been very dissatisfied (Fig. 10.10).

As social media impact travel planning, the change in respondent's choice during their last trip has been explored. One hundred and seventy six respondents (44%) indicated that their choice of destination changed during their last trip, 154 respondents (38.5%) showed that their choice of accommodation in a specific destination changed, and 70 respondents (17.5%) whole trip planning changed before making final decision (Fig. 10.11).

In general, 215 respondents (53.75%) are most likely to change their travel plan after searching for photos and videos shared by previous travelers about their experience. Meanwhile, 91 respondents (22.75%) change their travel plan once they are exposed to poor comments and feedback about a specific destination or a choice of accommodation. Also, 94 respondents (23.5%) change their travel plan based on fascinating comments that come from other social media users. Basically, negative or positive user-generated content (UGC) affects the planning of travelers (Fig. 10.12).

Moreover, the impact of information on social media on trip planning has also been questioned. Information on social media has been supportive of many travelers around the world in terms of trip planning and decision-making. Two hundred and seven respondents (51.75%) have received good support from available information on social media in order to make their trip planning decision. Also, 41 respondents (10.25%) have received maximum support. In general, this shows that the majority of respondents found information on social media useful to them for their trip planning. However, 122 respondents (30.5%) have received medium support from social media information, and 14 respondents (3.50%) have not received any support at all.

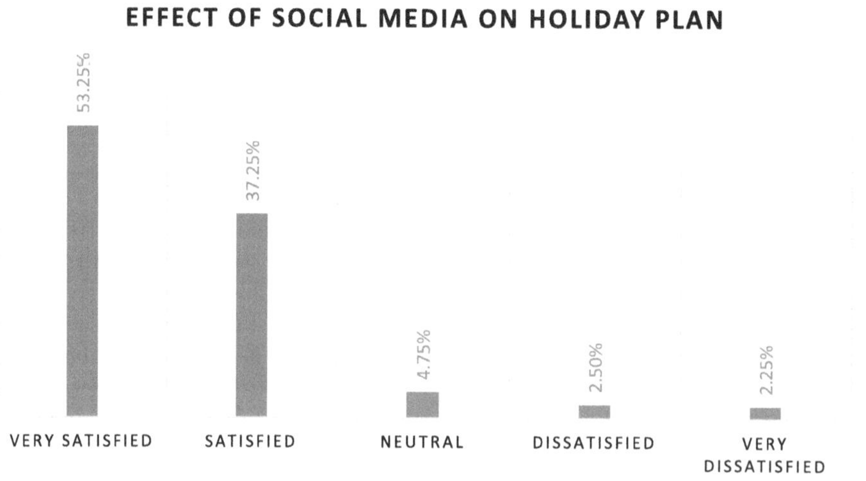

Fig. 10.10 Effect of social media on holiday plan

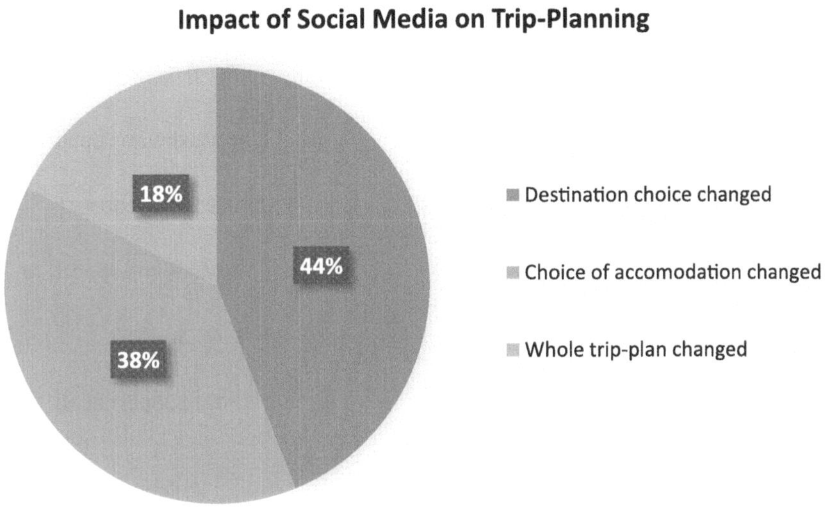

Fig. 10.11 Impact of social media on trip planning

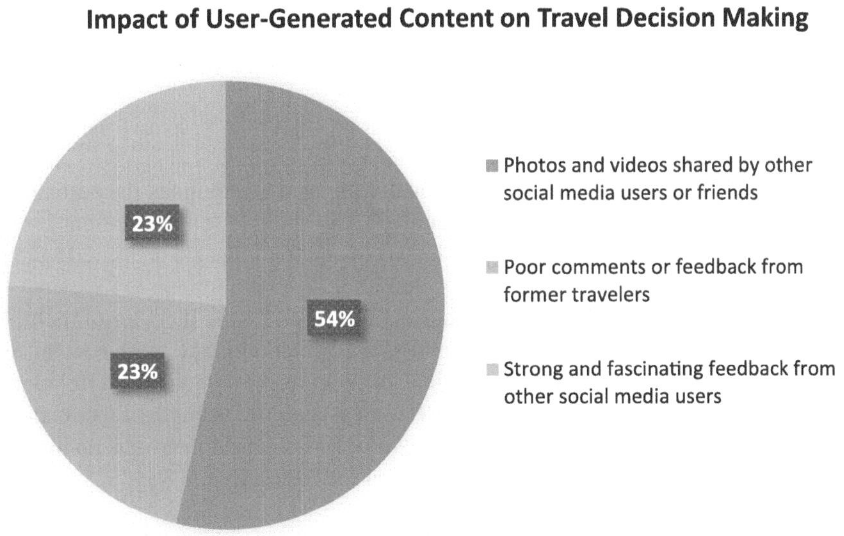

Fig. 10.12 Impact of user-generated content on travel decision-making

Furthermore, the other 16 respondents (4%) have not been able to identify the level of usefulness of social media information (Fig. 10.13).

To summarize this section, the researcher responded to the second research question, which is what are the demographic characteristics of travelers that are impacted by social media during each stage of travel planning and decision-making process?

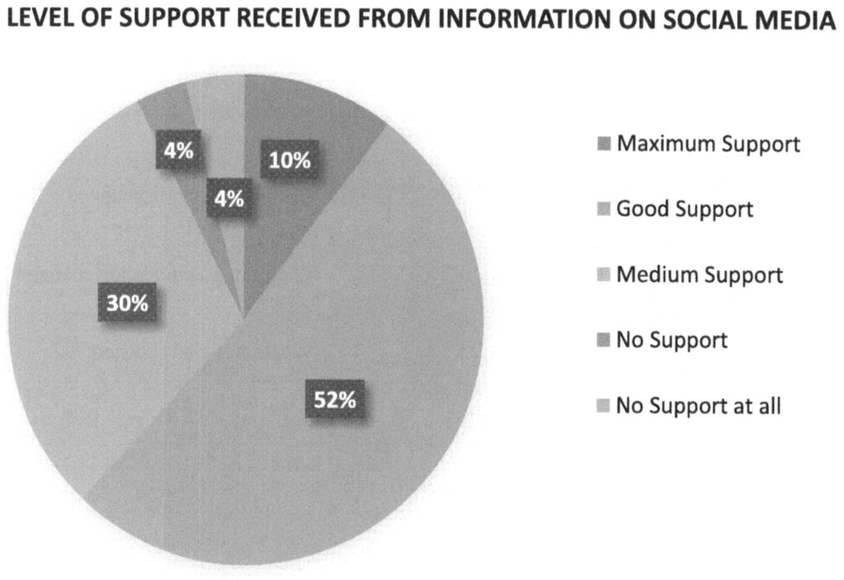

Fig. 10.13 Level of support received from information on social media

10.4.2 Canonical Correlation Analysis (CCA)

10.4.2.1 Overall

Canonical correlation is a form of statistical analysis that examines the correlation of two latent variables. In this type of analysis, the variable sets are presented as a dependent set of variables and independent set of variables that are measured against the indicators.

Canonical to Bhatia, correlation analysis (CCA) is a family member of multiple general linear hypotheses (MGLH). Canonical correlation is the most generalized family member of multivariate statistical techniques. In canonical correlations, despite having the primary purpose, which is measuring the strength of the relationship between two latent variables, it is also useful to understand the number of dimensions needed to account for the variables' relationship.

10.4.2.2 Canonical Correlation Using SPSS

In SPSS, canonical correlation (CC) is a MANOVA Command in which a set of variables has to be referred as "dependent," and the other set of variables has to be referred to as "covariates." It is available only in "Syntax," not from the SPSS menus.

10.4.2.3 Level of Significance

As within research using statistical techniques, the statistically significant level of functions of whose canonical correlation coefficients are typically beyond some level of 0.05 or above is the most common practice to determine the analysis. If any independent function is estimated to be insignificant, the relationship among those variables is not going to be interpreted. De Vaus and de Vaus (2013) argued that 0.6 scale is considered as an acceptable level of reliability of data. Also, according to Sekaran, the reliability of data rises as alpha approaches 1.0. On the contrary, the reliability of data decreases when the alpha reaches 0.6. In this case, the reliability is considered low with a 0.7 level of significance, while it is deemed to be acceptable with 0.8, or when it is above, it is considered as high.

However, many authors believe that using a single criterion, such as the level of significance, is very superficial. Alternatively, it is recommended that, at least, more than one criterion, in conjunction, to be used with another in order to decide the correct canonical function to be interpreted.

In this study, the canonical correlation analysis of the data has mainly produced three criteria, which are:

(Hakeem) the level of significance of functions
(Hakeem) the magnitude of the canonical correlations (CCM)
(Hakeem) the percentage of coefficient variance accounted from data sets (this is similar to multiple regression analysis *R2*)

Furthermore, the dependent set is the traveler's decision-making process that included (7) indicators to measure changes in the three phases of decision-making and travel planning.

V20, V421, and V22 are used to measure the changes in the three phases of travel decision-making process, while V23, V24, V25, and V26 are aimed at traveler's planning.

Independent variable set: The role of social media sites that include 19 indicators is labeled as V1 to V19: for the personal information of respondents is labeled as V1 to V6 and for social media usage and trust on social media for traveling is labeled as V7 to V15.

Table 10.3 indicates the eigenvalues of the dependent set of variables. The relative size of the eigenvalues reflects the variations in the canonical correlation. The first correlation is the largest as it is corresponding to the first eigenvalue, which is followed by all subsequent smaller eigenvalues of dependent variables.

In SPSS pack, several multivariate statistics are available, so as to test the null hypothesis and to prove that the canonical correlations are zero, which means that the variables under study have no linear relationship (Table 10.4).

Pillai's trace is the first test name of the three multivariate statistics calculated by SPSS, which is the sum of the squared canonical correlations. According to Table 10.3, Pillai's trace is $(0.54968)^2 + (0.47251)^2 + (0.40601)^2 + (0.38316)^2 + (0.31505)^2 + (0.22518)^2 + (0.16932)^2 = 1.01570$, which can be found in the section

Table 10.3 Eigenvalues and canonical correlations

Dependent Variables Root No.	Eigenvalue	Percentage of sum of eigenvalue	Cumulative Percentage	Canonical Correlation	Square Correlation
1	0.43297	33.74668	33.74668	0.54968	0.30215
2	0.28744	22.40416	56.15085	0.47251	0.22327
3	0.19738	15.38475	71.53559	0.40601	0.16485
4	0.17207	13.41178	84.94738	0.38316	0.14681
5	0.11019	8.58887	93.53624	0.31505	0.09926
6	0.05341	4.16329	97.69953	0.22518	0.05071
7	0.02951	2.30047	100.00000	0.16932	0.02867

Table 10.4 Multivariate test of significance

Test Name g of F	Value	Approx. F	Hypoth. DF	Error DF	Significance of F statistics
Pillai's	1.01570	3.39456	133.00	2660.00	0.000
Hotelling's	1.28299	3.59127	133.00	2606.00	0.000
Wilks'	0.32079	3.50356	133.00	2481.91	0.000

of output. This indicates that the correlation is highly significant at 99% level of significance, and there is a correlation between the variables under investigation.

Hotelling trace is the second test name of the three multivariate calculated by SPSS, which is very similar to Pillai's trace. Hotelling trace can be calculated by the sum of the values of (canonical correlation^2/ (1-canonical correlation^2)). For instance, for the first-dependent variable V43, the value is (0.54968^2 / $(1–0.54968)^2$). When the same calculation is repeated for the rest of six dependent variables as (0.47251^2 / $(1–0.47251)^2$) (0.40601^2 / $(1–0.40601)^2$) (0.38316^2 / $(1–0.38316)^2$) (0.31505^2 / $(1–0.31505)^2$) (0.22518^2 / $(1–0.22518)^2$) (0.16932^2 / $(1–0.16932)^2$), the sum is going to be equal to 1.28299. As a result, once more, the correlation will be highly significant.

Wilks' lambda is the third multivariate statistics calculated by SPSS, which is the product of the values of 1-canonical correlation. In this example, our canonical correlations are 0.54968, 0.47251, 0.40601, 0.38316, 0.31505, 0.22518, and 0.16932, so the Wilks' Lambda testing for all of the correlations is (1–0.54968) *(1–0.47251) *(1–0.40601) *(1–0.38316) *(1–0.31505) *(1–0.22518) *(1–0.16932) = 0.32079.

10.4.2.4 Interpretation of Raw Canonical Coefficients for Dependent and Independent Variables

The results of the raw canonical coefficients for dependent and independent variables are indicated in Table 10.5. The purpose of row canonical coefficients for covariates is to define the linear relationship between the dependent variables and

Table 10.5 Raw canonical coefficients for dependent and independent variables

Independent variables	Dependent variables						
	1	2	3	4	5	6	7
V1	−0.33749	−0.29980	−0.17049	0.31649	0.64565	0.32960	−1.11832
V2	−0.80185	0.08244	0.09538	0.59204	−0.29019	0.03537	0.12943
V3	0.14906	0.46299	−0.05846	−0.46674	0.01935	0.22241	0.58625
V4	0.11925	0.97980	0.60736	−0.18989	−0.01671	−0.00689	0.29012
V5	0.24020	0.37162	−0.12235	−0.05239	0.07584	−0.15075	0.21702
V6	0.28761	−0.00655	0.42704	0.08812	0.04331	0.29879	−0.38437
V7	0.10007	0.31656	−0.08693	0.04073	−0.00315	−0.18324	−0.26635
V8	−0.08871	0.26256	−0.13447	−0.28173	−0.01901	−0.10816	−0.20401
V9	0.23343	−0.08030	0.17502	0.25877	0.17222	0.45527	−0.05229
V10	0.00210	0.15202	−0.10629	0.00785	−0.09299	0.24389	−0.04580
V11	−0.20765	0.07049	0.25132	−0.23657	−0.23814	0.27257	0.05145
V12	−0.20057	−0.49329	0.27116	0.29945	−0.63305	−0.73354	−0.49353
V13	0.05751	0.18345	0.13586	−0.19901	−0.44288	0.96947	−0.01445
V14	0.09691	−0.27676	−0.11043	−0.17435	0.29657	0.19088	0.44074
V15	0.19165	−0.08326	0.18816	−0.51568	−0.03935	−0.49046	0.66150
V16	−0.10320	0.00384	0.11594	−0.01729	0.04463	0.14955	0.15944
V17	0.32698	−0.16773	−0.57087	−0.06620	−0.23681	0.35707	0.00692
V18	0.37274	−0.08190	0.25989	−0.67375	−0.53165	−0.02298	0.22175
V19	0.66694	0.39283	−0.19765	1.28493	−0.34280	−0.22007	0.55709

the independent variables. Interpretation of row canonical coefficients is a manner analogous to interpreting multiple linear regressions (linear regression coefficient).

For instance, for the first covariate, a one-unit increase in V1 leads to a 0.33749-unit decrease in D1, a 0.29980-unit decrease in D2, a 0.17049-unit decrease in D3, and a 1.11832-unit decrease in D7. This shows that there is a negative relationship between V1 with D1, D2, D3, and D7. On the contrary, there is a positive relationship between V1 with D4, D5, and D6. A one-unit increase in V1 will lead to a 0.31649-unit increase in D4, a 0.64565-unit increase in D5, and a 0.32960-unit increase in D6.

Regarding the second covariate, a one-unit increase in V2 will lead to a 0.8244-unit increase in D2, a 0.9538-unit increase in D3, a 0.59204-unit increase in D4, a 0.03537-unit increase in D6, and a 0.12943-unit increase in D7. This shows that there is a positive relationship between the age of respondents as social media users and usage of social media, specifically during-trip and post-trip stages as well as the change in travel planning. On the contrary, a one unit-increase in V2 will lead to a 0.80185-unit decrease in D1 and a 0.29019-unit decrease in D5. This indicates that there is a negative correlation between the age of respondents and pre-trip decision-making, as well as changes occurred in the respondent's last trip planning.

Regarding the third covariate, a one-unit increase in V3 will lead to a 0.14906-unit increase in D1, a 0.46299-unit increase in D2, a 0.01935-unit increase in D5, a 0.22241-unit increase in D6, and a 0.58625-unit increase in D7. This indicates that there is a positive correlation between the education level of respondents and the ability to use social media before-trip and during-trip stages, as well as making changes in a trip before making a final decision. On the other hand, a one unit-increase in V3 will lead to a 0.05846-unit decrease in D3 and a 0.46674-unit decrease in D4. The educational level has a negative correlation with the usage of social media in the post-trip stage and the effect of social media on holiday planning.

For the fourth covariate, a one-unit increase in V4 will lead to a 0.11925-unit increase in D1, a 0.97980-unit increase in D2, a 0.60736-unit increase in D3, and a 0.29012-unit increase in D7. According to these data, there is a positive relationship between employment status of travelers and usage of social media during all the three stages of the trip decision-making process and support received by information on social media for their last trip planning. Quite the opposite, a one-unit increase in V4 will lead to a 0.18989-unit decrease in D4, a 0.01671-unit decrease in D5, and a 0.00689-unit decrease in D6. This indicates that there is a negative relationship between the educational level of respondents as social media users and its impact on holiday planning, as well as changes, occurred in their last trip planning and social media impact before making the final decision for a holiday.

Regarding the fifth covariate, a one-unit increase in V5 will lead to a 0.24020-unit increase in D1, a 0.37162 increase in D2, a 0.07584-unit increase in D5, and a 0.21702-unit increase in D7. This shows a positive relationship between income of travelers and usage of social media in pre-trip and during-trip phases, as well as information collected on social media for the previous trip and changes occurred in their last trip. Contrary, there is a negative relationship between V5 with D3, D4, and D6, which means income does not have an impact on travelers in the post-trip stage and holiday planning. Also, income as a financial factor affecting travelers does have a negative relationship with the changes occurred in their last trip planning.

In the sixth covariate, a one unit-increase in V6 leads to a 0.28761-unit increase in D1, a 0.42704-unit increase in D3, a 0.08812-unit increase in D4, a 0.04331-unit increase in D5, and a 0.29879-unit increase in D6. However, it leads to 0.00655-unit decrease in D2 and 0.38437-unit decrease in D7. This shows that there is a positive relationship between the number of hours' social media used per day by travelers and its impact on the decision-making processes in the pre-trip stage and post-trip stage, as well as changes in holiday planning and online-generated content such as electronic word of mouth. However, there is a negative relationship between the hours' social media used during the trip stage, as well as the support received by the information collected on social media.

In the seventh variables, a one-unit increase in V7 leads to 0.10007, 0.31656, and 0.04073 units increase in D1, D2, and D4, respectively. However, a one-unit increase in V7 will lead to 0.08693, 0.00315, 0.18324, and 0.26635 unit decreases in D3, D5, D6, and D7, respectively. These variables indicate that there is a positive relationship between the reasons social media sites used and travel decision-making process in the pre-trip stage and during the trip stage, as well as its impact on holiday planning. On the contrary, there is a negative relationship between the reasons social media used and usage of social media in the post-trip stage and changes occurred in last trip planning by social media. Also, there is a negative relationship between the reason social media used and the maximum support received by information on social media, especially during their last trip.

In the eighth covariates, a one-unit increase in V8 will lead to a 0.26256-unit increase only in D2, while a one-unit increase in V8 will lead to 0.08871, 0.13447, 0.28173, 0.01901, 0.10816, and 0.20401 unit decreases in D1, D3, D4, D5, D6, and D7, respectively. This indicates the frequency of traveling by respondents' impact on social media usage and trust on social media for their trip planning and trip decision-making.

In the ninth covariate, a one-unit increase in V9 leads to 0.23343, 0.17502, 0.25877, 0.17222, and 0.45527 unit increases in D1, D3, D4, D5, and D6, respectively, but it leads to 0.08030 and 0.05229 unit decreases in D2 and D7, respectively. There is a positive relationship between the purpose of traveling and usage of social media in pre-trip and post-trip stages, as well as the effect of social media on their holiday planning, changes occurred in their last trip by reliance on social media and making changes before making a final decision.

Followed by the tenth covariates, a one-unit increase in V10 will lead to 0.00210, 0.15202, 0.00785, and 0.24389 unit increases in D1, D2, D4, and D6, respectively. Reversely, a one–unit increase in V10 leads to 0.10629, 0.09299, and 0.04580 unit decreases in D3, D5, and D7, respectively. According to this interpretation, there is a positive relationship between the source of information used and pre-trip and during-trip phases of trip planning, the level of satisfaction with social media on trip planning, and changes occurred in traveler's last trip planning based on social media information such as reviews and feedback. Moreover, there is a negative relationship between the source of information used for trip planning and usage of social media in post-trip phase changes occurred in holiday planning because of social media impact and maximum support received by social media's information.

Afterward, a one-unit increase in V11 leads to 0.07049, 0.25132, 0.27257, and 0.05145 unit increases in D2, D3, D6, and D7, respectively. A one-unit increase in V11 leads to 0.20765, 0.23657, and 0.23814 unit decreases in D1, D4, and D5, respectively. This indicates a positive relationship between the social media site used and its impact on the during-trip stage and post-trip stage of decision-making, the changes occurred before making the final decision based on reviews, comments, and feedback collected on social media, and the maximum support received by information on social media information. On the contrary, there is a negative relationship between social media site used and the pre-trip stage of decision-making, the travelers' satisfaction with social media usage for travel planning, and the changes occurred during the trip decision-making stages.

Subsequently, a one-unit increase in V12 leads to 0.27116 and 0.29945 unit increases in D3 and D4, respectively. There is a positive relationship between these two variables only, while the relationship between all other variables remains negative. The variables D1, D2, D5, D6, and D7 decrease by 0.20057, 0.49329, 0.63305, −0.73354, and 0.49353 units when there is a unit increase in V12. There is a positive relationship between social media usage after returning home and the duration spent on a trip. Also, there is a positive relationship between the duration of trip and the impact of social media on trip planning. However, there is a negative relationship between duration spent on a trip and usage of social media in pre-trip or during-trip stages, changes social media has made in trip planning, and social media content such as poor or strong comments, reviews, and feedback.

A one-unit increase in V13 leads to 0.05751, 0.18345, 0.13586, and 0.96947 unit increases in D1, D2, D3, and D6, respectively. Oppositely, it leads to 0.19901, 0.44288, and 0.01445 unit decreases in D4, D5, and D7, respectively. There is a positive relationship between the budget spent on a trip as social media users and three stages of decision-making, as well as the changes occurred during each stage after encountering with social media information. However, there is a negative relationship between the budget spent on a trip and social media usage during the trip, the changes occurred during a trip while using social media during all stages of decision-making, and maximum support received on social media information. This shows that a fixed budget does not change the plan even when maximum support is received from its information, specifically in the entire three stages of decision-making. In conclusion, the same interpretation goes to the rest of the variables in sequence.

10.4.3 Factor Analysis (Principal Component Analysis)

Factor analysis is an exploratory investigation that reduces the number of variables in a model to test the hypothetical relationship among the multivariate (Packages et al., 2020). The main goal of factor analysis is to identify the factors underlying the variable, where there is a possibility of having fewer factors compared to variables.

In this research, principal component analysis (PCA) is used.

With PCA, the solution is going to answer two main questions which are:

1. How many components or factors are necessarily extracted to represent the variables?
2. What do those components represent?

KMO and Bartlett's Test

Table 10.6 presents two tests that demonstrate the suitability of the collected data for carrying out a principal component analysis, which is a KMO test of sampling adequacy and Bartlett's test of sphericity.

Kaiser-Meyer-Olkin Measure of Sampling Adequacy

Table 10.6 KMO and Bartlett's tests

Kaiser-Meyer-Olkin measure of sampling adequacy		0.533
Bartlett's test of Sphericity	Approx. Chi-Square	1844.748
	df	325
	Sig.	0.000

The KMO is a statistical test that specifies the proportion of variance among variables that may be caused by underlying factors. High values close to 1.0 are considered useful with factor analysis, while values less than 0.50 are deemed unsuitable with factor analysis results.

Bartlett's Test of Sphericity

Bartlett's test studies the hypothesis that discloses the unrelated variables. Therefore, the data are considered inappropriate for structural detection. Like CCA test of significance, small values less than 0.05 indicate a weak level of significance, where factor analysis may not be useful with the data.

In this research, the table above presents the two tests designated to check the suitability of collected data for structural detection. The KMO value of 0.533 indicates that the sample is adequate to be used for PCA as it is close to 1, while the p-value of Bartlett's test of sphericity, which is 0.00, indicates a strong relationship among variables. This tests the null hypothesis that the correlation matrix is an identity matrix, so we may reject the null hypothesis and to state that the correlation matrix is not an identity matrix.

Communalities

Communalities present the amount of variance that every single variable is accounted for before and after extraction. Initial commonalities are the estimation of the variance in each variable accounted by all factors. For principal component extraction, the correlation is always equal to 1.000.

Table 10.7 presents high communalities, which come from the extracted components representing the relationship between variables. In communalities, when the principal components are low, there is a need for another component extraction, but the below values present acceptable extractions since the majority of values are above 0.5. Therefore, in this research, further analysis is going to be considered.

Extraction Method: Principal Component Analysis

Total Variance Explained

In this section, the total variance explained is displayed by the initial solution, extracted components, and rotated components.

In Table 10.8, the first table presents the eigenvalues in the (total) column, which indicates that the amount of variance is the original variables by each component. Followed by (% of variance) as the values are expressed as the percentage of variance, and they are accounted for by each given component. In the (cumulative %) column, the percentage of variance accounted for by first n components is given. For instance, the cumulative percentage for the third component is the sum of the percentage of variance for the second and third components. This is going to account for by all other components in a row.

In the correlation analysis, the sum of eigenvalues is equal to the number of components. In this analysis, the eigenvalues greater than 1 are requested to be extracted. Therefore, the three first principal components form the extracted solution.

The second section of the table shows the extracted components. They explain nearly 63% of the variability in the original ten variables, so the complexity of data

Table 10.7 Communalities

	Initial	Extraction
Usage of social media is affected by a personal factor, such as gender	1.000	0.598
Usage of social media is affected by a personal factor such as age	1.000	0.658
Usage of social media is affected by the education level	1.000	0.495
Usage of social media is affected by employment status of users	1.000	0.740
Usage of social media and traveling are influenced by the level of income of users	1.000	0.672
Trust on social media influence the number of hours social media used per day	1.000	0.715
The purpose social media used influence on the usage of social media	1.000	0.534
Frequency of traveling per year influence on the usage of social media	1.000	0.572
The purpose of traveling influence on the usage of social media	1.000	0.637
The source of information used influence on the last trip planning of travelers	1.000	0.604
Type of travel site used influence on trip planning of travelers	1.000	0.698
Duration of trip influenced on the last destination decision of travelers	1.000	0.675
The budget of the trip influenced the last destination decision of travelers	1.000	0.677
Shopping prioritized the last travel purpose of travelers	1.000	0.718
Having a leisure time prioritized the last trip of travelers	1.000	0.719
Adventure prioritized the last trip of travelers	1.000	0.569
Level of satisfaction on SM information influence on the usage of social media	1.000	0.607
E-WoM influence on trip planning	1.000	0.589
Travelers produce UGC after returning from a trip	1.000	0.708
Before a trip, usage of social media is influenced by the purpose SM used	1.000	0.665
During a trip, the usage of social media is influenced by the purpose SM used	1.000	0.628
After a trip, usage of social is influenced by the purpose SM used	1.000	0.589
Social media influenced an aspect of last holiday planning of travelers	1.000	0.617
Social media make changes in holiday planning	1.000	0.501
Photos, comment, reviews and feedbacks change destination decision	1.000	0.554
Social media support travelers to make a trip planning decision	1.000	0.567

set can considerably be reduced by using these components, with only a 37% loss of information.

The third section of the table shows the rotated extracted components, which is expressed in the cumulative percentage of variance. The difference here is that the variations are more evenly spread over the components. The big changes in the total values recommend us that the component matrix is easier to interpret compared to the unrotated matrix.

Scree Plot

The scree plot determines the optimal number of components. Usually, the eigenvalue of each component is plotted in the initial solution. Generally, the scree plot is given to extract the components on the steep slope. Furthermore, the components

Table 10.8 Total variance explained

	Initial eigenvalues			Extraction sums of squared loadings			Rotation sums of squared loadings		
F.	Total	% of Variance	Cumulative %	Total	% of Variance	Cumulative %	Total	% of Variance	Cumulative %
1	2.584	9.940	9.940	2.584	9.940	9.940	1.870	7.191	7.191
2	2.470	9.502	19.442	2.470	9.502	19.442	1.789	6.881	14.072
3	1.902	7.316	26.757	1.902	7.316	26.757	1.781	6.851	20.924
4	1.663	6.395	33.153	1.663	6.395	33.153	1.713	6.588	27.512
5	1.579	6.073	39.226	1.579	6.073	39.226	1.705	6.557	34.069
6	1.403	5.398	44.624	1.403	5.398	44.624	1.595	6.136	40.204
7	1.260	4.847	49.471	1.260	4.847	49.471	1.525	5.866	46.071
8	1.194	4.593	54.064	1.194	4.593	54.064	1.476	5.678	51.749
9	1.159	4.458	58.522	1.159	4.458	58.522	1.426	5.483	57.232
10	1.090	4.193	62.715	1.090	4.193	62.715	1.426	5.483	62.715
11	0.993	3.817	66.532						
12	0.937	3.606	70.138						
13	0.841	3.236	73.374						
14	0.813	3.125	76.500						
15	0.784	3.014	79.514						
16	0.724	2.785	82.299						
17	0.679	2.610	84.909						
18	0.625	2.405	87.314						
19	0.558	2.147	89.462						
20	0.516	1.983	91.445						
21	0.464	1.783	93.228						
22	0.412	1.586	94.814						
23	0.405	1.559	96.373						
24	0.369	1.418	97.790						
25	0.314	1.206	98.996						
26	0.261	1.004	100.000						

on the shallow slope contribute very little to the solution. In this case, the last big drop falls between 9 and 10 components. Therefore, using the first ten components is an easy choice (Fig. 10.14).

Rotated Component Matrix

The rotated component matrix determines the representation of each component. The rotated component matrix is the key output of principal components analysis, and it represents the loadings after rotation of factors.

Extraction Method: Principal Component Analysis

Rotation Method: Varimax with Kaiser Normalization

(a) Rotation converged in 15 iterations

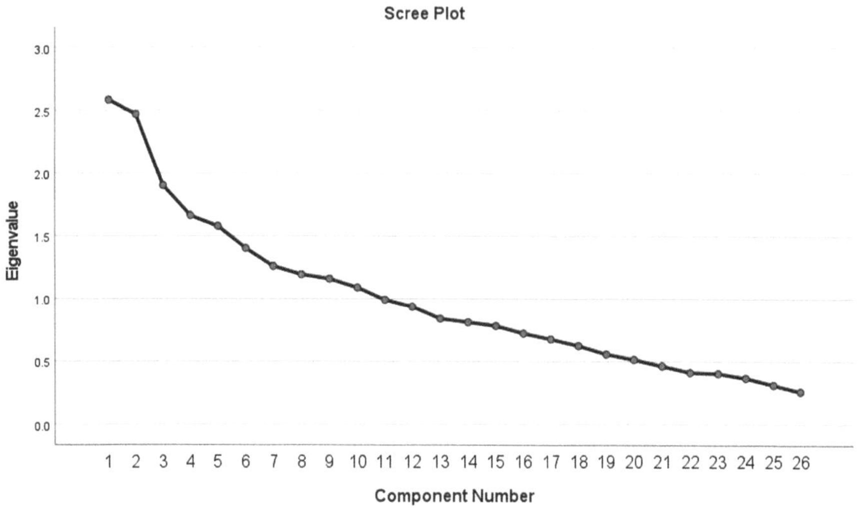

Fig. 10.14 Scree plot

Table 10.9 shows the rotated component matrix of (PCA) factor analysis. Twenty six variables related to the role of social media in destination decision-making are combined into 10 factors.

Factor 1 comprises the variable "Income Level of Social Media Users" with factor loadings of 0.700. This factor represents the impact of a personal factor, which is the level of income on social media usage and destination choice.

Factor 2 comprises the variable of "Education Level of Social Media Users" with factor loadings of 0.605. It represents the impact of the education level on the frequency of social media usage and the type of social media used.

Factor 3 comprises the variables of "frequency of travelling," "purpose of travelling," and "leisure holidays" with the factor loadings of 0.668, 0.715, and 0.581. These variables are closely related, which can be named as "Travelling Purpose" only.

Factor 4 comprises the variables of "Budget of the trip" and "'Duration of the trip" with the factor loadings of 0.691 and 0.775, respectively. These variables are also closely related and can be named as "Travelling Resources."

Factor 5 includes variables such as "Social media information," "E-WoM," and "Social media support for trip planning decision." The factor loadings are 0.574, 0.560, and 0.740, respectively. These three variables discuss the social media-generated information by users and its impact on other prospect users. Therefore, this component can be renamed as "UGC" user-generated content.

Factor 6 comprises the variable of "Shopping" with a factor loading of 0.783. This indicates that shopping could be a reason for arranging a trip by travelers.

Factor 7 contains the variable "Adventure" with a factor loading of 0.681. This is also a representation of a trip arrangement due to looking for adventure by travelers.

Factor 8 comprises the variables "Usage of social media after a trip" and "Usage of social media before a trip" with factor loadings of 0.652 and 0.767, respectively.

Table 10.9 Rotated component matrix

	1	2	3	4	5	6	7	8	9	10
Usage of social media is influenced by a personal factor such as gender	0.307	−0.004	0.241	0.351	−0.153	0.496	0.057	0.126	0.018	−0.180
Usage of social media is influenced by a personal factor such as age	0.510	0.359	0.090	−0.017	−0.119	−0.271	0.165	−0.108	0.336	−0.143
Usage of social media is influenced by education level	0.253	0.605	0.086	0.113	0.010	−0.016	−0.029	0.193	0.072	−0.002
The employment status of users influences the usage of social media	−0.818	0.075	0.011	−0.011	−0.235	−0.034	0.037	0.048	0.069	0.024
The level of income of users influences the usage of social media and traveling	0.700	0.235	0.039	0.053	−0.246	0.030	−0.197	0.059	0.114	−0.072
Trust on social media influence number of hours social media used per day	−0.013	−0.012	−0.169	−0.086	−0.023	−0.095	−0.075	−0.091	−0.799	0.128
The purpose social media used influence on the usage of social media	0.021	0.165	−0.012	0.280	0.068	0.264	−0.438	0.388	0.029	−0.105
Frequency of traveling per year influence on the usage of social media	−0.016	−0.080	0.668	−0.028	0.103	−0.013	−0.287	0.035	0.107	−0.111
The purpose of traveling influence on the usage of social media	0.080	0.144	0.715	−0.218	−0.081	0.015	0.114	0.010	0.136	0.112
The source of information used influence on the last trip planning of travelers	0.063	−0.545	−0.148	0.234	−0.026	0.115	0.366	0.220	0.114	0.131
Type of travel site used influence on trip planning of travelers	0.046	−0.763	0.077	−0.165	−0.055	−0.179	−0.163	0.106	0.085	−0.011
Duration of trip influenced on the last destination decision of travelers	−0.079	0.169	−0.113	0.691	0.312	0.105	0.193	0.032	0.028	−0.054
The budget of the trip influenced the last destination decision of travelers	0.102	0.056	−0.039	0.775	−0.036	−0.122	−0.077	−0.094	0.080	0.157

(continued)

Table 10.9 (continued)

	1	2	3	4	5	6	7	8	9	10
Shopping prioritized the last travel purpose of travelers	−0.135	0.045	−0.085	−0.059	0.206	0.783	−0.058	−0.103	0.098	−0.091
Having a leisure time prioritized the last trip of travelers	0.086	−0.059	0.581	0.291	0.118	−0.001	0.405	−0.152	−0.271	0.107
Adventure prioritized the last trip of travelers	−0.137	0.053	0.003	0.094	−0.120	0.044	0.681	−0.052	0.235	−0.018
Level of satisfaction on SM information influence on the usage of social media	0.063	−0.148	0.086	0.162	0.574	0.420	−0.091	0.068	0.167	0.038
E-WoM influence on trip planning	−0.219	0.202	0.394	0.055	0.560	0.032	−0.070	0.132	−0.021	0.067
Traveler’s generate UGC after returning from a trip	−0.222	−0.339	0.087	−0.088	0.231	0.038	0.138	0.652	−0.168	0.045
Before a trip, usage of social media is influenced by the purpose SM used	0.085	0.086	−0.037	−0.054	0.005	−0.056	−0.099	0.767	0.157	0.144
During a trip, usage of social media is influenced by the purpose SM used	−0.050	0.004	−0.031	−0.003	0.259	−0.130	0.119	−0.014	0.039	0.724
After a trip, usage of social is influenced by the purpose SM used	0.000	0.104	−0.218	−0.134	0.070	−0.142	0.450	0.210	−0.344	−0.351
Social media influenced an aspect of last holiday planning of travelers	0.078	0.161	0.051	−0.329	0.003	0.527	0.081	0.091	−0.159	0.396
Social media make changes in holiday planning	0.292	−0.168	−0.318	0.028	0.178	−0.089	0.205	0.016	0.446	0.070
Photos, comment, reviews and feedbacks change destination decision	−0.101	−0.091	0.050	0.125	−0.097	0.051	−0.134	0.227	−0.170	0.638
Social media support travelers to make a trip planning decision	0.072	0.021	−0.075	0.033	0.740	0.026	−0.036	0.033	−0.010	0.068

As these two variables are closely related, which discuss the usage of social media in two different stages of the decision-making process, the factor could be renamed as "pre-trip and post-trip stages."

Factor 9 does not contain any variable, while factor 10 comprises the variables of "Usage of social media during a trip stage" and "Review, feedbacks and comments" with factor loadings of 0.724 and 0.638, respectively, and it can be renamed as "During trip-stage."

The above factors of social media impact on travel decision-making are extracted from the factor analysis. The factors are renamed as "Income," "Education," "Purpose of Travelling," "Source for Travelling," "User-Generated Content," "Shopping," "Adventure," and "Decision Making Process Stages." These factors are measured on a nominal scale, which indicates the role of social media on holiday decision-making stages. The extracted components indicate that travelers are mainly influenced by the level of education they hold as well as their level of income in terms of using social media for trip planning. This is consistent with the results represented in the canonical correlation analysis. Also, the frequency of traveling and purpose of traveling such as leisure, shopping, and adventure determine the frequency and the type of social media used for a trip planning process. In addition to this, the budget of the trip which is influenced by the monthly income of travelers and the duration spent on a trip impact the usage of social media for a holiday travel planning. Last but not least, user-generated content and electronic words of mouth play a crucial role in decision-making.

10.5 Conclusions, Implications, and Recommendations

10.5.1 Conclusions

According to the review of literature, the complexity of traveler's behavior pushes marketers to develop strong marketing strategies based on the understanding of the customer's behavior. Therefore, this chapter heavily contributes to the tourism industry and other specific industries dealing with customer behavior in the area of information technology. IT development has triggered travelers to have full control over their demands and their fulfillment. Thus, current travelers have become more active rather than being passive in terms of making a holiday decision. Most of the existing studies are focusing on the impact of social media on the development of the tourism industry in the Kurdistan Region.

In contrast, this study provides a comprehensive picture of the impact of social media on consumer behavior in the tourism industry. This research is in relation to the study of Pop et al. (2022) that attempted to understand the role of social media sites and its impact on the last holiday planning of travelers. Consequently, it depicted the actual travel behavior rather than carrying out a theoretical study. By focusing on travelers residing in the Kurdistan Region, a market with national culture and characteristics, this study attempts to add discussion elevated by Tham et al. (2020) to address the differences about the usage of social media among different national markets.

This study also investigated the use of social media during different phases of the holiday planning process. Besides, the purpose and the extent social media used in each stage are found out, which is discussed in the next section (Summary of findings). This empirical contribution was meant to unfold and analyze the effect of social media sites on travelers, and then to discover new methods that will enhance the performance of tourism marketers in the Kurdistan Region. A discussion was made under the light of former scholars and tourism marketers who study the traveler's behavior in their local markets.

This research has been formulated under the travel decision-making process framework. Hence, the empirical data were collected based on the survey questionnaire. After that, it was analyzed using descriptive statistics, and statistical analysis methods such as CCA and PCA to ensure the accuracy of data and statistical analysis methods used. This research targeted 400 respondents on social media and tourism spots by using a judgmental (purposive) sampling technique.

10.5.2 Summary of Findings

In terms of social media and tourism behavior, the data gathered for this research are more up to date and present contemporary trends and growth compared to the previous literature. In addition, the data demonstrate a more advanced level of research, which is based on a macrolevel approach. Throughout the quantitative data collection, the three stages of the decision-making process of traveling are discussed. This perhaps suggests that the travel decision-making process is more extensive in terms of traveler's behavior. To some extent, the findings are consistent with the other researchers in another different context.

However, some slight and unexpected differences stem from social media when it comes to the context of the Kurdistan Region and Kurdish travelers. According to Chavez et al. (2020), it is astonishing how different aspects of traveler's behavior can interrelate and how social media differently influence various characters.

Moreover, this study reveals a strong relationship between social media and its impact on choosing a specific destination or accommodation, and the changes occurring in a holiday plan before a final decision to be taken. As the perceived level of influence on the choice of destination or accommodation increased by social media, it is more likely that there were more changes in the last holiday plan of respondents in terms of destination or accommodation selection.

Finally, the finding of this research is compared with the results of Chavez et al. (2020), who found that there are differences among various national markets in terms of the influence of social media on traveler's behavior. However, as aforementioned, the differences are indicated in the perceived level of trust, the perceived level of use, and the perceived level of influence of social media on destination or accommodation selection before making a final decision. Nevertheless, differences in relation to national cultures, social factors, or psychological factor are not examined in this research.

From the analysis, it was found that

1. Male and female are equal in terms of decision-making for a holiday plan in Kurdistan Region.
   (1) Compared to the study of Chavez et al. (2020), the female has been overrepresented in their research, and this might be due to gender differences in holiday-related roles (Masset et al., 2024).
2. University degree holders are the main active social media users and online content generators.
3. There is a positive relationship between the level of income earned and the usage of social media per day. The higher the income, the more social media is used during a day.
4. The level of education and the level of income earned per month influence the type of social media used. For example, users of LinkedIn tend to be more educated compared to users of Facebook.
5. The majority of users use social media 1 to 2 h per day.
6. The majority of social media users travel at least once per year.
7. In comparison with the study of Masset et al., 2024, in terms of education, the majority of social media users are university graduates who visit at least one social media page almost every day.
8. The frequent purpose of traveling is having a holiday and leisure time, specifically during summer breaks.
9. Social media has been the primary source of information and reliance for traveler's in the past year compared to other sources such as friend's suggestion or a company's promotion.
10. The traveler has used Booking.com the most compared to other travel applications.
11. The reason social media is used for travel planning is because of its ease of access to information.
12. The budget for a trip initially has been the main factor influencing a travel destination decision.
13. The duration spent on a trip has been the second factor influencing a travel plan.
14. Electronic word of mouth affects the travel planning in the Kurdistan Region.
15. Reviewing, providing feedback, and comments have not become a common activity among travelers in the Kurdistan Region, and the majority of respondents sometimes give feedback on their travel experience.
16. In this research, social media is predominantly used in the pre-trip stage, mainly to collect information about the selected destination and choice of accommodation. Also, in the finding of Wang and Yan (2022), social media is predominantly used before the trip stage to search for information.
17. During a holiday journey, social media is mostly used by travelers to share their travel experience with others.

18. After returning home, social media is used by travelers to provide feedback specifically about the tour services and accommodation.
19. On the contrary, according to the findings of Ţuclea et al. (2020), among the three stages of the travel decision-making process, social media is mostly used in the after-trip stage by travelers to share the travel experience with others.

    (1) During the trip stage, social media is to stay connected with family and friends.
    (2) In the trip stage, travelers use social media to seek information and ideas on leisure activities.

20. Social media positively changes holiday plan of travelers.
21. Social media primarily changes the destination choice of travelers, and then, it changes the choice of accommodation of travelers.

    (1) However, Wang and Yan (2022) presented that social media has made few changes in the original plan of travelers.

22. Photos and videos on social media have been more influential compared to other types of user-generated content, such as comments or feedback.
23. Social media has been supportive of the majority of respondents in terms of decision-making.

    (1) Wang and Yan (2022) stated that friends and relatives had been the most trustworthy source of information to travelers and then followed by information provided on various travel websites. At the same time, it is proved that traditional marketing has become the least trustworthy source of information to travelers.

10.5.3 Managerial Implications

As tourism behavior is quite a new field of study in many countries, the data collected for this research are an outstanding contribution to this field of knowledge. It supports the concept of social media as a provocative factor in the tourism industry. Nevertheless, this chapter has led to challenging questions that remain to be answered. Decision-making has always been considered as a very personal factor that depends on many intrinsic components.

The more various intrinsic elements considered, the more decision-making studies get complicated. Besides, external environmental factors also play a critical role in influencing decision-making. Due to the complexity of this topic, further aspects of this study could be explored in more depth.

First, this research provides insights into tourism industry practitioners in the Kurdistan Region, and this enables the travel organizations to harmonize their social media campaigns.

Second, this study also delivers preliminary indications that national markets behave differently in different aspects such as the usage of social media level, social media adoption, the scope of use, and the perceived level of trust on social media information. Therefore, tourism organizations should also study them before designing or implementing a social media campaign. Moreover, this study can also be applied to different geographic regions within a country due to various factors.

Third, "the during holiday stage" remained challenging to many researchers. In this stage, social media is mainly used for making connections with families and maintaining relationships with friends and others. Thus, providing feedback, reviewing, and making comments become the least preferred activity. This also obscures the result that providing feedback has not become a common activity among travelers in the Kurdistan Region.

Fourth, in terms of contextual differences between the Kurdistan Region and other developed countries, there are significant differences to be assessed. Therefore, there is a need for differentiation in social media campaigns aiming at attracting travelers from different regions.

Last but not least, the importance of social media has tremendously increased. However, tourism practitioners have not discovered the art of manipulating it yet, thus understand the full potential of their travel organizations.

10.5.4 Recommendation to Tourism Organizations

According to former Coca-Cola chief marketing officer, Sergio Zayman "traditional marketing is not dying, and it is dead".

With regard to the tourism industry, it is suggested that tourism and travel organizations make the most generous use of social media to be able to develop strong marketing strategies for their organizations. This is because the mass media advertisement is replaced with social media for marketing.

According to Dellarocas (2003), frequent interaction with traveler's is going to benefit tourism organizations and their reputation. Consequently, brand recognition will increase their profit margin.

10.5.5 Recommendations for Future Research

Due to the intricacy of this subject, it is recommended that future researchers study all aspects of this topic. Likewise, it is suggested that further investigation be undertaken into sociological, psychological, cultural, economic, and situational factors influencing social media users during the decision-making process.

Also, it is recommended that social media-related searches should be emphasized equally in all stages of the decision-making process rather than emphasizing one stage of decision-making only.

Also, taking into account the finding of this research in comparison with the findings of Wang and Yan (2022), it can be claimed that social media play different roles in decision-making among various tourism markets, and this is due to the contribution of cultural differences. As a result, a sufficient number of cross-cultural researches are required to validate this claim.

In addition, the current research has explored the impact of social media on travel decision-making based on different personal factors. However, further research is required to boost the confidence of this research in terms of the generalizability of the findings and results.

The impact of social media sites on traveler's behavior has been investigated in the developed countries by considering the case of their local market, comparing the case of their local market with another, emphasizing on one stage of travel planning or getting the case of one social media site or application. Therefore, it also is recommended that the future researchers investigate the relationship between social media and travel behavior in the same way in our local market by considering the specific cases to make this field of study as rich as possible. As a result, it is also going to support tourism organizations to understand our local market more in-depth.

Finally, it would also be exciting to conduct research on how organizations take advantage of cultural differences, as a result, to maximize the effectiveness of social media sites in generating profit.

10.5.6 Limitations

Although this study filled a research gap, yet, like any other research, some limitations remain.

- In terms of limitations, this study is based on one specific geographic context only. Thus, the findings of this research cannot be generalized or cannot be applied to other national markets with distant cultural differences.
- This study limited the sample to a specific criterion, which was the duration. The travelers of the past year have been a part of this study. This limits other travelers who might not have been able to travel in the past year due to a specific or personal reason. Also, the study limited the participants based on other criteria that only active social media users were included.
- This study explored the travel experience of leisure travelers only while other types of tourists have not been taken into account for this research.
- The sample consisted of past travelers and not the actual travelers, and this also can be considered as a limitation.
- In general, the term "consumer" or "customer" could not be associated with this study, and the term has interchangeably been used with other terms such as "traveler," "user," or "content generator."
- The generalization of the "travel decision journey" has also been considered a limitation in this study, as it lacks details concerning the selection of the final destination choice among different alternatives that might contain the evoked set.

- "The decision journey model" consists of untested relationships, which limits the collaborative decision processes, emotions, and socialization processes. Moreover, there is a lack of reflexive loop in this model. As a result, this model neglected the impact of the last destination choice in influencing future destination selection.
- Again, to assess the model's limitation, the "decision journey model" considers travelers as logical decision-makers and neglects interpersonal, family, and social influences.
- The term "post-purchase" is misused in the tourism marketing literature, and it is replaced by "post-experience."
- Another limitation that hindered this research was the outbreak of the pandemic virus (COVID-19) at the beginning of March 2020. The initial goal was to include the international tourists in the Kurdistan Region later in February to assess their travel experience as well. As a result, only the case of nationals of the Kurdistan Region had to be considered for this study.

Appendix 1

Questionnaire

Section 1: Personal Information

1.	Gender ☐ Male ☐ Female
2.	Age in years ☐ 18–24 years ☐ 25–34 years ☐ 35–44 years ☐ 45–54 years ☐ 55 and above years
3.	The highest level of Education ☐ Primary School ☐ High School ☐ Undergraduate ☐ Graduate ☐ Postgraduate
4.	Occupation ☐ Employed ☐ Self Employed ☐ Unemployed
5.	Income per Month in USD ☐ Less or equal to 500 USD ☐ Between 500 and 1000 USD ☐ Between 1,000 and 1500 USD ☐Between 1,500 and 2000 USD ☐Above 2000 USD Note: *For Iraqi nationals, exchange rate of 1200IQD can be used to provide your answer.*
6.	How often do you use social media per day? • Less than 1 h • 1–2 h • 2–3 h • 3 h and more • (it should be five option)

Section 2: Impact of Social Media on Traveling

1.	How often do you travel abroad per year? • Once a year • Twice a year • Three times a year • More than three times • Not sure
2.	What is the frequent purpose of your travel? • Leisure • Work • Family • Treatment • Others (please specify)
3.	Which of the following source of information do you rely on for your holiday planning? • Social media websites • Word-of-mouth • Travel agents or tour operators • Travel guides, TV programs, or advertisements • Official stated or destination websites
4.	Why do you use social media for searching information? • Reliability • Ease of access • Trust in the information • Multiple sources of information • Able to collect feedback from users with the similar interest • Others (please specify)
5.	Which of the below traveling social media application do you use the most for your trip planning? • TripAdvisor • Air bnb • Booking.com • Trivago • Others (please specify)
6.	What was the importance of following factors that helped you prioritize your destination last time you went on a trip abroad? • Duration of the trip • Budget of trip • Shopping • Leisure • Adventure 1. Very important 2. Medium important 3. Less important 4. Not important

7.	In general, how do you find the information gathered on social media? • Very satisfied • Satisfied • Neutral • Dissatisfied • Very dissatisfied
8.	I check on the past experience of other travelers on social media by checking their comments, reviews, and feedback after they have been to a specific destination. • Always • Sometime • Never
9.	Do you make comments, reviews, and feedback on a social media application or a page after your travel experience? • Always • Sometime • Never

Section 3: Social Media Usage Levels and Reasons for Use During the Holiday Planning Process

1.	Before a holiday travel, for what purpose do you use social media the most? • To search for a new destination • To collect information about the selected destination and accommodation • To review feedbacks and comments of other travelers
2.	During a holiday travel, for what purpose do you mainly use social media? • To stay connected with family and friends • To find holiday travel related information • To share and post my travel experience with others
3.	After your holiday travel, for what purpose do you use social media? • To provide comments about the destination • To share my travel experience with others • To provide feedback about the accommodation and tour services

Section 4: Social Media Influence on Holiday Plans

1.	Indicate your level of satisfaction with the following sentence "during holiday planning, social media affects my plan." • Very satisfied • Satisfied • Neutral • Dissatisfied • Very dissatisfied

2.	During your last holiday planning, what social media changed in your trip? • Destination choice changed • Accommodation choice changed • Whole trip plan changed before making final decision
3.	What make you to change your plan on social media before making final decision? • Poor comments and feedback from other travelers • Strong and fascinating feedbacks from others • Photos and videos shared by other social media users or friends
4.	Did information collected on social media support you to make a trip planning decision? • Maximum support • Good support • Medium support • No support at all • I am not sure

References

Adinegara, J., Suprapti, N. W. S., Yasa, N. N. K., & Sukaatmadja, I. (2017). Antecedents and consequences of tourist satisfaction: A literature review. *ASEAN Marketing Journal, 9*(2), 1.

Bessarab, A., Mitchuk, O., Baranetska, A., Kodatska, N., Kvasnytsia, O., & Mykytiv, G. (2021). Social networks as a phenomenon of the information society. *Journal of Optimization in Industrial Engineering, 14*(Special Issue), 17–24.

Boyd, D. M., & Ellison, N. B. (2007). Social network sites: Definition, history, and scholarship. *Journal of Computer-Mediated Communication, 13*(1), 210–230.

Chavez, L., Ruiz, C., Curras, R., & Hernandez, B. (2020). The role of travel motivations and social media use in consumer interactive behaviour: A uses and gratifications perspective. *Sustainability, 12*(21), 8789.

Cheung, M. L., Pires, G. D., Rosenberger, P. J., III, Leung, W. K., & Ting, H. (2021). Investigating the role of social media marketing on value co-creation and engagement: An empirical study in China and Hong Kong. *Australasian Marketing Journal, 29*(2), 118–131.

Chopra, I. P., Lim, W. M., & Jain, T. (2022). Electronic word of mouth on social networking sites: What inspires travelers to engage in opinion seeking, opinion passing, and opinion giving? *Tourism Recreation Research, 49*, 1–14.

Cicciola, E., Foschi, R., & Lombardo, G. P. (2014). Making up intelligence scales: De Sanctis's and Binet's tests, 1905 and after. *History of Psychology, 17*(3), 223.

Cochran, W. G. (1963). *Sampling techniques* (2nd ed.). Wiley.

Corral-Gonzalez, L., Cavazos Arroyo, J., & Josefa, G. M. (2023). Regenerative tourism: A bibliometric analysis. *Journal of Tourism, Heritage & Services Marketing, 9*(2), 41–54.

Dellarocas, C. (2003). The digitization of word of mouth: Promise and challenges of online feedback mechanisms. *Management Science, 49*(10), 1407–1424.

De Vaus, D., & de Vaus, D. (2013). *Surveys in social research*. Routledge.

Ellingson, L. L., & Sotirin, P. (2020). *Making data in qualitative research: Engagements, ethics, and entanglements*. Routledge.

Eraslan, L., & Kukuoglu, A. (2019). Social relations in virtual world and social media aggression. *World Journal on Educational Technology: Current Issues, 11*(2), 1–11.

Gretzel, U., & Yoo, K. H. (2017). Social media in hospitality and tourism. In *The Routledge handbook of consumer behaviour in hospitality and tourism* (pp. 339–346). Routledge.

Grover, P., Kar, A. K., & Dwivedi, Y. (2022). The evolution of social media influence-A literature review and research agenda. *International Journal of Information Management Data Insights, 2*(2), 100116.

Hakeem, I. (2013). *Impact of information and communication technology on goods' clearance operations in West Africa; A case study of Nigeria customs service clearance operations* (Master. Thesis. Master. Thesis.). University of Liverpool.

Hede, A. M., & Kellett, P. (2012). Building online brand communities: Exploring the benefits, challenges and risks in the Australian event sector. *Journal of Vacation Marketing, 18*(3), 239–250.

IOM. (2018). *Demographic Survey: Kurdistan Region of Iraq*. Retrieved from http://iomiraq.net/reports/demographic-survey-kurdistan-region-iraq

Jacobsen, W. C, & Forste, R. (2011). The wired generation: Academic and social outcomes of electronic media use among university students. *Cyberpsychology, Behavior, and Social Networking, 14*(5), 275–280.

Kapoor, P. S., Balaji, M., Jiang, Y., & Jebarajakirthy, C. (2022). Effectiveness of travel social media influencers: A case of eco-friendly hotels. *Journal of Travel Research, 61*(5), 1138–1155.

Karlovitz, T. J. (2020). The democratization of technology–and its limitation. In *Managing customer experiences in an Omnichannel world: Melody of online and offline environments in the customer journey* (pp. 13–25): Emerald Publishing Limited.

Khairi, M., & Darmawan, D. (2021). The relationship between destination attractiveness, location, tourism facilities, and revisit intentions. *Journal of Marketing and Business Research (MARK), 1*(1), 39–50.

Lehto, X. Y., Kirillova, K., Wang, D., & Fu, X. (2024). Convergence of boundaries in tourism, hospitality, events, and leisure: Defining the core and knowledge structure. *Journal of Hospitality & Tourism Research, 48*(3), 407–419.

Liu, X., Mehraliyev, F., Liu, C., & Schuckert, M. (2020). The roles of social media in tourists' choices of travel components. *Tourist Studies, 20*(1), 27–48.

Mainolfi, G., Lo Presti, L., Marino, V., & Filieri, R. (2022). "YOU POST, I TRAVEL." Bloggers' credibility, digital engagement, and travelers' behavioral intention: The mediating role of hedonic and utilitarian motivations. *Psychology & Marketing, 39*(5), 1022–1034.

Masset, J., Decrop, A., & Frochot, I. (2024). Videography in tourism research: An analytical review. *Tourism Management, 102*, 104869.

Matikiti-Manyevere, R., & Kruger, M. (2019). The role of social media sites in trip planning and destination decision-making processes. *African Journal of Hospitality, Tourism and Leisure, 8*(5), 1–10.

Miller, D. (2020). Social networking sites. In *Digital anthropology* (pp. 146–161). Routledge.

Nanjundeswaraswamy, T., & Divakar, S. (2021). Determination of sample size and sampling methods in applied research. *Proceedings on Engineering Sciences, 3*(1), 25–32.

Oliveira, T., Araujo, B., & Tam, C. (2020). Why do people share their travel experiences on social media? *Tourism Management, 78*, 104041.

Page, S. J., & Connell, J. (2020). The role of the public sector in tourism. In *Tourism* (pp. 280–299). Routledge.

Pasquinelli, C., Trunfio, M., Punziano, G., & Del Chiappa, G. (2023). Online tourism experiences: Exploring digital and human dimensions in in-remote destination visits. *Journal of Hospitality Marketing & Management, 32*(3), 385–409.

Pop, R.-A., Săplăcan, Z., Dabija, D.-C., & Alt, M.-A. (2022). The impact of social media influencers on travel decisions: The role of trust in consumer decision journey. *Current Issues in Tourism, 25*(5), 823–843.

Pung, J. M., Del Chiappa, G., & Sini, L. (2022). Booking experiences on sharing economy platforms: An exploration of tourists' motivations and constraints. *Current Issues in Tourism, 25*(19), 3199–3211.

Reinhardt, J. (2019). Social media in second and foreign language teaching and learning: Blogs, wikis, and social networking. *Language Teaching, 52*(1), 1–39.

Şengül, C., & Çora, H. (2020). Healthcare tourism in second decade of 21st century-a review of Turkey as the new global center for international patients. *Journal of Health Systems and Policies, 2*(1), 56–86.

So, K. K. F., Wei, W., & Martin, D. (2021). Understanding customer engagement and social media activities in tourism: A latent profile analysis and cross-validation. *Journal of Business Research, 129*, 474–483.

Spyridou, A. E., Christou, E., & Shin, D. (2022). Tourism destinations' online representation: A performance assessment. *International Journal of Technology Marketing, 16*(4), 318–331.

Tham, A., Mair, J., & Croy, G. (2020). Social media influence on tourists' destination choice: Importance of context. *Tourism Recreation Research, 45*(2), 161–175.

Thevenot, G. (2007). Blogging as a social media. *Tourism and hospitality research, 7*(3–4), 287–289.

Tsiakali, K. (2018). User-generated-content versus marketing-generated-content: Personality and content influence on traveler's behavior. *Journal of Hospitality Marketing & Management, 27*(8), 946–972.

Ţuclea, C.-E., Vrânceanu, D.-M., & Năstase, C.-E. (2020). The role of social media in health safety evaluation of a tourism destination throughout the travel planning process. *Sustainability, 12*(16), 6661.

Van Looy, A. (2022). Definitions, social media types, and tools. In *Social media management: Using social media as a business instrument* (pp. 21–50). Springer International Publishing.

Wang, H., & Yan, J. (2022). Effects of social media tourism information quality on destination travel intention: Mediation effect of self-congruity and trust. *Frontiers in Psychology, 13*, 1049149.

Part IV
Infrastructure and Agricultural Development

Chapter 11
Investigating the Impact of Risk Factors on Cost Estimate Inaccuracy Caused by Project Cost Overrun in the Kurdistan Region's Public Sector Construction Projects

Karwan Akram Ezzat

Abstract A construction project will be successful when it is delivered on time, is executed within the estimated budget, is according to required specifications, and satisfies the client or project owner. No matter how detailed the pre-planning phase of any construction project is, there should be stumbling in one way or another during the construction phase, for example, cost overruns, delivery and handover timing amendments, difficulties in providing resources, and qualitative deficiencies. Failure in construction projects is of high risk due to the large amount of finances invested and the involvement of different partners. The risk is mainly due to delays in delivery and cost overruns, which are considered the most common and damaging factors. In this research, seven risk factors are chosen to investigate their effects on project cost overrun. They are related to (1) the project, (2) the client or owner, (3) the design, (4) the contractor, (5) the materials and equipment, (6) the manpower, and (7) external factors. This chapter studies the identified risk factors that affect the accuracy of cost estimation. It also discusses best practices in calculating cost estimates. A mixed methodology is conducted; the empirical part in the form of a survey questionnaire examines the identified factors among those who are experts in different fields of specialties. An ordered logit probability model is estimated based on the seven main risk factors. To support the empirical findings, a qualitative study is performed in the form of interviews with five experts in the construction industry. The findings report that the highest risk causing cost overruns is contractor-related factors, followed by design-related factors. On the other hand, project-related factors, materials-related factors, and external factors tend to have the lowest risk of cost overrun.

K. A. Ezzat (✉)
Qaiwan Company, Qaiwan Mirador project, Erbil, Iraq

G. M. Muhamad, N. T. Khayyat (eds.), *Resource Management Performance: A Sectoral Analysis in the Post-Conflict Kurdistan Region of Iraq*, Perspectives on Development in the Middle East and North Africa (MENA) Region,
https://doi.org/10.1007/978-981-97-7725-9_11

Keywords Project cost overruns · Risk factors · Public sector · Construction projects · Kurdistan region

11.1 Introduction

The aim of any investment project is the product or service delivered to the client. Throughout the period of any project, whether unintentional or planned, the client's vision will be clarified in order for this vision to be implemented, and the final product to be delivered. These processes and planning occur, taking into consideration the scope of the project, timing and delivery, project budget, available resources, and other precautions ensuring the expected quality of the project (Amusan et al., 2018; Axmadjonovich, 2023).

Construction projects are known to be successful when they are delivered on time, are executed within the estimated budget, are according to required specifications, and satisfy the client or project owner (Wang et al., 2023). No matter how detailed the pre-planning phase of any construction project is, there should be stumbling in one way or another during the construction phase. For example, cost overruns, delivery, and handover timing amendments, difficulties in providing resources, and qualitative deficiencies.

During the planning and construction of any project, there has to be a critical phase, where the project is stumbled in a certain way. Wang et al. (2023) argue that most project delays occur during the construction phase, due to interference of invisible factors. Those factors affect the ongoing process of the project, and, mostly, the cost of the projects resulting in what is known as cost overruns (Sovacool et al., 2014).

Success or failure in the construction phase of the projects, especially large-scale projects, affects dramatically the companies' budgets. Methods of construction are affected by changeable factors that will result in the success, failure, or delay of construction projects. Examples of factors that contribute to the success or failure of construction projects are the qualifications of planners before and during the construction phase, supervision, administration, lack of inefficient distribution of resources, and other external factors (Gómez-Cabrera et al., 2023). Thus, poor performance and delays result in cost overruns.

Failure in construction projects is of high risk due to the large amount of finances invested and interference of different partners. The risk is mainly due to delays in delivery and cost overruns, which is considered the most common and damaging factors. It is worth mentioning that the case of cost overrun is present, although on different scales, in almost all construction projects (Gómez-Cabrera et al., 2023).

Cost overruns can be defined as the difference between the estimated cost of the project, the project budget, and the cost of executing the project after finalization (Vaardini et al., 2016). Cost overruns and project delays are mysterious and, mostly, unexpected. Cost overruns and delays negatively affect clients, contractors, consultants, income, and the general psychological status of all involved in the project. For this reason, it is vital to diagnose the common reasons for cost overruns in order to limit it, reduce the negative factors, and preserve the strategic goal of the project.

The cost estimation of any project resembles the recommended cost of the project. Shoar et al. (2023) explain the cost estimation of a project as the technical resolution of expected expenditures. The cost estimator depends, mostly, on available information and experience in delivering the best quality end product. Accuracy in cost estimation has a great deal of influence on the ongoing phase of the project and its result. It ensures that accurate estimation strengthens accounting and financing projects. In addition to that, risk and safety factors should be added to the cost estimation to obtain accurate figures.

The cost estimation should provide an understanding of the nature of the project, a full understanding of the cost of each phase, solutions to deal with expected risks, and other factors that contribute to the success of the project. This can happen when the estimator takes into consideration risk factors and the detailed study and breakdowns that can avoid or minimize falling into risks (Sayed et al., 2023).

Fundamental factors that affect the accuracy of cost estimation should be studied well to avoid falling into errors and mistakes. Sayed et al. (2023) mentioned that those primary items are found in the initial cost estimation that are presented in the beginning of the project. In addition to that, technical requirements, unclear specifications, and the unspecified needs of the clients also contribute in causing variations in the cost estimation.

In this research, a number of seven fundamental factors are chosen for further investigation, and these are (1) factors related to the project, (2) factors related to the client or owner, (3) factors related to the design, (4) factors related to the contractor, (5) factors related to the materials, machinery, and equipment, (6) factors related to manpower, and (7) external factors. The above seven fundamental factors should be tackled from three main angles: the client, the contractor, and the consultant.

This research studies the identified risk factors that affect the accuracy of cost estimations. In addition to that, it discusses best practices in methods for calculating projects cost estimations. Ali et al. (2023) consider a project successful if it is delivered on time, within the estimated budget, and according to international qualitative requirements. Muñoz-La Rivera et al. (2021) chose several factors related to cost estimation and put them under examination to see how they affect the cost estimation of projects. Changes and variations in the cost are a sign that more knowledge is needed in the cost estimation of each phase of the project.

Although achieving success is the goal, yet what is important is figuring out or estimating the actual cost of the project. Holm and Schaufelberger (2021) mentioned that the status of a project, if surpassed the estimated budget, is considered an international, general, or common case. Most cost overruns are found in the period of the construction of the project. This is to say that in the initial phase of the project, planning and designing phase, a lot of efforts are invested to achieve the best results but in the same time the goal should be to minimize expected risks.

It is possible to prevent or reduce risks during the phase of planning and designing by conducting a thorough study, using best practices, proposing best technical solutions, international codes and standards, implementing site surveys, and benefiting from past records. However, from a historical record, it is shown that even projects that are perfectly planned and studied are never executed the same way they were budgeted or planned. This is due to risks and uncertainties that occur during the construction phase (Holm & Schaufelberger, 2021).

Cost estimation during the planning phase is based on a set of information that is taken in a specific time, and also takes into consideration accumulated knowledge and cost substitutes (Santos & Cabral, 2008). Even though, it is rare that projects are executed within their estimated budgets. Any changes in the factors that contribute in the success of a project such as time, quality, terms, and specifications and resources will negatively affect the cost of the project. This is why the process of cost control and management is a challenge for the project manager and the whole working team.

This research aims at providing a thorough and detailed analysis for the elements and factors that contribute to the accuracy of projects cost estimation. The cost can be viewed in different ways, yet in this research, it is considered as the budget or the operational cost.

Two definitions for operation cost and budget are considered relevant to the current study; operation cost is defined in the Cambridge dictionary as the daily expenses of managing any institution, beneficiary project, or the needed cost to keep a firm running.[1] Budget on the other hand is defined in Collins Dictionary[2] as the cost of purchasing land, building, property, the cost of equipment and machinery to produce something, or offering a specific service.

This research focuses on the cost in terms of the "budget" through the following steps:

1. Diagnosing risk factors from a primary survey and using the seven identified factors to conduct a thorough and detailed survey.
2. From the survey, the identified factors are verified to find the common and relevant factors among those who are expert in different fields of specialties.

The most common questions among engineers that arise during the team work regular meetings are: What happened? Why does the actual cost surpass the estimated one? Was there any mistake or deficiency in the design? Was there a wrong scope followed in the planning phase? Was the estimated cost low? and many others?

In the KRI a project proposal should have the complete design and engineering drawing with the bill of quantities and cost estimate. At the signing stage of projects, all the agreed costs will be financed by the Ministry of Finance and paid in accordance with the project's progress. This means that the government will only make payments to the project at a specific time when the production and progress of the project are identified. Any delay in the financial request for the project will affect budget allocation. This will cause amendments in the timetable of the project and will have an increase in the cost estimate and, finally, lead to cost overruns.

[1] https://dictionary.cambridge.org/dictionary/english/cost

[2] https://www.collinsdictionary.com/dictionary/english/budget_1

In KRI, the government allows for an additional amount of up to 7% of the estimated cost of the project. This amount has been specified for any possible changes in the project as per the regulated change orders. According to the planning senior director of KRG, more than 50% of the projects are utilizing this reserve amount as a common practice.

Besides the mentioned above, other reasons cause cost overruns of projects. These are highlighted as follows:

1. The discrepancy between the actual plan agreed with the plan implemented. This may lead to delay in payments, which leads to delay in execution, which will affect the cost of contractors' change orders due to price differences and other administration expenses.
2. Additional projects that are not originally considered in the annual investment plan will affect the other projects' funding that are originally in the investment plan. This will indirectly affect the projects' cost overruns.
3. Project management and procedures such as not following the codes and common practices, not using the added values in the bill of quantities, and poor performance of the project team from the client and contractor's side will contribute to cost overruns.

Figure 11.1 and Table 11.1 highlight the differences between the actual budget allocated and the total budget spent. It is obvious from the figure that the total amount that has been spent is noticeably larger than the actual budget. This explains the cost overrun phenomenon in the KRI project implementation. The decline in 2010–2011 is due to political instability, especially, KRG cabinet Change and less number of awarded projects in the region.

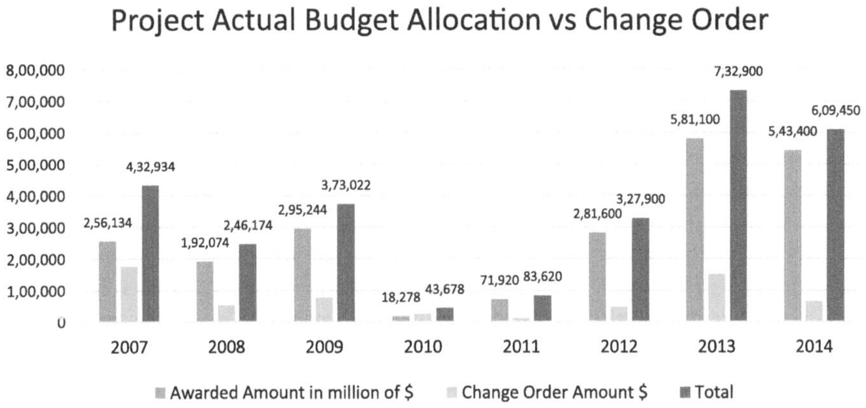

Fig. 11.1 Project actual budget allocation vs. change order. Source: KRG Directorate of Planning

Table 11.1 Project actual budget allocation vs. change order

No.	Year	No. of Project	Awarded amount USD	Change Order Amount USD	% Change
1	2007	115	256,134,000	176,800,000	69.00
2	2008	94	192,074,000	54,100,000	28.16
3	2009	72	295,244,000	77,778,000	26.34
4	2010	119	182,780,000	25,400,000	13.89
5	2011	43	71,920,000	11,700,000	16.26
6	2012	51	281,600,000	46,300,000	16.44
7	2013	64	581,100,000	151,800,000	26.12
8	2014	36	543,400,000	66,050,000	12.15
Total		594	2,404,252,000	609,928,000	25.36

11.2 Review of Previous Works

11.2.1 Capital Cost

The problem raised in a study conducted by Caffieri et al. (2018) is the limited research explaining how the public sector can ensure capital projects are completed within a given budget plan. The study recommends conducting complete and relevant research within the field of production planning of construction projects, through the use of the Strategic Asset Management Framework.

The framework was developed by the Western Australian State Government, and implemented to ensure capital projects were delivered within a percentage of their given budget. In other words, this framework was used to address efficient management of the "capital expenditure of assets" and identify reasons to the contribution of cost overrun in major capital projects.

The study concluded that major capital projects are expected to have cost increases, but suggest that future research could be able to further address the approaches used by governments to managing capital costs.

Bertisen and Davis (2008) conducted a feasibility study concerning the under-evaluation of the as-built capital cost of international mining projects. They reviewed 63 International mining projects and showed a clear average of 14% increase in completion cost higher than as calculated in the feasibility study. Bias, as defined by the authors, is the tendency of errors to be statistically different than zero which is the point on which the feasibility study was based.

The argument for determining this business considers the shortage of financing a project to expand the economics in a project tender, therefore, to obtain more funding. Approximately, the as-built capital cost of the majority of projects comes out of the estimated ±15% of the feasibility study in addition to the calculated bias. The authors further mentioned that all cost overruns in projects that are happening on average 1 of 13 of projects are more inaccurate when it comes to large-scale projects. They also concluded by the complete risk that is resulted from poor or uncertain capital cost estimation.

11.2.2 Factors Affecting Construction Projects Cost Estimates

11.2.2.1 Project Delay

In their research, Park (2021) addressed the limited studies presented on the understanding and acknowledgment of the intentionality of delays in projects. The research explains how intentionality plays an important role in the study of understanding project delays. The findings of the research, through the literature review, suggest that intentionality could play an important role in plans that are not developed properly which leads to project delays. In other words, the authors developed an understanding of project delays through the inclusion and acknowledgment of project delays, whether unintended, intended, or as an imaginary point of view.

Dahlin and Pesämaa (2021) addressed in their article that Norway, similar to other countries, faces cost and time overruns in construction projects caused by different factors affecting the end results. The authors discussed some factors that may cause delay which are insignificant like scheduling and planning, shortage in resources, making slow assessment, different parties poor coordination, poor quality control, incomplete design, objectives and goals not clear, and organization and administration differences. Their findings were summed by presenting a practical and qualitative connection between the problems and the solutions in terms of time schedule to assist clients, consultants, and contractors.

11.2.2.2 Cost Estimation Method

Cost estimation is the most significant primary procedure in any construction project. The construction cost estimate plays a great part in the research exertion in construction management (Tayefeh Hashemi et al., 2020).

Using a computerized management system instead of human expertise will minimize errors in cost estimation proposals. This will inspire researchers and industry specialists to use one unified progressed construction cost estimate, for all factors of design and the project's specification. Scientific reasoning for cost estimates used worldwide will provide a clear description of the estimator's biases and will raise the level of accuracy and clearness, shaping the accurate construction cost estimate to be led by a standard scale that leads to determining a rule of thumb, if other ways of cost estimate are not available. The above is essential for sorting, bunching, and standing the proposal of cost estimate.

Information systems project estimation costs and benefits is a stimulating effort and is infamously disposed to uncertainties and errors due to extensive use of evaluating the cost and benefits in obtaining serious business decisions (Venkataraman & Pinto, 2023). The accuracy of the costs and returns calculations should be measured as an important part of the information system execution planning, risk reduction, and imitation modeling of project results; ignoring this accuracy may lead to incorrect results on procuring information system.

11.2.2.3 Geographical Location and the Environment

Mbachu and Cross (2015) explained in their study that construction projects and the environment within which they are executed are multifaceted, active, and over-controlled. As an outcome, substantial inconsistencies are presented between preliminary contract values and final accounts for almost all projects. These differences highlight significant risks and uncertainty with values such as disputes, high cost of project finance, and low-profit margins. The study attempted to quantify and segregate them in terms of obligations, responsibilities, and liability in developing the process of building. The authors recommended that to prioritize the factors under each extensive group, project teams should address practically the priority factors mentioned above in terms of efficiency to modify project cost overruns and to confirm more reliable results in the project delivery phases.

According to Lukale (2018), project attributes, namely, project size, project type, and implementation period, nature of work, and contractor nationality, have no effect on cost overrun. The findings of the study concluded that there were cost overruns in the rural road projects in Kenya based on the review and assessment of 68 projects. Also, the findings of the study highlighted project size to being the major influential factor of cost overruns.

In their article Rahman et al. (2018) stated that the construction industry is one of the significant foundations to the development in any country's economic. But this industry has severe complications as there have been difficulties in project completion within specified time and cost. Hence, the authors evaluate the different risk factors resulting in time and cost overruns during the construction period. In their findings, the risk factors in the construction, design, and planning stages are related to other worldwide countries. Nevertheless, in the finishing stage, the risk factors in construction projects in Malaysia are more than in other countries. Probably it is because of the geology and the environmental variances in each country that may disturb/intrude on the factors in every stage of the project.

11.2.2.4 Construction Management

Amadi and Omotayo (2017) in their study argued that construction management research is a developing research field of study and does not necessarily have a recognized methodological orientation. With this being said, the study suggests that construction management research should build on theories and views of "related natural and social science research."

The study focuses on the "philosophical argument" in construction management within cost overrun research and understands the limits of previous methodological-related research. It reviews supportive literature on the problem of cost overruns in construction management projects. The findings of the study, upon examining the methodological and philosophical reasoning of cost overrun research, conclude that "positivist philosophies" do not adequately explain or provide better understanding of the factors in construction organizations that lead to the cost growth in projects.

11.2.2.5 Material Management

Tedla and Patel (2018) explored in their study that material management is an essential and fundamental part of every organization, as construction materials normally estimate the main measure for the total cost of a construction project. Insignificant management of construction projects can result in a substantial negative consequence with low outcomes, cost, and time overrun. According to the authors, delays in the delivery of materials are the main problem of poor material management.

The objective of the study was to investigate existing exercises in material management, to find the problem in construction material management, and to apply ABC (always better control) analysis and s-curve analysis. The information communication technology system, which could be one of the tools for refining material management, was not used efficiently because of ignorance in the construction industry.

11.2.2.6 Site Characteristics

Some construction sites may have some poor soil with water seepage condition which will result in limiting the access to them and finally elevate the estimated cost. The items that include ground preparation including layering, leveling, excavation, compaction, and others are influenced by poor ground conditions. In such cases, accurate cost estimations cannot be conducted unless a soil review test takes place. This kind of test can be achieved by taking several boreholes from different locations in the construction site prior to cost estimation in order to know the ground conditions (Sorvig & Thompson, 2018).

11.2.2.7 Risk Management

Akintoye and MacLeod (1997) cited in Diab et al. (2017) in their research tackled the risks in the industry of construction in terms of investigation, activities, practices, analysis, and management procedures. They concluded that risk management is a vital tool in order to reduce losses and boost profits. They also viewed construction risks as measures that directly impact the project aim, cost, time, and delivery. Risk management and analysis in the construction industry, generally, depend on perception, decision, and practice. Proper risk analysis and management techniques are rarely used due to the absence or lack of information. It is also related to suspicions on the appropriateness of these techniques for the activities of construction industry.

Raza and Khosravi (2015) in their article pointed out that construction is a risky and unsafe work due to the exceptional environment of activities involved and the uniformity of many sites' performances. They specified in their research eight main groups of factors: (1) society, (2) company organization, (3) project management, (4) supervision, (5) contractor, (6) site condition, (7) workforce, and (8) different characteristics. They concluded that more studies are essential to provide a better consideration of the relations between unsafe performance concepts and practical results, contest hypothetical norms, change/develop new functional theories, and create solid recommendations.

11.2.2.8 Competition

Liu et al. (2020) focused on the issue of competition and considered it as a main factor influencing cost estimates. They explained how some contractors when they realize high competition on a certain project simply switch their interests and seek for another work opportunity. Mostly contractors try to escape from some bids by issuing non-interest submittals to avoid expensive misfortune. In some cases, contractors lose large profits due to turning down a certain bid just to avoid the risk of losing in case of high competition.

Other studies indicate that scope precision and competency of the project manager will positively affect cost function, while disagreement between project members, inexperience of project manager, and shortage of information will affect negatively on cost function of public construction projects (Sinesilassie et al., 2018; Irfan et al., 2021; Moradi et al., 2020).

The idea of the imaginary is the knowledge about the planner, research in the future could discover the planner's character and their plans are illusory, and how imaginations will affect the execution of the project.

11.2.2.9 Interdependency of Causes

Steininger et al. (2021) conducted a study to explain cost overruns in infrastructure projects. The aim of their study was to develop a new theoretical framework and to apply it to Norwegian infrastructure projects. They conducted a literature survey and for their empirical study, they utilized a survey-based questionnaire. Their finding was that political, strategic, psychological, and competence-related aspects are the most influential factors in cost overruns. For their empirical part, they found that the initiation and planning stages are the most important parts of any project where the cost overruns occur.

In their article, Love et al. (2016) pointed out the reason behind derailing the delivery and increase in cost of infrastructure projects relating it to the growth in population. The main two reasons mentioned are, firstly, decisions that are taken based on preliminary designs and, secondly, due to the quantitative and qualitative changes during the construction phases. The aim of the study was to introduce a probabilistic approach, theory, to consider the interdependencies of causes. The study was not to provide solutions but to spread awareness and sow the seeds for the theory of probabilistic causation to control cost overruns in infrastructure projects.

11.2.2.10 Other Factors

A study was conducted by Eliufoo (2017) to identify the influencing factors of cost overruns in Tanzania building projects. In doing so the study empirically targeted the groups of respondents, namely, clients, consultants, and contractors. The respondents ranked the most perceived five determinants of cost overruns, an increase in cost of materials, errors and neglect in design, change in the scope of work, design change, and finally, change in specifications. The study further concluded that different public projects show that the causes of cost overruns are technical and stem from internal sources.

11.2.3 Cost Overruns

Cost overruns of projects have been widely studied. Below is the most relevant literature to the current study that investigates the effects of cost estimate accuracy on construction projects' cost overrun.

In order to increase the insight on the performance of Dutch transportation infrastructure projects regarding estimated and actual costs, Molinari et al. (2023) conducted a descriptive study to analyze the characteristics of Dutch projects regarding the costs. The findings reveal that the average cost overrun in projects in the Netherlands is 10% compared to 28% in projects around the world.

Korytárová and Hromádka (2020) employed the expected value method (EVM) measurement of infrastructure project risk, and they identified the main sources of risk in infrastructure projects. The authors suggested that for feasible infrastructure projects, the maximum cost overrun should not exceed 25% of the project cost estimate; in addition, the maximum time overrun should be about 30% of the project time estimate. The authors used the underground metro corridor in developing countries of South Asia as a case study.

In their findings, the amount of risks involved in the case study were many. If risks are not handled, the likelihood of not completing the project within the allocated time and cost frame will increase and hence negatively affect the efficiency and profitability of the organization.

Annamalaisami and Kuppuswamy (2021) have addressed in their article that the cost overrun of infrastructure projects actually leads to major financial difficulties for investors. The authors believe that the cost overrun scale of infrastructure projects has not been improved since a few decades ago, highlighting that no important knowledge has been acquired in reducing its unfavorable effects. Financial insecurity, uniqueness, difficulty, and time stress are the most common causes of cost overrun.

Manage large-scale transportation infrastructure projects is challenging due to common misrepresentation of the costs, which will lead to large cost overruns that frequently impend the whole project's feasibility (Cantarelli et al., 2013). The paper examines the descriptions of cost overruns; generally, four groups of descriptions are noted: technical, economic, psychological, and political. The political description is considered the main description for cost overruns. Agency theory is measured as the most motivating for political descriptions, and an eclectic theory is also considered possible. The level of the use and the difference in theories used in the literature are actually quite large. The article recommended that to search for other encouraging theories that help in taking better account of cost overruns, theories in political science and economics are valuable, in addition to research in contingencies and descriptions in regard to demand estimates.

The finding of those studies indicates that the reasons for a lack of consideration of the effect of systematic and complications of projects are as follows: Impractical cost targets, mistakes in a sequence of project scope, cost and estimated project period, uncertainties, and dishonesty. They concluded that cost overrun has a large deterioration in the enhancement and improvement of the knowledge area.

Ahiaga-Dagbui et al. (2017) explored the methodological weaknesses that are dominant in explaining cost overruns in infrastructure projects. They suggest moving from the traditional single-cause identification system to the so-called system thinking to address the interactions between multiple factors. Their findings emphasized the lack of a systems approach in cost overrun studies, while neglecting the overall look at the whole project system and how several variables dynamically interact. The purpose of the article was not to discredit previous works but rather to map out future directions for cost-overrun research.

In their study, Huo et al. (2018) measured the features of cost overruns in mega infrastructure projects in Hong Kong, and explored the needs of the cost overruns on the size of project, the type of project, and the duration of the project execution period.

As it is known that cost overruns frequently occur and have been considered a problem for the past 30 years, it is required that engineering management should have a deeper understanding of the process. This will result in influencing decision-makers and come up with successful projects through comparing between Hong Kong and worldwide studies along with other regional studies. It is suggested, in this chapter, to shorten the construction period in order to minimize opportunities for cost overruns to occur. In addition to that, it is proposed to adopt data mining methods to study and analyze more specific related factors and compare data to study relationships between different construction stages.

Gamil and Rahman (2018) identified 33 causes and 21 effects of cost overrun. The causes were mainly missing active communication between construction parties, absence of operative communication and policy and system, inadequate communication channels, and absence of communication strategy. The effects on the other hand were mainly time overrun, low output, amending and redesigning incidence, demoralized employees, and design faults.

11.2.4 Impact of Cost Overruns on Project Implementation

Mukuka et al. (2014) have pointed out that the construction industry is an important segment in the development and economic progress of South Africa.

The authors evaluate the construction experts for their awareness on the reasons of construction project cost overruns, and their significant consequences in the construction industry in Gauteng—South Africa.

Their findings showed the immaturity of contractors in the project, insignificant project management, poor planning, contractors' incompetence, inadequate financial study, lack of experienced workers, and poor workmanship are the main causes of cost overruns.

The study also exposed the increment of project cost because of extension of time, project's neglect, companies or firms' responsibility to liquidation, minimizing client's capital, not utilizing manpower resources, accountability of companies or firms to bad debt, and not using plants and equipment bought for the projects are the results for cost overruns during the construction phases.

According to Jarkas and Marenjak (2014), the main Objective of Clients, Consultants, Contractors, and Policy Makers in Kuwait is to improve the performance of Cost in Construction Projects, which can be monitored from the beginning of the contract process with minimum control. This could be achieved by identify, explore, and rank the causes of cost overruns.

The authors emphasized on examining and determining factors such as budget deficits, financing costs and debts, productivity and profit losses, and disputes and claims cases. The factors are considered the main determinants of construction cost overrun that lead to obtaining the relationship between the causes of cost overruns and the control, mitigation, and practical solutions of cost overruns.

A study conducted by Ansah et al. (2018) argues that delays often occur in almost every organization, especially in construction projects. However, the extent of delays in construction projects requires a serious valuation for the actual causes. Furthermore, their study explored causes of delay in the core setting of construction projects through "4P" framework analysis, namely, projects management, project-related, project participations, and procurement that are used for the progress evaluation and standard/target of the project.

In their article, Zidane and Andersen (2018) highlighted the point that projects regularly have time delays, due to several factors. The objective of the study is to classify the common delay factors from a literature survey, supplemented by delay factors in major Norwegian construction projects based on empirical data. The top 10 delay factors are design changes for the duration of the construction period/ change orders; payment delay of contractor(s); improper planning and scheduling; lack of site management and supervision; incomplete or poor design; insufficient/ inadequate contractor experience/methods of building and approaches; contractor's financial problems; sponsor/owner/client's financial difficulties; shortage in resources (human resources, machinery, and equipment); and lack in labor efficiency /productivity and poor of expertise.

Narayanan et al. (2018) conducted a study and categorized infrastructure projects into two types: major and mega infrastructure projects. Those two types can fall into one of these categories: road transport and highways, power, atomic energy, metro and urban development, petroleum, or petrochemicals.

Road transport and highway projects are found to have the highest time and cost overruns. Most mutual reasons for time and cost overruns are known as delay in land purchase, delay in property permission, law and order problems, price increase in general, high capital cost, poor/slow execution of contractor, and late supply of material and equipment.

Gunduz and Maki (2018) in their article pointed out that, as there are many studies to understand the factors associated with the cost overrun of projects, within the construction industry, they focused on identifying what were the most influential cost overrun factors. Through the assessment of relevant literature, the authors identified a list of 39 cost overrun factors. The findings indicate that factors such as schedule delay, improper planning and scheduling, frequent design changes, frequent changes to the scope of work, and inaccurate time and cost estimates of projects are among the most affective factors.

11.3 Research Design and Methodology

11.3.1 The Scope of the Study and Its Limitation

It is known that many factors contribute to causing cost overruns in construction projects. Each one of these factors has different or variable occurrence and affects the final cost of the project. This is to say that it is vital to identify both aspects of each factor which are the occurrence and impact on construction projects. In this way, the cost overruns on each of the industry and stakeholders will be identified.

This research study has its own limitations as any other study, lack of adequate secondary information and related documentation in the field of construction, and the unwillingness of some stakeholders to provide accurate information related to cost.

11.3.2 The Questionnaire

The questionnaire is considered the best genuine mechanism to assist the researcher in the primary data collection from the aimed participants of the study who are in the private and government sectors. It was significant to choose the aimed participants in the construction industry because of the awareness they have in identifying concerns associated with cost estimation and cost overruns, and the risk factors affecting cost estimate accuracy and its impact on project cost overruns in construction projects.

The questionnaire was designed in four parts as follows:

Part 1: Demographical part
Part 2: Addressed the ethical questions
Part 3: Contains seven major sections with 46 hypothesized risk factors
Part 4: Addressed the factors that impact project cost overruns

The questionnaire is attached in the Appendix.

11.3.3 Data Collection

This study has invested in different resources in order to come up with two kinds of documents: archived-based (secondary data) and respondents' data (primary data). In the latter type of document, respondents are collected through survey questionnaires distributed among stakeholders, i.e., clients, project owners, consultants, and contractors.

It is commonly known that two kinds of survey questions exist: closed-ended and open-ended. In this research, the questionnaire used both methods of survey questions. The archived-based documents were taken from completed projects through letters, payment documents, and project reports. The investigation of those documents was important in the identification of the problem of cost overruns.

Likert's scale along with five measures of agreement was implemented to receive statements from zero to four, as in the following section. The main two reasons for using this type of scale were, firstly, to simplify the process for respondents and, secondly, to ease the process of data collection.

Respondents' attitudes and feelings are taken into consideration when using the Likert's Scale by indicating the respondents' feelings regarding each question on a rating scale.

After identifying the variables that contribute to cost overruns, the respondents are asked whether they agree or disagree regarding those variables.

For this reason, the respondents were given the chance to express their feelings using the following indicators:

- No risk
- Low risk
- Average risk
- High risk
- Highest risk

The second phase, after respondents expressed their feelings of agreement, was to ask them about the risk factors that affect the accuracy of project cost estimates, each variable as shown below in the choices:

- No risk,
- Low risk,
- Average risk,
- High risk, and
- Highest risk

The stage afterward, after asking regarding the chance of occurrence for each variable, was to ask the respondents about the impact of each cause resulting in cost overruns using the choices; 15 potential factors that can cause project cost overruns have been identified below. To enable the evaluation of these factors and how they impact project cost overruns, a Likert scale of 1 to 15 was created. The scale will be used to rank the impact, with 1 being the most impactful and 15 being the least impactful.

When the data collection process is finished, the responsible party for cost overruns should be identified. This process is made possible as the questionnaires were made in a way that allows detailed data collection using matrix tables that are systematically prepared.

11.3.4 Sample Selection

The samples selected in this study were clients, consultants, and contractors that are directly related to the field of project construction. Due to lack of enough time and the risk of not receiving all the respondent's surveys, the researcher limits the sample size to 89 complete respondents. The sample size for the current study is within the range of acceptance for having a reliable outcome (Lakens, 2022).

Clients/ project owners and contractors (general contractors and building contractors) were selected from already running and active construction projects in Kurdistan/ Iraq. All clients, consultants, and contractors were randomly selected.

11.3.5 Data Collection Process

The research strategy will include a questionnaire for quantitative data collection. The type of questions within the questionnaire will be of closed-ended type, addressing the study objectives directly. The process of data collection of the survey questionnaire will include a face-to-face interview as well as sending the questionnaire by email. There are a variety of advantages when using email questionnaires, including but not limited to the low cost of collecting large amounts of information, respondents can answer at a convenient time, and less boundary burden as respondents who are continuously traveling can access the questionnaire anywhere.

Furthermore, phone interviews will be conducted for more flexibility and assurance of getting the needed data from respondents. Not forgetting that to get accurate and reliable information and data, the researcher should construct a detailed and well-studied questionnaire, and it should avoid the so-called leading questions. In other words, the researcher will be following Lydeard's (1991) proposal in forming the questionnaire as shown below:

- The scope of the investigation will be defined through a relevant literature review.
- The literature review will be the source from which the questions will be formulated.
- Test for reliability and validity.
- The errors along with their sources should be recognized through the validation process.

To receive qualitative data, the researcher will be using in-depth and detailed interviews to get important information that is related to the scope of the study. The researcher takes notes when interviewing the respondents. Ghauri and Grønhaug (2002) claimed that detailed and in-depth interviews are important for more accuracy, and clear picture can be obtained out of respondents, which is suitable for inductive research and studies.

The difficulty of in-depth interviews is how the researcher should construct the questions and the talk to keep the respondent focused on the scope of the study, and not let them stray away. To deal with this risk, the researcher should have a semi-structured interview, keep some level of understanding before conducting the interview, start the interview with some open-ended questions, and allow flexibility and changes in case new ideas might arise (Rabionet, 2011). The process of the interview is to get perspectives from the person being interviewed regarding the questions being asked or discussed.

In addition, the researcher supports the primary data received from interviews by secondary data collected from firms archives or available reports. The tools used in data collection will be continuously subjected to reliability and validity at several stages to guarantee consistency and integrity.

11.4 Data Analysis and Presentation of the Results

11.4.1 Description of Variables

11.4.1.1 General Information

Although the sampling procedure was randomly selected, the sample was associated with the construction industry in the KRI. A total number of 89 participants were involved in the survey (see Appendix for the questionnaire), out of which 23 were clients of construction projects, 36 were consultants, and 30 were contractors (see Fig. 11.2).

One of the causes that significantly affects the cost enhancement and effectiveness of construction projects is the experience of the involvement of stakeholders.

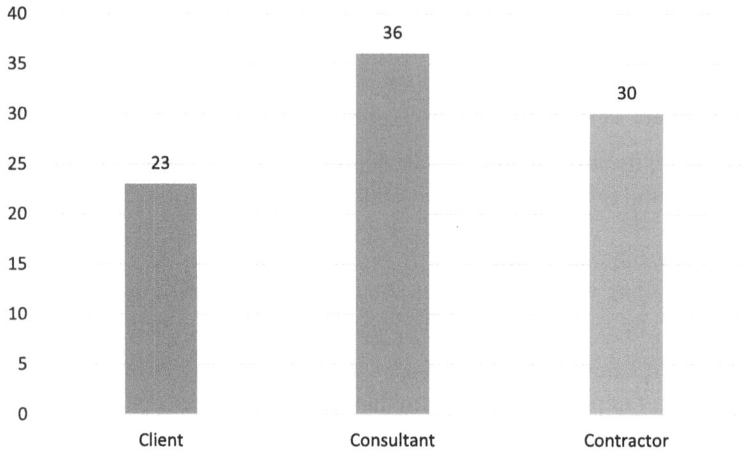

Fig. 11.2 Participants' job

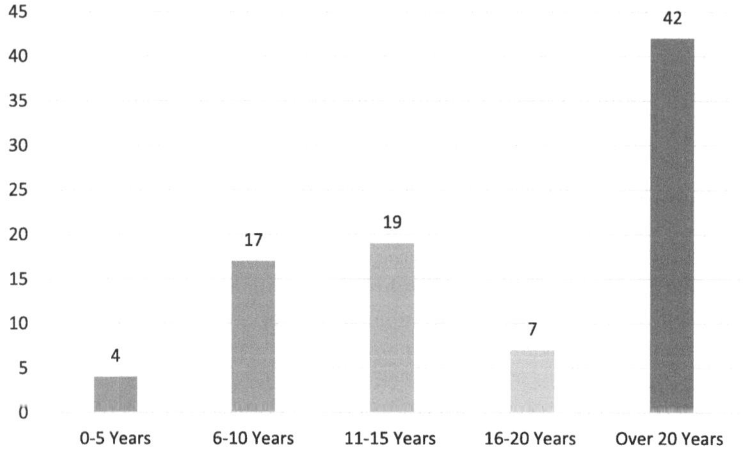

Fig. 11.3 Experience of involved stakeholders (no of years)

To evaluate this variable, participants were questioned about their professional experience while being in the construction industry. Almost 42% of the participants had experience of more than 20 years (See Fig. 11.3). Doloi et al. (2012), in a study on construction's qualification criteria, concluded that technical planning and controlling expertise of contractors is important to the success of any project.

The participants were questioned to classify the types of projects their respective organizations had executed. According to Fig. 11.4, it shows that 24% of the respondents had executed various kinds of engineering projects. The largest percentage, 39%, participated in projects that involved engineering fields of civil and structural,

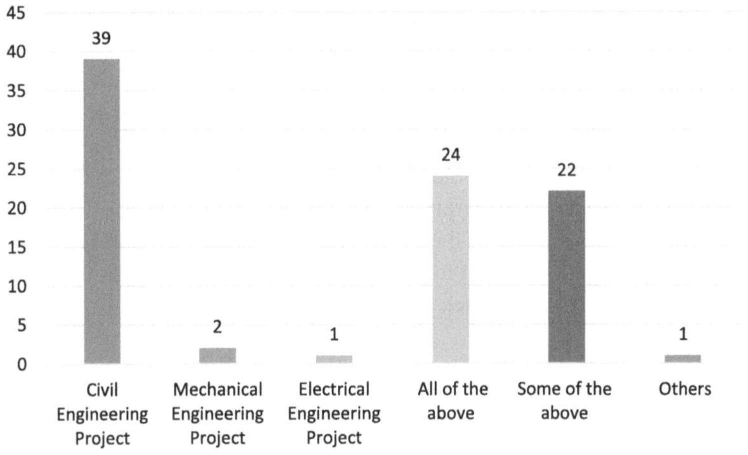

Fig. 11.4 Projects executed by participants

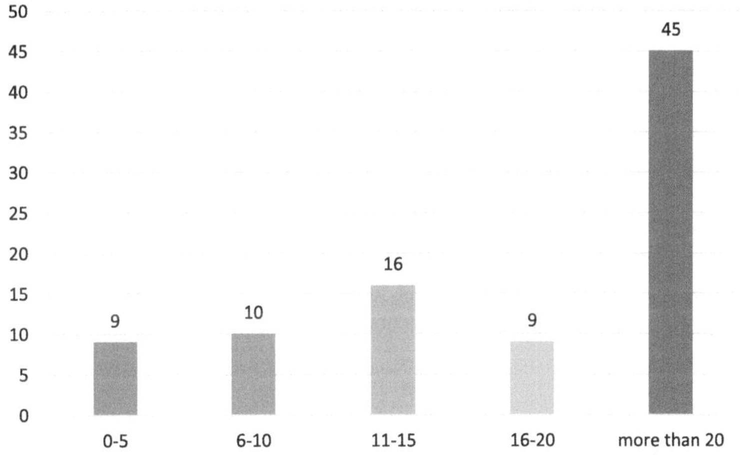

Fig. 11.5 Number of projects involvement by participants

and an additional 22% of the respondents showed that they were involved in other kinds of projects such as mechanical and electrical.

In addition, the participants were also asked about the number of strategic projects they were involved in for the last 10 years, and this will infer the participants' degree of professionalism in project execution (see Fig. 11.5).

11.4.1.2 Risk Factors Affecting the Accuracy of Project Cost Estimates

In this section, a summary statistic of the seven major risk factors will be presented. The respondents were asked to rank by using a Likert scale of 1 to 5, with 1 being the least impactful, and 5 being the most impactful of the substantial risk factors, classified under each of the seven major hypothesized risk factors, which may affect the accuracy of a projects cost estimate.

In the below sections, each of the seven major hypothesized risk factors will be analyzed to demonstrate the most important and least impactful risk that affect the accuracy of a project cost estimate.

Project-Related Risk Factors

According to Table 11.2, it is noticeable that 34%of respondents have ranked the risk factor characteristics of the project to high and highest risk, while 39% of the respondents ranked no and low risk. A total of 40% of the respondents have ranked the risk factor of additional cost due to additional work as high and highest risk, while 50% ranked this variable as no and low risk.

Regarding the change in the project's scope, 41% ranked it as high and highest risk, while 55% of respondents ranked it as no and low risk.

The risk factor communication among the various stakeholders has an impact on the practical side of the project; 59% of the respondents ranked at high and highest risk, while 30% of respondents ranked no and low risk.

Site condition is known from the start of the project so 60% of respondents ranked at high and highest risk, while only 36% of respondents ranked it as no and low risk.

Regarding the risk factor speed of decision making by the project team, 50% of respondents ranked high and highest risk which is logical as the delay in making decisions by the project team will lead to an increase in the project's period and cost, while 40% respondents ranked no and low risk.

Table 11.2 Project-related factors

Project-related factors	No	No risk %	Low risk %	Average risk %	High risk %	Highest risk %
Characteristics of the projects	89	17	22	27	27	7
Well-defined scope of the work	89	7	27	17	22	27
Additional cost due to various works	89	12	38	9	12	28
Project scope change	89	25	30	3	11	30
Communication among the various stakeholders	89	8	22	10	21	38
Site conditions: (location, topography, accessibility, existing and surrounding elements	89	7	29	3	29	31
Speed of decision-making by project team	89	11	29	9	12	38

According to Fig. 11.6, 54 respondents ranked the characteristics of the project as high and highest risk, while only 32 respondents ranked no and low risk. In total, more than 60% agree that the characteristics of the project are associated with the cost overrun.

An additional cost is due to additional work that is not specified in the original project plan that has high effect on changing the cost. Thirty-four respondents ranked this variable as low risk while 36 have ranked it as high and highest risk.

The change in the project's scope was ranked as low risk by 27; another 27 respondents ranked it as highest risk. From the figure mentioned, one can notice a variation in respondent's opinions about the degree of risk factors.

Communication among the various stakeholders has an impact on the practical side of the project; 53 respondents ranked at the highest risk and high risk, while only 27 respondents ranked low and no risk.

Site condition is known from the start of the project so the percentages, 54 respondents ranked highest risk and at high risk, while only 32 respondents ranked it as no and low risk.

Regarding the speed of decision making by the project team, 45 respondents ranked highest and high risk which is logical as the delay in making decisions by the project team will lead to an increase in the project's period and cost, while only 36 respondents ranked low and no risk.

The above is a partial answer to the research's first question: how does cost estimation accuracy impact construction projects' cost overruns?

Client-Related Risk Factors

Table 11.3 shows that the risk factor of project financing is the most significant factor, where 62% of respondents ranked at high and highest risk, while only 15% of respondents ranked no and low risk. Contractual terms and requirements show 42% of the respondents ranked high and highest risk and only 21% of the respondents ranked no and low risk. For pressure on estimators and engineers, 49% of the respondents ranked at high and highest risk, while 33% of respondents ranked no and low risk.

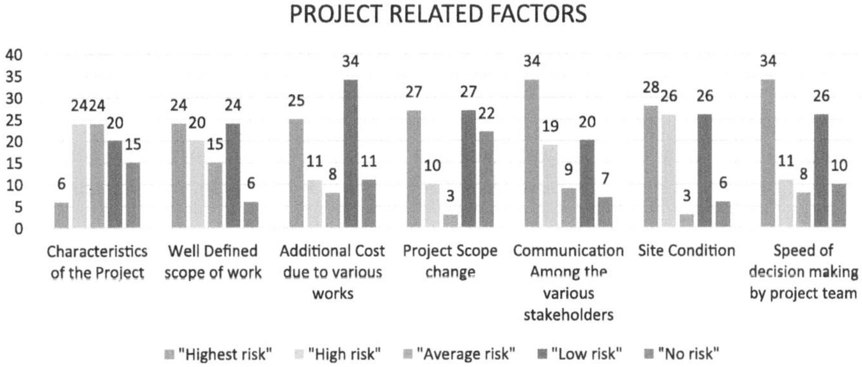

Fig. 11.6 Project-related risk factors

Table 11.3 Client-related risk factors

Client-related factors	No	No risk %	Low risk %	Average risk %	High risk %	Highest risk %
Project financing	89	8	7	23	46	16
Contractual terms and requirements	89	10	11	36	31	11
Pressure on estimators/engineers	89	7	26	19	42	7
Changing company policies and procedures	89	6	18	37	25	15
Executive bureaucracy in the client's organization	89	9	9	42	33	8
Communication among stakeholders	89	8	25	33	27	8
Estimating errors	89	6	12	27	33	22

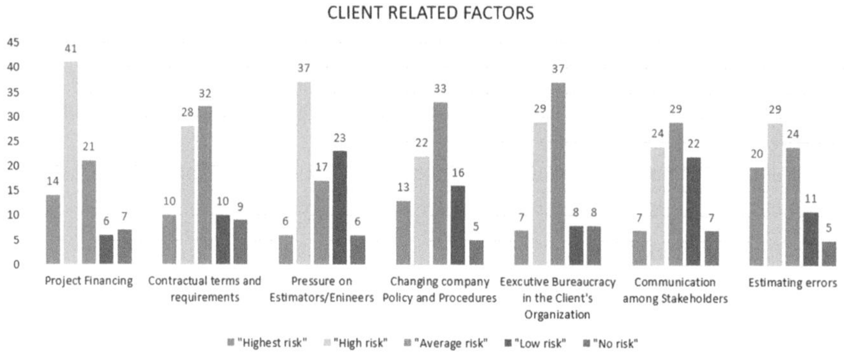

Fig. 11.7 Client-related risk factors

As for the risk factor of executive bureaucracy in the client's organization, 41% ranked high and highest risk, while only 18% of respondents ranked no and low risk as a reasonable percentage that affects the delay of project and cost increase.

Communication among stakeholders shows 35% of the respondents ranked high and highest risk, while 33% ranked no and low risk. For the risk factor estimating error, 55% of respondents ranked high and highest risk whereas only 18% of the respondents ranked no and low risk.

Figure 11.7 shows that project financing is an important factor; 55 respondents (60%) ranked at high and highest risk shows, while only 13 respondents ranked no and low risk.

For pressure on estimators and engineers, 43 respondents ranked at high and highest risk, while 29 respondents ranked no and low risk.

For estimating error, 49 respondents ranked high and highest risk, whereas only 16 respondents ranked no and low risk.

In executive bureaucracy in the client's organization, 36 respondents ranked high and highest risk, while only 16 respondents ranked no and low risk as a reasonable percentage that affects the delay of the project and cost increase.

The above is a partial answer to the research's second question which is, is cost estimation the main factor of cost overruns in construction projects?

Design-Related Risk Factors

Table 11.4 shows the risk factor experience of designers showing 71% of respondents ranked high and highest risk, while only 8% of respondents ranked no and low risk; this is an important factor that affects cost overruns and shows a significant difference.

The complexity of the project design shows 45% of the respondents ranked high and highest risk, while only 17% ranked no and low risk.

The risk factor delay of drawings and/or orders requested by the contractor shows that 51% of the respondents ranked high and highest risk, while only 15% of the respondents ranked no and low risk. Mistakes and omission in design shows 63% of the respondents ranked high and highest risk, whereas only 10% of the respondents ranked no and low risk; this is considerably a significant risk factor.

The accuracy of the survey shows 57% of the respondents ranked high and highest risk, while only 12% ranked no and low risk. Scope creep shows 35% of the respondents ranked high and highest risk, while 21% of the respondents ranked no and low risk.

Project location shows 30% of the respondents ranked high and highest risk, while 32% of the respondents ranked no and low risk. Inadequate/ nonexistent records show 47% of the respondents ranked high and highest risk, while only 21% ranked no and low risk.

According to Fig. 11.8, experience of designers shows 63 respondents ranked high and highest risk, while only 8 respondents ranked no and low risk. This is an important factor that affects cost overruns.

For mistakes and omission in design, 56 respondents ranked high and highest risk, whereas only 9 respondents marked no and low risk.

Table 11.4 Design-related risk factors

Design-related fACTORS	No	No risk %	Low risk %	Average risk %	High risk %	Highest risk %
Experience of designers	89	4	4	20	44	27
Complexity of the project design	89	8	9	38	29	16
Delay of drawings and/or order requested by the contractor	89	3	11	34	40	11
Mistakes and omissions in designs	89	1	9	27	38	25
Accuracy of survey	89	2	10	30	37	20
Scope creep	89	4	17	44	26	9
Project location	89	7	25	38	26	4
Inadequate/nonexistent records	89	3	18	31	31	16

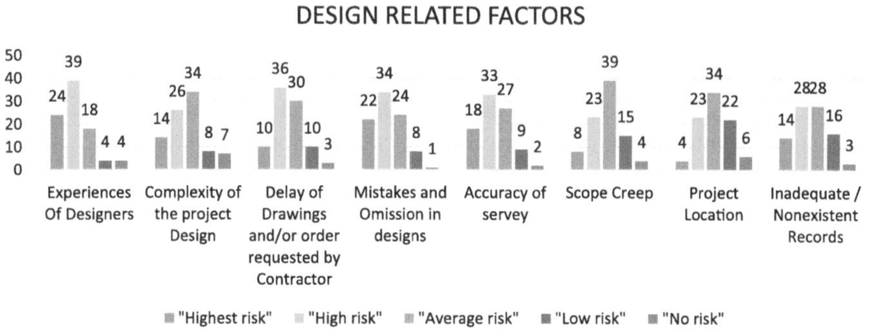

Fig. 11.8 Design-related risk factors

For delay of drawings and/or orders requested by the contractor and mistakes and omissions, 46 respondents marked high and highest risk, while only 13 respondents marked no and low risk.

In addition to all other factors causing cost overruns in Kurdistan, preliminary designs, studies, and reports can be considered as factor causing an increase in project finalization cost. This is because governmental institutes lack international standards and specifications, lack of experts, poor designing techniques and abilities, and the lack of design checks and auditing systems. Cost overruns in this case are due to:

- Estimated quantities do not reflect actual quantities.
- The need to modify construction items through removal, addition, improvement, expansion, and considering alternative solutions. This process leads to adding new items that did not exist in the preliminary design phase and cost estimates.

The above is a partial answer to the researcher's first question: how cost estimation accuracy impacts the construction projects' cost overruns?

Materials and Equipment Related Risk Factors

Table 11.5 shows the risk factor difficulties in obtaining materials in the local market 39% of the respondents ranked high and highest risk, while 31% of the respondents ranked no and low risk.

Material shortage shows that 53% of the respondents ranked high and highest risk, while only 19% ranked no and low risk; again, this factor is considered an important factor affecting delay in the project schedule.

The risk factor, fluctuations in the cost of materials and price change, shows that 48% of the respondents marked high and highest risk, while only 11% ranked no and low risk. Wrong materials purchased shows that 60% of the respondents ranked high and highest risk, while only 25% ranked no and low risk. Changes in material specifications show 38% of the respondents ranked high and highest risk, while only 17% ranked no and low risk. Long lead items show that 35% of the respondents ranked high and highest risk, while 20% ranked no and low risk.

Table 11.5 Material/equipment-related risk factors

Material/Equipment-related risk factors	No	No risk %	Low risk %	Average risk %	High risk %	Highest risk %
Difficulties in obtaining materials in local market	89	16	15	42	33	6
Material shortage	89	4	15	28	46	7
Fluctuations in the cost of material and price change	89	3	8	40	29	19
Wrong materials purchased	89	7	18	15	30	30
Changes in material specifications	89	6	11	45	26	12
Long lead items	89	4	16	45	28	7
Equipment availability	89	4	22	29	35	9
Wrong selection of equipment	89	2	17	29	29	22

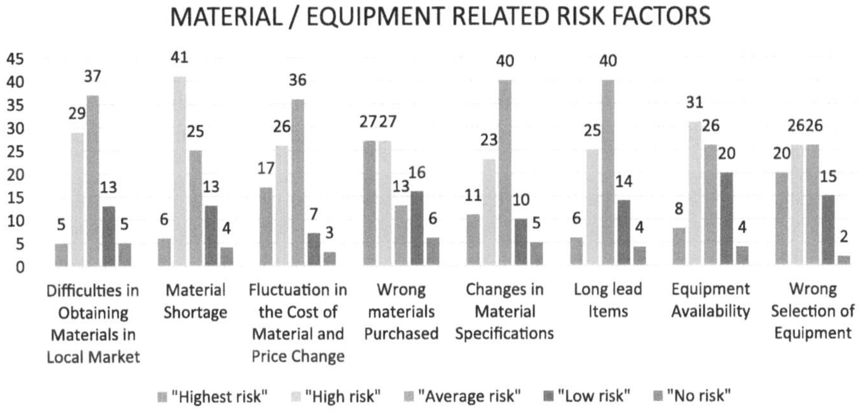

Fig. 11.9 Materials—equipment-related risk factors

Equipment availability shows that 44% of the respondents ranked high and highest risk, while 26% ranked no and low risk. The factor wrong selection of equipment shows that 51% of the respondents ranked high and highest risk, while only 19% ranked no and low risk.

Figure 11.9 shows that for material shortage, 47 respondents ranked high and highest risk with a percentage of (52%), while for the difficulties in obtaining materials in the local market, 34 respondents ranked high and highest risk, which is not accurate, as at present all types of materials are imported from different parts of the world.

For fluctuations in the cost of materials and price change 43 respondents (48%) marked high and highest risk, as all contracts are in Iraqi Dinar and the imported materials are in foreign currency; this will have a negative impact on the project and increase in cost.

The above are partial answers to the research's third question: what are the risk factors that affect the accuracy of cost estimates?

Contractor-Related Factors

Table 11.6 shows that for the availability of contractor resources 38% of the respondents ranked high and highest risk, while 21% ranked no and low risk.

The risk factor contractor experience in planning and execution of projects shows that 62% of the respondents ranked high and highest risk, while only 18% of the respondents ranked no and low risk. This is a significant factor causing cost overruns of projects in the construction industry.

The factor cash flow shows that 72% of the respondents ranked high and highest risk, while only 11% of the respondents ranked no and low risk. This is an important factor where most of projects will be affected directly and one of the major causes of cost overruns.

The risk factor of contractor bankruptcy shows that 69% of the respondents ranked high and highest risk, while only 10% of the respondents ranked no and low risk. Abuse of change order process shows 57% of respondents ranked high and highest risk, while only 11% of respondents ranked no and low risk. This is an important factor in addition to the above factors. Over time abuse shows 31% of the respondents ranked high and highest, while only 18% of the respondents ranked no and low risk.

Figure 11.10 shows that for contractor experience in planning and execution of projects 56 respondents ranked high and highest risk, while only 16 respondents ranked no and low risk.

The contractor bankruptcy shows that 62 respondents ranked high and highest risk, while only 9 respondents ranked no and low risk, and for the variable cash flow, 64 respondents ranked high and highest risk, while only 10 respondents ranked no and low risk; these two factors are common in Kurdistan due to lack of banking system and financial supervision compared with the European countries affecting the accuracy of project cost estimates, in addition to a fact that contractors depend on self-financing not on bank loans and facilities.

Table 11.6 Contractor-related factors

Contractor-related factors	No	No risk %	Low risk %	Average risk %	High risk %	Highest risk %
Availability of contractor resources	89	10	11	40	30	8
Contractor experience in planning and execution of projects	89	8	10	19	49	13
Cash flow	89	7	4	17	48	24
Contractor bankruptcy	89	4	6	20	21	48
Abuse of change order process	89	3	8	31	39	18
Over time abuse	89	6	12	51	21	10

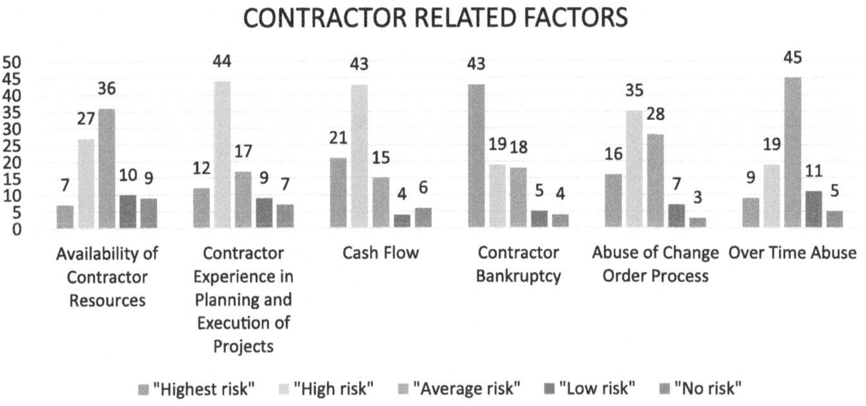

Fig. 11.10 Contractor-related factors

Table 11.7 Workforce-related risk factors

Workforce-related risk factors	No	No risk %	Low risk %	Average risk %	High risk %	Highest risk %
Skill level of crew members	89	3	11	24	49	12
Availability of labor crews	89	3	17	43	29	8
Low productivity	89	1	13	27	40	18
Labor office issues	89	5	24	36	26	9

For abuse of the change order process, 51 respondents ranked high and highest risk, while only 10 respondents ranked no and low risk; this is an important factor in addition to the above factors.

The above is a partial answer to the research's second and third questions: Is cost estimation the main factor of cost overruns in construction projects? And what are the risk factors that affect the accuracy of cost estimates?

Workforce-Related Factors

Table 11.7 shows that for the risk factor skill level of crew members 61% of the respondents ranked high and highest risk, while only 14% of the respondents ranked no and low risk. The factor availability of labor crews shows that 37% of the respondents ranked high and highest risk, while 20% ranked no and low risk.

In low productivity, 58% of the respondents ranked high and highest risk, while only 14% of the respondents ranked no and low risk, both factors affecting the progress of the project in the construction industry which will impact the cost overruns. The factor labor office issues shows 35% of the respondents ranked high and highest risk, while 29% of the respondents ranked no and low risk.

Figure 11.11 shows that for the skill level of crew members, 55 respondents (61%) ranked high and highest risk, while only 13 respondents ranked no and low risk, whereas for low productivity, 52 respondents (58%) ranked high and highest

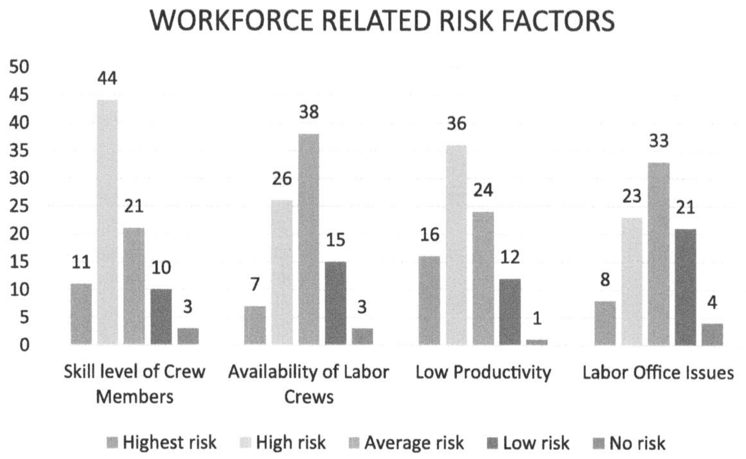

Fig. 11.11 Workforce-related factors

Table 11.8 External risk factors

External risk factors	No	No risk %	Low risk %	Average risk %	High risk %	Highest risk %
Weather concerns	89	3	27	50	13	6
Environmental concerns	89	6	29	54	7	4
Required state and local permits/ licenses	89	6	26	34	29	6
Force majeure	89	6	19	34	26	16
Changing codes and standards	89	11	15	40	26	8
Political factors	89	3	18	17	28	34

risk, while only 13 respondents ranked no and low risk, both factors affecting the progress of the project in the construction industry which will impact the cost overruns. The above is partial answer to the research's third question: what are the risk factors that affect the accuracy of cost estimates?

External Risk Factors

According to Table 11.8, the factor weather concerns shows only 19% of the respondents ranked high and highest risk, while 30% ranked no and low risk. The risk factor environmental concerns shows 11% of the respondents ranked high and highest risk, while 35% ranked no and low risk. For required state and local permits/ licenses, 35% of the respondents ranked high and highest risk, while 32% ranked no and low risk.

The factor force majeure shows 42% of the respondents ranked high and highest risk, while 25% ranked no and low risk. The risk factor changing codes and standards shows 34% of the respondents ranked high and highest risk, while 26% ranked no and low risk.

The risk factor in all the above items can be considered acceptable. Political factors results are 62% of the respondents ranked high and highest risk, while only 21% of the respondents ranked no and low risk. This factor has the highest impact on the construction industry in terms of suspension and delays. An example of that, the ISIS invasion of Mosul and other cities in Iraq had a huge impact on project delays and suspension in KRG and caused cost overruns.

The risk factor in all the above items can be considered acceptable. Political factors results are 55 respondents (61%) ranked high and highest risk, while only 19 respondents (21%) ranked no and low risk. This factor has the highest impact on the construction industry in terms of suspension and delays. An example of that is the ISIS invasion of Mosul and other cities in Iraq had a huge impact on project delays and suspension in KRG and caused cost overruns. The above is partial answer to the research's third question: what are the risk factors that affect the accuracy of cost estimates? (Fig. 11.12)

11.4.2 *Regression Analysis*

For the multivariate statistical method, the risk factors have been reduced to seven main factors. As such, seven latent variables are created, representing the group of original questions as recommended by Ture et al. (2007). To reduce the dimensionality of the variables, a mean score of the sub-variables is calculated through SPSS. Table 11.9 presents the descriptive statistics of the newly constructed latent variables based on the mean score approach.

According to Table 11.9, all of the variable's standard deviation is less than one, indicating that the data are mostly centered around the mean: in other words, a standard deviation, which is the square root of the variance measures on average the distance between the points (the data) and the mean. The smaller the distance, the less dispersed the data (Heshmati & Khayyat, 2014).

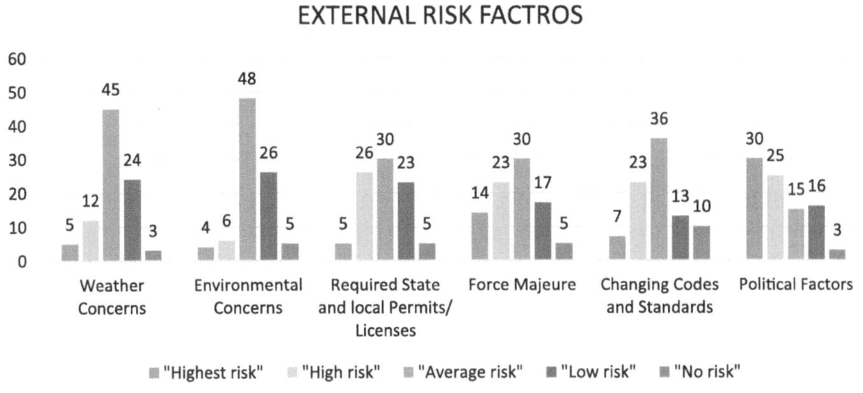

Fig. 11.12 External risk factors

Table 11.9 Descriptive statistics of mean of variables

Descriptive statistics						
	N	Minimum	Maximum	Mean	Std. deviation	Variance
Factors affecting project cost overrun	89	1.00	5.00	2.5169	1.02372	1.048
Project-related factor (PRF)	89	1.00	5.00	3.2360	0.69122	0.478
Client-related factor (CRF)	89	1.00	5.00	3.3258	0.86307	0.745
Design-related factor (DRF)	89	1.00	5.00	3.5000	0.73469	0.540
Material-related factor (MRF)	89	1.00	5.00	3.3764	0.83012	0.689
Contractor-related factor (COTRF)	89	1.00	5.00	3.5112	0.78689	0.619
Workforce-related factor (WRF)	89	1.00	5.00	3.3876	0.81447	0.663
External risk factor (erf)	89	1.00	5.00	3.0899	0.77446	0.600

Table 11.10 Frequencies of actual and predicted outcomes-ordered logit model

Predicted alternatives of risk factors that impact project cost overruns (COV)						
Actual alternatives	No risk	Low risk	Average risk	High risk	Highest risk	Total
COV	Y0 0	Y1 1	Y2 2	Y3 3	Y3 4	
Y0	19 (63%)	6	4	1	0	30
Y1	1	12 (63%)	2	2	1	19
Y2	2	4	12 (57%)	0	1	21
Y3	0	0	0	10 (77%)	0	13
Y4	0	0	0	0	2 (33%)	6
Total	22	22	18	13	4	89

An ordered logit probability model is estimated based on the latent variables described in Table 11.9 using SPSS. The dependent variable is the latent variable cost overrun (COV).

To examine how the specified model fits to explain the variations in the data, Table 11.10 presents the predicted versus actual frequencies and percentages based on the actual number of observations of each alternative.

According to the results reported in Table 11.9, the Likert no risk is the most chosen alternative by surveyors; the model has estimated 63% of the actual outcome. The second two highest frequency alternatives are low and average risk, and the model has estimated 62% and 57% of the actual outcome, respectively. To test the fit of the model, the predictive values for the five alternatives are calculated: (19 + 12 + 12 + 10 + 2)/89 = 61.8%, which implies that around 62% of the data fits well and is correctly predicted by the estimated ordered logit model.

To test the validity of the model, the chi-square statistics are reported from the estimation of a likelihood ratio (LR) of 97.75 with 10 degrees of freedom. This number is significantly above the standard chi-square critical value, indicating that the model is significant at 99% significance levels (Greene, 2008).

The results of the regression are reported in Table 11.11.

According to the results shown in Table 11.11, most of the variables are significant at different levels of significance; the order logit model performed well as all the variables are significant. Project-related factors, material-related factors, and external factors are all having negative coefficients, implying that these factors according to the results tend to have a lower risk of cost overrun than the other factors. Looking at the size of these negative coefficients, external-related factors have the largest coefficients in absolute value, indicating that this group of factors (i.e., the external factors) has more effects than the other ones on cost overrun. The largest risk of cost overrun variation is the group of client-related factors, with an estimated coefficient of 0.523 (with a 95% degree of significance), followed by the group of contractor-related factors, which is an estimated coefficient of 0.515 (with 90% degree of significant) and then the group of design-related factor, which has the estimated coefficient of 0.509 (with 99% degree of significant).

The workforce-related factor has the smallest positive coefficient, indicating that the positive effects of this group of factors on the cost overrun variation are relatively smaller compared to the other factors.

11.5 Summary, Conclusions, and Recommendations

In this research, the potential factors that affect the accuracy of cost estimation for construction projects are identified. The results of the analysis herein show that costs are affected by project quality, financial issues, market conditions, contractors, and some other characteristics. In this section, a summary of the research is drawn, a conclusion is presented, recommendations for future research are highlighted, and finally, limitations of the research are mentioned.

Table 11.11 Ordered logit model coefficients estimates

Variablel	Coefficient	Standard Error	b/St.Er.	lP[lZl > z]l
PRF1	−0.684	0.354	−1.933	0.053**
CRF1	0.523	0.277	1.886	0.059**
DRF1	0.509	0.332	1.533	0.001***
MRF1	−0.066	0.318	−0.209	0.013***
COTRF1	0.515	0.296	1.738	0.082*
WRF1	0.228	0.357	0.638	0.052**
ERF1	−0.746	0.329	−2.269	0.023**

Signiant level: * for 90%, ** for 95%, *** for 99%

11.5.1 Research Questions and Key Findings

The key findings of this research can be summarized as follows: In this research, a number of seven main risk factors that are related to the accuracy of projects' cost estimates have been designed and studied. In addition, a number of 15 risk factors that affect the project cost overruns are designed and studied.

For the empirical part of this study (i.e., the quantitative part), a survey questionnaire has been designed covering all risk factors mentioned above with their subfactors. A number of 89 respondents of the survey are obtained, and a description analysis in the forms of graphs and tables is presented in Sect. 11.4 about the mentioned factors. In addition to that, a regression analysis is conducted to further investigate the effects of those factors on the accuracy of cost overrun.

As per the questionnaire survey in this research, it was found that the highest risk causing cost overruns is contractor-related factors, followed by design-related factors. In terms of contractor-related Factors, we had the contractor experience taking the highest percentage in causing cost overruns. In addition, contractor cash flow, contractor bankruptcy, and the abuse of change orders also had high ranks in causing cost overruns, whereas design-related factors, complexity of the project design, delay of drawings, and mistakes and omissions in design were upon the most common factors causing cost overruns.

On the other hand, project-related factors, materials-related factors, and external factors were also important players in causing an excess in project cost as per the conducted questionnaire. For an example of those factors, change in project's scope and additional cost due to additional work were among the highest factors causing increase in projects cost. As for materials-related factors, the fluctuation in the cost of materials was among the highest factors leading to cost overruns.

11.5.2 Interviews

For further support to the stated research questions and for the empirical part of this research, an Interview process is conducted to represent a qualitative part of this study. Five interviews were conducted to target the core issues in this research as follows: A number of three governmental key persons and two engineers from the private sector. All the five interviewees were asked the same following questions:

1. How do you evaluate the current governmental system in dealing with construction projects in terms of time and cost control?
2. What are your recommendations in order to improve the governmental system in KRG in terms of planning and managing existing and future projects?
3. How do you evaluate the current private sector in terms of responsiveness to governmental policies and what do you recommend as improvements?

The way the questions were set was to first investigate and diagnose the deficiencies in the governmental sector that are causing project delays and cost overruns. The second aspect was to concentrate on what recommendations should be proposed for KRG to enhance and develop the way of managing construction projects. The third aspect was on what are the roles of the private sector and how they should be responsive and supportive of the governmental sector.

11.5.2.1 Interviewee A

Background: Deputy governor of Erbil, Civil Engineer with more than 30 years' experience in different sizes of construction projects.

How do you evaluate the current governmental system in dealing with construction projects in terms of time and cost control?

> As per my experience, very few projects are actually executed within the time frame planned for them. That is because many reasons for example, the governmental payment, installment, method is so rigid and slow which negatively affect contractors and finally will be reflected on the work pace and quality. In addition to that, too many vacations, holidays, feasts, and mostly Ramadan negatively impact the pace of work and delay projects. Also, amendments during the construction phase always negatively affect the completion of projects in addition to the increase in cost.

What are your recommendations in order to improve the governmental system in KRG in terms of planning and managing existing and future projects?

> I believe that the governmental sector should consider the following recommendations:

- Lay annual budget and plan for the near and far future in terms of construction projects
- Projects should be well studied in detail and scientific studies should be made for proper cost estimations
- Construction firms should be carefully selected with good reputations and experience in the construction field
- Obstacles should be omitted and unnecessary regulations and complications in governmental contracting policies
- The method of general invitation should be replaced with direct invitation method for firms with good reputation
- Carefully select firms and companies that are financially capable. In addition to that, those firms should have well experienced staff, numerous machineries, and resources.

How do you evaluate the current private sector in terms of responsiveness to governmental policies and what do you recommend as improvements?

> The private sector should make good use of time and not be limited by governmental working hours and working days in order to accomplish projects on time. The contractor should

use equipment and machinery that are weatherproof in order to cover more working days even in bad weather conditions.

In addition to that, the private sector should work on training their own staff technically through taking courses in construction methodologies and construction management. Those courses can be either given locally or abroad.

11.5.2.2 Interviewee B

Background: Director of the Technical and Planning Department in the Ministry of Construction and Housing /Erbil, Civil Engineer with 40 years' experience in Construction projects, Buildings, and roads.

How do you evaluate the current governmental system in dealing with construction projects in terms of time and cost control?

The percentage of projects that are subject to change orders is 89% and that is due to changes in project specifications, design amendments, changes in bills of quantities, materials prices variation, exported items price variation, and finally the incompliance between the design and the execution of the project. Some of the foreign construction firms commit mistakes in cost estimations due to the lack of proper local and site investigations, lack of local knowledge in terms of geography and weather conditions and poor knowledge in the local market. Mostly those mistakes occur in large-scale and strategic projects like roads, bridges, dams, and tunnels.

In addition to that, KRG lacks a specialized governmental institution dealing with strategic project designs like roads, bridges, tunnels, dams, and power generation projects. Even more, the experienced staff in governmental institutions change every 4 years in relation to any changes occurring in the governmental institutions which negatively affect project management. Young expertise and new employees are not interested and well prepared to manage ongoing projects in a professional manner.

What are your recommendations in order to improve the governmental system in KRG in terms of planning and managing existing and future projects?

In my opinion…

- The government should enforce and activate the 3 leveled-plan; the long-term plan of 15–25 years, the medium-term plan of 3–5 years, and the short-term plan of one year. The government should benefit from the results of those 3 planning levels for future studies in terms of construction projects
- The government should consult engineering consulting bureaus, and local and international firms to prepare budgetary studies, geological studies, designs, and project supervision in parallel with the governmental engineers and teams. Those private bodies should also train the governmental staff to elevate their abilities
- The government should work on improving the financial installment system in order not to cause delays in construction projects
- The government should encourage international construction firms to execute local projects and should offer them all facilitations in order to improve the level of projects

- The government should work on eliminating bureaucracy in its institutions in order to improve the quality of designs and tendering methods
- The government should apply a new and different method of evaluating consultancy bureaus, project managing firms, and construction firms
- The government should devise a way to transfer governmental employees into the private sector and encourage them to be trained with international firms
- The government should make use of experts in universities and the academic sector from those who have good theoretical experience to back up the practical experience of the governmental institutions' staff. Academic experts can assist in project designs, projects management, financial management, and budgetary studies for engineering projects
- For strategic and infrastructural projects like water projects, sewer, power, roads, dams, airports, tunnels and irrigation projects should be supervised by a third party. The third party preferred to be an international or foreign specialized supervision firm.

How do you evaluate the current private sector in terms of responsiveness to governmental policies and what do you recommend as improvements?

The private sector should not only be responsive to the rigid policies laid by the governmental institutes. On the other hand, the private sector should be suggestive and develop its capabilities in order to encourage our governmental institutes for better and higher levels of corporation.

In my opinion, our private sector lacks exposure to contemporary construction technologies introduced worldwide and is limited to what is considered locally accepted. They should adopt different methodologies in construction that can save time, save cost elevate the quality, and train their staff accordingly. In addition to that, the private sector should benefit from the free system of hiring, working hours, working days, and other to improve capabilities and experience.

11.5.2.3 Interviewee C

Background: Director of Planning department in council Minsters, civil Engineer with more than 35 Year experience in construction projects.

How do you evaluate the current governmental system in dealing with construction projects in terms of time and cost control?

For the past 4 years in KRG, a lot of construction projects were held or paused which negatively affected on their completion, supervision and payments installment. In order to resume those projects, it require approvals and release for allocated budgets. In addition to that, development in the field of construction is slow and is paralyzed in KRG. In KRG there is no certain law for contracting which we highly need to establish and develop. There is a law for contracting only in the federal government of Baghdad which is recognized by the Iraqi parliament. For the past 4 years, the budgetary law is placed on hold which caused a lot of delays for construction project accomplishment.

The method of categorizing construction companies in KRG should be reviewed as we have over 600 local construction firms in KRG classified as the first category. If that was compared to the eighties, in all of Iraq there were only 40 local construction firms classified as first category or grade.

The Ministry of Planning lacks a contracting plan and we do not have investment plans which, both, the Ministry of Finance need to prepare the annual budget and installment system. In conclusion, development projects are divided into 3 categories; engineering projects, services projects, and supply projects. In all of these 3 categories, we can clearly witness cost overruns.

What are your recommendations in order to improve the governmental system in KRG in terms of planning and managing existing and future projects?

We suggest to establish an independent center for design checks, studies, budgetary studies preparation, staff training and other. This center should function as an independent governmental unit and be related to the Ministry of Planning. This center should be responsible for preparing different kinds of engineering studies and technical reports for industries, factories, infrastructural projects, roads, and other projects that have significant financial income.

The construction projects should not be only studied in terms of technical requirements, the "value of engineering" aspect of them should be also taken into consideration. In addition to that, performance and cost should be studied hand in hand in which both are related to time factor, delivery, and final cost. The contracting unit and the execution unit in our governmental institution have little or no cooperation between them. Those two departments should be related and connected to each other and both do not follow the reports of the site engineer which end up in cost overruns and project delay.

There is a specific unit in the ministry of planning in KRG under the name of "engineering studies unit". This unit should be activated and supported as an independent unit and a new law for contracting in KRG should be established accordingly. Furthermore, we should work on establishing an independent unit responsible for creating and enforcing policies and regulations for construction projects. This unit should take the responsibility of monitoring, auditing, supervising and following up construction projects.

How do you evaluate the current private sector in terms of responsiveness to governmental policies and what do you recommend as improvements?

First of all the Contractors Union in KRG have no commitment towards construction projects. In addition to that, many local construction firms have no clear classification or categories, they lack experience in projects management and have poor financial capabilities. The financial capabilities of a construction firm are determined by the firm budget, the firm earnings in terms of equipment and staff and the current on-going projects. Furthermore, the local engineering consultancy bureaus which are established as per KRG engineers' union policy, should work on improving their capabilities through corporation with international consultancy bureaus.

11.5.2.4 Interviewee D

Background: Engineer and contractor with 20+ years of experience in the private sector.

How do you evaluate the current governmental system in dealing with construction projects in terms of time and cost control?

When work is suspended for a period of 1 to 3 years this will affect the quality of work so when the work is resumed the quality of work will not match the specifications that were laid from the beginning. In this case we will end up with exceeding the estimated cost and cause delay. In some cases, some supervising engineers with little experience are hired for supervision and projects handover. This situation affects the work a lot along with the slow and improper decisions made by the owner.

The systematic and rigid routine followed by governmental institutes in terms of contractors' payments causes delays in projects completion. In addition to that, the policy that is laid to classify and categorize contactors is not being well followed by the ministry of planning. Accordingly, this will negatively influence on the process of shortlisting during tendering and awarding.

What are your recommendations in order to improve the governmental system in KRG in terms of planning and managing existing and future projects?

In the case of turn-key projects contracts, contracts are not being made neutral and mostly support the owner interest and protects the owner rights. Because of this, the contractor is required to come up with a very accurate and detailed studies, quantities and estimations in order to avoid any disagreements during construction. Even though, during construction many items are added or quantities are increased with amending the initial agreement whereas when quantities are reduced the owner will reduce the agreed turn-key price. The project owner or any governmental sector should review the designs, specifications and quantities prior to project kick-off and in case there are any remarks or amendments, the contractor should be notified not in the middle of the construction phase. As an example to that, in some cases there are no soil tests conducted for a certain turn-key project and after the test is conducted new modifications will appear and the contractor should cover them.

How do you evaluate the current private sector in terms of responsiveness to governmental policies and what do you recommend as improvements?

I believe our private sector suffers from the following issues:

- When designs are incomplete or done only on a preliminary level, the contractor has to revise and complete the design then submit for the owner for approval. This issue takes time and cause cost overruns especially when items appeared that they were not considered.
- Foreign engineering consultancy offices do not take clear and immediate decisions, whereas they transfer the case to local bodies. In this system, the local body or supervising party considers the owner representative as the decision maker regardless his/her educational background.
- On a contractual level, contracts are not following and including all contractual conditions, work ethics, specifications and other between both parties. This, as usual, cause delay in the project and unexpected additional costs.
- All private construction company have issues with financing due to the poor local banking systems which lack facilitations in terms of financing, letters of credits and other services as the case in other developed countries. Unfortunately, due to

the absence of such banking services, the contractor depends on his/her current financial capabilities in cash.

11.5.2.5 Interviewee E

Background: University professor with high experience in engineering projects supervision and management.

How do you evaluate the current governmental system in dealing with construction projects in terms of time and cost control?

The law after 1956 began to change gradually in terms of implying the system of service contracts which made the contractor as a slave working for the owner. This aspect laid to decrease the quality of work and services offered by the contractor. The contractor in this case is having the intention to execute the work with minimum quality just to accomplish the project and get paid.

Governmental institutes have poor supervision and follow up system and that is because of the whole system and the lack of experience. The government is not training engineers and staffs enough to be capable of handling and supervising project so they may finish on time and within the estimated cost. Also governmental institutes have a law level of corporation with third parties and consultation bodies in order to assist them follow up and supervision.

What are your recommendations in order to improve the governmental system in KRG in terms of planning and managing existing and future projects?

A construction projects is composed of 3 elements; land, budget and a concept or an idea. Usually in construction projects, the designer and the developer work hand in hand to find an investor which is a bank or any financial institution. In this process the project will be executed professionally and smoothly. I believe our governmental institutes should adopt the following recommendations:

- Should adopt the institutional mentality which is lacking most of our governmental institutions.
- Priorities should also be set in all strategic and development projects.
- Every ministry should have its own planning department that functions as an independent unit responsible for supervision, planning, design and follow up.
- The master plan for development projects should be set and laid by the ministry of planning in coordination with the ministries and taking into consideration their requests.
- The collective work method should be applied in all our ministries for development and construction projects and we should go back to the former laws before the civil law introduced in 1956. The law before 1956 was fairer for contractors and in the same time protects the rights of the government contractually in away both parties have duties and responsibilities.

- Third parties as independent units should be involved with a role specifically for supervision and follow up. The same party, the third party, can also be responsible for the phase of testing and commissioning.

How do you evaluate the current private sector in terms of responsiveness to governmental policies and what do you recommend as improvements?

I believe that projects and mostly large scale projects are being awarded for firms not based on their profiles, experience, executed projects and background. This is because our governmental institutes do not have clear data base that categorizes construction firms as per their abilities and qualifications. KRG government should work on re-studying private construction firms and the way that have been categorized and follow the direct invitation system in tendering accordingly.

Governmental institutions should device some laws that facilitate payment methods for contractors and not follow the slow and rigid polities. In addition to that, they should work on encouraging our local banking system to offer facilitations in terms of financing.

On the other side, our private sector should work seriously on improving their technical skills through hiring qualities staff, training courses, affiliation with international firms and adopting up-to-date construction technologies in terms of time and cost saving.

11.5.3 Recommendations and Policy Implications

The recommendations fall into two major parts: The first part is mostly concerned with governmental institutions (Public Sector) after diagnosing the deficiencies in the system followed in dealing with construction projects. The other part focuses on the private sector and what recommendations are suggested in order to elevate the quality of the offered services and responsiveness to the governmental sector.

In terms of KRG governmental institutes (Public Sector), the main recommendation is to work on eliminating the bureaucracy in the existing system. This step will allow the introducing of more flexible methods in dealing with construction projects. Those methods will cover the sector of financing construction projects, installment methods, contracts, project management, supervision and follow-up, and testing and commissioning. In addition to that, will allow more interference and support for third parties and international consultation bodies to take part in the process. All those procedures and development will, at the end result, have a positive impact on construction projects in terms of time, quality and cost control.

At the other hand, the private sector will benefit from the elimination of bureaucracy in terms of time-saving, less procedures, more flexible system and fairer tendering system. Yet, the private sector should also work continually on developing local abilities in terms of staff, machinery and technological methods of construction. The private sector should also start adopting construction mentality that is toward sustainability and energy saving which might increase the initial cost but save a lot on the long run. Exposure to up-to-date construction and project management systems requires efforts in terms of training, joint ventures with international firms, and continuous improvement of the local staff.

11.5.4 Recommendations for Further Research

There are a number of areas that were mentioned without details, or problems were highlighted without proposing detailed solutions. Each point of those can be studied in details and get full analysis for it and propose a way of customizing it to project cost accuracy.

For example, for each main risk factors an open-ended question would be of benefit so the surveyor expresses her opinion in more broad sense.

In addition, this study recommends further investigation on how cost estimation accuracy of a construction project can be minimized or for some projects can be eliminated. Classifying the projects based on type for example infrastructure projects, feasibility studies, dams, and tunnels projects would be interesting if evaluated separately by the identified risk factors. For Future research, one should take into consideration taste, quality requirements, and material factor prices may impact the cost situation and magnitude of cost overrun. These fine details required independent separate studies.

11.5.5 Limitations

There have been a number of limitations in this research and below are the main ones:

- Sample size: Despite the low number of sampled population, the targeted staff and the response rate should give representative results, as they were purposively selected from different entities and in different managerial levels. This may not give exact representation of reality, but it should be close to it.
- Data collection process: It was highlighted above that interviews were conducted with people who are directly involved in project management and who are fully aware of it and this is a positive point. On the other hand, this could be an environment of being bias toward their work, as they are part of construction project management.
- Data: Although the plan was to collect data from primary and secondary resources, it ended up collecting the data only from primary resources. The reason behind this change in plan was due to primary data are direct to the point and summarized many unnecessary repetitive details in secondary sources.

Appendix: Survey Questionnaire

Section 1: General Information (Demography)

1. Which of the following best describe your job function?

☐ Client
☐ Consultant
☐ Contractor

2. How many years of Experience do you have?

☐ 0–5 Years
☐ 6–10 Years
☐ 11–15 Years
☐ 16–20 Years
☐ More than 20 Years

3. How many projects have you been involved in?

☐ 1–5
☐ 6–10
☐ 11–15
☐ 16–20
☐ More than 20

4. What type of projects have your organization executed?

☐ Civil Engineering Project
☐ Mechanical Engineering Project
☐ Electrical Engineering Project
☐ Structural Engineering Projects
☐ All of the above
☐ Some of the above
☐ Others

2. Participation Consent and Ethics

This Section will be used to confirm your voluntary participation in this survey and ensure highest ethical standards are maintained

5. Was the goal of this research clearly explained to you?

☐ No
☐ Yes

Other (please specify): ----------------------------

6. Were you coaxed or promised any benefits to participate in this survey?

☐ No
☐ Yes

If your answer is yes, explain: ----------------------------

7. Is your participation in this survey voluntary?

☐ No
☐ Yes

If your answer is No, explain: ----------------------------

3. Risk Factors that Affect the Accuracy of Project Cost Estimates

A. Project-Related Factors

#	Factor	No risk	Low risk	Average risk	High risk	Highest risk
A.1	Characteristics of the Project (nature, complexity, size)					
A.2	Well-Defined Scope of Work					
A.3	Additional Costs due to variations works					
A.4	Project Scope Change					
A.5	Communication among the various Stakeholders					
A.6	Site conditions: (Location, topography, accessibility, existing and surrounding elements)					
A.7	Speed of Decision making by Project Team					

B. Client-Related Factors

#	Factor	No risk	Low risk	Average risk	High risk	Highest risk
B.1	Project Financing					
B.2	Contractual terms and Requirements					
B.3	Pressure on Estimators/Engineers					
B.4	Changing Company Policies and Procedures					
B.5	Executive bureaucracy in the client's organization					
B.6	Communication among Stakeholders					
B.7	Estimating Errors					

C. Design-Related Factors

#	Factor	No risk	Low risk	Average risk	High risk	Highest risk
C.1	Experience of Designers					
C.2	Complexity of the project design					
C.3	Delay of drawings and/or order requested by the contractor					
C.4	Mistakes and omissions in designs					
C.5	Accuracy of Survey					
C.6	Scope Creep					
C.7	Project Location					
C.8	Inadequate/nonexistent records					

D. Material/Equipment-Related Risk Factors

#	Factor	No risk	Low risk	Average risk	High risk	Highest risk
D.1	Difficulties in obtaining materials in local market					
D.2	Material Shortage					
D.3	Fluctuations in the cost of material and price change					
D.4	Wrong materials Purchased					
D.5	Changes in Material Specifications					
D.6	Long lead Items					
D.7	Equipment Availability					
D.8	Wrong Selection of Equipment					

E. Contractor-Related Factors

#	Factor	No risk	Low risk	Average risk	High risk	Highest risk
E.1	Availability of Contractor Resources					
E.2	Contractor Experience in Planning and Execution of Projects					
E.3	Cash Flow					
E.4	Contractor Bankruptcy					
E.5	Abuse of Change Order Process					

#	Factor	No risk	Low risk	Average risk	High risk	Highest risk
E.6	Over Time Abuse					

F. Workforce-Related Risk Factors

#	Factor	No risk	Low risk	Average risk	High risk	Highest risk
F.1	Skill level of Crew Members					
F.2	Availability of Labor Crews					
F.3	Low Productivity					
F.4	Labor Office Issues					

G. External Risk Factors

#	Factor	No risk	Low risk	Average risk	High risk	Highest risk
G.1	Weather Concerns					
G.2	Environmental Concerns					
G.3	Required State and local Permits/ Licenses					
G.4	Force Majeure					
G.5	Changing Codes and Standards					
G.6	Political Factors					

4. Risk Factors that Impact Project Cost Overruns

Fifteen Potential Factors that can cause project cost overruns have been identified below. To enable the evaluation of these factors and how they impact project cost overruns. A Likert scale of 1–15 was created below. The scale will be used to rank the impact with 1 being the most impactful and 15 being the least impactful.

Factors Affecting Project Cost Overruns

#	Factor	Rank/Scale														
		first	second	third	fourth	fifth	sixth	seventh	eighth	ninth	tenth	eleventh	twelfth	thirteenth	fourteenth	fifteenth
1	Characteristics of the project															
2	Scope change															
3	Effective communication among the stakeholders															
4	Site conditions															
5	Contractual terms and conditions															
6	Estimating error															
7	Mistakes and omission in designs															
8	Accuracy of survey															
9	Project Location															
10	Abuse of change order process															
11	Wrong material purchased															
12	Labor Office rules and regulations															
13	Equipment Availability															
14	Weather Concerns															
15	Required state and local permits															

References

Ahiaga-Dagbui, D. D., Love, P. E., Smith, S. D., & Ackermann, F. (2017). Toward a systemic view to cost overrun causation in infrastructure projects: A review and implications for research. *Project Management Journal, 48*, 88–98.

Akintoye, A. S., & Macleod, M. J. (1997). Risk analysis and management in construction. *International Journal of Project Management, 15*, 31–38.

Ali, A. H., Elyamany, A., Ibrahim, A. H., Kineber, A. F., & Daoud, A. O. (2023). Modelling the relationship between modular construction adoption and critical success factors for residential projects in developing countries. *International Journal of Construction Management*, 1–12.

Amadi, A. & Omotayo, T. 2017. Positioning cost overrun research in the philosophical debate: A case for critical realism.

Amusan, L. M., Afolabi, A., Ojelabi, R., Omuh, I., & Okagbue, H. I. (2018). Data exploration on factors that influences construction cost and time performance on construction project sites. *Data in Brief, 17*, 1320–1325.

Annamalaisami, C. D., & Kuppuswamy, A. (2021). Managing cost risks: Toward a taxonomy of cost overrun factors in building construction projects. *ASCE-ASME Journal of Risk and Uncertainty in Engineering Systems, Part A: Civil Engineering, 7*, 04021021.

Ansah, R. H., Sorooshian, S., & Mustafa, S. B. (2018). The 4ps: A framework for evaluating construction projects delays. *Journal of Engineering and Applied Sciences, 13*, 1222–1227.

Axmadjonovich, Q. S. (2023). Effective organization of investment projects in industrial enterprises. International Journal of Research. In Commerce, It, Engineering and Social Sciences. Issn: 2349-7793 Impact Factor: 6.876, 17, 7–11.

Bertisen, J., & Davis, G. A. (2008). Bias and error in mine project capital cost estimation. *The Engineering Economist, 53*, 118–139.

Caffieri, J. J., Love, P. E., Whyte, A., & Ahiaga-Dagbui, D. D. (2018). Planning for production in construction: Controlling costs in major capital projects. *Production Planning & Control, 29*, 41–50.

Cantarelli, C. C., Flybjerg, B., Molin, E. J., & Van Wee, B. (2013). Cost overruns in large-scale transportation infrastructure projects: Explanations and their theoretical embeddedness. *Arxiv Preprint Arxiv, 1307*, 2176.

Dahlin, P., & Pesämaa, O. (2021). Drivers of cost and time overruns: A client and contractor perspective. *Organization, Technology & Management In Construction: An International Journal, 13*, 2374–2382.

Diab, M. F., Varma, A., & Panthi, K. (2017). Modeling the construction risk ratings to estimate the contingency in highway projects. *Journal of Construction Engineering and Management, 143*, 04017041.

Doloi, H., Sawhney, A., Iyer, K., & Rentala, S. (2012). Analysing factors affecting delays in Indian construction projects. *International Journal of Project Management, 30*, 479–489.

Eliufoo, H. (2017). Project team perception of causes of building cost overruns: A reflection in Tanzania. *Journal Of Civil Engineering And Architecture, 11*, 149–158.

Gamil, Y., & Rahman, I. A. (2018). Identification of causes and effects of poor communication in construction industry: A theoretical review. *Emerging Science Journal, 1*, 239–247.

Ghauri, P., & Grønhaug, K. (2002). *Research methods in business studies: A practical guide, (in 1995)*. Pearson Education.

Gómez-Cabrera, A., Gutierrez-Bucheli, L., & Muñoz, S. (2023). Causes of time and cost overruns in construction projects: A scoping review. *International Journal of Construction Management*, 1–19.

Greene, W. H. (2008). The econometric approach to efficiency analysis. *The Measurement Of Productive Efficiency And Productivity Growth, 1*, 92–250.

Gunduz, M., & Maki, O. L. (2018). Assessing the risk perception of cost overrun through importance rating. *Technological and Economic Development of Economy, 24*, 1829–1844.

Heshmati, A., & Khayyat, N. T. (2014). Analysis of landmine fatalities and injuries in the Kurdistan region. *Journal of Interpersonal Violence, 30*, 2591–2615.
Holm, L., & Schaufelberger, J. E. (2021). *Construction cost estimating*. Routledge.
Huo, T., Ren, H., Cai, W., Shen, G. Q., Liu, B., Zhu, M., & Wu, H. (2018). Measurement and dependence analysis of cost overruns in Megatransport infrastructure projects: Case study in Hong Kong. *Journal of Construction Engineering and Management, 144*, 05018001.
Irfan, M., Khan, S. Z., Hassan, N., Hassan, M., Habib, M., Khan, S., & Khan, H. H. (2021). Role of project planning and project manager competencies on public sector project success. *Sustainability, 13*, 1421.
Jarkas, A. M., & Marenjak, S. (2014). Significant contributors to construction cost overruns: Findings of Kuwait. *International Journal Of The Built Environment and Asset Management, 1*, 193–220.
Korytárová, J., & Hromádka, V. (2020). Risk assessment of large-scale infrastructure projects—Assumptions and context. *Applied Sciences, 11*, 109.
Lakens, D. (2022). Sample size justification. *Collabra. Psychology, 8*, 33267.
Liu, J., Yi, Y., & Wang, X. (2020). Exploring factors influencing construction waste reduction: A structural equation modeling approach. *Journal of Cleaner Production, 276*, 123185.
Love, P. E., Ahiaga-Dagbui, D. D., & Irani, Z. (2016). Cost overruns in transportation infrastructure projects: Sowing the seeds for a probabilistic theory of causation. *Transportation Research Part A: Policy and Practice, 92*, 184–194.
Lukale, A. M. (2018). *Determinants of cost overruns in rural roads infrastructure projects in Kenya*. Strathmore University.
Lydeard, S. (1991). The questionnaire as a research tool. *Family Practice, 8*, 84–91.
Mbachu, J. I., & Cross, C. (2015). Key drivers of discrepancies between initial and final costs of construction projects in New Zealand. *Proj Manage Inst Pm World J., Iv*, 1–11.
Molinari, L., Haezendonck, E., & Mabillard, V. (2023). Cost overruns of Belgian transport infrastructure projects: Analyzing variations over three land transport modes and two project phases. *Transport Policy, 134*, 167–179.
Moradi, S., Kähkönen, K., Klakegg, O. J., & Aaltonen, K. (2020). A competency model for the selection and performance improvement of project managers in collaborative construction projects: Behavioral studies in Norway and Finland. *Buildings, 11*, 4.
Mukuka, M., Aigbavboa, C., & Thwala, W. (2014). Construction experts' perception on the causes and effects of cost overruns in Johannesburg, Gauteng Province, South Africa. The 2014 (5th) international conference on engineering, project, and production management, 349.
Muñoz-La Rivera, F., Mora-Serrano, J., & Oñate, E. (2021). Factors influencing safety on construction projects (Fscps): Types and categories. *International Journal of Environmental Research and Public Health, 18*, 10884.
Narayanan, S., Kure, A. M., & Palaniappan, S. (2018). Study on time and cost overruns in mega infrastructure projects in India. Journal of the Institution of Engineers (India)*:* Series A, 1–7.
Park, J. E. (2021). Schedule delays of major projects: What should we do about it? *Transport Reviews, 41*, 814–832.
Rabionet, S. E. (2011). How I learned to design and conduct semi-structured interviews: An ongoing and continuous journey. *Qualitative Report, 16*, 563–566.
Rahman, I. A., Ismail, I. B., & Jaber, M. M. (2018). Risk assessment of time and cost overrun factors throughout construction project lifecycle: Pilot study. *International Journal Of Engineering & Technology, 7*, 717–723.
Raza, M. Q., & Khosravi, A. (2015). A review on artificial intelligence based load demand forecasting techniques for smart grid and buildings. *Renewable and Sustainable Energy Reviews, 50*, 1352 1372.
Santos, F. R. S. D., & Cabral, S. (2008). Fmea and Pmbok applied to project risk management. *Jistem-Journal Of Information Systems and Technology Management, 5*, 347–364.
Sayed, M., Abdel-Hamid, M., & El-Dash, K. (2023). Improving cost estimation in construction projects. *International Journal of Construction Management, 23*, 135–143.

Shoar, S., Yiu, T. W., Payan, S., & Parchamijalal, M. (2023). Modeling cost overrun in building construction projects using the interpretive structural modeling approach: A developing country perspective. *Engineering, Construction And Architectural Management, 30*, 365–392.

Sinesilassie, E., Tabish, S., & Jha, K. (2018). Critical factors affecting cost performance: A case of Ethiopian public construction projects. *International Journal of Construction Management, 18*, 108–119.

Sorvig, K., & Thompson, J. W. (2018). *Heal injured soils and sites. Sustainable landscape construction*. Springer.

Sovacool, B. K., Gilbert, A., & Nugent, D. (2014). An international comparative assessment of construction cost overruns for electricity infrastructure. *Energy Research & Social Science, 3*, 152–160.

Steininger, B. I., Groth, M., & Weber, B. L. (2021). Cost overruns and delays in infrastructure projects: The case of Stuttgart 21. *Journal of Property Investment & Finance, 39*, 256–282.

Tayefeh Hashemi, S., Ebadati, O. M., & Kaur, H. (2020). Cost estimation and prediction in construction projects: A systematic review on machine learning techniques. *SN Applied Sciences, 2*, 1703.

Tedla, Y., & Patel, D. (2018). Assessing problems of construction material management in residential project: Case study. *International Journal Of Emerging Technologies And Innovative Research Jetir*. Jetir.

Ture, M., Kurt, I., & Akturk, Z. (2007). Comparison of dimension reduction methods using patient satisfaction data. *Expert Systems with Applications, 32*, 422–426.

Vaardini, S., Karthiyayini, S., & Ezhilmathi, P. (2016). Study on cost overruns in construction projects: A review. *International Journal of Applied Engineering Research, 11*, 356–363.

Venkataraman, R. R., & Pinto, J. K. (2023). *Cost and value management in projects*. Wiley.

Wang, T., Xu, J., He, Q., Chan, A. P., & Owusu, E. K. (2023). Studies on the success criteria and critical success factors for mega infrastructure construction projects: A literature review. *Engineering, Construction And Architectural Management, 30*, 1809–1834.

Zidane, Y., & Andersen, B. (2018). The top 10 universal delay factors in construction projects. *International Journal of Managing Projects in Business, 11*, 650–672.

Chapter 12
What Determines Household Electricity Consumption?

Dilveen D. Mustafa

Abstract The capacity to predict the immediate changes in electricity demand in a region and the factors that drive them are increasingly important to electricity system operators, particularly in the deregulated power system environment. In addition to its price, modeling residential electricity consumption (REC) involves millions of households and depends on numerous variables, such as temperature, income, household size, new energy technologies, users' responses to pricing, and the level of investments made by utilities for energy savings and demand-response programs, as well as management strategies built on the relationship between energy price response and energy improvements. This study investigates the factors affecting residential electricity consumption in the Kurdistan Region of Iraq. The study of the determinants of household demand for electricity has a dual purpose: firstly, to determine the important variables that play roles in electricity consumption through econometric modeling of households' electricity consumption, allowing us to analyze the possible impact of family behavioral changes on their electricity consumption, promoting its rationalization, efficiency, and hence reducing the electricity demand; secondly, the knowledge of these determinants will allow planning and development entities to benefit from the useful information for their decision-making to design strategies for rational electricity consumption, establish intervention strategies according to identified variables, and formulate and implement targeted campaigns to inform and educate in order to promote advances and changing habits of its users, to reduce the electricity demand.

Keywords Electricity demand · Electricity consumption · Efficiency · Kurdistan region

D. D. Mustafa (✉)
Vision Education, Erbil, Iraq

G. M. Muhamad, N. T. Khayyat (eds.), *Resource Management Performance: A Sectoral Analysis in the Post-Conflict Kurdistan Region of Iraq*, Perspectives on Development in the Middle East and North Africa (MENA) Region,
https://doi.org/10.1007/978-981-97-7725-9_12

12.1 Introduction

The capacity to predict the immediate changes in electricity demand in a region and the factors that drive them is increasingly important to electricity system operators, particularly in the deregulated power system environment (Khayyat, 2015; Santiago et al., 2021). In addition to its price, modeling residential electricity consumption (REC) involves millions of households and depends on numerous variables, such as temperature, income, household size, new energy technologies, users' responses to pricing, and the level of investments made by utilities for energy savings and demand-response programs, as well as management strategies built on the relationship between energy price response and energy improvements (Wang et al., 2020).

Data on electricity consumption and its correlation with these variables are made available by smart meter records, through extensive econometric models and sophisticated consumer survey techniques. These techniques are presented as flexible, low-cost, and available options without centralized records, but with several print possibilities on residential demands, data on the progress of regulatory and market restructuring policies, and in particular, the implementation of price response programs, in their successes or failures (Andersen et al., 2021).

Since the internal conflicts and consequences of the Gulf War in 1991, the Kurdistan Region of Iraq had centered its attention on providing basic necessities to its people. Throughout the years, there has been much attention on providing these necessities such as energy consumption in the form of electricity (along with other essentials as well). In spite of this focus, little attention and studies on the determinants of electricity consumption have been conducted.

In 1998, the providing of electricity was in a poor state; distributions were so weak that households had access to electricity for only 3–5 h per day, with some areas receiving either less than this or none at all (UNDP, 2008; Jamal et al., 2021). Through a $450 million dollar project, supported by the UNDP, the Ministry of Electricity in the Kurdistan Region, and Japan, electricity improved rapidly and effectively. By 2013, households were provided with nearly 20 h of electricity throughout all districts, cities, and towns in the Kurdistan Region of Iraq (UNDP, 2008).

Although deemed to be a public good in theory, in practice, electricity in the KRI is more falling under the category of being a private good. As common practice and understanding shows that electricity, to a large extent, is a public good and should be provided as a basic necessity by a government. Households in the Kurdistan Region more so rely on the private sector for the providing of electricity, which results in electricity being a private good rather than a public good. The reason why electricity is a private good rather than a public good is that the electricity sector used to fall under full government control, but in due time, it struggled to provide electricity to households, failing to meet the demands of people and in turn creating the opportunity for households to invest in the private sector to meet their demands and needs.

A pure public good is a good that has no competition in its consumption (non-rival), and one's consumption of a good has no effects on another individual's good consumption (non-excludable) (Gruber, 2007). An impure public good is a good that falls under the category of both non-rival and non-excludable, but only to a certain extent. Through the KRI's 20-year project on improving electricity, funded and controlled by the private sector and foreign assistance, the improvements in electricity were evident. With improvement in electricity being drastic, many households continue to use alternatives such as gas for cooking rather than electricity.

Improvements in the KRI's electricity sector provided to households have shown significant results. However, despite the improvements in the distribution of electricity, the electricity sector in the KRG is unable to provide the contributing factors affecting how much a household uses this energy.

Determining the factors that contribute to electricity consumption is necessary since it provides an indication as to how a household uses what source of energy whether it is biomass in the form of wood, gas for cooking, or provided electricity. Having these factors assessed, this study can provide an interpretation on how much energy is over or under-consumed and confront the issues accordingly.

One of the main predicaments of achieving the determining factors of energy consumption is categorizing how much a household consumes in each energy category. For instance, a household may use gas for cooking, electricity for air conditioning, wood for a fireplace, or kerosene for heating and cooking. This predicament is also followed by the inconsistency and lack of recorded consumption for households. According to an article submitted by the World Bank, the use of electricity and its consumption among households has left effects of electricity theft, issues with the distribution of electricity and insufficiency in recordings, and collection of electricity bills (The World Bank, 2009; The World Bank, 2016).

The purpose of this research is to help classify what variables affect the extent of electricity consumption and help in providing a clearer understanding of the energy consumption behavior in households across Erbil.

12.2 Literature Review

Throughout this study, the use of qualitative research and other conducted studies will help in examining and determining the factors which influence the household electricity consumption. Several research and reports have been dedicated to this matter that will serve as a useful comparison for household electricity consumption in the KRG.

The following literature reviews will show relevance to the study in supporting and evidencing the factors of consumption in regard to electricity in households. The devising of this section will help in filling in the gaps, which is the lack of knowledge and awareness on the topic of discussion.

12.2.1 Climate and Economic Impact on Energy Consumption

During an economic growth period (1970s and onward) in Hong Kong, China, there was a rise in the standard of living and a major increase in electricity consumption. A rise in consumption of electricity raised many questions and studies because Hong Kong relied mainly on energy sources such as oil and coal. Lam (1998) observed 23 years (1971–1993) and linked the relationship between residential electricity consumption, economic variables, and climate factors while considering the factors of influence such as household income and size, electricity pricing, and cooling degree days (Kostakis, 2020).

The consumption of this energy also varies according to season (influenced by climate condition) and annually (factors such as economics, social, and demographics). In assessing the heating and cooling requirements and demonstrating the impact of weather on electricity, Du et al. (2020) used degree-day statistics and techniques that involved key weather parameters. By observing previous work on weather data, the study identified three major variables that are temperature, moisture content, and solar radiation. These explained the effects of cooling requirements and selected three termed variables as follows:

- Cooling degree days (CDD): indicating the cooling requirement for a particular location
- Latent enthalpy days (LED): indicating the amount of energy needed to remove excess moisture form outdoor air and lower humidity to meet indoor levels
- Cooling radiation days (CRD): measures the building cooling load that results from unwanted solar radiation during summer months

These variables were used in a multiple regression to model the monthly electricity consumption and to understand the dominant variable CDD/the finding revealed that seasonal variation can be explained by the variations in the three variables CDD, LED, and CRD. These results implied that climate change influences electricity consumption, and seasonal variations influence the extent of consumption. Factors of further influence were social, economic, and demographic conditions that contributed to the increasing level of electricity consumption in Hong Kong.

Berardi and Jafarpur (2020) examined the relationship between climate change and energy consumption, focusing on the impact of temperature variations on energy demand. It synthesizes findings from multiple studies that analyze historical data and model future scenarios to predict changes in energy consumption patterns due to climate change. The study found that both heating and cooling degree days significantly influence energy demand. In colder climates, energy demand increases for heating, while in warmer regions, cooling needs drive up electricity consumption. Moreover, the study found that seasonal temperature variations have a direct impact on energy consumption, with peak demand observed during extreme weather conditions (e.g., heat waves and cold snaps). Other factors such adaptation and mitigation strategies are important factors to implement energy-efficient technologies for climate change mitigation.

Ekonomou and Halkos (2023) explored the intricate relationship between economic growth and energy consumption, analyzing how economic development drives energy demand and how energy consumption, in turn, influences economic performance. Economic growth and energy consumption are closely linked and managing this relationship is key to achieving sustainable development. Policymakers should heavily observe both economic and environmental factors to foster growth without compromising energy sustainability.

12.2.2 Electricity Demand: End-Use Consumption

By combining the effects of household electric appliances and end-uses such as space, heating, and lighting, the research aims to find a method for estimating end-use consumption, Andersen et al. (2021) have conducted a research on metering data on total electricity consumption for different end-uses in Denmark. To calculate the end-use consumption of electricity, the authors use two major techniques: the engineering model and the econometric model.

The engineering model consists of engineering knowledge regarding technical and constructional features of different houses and the influence of these features on energy demand. The model also presents various equations and parameters that require obtaining information for input values of these parameters from other sources. The limitation of this model was the excessive use of equations that require calibration due to the lack of information and uncertainty in numerical data.

On the other hand, to assess the econometric model it requires information on which a particular appliance or a number of appliances a household possesses and socioeconomic characteristics. The research compared the two models and the results from the engineering model estimated that consumption was higher in households that used space and water heating. The econometric model estimated significantly higher electricity consumption with households that used electric appliances such as electric heaters, hair dryers, dishwashers, and TVs., compared to those who did not.

12.2.3 Understanding Energy Consumption

Energy consumption in households is a multifaceted issue affected by several factors, including socioeconomic status, household size, type of dwelling, climatic conditions, and behavioral patterns. Understanding these factors is crucial for developing strategies to improve energy efficiency and reduce environmental impact.

Energy consumption in households is a critical area of study due to its significant impact on both economic and environmental dimensions. In researching energy consumption, Huebner et al. (2016) explained the effects of different variables according to electricity consumption with gas-fueled space and water heating. In this study, a regression model was run on four models to test each variable for the existence of multicollinearity (occurs when a variable can be linearly predicted) in dwellings. While the dependent variable was the annualized electricity consumption in kilowatts per hour; the independent variables included the building variable and their frequencies, socio-demographic variables, appliances and lighting, and other occupant variables.

First, an OLS regression was performed per variable. When there was suspicion of collinearity, variance influence factors (VIF) were tested. VIF indicates how much the variance of an estimated regression coefficient increases if the explanatory variables are correlated. A value of VIF = 1 shows the variables being uncorrelated but the results for this test showed the value of VIF being larger than 3.3 and this resulted in using a Lasso regression. This regression is a linear model used to calculate regression coefficients by setting these coefficients to zero to eliminate irrelevant variables and to minimize the usual sum of squared errors.[1]

In the final steps of the research, the separate models of regression were combined to test for increments. Having combined the models one at a time the results of these proved that there was a 35% variability in electricity consumption explained by the four main variables (building variables, socio-demographics, appliances, lighting, and other occupant variables). The finding revealed that multicollinearity is an issue in analyzing electricity consumption data, appliance ownership, and its uses are most important in understanding electricity consumption, household size is likewise a significant predictor.

When it comes to the different uses of fuel in households, few literature has touched upon this subject (Van der Kroon et al., 2014; Ahmad & Zhang, 2020). For example, James et al. (2020) assessed the pattern of fuel used for cooking in households to determine the association between the types of fuel used and socio-demographic characteristics.

Stoner et al. (2021) used a novel modeling approach to provide detailed global, regional, and country estimates of the percentages and populations mainly using several fuel categories (electricity, gaseous fuels, kerosene, biomass, charcoal, coal). The finding was that 53% of the global population mainly used polluting cooking fuels in 1990, dropping to 36% in 2020. In urban areas, gaseous fuels is still dominant, with a growing reliance on electricity; in rural populations, high levels of biomass use persist alongside increasing use of gaseous fuels.

[1] Ibid.

12.2.4 *Feedback on Household Electricity Consumption: A Tool for Saving Energy?*

A research conducted by Fischer (2008) serves as an essential reminder of the importance of consuming electricity responsibly or how electricity conservation is not limited to the act of using electricity but starts with choosing and purchasing energy-using appliances like a TV set, washing machine, computer equipment, or electric heater.

In each of these activities, conservation means a different set of behavioral modifications. This goes to show that although it is difficult to conserve or even measure electricity consumption, many factors that go unnoticed are still very relevant.

This study highlighted a vital theory called environment psychology that contains models to explain and understand environment-related behavior and what factors may change it. Linking environmental behavior and electricity, the model used by Zelenski and Desrochers (2021), helps explain why it is necessary to reduce electricity consumption and how it could be achieved. Firstly, the model presents a term called "environmentally detrimental habits" that arise from habitual actions (day-to-day behavior) such as switching on the TV, lights, stove, and other day-to-day electricity appliances. This model mainly suggests that if an impact or a change was intended, then there must be a switch from habitual behavior to a *conscious decision*.

The conscious decision is proposed as a three-step course where the first is realizing an issue is actually at hand, the second for an individual to come to the belief that they contribute to this issue, and the final step is for the individual to understand that this issue is their responsibility and have an area of influence. The depiction of this model shows great significance, especially in areas such as Kurdistan, where consumers of electricity often do not realize the possible issues that arise from neglecting or irresponsibly consuming electricity.

12.3 Methodology

The methodology section presents the methods of research that are categorized into two different sections. The first section is the descriptive statistics section, which will outline and summarize the data collection and methods. The second section will comprise the model descriptor, where the independent and the dependent variables will be detailed. This part will also depict the methods used in conducting the data collection. The use of primary and secondary data has been used in the collection and interpretation of data for the sole purpose of ensuring an understanding of the electricity consumption of households.

12.3.1 Descriptive Statistics

The data in this study was collected from the KRG Ministry of Electricity based on the electricity bills of 25 houses in Erbil, the capital city of the KRI. The households contributed to a questionnaire that served as the guideline for the descriptive statistics and for ascertaining the dependent and independent variables. Households were asked in a survey a wide range of questions regarding their electricity consumption behavior, the number, and uses of electricity appliances, the household's income range, as well as the size (in meters squared) and age of the building.

The questionnaire consisted of 13 questions and was further combined with each household's previous electricity consumption data in KWH and the amount that was paid according to KW/hr., in Iraqi Dinar. The recordings of the data were constructed by putting the household consumption of KWH against all the answers to the questionnaire for every 3 months during the years 2013 until 2017 which totaled into a 6-period observation for every household.

A panel data was constructed, where the untested model is presented in the table below (Table 12.1). The dependent variable refers to the variable that is influenced by other factors in the test and is completely dependent on the other independent variable to predict its values.

The dependent variable of the test is the cost each household pays for their electricity consumption. The independent variables are measured for further comparison to test their significance. The independent variables of this data are the results from questions 1 to 13 (of the survey), creating 13 independent variables in the regression analysis.

12.3.2 Model Descriptor

With 568 observations in total, the panel data facilitates the estimation of the regression equations to be:

$$\begin{aligned}\log(\text{cost}) = {} & \alpha_0 + \alpha_1(\text{hhmbrs}) + \alpha_2(\text{hhadults}) + \alpha_3(\text{hhrooms}) + \alpha_4(\text{hhage}) \\ & + \alpha_5(\text{hhm}^2) + \alpha_6(\text{income}) + \alpha_7(\text{lightbulbs}) + \alpha_8(\text{numbrelecapp}) \\ & + \alpha_9(\text{elecappuseage}) + \alpha_{10}(\text{energy}) + \alpha_{11}(\text{season}) \\ & + \alpha_{12}(\text{elecappovernight}) + \alpha_{13}(\text{elecapponly}) + \varepsilon_t\end{aligned}$$

Table 12.1 Descriptive statistics of the variables

Variable	Mean	Std. Dev.	Minimum	Maximum	Cases
ID	12.9208	7.52907	1	25	568
YEAR	2015	133.463	2013	2017	568
READ	29.8347	23.2924	0	219.4	568
COST	96.1812	188.995	0.25	2129.25	568
Q1	5.42077	2.24529	2	13	568
Q2	4.30106	2.08358	2	11	568
Q3	7.54401	1.37943	5	9	568
Q4	17.4419	13.267	2	54	568
Q5	222.289	87.1033	100	450	568
Q6	2.37324	1.47099	0	5	568
Q7	1.83451	0.468484	0	2	568
Q8-1	1.48239	0.639422	1	4	568
Q8-2	0.961268	0.368868	0	2	568
Q8-3	1.08803	0.283586	1	2	568
Q8-4	0.447183	0.497641	0	1	568
Q8-5	1.38028	0.485884	1	2	568
Q8-6	1.21831	0.413463	1	2	568
Q8-7	4.23239	2.42246	0	8	568
Q8-8	1.84683	0.809636	0	3	568
Q8-9	0.545775	0.498339	0	1	568
Q8-10	0.334507	0.472234	0	1	568
Q9-1	0	0	0	0	568
Q9-2	0.880282E-01	0.283586	0	1	568
Q9-3	0.373239	0.484091	0	1	568
Q9-4	0.59331	0.491649	0	1	568
Q9-5	0	0	0	0	568
Q9-6	0	0	0	0	568
Q9-7	0.133803	0.34074	0	1	568
Q9-8	0.387324E-01	0.193127	0	1	568
Q9-9	0.832746	0.373531	0	1	568
Q9-10	0.776408	0.417019	0	1	568
Q10	5.08099	1.63098	1	6	568
Q11	2.24296	2.43087	0	5	568
Q12	0.922535	0.267563	0	1	568
Q13	0.257042	0.437388	0	1	568

A simpler representation of the estimated multiple regression with 13 independent variables may be presented as such:

$$\begin{aligned}\hat{Y} = \hat{\alpha}_0 + \hat{\alpha}_1 x_{1+} \hat{\alpha}_2 x_2 + \hat{\alpha}_3 x_3 + \hat{\alpha}_4 \\ + \hat{\alpha}_5 x_5 + \hat{\alpha}_6 x_6 + \hat{\alpha}_7 x_7 + \hat{\alpha}_8 x_8 \\ + \hat{\alpha}_9 x_9 + \hat{\alpha}_{10} x_{10} + \hat{\alpha}_{11} x_{11} + \hat{\alpha}_{12} x_{12} \\ + \hat{\alpha}_{13} x_{13} + \varepsilon_t\end{aligned}$$

By replacing the variables from the first equation, the variables in the second equation signify α_0 as the intercept, and α are the parameters associated with x. $\alpha_1\, x_1$ represents the total number of members in all the households, $\alpha_2\, x_2$ is associated to how many members in the households are above the age of 18, $\alpha_3\, x_3$ represents the number of rooms the households comprise of while $\alpha_4\, x_4$ denotes the age of the building in years, $\alpha_5\, x_5$ is the recorded measure of the size of the house building in meters squared, $\alpha_6\, x_6$ refers to the range of the total income the household receives (on a yearly basis), $\alpha_7 x_7$ indicated what type of light bulbs the households were aware of using (traditional or energy saving), $\alpha_8\, x_8$ referred to the specific appliances as well as how many of each of those appliances were in the possession and use of the households, $\alpha_9\, x_9$ represents whether these electric appliances were used on a daily basis, $\alpha_{10}\, x_{10}$ is the variable indicating whether the households used energy sources other than electricity, $\alpha_{11}\, x_{11}$ refers to the season households assumed they consumed the most electricity, $\alpha_{12}\, x_{12}$ associated to leaving any electric appliances working overnight/ throughout the entire day and the final variable $\alpha_{13}\, x_{13}$ was an opinionated question on whether households were willing to switch over to electricity appliances only, finally $\mathcal{E}_t$ represents the residual variable that will represent variables other than those listed that affect the dependent variable (Wooldridge, 2013).

The panel data model comprises many tests that will be further scrutinized below, however, the main three models and tests that are relevant to this research are the Classical model, the Autocorrelation model (one way), and the Random Effects Model. The OLS regression without group dummy variables was estimated first (refer to Appendix: *Original Descriptive Data*). OLS regressions are used to estimate the parameters of $\alpha_{1,}$ $\alpha_{2,}$ and so forth to predict new values for the variables (Table 12.2).

The OLS without dummy variable test estimates the $k + 1$ that's chosen to minimize the sum of squared residuals which is shown as:

$$\begin{aligned}\hat{Y} = \hat{\alpha}_0 + \hat{\alpha}_1 x_{1+} \hat{\alpha}_2 x_2 + \hat{\alpha}_3 x_3 + \hat{\alpha}_4 \\ + \hat{\alpha}_5 x_5 + \hat{\alpha}_6 x_6 + \hat{\alpha}_7 x_7 + \hat{\alpha}_8 x_8 \\ + \hat{\alpha}_9 x_9 + \hat{\alpha}_{10} x_{10} + \hat{\alpha}_{11} x_{11} \\ + \hat{\alpha}_{12} x_{12} + \hat{\alpha}_{13} x_{13} + \varepsilon_t\end{aligned}$$

$$\sum_{i=1}^{n} \left(\hat{y}_I - \hat{\alpha}_0 - \hat{\alpha}_1 x_{i1} - \hat{\alpha}_2 x_{i2} - \hat{\alpha}_3 x_{i3} - \ldots - \hat{\alpha}_{13}\ x_{i13}\right)^2$$

Table 12.2 OLS without group dummy variables

Variable	Coefficient	Std. Error	P[|Z| > z]	Mean of X
Q1	0.32679	0.079736	0	5.424354
Q2	−0.70665	0.209159	0.0007	4.309963
Q3	0.99549	0.328257	0.0024	7.54797
Q4	−0.02005	0.010195	0.0493	17.52399
Q5	−0.00042	0.001807	0.8162	222.6568
Q6	0.552773	0.105851	0	2.378229
Q7	−1.08491	0.389342	0.0053	1.833948
Q8-1	−0.54674	0.22987	0.0174	1.483395
Q8-2	0.697818	0.318321	0.0284	0.961255
Q8-3	−0.00833	0.491557	0.9865	1.088561
Q8-4	−3.53034	0.803329	0	0.448339
Q8-5	−2.981	0.5635	0	1.381919
Q8-6	2.06846	0.490018	0	1.219557
Q8-7	−0.33684	0.112085	0.0027	4.236162
Q8-8	−0.37967	0.351653	0.2803	1.848708
Q8-9	−0.70363	0.461785	0.1276	0.54797
Q8-10	3.342615	0.619299	0	0.335793
Q10	−0.2393	0.068013	0.0004	5.081181
Q11	0.105109	0.06908	0.1281	2.254613
Q12	−1.01541	0.691645	0.1421	0.922509
Q13	−0.08795	0.243731	0.7182	0.258303
Constant	5.246559	1.66367	0.0016	

The second test is OLS with Group Dummy Variables. Dummy variables are important to test to indicate whether other variables, aside from the independent variables listed, affect and influence the dependent variables (Appendix: 2.3 Ordinary Least Square with Group Dummy Variable). Moreover, if they show an influence, it will indicate how significant its influence is.

The third test is the Random Effect model, when testing for this model, we assume that the dependent variables are uncorrelated with the independent variables and there are no fixed effects (Appendix: 2.4 Random Effect Model). Following this test, this study runs the Random Effect Model with an AR1 model to test the values and effects of the error term based on the parameters (Appendix: 2.5 Random Effect Model AR (1)).

The Classical Linear Regression Model assumes that the variables are predictable while predicting the dependent variables based on the independent variables (Appendix: 2.6 Classical Linear Regression Model) (Khayyat & Heshmati, 2014). An autocorrelation test was used to find repeated patterns that may cause fluctuations between the mean and the variance (Appendix: 2.7 Autocorrelation Model). The following test of Least Square with Group and Period Effect Model is to combine the period (years and months) and groups of similar data for interpretation (Appendix: 2.8 LS with group and period effect model). The final test of the

Table 12.3 OLS with panel-corrected covariance matrix

LHS = ONE	Mean	= 3.662468
	Standard deviation	= 1.434121
WTS = none	Number of observations	= 568
Model size	Parameters	= 21
	Degrees of freedom	= 547
Residuals	Sum of squares	= 959.8821
	Standard error of e	= 1.324693
Fit	R-squared	= 0.1768794
Model test	F[20, 547]	= 0.1467836
Diagnostic	Log-likelihood	= 5.88 (0.0000)
	Restricted (b = 0)	= −954.9688
	Chi-sq. [20] (prob)	= 110.556 (0.0000)

descriptive statistics is the Ordinary Least Squares Regression with the Panel-corrected covariance matrix (Appendix: 2.9 OLS with Panel-corrected covariance matrix) (Table 12.3):

12.4 Discussion of Results

12.4.1 Data Collection

This research will comprise of collective textual analyses of primary and secondary sources that include books, articles, reports, and collected data. The prospect of this research will focus on the literature reviews and collected data to deduce conclusions that will also be based on existing theories. The use of other forms of data have been involved such as surveys administered to specific households and data received from the Ministry of Electricity, in Erbil. The most vital usage of the study is from the conducted descriptive statistics that provide this research with useful numerical results. These approaches are deemed the most reliable methods in explaining the research question and testing the hypothesis.

12.4.2 Research Design

With various forms of research collection and design available, the main focus for this research has been on the use of quantitative data. Throughout the course of assembling this research, the emphasis was on the electricity consumption in 25 households. The data was obtained from the electricity bills of each of these households in Erbil, where the electricity bills were traced to attain the previous electricity consumption for the past 5 years.

Subsequent to this, the same 25 houses participated in a questionnaire which surveyed the manner of each household's utilization of electricity. After completing the questionnaire the results, along with the information received from the Ministry of Electricity on the household electricity bills, were recorded and estimated according to panel data models.

12.4.3 Results

This section will consist of interpreting the results depicted in the previous section while referring to the previously conducted questionnaire. Although the questionnaire and regression, there includes Q9 and α_9, the coefficient is disregarded since it is unimportant in the descriptive statistics. The following results are based on the relationship of the independent and dependent variables based on the regression of:

$$\begin{aligned}\hat{Y} = \hat{\alpha}_0 + \hat{\alpha}_1\, x_{1+}\, \hat{\alpha}_2\, x_2 + \hat{\alpha}_3\, x_3 + \hat{\alpha}_4\, x_4 \\ + \hat{\alpha}_5\, x_5 + \hat{\alpha}_6\, x_6 + \hat{\alpha}_7\, x_7 + \hat{\alpha}_8\, x_8 \\ + \hat{\alpha}_9\, x_9 + \hat{\alpha}_{10}\, x_{10} + \hat{\alpha}_{11}\, x_{11} \\ + \hat{\alpha}_{12}\, x_{12} + \hat{\alpha}_{13}\, x_{13} + \varepsilon_t\end{aligned}$$

OLS With and Without Dummy Variable

While dummy variables test for the absence or presence of an outlying effect, we test the OLS with group dummy variables and without. The *R*-squared of the test is deemed an unreliable source in the tests and therefore will not be analyzed throughout. However, the coefficients will signify separate relationships between the independent and dependent variables that are reliable for interpretation.

The first variable of Q1, in the test with no dummy variable, has a positive coefficient of 0.22477077. This means that for every unit of increase in the cost (how much a household pays for electricity KWh in IQD), there is a 0.22% increase. This also signifies that the number of households living in a house has little significance. The coefficient with the dummy variable testing for the presence of an outlying effect shows a coefficient of 0.85, resulting in any unit of increase of cost (Y), there is an equivalent increase of 0.85% in the number of members living in a household.

The second coefficient for both tests shows similar results. The coefficient without the dummy variable shows −0.45, this indicates that any decrease in the cost leads to an increase of −0.45 in Q2 being the number of members who are aged 18 and above. The coefficient with the dummy variable is 0 resulting in any increase or decrease in the cost leads to a 0 increase or decrease in Q2. With these results, it can be verified that the number of adults in a house is irrelevant which could be because adults are more conscious of their consumption of electricity.

The coefficient of no dummy variable test shows a significance of 0.71%. This expresses that an increase in cost leads to a 0.71 increase in Q3 which is the number of rooms the houses comprise of. The test with the dummy variable shows an even greater influence of 1.67%. This is interpreted as a considerable influence where one-unit increase in cost is met with a 1.67 increase in Q3. Evidently, the number of rooms in a house contributes to an increase in electricity consumption since the more rooms a house has, the more electric appliances it requires (lights, cables, A/C, etc.).

The fourth variable Q4 refers to how old a house building is. The OLS without dummy variable shows a coefficient of −0.01, this results in any decrease in the dependent variable is an increase of −0.01% in $\alpha_{4.}$ The LS with group dummy variable has a coefficient of 0 therefore for any increase in cost there is a zero percent increase in the independent variable. From both tests it is evident that the age of the house building indeed has no significance on the household members using electricity; in fact, it shows a negative relationship in the first test. This indication is reasonable since no matter how old a house is, the general electric necessities such as refrigerators, A/C, and washing machines will almost always be present.

In the OLS without a dummy variable, the coefficient is of little significance at −0.0009 which indicates any decrease in the cost leads to a −0.0009 increase. Q5 is the house size, measured in meters squared. The test with a dummy variable signifies a coefficient of −0.05 meaning for any decrease in the cost of consuming electricity, there is an increase by −0.05. Throughout this research, Q5 was estimated to be an influential variable, assuming that the larger the house, the more electricity it would require. This was proved to be unfitting, and the underlying reason is because even though a house may be large it would not necessarily mean they double their electrical appliances. Light bulbs make a minor contribution, therefore, are disregarded as compared to air conditioning or refrigerators. In most cases, many of the houses no matter their size all comprised of either one or two significant electric appliances such as a water heating system and washing machines.

The variables following Q5 were all estimated under a fixed parameter and therefore the coefficients of Q6 until Q13 were estimated at value zero.

Random Effects Model

The random effects model is of value to indicate since it allows for differences in the variables as the test accounts for variability (Table 12.4).

The first variable has a coefficient of 0.22, referring to, "Appendix: *Questionnaire*" it signifies that for any one unit of increase in the cost, there is a 0.22% increase in

Table 12.4 Random effects model: v (i, t) = e (i, t) + u (i)

Estimates:	Var[e]	= 0.164488D + 01
	Var[u]	= 0.125595D-01
	Corr[v (i,t), v (i, s)]	= 0.007578
Lagrange Multiplier Test vs. Model (3) = 11.34		
(1 df, prov value = 0.000757)		
(High values of LM favor FEM/REM over CR model.)		
Baltagi-Li form of LM statistic = 1.69		
	Sum of squares	0.941438D + 03
	R-squared	0.192696D + 00

the relativity of the number of people living in a house. From this, we can interpret that the members of a household make a contribution to the electricity consumption of the household.

Although the second variable refers to the members of the house who are aged 18 and above, its coefficient from the random effects test shows a negative correlation of −0.45. For every decrease in the unit of cost, there is an opposite correlation of an increase of −0.45%. This also signifies that even though the total number of people in a household is significant, the number of people aged 18 and above shows an adverse significance.

The variable of Q3 has a coefficient of 0.72, where the number of rooms a house comprises is of significance. In other words, for any increase in the cost of consuming electricity, there is an increase of 0.72%. As seen in the test for the dummy variable, the number of rooms indeed contributes to an increase in electricity consumption. The more rooms a house contains, the more the likelihood of having more air conditioning and lights present.

The next two variables Q4 and Q5 both have a negative coefficient of −0.016 and −0.0009. For both tests of random effect, any decrease in the cost leads to an increase by −0.016% for the age of the house and −0.0009% for the size of the house building in square meters. According to this, we deduce that the age of the building and the size are insignificant.

The random test for the variable Q6 has a coefficient of 0.42. Indicating that an increase in the cost leads to an increase in the variable's coefficient by 0.42%. Showing a positive relationship with significance, the total income of a house is evident to be a factor determining its electricity consumption. The next variable of Q7 shows an opposite correlation of having a coefficient of −1.17. Any one-unit increase in the cost indicates an increase of −1.17%. Also meaning that the type of light a house uses whether energy saving or traditional incandescent light bulbs are irrelevant and do not contribute in determining household electricity consumption.

The next variables are under the same concept of examining the types of electric appliances a household possesses, having already noting the number of each appliance. The coefficient being −0.33 shows that possessing a refrigerator has a negative relationship with the consumption and cost of electricity and for any unit decrease of the dependent variable there is an increase by −0.33%. Q8-2 with the measure of 0.52 indicates for any increase in cost per unit there is an increase of 0.52 in houses possessing freezers. Q8-3 also shows a positive but insignificant coefficient of 0.04, implying for any increase of one unit in cost there is an increase of 0.044% in possessing a washing machine. Q8-4 shows a negative coefficient of −2.4, this is negatively significant revealing that not many houses possess a dishwasher therefore it does not affect the consumption of electricity. Furthermore, this may be linked to the coefficient of income, where mostly high-income earning families possess dishwashers.

Since all the houses possess a water pump, the coefficient of Q8-5 is questionable for having a negative relationship of −2.6. For any one-unit decrease in the cost, there is a significant increase of −2.6%. A water heating system shows great significance of 1.7, where all houses own a water heating system that is mostly used during the winter. Therefore, for the variable of Q8-6, any increase in the dependent variable is an increase of 1.7% in the independent variable.

The coefficients of Q8-7 and Q8-8 are similar with values of −0.23 and −0.22 both showing negative significance to air conditioning and television. This seems slightly misleading since the houses that possess air conditioning use it due to the weather conditions. What was discovered during this research was that houses used air conditioning mostly in the summer and some would even use it occasionally. This is because almost all the houses use coolers that are filled with water and use minimal amounts of electricity. Therefore, any decrease in the unit of Y, shows an increase of −0.23 in Q8-7. In Q8-8 there is a decrease in the dependent variable for any increase in variable of the number and possession of televisions.

Following these, the variable Q8-9 also shows a negative correlation between the dependent and independent variable −0.77 in the possession of microwaves. A decrease of the cost is an increase by 0.77% in Q8-9 since few houses used microwaves and even those that did report to not using it on a daily basis. For the final variable Q8-10 being the possession of an electric oven and stove the coefficient showed to be 2.7. This signifies that an increase in cost is a 2.7% increase in the variable. Even though a few houses did not possess this, newly electric appliance houses reported to noticing that electric stoves are more energy consuming as compared to using gas for the stove.

In the variable of Q10, the coefficient is −0.25 where the majority of houses reported using a mixed energy strategy. Thus, for a decrease in the cost of electricity, there is an increase of −0.25. The next variable of Q11 shows a slight significance of 0.11. This not only signifies that any increase in the unit of cost results in a 0.11% increase but also houses by the majority reported that the most electricity they consumed was during the summer. The variables coefficient of Q12 and Q13 were −0.53 and −0.12. These variables were open-ended questions in which Q12 referred to houses leaving electric appliances working overnight, showing little increase per decrease in cost. While Q13 showed that the majority of houses denied wanting to switch to only electric appliances, preferring a mixed energy consumption.

Autocorrelation Model

An autocorrelation model in this case was used for finding repeated patterns that may cause fluctuations between the mean and the variance and basing these to interpret the independent variables (Table 12.5).

Table 12.5 Panel data analysis of LCOST [one way]/autocorrelation model

Autocorrelation model	RHO = 0.000000		
Unconditional ANOVA (No regressors)			
Source	Variation	Deg. Free.	Mean square
Between	234.875	23	10.212
Residual	757.791	518	1.46292
Total	992.666	541	1.83487

The first coefficient, Q1 has a value of 0.32, signifying for every unit increase in cost there is an increase in the variable by 0.32%, making it a significant factor in the determinants of electricity consumption. Q2 is −0.7 where there is a negative relationship between the independent and dependent variables; any unit of decrease in the dependent variable is met with the same unit increase by −0.7% in Q2. The number of rooms, the variable Q3, shows significance levels of 0.99, which has been evident in the previous tests as well where there is a 0.99% increase per unit of increase in the dependent variable.

The coefficients of Q4 and Q5 identically have values of −0.02 and −0.0004, these both show no significance as any decrease leads to an increase of −0.02% and −0.0004. In previous tests as well according to the results we disregard the age and size of the house for determining if they are factors of electricity consumption.

Following this is the coefficient of variable Q6 with a value of 0.55, referring to household income. This shows significance and a positive increase and relationship between the independent (income) and dependent (cost) variables. Subsequent to this is the coefficient of Q7 of value −1.08, resulting in a major opposing relationship between cost and the sort of lights. Therefore, for the decrease of the cost in units, there follows an increase of −1.08.

Classifying all of Q8, the negatively associated variables are Q8-1 (refrigerator), Q8-4 (dishwasher), Q8-5 (water pump), Q8-7 (air conditioning), Q8-8 (television), and Q8-9 (microwave). The coefficients associated with these accordingly are −0.5, −3.5, −2.9, −0.33, −0.37, and −0.7, which signifies that any unit of decrease of the dependent variable leads to an increase according to each value in percentage. Although Q8-3 is also a negative coefficient, it is valued at −0.008, implying that washing machines although are not considered significant, are of value for explanation.

Freezers showed a coefficient of 0.69, signifying that any increase in the cost leads to a 0.69% in Q8-2. The coefficient of Q8-6 is 2.06 showing that there is high significance in regard to electricity consumption for households possessing water heating systems. Lastly, Q8-10 is valued at 3.34, showing the most significance than all the other electric appliances.

Even though all the houses expressed that they used a mixed energy source, the coefficient of the variable Q10 is −0.23 which is interpreted as an increase of −0.23 in the independent variable following the decrease in the dependent variable. Many houses admitted to using the most electricity during the summer therefore the value of variable Q11 is 0.15 where any increase in the cost is met with an increase of 0.15%. Q12 and Q13 both are presented with negative coefficients of −1.01 and −0.08 which indicates they have a negative relationship with the dependent variable.

OLS with Panel-Corrected Covariance Matrix

The final test of the descriptive statistics is the Ordinary Least Squares Regression with the panel-corrected covariance matrix (Table 12.6).

The OLS corrected covariance matrix is the final test which is perceived to be the most reliable since it corrects the determining factors of the relationship between the variables. Similar to the previous tests, the coefficient of Q1 has a positive

Table 12.6 Ordinary least squares regression with panel-corrected covariance matrix

LHS=ONE	Mean	= 3.662468
	Standard deviation	= 1.434121
WTS = none	Number of observs.	= 568
Model size	Parameters	= 21
	Degrees of freedom	= 547
Residuals	Sum of squares	= 959.8821
	Standard error of e	= 1.324693
Fit	*R*-squared	= 0.176879
	Adjusted *R*-squared	= 0.146784
Model test	F[20,547](prob)	= 5.88(0.0000)
Diagnostic	Log-likelihood	= −954.969
	Restricted (b = 0)	= −1010.25
Chi-sq[20](prob)	= 110.56 (0.0000)	

relationship with the dependent variable and has a significant value of 0.28. Hence any increase in the cost of electricity leads to an increase of Q1 by 0.28%.

Likewise, the variable of the number of members in a house aged 18 and above has a negative coefficient of −0.97. Q2 shows insignificance and a negative relationship between Q2 and the dependent variable. From this test and the previous ones, it is evident that the number of rooms a house comprises of has a large influence on determining electricity consumption among households. With the coefficient of Q3 being 1.67, an increase per unit in the cost of electricity indicates a 1.67% increase in Q3.

The coefficient of Q4 and Q5, the house age and size are both insignificant in value, −0.002 and −0.001, and have a negative relationship with the dependent value. Even though we can conclude that the age and size of the house are irrelevant, evidently the household income is of significance by 0.43. Although it is not a huge contributing factor, it indicates any increase in the cost is a likewise increase by 0.43% in Q6.

Q7 and Q8-1 are both insignificant by −0.12 and −0.56 therefore the decrease in the cost leads to an increase in the two variables accordingly. The variables of Q8-2 and Q8-3 shows the possession of freezers and washing machines to be of great influence by 0.43 and 1.17. While Q8-4 and Q8-5, the dishwasher and water pump, show to have a negative correlation where any decrease in the cost leads to an increase by −4.1% and −2.1%.

Q8-7 (A/C) and Q8-8 (TV) are also negatively correlated, while Q8-6 (water heating system) shows great significance, as well as Q8-9 (microwave) and Q8-10 (electric oven and/or stove), have large impacts on the determinants of electricity consumption.

The Q10 variable refers to the mixed energy sources that households use other than electricity, and although all the houses used a mixed source, the coefficient of the variable is −0.09. This translates that even though houses use different energy sources, it is not significant in regards to the electricity consumption determinants. On the other hand, variable of Q11, representing the season, households thought they used the most electricity, showing a coefficient of 0.20. This value is of significance for which any increase in the cost of electricity is a 0.20% increase in Q11.

Following this, the results of Q12 are notable since many of the houses admitted to leaving lights working all throughout the day and night, the coefficient of this variable shows a negative correlation of −1.9. This variable is disregarded according to the final test after signifying its effects on the dependent variable. The final variable Q13 has a positive relationship with the cost but is of very little significance, valued at 0.07. Therefore, any increase in the dependent variable of the cost is an increase by 0.07% in the independent variable.

12.5 Conclusion and Recommendation

12.5.1 Conclusion

The purpose of this paper was to showcase the relationship of household factors, such as household size, income, electric appliances, and its effects on electricity consumption. By collecting information on electricity consumption for 25 households and testing various models based on the information, it was evident that in many cases the independent variables did in fact influence the dependent factors, showing their significance. Throughout this research, it was discovered that houses in Erbil mostly used a mixed source of energy in their everyday lives. With this being evident, many of the households admitted to overusing electricity in instances of leaving unnecessary electric tools working. In assessing the determinants of electricity consumption in households, we attain an understanding of how households use their electricity and with this valuable information we can further enhance the distribution and provision of electricity across the region.

Having completed the interpretation of the behavior of household electricity consumption and the panel data, this study has served as a guideline as to what influences a house's behavior toward energy consumption. A prominent point that stood out during this research was that many households even when consuming a fair amount of electricity were paying little amounts in IQD. Other houses admitted to leaving on many lights all throughout the day and night. Appropriate and heavily regulated electricity pricing should become customary until houses are familiar with proper electrical consuming and spending.

Although these may seem like minor issues, this number of houses adds up and can cause drastic detrimental damages to the electricity sector. An additional problematic area that was discovered during this research was electricity theft in households. Households admitted to adjusting their electricity readings by altering these readings from the electricity box available in every house. Although it is difficult to track down electricity theft, houses should not have easy access to adjusting their readings.

The existing literature available on the determinants of electricity consumption in Kurdistan is insufficient. More progress is necessary in this area, as it is important to have studies to be continuously updated in the electricity sector. Even though this research looked at reliable research conducted in other countries, the same interpretations and results are unfortunately not applicable to the Kurdistan Region.

From the outcomes of the result section, many factors became evident in determining what causes a household to consume more or less electricity. Income and the number of rooms were a prevailing variable as was the season that households revealed they used the most electricity. Even though a mixed source of energy is assumed to aid in less electricity consumption, this was in fact not the case. Although a progressive system of charging households based on their consumption is present, there are still many ghost consumers. Many households are unaware of appliances that may be energy saving and this lack of information may cause them to pay more in electricity bills despite them receiving a low income. Information asymmetry is a prominent issue that should be addressed in order to improve the conditions of electricity provision from the Ministry of Electricity and the consumption in households.

The electricity sector is a vital and vast sector where any adjustments will take many years, but these reformations are paramount. Many housing areas in Erbil provide 24 h of electricity from the private sector, but many houses also suffer from the lack of electricity, especially during the harsh summers. Overcoming information asymmetry and preventing electricity theft are the most fundamental in order to improve electricity consumption in households.

12.5.2 Limitations

The main limitation that was faced while putting together this research study was the absence of existing information and studies regarding electricity in the Kurdistan Region. This served as a major obstacle which also made the collecting of electricity bills per household just as difficult. This is why a great amount of emphasis on this research was invested in other research and papers conducted in various other countries. An additional limitation that was faced was regarding the collection of household electricity bills where some households refused to offer past receipts of their consumption of electricity in fear of being investigated for electricity theft. Furthermore, the data was also doubtful in its recordings, as many of the recordings of electricity consumption seemed uncanny.

Appendix

Appendix 1: Questionnaire

1. How many members live in this household?
2. How many of these members are aged 18 and above?
3. How many rooms does your household comprise?
4. In years, how old is your house (on estimate)?
5. How many square meters is the house building?

   - 50–100 m^2
   - 100–200 m^2
   - 200–300 m^2
   - 300–400 m^2
   - 500–600 m^2
   - 600 m^2 and/or more

6. What is the total income range of the household?

   - $500–$1000
   - $1000–$2000
   - $2000–$3000
   - $3000–$4000
   - $4000–$5000
   - $5000 and/or more

7. What kind of light bulbs does your household use?

   - Traditional incandescent light bulb
   - Energy saving incandescent
   - Combination
   - I don't know

8. Which electric appliance(s) does your household use (specify if there includes more than one)?

   - Refrigerator (with freezer)
   - Freezer
   - Washing machine
   - Dishwasher
   - Water pump
   - Water heating system
   - Air conditioner
   - Television
   - Microwave
   - Electric oven and/or stove

9. Of the appliances your household possesses, which of these appliances are used on a daily basis?
    - Refrigerator (with freezer)
    - Freezer
    - Washing machine
    - Dishwasher
    - Water pump
    - Water heating system
    - Air conditioner
    - Television
    - Microwave
    - Electric oven
10. What energy source other than electricity does your household use (refer to Q 13)?
    - Firewood
    - Gas (for cooking/ for heating)
    - Kerosene
    - Diesel
    - Other (specify)
11. In which season do you think this household consumes the most electricity?
    - Summer (May–September)
    - Autumn (October–November)
    - Winter (December–February)
    - Spring (March–April)
12. Are lights or other electricity consuming devices (other than those specified above) left working overnight (or consistently during the day). If yes, specify what devices they are (e.g. lights, chargers, TV, and a/c)
    - Yes,
    - No.
13. (For households using mixed energy) :
    - Would you be willing to switch over to only electric appliances and pay according to how much electricity you consume?
        - Yes.
        - No.

Appendix 2: Descriptive Statistics

2.1 Descriptive Statistics of the Variables

Variable	Coefficient	Standard error	b/St.Er.	P[|Z| > z]	MeanofX
Q1	0.32679	0.079736	4.098	0	5.424354
Q2	−0.70665	0.209159	−3.379	0.0007	4.309963
Q3	0.99549	0.328257	3.033	0.0024	7.54797
Q4	−0.02005	0.010195	−1.966	0.0493	17.52399
Q5	−0.00042	0.001807	−0.232	0.8162	222.6568
Q6	0.552773	0.105851	5.222	0	2.378229
Q7	−1.08491	0.389342	−2.787	0.0053	1.833948
Q8-1	−0.54674	0.22987	−2.378	0.0174	1.483395
Q8-2	0.697818	0.318321	2.192	0.0284	0.961255
Q8-3	−0.00833	0.491557	−0.017	0.9865	1.088561
Q8-4	−3.53034	0.803329	−4.395	0	0.448339
Q8-5	−2.981	0.5635	−5.29	0	1.381919
Q8-6	2.06846	0.490018	4.221	0	1.219557
Q8-7	−0.33684	0.112085	−3.005	0.0027	4.236162
Q8-8	−0.37967	0.351653	−1.08	0.2803	1.848708
Q8-9	−0.70363	0.461785	−1.524	0.1276	0.54797
Q8-10	3.342615	0.619299	5.397	0	0.335793
Q10	−0.2393	0.068013	−3.518	0.0004	5.081181
Q11	0.105109	0.06908	1.522	0.1281	2.254613
Q12	−1.01541	0.691645	−1.468	0.1421	0.922509
Q13	−0.08795	0.243731	−0.361	0.7182	0.258303
Constant	5.246559	1.66367	3.154	0.0016	

2.2 Ordinary Least Square without Group Dummy Variable

Ordinary least squares regression		
LHS = LCOST	Mean	= 3.662468
	Standard deviation	= 1.434121
WTS = none	Number of observations	= 568
Model size	Parameters	= 22
	Degrees of freedom	= 546
Residuals	Sum of squares	= 941.4255
	Standard error of e	= 1.313097
Fit	R-squared	= 0.1927064
	Adjusted R-squared	= 0.1616566

Ordinary least squares regression		
Model test	F[21, 546]	= 6.21 (0.0000)
Diagnostic	Log-likelihood	= −949.4548
	Restricted (b = 0)	= −1010.25
	Chi-sq. [21] (prob)	= 121.59 (0.0000)

Panel data analysis of LCOST [one way]			
Unconditional ANOVA (no regressors)			
Source	Variation	Degree of freedom	Mean square
Between	231.858	25	9.27433
Residuals	934.292	542	1.72379
Total	1166.15	567	2.0567

Variable	Coefficient	StandardError	b/St.Er.	P[|Z| > z]	MeanofX
Q1	0.224771	0.084809	2.65	0.008	5.420775
Q2	−0.45115	0.221842	−2.034	0.042	4.301056
Q3	0.71574	0.347438	2.06	0.0394	7.544014
Q4	−0.01618	0.010653	−1.519	0.1289	17.4419
Q5	−0.0009	0.001918	−0.471	0.6374	222.2887
Q6	0.427149	0.112173	3.808	0.0001	2.373239
Q7	−1.18515	0.409506	−2.894	0.0038	1.834507
Q8-1	−0.33441	0.243415	−1.374	0.1695	1.482394
Q8-2	0.537064	0.333428	1.611	0.1072	0.961268
Q8-3	0.035139	0.519875	0.068	0.9461	1.088028
Q8-4	−2.72583	0.850539	−3.205	0.0014	0.447183
Q8-5	−2.62663	0.595936	−4.408	0	1.380282
Q8-6	1.709122	0.519933	3.287	0.001	1.21831
Q8-7	−0.22924	0.11908	−1.925	0.0542	4.232394
Q8-8	−0.20538	0.36928	−0.556	0.5781	1.846831
Q8-9	−0.79974	0.484733	−1.65	0.099	0.545775
Q8-10	2.794919	0.656615	4.257	0	0.334507
Q10	−0.25374	0.071238	−3.562	0.0004	5.080986
Q11	0.113188	0.073345	1.543	0.1228	2.242958
Q12	−0.51994	0.731406	−0.711	0.4772	0.922535
Q13	−0.12818	0.258997	−0.495	0.6207	0.257042
Constant	5.730914	1.751638	3.272	0.0011	

2.3 Ordinary Least Square with Group Dummy Variable

Ordinary least squares regression		
LHS = LCOST	Mean	= 3.662468
	Standard deviation	= 1.434121
Residuals	Sum of squares	= 934.2916
	Standard error of e	= 1.339129
Fit	*R*-squared	= 0.1988238
	Adjusted *R*-squared	= 0.1280865
Model test	F [46, 521] (prob)	= 2.81 (0.0000)
Diagnostic	Log-likelihood	= −947.2946
	Restricted (b = 0)	= −1010.250
	Chi-sq. [46] (prob)	= 125.91 (0.0000)
Estimated autocorrelation of e (i, t) 0.404270		

Estimated group	Fixed effects coefficient	Standard error	*t*-ratio
1	−2.06646	0.24449	−8.45213
2	2.79601	0.27335	10.22873
3	−4.79469	0.26783	−17.9023
4	−1.97287	0.27923	−7.06546
5	1.50521	0.27923	5.39062
6	−1.39423	0.25772	−5.40994
7	−2.65658	0.29944	−8.87187
8	−1.98716	0.25307	−7.85215
9	−5.47505	0.25772	−21.2446
10	−4.19218	0.29944	−14.0002
11	−6.93136	1.33913	−5.17602
12	−3.63957	0.29222	−12.4548
13	−3.37923	0.32479	−10.4045
14	4.58528	0.2855	16.06036
15	−10.6653	0.25772	−41.3838
16	−0.09413	0.27335	−0.34435
17	11.32654	0.34576	32.75823
18	−2.59353	0.29222	−8.87521
19	7.52805	0.2855	26.36767
20	6.21772	0.27923	22.26756
21	3.31833	0.24867	13.34429
22	−0.74354	0.26783	−2.77622
23	7.15584	0.26783	26.71826
24	0.17344	0.25772	0.672993
25	−5.29489	0.29222	−18.1194
26	−6.93136	1.33913	−5.17602

2.4 Random Effects Model

Random effects model: v(i,t) = e(i,t) + u(i)
Estimates: Var [e] = 0.164488D + 01
Var [u] = 0.125595D-01
Corr [v(i,t),v(i,s)] = 0.007578l
Lagrange Multiplier Test vs. Model(3) = 11.34
(1 df, prob. value =0.000757)
Sum of squares 0.941438D + 03
R-squared 0.192696D + 00

Variable	Coefficient	Standard Error	b/St.Er.	P[lZl > z]	Mean of X
Q1	0.223908	0.090169	2.483	0.013	5.420775
Q2	−0.45346	0.233706	−1.94	0.0523	4.301056
Q3	0.72156	0.364762	1.978	0.0479	7.544014
Q4	−0.01571	0.011261	−1.395	0.163	17.4419
Q5	−0.00093	0.002033	−0.455	0.6489	222.2887
Q6	0.424711	0.118856	3.573	0.0004	2.373239
Q7	−1.17074	0.431188	−2.715	0.0066	1.834507
Q8-1	−0.33335	0.255957	−1.302	0.1928	1.482394
Q8-2	0.525788	0.34979	1.503	0.1328	0.961268
Q8-3	0.04891	0.548465	0.089	0.9289	1.088028
Q8-4	−2.72551	0.891943	−3.056	0.0022	0.447183
Q8-5	−2.61636	0.629157	−4.159	0	1.380282
Q8-6	1.711218	0.547987	3.123	0.0018	1.21831
Q8-7	−0.23067	0.126061	−1.83	0.0673	4.232394
Q8-8	−0.22002	0.386658	−0.569	0.5693	1.846831
Q8-9	−0.77873	0.510276	−1.526	0.127	0.545775
Q8-10	2.796668	0.690795	4.048	0.0001	0.334507
Q10	−0.25017	0.075176	−3.328	0.0009	5.080986
Q11	0.114641	0.077683	1.476	0.14	2.242958
Q12	−0.53932	0.77253	−0.698	0.4851	0.922535
Q13	−0.12235	0.275151	−0.445	0.6566	0.257042
Constant	5.67027	1.844043	3.075	0.0021	

2.5 Random Effect AR (1) Model

Random effects model: v(i,t) = e (i,t) + u (i)
AR1 model: Autocorrelation rho = 0.000000
Estimates: Var[e]*(1-rho)^2 = 0.139814D + 01
Var[u]*(1-rho)^2 = 0.116057D-03
Corr[v(i,t),v(i,s)] = 0.000083
Lagrange Multiplier Test vs. Model(3) = 12.18
(1 df, prob. value = 0.000482)
(High values of LM favor FEM/REM over CR model.)
Baltagi-Li form of LM statistic = 11.49
Original: Var [e] = 0.139814D + 01
Var[u] = 0.116057D-03
Sum of squares 0.952222D + 03
R-squared 0.184692D + 00

Variable	Coefficient	Standard error	b/St.Er.	P[|Z| > z]	Mean of X
Q1	0.326789	0.078173	4.18	0	5.424354
Q2	−0.70665	0.205035	−3.446	0.0006	4.309963
Q3	0.99549	0.321771	3.094	0.002	7.54797
Q4	−0.02005	0.009994	−2.006	0.0449	17.52399
Q5	−0.00042	0.001772	−0.237	0.8126	222.6568
Q6	0.552772	0.103772	5.327	0	2.378229
Q7	−1.08491	0.381669	−2.843	0.0045	1.833948
Q8-1	−0.54675	0.225332	−2.426	0.0152	1.483395
Q8-2	0.697823	0.312034	2.236	0.0253	0.961255
Q8-3	−0.00833	0.481877	−0.017	0.9862	1.088561
Q8-4	−3.53034	0.787443	−4.483	0	0.448339
Q8-5	−2.98101	0.552407	−5.396	0	1.381919
Q8-6	2.068465	0.480358	4.306	0	1.219557
Q8-7	−0.33684	0.109881	−3.065	0.0022	4.236162
Q8-8	−0.37967	0.3447	−1.101	0.2707	1.848708
Q8-9	−0.70363	0.452686	−1.554	0.1201	0.54797
Q8-10	3.342621	0.607076	5.506	0	0.335793
Q10	−0.2393	0.066675	−3.589	0.0003	5.081181
Q11	0.10511	0.067723	1.552	0.1206	2.254613
Q12	−1.01541	0.678036	−1.498	0.1342	0.922509
Q13	−0.08795	0.238951	−0.368	0.7128	0.258303

Variable	Coefficient	Standard error	b/St.Er.	P[|Z| > z]	Mean of X
Constant	5.246566	1.630878	3.217	0.0013	

2.6 Classical Linear Regression Model

Test Statistics for the classical model				
	Model	Log-likelihood	Sum of squares	R-squared
(1)	Constant term only	−1010.25	0.1166149982D + 04	0
(2)	Group effects only	−947.295	0.9342916492D + 03	0.198824
(3)	X-variables only	−949.455	0.9414254669D + 03	0.192706
(4)	X and group effects	−947.295	0.9342916492D + 03	0.198824
(5)	X ind. and time effects	−929.851	0.8786322477D + 03	0.246553

Hypothesis test:

	Likelihood ratio test			F test			
	Chi-squared	d.f.	Prob.	F	Num.	Denom.	P value
(2) vs. (1)	125.911	25	0	5.38	25	542	0
(3) vs. (1)	121.591	21	0	6.206	21	546	0
(4) vs. (1)	125.911	46	0	2.811	46	521	0
(4) vs. (2)	0	21	1	0	21	521	1
(4) vs. (3)	4.321	25	1	0.159	25	521	1
(5) vs. (4)	34.888	30	0.24675	1.037	30	491	0.41495
(5) vs. (3)	39.208	56	0.95689	0.627	56	491	0.98411

2.7 Autocorrelation Model

The Autocorrelation Model/Panel Data Analysis of LCOST:

Variable	Coefficient	Standard error	b/St.Er.	P[|Z| > z]	Mean of X
Q1	0.32679	0.079736	4.098	0	5.424354
Q2	−0.70665	0.209159	−3.379	0.0007	4.309963
Q3	0.99549	0.328257	3.033	0.0024	7.54797
Q4	−0.02005	0.010195	−1.966	0.0493	17.52399
Q5	−0.00042	0.001807	−0.232	0.8162	222.6568
Q6	0.552773	0.105851	5.222	0	2.378229
Q7	−1.08491	0.389342	−2.787	0.0053	1.833948
Q8-1	−0.54674	0.22987	−2.378	0.0174	1.483395
Q8-2	0.697818	0.318321	2.192	0.0284	0.961255

Variable	Coefficient	Standard error	b/St.Er.	P[|Z| > z]	Mean of X
Q8-3	−0.00833	0.491557	−0.017	0.9865	1.088561
Q8-4	−3.53034	0.803329	−4.395	0	0.448339
Q8-5	−2.981	0.5635	−5.29	0	1.381919
Q8-6	2.06846	0.490018	4.221	0	1.219557
Q8-7	−0.33684	0.112085	−3.005	0.0027	4.236162
Q8-8	−0.37967	0.351653	−1.08	0.2803	1.848708
Q8-9	−0.70363	0.461785	−1.524	0.1276	0.54797
Q8-10	3.342615	0.619299	5.397	0	0.335793
Q10	−0.2393	0.068013	−3.518	0.0004	5.081181
Q11	0.105109	0.06908	1.522	0.1281	2.254613
Q12	−1.01541	0.691645	−1.468	0.1421	0.922509
Q13	−0.08795	0.243731	−0.361	0.7182	0.258303
Constant	5.246559	1.66367	3.154	0.0016	

2.8 Least Square with Group and Period Effects Model

Least Squares with group and period effects		
Ordinary least squares regression		
LHS = LCOST	Mean	= 3.662468
	Standard deviation	= 1.434121
WTS = none	Number of observs.	= 568
Model size	Parameters	= 77
	Degrees of freedom	= 491
Residuals	Sum of squares	= 878.6322
	Standard error of e	= 1.337713
Fit	*R*-squared	= 0.246553
	Adjusted *R*-squared = 0.1299298	
Model test	F[76,491](prob) = 2.11(0.0000)	
Diagnostic	Log-likelihood = −929.8507	
	Restricted(b = 0) = −1010.250	
	Chi-sq[76](prob) = 160.80 (0.0000)	
Estd. Autocorrelation of e(i,t) 0.419231		

Variable	Coefficient	Standard Error	b/St.Er.	P[|Z|>z]	Mean of X
Q1	0	...... (Fixed Parameter).......			
Q2	0	...... (Fixed Parameter).......			
Q3	0	...... (Fixed Parameter).......			
Q4	0	...... (Fixed Parameter).......			
Q5	0	...... (Fixed Parameter).......			

Variable	Coefficient	Standard Error	b/St.Er.	P[|Z|>z]	Mean of X
Q6	0	...... (Fixed Parameter).......			
Q7	0	...... (Fixed Parameter).......			
Q8-1	0	...... (Fixed Parameter).......			
Q8-2	0	...... (Fixed Parameter).......			
Q8-3	0	...... (Fixed Parameter).......			
Q8-4	0	...... (Fixed Parameter).......			
Q8-5	0	...... (Fixed Parameter).......			
Q8-6	0	...... (Fixed Parameter).......			
Q8-7	0	...... (Fixed Parameter).......			
Q8-8	0	...... (Fixed Parameter).......			
Q8-9	0	...... (Fixed Parameter).......			
Q8-10	0	...... (Fixed Parameter).......			
Q10	0	...... (Fixed Parameter).......			
Q11	0	...... (Fixed Parameter).......			
Q12	0	...... (Fixed Parameter).......			
Q13	0	...... (Fixed Parameter).......			
Constant	3.662468	0.056129	65.251	0	

Estimated fixed effects		Full sets of effects	normalized to sum to 0
Group	Coefficient	Standard Error	*t*-ratio
1	0.14817	0.23769	0.62337
2	−0.32503	0.26723	−1.21628
3	0.44199	0.26159	1.68963
4	1.56299	0.27323	5.72048
5	−0.0099	0.27323	−0.03624
6	0.44081	0.25125	1.75448
7	−0.86641	0.29381	−2.94891
8	1.07936	0.24649	4.37884
9	0.51567	0.25125	2.05243
10	0.57369	0.29381	1.95259
11	−0.51616	1.33653	−0.3862
12	−0.57453	0.28647	−2.00557
13	0.51048	0.31955	1.5975
14	−0.37488	0.27962	−1.34065
15	0.00346	0.25125	0.01378
16	0.65583	0.26723	2.45418
17	−0.38249	0.3408	−1.1223
18	−0.40317	0.28647	−1.40741
19	−1.23101	0.27962	−4.40239
20	−0.04307	0.27323	−0.15765
21	−0.39123	0.24198	−1.61679
22	0.17193	0.26159	0.65726

Estimated fixed effects		Full sets of effects	normalized to sum to 0
Group	Coefficient	Standard Error	*t*-ratio
23	−0.77856	0.26159	−2.97628
24	−0.58616	0.25125	−2.33298
25	−0.57905	0.28647	−2.02134
26	−0.51616	1.33653	−0.3862

Estimated Fixed Effects—Full sets of effects, normalized to sum to 0			
Period	Coefficient	Standard error	*t*-ratio
1	0.62012	0.41928	1.479
2	−0.04164	0.39941	−0.10426
3	−0.11841	0.3408	−0.34745
4	0.3291	0.35309	0.93208
5	0.83323	0.36674	2.27196
6	−0.22777	0.32968	−0.69087
7	0.72261	0.3408	2.12031
8	−0.04773	0.30172	−0.15819
9	−0.99767	0.31955	−3.1221
10	0.24695	0.29381	0.84053
11	−0.11382	0.28647	−0.39732
12	0.04762	0.27323	0.17428
13	−0.24105	0.30172	−0.79895
14	−0.66674	1.33653	−0.49885
15	0.22786	0.29381	0.77553
16	−0.22793	0.28647	−0.79566
17	0.18055	0.28647	0.63025
18	−0.20904	0.30172	−0.69283
19	−0.18715	0.26723	−0.70034
20	0.11453	0.28647	0.39979
21	−0.15064	0.28647	−0.52587
22	−0.51457	0.28647	−1.79627
23	−0.09863	0.27323	−0.36097
24	0.06398	0.27323	0.23416
25	0.20168	0.26723	0.75473
26	0.0833	0.28647	0.29078
27	−0.12682	0.30172	−0.42034
28	−0.0279	0.27323	−0.10212
29	−0.01728	0.27323	−0.06325
30	0.21026	0.35309	0.59549
31	0.25292	0.32968	0.76717

2.9 OLS with Panel-Corrected Covariance Matrix

OLS with panel-corrected covariance matrix		
Ordinary least squares regression		
LHS=ONE	Mean	= 3.662468
	Standard deviation	= 1.434121
WTS = none	Number of observs.	= 568
Model size	Parameters	= 21
	Degrees of freedom	= 547
Residuals	Sum of squares	= 959.8821
	Standard error of e	= 1.324693
Fit	R-squared	= 0.176879
	Adjusted R-squared	= 0.146784
Model test	F[20,547](prob)	= 5.88(0.0000)
Diagnostic	Log-likelihood	= −954.969
	Restricted(b = 0)	= −1010.25
Chi-sq[20] (prob)=	110.56 (0.0000)	

Variable	Coefficient	Standard Error	b/St.Er.	P[|Z| > z]
Q1	0.281713	0.056575	4.979	0
Q2	−0.97682	0.106815	−9.145	0
Q3	1.671079	0.130291	12.826	0
Q4	−0.00258	0.009381	−0.275	0.7833
Q5	−0.00115	0.001798	−0.638	0.5234
Q6	0.432954	0.09806	4.415	0
Q7	−0.12046	0.114757	−1.05	0.2939
Q8-1	−0.5628	0.196409	−2.865	0.0042
Q8-2	0.438996	0.40265	1.09	0.2756
Q8-3	1.175767	0.248921	4.723	0
Q8-4	−4.1584	0.561655	−7.404	0
Q8-5	−2.93746	0.51337	−5.722	0
Q8-6	2.263365	0.396238	5.712	0
Q8-7	−0.47093	0.068117	−6.914	0
Q8-8	−1.16422	0.151272	−7.696	0
Q8-9	0.402234	0.274569	1.465	0.1429
Q8-10	3.680685	0.455883	8.074	0
Q10	−0.09149	0.046205	−1.98	0.0477
Q11	0.201068	0.068718	2.926	0.0034
Q12	−1.9576	0.330269	−5.927	0
Q13	0.077296	0.177996	0.434	0.6641

References

Ahmad, T., & Zhang, D. (2020). A critical review of comparative global historical energy consumption and future demand: The story told so far. *Energy Reports, 6*, 1973–1991.

Andersen, F., et al. (2021). Residential electricity consumption and household characteristics: An econometric analysis of Danish smart-meter data. *Energy Economics, 100*, 105341.

Berardi, U., & Jafarpur, P. (2020). Assessing the impact of climate change on building heating and cooling energy demand in Canada. *Renewable and Sustainable Energy Reviews, 121*, 109681.

Du, K., et al. (2020). Climatic impact on China's residential electricity consumption: Does the income level matter? *China Economic Review, 63*, 101520.

Ekonomou, G., & Halkos, G. (2023). Exploring the impact of economic growth on the environment: An overview of trends and developments. *Energies, 16*(11), 4497.

Fischer, C. (2008). Feedback on household electricity consumption: A tool for saving energy? *Energy Efficiency, 1*(1), 79–104.

Gruber, J. (2007). *Public finance and public policy*. Massachussetts Institute of Technology.

Huebner, G., et al. (2016). Understanding electricity consumption: A comparative contribution of building factors, socio-demographics, appliances, behaviours and attitudes. *Applied Energy, 177*, 692–702.

Jamal, M., et al. (2021). *Iraqi electricity sector overview*. KAPITA's Research team.

James, B. S., et al. (2020). Household cooking fuel use and its health effects among rural women in southern India—A cross-sectional study. *PLoS One, 15*(4), e0231757.

Khayyat, N. T. (2015). Literature on energy demand. *Energy Demand in Industry: What Factors Are Important?* 31–45.

Khayyat, N. T., & Heshmati, A. (2014). *Production risk, energy use efficiency and productivity of Korean industries*.

Kostakis, I. (2020). Socio-demographic determinants of household electricity consumption: Evidence from Greece using quantile regression analysis. *Current Research in Environmental Sustainability, 1*, 23–30.

Lam, J. C. (1998). Climatic and economic influences on residential electricity consumption. *Energy Conversion and Management, 39*(7), 623–629.

Santiago, I., et al. (2021). Electricity demand during pandemic times: The case of the COVID-19 in Spain. *Energy Policy, 148*, 111964.

Stoner, O., et al. (2021). Household cooking fuel estimates at global and country level for 1990 to 2030. *Nature Communications, 12*(1), 5793.

The World Bank. (2009). *Reducing technical and non-technical losses in the power sector*. Background Paper for the World Bank Group Energy Sector Strategy, The World Bank.

The World Bank. (2016). *The Kurdistan region of Iraq – Reforming the economy for shared prosperity and protecting the vulnerable* (Vol. 2). Main report (English). World Bank Group.

UNDP. (2008). *Electricity sector reconstruction project in Kurdistan region: Stage II*.

Van der Kroon, B., et al. (2014). The impact of the household decision environment on fuel choice behavior. *Energy Economics, 44*, 236–247.

Wang, Q., et al. (2020). Does urbanization lead to less residential energy consumption? A comparative study of 136 countries. *Energy, 202*, 117765.

Wooldridge, J. M. (2013). *Introductory econometrics: A modern approach*. South-Western Cengage Learning

Zelenski, J. M., & Desrochers, J. E. (2021). Can positive and self-transcendent emotions promote pro-environmental behavior? *Current Opinion in Psychology, 42*, 31–35.

Chapter 13
The Role of Agricultural Production on the Economy of the Kurdistan Region

Dery Hoger Shalli

Abstract The agriculture sector contributes highly to the national product of many countries around the world as it is counted as an issue of national security by being self-sufficient to produce enough food for the population. Kurdistan Region of Iraq (KRI) has immense landscapes, water resources, and wilderness to raise farm animals, and it has been counted as one of the most fertile lands in the area. It used to be a food basket for the rest of Iraq. This study examines the role of the agriculture sector in the economy of the Kurdistan Region. Particularly, we address the performance status of agricultural production and obstacles of underdevelopment of agriculture sector in KRI. Information has been collected by summarizing the existing statistical data on agricultural production and its related activities and its role in promoting the economy of the KRI. The findings report huge non-utilized resources in the agriculture sector that can be used to increase the level of production in the sector significantly, which may lead to higher national income and more employment generation. Further results elucidate that domestic agricultural production value has increased compared to previous years, while less investment capital has been allocated for the agriculture sector compared to other sectors. Therefore, the Kurdistan Regional Government (KRG) should undertake effective strategies to promote this sector to increase the national income and more employment generation.

Keywords Agriculture economics · Agricultural production · Kurdistan Region

D. H. Shalli (✉)
Crescent Petroleum/Dana Gas, Sulaymaniyah, Iraq
e-mail: dfaraj@crescent.ae

G. M. Muhamad, N. T. Khayyat (eds.), *Resource Management Performance: A Sectoral Analysis in the Post-Conflict Kurdistan Region of Iraq*, Perspectives on Development in the Middle East and North Africa (MENA) Region,
https://doi.org/10.1007/978-981-97-7725-9_13

13.1 Introduction

Agriculture Economics examines the issues by which natural resources and human resources can be economically achieved. The agriculture economy and the general economy are highly interlinked since the objectives of the agricultural economy are not fundamentally different from the objectives of the origin from which it is derived. However, the agricultural economy is primarily concerned with knowledge of the activities of the owners of agriculture and their welfare, so it seeks to find appropriate solutions to agricultural problems. The agriculture sector cannot grow and develop without the development and growth of other economic activities (Norton et al., 2021). In other words, the agricultural economy is complementary to the general economy and is not different from it, but it is more than the general economy by focusing on the technical and applied agricultural sciences.

All through history, cultivating has been one of the principles of autonomous factors that draw out the lives of individuals on earth. It is seen as an effective way to undertake the issue of national security. Obviously, the role of the agriculture sector in determining the economic level of a country is undeniable. Therefore, the process of developing agriculture should be considered as the prime tool toward economic sustainability (Guth et al., 2020). Many scholars believe that the agricultural sector is an important source of total growth in almost all countries (Muhamad, 2024). This is due to the daily need for agriculture products in the market.

The agriculture sector can be seen as one of the main economic instruments that contribute to the national economy and food security linked to national security (Kogo et al., 2021). Achieving food security depends mainly on the provision of food from local agricultural production. The revival of the agricultural sector is contributing to the diversification of the economy, poverty alleviation, improved trade balance, and the movement of most of its associated sectors, both directly and indirectly (Norton et al., 2021). In other words, the development of the agricultural sector contributes to combating unemployment, reducing the volume of imports, developing and promoting the social, and strengthening the national economy. The development of the agricultural sector is also reflected positively in improving the environmental situation.

Many countries worldwide pay more attention to priority bases to raise the productivity of the agriculture sector due to its share in GDP. The agriculture sector contributes to the national income of many developing countries, and it is counted as the provision of the raw material for the various industries (Abidin et al., 2022). The agriculture sector forms a source of food and raw materials, absorbs great labor, and contributes significantly to the overall economy. In many developing countries, the agriculture sector provides employment opportunity to a large scale of citizens in rural areas to strengthen incomes and reduce poverty (Ayoo, 2022; Peskett et al., 2022). It also contributes to the provision of intermediate inputs for many industries (Abidin et al., 2022). It contributes to obtaining financial resources through return exports of agricultural commodities (Bezpartochnyi et al., 2022).

Despite the great efforts of many countries and their growing interest in agricultural development issues and the availability of land, human, water, and material resources, this sector faces many problems and obstacles in developing countries.

In the Kurdistan Region, agriculture still remains a great barrier in the face of progress and development despite having immense landscapes, and it has been counted as one of the most fertile lands in the area (Daneshmehr & Nasrollahizadeh, 2024). Like other developing countries, the region has not been able to generate enough agricultural goods to cover its needs. Thus, the development of the agricultural sector and the provision of food security remain a key issue in the strategy of economic and social development of the KRI and are among the most important challenges that the region has been facing. These challenges have become more intense to coincide with the aftermath of a difficult global economic crisis and rising prices for major food commodities worldwide, especially during the COVID-19 pandemic and the war in Ukraine (Dilshad et al., 2023; Muhamad, 2024). The rise is expected to continue over the next decade, in light of climate change and increased demand for food commodities by fast-growing economies, as population growth continues and energy prices continue to rise (Hemathilake & Gunathilake, 2022).

The study is conducted aiming to achieve an understanding of the contribution of agriculture production to the national economy of the Kurdistan Region. We also investigate the amount of agriculture consumption and the region's requirement for agricultural goods and the problems and challenges that hinder the growth and development of agriculture in the region. The findings can be utilized as a source of perspective for measuring the effectiveness of this sector to reduce poverty and increase employment. It also offers empirical messages for the policymakers in Kurdistan about new strategies that have been implemented in other countries as success stories.

This chapter uses the data from the Ministry of Agriculture on overall agricultural production and strategies to improve the economy. It was a challenge for the researcher to cover the overall value of agricultural production from various years, which required a lot of time. Another challenge was the data collection regarding the share of agriculture to the gross domestic product and employment generation. In view of this circumstance, the researcher has approached specialized people within the Ministry of Agriculture and Water Resource, Ministry of Planning, KRSO, and BOI.

The remaining sections are presented as follows: the next section provides an overview of the agricultural sector in the KRI including a historical background of agriculture sector, the characteristics, and obstacles in the Kurdistan Region. Section 13.2 gives a general overview about the agriculture sector in the Kurdistan region of Iraq. Section 13.3 focuses on the role of agriculture in the economy. It also offers some case studies from literature. Section 13.4 provides the methodology of the chapter and discusses the analysis and the results and Sect. 13.5 concludes and offers some policy advise.

13.2 An Overview of the Kurdistan Region's Agriculture Sector

Kurdistan Region has a long history of agriculture production, and it is known as a nest of humanity and civilization in the area. The earliest people of Kurdistan departed from the mountains to live on harvesting agriculture. According to historical evidence, Charmo village has been counted as the most ancient agricultural residence in the new Stone Age (USAID, 2008). For a long time, the people in this area were busy with farming, particularly wheat, lentils, barley, and chickpeas. They also had domestic animals such as goats and pigs. The Saddam Hussein's Iraqi government ordered the confiscation of lands, burning of forests, and switching peasants from farmers to service workers. This led to the collapse of the agricultural sector and the decline of self-sufficiency to importing countries. However, after the Kurdish uprising in 1991, many people rebuilt their villages as most of them were busy with agricultural projects.

In today's world, despite technological development, trade openness, and accessible international transportation, nations are struggling to be self-sufficient by producing enough food for domestic consumption (Muhamad, 2024). Throughout economic history, there has not been a single country that has been transformed from economic stagnation to the starting stage without having achieved a significant amount of improvement in agricultural production (Hrustek, 2020; USAID, 2008). Kurdistan Region has vast landscapes and wilderness to raise farm animals, has plenty of water, and is one of the most fertile lands in the area (USAID, 2008). Yet, most of the foods and products consumed in Kurdistan are imported from Iran and Turkey while almost anything grown in those countries could be raised here too. Consequently, farming in the region has become the poor man's profession as it is ignored by leadership (Daneshmehr & Nasrollahizadeh, 2024; Muhamad, 2022). This has made the food security of the region volatile. The biggest risk facing the region, similar to many nations, is the lack of food sustainability, and it is impossible to prevail without adopting a developed agricultural system. Therefore, having a sustainable plan to guarantee daily life food is necessary.

Over the past years, the Kurdistan Regional Government (KRG) developed several strategies in the hope of improving agriculture and infrastructure and attracting foreign investors to come and invest in the region. As a result, some of the sectors like oil and construction developed very well, yet many other sectors including agriculture stayed vulnerable and did not improve. This necessitates the promotion

Table 13.1 Cultivable land in KRI (in hectares)

Land	Total area	Total cultivatable land	Percentage of total area
Sulemanyah	1,514,120	626,280	41%
Duhok	931,398	301,542	32%
Erbil	1,042,808	291,999	28%
Total	3,488,326	1,219,821	34.97%

Source: author's investigation.

of the agriculture sector by valuing the local products as an inducement for the development of agriculture production, which may contribute to creating more job opportunities for the local people in the region.

The total land area in Kurdistan Region is 3,488,326 ha of which only around 35% is cultivable. Table 13.1 reports cultivable land in KRI of which Sulaymaniyah governorate has the largest area accounts for 41%. These figures marked Iraq to be the second cultivated area in the Middle East in 2019 after Iran (Puri-Mirza, 2024).

In general, crop production is the major source of livelihood for most of the farmers, particularly wheat and barley serving as the two major crops of cultivation in the region. The wheat areas in the region occupy about 567,625 ha of land and produce approximately 500,000 tons each year. While the region has not achieved self-sufficiency, wheat planted area recorded 2% increase in 2016–2017 compared to 2012–2013. Wheat planted area has different records across Kurdistan region's governorates (Statistics Office, 2018). However, the report indicated that the region has achieved only 8% self-sufficiency in terms of corn production and 11% self-sufficiency of oat production. Accordingly, these two types of crops offer potential investors a strong opportunity for success as both represent critical areas of demand in the region. There is also a high demand for rice as it is a preferred crop, and it is becoming the basic staple of the Kurdish people.

The KRG attempts to expand its capabilities to correspond to the present demand of water supply. The region depends most on rain and its groundwater resources for cultivation. Therefore, more infrastructure developments are required in this area. There are still issues relating to water shortages as there are no water recycling plants in the region and no systems in operation for treating wastewater. As such, as reported in Table 13.2, the KRG has put in a pipeline the development of water resources and investment of $3 billion from 2012 to 2020.

Despite the opportunities of the agriculture sector in Kurdistan Region, investment in this sector compared to other sectors is few. This is mainly due to resource curse, which undermines the competitiveness of the non-oil sectors (Abdullah & Gray, 2022; Muhamad, 2023; Muhamad et al., 2020, 2021). Table 13.2 reports some facts on Kurdistan's agriculture sector. Accordingly, the contribution of the sector into the GDP is 10%, while many of the agricultural services has been subsidized

Table 13.2 Data on agriculture

Contribution to GDP	10%
Investment (2013–2020)	$1.2 billion
Total Investment (2006–2013)	$677 million
Population relies on agriculture	9%
The KRG's subvention (annual)	$250 million
Workforce	7%
Projected Investment (Water) (2013–2020)	$3 billion

Source: authors' investigation.

and costed 3.66% of the KRG budget from 2010 to 2013 (Muhamad, 2022). The KRG, to reduce oil dependency, has put investment to support agriculture; the total investment of agriculture from 2006 to 2013 has reached $677 million, and it's projected to reach to $1.2 billion for 2013–2020. Despite relatively small financial support, around 9% of the total population of the region relied on agriculture and 7% of the total workforce worked in that sector.

13.2.1 Geography of the Kurdistan Region

The Kurdistan Region of Iraq is located in the southwestern part of Asia, where it extends between latitude 34° and 37° North and longitude 41° and 64° east. The Kurdistan Region is considered to be within the northern temperate zone. It belongs to the Mediterranean climate. The region is divided into three levels in terms of rainfall, which ranges from 350 to 1200 mm. The Kurdish people have lived in this geographical area for thousands of years and are known for their agricultural and natural resources. As a result of the ongoing repression, displacement, and destruction of the infrastructure of the region since 1961, which culminated in 1988, where more than 4000 villages were abandoned (Bozarslan et al., 2021). They were forced to live in forced housing complexes as well as the destruction of water resources, agriculture, and planting them with millions of mines that continue to pose a danger and a hindrance to their rehabilitation. Agricultural activity generally has many characteristics distinct from other economic activities such as high sensitivity to the natural and seasonal nature of the activity, the specificity of agricultural management, and the linkage of the activities of this activity to the provision of basic human needs and food security. All of which are influenced by policies adopted at various stages of development in this sector.

Water resources are the main determinants of food security and water security, and the process of agriculture depends mainly on them. The region is characterized by abundant water and multiple sources for its area where surface and groundwater are available, and rain and snow fall in various areas of the region. The region is divided into three levels in terms of the amount of annual rainfall fall from 250 to 1200 mm. Snow gathers and covers some mountain peaks most of the year. The other water resources are rivers and wells.

13.2.2 The KRG Policies and Strategic Plan for the Agriculture Sector

During the fifth Cabinet of the KRG, the idea of the strategic plan to renovate previous abilities in the agriculture sector was addressed. With the participation of the water resources sector, trade, and food industries, the local government has been implementing the 5-year plan in 2009 to support the agriculture sector in the region. However, the lack of sufficient budget has caused to destroy many of the objectives that have been set to renovate the sector. The KRG seeks to encourage citizens to move back to their villages and resume farming. However, the process has not yet developed the legal framework and policies to facilitate this process. At the same time, there is general support for the local government's objective of encouraging people to return to their villages.

The KRG established "2020: Vision for the Future" and set four sector priorities (roadmap of reform) including agriculture sector to develop the local production. The financial crisis has affected the agricultural sector in general. However, this can be seen as an opportunity to take advantage of this crisis. Currently, most people have lost their source of income, and some people go to villages to work in the agricultural sector. This also leads to the increased capital formation in society through investment in the agricultural sector. It contributes to the expansion of the productive base of the national economy as well as directing part of the capital to invest in other sectors. Agricultural investment is also an important source that can be relied on to obtain foreign currency through the export of agricultural products and the reduction of imports. Therefore, any limitation of agriculture sector will affect the progress of other economic sectors.

The KRG within the vision for the future 2020 has set priorities on the agriculture sector to encourage more local and foreign investment. The Government believes that the agriculture sector can be seen as a potential tool to play a remarkable role in supporting the development of the region's economy. Based on the KRG's Ministry of Planning (MOP), the Kurdistan Region has combined 1.5 million hectares of irrigated lands for agriculture. At the same time, the region has a diversified population of livestock and a proper environmental provision that has allowed for the development of different types of agricultural goods. These are indicators that the agriculture sector can highly contribute to shaping the future of the region.

Agriculture in the Kurdistan Region has limited growth for nearly 25 years, mainly due to decades of conflict and war. However, the KRG's share of budget from the Iraqi government and the KRG's policy to expand public sectors have critically affected the intention of farmers to stay in the sector. For example, in 2003, about 35% of the people in the region relied on the agriculture sector as the source of livelihood, while this percentage dropped to only 9% by 2012 (Mazid, 2015).

The KRG has several startegic plans in place such as the 5-year strategic plan from 2008 to 2013 of self-sufficiency for agriculture production and food security and the Ministry of Planning 3-year strategic plan to promote food security, economic prosperity for its farmers, and identified the ambitious target of becoming a major producer and exporter of new agriculture and food products, but the outcome was disappointing.

The KRG's Government sees the improvement of some sectors as the major element for the development of the region's economy such as agriculture sector, tourism, manufacturing, and industry. Therefore, the Government has prioritized foreign investment in specific sectors to facilitate maximum growth and development. In accordance with these goals, the Board of Investment has implemented alluring incentives to the investors, including the provision of land-plots for subsidized lease. To accommodate these agricultural projects, the KRG has allocated more than 13 million square meters of land.

Currently, the region has set-up strategic opportunities as a strong local producer of vegetable fruits such as potatos, cucumbers, tomatoes, peppers, eggplant, onions, watermelon, and other products. Among all those products, potatoes have recorded an impressive growth rate; potato production levels increased 50-fold from 12,000 tons in 2009 to more than 600,000 tons currently. This development not only provided self-sufficiency in those agricultural products but also has made the region to be successfully exporting a number of products to other countries. The main policy of the region is investing in dams, technology, and access to new markets to fully achieve self-sufficiency or even becoming a greater producer and exporter of agricultural goods.

13.2.3 Obstacles of Agriculture Growth in the KRI

The agriculture sector depends on various physical or economic factors. For example, agricultural typology is highly linked to the natural environment and hence, people without technology tools have less control over success or failure of the agricultural development. The most prominent ones are water utilization, soil or plant nutrient requirements, and market competition and policies, all of them interact with and are impacted by climatic conditions (Abd-Elmabod et al., 2020). Weather and climate are interwoven into the social and economic context. Agriculture in the Kurdistan Region as in any other place is determined by physical and economic factors.

13.2.3.1 Water and Climate

Obviously, the climate is characteristically monsoonal with changing the season in the most countries in the world (Abd-Elmabod et al., 2020; Anderson et al., 2020). In the Kurdistan Region, winter starts from December and ends in March, which is followed by a spring from March to the end of May. Then from June and up to the beginning of October is the summer with almost no rain. Hence, the agricultural activities are highly connected to the seasonal variations in the distribution of climatic elements in KRI. Accordingly, the productions and cropping pattern differ from development place to one another and season to season. Agriculture in developing countries depends on rainfall and seasonal rain that can only be used within a specific period of time and for the cultivation of only one crop. Rainforest farming is the prevailing world, but because of the presence of Kurdistan within the regional climate, does not always have a high proportion of rainfall. Rainwater is often unstable and often unreliable. The average annual rainfall in KRI is less than 500 millimeters; this is to the fact that rain-fed agriculture is different from place to another. Rainforest farming is unstable where the quantity of rainfall fluctuates between years.

The climate additionally influences immature farming area, particularly on deciding the rate of warmth and dampness required for a specific sort of item or plantation. Without appropriate water system and watering, for instance, a few spots are only difficult to attempt estates in because of dryness. The additional low temperature brings about restricting impacts on plant developing and advancement as water utilization is hindered when the dirt temperature is low since water is thicker at low temperature and less portable and the cellular material is less porous.

13.2.3.2 Low Agricultural Income

The efficiency of agricultural operation depends highly on the generation of agricultural income. The collection of some of some agricultural characteristics, without doubt, will lead to lower income in agricultural production. Sometimes, agricultural production in Kurdistan Region, especially during the summer, is often unable to cover the cost price. The excess of income over costs does not cover the living expenses of the rural household, so it decreases the standard of living of the majority of the rural population. The remaining income, after paying all expenses consumption, does not meet the requirements of investment in the agricultural sector. This is often spent on improving consumption or reserve savings to cover social obligations. Even those with high incomes prefer to spend their savings in the city where they live. This is why there is a gradual deterioration of agricultural production as this sector becomes a burden on the state budget rather than an aid to improvement. Unless the state intervenes to establish the required investment projects and follow-up implementation, the percentage of agricultural income contributed to national income is low (Muhamad, 2024). In addition, the Government can support their production process within the country or even export them to other countries. In the previous years, many farmers have left their jobs and migrated to cities due to the fact that agriculture is an unprofitable economic activity in the region.

13.2.3.3 Soil and Land Topography

The soil is a significant inhibitory physical factor that is faced by the farmers in the agricultural plants. Even the soil itself is influenced by various factors such as the nature of the soil, steepness, and length of the slope, climate, particularly by rainfall. Improvement of farming is straightforwardly identified with the example of land geography. For instance, in level geography, crops must be profitable when they are planted in straight lines, dissimilar to bumpy geologies where harvests are to be planted nearby the slopes on a level plane since it controls the level of disintegration happening to rural terrains and its impacts on utilizing systems and apparatuses for development.

13.2.3.4 Market Economy

Liverpool-Tasie et al. (2020) illustrated that the most important challenge is to bring small farmers into value chains as profitable partners and link them to markets. The market is the fundamental point of socio-economic life (Nugroho, 2021). Marketing is one of the stimulating elements of the development process of agriculture sector in all the countries around the world. Accordingly, the expansion of market facilities is interlinked with sufficient transport networks from one point to another. With the availability of a good marketing function for the agricultural commodities in any place of production demand, production can later be transported efficiently and effectively. Due to the non-availability of marketing element in the Kurdistan Region of Iraq, the agricultural production has become damaged. Nevertheless, this has given a negative point to discourage the peasants from continuing with farming in the region. Despite the new way of marketing, the farmers in the region sell their agricultural products by following a classical way of marketing as they use a daily package process. In many cases, with the price elasticity, the farmers bring their commodities to the market in light vehicles and sell the products on the same day. They do not have a special place to store their agricultural goods for a week. Hence, they have local customers as well as those who come from other close districts. For this constraint, many farmers have faced various obstacles as their agricultural commodities may not be brought to all the markets. Additionally, they can reach distant markets for the transaction of their agricultural goods.

13.2.3.5 Crop Waste and Pollution

Several studies reported the loss of agricultural yields at fields (Liliane & Charles, 2020; Norton et al., 2021; Nugroho, 2021). Accordingly, 40% of agricultural crops in developing countries are lost at the level of farms and fields due to pollution, various plant diseases, insects, and various weeds. Thus, controlling pests and diseases affecting agricultural crops has become a working priority in the field of agricultural, and there is no doubt that the use of pesticides assists the process to control pests.

13.2.3.6 The Minimum Use of Technology

The low technological level in agriculture leads to low productivity within the agriculture field. Developing countries are primarily dependent on production of simple or conventional technology (Takahashi et al., 2020). In other words, agriculture in such countries depends more on human or animal manual labor from being dependent on machinery and equipment such as tractors, harvesters, and various machinery on advanced technology. Also, this coupled with the poor use of fertilizers, pesticides, and improved seeds. Hence, all these will negatively affect the amount of agricultural production, so that agriculture is limited to achieving sufficiency. Nevertheless, the Kurdistan Region has begun to benefit more and more since early 2005 with modern inputs of production and technology using more fertilizers and also began to expand the introduction of axial spraying technology as well as watering drip, which is on its way to spread more.

13.2.3.7 Waste of Agricultural Resources

Agricultural land is the most important element in increasing production. In many countries, agricultural lands have been used for housing and other related developments, especially if we know that the proportion of population increase in developing countries is high (Güneralp et al., 2020). Despite the relative stability of the area, agricultural world compared to the continuous increase in population, agricultural lands are subject to multiple images of depletion and decrease. By the time, this will lead to a deepening of the gap between the possibilities of providing food on the one hand and the continuing population growth on the other, many of the irrational practices of using land within the framework of agricultural activity have led to a reduction in productivity to the extent that large areas are not able to be used.

13.3 The Role of Agricultural Activities in the Economy

The agriculture sector contributes highly to the national product of many developing countries. This contribution depends on the different potential agricultural resources available from one country to another. There are countries for which agricultural production has contributed more than 50% of the gross national product, reflected in the high contribution of agricultural output in the economic development of those countries (Miah et al., 2020). The role of agriculture in contributing to the economies of developed countries has decreased over time, mainly due to the growth of non-agricultural sectors such as the service and industrial sectors. Similarly, in some developing countries, the oil and mining sectors have emerged as major contributors to the economy, further reducing the significance of agriculture. However, agricultural output remains an important part of the national product of developed countries where they export many food commodities (Smith & Glauber, 2020). The agricultural activities aim to provide food to meet the needs of citizens as economic development leads to an escalation in demand for agricultural goods in order to meet the increase in the population, on the one hand, and the high level of consumption, on the other hand, as a result of increasing income.

Kołodziejczak (2020) indicated that the agricultural sector provides the industry and other actors with the surplus labor available in the sector as a result of the growth of the rural population and the introduction of technological progress. The introduction of mechanization and increasing the productivity of the work leads to an increase in productivity in the countryside. It also reduces the number of people required to provide for the needs of the population and leads to the emergence of surplus labor in the agricultural sector and converting them to the industrial sector to feed industries cheap labor, which increases production and reduces costs. Based on this, it can be stated that the agriculture sector increases the level of production efficiency of human resources and increases their efficiency and productivity.

Delpasand et al. (2020) and Pawlak and Kołodziejczak (2020) explained the contribution of agriculture sector to the development of the industrial sector by providing raw materials to the industrial sector. Further, it contributes to the development of many food industries through which the absorption of surplus agricultural production and food storage and transport to different places. It also contributes to the conservation and improvement of prices of agricultural commodities and the provision of food commodities for the population. On the other hand, it creates a balance between the supply and demand of agricultural goods, which in turn leads to the interests of producers and consumers. In addition to the above, agriculture provides herbs and medicinal plants for the pharmaceutical industry, which emphasizes the importance of agriculture in the development of this type of industry and contribute to improving the health status of members of (Ahad et al., 2021; Pawlak & Kołodziejczak, 2020).

Several studies explained the contribution of agriculture into economic development (Ferreira et al., 2022; Miah et al., 2020; Pawlak & Kołodziejczak, 2020). The agricultural sector contributes to economic development by expanding the market to the finished industrial products. The increase in agricultural production leads to increasing agricultural incomes, modernizing the countryside and bringing the countryside close to the city. This, in turn, leads to the promotion and development of the process of industrialization in addition to increasing the incomes of farmers and leads to a shift in the pattern of agricultural production.

13.3.1 Characteristics of Agriculture Sector

The land may be limited in size and may be subject to increase through reclamation and increased productivity by applying modern technologies and transforming them into fertile land and regulating their mineral, organic, aquatic, and aerobic feeding, and may be reduced by erosion, salinity or poor exploitation (Liu et al., 2020). Most agricultural products are foodstuffs that are consumed once as opposed to industrial products.

According to Liu et al. (2020), Niho (1974) agricultural capital is classified economically in fixed capital, which represents the value of the means of agricultural production. These include the land, its facilities, trees, animals, machinery, and other improvements, and the revolving capital (current operating costs) raw materials, labor, fuel, oil and grease, and an imbalance between the former capital leads to a reduction in profit or loss opportunities. Generally, the per capita income is weak due to poor agricultural productivity compared with industrial production, and the large disparity between the incomes of different agricultural groups in their investment methods (irrigated or rain-fed agriculture, large or small farms) and income instability due to climate and natural factors. Manpower in agriculture refers to the population capable of working in agriculture; those who are between the ages of 15 and 65 years. The agricultural labor force is divided into a working human force, which is economically active in agriculture and a disabled human force with an ability to work in agriculture, which is high in many countries of the world (Zaika & Gridin, 2020).

Kołodziejczak (2020) reported that agricultural economic development requires balanced growth between agriculture and industry, and increased agricultural production is essential for economic development. It is generally recommended that priority should be given to agriculture in a country that wishes to develop its economy in accordance with its environmental conditions (Streimikis & Baležentis, 2020). Agriculture has another key role in the production of export agriculture and the combination of hard currency necessary to purchase manufacturing supplies. The overall dependence on one export crop or a few export crops makes the national economy vulnerable to shocks due to global price fluctuations (Vatsa & Miljkovic, 2022). Therefore, a plan to diversify agricultural crops must be included since crop diversification may have triple impacts on economic stability, environmental impacts, and loss of biodiversity (Hufnagel et al., 2020). Nevertheless, agriculture is the main industry covering the import of investment goods, intermediates, raw materials, and fuel, which are the mainstays of economic development.

13.3.2 The Importance of Agriculture Development

In general, developing nations are characterized by low per capita income. Although real per capita income gives us the best measure of differentiation between countries, it remains insufficient for the analytical study of underdevelopment and economic development. According to Arendonk (2015), the most common feature of developed and developing countries relies primarily on meeting the needs of its citizens, where it is believed that developing countries are agricultural countries while the developed countries are industrialized countries. Therefore, the agricultural sector accounts for a large number of economic activities in the developing countries. This is in contrast to the developed countries, which, according to their structural nature, contribute to economic development as a continuous process of improving the standard of living (Qaim, 2020). Furthermore, it contributes to the provision of financial resources to be used to cover the needs of the industry in many developing countries. Therefore, the agricultural sector is considered one of the main sectors in developing countries due to the role played by this sector in the economic and social life such as absorbing the labor force or contributing to the formation of national income (Ayoo, 2022; Peskett et al., 2022). Given the different circumstances of each country, there is growing recognition that the existence of a strong agricultural sector and growth is imperative and indispensable for economic development. The increase in the rate of industrialization requires the provision of labor, the provision of raw materials, and even capital, and of course, the task of the agricultural sector is to meet these requirements (Abidin et al., 2022).

However, in most developing countries, agriculture is still lagging behind and inefficient because it has not been given adequate attention in carrying out economic development projects (Rahman et al., 2022). Given the belief that industrial development is an effective factor in economic development and that progress is synonymous with industrialization. For this reason, it has devoted great attention to the industry, and in turn, has failed to develop its cultivation and modernization.

The obstacles that have been discussed extensively in the literature are the inability of the agricultural finance agencies, the lack of irrigation, and drainage methods. Pawlak and Kołodziejczak (2020) explained several issues within the agriculture system in developing countries including the productive relations of land ownership or the relationship between their owners and tenants and the ignorance of farmers about the issues related to their activities in terms of production and marketing. In this regard, developing countries need to draw attention to the danger of neglecting agriculture in economic development projects and its focus on projects that have fixed social capital (Arendonk, 2015). The attraction of such projects to economic development is that they respond to the aspirations of the public and are thus an effective means of publicity and are often supported and easily assisted by international bodies. The neglect of such projects costs the country the loss of external resources that are most needed to support its economic activity. Therefore, the developed countries should move toward the promotion of such projects in line with the needs of growth, but without neglecting the agricultural sector.

In order to start this process, the resources available should be exploited, even if they are simple but efficient and effective. It is necessary to increase the available resources, develop productive services, and introduce the most advanced technology in the production process (Ferreira et al., 2022; Guth et al., 2020). Thus to accomplish this goal, it is crucial for the authorities to put their economic policies and regulatory and institutional frameworks in line with the needs and requirements of the development process to ensure that they have the momentum toward the target.

13.3.3 The Effect of Agricultural Growth on Unemployment and Poverty

The agriculture sector is well known to be one of the major contributors to reduce unemployment and poverty rate within many regions in the world. The trend of agricultural growth in developing countries has multiple dimensions, especially between poverty and unemployment rate (Ayoo, 2022).

Obviously, the unemployment rate has a direct impact on poverty as it has been identified as one of the major causes of poverty (Akhmad et al., 2022). Indeed, in most developing countries, government officials and policymakers are seeking to improve the agriculture sector in order to reduce unemployment and poverty (Ayoo, 2022). They also stated that the governments should encourage the farmers to increase agricultural production as this will create more employment within the community, and as a result it reduces poverty.

The agriculture sector has been one of the key essentials to employment generation all over the world. Agricultural communities are characterized by high rates of labor availability, making them a major home for human energy and having more job opportunities for local people. The agriculture sector can attract considerable foreign companies to open new markets (Magdalena & Suhatman, 2020). Hence, it increases the job opportunities for the local people in this sector. Pawlak and Kołodziejczak (2020) indicated that the agriculture sector provides different sectors with raw materials and gives opportunities to the local people to be employed. The availability of effective strategies of agricultural investment will impact faster with the overall employment and boost the country's economy. Industrial progress and the consequent expansion of services and other non-agricultural sectors are creating a growing demand for the labor force, while the percentage of agricultural workers is declining due to the adoption of advanced methods and the mechanization of rural work, especially in the advanced stages of economic development. This will certainly lead to an increase in the output of the worker and consequently the downward trend of the agricultural labor force. On the other hand, agriculture may be a source of labor for other sectors if the growth of the agricultural population is higher than that of the non-agricultural population (Arendonk, 2015). Therefore, more attention to other sectors is always in the case of continuous expansion and demand for labor.

13.3.4 Strategically Support Policies of Agricultural Production

Most governments support agricultural production in various forms in the time of economic crises or shocks in the agriculture sector. Support may be aimed at stimulating production indirectly by encouraging exports through the use of multiple means such as export duty exemptions or production taxes. Sometimes, subsidies have been paid to exporters to enable them to export their goods at lower prices. This means that they contribute at a lower cost than competing in foreign markets to get the support from the foreign currency to support the trade balance. The government is willing to intervene in market forces by recognizing economic priorities that it believes are important.

For the above reasons, support was used for the development of the agricultural sector in developing and developed countries in order to establish a relatively competitive foreign agricultural base. This subsidy represents real expenditure from the state budget and takes the greatest value from the forms of subsidies. It includes the sale of consumer goods at prices below their international prices as well as the sale of locally produced goods at prices below their production costs (Zhang et al., 2021).

This type of support focuses on commodities and foodstuffs such as wheat flours and other food than other consumer goods as clothing.

One of the support focuses on commodities and foodstuffs. In this type of subsidy, the state pays part of the cost of agricultural inputs such as chemical fertilizers, pesticides, fodder, veterinary medicines, and so on. The state also provides a number of subsidies for intermediate goods used in other economic sectors such as the housing and construction sector as well as cement and reinforcing steel. The state subsidizes the price differences between the selling price and the cost price of inputs and intermediate goods (Lencucha et al., 2020; Zhang et al., 2021).

Another type of subsidy is the exemption of some new projects of taxes for a certain period of time. This type of subsidy is the sale of goods at reduced prices. These commodities may be consumer or intermediate produced by public sector companies and are forced to sell at prices much lower than similar prices of imported goods or less than prices which the consumer is willing to pay (Heyl et al., 2022).

The high prices due to price support policy encourage the expansion of subsidized crop cultivation, resulting in increased production and improved living conditions for producers. Increasing production facilitates supports the state in securing the needs of the food population and achieves a stable storage policy that compensates for imports from the global market and the elimination of economic dependence. Furthermore, the price support policy provides the required rate of accumulation for the development of agriculture such as the purchase of new machinery and the use of modern technologies that result in increased productivity and production (Zhang et al., 2021).

However, the subsidization policy can have several disadvantages. The policy of subsidizing the final output may cause other issues, such as higher prices for agricultural products for the consumers. This will appear especially in countries that do not follow the policy of supporting consumer prices and decreases between the interest of the product and consumer interest. While in this case, such a policy is beneficial to the product, it is harmful to consumers who have allocated a high proportion of their income to purchase food.

Another disadvantage of this policy is that it leads to an increase in government expenditure, which burdens the state budget, and this may be at the expense of other economic activities, as well as the increase in government expenditures lead to an increase in overall demand and then a significant increase in the overall level of prices (Sane et al., 2021).

13.3.5 Success Cases: Country Examples

The literature highlights the need for successful and sustainable agriculture in developing countries. The agriculture sector is integrated with different dimensions of development and policymaking and include relevant stakeholders. Agriculture has a significant role in the economy of developing countries. Agriculture is a primary source in most developing countries. It is also the main source of employment. Therefore, the protection of the agricultural sector in developing countries and the basic resources of its components are essential, especially if we know that developed countries constantly seek to fight and compete in international trade. The improvements within the agricultural sector received wide attention at all levels. Many countries have come to the realization that they have an opportunity to develop this sector to a new level.

Furthermore, regional and global developments topped the concerns of stakeholders to engage more in the agricultural economy. The issue of rural development is one of the sensitive issues facing the Kurdistan Region's agriculture because of its economic, political, environmental, and social dimensions. All these are closely related to the agricultural sector, and its surrounding internal and external factors directly affect its performance in food production and increase income for a nation. In this section, we look at some success story in developing countries.

13.3.5.1 The Case of Vietnam

Vietnam has experienced a fast economic development in total having 5.8% per capita income grwoth from 1990 to 2010 and also grew quickly in almost all the sectors including finance, industry, and agriculture (Huy, 2021; Huynh et al., 2021). Between 1990 and 2010, the average agricultural growth per year was counted as one of the best performance rates in the world during that period. The overall productivity growth was also very fast, at 3.1% per annum during 1991 to 2000 and 2.4% per annum during the period from 2001 to 2009 (Fuglie, 2012).

The agriculture sector in Vietnam has been the major contributor to economic development of the country. The sector provided the largest job opportunities in the country, employing 53% of the total workforce in 2009 (Tuan Anh et al., 2020). The major growth of the sector came from increased yields in which rice has increased by 50%, but yields of maize, rubber, cashew nuts, and cassava have more than doubled. However, the harvested area has also increased. Maize and rubber areas have more than doubled, the area under cashew nuts has increased more than three times, and the area planted with coffee has increased 60 ha in 1990 to more than half of the eight times by 2008. Aquaculture production has also grown very rapidly, reaching about 12% a year since 1990 (De Brauw, 2020; Nguyen et al., 2024).

The land distribution in Vietnam is relatively equal compared to most countries; growth in yield has benefited many smallholders (McCaig & Pavcnik, 2013). Growth in harvested areas has also increased demand for labor, a major asset of the poor. This growth model contributed to rapid reductions in poverty and undernourishment. Vietnam has already achieved many of the agricultural development goals. Market-oriented agricultural households have benefited to a large extent, especially during the 1990s, with the poverty rate reducing 40% in 5 years period.

13.3.5.2 The Case of Tanzania

The agricultural sector in the Republic of Tanzania grew at an average annual rate of 3.8% between 1990 and 2010, placing it among the top 15 agricultural sectors worldwide in terms of performance during that period (Fuglie, 2012). However, the prevalence of undernourishment initially increased and remained steady during the past 20 years and progress in reducing stunting and poverty has been very slow, indicating that rapid agricultural growth is not sufficient and of itself to improve nutrition. The growth of production in agriculture during the last 20 years was primarily due to an increased harvested area, while only a small amount of yield was achieved. Four-fifths of the harvested area was planted with eight crops: maize, dry beans, peanuts, rice, bananas, coconuts, sorghum, and cassava. But yields from maize, coconuts, sorghum, and cassava have declined over the past two decades, while yields from rice have only increased slightly. Crop decline may be a reflection of the expansion of marginal land with lower soil fertility and crop potential. While the overall productivity growth of the factors of production in agriculture was positive, reflecting the dependence on land expansion, it was not particularly notable during that time (Wineman et al., 2020)—it averaged 0.4% per year between 1991 and 2000 and 0.1% from 2001 to 2009 (Fuglie, 2012). The growth model of land expansion raises questions about its sustainability. In addition, the extent to which the poor benefit from the dependence on the extent of the extra land fertility used in agriculture and the extent to which the poor have access to it. There has been some rapid growth in cotton exports and follow-up in recent years, both of which are smallholder crops (Kulaya, 2020). A growth strategy focused on maize, root crops, legumes, and oilseeds would be more effective in reducing poverty and undernourishment because these crops are grown more widely by poor farmers and play a large share of poor budgets (Wineman et al., 2020). If this growth strategy is to be pursued, it is necessary to increase expenditure on agricultural research and extension processes that focus on these crops.

Maulu et al. (2021) studied the role of agriculture in reducing poverty in Tanzania with a certain emphasis on the role of agricultural within the overall economy. The study explained the investable role of agriculture in reducing aggregate poverty among rural population of Tanzania. Tanzania is one of the poorest countries in the world with $3050 a per capita income. The base for improving the economy and reducing the poverty rate is linked to the design of effective agricultural and rural development strategies. This is because agriculture sector has generated about 30% of GDP in recent years and employing around 66% of labor force in Tanzania. At the same time, agriculture production accounts for three-quarters of business exports and from a macroeconomic perspective, it is counted as a source of livelihood to nearly 80% of the total population.

13.3.5.3 The Case of Nigeria

Several studies examined the contribution of agriculture to economic growth in Nigeria (Grove, 2023; Olomu et al., 2020). They emphasized the role of agriculture as an engine of growth that contributes to the development of other sectors. They have established a relationship between agriculture production and economic growth. While they reported evidence on the positive and consistent contribution of agriculture sector to the economic growth in Nigeria, they reaffirm the agriculture's importance in the economy. For instance, Tochukwu et al. (2021) reported that 70% of the total population in Nigeria is employed within the agriculture sector. The resilience of the sector is a clear example of its ability to recover more quickly than other sectors from shocks and economic recession. The growth in agriculture is overly dependent on the growth of crop production as it contributes the most to agriculture production in the country. Hence, the economic growth in this country will be almost impossible to perform without developing the agriculture sector.

13.3.5.4 Other Cases

A study was undertaken by Arendonk (2015) as a case study about the share of agriculture in overall GDP and employment in China, Indonesia, the Netherlands, and the United States. As economic growth of countries proceeds, the role of agriculture sector in GDP and employment changes as it is high but declining in developing countries, while it is low but more stable within the developed countries. The study indicated that the position of agriculture sector in the economy seems more

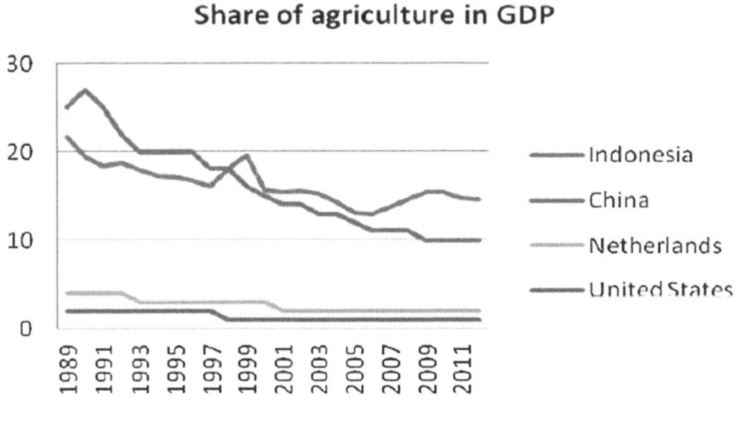

Fig. 13.1 Agriculture shares in GDP development over time (Source: Arendonk 2015)

influential in developing countries, however, is less important in developed countries. Based on the results, the agricultural production in the Netherlands and the United States is smaller than in Indonesia and China. Both developed countries of Indonesia and China involve in slowly transitioning toward the stage of the United States and the Netherlands. As illustrated below in Fig. 13.1, the share of agriculture reduces quickly in the period 1989–2011 in Indonesia and China, whereas there is a slow decline within the same period in the United States and the Netherlands.

13.4 Analysis of Agricultural Development in the Kurdistan Region

We collected data from various sources on the agriculture sector, namely the Ministry of Agriculture and Water Resource (MAWR), Ministry of Planning (MoP), Kurdistan Region Statistical Office (KRSO), and Board of Investment (BOI). The data were analysed through the use of Excel and presented in an understandable way by using graphs, figures, and tables. The objective of this chapter is to find out the agriculture production and its role in economic development.

13.4.1 Consumption of Agricultural Food Commodities

Consumption is defined as a demand to satisfy human needs. It is also known as the end-use of food commodities in its final form. Consumer food demand is the determinant and final guide of economic activity in different societies. We investigated different and most prioritized aspects of food consumption in terms of different levels. The importance of the consumption study stems from its being one of the pillars of the economic balance. In this case, if the food consumption changes, a change in the volume of food production or supply of food commodities should be achieved if the region wants to rebalance the economy once again.

Table 13.3 shows an increase in the rate of some of the most important consumer goods and a decrease the rate of production of some others. With an average of agriculture production reaching 2,184,797 tons from 2014 to 2016, and the region's requirement or the consumption rate of goods has reached 2,251,786 in total.

In addition, the table shows that the Kurdistan Region needs to import most of the agricultural goods as they are inefficient. Accordingly, the region is self-efferent in the only minimum of agricultural products, and they can be exported which are wheat, potato, and squash.

Figure 13.2 shows agricultural productions volumes during the past years compared to region's requirement. Some basic products recorded the highest level of increase. For example, wheat production doubled between 2014 and 2016, highly exceeding the region's consumption requirement.

Table 13.3 Consumption and regions requirement of food from (2014–2016) (in tons)

Product	2014	2015	2016	Average 2014–2016	Mean of the region's requirement	Self-sufficiency
Wheat	844,585	1,097,427	1,686,784	1,209,599	650,000	1.860922
Chicken meat	69,568	81,513	99,738	83,606	128,000	0.653172
Eggs	48,200	48,611	15,400	37,404	48,000	0.77925
Red meat	66,000	68,000	71,500	68,500	77,126	0.888157
Milk	226,128	25,200	260,000	170,443	439,192	0.388083
Tomato	64,782	60,772	86,205	70,586	133,736	0.527801
Potato	123,334	150,383	276,104	183,274	80,340	2.28123
Onion	59,491	47,501	61,497	56,163	58,258	0.964039
Eggplants	21,584	21,948	42,514	28,682	37,466	0.765547
Squash	15,778	16,630	20,798	17,735	17,267	1.027104
Cucumber	58,656	66,442	56,607	60,568	169,069	0.358244
Other vegetables	131,393	140,060	126,200	132,551	146,641	0.903915
Apple	7006	16,806	4078	9297	52,332	0.177654
Grape	6486	11,451	15,690	11,209	65,038	0.172345
Pomegranate	21,419	24,851	19,807	22,026	65,304	0.337284
Peach	9245	9707	4106	7686	18,472	0.416089
Other Fruits	6768	16,445	10,635	11,283	58,055	0.19435
Fish	2175	4000	4730	3635	6000	0.605833
Honey	800	853	0	551	1490	0.369799
Average	178,5412	1,910,615	2,864,409	2,184,797	2,251,786	–

Source: author's investigation.

It is obvious that the agricultural production for some of the prioritized products has increased, however, the region has not reached a point for self-sufficiency for most of the agricultural goods. This gives a meaning that the region is still in need of importing agricultural goods from abroad. However, the region has potential in exporting some agricultural goods, such as wheat, potato, and squash. Wheat production has remarkably increased from 844,585 tons in 2014 to 1,686,784 tons in 2016. In 2024, this figure has dramatically raised to cultivating approximately 2.9 million donums of land with an expected yield of 2.5 million tons, which is highly exceeding the region's consumption requirement. This aligns with the Kurdistan 2020 Vision for Agriculture and Agro-industry, which foresees the KRI to be a major food and agricultural producer and exporter of wheat, vegetables, fruit, meat, dairy, and poultry in the wider region and beyond.

Similarly, the production of potatoes has doubled from 123,334 tons in 2014 to reach 276,104 tons in 2016, and in 2023 potato production reaches 600,00 tons with revenues estimated at $500 million. Nevertheless, the region's requirement is only 80,340 tons. The reason for such success is due to an increasing number of KRI citizens moving to rural areas to pursue agricultural business. Over the past, a large number of people in urban areas lost their jobs because of economic instability in

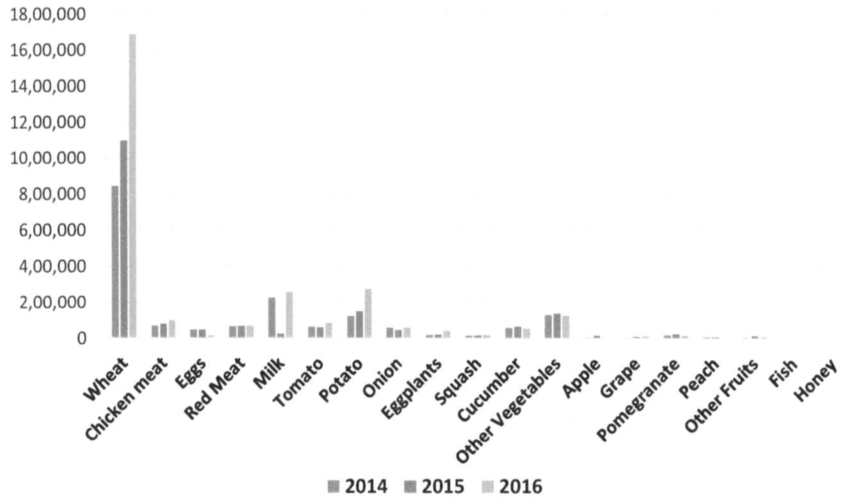

Source: Author's investigation.

Fig. 13.2 Level of agriculture production from 2014 to 2016 in KRI (tons) (Source: author's investigation)

Table 13.4 Distribution of urban and rural population in KRI from 2003 to 2012

Year	Urban	Percentage	Rural	Percentage	Overall
2003	2,123,272	74.2	738,429	25.8	2,861,701
2004	2,621,114	73.22	958,802	26.78	3,579,916
2005	2,701,232	73.07	995,564	26.93	3,696,796
2006	2,783,620	72.92	1,033,706	27.08	3,817,326
2007	2,868,271	72.77	1,073,258	27.23	3,941,529
2008	3,062,505	72.93	1,136,526	27.07	4,199,031
2009	3,676,390	78.24	1,022,392	21.76	4,698,782
2010	3,882,568	81	910,724	19	4,793,292
2011	3,989,760	81	935,869	19	4,925,629
2012	4,097,798	81	961,212	19	5,059,010

Source: author's investigation.

the region and moved to rural areas to work in the agriculture sector. A further reason is the KRG support to the farmers and producers, which started competing with Iranian and Turkish agricultural products. Nevertheless, there are still other products that are imported from abroad to fulfill the region's requirement such as milk, tomato, cucumber, and some other fruits and vegetables.

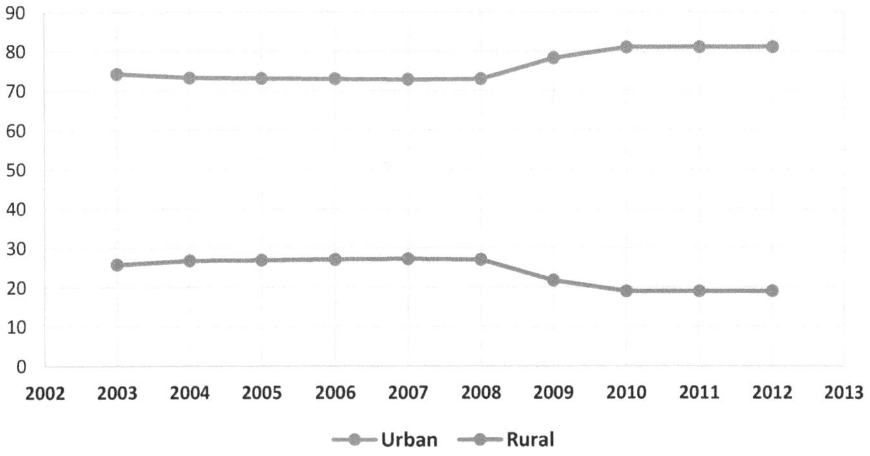

Fig. 13.3 Urban and rural population in KRI from 2003 to 2012

13.4.2 Human Capital and Agriculture Production

Most agricultural operations depend heavily on the labor force and the use of new technologies. The Kurdistan Region has a relatively large human mass, and a large size of the population of the region has worked in the agriculture sector as the main source of livelihood. Table 13.4 shows the distribution of the urban and rural population in the Kurdistan Region during the period 2003–2012. As can be seen, the rural population has declined by 7% in 10 years mainly because of imbalance between the economic sectors, specifically between public and private sectors.

Figure 13.3 shows that the Kurdistan Region in 2010, 2011, and 2012 had the highest percentage of the urban population, which amounted to about 81%. On the other hand, the lowest proportion of the rural population amounted to about 19%. The continuous decline of the rural population, in general, is observed mainly due to the government's lack of interest in rural areas, low level of income in those areas, mass recruitments by the public, and increased migration from rural to urban.

13.4.3 Employment in Agriculture Sector

For the size of the unemployment rates among the three governorates, Fig. 13.4 shows the unemployment rate at the governorate level in the Kurdistan Region. As it is illustrated, the unemployment rate was 14% during 2008 and 2014 and it has reduced the lowest during 2011-2-12 and once again increased to 25% in 2016 due to the emergence of ISIS in 2014 and the financial crisis that the region was facing following oil prices drop.

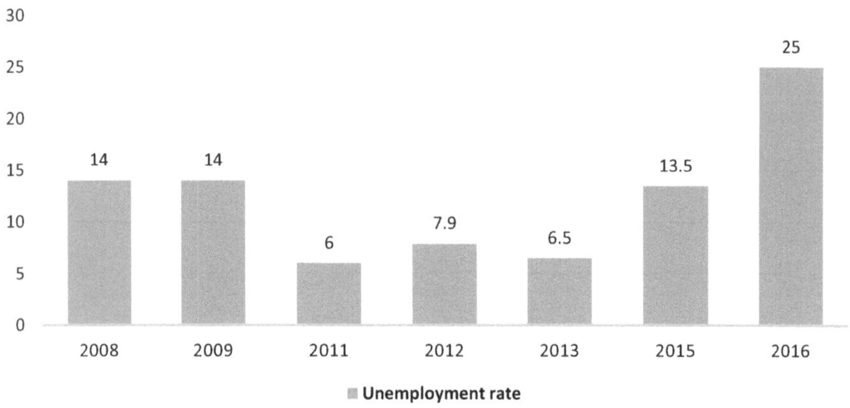

Source: Authors' investigation

Fig. 13.4 Unemployment rate in KRI from 2008 to 2016 (Source: authors' investigation)

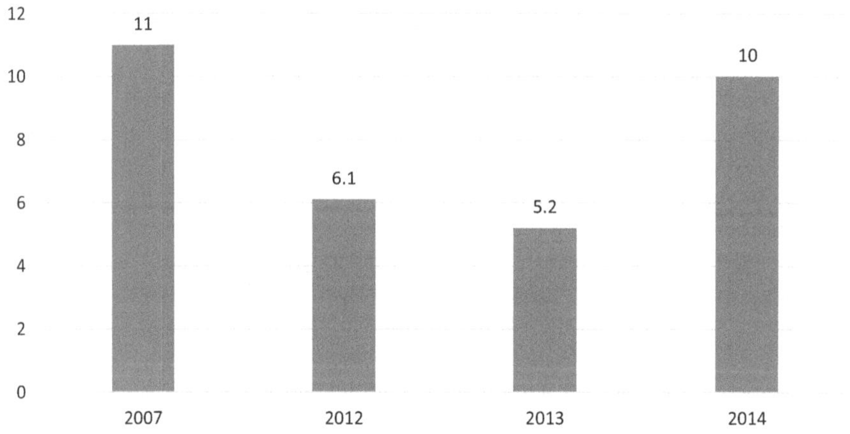

Source: Authors' investigation

Fig. 13.5 Unemployment rate in agriculture sector in KRI from 2007 to 2014 (Source: authors' investigation)

As it is shown in Fig. 13.5, the employment in agriculture in the Kurdistan Region has been fluctuating due to the economic status for a specific time period. The figure reveals that employment in agriculture was 11% in the Kurdistan Region. In contrast, the rate of employment in agriculture has largely decreased to only 6.1% in 2012 and 5.2% in 2013. Once again, the percentage of employment within the agriculture sector has increased to 10% in 2014.

The rural agriculture sector plays an important role in reducing rural unemployment rates and overall unemployment in the region as a whole. The rate of employment is highly linked to the economic status of the Kurdistan Region. As it is indicated in the figures, a large portion of the KRI's population relying on agriculture sector was 10% in 2007. However, the flourishing economic status of the region during 2009–2013 caused a reduction in employment in the agriculture sector to only 6.1% in 2012 and 5.2% in 2013. This is due to a large portion of people from the rural area having migrated to urban cities, and they were encouraged by the local Government to work as public servants. But the economic crisis during the last few years has had a positive influence on persuading the farmers to go back to their villages and precede agricultural planting and cultivation.

13.4.4 Agriculture Investment

Agricultural investment plays a prominent role in expanding capacity and improving productivity and development in various fields for the economy. This is particularly true in terms of agricultural development in general and in particular foreign direct investment (FDI) as a means of covering the funding gaps experienced by some underdeveloped economies.

According to the Kurdistan Regional Investment Authority, the volume of investment in the region during the years 2006–2018 are as follows (Fig. 13.6):

The total number of approved investment projects in the region reached 791 projects during the years 2006–2018, of which 714 projects invest in local capital and 31 joint ventures and 46 projects with foreign capital. Both industry and housing sectors are coming as the first and second sectors for their large allocation of capital

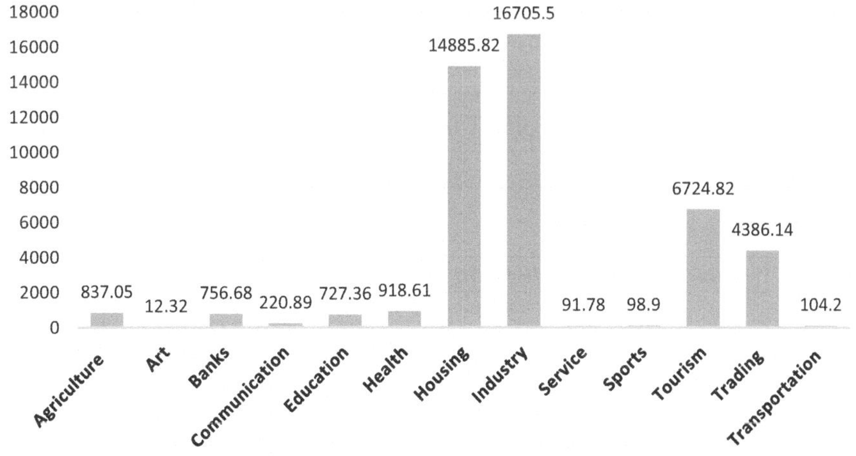

Source: Data from Board of Direct Investment (BOI), 2018.

Fig. 13.6 Invested capital by sectors in KRI from 2006 to 2018 ($ million) (Source: data from Board of Direct Investment (BOI), 2018)

Table 13.5 Agricultural investment in KRI from 2006 to 2018

	No. of projects	Capital in dollar	Area in donum	Sector capital (%)
Erbil	16	243,291,709	6753	1.24
Sulaymaniyah	5	19,367,385	2936	0.52
Duhok	9	574,392,972	89	0.04
Average	30	837,052,066	9778	1.80

Source: authors' investigation.

by $16 billion and $14 billion. On the other hand, $837 million was invested in agriculture out of 46 billion.

Table 13.5 shows the number of agricultural licensed projects approved by the Board of Investment from 2006 to 2018. In overall, $837,052,066 was invested for the total of 30 projects in Kurdistan Region. The area in donum reached 9778 in total and with the sector capital only reaching 1.8% for all three governorates and 98.2% for the rest of the sectors. This is highly off-track with the level of covering the gap between the required plan of the Ministry of Agriculture and government investments in this sector. In terms of the inter-sector activities, investments in the industrial sector, although relatively high, have not been able to increase the role of this sector in generating GDP.

Most foreign and domestic investments went to areas that yielded fast and guaranteed returns. Therefore, a large part of the investments is directed to non-agricultural sectors such as general trade and general contracting, construction of buildings, and real estate projects. However, the current diversification policy of the KRG has caused to increase inward investment in the region's agriculture from 1.5% to over 10% in 2022. Despite relative development of the sector and launching several agricultural and food security projects in the region, the KRG needs to build strong industrial and agricultural infrastructure through encouraging foreign and domestic investments, particularly the agriculture sector. The KRG should benefit from international expertise in agriculture, irrigation, livestock, and poultry farming, and the production and processing of food products to help secure growth and sustainable agricultural development that contribute to the achievement of food security.

13.4.5 Agriculture Production in KRI

Through our review of the figures and statistics that focused on the levels of production and productivity of the agro-food sector in its fields, the data have confirmed an increase in agricultural products compared to previous years. Specifically, the agricultural sector witnessed fluctuations in regard to the level of production.

Table 13.6 and Fig. 13.7 present the total agricultural production in the Kurdistan Region from 2007 to 2016. The total agricultural goods in KRI were 1,996,798 tons in 2007. While the level of production has witnessed a decrease between 2011 to

Table 13.6 Average agriculture production by governorates over 2007–2016 (tons)

Year	Erbil	Duhok	Sulaymaniyah	Garmian	Total
2007	888,146	410,164	479,696	218,791	1,996,798
2008	466,793	308,621	135,631	209,846	1,120,891
2009	975,431	534,643	254,356	352,795	2,117,225
2010	385,911	607,762	89,259	39,424	1,122,356
2011	333,088	239,464	134,538	33,377	740,466
2013	394,644	289,104	201,871	56,173	941,792
2014	150,680	124,338	224,909	12,358	512,285
2015	275,483	158,789	374,231	143,843	952,346
2016	1,188,817	427,594	1,069,116	208,197	2,893,724

Source: author's investigation.

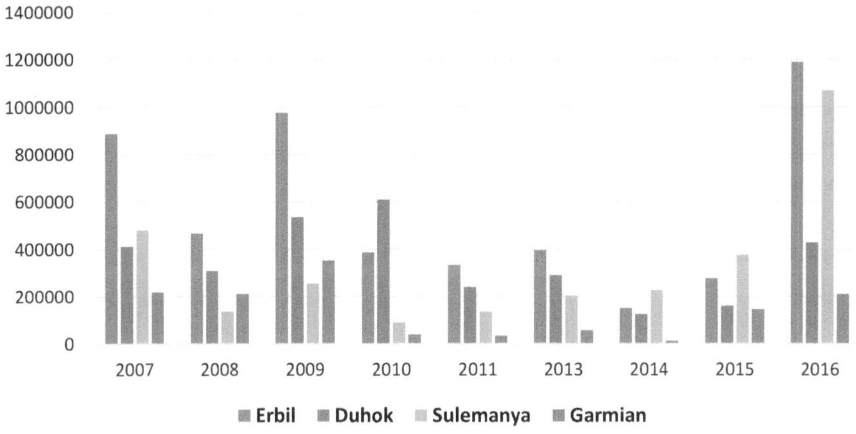

Fig. 13.7 Agriculture production in KRI from 2007 to 2016 (tons)

2015 compared to the previous years with a mean of 941,792 tons. This shows that the existence of the food gap in both vegetable and animal areas has decreased gradually due to more productivity in the agricultural sector. Agricultural development is not only achieved through the provision of modern production inputs and by the development and upgrading of human resources, which uses these resources but also requires all measures that will improve agricultural production and productivity in the context of overall economic development.

In 2016, agricultural production has increased by reaching 2,893,724 tons. Further, as has shown in the figure, Erbil comes first in agricultural production compared to other provinces and areas in the region.

Table 13.7 presents the level of importing agricultural goods versus the local production of vegetables over 2007–2016. Due to an increase in the demand for agricultural products, the consumption of the goods has increased during the years 2007–2016. Further, the percentage of import consumption has dropped from 60%

Table 13.7 The Consumption amount and the percentage of local production and import over 2007–2016 (tons)

Year	Local	Percentage	Import	Percentage	Consumption amount
2007	295,984	40	438,577	60	734,561
2008	355,220	46	423,392	54	780,620
2009	325,622	44	416,876	56	742,498
2010	363,115	35	668,473	65	1,031,588
2011	468,451	48	707,062	52	1,175,513
2013	481,367	49	492,744	51	974,111
2014	475,017	48	506,777	52	981,794
2015	503,835	51	491,040	49	994,875
2016	646,193	55	520,478	45	1,166,670

Source: author's investigation.

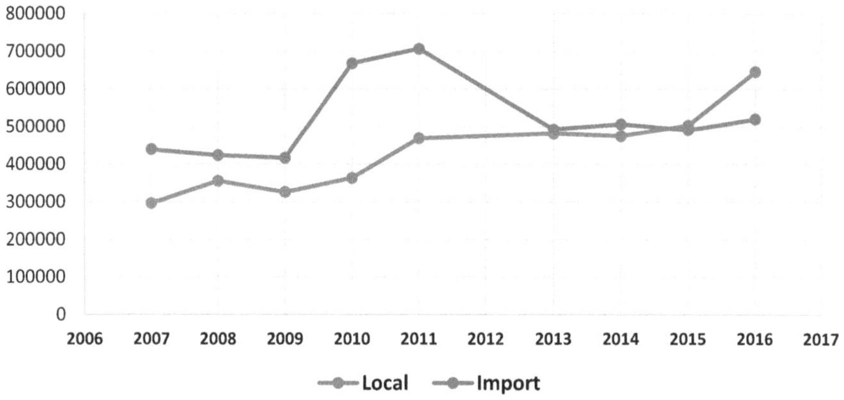

Source: Authors' investigation

Fig. 13.8 Importing vs. local production of vegetable from 2007 to 2016 (tons) (Source: authors' investigation)

in 2007 to 45% in 2016. A possible reason lies in an improvement in the agriculture sector, and this leads to more agriculture production.

Figure 13.8 reveals the increase in domestic production between the periods 2007 until 2016. In 2007, the local production of agriculture goods was only 295,984 tons, representing 40% of the total, while the importing of goods were 438,577 tons during the same year with a percentage of 60%. Additionally, during 2016, the level of agricultural production has witnessed an increase to 646,193 tons with the percentage of 55%. During the same year, the amount of total consumption of agriculture goods reached 1,166,670 tons.

Table 13.8 provides detailed statistical information on the overall planting agricultural area in the Kurdistan Region over 2007–2016. The years 2007 and 2008 saw the highest activity in planting agricultural products, covering an area of 4407572 donums and 3903592, respectively. However, the total planted area

Table 13.8 Planted agricultural area in KRI from 2007 to 2016 (donum)

Year	Erbil	Duhok	Sulemaniyah	Garmian	Total
2007	1,657,559	904,513	968,252	877,248	4,407,572
2008	1,822,203	799,647	361,884	919,858	3,903,592
2009	1,669,799	87,692	82,927	11,674	1,852,092
2010	1,373,576	1,105,501	60,813	16,798	2,556,688
2011	31,775	96,241	71,117	14,465	213,598
2013	1,385,106	966,882	809,722	234,713	3,396,423
2014	201,935	52,871	36,113	15,488	306,407
2015	211,843	542,689	43,217	23,511	821,260
2016	1,648,867	814,346	368,682	368,682	3,200,577

Source: KRG Ministry of Agriculture and Water Resources, Unpublished Official Records 2018.

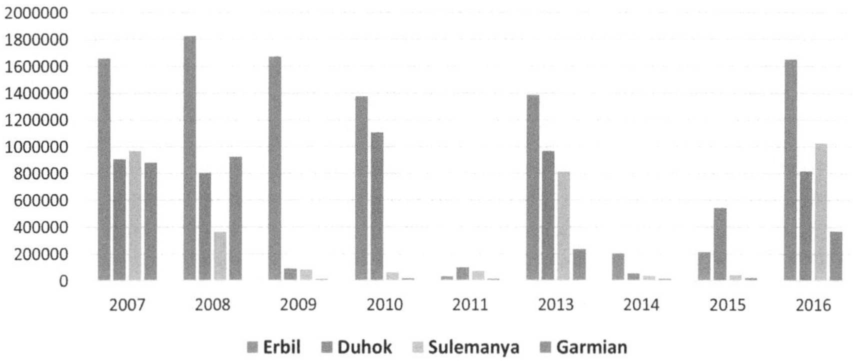

Source: KRG Ministry of Agriculture and Water Resources, Unpublished Official Records.2018.

Fig. 13.9 Agricultural area by Governorates from 2007 to 2016 (donum) (Source: KRG Ministry of Agriculture and Water Resources, Unpublished Official Records 2018)

dropped significantly in 2011 to only 213,598 donums. It has since increased and in 2016, the total planted area reached 3200577 donums. Although the area of agriculture planting has dropped significantly, agriculture production has increased. Thus, increasing the productivity of the land is to improve the conditions of cultivation in terms of selection of crops that correspond to the nature of the land and the selection of seeds and pest control.

Figure 13.9 presents the total agricultural area by governorates from 2007 to 2016. Erbil was coming first in planting a large area for agriculture, as it has reached a pick in 2008 by providing 1,822,203 donums, while Garmany came last for planting agricultural area by 11,674 donums in 2009. As it is clearly shown in the figure, the planted area for agricultural goods in 2011 has dropped compared to the previous and coming years it was counted as the most inactive year. The possible reasons for this fluctuation in the planted area by governorates are due to the availability of suitable land and the investment status in agriculture.

Nevertheless, rural–urban migration has been the most challenging factor facing the region's agricultural development plans and programs over the past years. It also results in increasing agricultural production costs and decreasing investment in the agriculture sector. The main reason for this migration is the rise in wages in urban areas, where there are abundant employment opportunities in other sectors. This is in addition to the large disparity in the level of health, education, and social services between rural and urban areas.

13.4.6 Share of Agriculture in National Economy of the KRI

Figure 13.10 provides the proportion of the contribution of the agriculture sector to the national economy of the Kurdistan Region during 2007–2014. The figure shows a notable fluctuation within the share of agriculture to the national income of the region. The share of agriculture contributing to the national economy was 6% in 2007 and 7% in 2009, while this contribution dropped largely to 3% in 2008, 2012, and 2014 and counted as inactive years. However, the share of the agriculture sector has reached a peak by 2013 to around 17%. This fluctuation has continued experiencing drop down to 3.1% in 2014 and rapid increase to 10% in 2017.

One possible reason for witnessing a rise in the share of agriculture sector in GDP is that as the region was facing a financial crisis during the last years; many families went back to their villages to provide a source of income for their families. In other words, during this period, a reverse-migration has happened from urban to

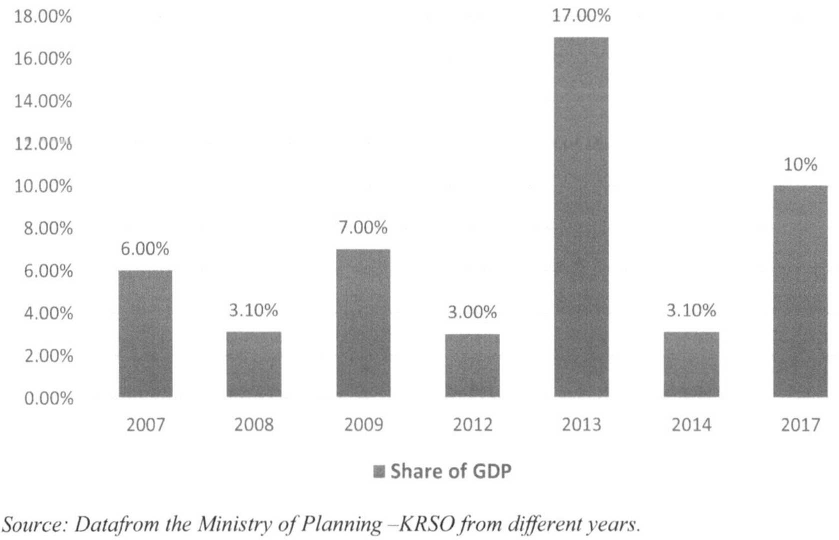

Fig. 13.10 Share of agriculture to the economic growth in KRI during 2007–2014 (GDP) (Source: Data from the Ministry of Planning—KRSO from different years)

rural areas. Having said that, one cannot ignore the constructive policies put in place by the KRG to safeguard the region's agricultural products from the neighboring countries' cheap imports. These figures remind us that the Kurdistan Region is capable of increasing its agricultural products if suitable policies were in place.

13.5 Conclusion and Policy Recommendation

The agriculture sector of the Kurdistan Region highly contributed to supporting economic growth, generating employment, enhancing food security, and being the source of livelihood for many people. The region has long relied on imports of most of the agricultural foods and has not been able to produce all the agricultural needs. The importation of food is mainly due to the lack of balance between the quantities produced and the need for food. While the KRG has currently focused on a diversified strategy, agricultural development requires an integrated system that seeks to provide the reasons for sustainable agricultural development that contributes to the achievement of more agricultural production and promote the economic growth.

Over the past years, the KRG developed several strategies in the hope of improving agriculture and infrastructure and attracting foreign investors to come and invest in the region. However, the oil industry, construction, and service sectors attracted almost all the investment, yet many other sectors including agriculture stayed vulnerable and did not improve well.

The region has suitable weather but is divided into three levels in terms of rainfall, which ranges from 350 to 1200 mm. Rainfall is the main source of various types of water resources on the surface of the earth. It is the main factor in agricultural production and agricultural crops. The KRG attempts to expand its capabilities to correspond to the present demand of water supply by building dams.

The analysis reported the presence of fluctuations in agricultural and food production in both the vegetable and animal sectors in the Kurdistan Region based on the economic status of the region. This instability has negatively affected the agricultural capacity of the region causing a large gap between demand and supply for agricultural products, making the sector vulnerable to employment, and consequently the productivity of the sector was not expected.

The agricultural production has increased gradually in terms of quantity and value due to increase in the demand for foodstuffs, support of the government to the sector, and change in preference of the population toward more local foods rather than imported ones. Improvement in the income of farmers has a profound role in the development of the sector since the government helped them in marketing of their products. As such, increasing agricultural production is imperative that the development of the sector and self-sufficiency are secured.

However, the Kurdistan Regional Government can't support further production of the agriculture sector through the following strategies: the KRG can support the increase in harvested areas to promote agriculture production. There are many non-cultivated lands that can be used as rainfed land or can come under irrigation, considering the fact that the region is in a good situation in terms of water resources. The KRG can support increasing yields through improvement in productivity, which mainly comes from using better technology or high-yield seeds by the farmers. The KRG must support employment in the agriculture sector and returnees to villages and rural areas. This must include rural development to increase agricultural production capacity in the country by paying attention to human development, especially in relation to employment. In particular, this includes the development of smallholder farming systems, support for rural women, assistance to farmers, reducing income inequalities between urban and rural areas, advancing health and education services, improving the well-being of rural populations, and expanding training programs for agricultural activities.

There is poor marketing of agricultural products in the Kurdistan Region due to the lack of access to the market and also the deterioration of roads and transportation. This does not encourage raising the level of agricultural production and guaranteeing a minimum income for agricultural producers on the one hand and the lack of agricultural reservoirs and fruit and vegetable crops on the other hand. Support in these areas will affect the productivity of the sector.

References

Abd-Elmabod, S. K., Muñoz-Rojas, M., Jordán, A., Anaya-Romero, M., Phillips, J. D., Jones, L., et al. (2020). Climate change impacts on agricultural suitability and yield reduction in a Mediterranean region. *Geoderma, 374*, 114453.

Abdullah, S., & Gray, T. (2022). Political constraints on economic diversification in the Kurdistan Region of Iraq. *Energy Policy, 171*, 113274.

Abidin, I. S. Z., Haseeb, M., & Islam, R. (2022). Impact of agricultural irrigated land and raw material import, labor force and capital formation on rice production: Evidence from the Malaysian economy. *Cuadernos de Economía, 45*(127), 106–112.

Ahad, B., Shahri, W., Rasool, H., Reshi, Z., Rasool, S., & Hussain, T. (2021). Medicinal plants and herbal drugs: An overview. *Medicinal and Aromatic Plants: Healthcare and Industrial Applications*, 1–40.

Akhmad, A., Amir, A., Saleh, S., & Abidin, Z. (2022). Effectiveness of regional government expenditure in reducing unemployment and poverty rate. *European Journal of Development Studies, 2*(4), 90–99.

Anderson, R., Bayer, P. E., & Edwards, D. (2020). Climate change and the need for agricultural adaptation. *Current Opinion in Plant Biology, 56*, 197–202.

Arendonk, A. V. (2015). *The development of the share of agriculture in GDP and employment: A case study of China, Indonesia, the Netherlands and the United States*. Wageningen University, Leibniz Institute of Agricultural Development in Transition Economies.

Ayoo, C. (2022). Poverty reduction strategies in developing countries. *Rural development-education, sustainability, multifunctionality* (pp. 17–57).

Bezpartochnyi, M., Britchenko, I., & Bezpartochna, O. (2022). Financial losses of Ukraine's agricultural exports and ensuring food security during martial law. *VUZF Review, 7*(2), 193.

Bozarslan, H., Gunes, C., & Yadirgi, V. (2021). *The Cambridge history of the Kurds*. Cambridge University Press.

Daneshmehr, H., & Nasrollahizadeh, B. (2024). Investigating the Contexts, Causes, and Consequences of Underdevelopment in Kurdistan Province (A grounded theory in the field of agriculture). *Iranian Journal of Agricultural Economics and Development Research.*

De Brauw, A. (2020). Seasonal migration and agricultural production in Vietnam. In *Migration, transfers and economic decision making among agricultural households* (pp. 114–139). Routledge.

Delpasand, M., Bozorg-Haddad, O., & Loáiciga, H. A. (2020). Integrated virtual water trade management considering self-sufficient production of strategic agricultural and industrial products. *Science of the Total Environment, 743*, 140797.

Dilshad, Z. Z., Ahmed, S. O., & Rahman, B. (2023). The effect of COVID-19 on the Kurdistan Region Government (KRG) economy. *Journal of the Knowledge Economy*, 1–16.

Ferreira, V., Almazán-Gómez, M. Á., Nechifor, V., & Ferrari, E. (2022). The role of the agricultural sector in Ghanaian development: A multiregional SAM-based analysis. *Journal of Economic Structures, 11*(1), 6.

Fuglie, K. O. (2012). Productivity growth and technology capital in the global agricultural economy. In *Productivity growth in agriculture: An international perspective,* 335.

Grove, A. T. (2023). Population densities and agriculture in northern Nigeria. In *Essays on African population* (pp. 115–136). Routledge.

Güneralp, B., Reba, M., Hales, B. U., Wentz, E. A., & Seto, K. C. (2020). Trends in urban land expansion, density, and land transitions from 1970 to 2010: A global synthesis. *Environmental Research Letters, 15*(4), 044015.

Guth, M., Smędzik-Ambroży, K., Czyżewski, B., & Stępień, S. (2020). The economic sustainability of farms under common agricultural policy in the European Union countries. *Agriculture, 10*(2), 34.

Hemathilake, D., & Gunathilake, D. (2022). Agricultural productivity and food supply to meet increased demands. In *Future foods* (pp. 539–553). Elsevier.

Heyl, K., Ekardt, F., Sund, L., & Roos, P. (2022). Potentials and limitations of subsidies in sustainability governance: The example of agriculture. *Sustainability, 14*(23), 15859.

Hrustek, L. (2020). Sustainability driven by agriculture through digital transformation. *Sustainability, 12*(20), 8596.

Hufnagel, J., Reckling, M., & Ewert, F. (2020). Diverse approaches to crop diversification in agricultural research. A review. *Agronomy for Sustainable Development, 40*(2), 14.

Huy, D. T. N. (2021). Banking sustainability for economic growth and socio-economic development–case in Vietnam. *Turkish Journal of Computer and Mathematics Education (TURCOMAT), 12*(2), 2544–2553.

Huynh, H. T., Nguyen, P. V., Trieu, H. D., & Tran, K. T. (2021). Productivity spillover from FDI to domestic firms across six regions in Vietnam. *Emerging Markets Finance and Trade, 57*(1), 59–75.

Kogo, B. K., Kumar, L., & Koech, R. (2021). Climate change and variability in Kenya: a review of impacts on agriculture and food security. *Environment, Development and Sustainability, 23*(1), 23–43.

Kołodziejczak, W. (2020). Employment and gross value added in agriculture versus other sectors of the European Union Economy. *Sustainability, 12*(14), 5518.

Kulaya, P. M. (2020). *The role of government intervention on agricultural growth in Tanzania: Case of cotton.* The Open University of Tanzania.

Lencucha, R., Pal, N. E., Appau, A., Thow, A.-M., & Drope, J. (2020). Government policy and agricultural production: A scoping review to inform research and policy on healthy agricultural commodities. *Globalization and Health, 16*(1), 11.

Liliane, T. N., & Charles, M. S. (2020). *Factors affecting yield of crops. Agronomy-climate change and food security*, 9.

Liu, J., Wang, M., Yang, L., Rahman, S., & Sriboonchitta, S. (2020). Agricultural productivity growth and its determinants in south and southeast asian countries. *Sustainability, 12*(12), 4981.

Liverpool-Tasie, L. S. O., Wineman, A., Young, S., Tambo, J., Vargas, C., Reardon, T., et al. (2020). A scoping review of market links between value chain actors and small-scale producers in developing regions. *Nature Sustainability, 3*(10), 799–808.

Magdalena, S., & Suhatman, R. (2020). The effect of government expenditures, domestic invesment, foreign invesment to the economic growth of primary sector in Central Kalimantan. *Budapest International Research and Critics Institute-Journal (BIRCI-Journal), 3*(3), 1692–1703.

Maulu, S., Hasimuna, O. J., Mutale, B., Mphande, J., & Siankwilimba, E. (2021). Enhancing the role of rural agricultural extension programs in poverty alleviation: A review. *Cogent Food and Agriculture, 7*(1), 1886663.

Mazid, A. (2015). *Status of wheat production in Kurdistan region of Iraq: Results of baseline survey*. Japan International Cooperation Agency (JICA) and International Center for Agricultural Research in Dry Area (ICARDA).

McCaig, B., & Pavcnik, N. (2013). *Moving out of agriculture: Structural change in Vietnam.*

Miah, M. D., Hasan, R., & Uddin, H. (2020). Agricultural development and the rural economy: The case of Bangladesh. *Bangladesh's economic and social progress: From a basket case to a development model*, pp. 237–266.

Muhamad, G. M. (2022). Private sector development analysis in post-conflict kurdistan region of Iraq. *UKH Journal of Social Sciences, 6*(2), 19–32.

Muhamad, G. M. (2023). *Reducing natural resource dependency for economic growth in resource rich countries*. Springer Nature.

Muhamad, G. M. (2024). The technological effects of renewable and non-renewable energy on agricultural productivity in developed countries. *International Journal of Empirical Economics*. https://doi.org/10.1142/S2810943024500082

Muhamad, G. M., Heshmati, A., & Khayyat, N. T. (2020). The dynamics of private sector development in natural resource dependent countries. *Global Economic Review, 49*(4), 396–421.

Muhamad, G. M., Heshmati, A., & Khayyat, N. T. (2021). How to reduce the degree of dependency on natural resources? *Resources Policy, 72*, 102047.

Nguyen, T. H., Doan, Q.-V., Khan, A., Derdouri, A., Anand, P., & Niyogi, D. (2024). The potential of agricultural and livestock wastes as a source of biogas in Vietnam: Energetic, economic and environmental evaluation. *Renewable and Sustainable Energy Reviews, 199*, 114440.

Niho, Y. (1974). Population growth, agricultural capital, and the development of a dual economy. *The American Economic Review*, 1077–1085.

Norton, G. W., Alwang, J., & Masters, W. A. (2021). *Economics of agricultural development: World food systems and resource use*. Routledge.

Nugroho, A. D. (2021). Agricultural market information in developing countries: A literature review. *Agricultural Economics/Zemedelska Ekonomika, 67*(11).

Olomu, M. O., Ekperiware, M. C., & Akinlo, T. (2020). Agricultural sector value chain and government policy in Nigeria: Issues, challenges and prospects. *African Journal of Economic and Management Studies, 11*(3), 525–538.

Pawlak, K., & Kołodziejczak, M. (2020). The role of agriculture in ensuring food security in developing countries: Considerations in the context of the problem of sustainable food production. *Sustainability, 12*(13), 5488.

Peskett, L., Slater, R., Stevens, C., & Dufey, A. (2022). *Biofuels, agriculture and poverty reduction*: ODI.

Puri-Mirza, A. (2024). *Cultivated area in the Middle East as of 2019, by country (in 1,000 hectare).* Retrieved 4/5/2024, from Statista https://www.statista.com/statistics/1305065/middle-east-cultivated-area-by-country/

Qaim, M. (2020). Role of new plant breeding technologies for food security and sustainable agricultural development. *Applied Economic Perspectives and Policy, 42*(2), 129–150.

Rahman, M. M., Khan, I., Field, D. L., Techato, K., & Alameh, K. (2022). Powering agriculture: Present status, future potential, and challenges of renewable energy applications. *Renewable Energy, 188*, 731–749.

Sane, M., Hajek, M., Nwaogu, C., & Purwestri, R. C. (2021). Subsidy as an economic instrument for environmental protection: A case of global fertilizer use. *Sustainability, 13*(16), 9408.

Smith, V. H., & Glauber, J. W. (2020). Trade, policy, and food security. *Agricultural Economics, 51*(1), 159–171.

Statistics Office. (2018). *Winter crops 2016-2017* [Press release]. Retrieved from https://krso.gov.krd/archived/articles/051118122505.pdf

Streimikis, J., & Baležentis, T. (2020). Agricultural sustainability assessment framework integrating sustainable development goals and interlinked priorities of environmental, climate and agriculture policies. *Sustainable Development, 28*(6), 1702–1712.

Takahashi, K., Muraoka, R., & Otsuka, K. (2020). Technology adoption, impact, and extension in developing countries' agriculture: A review of the recent literature. *Agricultural Economics, 51*(1), 31–45.

Tochukwu, O. R., Omoyele, O. S., Olanipekun, W. D., & Aderemi, T. A. (2021). Is agriculture still a strong force in employment generation in Nigeria? An empirical investigation. *EuroEconomica, 40*(2).

Tuan Anh, N., Gan, C., & Anh, D. L. T. (2020). Does credit boost agricultural performance? Evidence from Vietnam. *International Journal of Social Economics, 47*(9), 1203–1221.

USAID, I. (2008). *Kurdistan region: Economic development assessment*. United States Agency for International Development.

Vatsa, P., & Miljkovic, D. (2022). Energy and crop price cycles before and after the global financial crisis: A new approach. *Journal of Agricultural Economics, 73*(1), 220–233.

Wineman, A., Jayne, T. S., Isinika Modamba, E., & Kray, H. (2020). The changing face of agriculture in Tanzania: Indicators of transformation. *Development Policy Review, 38*(6), 685–709.

Zaika, S., & Gridin, O. (2020). Human capital development in the agricultural economy sector. *Technology Audit and Production Reserves, 1*(4), 51.

Zhang, R., Ma, W., & Liu, J. (2021). Impact of government subsidy on agricultural production and pollution: A game-theoretic approach. *Journal of Cleaner Production, 285*, 124806.

Chapter 14
Agriculture Employment and Economic Growth in the Kurdistan Region of Iraq

Ribaz Chato Biro

Abstract The Kurdistan Region in Iraq (KRI) is naturally blessed with agriculturally fertile land areas, water supplies, and favorable weather. However, the region's agricultural sector substantially declined due to the first Gulf War and the subsequent embargo period. In KRI, the agriculture industry is undiversified, production costs are high, and there is no clear policy protecting domestic producers. Aside from the difficulties farmers have in gaining access to markets, financing, and supplies, food production needs to compete with imported items with generally cheaper pricing. Turkey and Iran, whose goods have filled Iraqi markets, are the primary competitors for Kurdish farmers. KRG's inability to design an effective homegrown national food supply policy and business people's greed and use of food import and distribution as a channel of money laundering effectively marginalized the agriculture sector. The radical reforms in trade, production, distribution, and employment are unavoidable due to the contribution of agriculture to GDP, the expansion of the service industry, the advancement of digital technologies, the enhancement of capital formation, and the increase in the skilled workforce. The economic growth strategies for Iraqi Kurdistan include two main goals: employment generation and the reduction of revenue inequity. This study assesses how the agriculture industry contributes to achieving these goals. A mixed method technique is used to collect and analyze data on agricultural production, agriculture added value to the GDP, and the number of farmers as unbalanced panel data for the years 2012, 2013, and 2018 have been employed to analyze a wider range of data and get a better result. Pooled OLS, fixed-effects, and random-effects techniques were used to estimate the relations between GDP growth and agriculture employment in the region. Findings demonstrate that although the agricultural industry has a strong capability of pro-

R. C. Biro (✉)
Economic Research Center, Soran University, Erbil, Iraq

Aynda Private Technical Institute, Erbil, Iraq
e-mail: ribaz.biro@soran.edu.iq

G. M. Muhamad, N. T. Khayyat (eds.), *Resource Management Performance: A Sectoral Analysis in the Post-Conflict Kurdistan Region of Iraq*, Perspectives on Development in the Middle East and North Africa (MENA) Region,
https://doi.org/10.1007/978-981-97-7725-9_14

ducing jobs and wealth, quality concerns are required for agriculture to promote productivity and employment and provide higher food security.

Keywords Job creation · Agriculture sector · Income distribution · Economic development · Iraqi Kurdistan

14.1 Introduction

Around the world, concerns about employment and job development continue to dominate the discussion. High-income nations deal with persistent unemployment brought on by economic slumps and ongoing financial turmoil, which affects both authorities and the population. People in middle-income nations are worried that development has left out significant portions of the population, increasing economic disparity and alienating meaningful social clusters. The main point of inclusive growth and eradicating poverty in low-income nations is the production of jobs (Dev, 2003).

Worldwide, sustainable agriculture and poverty eradication are closely related. Studies have revealed that agriculture reduces poverty in many economies by almost three times more effectively than other industries.

Agriculture investment generates a sizable amount of employment upstream and downstream of the food supply chain because it represents one of the most employment industries. According to studies, nations with more equitable income distribution have better growth elasticity of poverty, with a 1% rise in per capita expenditure connected with an estimated 2–3% drop in the poverty levels (Sudhir, 2003).

In order to meet its population's demands, Iraq has been a small-scale food producer. The Kurdistan region produces most of the country's wheat and barley. In contrast, much of the country's vegetable production is concentrated alongside rivers and in places where irrigation is accessible (Abramzon et al., 2016).

Iraq's temperate upland geography and dry areas with access to groundwater were ideal for fruit and date farms (Gibson et al., 2012). Nevertheless, during the past few decades, Iraq and the Kurdistan Region of Iraq (Abramzon et al.) have become significant food importers. The population's ability to be fed through agriculture and its contribution to the economy have been severely harmed by misguided modernist strategies, bloody war and conflict, and low-cost food imports (Eklund et al., 2016).

International organizations stress that the food and agricultural industry in Iraq and the Kurdistan Region in Iraq (KRI) can significantly contribute to rural employment and income creation, saying that it might add value to economic and political stability. These organizations include the World Bank Group (or World Bank, WB), the United Nations Development Programme [UNDP; Ministry of Planning & Ministry of Agriculture and Water Resources (KRG)], and the Food and Agricultural Organization [UNDP; Ministry of Planning & Ministry of Agriculture and Water Resources (KRG)].

Although national authorities and multinational corporations see agriculture as a possibly thriving industry in Iraq and the KRI, they find the food industry is now organized unsatisfactory. The critical concern they point out is poor infrastructure, which they connect to the fact that small-scale farmers control primary agriculture and are, reputedly, unskilled and unwilling to make investments (Eklund et al., 2017).

This research aims to investigate the relationship between agriculture production, job creation, and economic growth in the KRI. Thus, it applies primary and secondary data-gathering methods, including qualitative and quantitative test techniques. Data on agricultural production, agriculture added value to the GDP, and several farmers for the KRI as unbalanced panel data for the years 2012, 2013, and 2018 have been employed to analyze a wider range of data and get a better result.

Pooled OLS, fixed-effects, and random-effects techniques were used to estimate the relations between GDP growth and agriculture employment in the region. The data have been acquired from several Ministries and supplemented with additional research and evaluations carried out by NGOs, multilateral entities, Kurdistan Region Statistics Office ((KRSO)), and farmers. The study focused on the four KRI provinces of Erbil, Sulaymaniyah, Duhok, and Halabja.

14.2 Literature Review

Most global economies tended to be primarily agro-based and changed through time. The proportion of agribusiness in an economy has constantly decreased as trade relations, economic development, and technological advancements have made it possible for economies to diversify and undergo modernization. More remarkable advancements in non-agricultural industries attracted enough human resources that the proportion of agricultural employment decreased.

The disparity in income and output between agricultural and non-farm industries was the driving cause behind the migration of workers from agriculture. The birth and mortality rates in rural regions, migration, and the volume and labor requirements of sectors rising faster than agriculture each affected whether the agricultural workforce increased or decreased in total numbers as the industry's similar part of the economy decreased (de Janvry & Sadoulet, 2010; Oluwatayo & Ojo, 2016).

The productivity gap between sectors is very high by historical standards across many African nations. Agriculture's contribution to the continent's GDP has decreased from 21% in 1961–1970 to around 14%, even though this covers South Africa and the nations that produce minerals. In the remaining nations, agriculture accounts for a quarter and a third of GDP but employs between two-thirds and three-quarters of the working population, excluding South Africa and the mineral suppliers (World Bank, 2012).

This data shows a two-to-one job satisfaction difference between non-farming and agricultural industries. With such a significant differential, one would assume that workers would leave agriculture quickly, while those who stayed would become more productive. Most young people are abandoning Africa's fields; 40% of the continent's population now resides in urban centers, and this pattern is anticipated to grow. However, revenues from exploiting natural resources, urban development, and services have increased the economy without substantially removing agricultural employees. Even under the most optimistic forecasts, the percentage of young Africans that can be integrated into services and manufacturing occupations is likely far lower than that of individuals currently joining the workforce in rural regions (World Bank, 2012).

According to a technical report by World Bank (2018), growing the agricultural sector might be essential to reducing poverty because of its high rates in rural Jordan and Lebanon (rural poverty rates in Jordan are 17%, while North Lebanon and Bekka can reach 36–40%). The economies of Jordan and Lebanon both depend on agriculture and food. The agricultural and food industry employs 20–25% of the population living in Jordan and Lebanon. Although core agriculture only provides a minor portion of both nations' earnings (about 4% of the GDP of both countries) while indirect impacts (the food industry) are taken into account, agriculture contributes 25–30% of the GDPs of these countries.

The value added to agriculture and its percentage of the GDP has increased in Jordan; from 2011 to 2016, by 40 and 24%, respectively, compared to the corresponding overall average between 2000 and 2010. Over the previous 5 years, Jordan's agricultural output increased by double digits, peaking at a growth rate of 16% in 2015. In Lebanon, the agricultural contribution increased by 24% from the average value between 1991 and 2000 to US$ 1.56 billion (constant 2010) over 2011–2016, despite a decline in its GDP contribution.

In a study, Castro (2015) demonstrated that in the past few decades, compared to other major industries in Brazil and the agricultural sectors of other countries, agriculture has been an oasis of economic growth triumph. Trade openness has emerged as a significant contributor to the increase of crop production in recent years, which can be a valuable perspective for other major Brazilian industries that stayed reasonably close to the business. Agriculture labor productivity in Brazil is an employment creator, unlike the significant macroeconomic modernization of other countries.

Agriculture performance has the potential to increase further. Brazil's review reveals that agriculture production may rise higher without further consuming natural resources or raising GHG emissions. Therefore, agricultural economic growth in Brazil maintains its significant upward pattern while being ecologically responsible, creating employment, and improving livelihoods for the rural poor.

The literature reviewed provides a comprehensive basis for understanding the complex relationship between agricultural employment and economic growth, which is highly relevant to the research's aim. Strategic investment in agriculture sector boosts economic development, weakens poverty, and elevates sustainable development, as mentioned in the examples of Brazil, Lebanon, and Jordan.

Accordingly, the previous studies pave the way for investigating the KRI's agriculture sector, particularly in finding the balance between sustainable development and the agricultural workforce. Thus, the review sets the point for an in-depth exploration of how agricultural employment could play a prominent role in KRI's economic development and provide a higher share of prosperity and economic stability.

14.3 Methodology

14.3.1 Data Presentation

The Kurdistan Region of Iraq is an autonomous region within the Federal Republic of Iraq. It consists of four northern governorates of Iraq, including Erbil, Sulaymaniyah, Duhok, and Halabja, as well as Garmian Independent Administration. The Kurdistan Regional Government [UNDP; Ministry of Planning & Ministry of Agriculture and Water Resources (KRG)], which is located in the capital Erbil, is the entity that runs the region in collaboration with the central government of Baghdad.

According to the Iraqi constitution of 2005, the KRI can have its governing branches, such as executive, legislative, and judiciary branches, with the possibility of having its education, health, and security policies, the management of natural resources, regional budget, and infrastructure development (Phillips & Kouchner, 2015).

Between latitudes 34° and 37° and longitudes 41° and 46° is where the KRI is placed. The population was about 6.2 million in 2020, with an annual growth rate of about 3%. By 2030, it is predicted that there will be 7.65 million people living there, which makes up about 15.3% of all Iraqis (40.2 million residents). The percentage of the people residing in urban agglomerates is 83% in Erbil, 74% in Duhok, and 85% in Sulaymaniyah, making up the bulk of the KRI population (81.6%). The rapid pace of urbanization is ascribed to economic turmoil and political unrest, such as the Gulf War, the Iran-Iraq War, and the new Iraq after 2003 ((KRSO), 2018a).

The entire area encompasses roughly 40.6 thousand square kilometers, consisting of the most arable land in Iraq and hills and mountains. The western border is with Syria, the northern border with Turkey reaches the Taurus Mountains, and the eastern border is with Iran. Due to the impact of extreme rainfall and eroded sandstones that the heavier plant cover has altered, the KRI is distinguished by its rich and fertile soil types, including non-saline clay and loam kinds. The primary rain-fed farming regions are the lowlands and valleys.

The KRI has 1,535,794 ha (6,143,176 dunums) of arable land. In addition, it is estimated that the entire area irrigated by ponds, deep wells, and small and large irrigation facilities is 327,428 ha (1,309,712 dunum), less than 22% of the total area that is suitable for irrigation. Although the region possesses a visible abundance of water, the unproductivity and mismanagement issues persist. A key source of water is the massive aquifers in the KRI, which make up a significant portion of the expected 38 billion cubic meters of groundwater that flow annually ((KRSO), 2012).

The KRI has 6.1 million dunums of total arable land, 4,292,306 dunums of natural and artificial forests, 229,037 dunums of orchards, and 4,892,779 dunums of irrigated and natural pasture (see Fig. 14.1). These factors and the region's geographic location make agriculture possible for various agricultural crop production.

In 2015–2017, the overall amount of rain-fed land in the KRG was 4,833,466 dunum, or 79% of the total cultivated area, whereas the total amount of irrigated

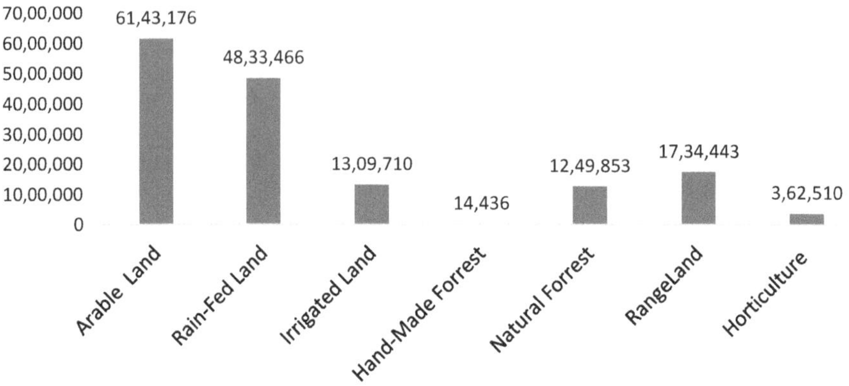

Fig. 14.1 Agriculture lands in Kurdistan Region in Dunum. Source: UNDP (2019) (UNDP; Ministry of Planning & Ministry of Agriculture and Water Resources (KRG), 2019)

land was 1,309,710 dunum or just 21% of the total cultivated area. The rain-fed region includes 15% non-guaranteed, 35% semi-guaranteed, and 50% guaranteed rain-fed land. In essence, the climate, rich soil, high precipitation relative to the center and south of Iraq, and availability of significant water sources like the Khabur, Sirwan, and Awa Spi rivers make Kurdistan's geographic location ideal for agriculture. In addition, these rivers provide 29.77 billion m^3 of water per year, in addition to 3662 springs and 68 soil dams with a storage capacity of 14 million m^3 (UNDP; Ministry of Planning & Ministry of Agriculture and Water Resources (KRG), 2019).

While worldwide norms call for roughly 10% of the budget, less than 4% of the KRG's budget has been set aside for agriculture during the previous few years. The value added of the agriculture sector to the KRG's GDP of 2018 is only 3.3%, which is a low proportion for a leading sector of an economy (see Fig. 14.2) ((KRSO), 2022).

The KRG has promoted local and international investments in aid of the farming community on a practical and financial level to promote agricultural growth. Yet, only 1.7% of total local foreign investment is dedicated to the agriculture sector, which is low ((BOI), 2021). Moreover, to promote the agriculture industry and attract more international investment, the KRG has prioritized the growth of its agricultural sector.

The growth of agricultural production in all of its facets is a focus for the Ministry of Agriculture, which has set idealistic aims to become a leading supplier and exporter of wheat, vegetables, fruit, meat, dairy, and poultry to the Middle East and North Africa (MENA) area and beyond. These long-term goals include achieving self-sufficiency from food production to the region's food security. Additionally, the MOP has put in place a three-pronged strategy for the industry's long run:

- Enhancing the economic well-being of its farmers
- Enhancing the food security of the Kurdistan Region's residents
- Enhancing wealth through the export of innovative agricultural and food products

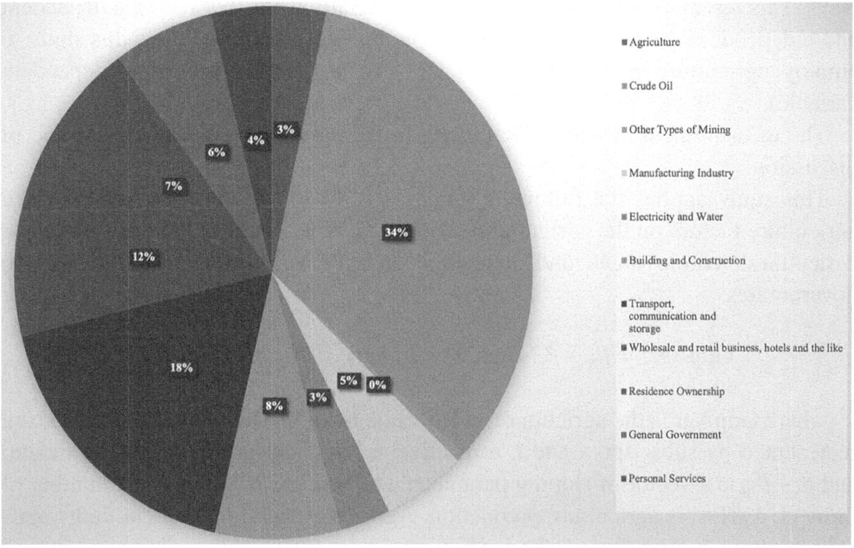

Fig. 14.2 Percentage of value added by sector to the KRG's GDP 2018. Source: (KRSO) (2022)

As a result, it is critical to illustrate the state of the agriculture industry now and to offer the essential direction for increasing productivity and ensuring the long-term viability of KRI's agricultural output (Sakina et al., 2022).

14.3.2 Empirical Model

This study employs the panel data of three KRI's provinces and one independent administration (Erbil, Sulaymaniyah, Duhok, and Garmian) over three time periods in 2012, 2013, and 2018, resulting in 12 observations to determine the nexus between employment in the agriculture industry and economic growth of the Kurdistan Region. The data and variables are obtained from the KRG Ministry of Agriculture and Water Resources, the KRG Board of Investment, and the KRG Bureau of Statistics. The four agriculture-related indicators are described below:

- GdpAgr: agriculture added value to the GDP
- NumFar: number of farmers
- AgrPro: total agricultural production (Griffith)
- AgrInv: capital investment in agriculture

The dependent and independent variables are essential to this study's outcome and the accuracy of its econometric models and estimation results. Based on theory and the available data, various factors for the independent variables have been added. The independent variables influence the dependent variables in multiple ways. This research is conducted to determine relationships between the dependent and independent variables. In addition, economic development forges this study to employ agriculture added value to GDP as the primary indicator (dependent variable).

The measurement of economic growth in the agriculture industry is a topic of discussion.

This study applies the following model (Eq. 14.1), which integrates the three agriculture factors on the agricultural share of GDP to estimate the nexus between agricultural employment and economic growth controlling for the sample governorates.

$$\mathrm{GdpAgr}_{\mathrm{it}} = \beta_0 + \beta_1 \mathrm{NumFar}_{\mathrm{it}} + \beta_2 \mathrm{AgrPro}_{\mathrm{it}} + \beta_3 \mathrm{AgrInv}_{\mathrm{it}} + e_{it} \tag{14.1}$$

where GdpAgr is the agriculture added value to GDP. Governorates and time are represented by subscripts i and t, respectively. β_0 is constant intercept-coefficient, and β_1 - β_{16} is a vector of sloping parameter coefficients. NumFar is the number of farmers, AgrPro is agriculture production, AgrInv is capital investment in the agriculture sector, and finally, e is the random error term assumed to have zero mean and constant or homoscedastic variance.

For accurate estimations, choosing the right estimating approach is crucial. This study uses an unbalanced panel data estimation approach to quantify how institutions affect economic development. Since it enables many cross-sections and periods and offers a more accurate and robust estimation, the panel data estimation approach is considered a practical analytical approach. Moreover, this research applies the pooled OLS, fixed-effects model, and random-effects (RE) model and selects the appropriate model to analyze the results based on evaluating the key statistics and comparing the performance of three applied models.

14.4 Results

The 12 observations from three governorates and one independent administration for the time periods of 2012, 2013, and 2018 comprise the data set for the final empirical model estimation of economic growth. Research data's descriptive summary statistics display data points like means, the lowest minimum value, the most significant maximum value, and standard deviations as a data dispersion measure.

Results from Table 14.1 summarize key statistics for the variables that are already described. The statistics provide a precise description of central tendencies and variabilities of the variables in our analysis. This analysis reveals some intriguing trends. While factors like GDP and the value of agriculture itself show moderate variation, the number of farmers, agricultural output, and investment levels exhibit significant fluctuations across regions. Interestingly, agricultural investment demonstrates the most dramatic range, highlighting the substantial disparities in financial resources dedicated to farming.

Table 14.1 Summary statistics of the variables, NT = 4 × 3 = 12 observations

Variable	Variable name	Mean	Minimum	Maximum	Standard deviation (n)
GdpAgr	GDP, Agriculture added value	7.9666	3.1	17.5	7.0413
NumFar	Number of farmers	9690	247	26,060	7636.058
AgrPro	Agricultural products	237,559	5150	437,798.2	141,358.1
AgrInv	Agricultural capital investment	0.4425	0	1.07	0.4067638

Table 14.2 Correlation coefficient of variables, NT = 12 observations

	GdpAgr	NumFar	AgrPro	AgrInv
GdpAgr	1.000			
NumFar	−0.0417	1.000		
AgrPro	−0.0374	0.0363	1.000	
AgrInv	0.2377	0.1127	−0.0934	1.000

The results of the correlation matrix (see Table 14.2) reveal that GDP from agriculture (GdpAgr) exhibits a positive correlation with agricultural capital investment (AgrInv) (correlation coefficient of 0.2377). This suggests that regions with higher agricultural output tend to attract more investment in capital assets. Conversely, the number of farmers (NumFar) shows a weak negative correlation with GdpAgr (−0.0417), implying that as agricultural productivity increases, the need for a large workforce decreases slightly. Additionally, the correlation between agricultural products (AgrPro) and capital investment is negative (−0.0934), indicating that higher production levels do not necessarily translate to proportionally increased investment.

To comprehensively investigate the influence of agriculture and employment on the economic development of the Kurdistan Region of Iraq over the period of 2012–2018, this study employs a rigorous analytical framework. We begin by testing the model presented in Eq. (14.1) through the application of linear pooled OLS, fixed-effects, and random-effects estimation methods.

According to the regression analysis and as indicated in Table 14.3, model selection is based on assessing key statistics and comparing the performance of the pooled OLS, fixed-effects, and random-effects models. The *R*-squared value measures the amount of variance in the dependent variable that can be predicted using the independent variables. Higher R-squared values generally indicate a better fit of the model to the data. For the combined OLS model, the R-squared value is 0.4495.

The fixed-effects model has an R-squared value of 0.3790, while the random-effects model matches the pooled OLS with an R-squared value of 0.4495. From these values, the pooled OLS and random-effects models have the same R-squared value, which is higher than that of the fixed-effects model, suggesting that these models explain the variance in GDP agriculture added value better.

Evaluating the significance of the coefficients across models helps understand which model better captures the relationships between the variables. For NumFar,

Table 14.3 Empirical results of panel data regression, dependent variable is agriculture added value to GDP

Variables	Pooled OLS (robust)			Fixed effects			Random effects		
GdpAgr	Coefficient	Std. err.	*P*-value	Coefficient	Std. err.	*P*-value	Coefficient	Std. err.	*P*-value
NumFar	−0.0006516	0.0002951	0.058	−0.0006682	0.0003019	0.069	−0.0006516	0.0002951	0.027
AgrPro	0.0000343	0.0000161	0.066	0.0000562	0.0000225	0.047	0.0000343	0.0000161	0.033
AgrInv	−0.1040489	5.168598	0.984	–	–	–	−0.1040489	5.168598	0.984
_cons	6.187286	3.706676	0.134	1.090498	5.585886	0.852	6.187286	3.706676	0.095
No. of observations		12			12			12	
R-Squared		0.4495			0.3790			0.4495	
Corr (*u*-*x*)		6.1259			−0.5980			0 (assumed)	

the pooled OLS model has a *p*-value of 0.058, the fixed-effects model has a p-value of 0.069, and the random-effects model has a *p*-value of 0.027.

For AgrPro, the pooled OLS model has a *p*-value of 0.066, the fixed-effects model has a *p*-value of 0.047, and the random-effects model has a *p*-value of 0.033. For AgrInv, the pooled OLS and random-effects models have a *p*-value of 0.984, while it is not included in the fixed-effects model. The random-effects model shows the highest statistical significance for the NumFar and AgrPro coefficients, which suggests it provides more reliable estimates for these variables.

Consistency in the magnitude and direction of coefficients across models indicates robustness in the relationships being studied. The coefficients for NumFar and AgrPro are relatively consistent in magnitude and direction across the pooled OLS and random-effects models. The fixed-effects model, while controlling for individual-specific effects, does not significantly alter the coefficients, suggesting that the unobserved individual-specific effects are not strongly influencing the relationship.

Given the higher R-squared value, the statistical significance of the coefficients, and the consistency of the results, the random-effects model appears to be the most appropriate choice for this analysis. It balances the efficiency of estimation while accounting for both within-entity and between-entity variations, making it a robust model given the data and results at hand. Generally, based on the available results, the random-effects model is selected as it provides a better fit (higher R-squared value), more statistically significant coefficients, and consistent estimates, making it suitable for analyzing the impact of the number of farmers, agricultural products, and capital investment on the economic growth of the Kurdistan region.

The selected model includes 12 observations, and the R-squared value is 0.4495, indicating that approximately 44.95% of the variability in GDP is explained by the independent variables. The correlation (Corr $(u\text{-}x)$) is assumed to be 0, as per the assumptions of the random-effects model. According to the table and empirical findings, the regression results with a particular focus on the random-effects model results are as follows:

The coefficient for NumFar is −0.0006516, accompanied by a standard error of 0.0002951 and a p-value of 0.027. This indicates a statistically significant negative relationship between the number of farmers and GDP agricultural added value, with a relatively low standard error suggesting a precise estimate.

For AgrPro, the coefficient is 0.0000343, with a standard error of 0.0000161 and a p-value of 0.033. This reflects a statistically significant positive relationship between agricultural products and GDP development. The low standard error again points to a precise estimate.

The coefficient for AgrInv is −0.1040489, with a standard error of 5.168598 and a *p*-value of 0.984. This very high *p*-value indicates that the relationship between agricultural investment and GDP per capita is not statistically significant in the random-effects model.

The intercept (_cons) is 6.187286, with a standard error of 3.706676 and a *p*-value of 0.095. This suggests that when all independent variables are zero, the GDP is not significantly different from zero at the 5% significance level, though it approaches significance at the 10% level. In general, Table 14.3 provides a comprehensive overview of our regression results, demonstrating the statistically significant impact of agricultural production and the existence of farmers on GDP growth in the KRI.

14.5 Discussion

Agriculture is a human invention; thus, any regulation must consider how individuals make choices to be effective. Many rural communities rely heavily on agriculture for their livelihoods. Since the first Gulf War and sanctions, the agricultural sector in the KRI has dramatically worsened. The region has been impacted by rising military expenditure and the flood of Syrian refugees following ISIL's invasion. Host areas are dealing with severe economic and social difficulties in the whole region.

However, the industry faced several issues due to the financial crisis, including a lack of field machinery and agricultural equipment, a shortage of high-quality crops and chemicals, and an investment shortage. The industry is now seen as the core of the economy's recovery. It can significantly contribute to fostering the extension of the domestic economy as a consequence of the growth that took place in various agricultural facets (Jongerden et al., 2019).

These farming activities in KRI include growing sunflowers, wheat, barley, rice, and other legumes like chickpeas and lentils. Moreover, farmers consider raising animals like cattle, sheep, goats, and chickens for their livelihoods. The agriculture industry has a big piece of the cake in creating job opportunities, particularly in rural areas.

Due to the low income level in agriculture, some families consider working in the public and private sectors. Other farmers in KRI receive extra money directly from the KRG, such as through pensions, ex-peshmerga status, being a former political prisoner, or from martyrs' relatives. Parents want their children to pursue job prospects in the public service or good revenue commercial sectors, such as the medical sector, because new generations do not appreciate working in agriculture (World Bank, 2016).

Families divide family labor into different types of work while also using outside labor; certain family members engage on the farm, whereas others serve as public employees or in the private sector. The farm serves as a significant income stream for some households while serving as a backup plan for others during economic hardship when they cannot support themselves in the urban environment. Farmer families may implement different financing tactics even if one of the aims is to increase job possibilities in the agriculture sector (Beer, 2017).

Local farmers support the whole agricultural industry in the KRI. They are the most prominent employment source in rural regions and the second-largest employer in the nation. Due to its labor-intensive nature, Iraq's agricultural industry can easily accommodate enormous quantities of labor in all stages of the value chain. The evidence further reveals that every new job produced in agriculture creates 0.8 jobs in non-agriculture and that a 1% rise in the agriculture GDP leads to a 1.2% growth in total employment, compared to only 0.35% for the industrial sector.

Additionally, if agricultural growth is coupled with efficient resource management across families, this might improve children's nutritional and health conditions. The farming industry is essential for political and economic stability because of its contribution to establishing (rural) jobs and increasing revenue (Aziz, 2017).

According to a report Mohammed (2020), productivity is one of the significant issues facing Iraqi agriculture. Farmers' inexperience and out-of-date methods are blamed for this low production. Local authorities and foreign experts now attribute the low capacity of the agri-food industry to old agricultural methods, a shortage of farmer skill sets, the tiny size of the farms, and the farmers' unwillingness to keep investing.

Additionally, farmers are considered to lack entrepreneurial abilities and to be driven primarily by a strong survival mentality in the rhetoric of authorities, and the small scale of the properties is regarded to hinder the adoption of new technologies. Therefore, it was believed essential to open the industry up to entrepreneurs and investors.

In 2013, the Iraqi Ministry of Agriculture made provisions for subsidizing land leasing to foreign agro-industrial businesses to link the agricultural sector to global capital through investment law. The Central Government of Baghdad and KRG started along a neoliberal path that eventually supported open markets, corporate agribusiness, and the deletion or drastic reduction of subsidies. Consequently, neither the government nor the market provided enough assistance to the agriculture industry. The infrastructure for processing capability, food, quality control, and applied research also collapsed along with the facilities and operation of alteration.

According to statistics on Iraq and the Kurdistan Region, 7% of urban families and nearly 50% of rural families own agricultural land. According to a study taken in the KRI, up to 74% of rural families are involved in agriculture. Men remained working in agriculture at a rate of 16% in 2017, up from 13% in 2000. At the same time, women were engaged at a rate of 44% in 2017, up from 26% in 2000 (see Table 14.4) (Marsland, 2017).

These statistics show that agribusiness is providing additional room for females. The fact that migrant labor appears to be a significant source of agricultural labor in the KRI and Iraq is not demonstrated by these figures. However, there are migrant laborers from Bangladesh and Egypt; Yezidi, who have been forcibly displaced in Kurdistan, supply most of the intensive agricultural workers in the KRI. In harvest

Table 14.4 Men and women's contribution to agriculture

Date	Men (%)	Women (%)
2000	13	26
2017	16	44

Source: Marsland (2017)

season, most internally displaced Yezidi agricultural laborers are young men and women who mainly pick chickpeas and potatoes for seven US dollars per day.

According to a study conducted by Jongerden et al. (2019), many of the farmers' kids were not motivated to farm and preferred city life and work for the government, where there is social security. However, in difficulties such as during the post-2014 turmoil, when the poverty rate increased from 3% in 2013 to 12% in 2015, many turned to farmland as a backup plan. However, a significant deterrent to individuals residing in rural areas is the absence of infrastructure, particularly essential educational and medical services. This matter points to a systemic issue with both succession and labor employment. Moreover, it makes it more difficult for farmer households to make rural life sustainable and inherit the lifestyle to the next generation.

Data from the previous seven decades show a substantial fall in the population of rural areas, although this trend stabilized after 1990. Almost 29% of Iraq's inhabitants of over 40 million live in rural regions, compared to just about one million (or 18.4%) of the KRI's population of six million. Nevertheless, throughout the past three decades, the number has remained relatively steady (Table 14.5). Population growth in rural regions has remained constant in real terms (by 2.6% annually) but at a slower rate than in metropolitan areas (3.1%) (Development-Indicators, 2023).

Major parties and individual politicians in Iraq and the Kurdistan Region have used employment in the public sector to build patron-client relationships and gain influence. Although most of its infrastructure has been destroyed, the government remains the largest employer, estimated to be around 42% of all jobs in the country. However, this percentage is significantly 47% in KRI. As a result, Iraq's Central and Regional governments use quite a sizable oil income to cover the cost of public sector wages (World Bank, 2017).

The KRI depends heavily on oil, much like the rest of Iraq does. The distribution of oil earnings in the region is influenced by major parties, who also control the economy. The public sector, which has evolved into the favored job market, is the primary tool for their allocation. The authorities and their followers in this economy need budgets, the former to preserve and widen their power network and the latter to sustain and boost consumerism. Despite the public sector's growth as a way to

Table 14.5 Rural population in Iraq (including KRI) 1960–2021

Date	Total population	Rural population	% of the total population	Annual % change
1960	7,289,760	4,162,522	57.101	Unavailable
1970	9,917,983	4,348,637	43.846	1.009
1980	13,653,354	4,707,538	34.479	1.0083
1990	177,419,113	5,276,946	30.294	3.0711
2000	23,497,585	7,402,680	31.504	2.8334
2010	29,741,976	9,189,379	30.897	2.2217
2021	41,187,654	11,893,008	28.881	1.5716

Source: Development-Indicators (2023)

foster patronage relationships, around 20% of all jobs in Iraq are still in the agricultural sector with a bigger share of males (Fig. 14.3) (Heshmati & Auzer, 2018).

With only 6% of jobs in farming in the KRI, this statistic is shockingly low; 23,160 farmers grow summer crops (see Table 14.6) ((KRSO), 2014), and 68,704 grow winter crops (see Table 14.7) ((KRSO), 2018b). Considering the significantly higher percentages of the rural population, this looks to be a result of the excessively high degree of governmental patronage and centralization as well as a shortage of jobs in the agriculture sector, which should be addressed by developing the sector. However, this would be a skewed interpretation given how many people in rural areas engage in small subsistence agriculture, which is not counted as jobs.

Some political conditions resulted in the migration of farmer families to the urban areas, such as the destruction of 4500 villages in Kurdistan, the reallocation of the Kurdish rural population to the southern cities of Iraq in 1987–88, and economic and social ones. Consequently, the KRI changed its position from a producer to a consumer region. In addition to the difficulties farmers face in gaining access to markets, financing, and supplies, local agricultural output faces intense competition from imported items with considerably lower prices. Turkey and Iran, whose goods have swamped Iraqi markets, are the primary competitors for local farmers (Dixit & Ahmed, 2019).

This dependence was not removed when the major Kurdish political parties took advantage of the chance to form an autonomous zone under international protection in 1991 following the Gulf War. Instead of rebuilding the rural and renewing agriculture, oil wealth was utilized to build up patron-client relationships through a booming governmental sector (Frappi, 2016).

Accordingly, the renewal of the agriculture industry promised by succeeding administrations over the previous few decades has stayed a fake hope. Since the crisis in 2014 caused by the war with the Islamic State (IS), the flow of IDPs and the KRG's consideration of political rather than economic issues along with lower oil

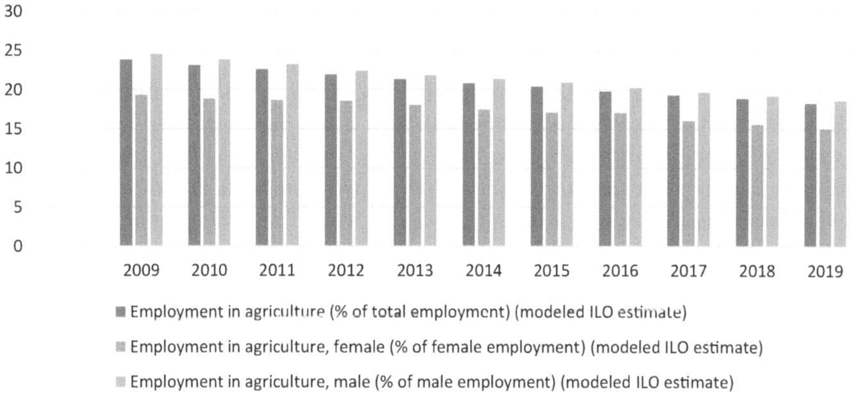

Fig. 14.3 Employment in agriculture in Iraq and KRI, 2009–2019 (% of total employment). Source: Development-Indicators (2023)

Table 14.6 No. of villages and summer crop farmers by KRI's governorates 2013

Governorate	No. of villages	No. of farmers
Erbil	630	5085
Sulaymaniyah	1025	11,385
Duhkk	775	5981
Garmian	80	709
KRI	2510	23,160

Source: (KRSO) (2014)

Table 14.7 Number of villages and winter crop farmers by KRI's governorates 2017

Governorate	No. of villages	No. of farmers
Erbil	1423	20,169
Sulaymaniyah	1674	26,060
Duhok	1442	11,458
Halabja	122	3257
Garmian	409	7760
KRI	5070	68,704

Source: (KRSO) (2018b)

prices as well as Iraqi reaction to the KRG independence referendum—cutting the annual share of the budget worth about 17% of the region's revenue—urban joblessness has encouraged people to return to the agriculture sector (Mirkhan, 2018).

The critical piece of the big puzzle that enables the farmers to improve their productivity is their knowledge of the production system. A better-educated farmer increases food output, makes it safer, and enhances the ecosystem in which it is produced.

Several studies demonstrated that the lack of advanced technology is a significant issue that hinders the development of the agriculture sector (Griffith, 2022; van Harold & Woodard 2017; Hickson, 2022). For the success of technology transfer in Kurdistan, agricultural professionals need to be capable of translating complicated agricultural challenges into statements that even farmers with limited education can learn and accept the new techs. Farmers' overall lack of knowledge significantly raises the demand for leading technology transfer institutions. It is found that the significance of technology transfer is critical (Heshmati, 2007).

According to Omar Bali & Zarea (2018), the KRG's agricultural industry is a crucial part of the country's economy, although it has been impacted by violence, poor management, and policy disruptions. Sustainable agriculture development forces producers and other stakeholders in the agricultural industry to be capable of dealing with the legacy of the old models and several future uncertainties, such as political unrest, market volatility, and climate change. Thus, by overcoming the following challenges, the agriculture industry would be a sector that can create many job opportunities:

- Diversification of the national economy from oil dependency to no-oil production
- Adoption of a vast public reform that provides more room for the agriculture industry

- Improvement of rural areas and their access to the banking system
- Advancement of university education
- Facilitation of technology transfer
- Expansion of the cultivated area to encourage private sector participation
- Provision of better services to the sector by further investments
- Consider adding rural fairs and agritourism
- Bring financial liquidity in rural areas by using financial institutions and microfinance (credit unions)

14.6 Conclusion and Policy Recommendations

14.6.1 Conclusion

The agriculture industry in KRI is undiversified, and production costs are high. Due to the region's political and economic uncertainty, it is imperative to increase self-sufficiency and avoid relying on trade with other nations. Nevertheless, the continuous hostilities, the migration of IDPs from conflict zones, and the substantial number of Syrian refugees have exerted demand and competition on the region's limited resources.

In addition to the difficulties farmers face in gaining access to markets, financing, and supplies, local agricultural output faces intense competition from imported items with considerably lower prices from Turkey and Iran, whose goods have swamped Iraqi markets. This study found that it is related to the region's history of blockades, invasions, and chemical assaults, and the curse of natural resources transformed the KRI from a provider of agricultural products to a buyer. However, it is mentioned that the modernization of the agriculture sector is vital to prevent any economic or humanitarian catastrophe.

Other findings demonstrated that the agriculture sector of KRI possesses most of the required elements for development, including good soil, underground water wells, a suitable temperature, and a workforce. Moreover, the findings demonstrate the statistically significant impact of agricultural production and number of farmers on GDP growth in the KRI.

Furthermore, to encourage local industry and increase regional and international exports, unprecedented steps should be taken into consideration in the agriculture sector. In addition to helping local farmers, adopting evidence-based practices in agricultural production would lessen dependency on imports and generate employment in urban regions, which will help boost the economy. In general, this study examined such viewpoint and suggests that market, labor, and a lack of appropriate state assistance are the primary issues the agricultural sectors of the KRI are now facing.

14.6.2 Policy Recommendations

The following recommendations intend to overcome the difficulties the KRI agricultural sector faces and open the door for its growth and modernization. Through the implementation of these initiatives, the region has the potential to boost agricultural productivity, generate a more significant number of employment prospects, diminish reliance on imports, and boost total prosperity. The joint endeavors of the authorities, the businesses, and various stakeholders are imperative to successfully execute these strategies and guarantee the long-term viability of the agricultural industry in the Kurdistan Region of Iraq.

It is imperative to enact a comprehensive array of policies to foster the growth and development of the agriculture sector in the Kurdistan Region of Iraq to create a robust and diverse job market. Initially, the government must give precedence to the diversification of the national economy, thereby shifting its reliance on oil toward adopting and promoting non-oil manufacturing.

This objective can be attained by implementing strategic public modifications that establish a conducive atmosphere for the expansion and development of the agricultural sector. Simultaneously, enhancing rural areas' conditions and facilitating their access to banking services is vital.

The provision of financial integration in rural areas will facilitate enhanced credit accessibility for farmers, enabling them to invest in contemporary cultivation techniques and technological advancements.

Furthermore, the progression of higher education in agricultural fields holds significant importance. By allocating resources toward developing farm education and training programs within universities, it is possible to nurture a proficient workforce with the necessary skills to propel innovation and facilitate the modernization of agriculture. To foster increased engagement, it is recommended that students pursuing agricultural studies be offered various incentives, including scholarships and financial assistance.

Furthermore, it is imperative to facilitate the technology transfer process in agriculture. Collaborations with established agriculture-based countries or private enterprises can introduce sophisticated farming methods and equipment specifically adapted to the particular circumstances of the Kurdistan Region of Iraq (Abramzon et al.).

In addition, to promote private sector involvement, the government must prioritize the expansion of cultivated land and offer incentives, tax exemptions, and simplifying regulatory processes to attract private investments in the agricultural sector. Meanwhile, resources of farming services, encompassing water supply, transportation, storage, and manufacturing infrastructure, are essential for enhancing the efficacy and output of the complete agricultural industry. Furthermore, implementing strategies to encourage rural fairs and agritourism initiatives can improve farmers' financial prospects while generating supplementary employment prospects within the hospitality and service industries.

To attain independence in food production and diminish dependence on imported goods, the KRI must formulate strategies that assist local farmers by implementing grants, price support, and special access to markets for domestically produced goods. Promoting sustainable agricultural practices to maintain environmental sustainability and make the most efficient use of resources is crucial.

The facilitation of market expansion and the advancement of exports of domestic farm goods necessitate the implementation of marketing initiatives, participation in business exhibitions, and establishing of collaborative relationships via global purchasers.

In summary, the agricultural sector in the Kurdistan Region of Iraq encounters notable obstacles. However, by adopting these comprehensive policies, it has the potential to evolve into a prosperous industry that fosters job creation and bolsters the region's economic advancement. The effective change and long-term progress of agriculture in Iraq's Kurdistan Region necessitates interaction among the public and private sectors and other interested parties.

Resources

Abramzon, S., Burger, N., Glick, P., Kumar, K. B., Montemayor, C. K., Mejia, N., et al. (2016). Agriculture. In *Calculating the gross regional product of the Kurdistan Region—Iraq* (pp. 7–10). RAND Corporation.

Aziz, S. (2017). *The economic system(s) of the Kurdistan Regional Government, Iraq* (pp. 103–122).

Beer, S. (2017). *The United States' program for agriculture in Post-Invasion Iraq*.

(BOI), B. o. I. (2021). *List of licensed projects in Kurdistan Region*. Retrieved from https://govkrd.b-cdn.net/OtherEntities/Board%20of%20Investment/English/Publication/Licensed%20Projects/List%20of%20Licensed%20Projects%20in%20Kurdistan%20Region.pdf

Castro, C. D. (2015). *Agriculture in Brazil's Southeast Region: Limitations and future challenges to development*.

de Janvry, A., & Sadoulet, E. (2010). Agricultural growth and poverty reduction: Additional evidence. *The World Bank Research Observer, 25*(1), 1–20. Retrieved from http://www.jstor.org/stable/40649308

Dev, S. M. (2003). Agriculture, employment and social sector neglected. *Economic and Political Weekly, 38*(14), 1353–1356. Retrieved from http://www.jstor.org/stable/4413395

Development-Indicators, W. (2023). *Rural population in Iraq 1960–2021*. Retrieved from https://databank.worldbank.org/source/world-development-indicators. Retrieved October 12th from World Bank https://databank.worldbank.org/source/world-development-indicators

Dixit, P., & Ahmed, R. (2019). Diversification of economy – An insight into economic development with special reference to Kurdistan's oil economy and agriculture economy. *Russian Journal of Agricultural and Socio-Economic Sciences, 85*, 395–404. https://doi.org/10.18551/rjoas.2019-01.48

Eklund, L., Persson, A., & Pilesjö, P. (2016). Cropland changes in times of conflict, reconstruction, and economic development in Iraqi Kurdistan. *Ambio, 45*(1), 78–88. https://doi.org/10.1007/s13280-015-0686-0

Eklund, L., Abdi, A., & Islar, M. (2017). From producers to consumers: the challenges and opportunities of agricultural development in Iraqi Kurdistan. *Land, 6*(2), 44. Retrieved from https://www.mdpi.com/2073-445X/6/2/44

Frappi, C. (2016). *Oil and state building in Iraqi Kurdistan* (pp. 91–121).

Gibson, G. R., Campbell, J., & Wynne, R. (2012). Three decades of war and food insecurity in Iraq. *Photogrammetric Engineering and Remote Sensing, 78*, 885–895. https://doi.org/10.14358/PERS.78.8.895

Griffith, W. H. (2022). Agriculture. In *Economic development of caricom* (pp. 19–54). Anthem Press.

Heshmati, A. (2007). *Review of the recent trends in development economics research: With experience from the federal region of Kurdistan*: Bonn.

Heshmati, A., & Auzer, K. (2018). The role of natural resources in Kurdistan Regional Government's economic development. *UKH Journal of Social Sciences, 2*, 1–14. https://doi.org/10.25079/ukhjss.v2n1y2018.pp1-14

Hickson, C. (2022). Innovation for agricultural adaptation in Africa *the case for a political declaration at COP27*. Retrieved from http://www.jstor.org/stable/resrep40597

Jongerden, J., Wolters, W., Dijkxhoorn, Y., Gür, F., & Öztürk, M. (2019). The politics of agricultural development in Iraq and the Kurdistan Region in Iraq (KRI). *Sustainability, 11*(21), 5874. Retrieved from https://www.mdpi.com/2071-1050/11/21/5874

(KRSO), K. R. s. S. O. (2012). *Agricultural areas in the governorates of Kurdistan Region*. Retrieved from Erbil - Kurdistan Region of Iraq:

(KRSO), K. R. s. S. O. (2014). *Summer crops agriculture report planting year 2013* (ID Number 32). Retrieved from Erbil, Kurdistan Region of Iraq: https://krso.gov.krd/content/upload/1/root/e104.pdf

(KRSO), K. R. s. S. O. (2018a). *Demographic Survey of Kurdistan Region of Iraq*. Retrieved from https://krso.gov.krd/content/upload/1/root/e61.pdf

(KRSO), K. R. s. S. O. (2018b). *Winter crops planted area survey in Kurdistan Region Area, yield, production, expenditure 2016–2017*. Retrieved from https://krso.gov.krd/content/upload/1/root/e52.pdf

(KRSO), K. R. s. S. O. (2022). *Measuring the GDP of Kurdistan Region of Iraq for the Year of 2018*. Retrieved from https://krso.gov.krd/en/statistics/gdp

Marsland, N. (2017). *Iraq - Agriculture damage and loss needs assessment*. Retrieved from Rome, Italy

Mirkhan, H. (2018). Iraqi Kurdistan referendum and its implications. *UKH Journal of Social Sciences, 2*, 17–18. https://doi.org/10.25079/ukhjss.v2n1y2018.pp17-18

Mohammed, S. (2020). Economic crunch revives farming in Soran. Retrieved from https://www.rudaw.net/english/business/050720201

Oluwatayo, I. B., & Ojo, A. O. (2016). Is Africa's dependence on agriculture the cause of poverty in the continent? An empirical review. *The Journal of Developing Areas, 50*(1), 93–102. Retrieved from http://www.jstor.org/stable/24737338

Omar Bali, A., & Zarea, H. (2018). The challenges of firms in Iraqi Kurdistan economy in the light of strategic acquisition theory (pp. 245–262).

Phillips, D. L., & Kouchner, B. (2015). *The Kurdish spring: A new map of the middle*. Transaction Publishers.

Sakina, M., Salih, D., & Mohamad, T. (2022). *The role of agricultural extension to facing agricultural risks in sulaymani governorate- Kurdistan Region - Iraq. 14*. https://journal.djas.uodiyala.edu.iq/index.php/dasj/article/view/3475

Sudhir, J. M. (2003). Agriculture and unemployment. *Economic and Political Weekly, 38*(15), 1463–1466. Retrieved from http://www.jstor.org/stable/4413428

UNDP; Ministry of Planning & Ministry of Agriculture and Water Resources (KRG), F., USAID (2019). *Review of the agricultural sector in The Kurdistan Region of Iraq analysis on crops, water resources and irrigation, and selected value chains*. Retrieved from Erbil, Kurdistan Region of Iraq https://info.undp.org/docs/pdc/Documents/IRQ/Agricultural%20Study%20-KRI%202019.pdf.

van Harold ES, & Woodard J (2017). *Innovation in agriculture and food systems in the digital age*. The global innovation index, World Intellectual Property Organisations (pp. 97–104). Retrieved from https://www.wipo.int/edocs/pubdocs/en/wipo_pub_gii_2017-chapter4.pdf

World Bank. (2012). *Land administration and reform in Sub-Saharan Africa: From piloting to scaling up*. Retrieved from Washington, DC

World Bank. (2016). *The Kurdistan Region of Iraq—Reforming the economy for shared prosperity and protecting the vulnerable*. Retrieved from Washington, DC

World Bank. (2017). *Iraq, systematic country diagnostic, Report No. 112333-IQ*. Retrieved from Washington, DC

World Bank. (2018). *The role of food and agriculture for job creation and poverty reduction in Jordan and Lebanon Agricultural Sector*. Retrieved from https://documents1.worldbank.org/curated/en/325551536597194695/pdf/Agricultural-Sector-Note-Jordan-and-Lebanon.pdf

Part V
Summary, Conclusion and Policy Implications

Chapter 15
Integrating Resource-Based Strategies for Sustainable Growth

Nabaz T. Khayat and Goran M. Muhamad

This book attempted to explain the experiences, challenges, and opportunities for the post-conflict Kurdistan region of Iraq (KRI). The resource-based sectoral analysis reported several challenges, including, but not limited to, mismanagement of natural resources, poor institutional quality, reliance on oil and gas and imported products, and an undiversified economy. However, the region's rich history, cultural heritage, and economic and geopolitical position can stand at a crossroads in its economic development and hold immense potential for economic transformation and further growth. As we conclude our exploration of the resource-based economy for the Kurdistan region of Iraq, it becomes clear that the efficient management and strategic utilization of resources are essential to sustainable growth and development.

This book has provided a comprehensive analysis across three distinct yet interconnected parts, shedding light on various dimensions of resource-based strategies. The first part covered several studies related to resource management and development in the KRI, encompassing political economy, the interplay between resource wealth and tax revenue, and the role of business and international organizations in KRI development. The second part explored several strategies for resource-based KRI, such as leadership, technology, and social media, which are essential in its

N. T. Khayat (✉)
Brandenburg University of Technology, Cottbus-Senftenberg, Germany

Technology Management, Economics, and Policy Program, College of Engineering, Seoul National University, Seoul, Korea (Republic of)
e-mail: nabaz@snu.ac.kr

G. M. Muhamad
Economic Research Centre, Soran University, Soran, Iraq

Economic and Finance Department, University of Kurdistan Hewler, Erbil, Iraq
e-mail: goran.mustafa@ukh.edu.krd

G. M. Muhamad, N. T. Khayyat (eds.), *Resource Management Performance: A Sectoral Analysis in the Post-Conflict Kurdistan Region of Iraq*, Perspectives on Development in the Middle East and North Africa (MENA) Region,
https://doi.org/10.1007/978-981-97-7725-9_15

development process. The final part of this book considered energy and natural resource management, including oil and gas, electricity, and agricultural resources.

15.1 Synthesis of Key Insights

15.1.1 Resource Management and Development

In the first part, we delved into the foundational aspects of resource management and development. We examined how effective management practices optimize resource utilization and drive economic growth. The main conclusion of this part is summarized as follows:

- The oil state formation model of the KRG failed due to its geopolitical condition and the way the KRG managed oil extraction and export, resulting in a political curse.
- A further reason was the economic model of the region, which has not ensured the welfare of its citizens. An alternative approach would be to establish a new economic model that emphasizes economic diversification and economic governance and reinforces institutions.
- The KRI's political economy of hydrocarbon faced several turbulences in recent years, mainly the continual internal political divisions, regional pressure, and the decision made by the International Court of Arbitration (ICC) in Paris, and ruled the Federal Government of Iraq's favor against the Kurdistan Region's independent crude oil exports through Turkey in March 2023.
- This study calls for the KRI's ruling parties to bring a robust energy vision and institutionalize system-wide patterns of governance so that the global economic market looks exuberantly forward to the Kurdistan Region during the Russian-Ukrainian war.
- The lucrative revenue from oil and gas caused deprioritization of other revenues, such as taxes, and resulted in undermining the KRG's accountability. As such, to support sustainable fiscal practices, the KRG should commit to counterbalancing the negative impacts of resource dependence by enhancing tax revenue mobilization.
- International organizations contributed to the development of the region, and their performance relied on several factors, namely, competitive advantage, human capital, and technology. The KRG may enhance the growth and performance of international organizations by improving their productivity through a set of rules and regulations.

The key takeaways of this part included:

- Establish a new model of economy that promotes economic diversification
- The importance of sustainable resource extraction and consumption

- Innovative approaches to resource management that enhance productivity
- The role of policy and regulation in ensuring equitable resource distribution
- A new energy vision that addresses the major contemporary hydrocarbon issues within Iraq

15.1.2 Resource-Based Strategies for Development

The second part of this book focuses on how resource-based strategies are essential for navigating the complexities of the modern economy. We explored various sectors, including leadership, the role of Information and Communication Technology (ICT) in HR, and social media impact. The major conclusions of this part are:

- Business Membership Organizations have not historically performed well in the KRI to promote a better business environment, mainly because they are weakly organized and highly politicized. There is a need to prepare a strategic plan that defines the BMO's future vision, strategic orientations, and role in achieving the national and local goals and preparing annual implementation work plans.
- The differences in the performance of leaders in the private sector compared to the public sector in the KRI were considered. The differences revealed that the public sector workplace is not designed to be competitive. The KRG should induce an evaluation and assessment system that examines the behaviors of public managers to make their leadership best deal with the recent awareness of the workforce and managing resources.
- We discussed how much Information and Communication Technology (ICT) contributes to increasing the performance level of HRM staff in higher education institutions in the Kurdistan Region of Iraq. While the level of ICT usage in KRI is not at that level where the individuals of HRM are well aware, the finding suggested positive effects of ICT on the performance level of HRM staff in KRI higher education institutions.
- We looked at the relationship between the travel decision-making process and social media, especially from the point of view of Kurdish travelers. We found evidence that social media has an essential role as the source of information to help travelers in every stage of travel decision-making in the Kurdistan Region. Nevertheless, a strategy with a model of the travel decision-making process through the use of social media is needed to execute marketing strategies that are more focused on the consumers.

- Increasing travel to the region will significantly contribute to economic development in several ways: (1) tourism revenue, which is considered a major economic driver; (2) infrastructure development, which is investment in infrastructure such as airport facilities, roads, hotels, and restaurants that follows the increase in tourism; (3) job creation, as tourism generates employability; (4) fostering cultural exchange and preservation through interactions with local traditions, arts, and cuisine; (5) economic diversification through the provision of alternative sources of income from unique natural, historical, and cultural assets; (6) increase in tax revenue; (7) encouraging small business growth and entrepreneurial activities as locals start small businesses to cater to tourism/s needs; and (8) increased travelers will improve the quality of life through enhanced infrastructure, better services, and cultural revitalization.

Highlights from this section include:

- Leadership: The need for visionary leadership that can align resource management with long-term strategic goals
- ICT in HR: The transformative effects of information technology on human resource management, enhancing productivity and employee satisfaction
- Social Media Impact: The influence of social media on consumer behavior and how businesses can leverage this to optimize resource-based marketing strategies

15.1.3 Energy and Natural Resource Management

The third part of this book emphasizes the critical energy and agriculture sectors, highlighting their significance in a resource-based economy. We concluded the following:

- The Kurdistan Region's infrastructure projects were associated with several risks resulting in projects' cost overruns. The main reason for this was the discrepancy between the actual plan agreed with the plan implemented. The KRG is required to be involved by eliminating the bureaucracy in the public sector government institutions and allowing the introduction of more flexible methods in dealing with construction projects.
- We investigated the relationship of household factors, such as household size, income, electric appliances, and its effects on electricity consumption. While houses in Erbil used a mixed source of energy in their everyday lives, they were overusing electricity in instances of leaving unnecessary electric tools working. Information asymmetry is a prominent issue that should be addressed in order to improve the conditions of electricity provision from the Ministry of Electricity (KRG) and the consumption in households.
- The role of the agriculture sector in the economy of the Kurdistan Region was examined, specifically issues with the underdevelopment of the agricultural sector. The main issues that effectively marginalized the sector are KRG's inability to design an effective homegrown national food supply policy, business people's greed, the use of food import, and distribution as a channel of money laundering.
- There were essential non-utilized resources in the agriculture sector that can be used to increase the level of production in the sector. The KRG should undertake effective strategies to promote this sector to increase the national income and more employment generation.

The main key points were:

- Sustainable energy management practices that balance economic growth with environmental stewardship
- The role of renewable energy sources in reducing dependence on nonrenewable resources
- Strategies for sustainable agriculture that increase food security, enhance soil health, and support rural economies

15.2 Integrating Insights for Holistic Development

Bringing together insights from these three parts, it is evident that a holistic approach to resource-based strategies is essential. The integration of effective management practices, strategic leadership, advanced IT solutions, and responsive social media strategies may create a resilient and adaptive economy. Additionally, economic diversification strategy and sustainable practices in energy and agriculture are crucial for long-term viability.

15.3 Policy Implication for the Kurdistan Regional Government

Given the unique context and opportunities within the Kurdistan Region, the following policy recommendations are tailored to enhance the region's resource-based economy:

1. Strengthening Institutional Frameworks:
   (a) Establish robust regulatory frameworks to ensure sustainable extraction and management of natural resources.
   (b) Create specialized agencies to oversee the implementation of resource management policies and monitor compliance.
   (c) Establish economic governance to make collective economic actions within institutions aiming at improving economic performance in different conditions.
   (d) Make a radical change in its administration and resource management, in particular the cohesiveness of political institutions, potential development of transparency, and investment in the institutional power of the government rather than political power.
2. Apply an Economic Diversification Strategy

(a) Downsizing the public sector and expanding opportunities for the private sector are principal acts for securing a diversified economy, and thus strengthening the status of KRG.
(b) Establishing a proper and fair tax system to reduce natural resource revenue dependency, thus deriving long-lasting economic stability and strengthening the government's accountability.
(c) Establishing a flexible tax regime that has both implications for its fiscal revenue and incentivizes significantly the effective engagement of the private sector.
(d) Establish an effective anti-dumping strategy to support the current agricultural initiative development and diversification strategy and get rid of the overdependence on imported products, thereby strengthening the fiscal capacity of the KRG.

3. Energy Policy

(a) Formulate a new energy vision and manifest to maintain KRI's national security.
(b) Find new cooperation, apply a balanced strategy to build trust and relationship with Baghdad, and actively engage and strategically position itself on the regional chessboard.
(c) Empower fiscal sovereignty by targeting natural gas policy to domestic use since the global demand for fossil fuel energy will gradually decline as many of the developed nations have a net zero emissions target policy and an alternative cost-effective strategy.

4. Promoting Renewable Energy

(a) Encourage investments in renewable energy sources such as solar, wind, and hydroelectric power to diversify the energy mix and reduce reliance on fossil fuels.
(b) Implement incentives for businesses and households to adopt renewable energy technologies.
(c) Fostering innovation and research.

5. Advancing ICT in Human Resource Management

(a) Support the integration of advanced IT solutions in public and private sector HR practices to improve efficiency and workforce management.
(b) Offer training programs to equip HR professionals with the skills needed to leverage IT effectively.

6. Leveraging Social Media for Economic Development:

(a) Utilize social media platforms to promote local businesses and attract foreign investments.
(b) Develop digital marketing strategies to boost tourism and showcase the cultural and natural heritage of the Kurdistan Region.

7. Sustainable Agriculture Practices
    (a) Implement policies that support sustainable farming techniques to improve crop yields and soil health.
    (b) Provide financial and technical assistance to farmers to adopt modern agricultural practices.
8. Fostering Innovation and Entrepreneurial Activities
    (a) Create innovation hubs and incubators to support startups and entrepreneurs focused on resource efficiency and sustainability.
    (b) Offer grants and funding opportunities for innovative projects that align with resource-based strategies.

15.4 Future Directions for the Kurdistan Region of Iraq

Looking ahead, several key areas warrant further exploration and development:

- Innovative Technologies: Continued investment in R&D to develop technologies that enhance resource efficiency. In addition, it is recommended to encourage public–private partnerships to accelerate the adoption of innovative technologies.
- Policy Frameworks: Strengthening policy frameworks to support sustainable resource management and equitable distribution and enhance regulatory oversight to ensure compliance with environmental standards and resource management policies.
- Global Collaboration: Fostering international cooperation to address global resource challenges, sharing best practices, and developing joint solutions. Furthermore, the KRG should make more efforts to engage with international organizations and forums to align regional strategies with global sustainability goals.
- Human Capital Development: Invest in capacity-building programs to develop a skilled workforce that can drive the region's resource-based economy and promote lifelong learning and continuous professional development to keep pace with evolving industry demands.
- Economic Diversification: Economic diversification will reduce dependency on a few key resources, fostering resilience against market fluctuations. This will also pave the way for the growth of non-resource sectors such as tourism, manufacturing, and services.
- Infrastructure Development: Invest in infrastructure projects that support resource-based industries, such as transportation, logistics, and communication networks, and ensure that infrastructure development is aligned with sustainability principles to minimize environmental impact.

15.5 Final Thoughts

In conclusion, the journey through the resource-based economy reveals the intricate interplay between various sectors and strategies. By embracing a resource-based approach, we can pave the way for a sustainable, inclusive, and prosperous future. The insights gained from this book serve as a foundation for policymakers, business leaders, educators, and researchers to continue advancing our understanding and implementation of resource-based strategies. Together, we can ensure that our resources are managed wisely, benefiting current and future generations.

For the Kurdistan Region, the integration of tailored policy measures and strategic initiatives can unlock significant potential for economic growth and development. By managing resources wisely and fostering innovation, the region can ensure that its resources benefit current and future generations. Together, we can build a resilient and dynamic economy that thrives on sustainable practices and forward-thinking strategies.

SPRINGER NATURE

GPSR Compliance

The European Union's (EU) General Product Safety Regulation (GPSR) is a set of rules that requires consumer products to be safe and our obligations to ensure this.

If you have any concerns about our products, you can contact us on ProductSafety@springernature.com

In case Publisher is established outside the EU, the EU authorized representative is:

Springer Nature Customer Service Center GmbH
Europaplatz 3
69115 Heidelberg, Germany

The manufacturer's authorised representative in the EU is Springer Nature Customer Service Centre GmbH, Europaplatz 3, 69115 Heidelberg, Germany. If you have any concerns regarding our products, please contact ProductSafety@springernature.com

Printed and bound by CPI Group (UK) Ltd, Croydon, CR0 4YY
01/10/2026
02225909-0015